PENGUIN BOOKS

THE MAKING OF THE BRITISH LANDSCAPE

'Tells the British experience from the ground upwards. Pryor
strips away layers of the landscape, and with each new layer
reveals something new about how generations of Britons
have lived . . . a warm and personable writer'
Dan Jones, *The Times*, Books of the Year

'Sweeping and extremely readable'
Country Life, Books of the Year

'A splendid narrative, each paragraph offering a new
nugget of information or insight'
Mark Horton, *The Times Literary Supplement*

'By any standards a major addition to our grasp of the subject . . .
There is no period in our own history in which Pryor does not
have something interesting and new to say'
Paul Johnson, *Spectator*

'The book successfully undermines several cherished landscape
myths. Global warming does not account for the disappearance
of the thriving borough of Dunwich in Suffolk, with its churches,
friaries and markets. Legal and economic changes had a far
stronger hand than the Black Death in depopulating medieval
villages . . . A physical Britain, however, complete with the
bumps, scars and scratches made by the past, is a common
inheritance. As this generously informative and challenging
book emphasizes, it is up to us all to ensure that such precious
marks remain visible and meaningful'
Jonathan Keates, *Sunday Telegraph*

'From the sprawling fields of East Anglia, to the mountains of the Pennines and the waters of the Lake District, humans have had a greater influence on their surroundings than we may think . . . a dynamic story lurks beneath the surface. Comprehensive and full of juicy facts, Pryor discusses everything from the gardens of stately homes to the influence of landscape poetry, medieval open-field farming and the modern planning system. He loves everything about Britain . . . The landscape is our story as told by us and as such we should do everything within our power to cherish it'
Rob Sharp, *Independent*

'This magisterial history of the British landscape turns out to be utterly accessible, a chronicle of foible and failure, family and fortune, the unwritten account of ordinary men and women, recorded only in the forms of the land itself . . . in this book Pryor draws them into one enticing new whole'
Adam Nicolson, *Scotsman*

ABOUT THE AUTHOR

Former president of the Council for British Archaeology, Dr Francis Pryor has spent thirty years studying the prehistory of the Fens. He has excavated sites as diverse as Bronze Age farms, field systems and entire Iron Age villages. He appears frequently on TV's *Time Team* and is the author of *Seahenge*, as well as *Britain BC* and *Britain AD*, both of which he adapted and presented as Channel 4 series.

FRANCIS PRYOR

The Making of the British Landscape

*How We Have Transformed the Land,
from Prehistory to Today*

PENGUIN BOOKS

PENGUIN BOOKS

Published by the Penguin Group
Penguin Books Ltd, 80 Strand, London WC2R ORL, England
Penguin Group (USA), Inc., 375 Hudson Street, New York, New York 10014, USA
Penguin Group (Canada), 90 Eglinton Avenue East, Suite 700, Toronto, Ontario, Canada M4P 2Y3
(a division of Pearson Penguin Canada Inc.)
Penguin Ireland, 25 St Stephen's Green, Dublin 2, Ireland (a division of Penguin Books Ltd)
Penguin Group (Australia), 250 Camberwell Road, Camberwell, Victoria 3124, Australia
(a division of Pearson Australia Group Pty Ltd)
Penguin Books India Pvt Ltd, 11 Community Centre, Panchsheel Park, New Delhi – 110 017, India
Penguin Group (NZ), 67 Apollo Drive, Rosedale, Auckland 0632, New Zealand
(a division of Pearson New Zealand Ltd)
Penguin Books (South Africa) (Pty) Ltd, 24 Sturdee Avenue, Rosebank, Johannesburg 2196, South Africa

Penguin Books Ltd, Registered Offices: 80 Strand, London WC2R ORL, England

www.penguin.com

First published by Allen Lane 2010
Published in Penguin Books 2011
005

Copyright © Francis Pryor, 2010

The moral right of the author has been asserted

Typeset by Ellipsis Books Limited, Glasgow
Printed in Great Britain by Clays Ltd, St Ives plc

A CIP catalogue record for this book is available from the British Library

978-0-141-04059-2

www.greenpenguin.co.uk

MIX
Paper from
responsible sources
FSC
www.fsc.org
FSC™ C018179

Penguin Books is committed to a sustainable
future for our business, our readers and our planet.
This book is made from Forest Stewardship
Council™ certified paper.

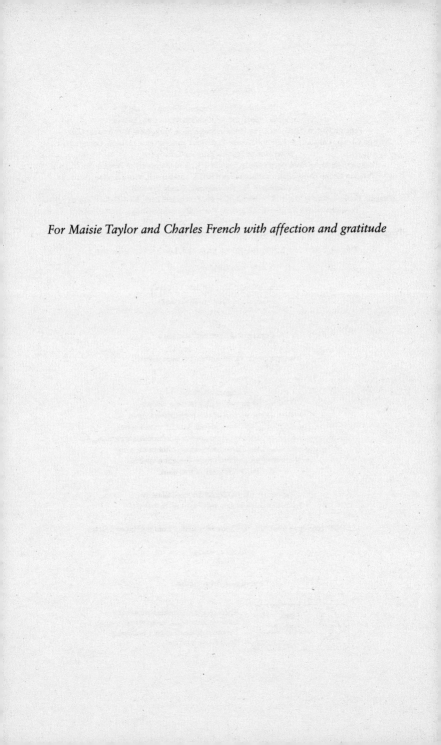

For Maisie Taylor and Charles French with affection and gratitude

Contents

CONTENTS

Acknowledgements

Dr Mike Nevell gave me numerous publications and references on his important work on the industrialization of Tameside and gently helped me understand some of its complexities; he has also kindly read the post-medieval chapter. Professor Mick Aston was a constant source of advice and encouragement and generously gave me free access to his enormous photographic archive; he also went through the manuscript and pointed out many inaccuracies and omissions. Mark Edmonds has also been kind enough to read through the manuscript and gave me photographs of Langdale in the Lake District. Marilyn Palmer and David Crossley were more than generous with their time and made special efforts to guide me through the fascinating maze that is industrial archaeology. David Cranstone has also shared his huge knowledge of matters industrial and Bill Bevan has helped me with advice on Sheffield and the uplands around it.

John Schofield at English Heritage conducted me around Second World War defences when we were filming *The Real Dad's Army* for Channel 4. My brother Felix and sister Caroline have been very helpful on a number of specific occasions, Felix being particularly good when it came to John Clare and William Wordsworth. My brother-in-law Nigel Smith kindly read through a draft of the manuscript and made many constructive suggestions. Keeping it in the family, my niece Anra Simpson and her husband Pete helped me around Brighton and its charming Lanes. Neil Rhind provided me with information about Blackheath and Shooters Hill, south-east London, and my old friend Mark Lloyd-Price found me material on chalk streams. Dr Martin Bell (University of Reading) was his usual generous self: he helped me understand the modern and prehistoric

Severn Levels and took me to some of the extraordinary sites he and his team have discovered.

Tim Taylor and several un-named directors were civilized enough to look the other way when occasionally I would steal away from the set of *Time Team*, with a camera concealed in my hat; Tim also gave me kind permission to use material from several *Time Team* shoots. Stewart Ainsworth made many useful comments, especially about landscapes in the Cheviot Hills.

Many of my photographic expeditions were made very much more pleasant when Maisie and I were able to arrange short holidays in Vivat Trust properties, some of which feature in this book (The Temple at Badger Dingle, Shropshire; Barns Tower, Peebles; and Church Brow Cottage, Kirkby Lonsdale, Cumbria).

Finally I would like to acknowledge my agent Bill Hamilton and the team at Penguin: my editors, Georgina Laycock and Michal Shavit, designers Lisa Simmonds and Alastair Richardson, editorial assistant and picture researcher Caroline Elliker, cartographer Alan Gilliland, production controller Rita Matos and editorial manager Richard Duguid. The large manuscript was ably copy-edited by Elizabeth Stratford. The index was compiled by Auriol Griffith-Jones.

It is usual to thank one's wife in the Acknowledgements; indeed, one day I would love to end this section with the words 'and special thanks to my dear wife Maisie, who has had to live with this book for a fortnight'. In the event, it was rather longer than that – and my thanks to her are heartfelt.

Preface

Many readers will be aware that the title of this book is a respectful nod in the direction of W. G. Hoskins's classic, *The Making of the English Landscape*, which was published in 1955. At that time scholars believed they knew rather more than was actually the case. In the middle of the twentieth century it was also still possible to paint a convincing picture with a broad brush. However, in the five subsequent decades research has revealed a great deal more, and as a consequence we now realize just how little we do in fact understand about the achievements of our ancestors. Broad brushstrokes are fine in their way, but there is a very great danger that they might paint out and obscure the real picture – or pictures.

The pace and volume of recent research has provided so much high quality material that no two individuals would ever agree on what might now constitute a 'standard' or balanced account of Britain's landscape. For a few months I briefly chased after this ideal, but realized the task was impossible, and opted instead for a personal account of what I believe to be the main themes of an extraordinarily exciting story. This has meant that I have included places and topics that some might consider trivial and have inevitably omitted sites and events that others would regard as essential. I have taken as my guide for selection the wise advice of David Collison, the distinguished documentary film director who would often say to me: 'Very good, Francis, but does it advance our story?' Nine times out of ten my bright ideas failed that simple test. So although I have made huge efforts to be factually correct, I am aware that this is certainly no textbook and should never be treated as such.

The British Isles are remarkable for the variety and richness of their landscapes. This was brought home to me when I lived and worked in Toronto in the 1970s. There, if you wanted to sample mountain scenery you had to drive for five days before you reached the foothills of the Rockies. The Prairies were vast beyond imagining and the huge areas of birch tree scrub and open country that comprised the sub-arctic Canadian Shield were indeed starkly beautiful, but interminable. The Great Lakes were, if anything, too great. You could have dropped the entire English Lake District into Lake Superior and still have room to sail a navy.

I suppose it boils down to a simple question of scale: the British landscape is human-sized. Like the motto of England's smallest county, Rutland, there is *multum in parvo* (much in little). So from my house in the Fens near the Wash, I can eat breakfast, take photographs of the Peak District before lunch, then head across the distinctive landscapes of the Trent Valley and the Vale of York, cross the North Yorkshire Moors and finish up with a pint of bitter and an excellent supper in the White Horse and Griffin, by the North Sea, at Whitby.

The human scale of the British landscape belies its enormous complexity, which we have only really begun to appreciate in the past fifty or so years. But as archaeologists and historians increasingly discover, the sad fact remains that less and less land is available for study. Vast housing estates, sprawling gravel quarries, new towns, motorways, airports and, worse than anything else, modern intensive farming are eating away at this huge resource of potential knowledge. In the simplest possible terms, the intimate scale of the British landscape and the huge size of the British population mean that the one is inevitably threatened by the other. This is a theme I shall return to from time to time, but it is not my intention here to write an archaeological *Silent Spring*: a dirge that bemoans the passing of the British landscape. Even at this time of unparalleled destruction, I think that would be premature, because so much still survives and some of it in remarkably good condition, albeit covered by an ever-growing cloak of filthy litter.[1]

Almost the entire British landscape has been transformed at some time by man. Even such seemingly permanent things as ancient woodlands have at some point in their lives been manipulated by humans. This means that people are increasingly realizing that drystone walls, trackways, crumbling bricks and earthen burial mounds are as important as – if less cuddly than – our feathered and furry friends. But unlike trees, hedges or animal populations, once destroyed, lost features of the man-made landscape can never be replanted or reintroduced.

Today, in the twenty-first century, many of us live increasingly mobile lives. We live where we work, or, speaking as someone who is self-employed, we live where the work is to be found. Many British people today have relatives scattered not only across all four countries of the British Isles, but across Europe and indeed, much further afield into Asia, America or Australia. The idea of the romantic drifter wandering along the highway of life, with nothing to keep him company except a hungry dog and an old guitar, is fine when one is a teenager living safely at home. But when the moment comes to embark on the real journeys of life, roots become increasingly important.

Human beings are social animals and we all need to feel that we belong to a larger community. More than that, I believe we also need to feel that a particular community is somehow greater than the sum of its component parts. So a community centred on a parish church is more than just a priest and a few churchwardens. It is heir to dozens of generations of priests and benefactors, often going back to Saxon or Norman times. This link with the past gives this otherwise insignificant community not just legitimacy, but a measure of prestige and influence too. Such local or regional institutions 'punch above their weight', because of their close associations with an area's history.

Places matter to people, because they were almost entirely created by humanity. The geological and geomorphological[2] foundation of a particular location, the rocks, mountains, rivers, lakes and coastlines were the long-term products of natural processes, over millions and millions of years. The results of these processes will undoubtedly have affected the way human communities developed their settlements and landscapes, but it would be a great mistake to suppose that such purely practical considerations were the only, or even the most important, factors to influence those developments. The study of landscape history has shown that human relationships, patterns of trade and commerce, religion, warfare and politics have had a far greater effect on the making of the British landscape than landforms alone.

I believe this is one reason why urban and rural landscapes fascinate us so much. We are naturally inquisitive about our surroundings. In some instances this curiosity can be satisfied with anger: by discovering why some halfwit decided to erect that 1920s cinema (sadly, now a listed building) that still obscures the best view of a cathedral. But in most cases our enquiries are less readily answered. Why, for example, was the cathedral built there in the first place? These are the sort of questions that follow from the need to acquire or accumulate a sense of place. In my experience that process can take a lifetime and lead to a wealth of new relationships, with both people and places.

The acquisition of an informed sense of place does not have to be a professional or a scholarly pursuit, although it will have to rely heavily on the work of such specialists. But there is a big difference between looking and seeing. Without some basic understanding of the story lying behind the making of the British scene, one may look at a landscape and appreciate nothing.

No written account can ever compete with the real thing: the fields and houses, or streets and factories are out there in front of you; but information about how they developed through time will fire them with new life. Little details, like the large rectangular windows in the upper storeys of certain nineteenth-century working-class houses in Nottinghamshire, become far more interesting when one learns that these upstairs rooms were the workshops of small-time lace-makers and frame-knitters in the days before electric light.[3] Given such knowledge, the odd-looking windows then cease to be even slightly peculiar, as one's imagination tries to picture what went on behind them. Suddenly a series of rather drab buildings that one may have driven past dozens of times before acquires an entirely new and unexpected meaning.

The story of the development of the British landscape is not a single coherent narrative. Instead there are numerous themes and sub-plots that criss-cross and intertwine, rather like a climbing wisteria or grapevine. Chronology might be seen as the framework across which they scramble. I have tried to follow what I consider to be the principal strands of the story in the main body of the text, but I am also aware that these themes are only a part of the whole. By and large these are the themes that interest me; people from different backgrounds will doubtless find other aspects of interest and I have tried to include sufficient references for them to chase up.

We all experience landscapes for ourselves and I cannot dictate which are the most significant or important. Having spent most of my working life around the Fens, I will not apologize for including many views of that region. For me, for example, the construction of the first mosques in Peterborough was actually more significant than the opening of the magnificent gilded building in Regent's Park, London. So I have included a Peterborough example in a setting that owes its origins to the railway, from which the mosque can be glimpsed, lighting up the otherwise drab urban scene on a summer's afternoon.

I have always taken the view that in prehistoric and historic times people's beliefs, hopes and aspirations were as important to them when taking decisions as were purely practical considerations.[4] So the layout of Bronze Age farms and fields might owe as much to the orientation of the sunrise, or to the location of long-respected burial mounds, as to simple agricultural factors. In most cases it will be a combination of the two. On Channel 4's *Time Team* I am often teased by other members of the team for seeing 'ritual' behind everything. I leave it for others to decide whether or not this is entirely fair, but I must warn readers that although I do not disregard such things in the present work, any attempt to reconstruct past landscapes must rely heavily on archaeological and historical evidence for relatively mundane aspects of the ancient world, such as field boundaries, trackways and changing patterns of land tenure. In such circumstances it is often difficult to see an overtly spiritual dimension – which is not, of course, to say that it was never there. Perhaps it still lurks in the alignment of the towns and streets of our ancient cities, that often follow the 'grain' of Roman and earlier landscapes. Maybe. But in each case it must be demonstrated, and never assumed. As we shall see later, many surviving grid-like town plans within ancient walled Roman towns are actually the result of much later, Saxon, rather than Roman town planning.

At this point I should come clean about my own approach to the landscape. There are two traditional approaches to the man-made landscape: one historical, the other archaeological. The former approaches a given landscape by way of documents, whereas the latter takes the evidence on the ground as its starting point. Very sadly, it is still possible to find historical books purporting to explain landscape change that simply ignore archaeology.[5] Today most specialists try to study their landscapes using a combination of both approaches, but our own personal backgrounds will usually lie in one or other of the two camps.

My background is archaeological. For some thirty years I surveyed and excavated pre-Roman landscapes around the edges of the Fens.[6] I soon learnt, however, that the key to understanding the way these pre-Roman landscapes might have functioned lay in much later, post-Roman, times. The more I read about research by historians of the Middle Ages into the working of the many Fenland abbeys and priories, the more I began to understand the relationship between wetland and dryland, pasture and arable. This in turn opened my eyes to the richness and diversity of Fenland landscapes, which I had been brought up to see as impoverished and rather 'marginal' (an imprecise and pejorative term that is best avoided in the study of landscape history). This perceived 'marginality' was emphasized when Fen landscapes were compared, for example, with the prehistoric wealth of areas such as Salisbury Plain. We now realize that both areas were rich in their own ways and that the Fens and their margins were part of the economic heartland of Bronze and Iron Age Britain. Part of my journey towards this new understanding of the region I had chosen to study was a result of long discussions with landscape historians who thoroughly understood the working of the medieval Fens. So although my own background is in prehistoric archaeology, I have the greatest possible respect for what the historian can contribute.

I have another string to my bow which has helped me understand how some pastoral landscapes might have worked.[7] It all began about twenty years ago when I was sold five sheep by the County Archaeologist of Norfolk, Peter Wade Martins. At the time he warned me that keeping sheep could become addictive – he had a substantial flock himself – but I failed to heed his warnings. In those days we lived in a farmhouse near the medieval village of Parson Drove, in the Fens outside Wisbech, in Cambridgeshire. Parson Drove is one of a series of long, thin or 'linear' villages that were established as part of planned developments that can be dated by scatters of fourteenth-century pottery in the fields around the village.[8]

Our house was within the two dykes (ditches) that defined the course of a medieval droveway known as the Seadyke, which was used for driving livestock from the fen towards markets in Wisbech. The back of the house looked across a series of large rectangular fields that were drained in medieval times and have changed little since then. The draining was quite a massive undertaking, part of a much wider scheme that brought large areas of slightly elevated land around the Wash into agriculture. The symbols of the prosperity of the medieval Fens can still be seen in the cathedrals of Ely and Peterborough and some of the finest churches in the whole of Europe. Even so, the myth still persists that the Fens were drained by the Dutch in the seventeenth century. The history of Britain's landscape is rich in such persistent myths and I shall do my best to debunk some of them.

In 1993 we moved ten miles north, just across the county line into Lincolnshire, where we manage a flock of about 130 pure-bred Lleyn ewes. That short move has brought us onto a very different landscape. Here the soil is slightly heavier and more moisture-retentive, which suits us well, given the steady increase in summer temperatures. We are in a different drainage area, where water in the dykes is maintained at a higher level. These subtle differences are crucially important, and it took us the best part of ten years to accumulate the knowledge we needed to make the change, which has been most worthwhile. Our new land, like that of our old farm, was drained for pasture in medieval times and we are surrounded by some of the finest medieval parish churches in the country, all built on the proceeds of wool. Today, sadly, our sheep are exceptional: as I write, the fields around us are largely given over to winter wheat and oilseed rape, both crops that can be grown almost anywhere.

As we shall see, the story of the British landscape is rarely straightforward and even regions as seemingly homogeneous as the Fens do actually have distinctive sub-regions within them, which only start to make sense when examined closely. The differences between, for example, peat (or Black Fen) and silt (or Marshland Fen) are fundamental, although to an outsider both types of landscape appear equally flat and, to some, boring. When confronted with the frequent accusation that flatlands are dreary, I like to reply with Sir Harry Godwin's riposte. Sir Harry was the leading palaeobotanist of his day, who had established his reputation with research into the ancient Fens. Towards the end of his life he published a popular book on the subject, the introduction to which boasts some wonderfully evocative writing about the hugeness of Fenland skies and the fondness Fen people have for their landscape. It includes this splendid quote: 'As one [fenman], unexpectedly communicative, explained to me: "any fool can appreciate mountain scenery but it takes a man of discernment to appreciate the Fens".'[9]

It also helps if one understands a bit about farming. Only then can one appreciate what a huge difference the various types and conditions of soil can make – and it is not just a matter of 'good' or 'poor' soil. One must ask: good or poor for what? Good soil for grassland must be heavy enough to retain moisture in summer, and have appropriate levels of copper and other trace elements, whereas good soil for arable must be light enough to plough well, but not to dry out during that crucial period in spring and early summer when wheats and barleys do their main growing. Farming is a complex business that should not be left to agronomists and soil scientists alone. The care of the soil requires the experience of good all-round farmers as well, but, sadly, they are leaving the land in their thousands. It is a worrying tendency that one sees in other aspects of modern life, and I have heard it described by the unlovely neologism, 'de-skilling'. Once the regional traditions of farming experience and expertise have been lost, 're-skilling' that takes into account the very subtle differences of the landscape will probably be impossible, or at best very slow and inefficient. I fear that in the not-too-distant future the largely urban population of Britain will have cause to regret the rapid collapse of the family farm, a collapse which has been such a sad feature of the very first years of the twenty-first century. The effects are visible in parts of upland landscapes today, where untended and ungrazed fields are being colonized by birch and hawthorn scrub.

Although my own background is as an archaeologist, prehistorian and sheep-farmer, I have decided to write this book from a slightly different perspective. Over the last two or so decades, and in common with many others, I have come to favour an approach to the past known simply as landscape history. I shall discuss what I mean by that in the Introduction.

Most measurements are expressed in metric, but I sometimes write as a farmer rather than a historian and some traditional imperial measurements appear at these points, or where imperial is more appropriate in the historical context. Readers should note that a hectare = 2.47 acres; a metre = 3.28084 feet or 1.09361 yards; a kilometre = 0.621371 miles; and a bushel = 8 gallons or 36.4 litres.

Sutton St James, Lincolnshire
August 2009

The Making of the British Landscape

Introduction

Landscapes are an expression of the here and now. But as I walk through them I am constantly reminded of their diverse histories by numerous and always unexpected clues. It is rather like meeting a new person for the first time. Your initial impression is certainly important: do you like him or her? Do they have a pleasant or an untrustworthy face? But then you automatically start to pick up other hints, usually about their past, that their words and body language transmit. These clues allow you, unconsciously, to place the person in some kind of context; they flesh out appearance with character and allow you to disregard, or excuse, superficially irritating characteristics, such as an exaggerated accent or silly mannerisms. Without them your new acquaintance lacks substance or indeed humanity: you might as well be talking to a cardboard cut-out.

I do not want to extend this metaphor too far, but for many people the landscape is something only to be appreciated at that first superficial level. Indeed, this was the case until very recently: landscapes were either beautiful, ugly or dull, and were best appreciated from well-known viewpoints. So if we are to get more out of our surroundings we must first learn to pick up those clues that are instinctive in human relationships.

Learning to do this is not a long process, but it does take effort and time. As a student I walked the fields around our house in the chalk hills of Hertfordshire with my eyes down, busily picking up flint tools, the evidence of Neolithic and Bronze Age settlement. Today when I walk those same hills I still keep an eye out for flints (flint-spotting becomes a lifelong habit), but I am also interested in the way hedge-lines have changed and how the lower parts of dry valleys are starting

3

to fill up with soil, through intensive agriculture. These things are only interesting if you understand what might have gone before; if you want to understand the landscape you cannot ignore the past.

There can be other reasons for an interest in landscape history. Some might want to understand more about their own immediate surroundings. Perhaps it was where they were brought up, or where they liked to take their holidays, but the thought that the suburban street where they now live could have any intrinsic interest may not have occurred to them. This is probably because we tend not to think of towns as being part of the landscape, but of course they are. The modern industrial urban landscape was a concept whose origins lay in the eighteenth and nineteenth centuries, and although modern towns appear very different from those of the past they still have to face the same problems of housing and employment, which by and large they do successfully. Their story or, more accurately, their stories are fascinating and require telling. Each story, however, will be different, depending on who is spinning the tale.

Landscapes cannot be changed or created overnight. They are the result of long-term processes and they provide a yardstick against which one may judge the present. Today towns, cities and suburbs provide homes for nine out of ten people in Britain. We talk about 'urban sprawl' as if it was a giant jellyfish that oozed its way across the neat and efficient patchwork quilt of the rural landscape. In actual fact such 'sprawl' – 'conurbation' is a better word without the unpleasant overtones – is a remarkably efficient means of housing and employing the huge population of Britain. It is so efficient that in England (the most urban of the three countries of mainland Britain) over 90 per cent of the population live in just 8.3 per cent of the total land area.[1] In other words, 91.7 per cent of England is still rural, in theory at least. So when people bemoan 'urban sprawl' they should be reminded that without it there would be precious little countryside left.[2]

If you enjoy a landscape you are halfway towards an understanding of it. But learning how to 'read' one with any competence or facility can take years of practice and study. Landscapes are rarely, if ever, simple. They may be as complex as the succession of people and cultures that fashioned them. I believe 'landscape history' offers the best way to understand how the current landscapes of Britain came into existence, how they developed, and finally why they appear as they are today. As a first step, I must define what I mean by the word 'landscape'.

Most of us know what we mean when we use the term, but unlike other descriptive terms, 'landscape' can imply different things to different people. To a farmer the landscape consists of soil types with various drainage and nutritional characteristics; to an engineer it poses load-bearing and other challenges that might require bridges or tunnels; to the tourist it includes views and viewpoints. The term is rarely used to refer to urban, suburban or industrial scenes, nor to airfields or coastal defences, yet to the landscape historian all of these – and many others besides – are important. It all depends on the periods and the problems being examined. The trade in salt in the late Bronze Age could effectively be examined in parts of southern Lincolnshire, whereas the landscapes of defence adopted by General Sir Edmund Ironside in 1940 must involve the entire island of Britain.

The word 'landscape' was introduced to the English language from the Netherlands, probably in the sixteenth century, where it was a painter's term that referred essentially to a pleasing view.[3] The archaeological use of the word has roots ultimately in the works of nineteenth-century researchers, particularly General Pitt-Rivers (see page 50 for more). The landscapes that archaeologists and landscape historians study are essentially products of human efforts, combined with natural features of the terrain, which together give certain regions a distinctive character. That is as close as we can get to a definition. The big difference between a modern understanding of the word and its use in the eighteenth and nineteenth centuries is that today we would include all components of a landscape and not just the picturesque rustic bits, such as 'Constable Country', the Lake District or Snowdonia.

SOLID GEOLOGY AND LANDFORM

I have read many times that the landscapes of Britain have been 'painted' by man on a 'canvas' provided by geology. Laying aside the originality of such metaphors, it is not as simple as that. Geology is continuing to this day: every time there is a rockslide in Snowdonia, or heavy rainfall causes layers of flood clay to be deposited over the floodplains of south-eastern England, these are geological processes. So the relationship of landscape to geology is still in progress. Although it would be a mistake to see geology as static, we can observe its effects at two levels. The earliest rocks that provide the bedrock of Britain probably formed sometime around 1,000 million years ago and that process has been carefully plotted through the various eras of geological time until about 2.5 million years ago. The rocks that formed during this vast epoch of time are generally referred to as Solid Geology. From about 2.5 million years ago, during the Pleistocene era, northern Europe was gripped by many ages of ice interspersed with warm spells. This process of freezing and thawing gave rise to a new series of geological deposits, such as the gravels and boulder-clays that form the subsoil of much of lowland Britain. These much later Ice Age deposits are known as Drift Geology and they affected the form of the British landscape as much as the older Solid rocks.

The landscapes of Britain are as complex as the geology beneath them. It would be a mistake, however, to assume that geology simply dictates the form of the landscapes that humans have created on its surface. Indeed, nothing could be further from the truth, and the relationship of the one to the other is complex and can only be understood on a case-by-case basis. Having said that, there is undoubtedly a clear difference in the geology and the landforms of landscapes on the east and west sides of Britain. This distinction led the archaeologist Cyril Fox to describe the 'personality' of Britain as being divided into highland and lowland zones.[4] The highland zone was to the north, west and south-west, the lowland mainly to the east of the higher ground. As we shall see shortly, this distinction reflects the antiquity and immense complexity of Britain's geological history.

I studied geology at A Level, and when I compare my old textbooks with what is being written today,[5] I might as well be looking at another subject. Back in the early 1960s the intellectual revolution caused by the discovery of plate tectonics had yet to affect education, where the history of geology was essentially a successional tale of oceans and periods of mountain formation that seemed to make little coherent sense. Incidentally, the word 'tectonic' refers to building or construction and reflects the fact that the plates are an integral part of the construction or structure of the earth's crust. We now understand that the formation of the bedrock of Britain was the result of complex interactions between the different plates that together comprise the outer crust of the earth. These plates are floating on a hot core of viscous liquid rock, known as magma when it gushes into our world during volcanic eruptions. When the plates collided, the mind-boggling energy released by their impact gave rise to the volcanoes and mountain ranges that have subsequently been worn down to form the hills and plains of our modern landscape.

The result of these many geological events and processes is a pattern of Solid Geology where the older, harder sedimentary and volcanic rocks, such as those of the Cambrian (545–485 million years ago) and Ordovician (485–445 m.y.) eras occur to the west, facing the Atlantic Ocean. This contrasts with more recent and softer sedimentary rocks, such as the chalks and limestones of the Jurassic (200–142 m.y.) and Cretaceous (142–65 m.y.) eras which are found on the eastern side. The latter are far less weather- and water-resistant and through time have eroded down to form the undulating downs, wolds, plains and wide valleys so characteristic of south and east Britain.

The geological formations of Britain are broadly arranged NW–SE. The northern and western parts of Britain are composed of harder and generally much older rocks that are more resistant to natural erosion. These have given rise to the uplands, high moors and mountains of Scotland, Wales and northern England. Many of these landscapes are quite acidic and where drainage is poor, bogs mostly of *Sphagnum* moss can develop, fed directly by rainfall.[6] These landscapes are broken up by steep-sided valleys with fast flowing rivers that rapidly flood when rain drains off the surrounding hills. The peninsula of southwestern England, mainly comprising Devon and Cornwall is also composed of ancient rocks such as granite, millstone grit and Old Red Sandstone, but the landscapes here are lower-lying and sharper than those further north, as they have not been affected by recent glacial action.

The great swathe of lowland Britain, very roughly all land south and east of a line from the Humber to the Bristol Channel is formed on softer, and younger, bedrocks of clays, sand and sandstones, limestone and chalk, mostly formed from Jurassic times. Here river valleys are wide and flat and hills are more undulating than precipitous. The contrast between south-east and north-west in England is mirrored in Scotland, where the countryside of the southern Lowlands and Kingdom of Fife contrasts with that of the Highlands and Islands. Similarly the east coasts of both Scotland and England tend to be more gently sloping and have fewer cliffs, islands and rocky promontories.

ICE AGES AND THE LANDSCAPE

We tend to think of the Ice Ages as being invariably cold, but in actual fact the sheets of ice were interspersed with warm periods when sometimes the temperature could be as warm, or indeed warmer than it is today. It was during these warmer inter-glacial periods that most of the huge areas of sand and gravel that occur in most lowland river valleys were laid down. Rivers became an extremely important agent of change in those warmer times.

The contrast between highland and lowland landscapes can most clearly be seen in the form of river valleys. The basic difference between the two reflects the speed with which the river water flows and its ability, or not, to carry silt and clay particles in suspension. The simple rule is that the faster water flows the more material it can carry; as the flow slows down this material is deposited on the river or flood-plain floor in the form of flood-clays, known as alluvium. In the uplands the valley sides are steep and the rivers are swift to swell after heavy rain. They become forces of erosion, when in spate, scouring-out their valleys and the water flowing into them, especially if it comes off freshly ploughed land, is pale brown and rich in eroded topsoil. In the lowlands rivers take longer to respond after heavy rain, but when they do their waters will burst through low natural banks and spread across wide floodplains, where they deposit thin layers of river-borne flood-clays, which accumulate on the ground as thick blankets of alluvium. The mechanics of the process are simple: as the water spreads out across wide floodplains it naturally loses velocity and the fine alluvium particles carried in suspension fall to the riverbed. In the ultra-lowland, flat and often artificially drained landscapes fringing the North Sea, river levels can take days to respond to rainfall inland, but when they break through their artificial banks their waters can flood immense tracts of land.

Glaciers and other natural forces changed the landscape significantly during the Ages of Ice, but these processes of change did not stop when the Ice Ages ended, some 10,000 years ago. Frost, wind and rain continue to alter our surroundings, and not always in subtle ways. Floods, for example, can cause devastation, and their frequent aftermath, glutinous deposits of flood-clay, can make the business of clearing up even more difficult. The situation today is being made worse by intensive farming, which has removed woods and hedgerows, the roots of which would have prevented soil from being washed into rivers in the first place.[7]

Many of the river valleys of upland and lowland Britain have been scoured out and enlarged by glacial action during the many Ice Ages of the Pleistocene period, from 2.5 million to 10,000 years ago. Many of the very wide river valleys of the British lowlands, too, where rivers meander their way across huge flat gravel floodplains, were actually formed by ice action in the Pleistocene period. One of the largest river valleys in Britain is the vast plain of the River Ouse in Bedfordshire, which seems to take about ten minutes to cross in a train travelling at 125 m.p.h., yet when one visits the actual river it is remarkably small and does not seem to 'deserve' such a huge floodplain. The fact that the form of the landscape altered far more dramatically in the Ice Ages than today also helps to explain why the transition between upland and lowland can appear to happen so quickly: one moment the river is a bubbling torrent, the next it is lazily snaking through flat floodplain pastures.

The Ice Age glaciers of the Pleistocene period probably had the greatest effect on the form of the British landscape. Glaciers are natural phenomena, of vast motive power. They consist of millions of tons of ice which carry and push huge rocks which slowly grind or scour away the sides of steep or V-shaped valleys, to give them a softer, rounded open U-shaped profile. The load of rocks they carry is deposited on the ground as they pass and when finally they melt. Isolated rocks lost in passing are known as 'erratics', but when the glaciers start to retreat as conditions grow warmer the entire load of transported clay and rocks is dumped to form a 'terminal moraine'. Terminal moraines can block whole valleys and can have a major effect on the formation of subsequent landscapes. A large moraine formed in the lower parts of the Vale of Pickering, in Yorkshire, and a lake formed upstream of it. The shores of the lake were fringed with some of the earliest post-glacial settlements in northern Europe, including the key earlier Mesolithic site of Star Carr.

Other glacial and periglacial effects include the boulder-clays or 'till' (a preferable term, as boulder-clay does not necessarily include boulders), a deposit which is laid down beneath the clay and is often found in chalk landscapes, where it provides unexpectedly damp and acid conditions. During the Devensian, the last major cold stage of the Pleistocene Ice Ages, most of east Yorkshire, Lincolnshire and the Fenland basin was a large lake fed by glacial run-off. The Breckland sands of central-south Norfolk were laid down by wind-blow at this time. Similar wind-blown sand occurs on the bed of the North Sea between East Anglia and the Low Countries.

TEMPERATURE, ICE AND VEGETATION

Although man has undoubtedly been the major influence in the formation of Britain's diverse landscape, geology, drainage and climate have also played an important role.[8] Soil types, too, have influenced the sort of plants that grow in particular areas. Most British plants tend to prefer their soils either alkali (limestone or chalky) or acid (usually sandy or volcanic). Trees such as beech and ash prefer alkali soils; oaks, sycamore, yew, birch and lime, for example, can also tolerate more acidic conditions, whereas most pines and rhododendrons (an introduced plant) like acidic soils. We see similar preferences among the common hedgerow shrubs, and with a little practice one can make a reasonably accurate guess at the local geology simply by observing the surrounding vegetation. Similarly, drainage will have a major bearing on the plant communities in a given landscape, with trees like alder and willow dominating very wet regions; damp, as opposed to wet landscapes will favour horse chestnuts, hazel, limes and hornbeam. Beech will not tolerate poor drainage and hawthorn, scrubby oaks, juniper and pines can thrive in even the driest and most exposed of landscapes.

Fig. 0.1 Woods of Scots pines at Ockham Common, near Cobham, Surrey. These trees and the bracken at their feet are typical of acidic sandy soils.

THE REGIONS OF BRITAIN

I take a less closely defined view of the highland and lowland zones than pre- and post-war archaeologists, who tended to see them as contained or inward-looking phenomena. I prefer two loosely defined provinces, whose flexible boundaries have always been determined by culture rather than climate I believe this contrast was one of the main characteristics, and creative forces behind, the social development of the British Isles. The North Sea province, which consisted of the Scottish and English east coast, extended across to the Pennines, through the Midlands, to the south coast around Dorset. The contacts here were with Scandinavia, the Low Countries, France and Germany. This contrasted with an Atlantic province to the west, which included Ireland, the Western Isles, the Isle of Man, Devon and Cornwall – an area previously labelled by E. G. Bowen 'the Western Seaways'.[9] Bowen saw close ties between those regions and neighbouring parts of Europe, especially Brittany, Spain and Portugal. In a recent and comprehensive reworking of the subject, Barry Cunliffe has arrived at much the same view.[10]

We know today that the development of the cultures, landscapes and societies of the British Isles happened through interaction rather than in isolation. We also know that travel and communication both within and beyond Britain was a regular feature from at least 3000 BC. By 2000 BC plank-built ships were being made that were perfectly capable of crossing the English Channel and the North Sea.[11] A number of recent discoveries – for example, the burials found near Stonehenge – have shown that some of the inhabitants of Britain actually grew up

Fig. 0.2 Professor Dudley Stamp's map of the regions of Britain, published in 1946. The heavy line indicates the boundary between highland and lowland Britain. The dotted areas plot coal measures, of which more on page 13.

in central Europe. Numerous finds of Continental bronzes bear this out, and the close similarity of their burial rites show that Bronze Age people on either side of the Channel must have been in frequent personal contact.

Throughout most of prehistory the two zones were probably of similar importance and provided each other with the competitive stimuli that might partly explain the vigour of pre-Roman culture in Britain. However, after the final conquest of Gaul by Caesar in 51 BC cross-Channel connections to the West Country ceased and the centre of gravity shifted to Essex, Kent and the south-east, where it has remained ever since. The Vikings subsequently complicated the picture when they settled in Ireland and along the north-west coast of Scotland. Generally speaking, the two halves of Britain remained on friendly terms, even if sometimes this relationship required the erection of monuments like Offa's Dyke. Only recently, however, and with communications so vastly improved, has the Atlantic–North Sea cultural contrast started to disappear. Perhaps its best expression is still to be found in regional accents and dialects.

It has long been recognized that Britain is composed of a series of distinctive regions and that in most cases these follow the broad highland–lowland division. Although there are inherent problems in broad-brush schemes, I personally prefer the rather impressionistic map drawn up in 1946 by Dudley Stamp, then Professor of Geography in the University of London.[12] In those days, of course, coal was still of vital importance, which explains why the coal measures are plotted onto a map that is otherwise mostly based on human or cultural geography. Stamp's map can still be controversial. Take the central Lowlands of Scotland; here many would see two quite distinct regions, to east and west, with roots extending back to the Picts and Gaels. I can also think of many residents of Essex who would be annoyed to learn that they lived in the London Basin, rather than in East Anglia.

W. G. HOSKINS AND THE DEVELOPMENT OF LANDSCAPE HISTORY

The academic study of landscape history is a relatively recent phenomenon, whose origins are often attributed to a single book: *The Making of the English Landscape* by Professor W. G. Hoskins, published in 1955. It has remained in print for more than half a century. As major academic milestones go, *The Making* was unusual. It was a slim volume, written in a relaxed conversational style and copiously illustrated with many fine photographs. It had an enormous effect.[13] The story it told was that of England, as it was preserved in fields, farms, roads, buildings, towns and villages. Having read Hoskins several times, both as a student and after graduation, my life has been hugely enriched. After a session spent within the pages of *The Making*, I feel as if I have enjoyed a walk through a sublime landscape in the company of a great poet. In actual fact some of Hoskins's views were reactionary in the extreme. He detested much of the modern world, for example, and his writing often seemed to hark back to a non-existent rural idyll. It is now clear that Hoskins's work had its roots in the Romantic tradition of landscape appreciation, as exemplified by poets such as Wordsworth.[14]

Hoskins's work took me away from the narrow confines of prehistory that academic discipline had necessarily imposed upon me.[15] This is understandable if one bears in mind that I had been brought up in a somewhat self-consciously scientific tradition of academic prehistory, known in the mid-1960s as the 'New Archaeology'. This approach to the subject was a reaction against many of the intuitive, seemingly commonsensical views of pre-war archaeologists and historians. 'New Archaeologists' wanted to approach the past more as a scientific experiment, because they recognized that ancient people did not think as we do today. Accordingly, they argued, we should act more as anthropologists, who would approach a particular group of people knowing nothing about them at all. Even working in this methodical manner, many mistakes were made, which merely proves that both anthropology and archaeology are humanities and will never be sciences. Despite the acknowledged shortcomings of the anthropological approach, it was widely recognized that this was a far better way of working than simply assuming, for example, that priests in the Middle Ages organized the social life of their parishes in the same way as a modern vicar. In reality the two were worlds apart, and if there were links they should be demonstrated and not taken for granted. So perhaps I should now come clean and admit at the very outset that, although I adored reading Hoskins, I have nonetheless remained true to my prehistorian's training.

Hoskins did, however, teach me to look at my surroundings with much closer attention. As I walked through the countryside I could ponder at length on the meaning of what I passed: was that sunken green lane over there cut off in the nineteenth century during the Enclosure Movement, or had it gone out of use much earlier? Could its origins go back before the Middle Ages, to Saxon times? My curiosity was now aroused by all of my surroundings, not just at weekends on trips out into the country, but also on the daily journey to work as I drove past the various layers of suburban houses that ringed the city of Peterborough. These buildings reflected its long history, first as a medieval monastic town, then as a regional market centre, then a major railway town and finally as an industrial city. Hoskins showed me that Victorian terraced housing or old canals choked with supermarket trolleys were as important in their own way as places like Stonehenge. His book effectively democratized access to the past.

Hoskins's main thesis was that the landscape was there to be 'read'. If one examined it closely one could 'read' or detect evidence for earlier landscapes that had subsequently been replaced or adapted. This approach has been likened to a palimpsest, faint traces of original writing visible in parchment that has been reused. Sometimes, the landscape, like manuscript palimpsests, can reveal multiple episodes of use and reuse. Hoskins stressed the importance of combining evidence produced by an archaeological examination of the landscape itself with a study of historical records, such as maps, parish registers, deeds and so forth.

Hoskins was writing in the post-war era. Soon, however, the growing number of archaeologists influenced by the New Archaeology would be less keen to invoke invasions and other external influences to explain changes observed in the field. In the 1970s the emphasis was increasingly on regional change and development 'from within', rather than on sudden and abrupt shifts, imposed by external forces or influences. These new research projects also required high-quality and detailed field survey, documentary research and excavation, which the writing of *The Making* anticipated. In some respects it was years ahead of its time; yet in others it was already very old-fashioned. This tension is perhaps what makes it still such a good read.

MODERN TECHNIQUES IN LANDSCAPE ARCHAEOLOGY

During the past three or four decades a number of science-based and other survey techniques have become available to landscape historians and archaeologists, and these have provided a wealth of new evidence, particularly about the landscapes of pre-Roman Britain. I do not want to linger too long on technicalities, but it is important to note just how much modern technology can achieve.

It is probably fair to say that our current understanding of the antiquity of the British landscape owes more to aerial photography than to any other single factor. Its roots lie in the First World War when first balloons, and then aeroplanes, were used by both sides to direct artillery fire and assess its effects. Photographs of the shattered land surface became increasingly important to the officers of military intelligence, and techniques of aerial photographic reconnaissance improved rapidly. After the war archaeologists who had acquired these new skills soon put them to effective use.[16]

Aerial photographs are of two types: verticals and obliques. Oblique views show minor undulation very clearly, especially in snow, or when the angle of the sun is low, in mid-winter, early in the morning or late in the evening. Marks in growing crops are often best seen in oblique views, too. Cropmarks are simply patches of rapid growth where the roots of certain crops, principally cereals, can reach down into water-retentive strata and cause the crop to grow faster and more luxuriantly. So plants growing directly above ancient ponds, ditches or pits will show as dark marks when viewed from the air. Sometimes a good photograph of cropmarks can reveal about 80 per cent of what lies hidden beneath the surface. Usually such clear and comprehensive marks only form on light, thin soils – and in dry years. Most often, too, only the larger pits and ditches will show as cropmarks, leaving the smaller post-holes and gullies to be revealed by excavation. Vertical photographs are usually taken for other purposes, such as military reconnaissance, or nowadays as part of routine map-making and they are best used in conjunction with oblique views, to provide links between areas surveyed in greater detail.

Aerial photography is just part of a larger spectrum of survey techniques, known collectively as remote sensing. Today these can also involve various forms of satellite imaging.[17] Like aerial photography, remote sensing comes in two forms: aerial and land-based. Aerial remote sensing today includes conventional photography and the use of heat-sensitive (for example, false colour infrared) and other film media.[18] It also includes a range of new techniques based around radar. One of these, known as LIDAR (Light Detection and Ranging) is

Fig. 0.3 An oblique aerial view of medieval ridge-and-furrow fields near the village of Naseby, Northamptonshire. This photograph is an excellent example of how subtle surface features can be brought out by careful use of low-angle sunlight, in this instance aided by a light covering of snow.

Fig. 0.4 A vertical aerial photograph of cropmarks on land about to be quarried for gravel at Mucking, near Thurrock, Essex. The light gravel soils of this important site especially favour the formation of cropmarks, as revealed in this remarkable photograph. It shows the double concentric ditches of the Bronze Age South Rings; overlying these are the rectangular ditches of Romano-British farmyards and buildings. The darker spots are either wells or early Saxon sunken-floored houses and the small circular ditches are the eaves-drip gullies (gutters at ground level) belonging to Iron Age roundhouses.

beginning to prove very useful. LIDAR images are capable of mapping very slight undulations on the ground surface and are not dependent on low light angles, as was the case with oblique conventional photography. It has proved particularly useful in the mapping of complex sites, such as ruined towns and in the detection of buried features that protrude just above the surface.

So the technology behind modern landscape research has come a long way from an eighteenth-century painter's appreciation of a view. But these advances do not invalidate aesthetic or historical approaches. There is room for all, because the landscape is about the diversity of the marks that mankind has made on the world. When confronted with such an extraordinarily rich source of information only a fool would presume to say that one particular approach was the right one.

I

Britain After the Ages of Ice

(10,000–4500 BC)

Our story will start, as it will end, at a time of major climatic change. Never before have we needed so much to understand what happens when the world around us grows inexorably warmer and our once-stable surroundings are replaced by something different. But it is not enough to learn about the physical mechanisms of climate change, of global warming and of sea-level rise alone. We must also try to understand how our landscape will be affected and how human societies are likely to respond to such changes. Perhaps for the very first time it is now becoming apparent that the survival and adaptation of human societies will depend on the way that scientific disciplines, such as meteorology, geology and physics, can combine with humanities such as archaeology, sociology, political science and history.

Art and science must come together just as much when we look back as when we look forward; and we may be able to use our current approach to the distant past as a model for confronting the challenges of the near-future. I have studied human prehistory for many years and I have noticed that science becomes increasingly important as one moves back in time. For a start, there are absolutely no written records of any sort prior to about 3000 BC, when the first writing appears in western Asia. So we have to rely on other means, such as radiocarbon dating, to provide us with chronology. Climate and sea levels can be reconstructed using scientific procedures that involve physics, biology and chemistry. Archaeologists who study these more remote periods also have to be competent in both geomorphology and soil science and most, too, have a good grasp of physical anthropology – the science that studies the evolution of human beings. It would be wonderful if such a breadth of vision allied with close academic collaboration could become a routine part of current debates over climate change, which so often become bedevilled by single-issue politics.

While it is important to approach the past and the future from both sides of the artificial arts–science divide, there are other reasons why we should break down the intellectual barriers that have become such an accepted part of the modern world. I believe that a balanced and rounded appreciation of the past enhances our respect for humanity, both dead and alive. The more I learn about the way ancient human societies adapted to and changed their surroundings, the greater my respect for them grows. My sense of humility is increased when I look around and see how different communities are coping with sometimes impossible conditions, whether it be in parts of sub-Saharan Africa, the floodplains of Bangladesh or indeed some inner cities in Britain.

But there are dangers in relying too heavily on anthropology and other studies of modern societies when we examine the very remote past. Ten or fifteen thousand years ago, for example, not just the landscape and climate but the way people thought about themselves were so very different. There is a danger, too, of circularity along the lines, 'if it cannot be done today, then it couldn't have happened in the past'. My argument against that is simply to suggest a visit to Stonehenge. We could never have conceived and created that place today and it is very hard indeed to find a good parallel for it in the vast literature devoted to tribal societies. We must be creative about the past as much as the future. Sometimes we must hope that the vast quantity of archaeological and scientific information we excavate from the soil will somehow speak to us and allow our imaginations to reveal new insights that may, or may not, be 'real'; we shall probably never know which. But I do not think that matters, because the process of investigating prehistory is valid in its own right for what it tells us about ourselves and our capabilities.

Such breadth of vision is certainly needed when we turn to the story of the landscape towards the end of the Ice Age. Everything was very different then. For a start, Britain was not yet an island and most of the North Sea did not yet exist. It was also bitterly cold. So how did the communities of the region cope with the rapid global warming that happened at the end of that final glacial period? To approach the problem we must briefly go back a little further, to the latter part of the Ice Age, around half a million years ago.

THE LATER ICE AGE

The maximum extent of Ice Age ice happened 478,000–423,000 years ago, when glaciers extended across what was later to become the island of Britain as far south as the Bristol Channel and then eastwards following a line just north of the M4, towards London and south Essex.

Fig. 1.1 Map showing the southerly extent of ice during the two major cold stages of the Pleistocene Ice Age. Ice and glaciers of the Anglian cold stage (478,000–423,000 years ago) extended across Britain and Ireland as far south as the Bristol Channel and eastwards towards London and south Essex. During the last glacial, or Devensian cold stage (122,000–10,000 years ago), ice covered all Scotland, most of Ireland and Wales, and parts of north-west and eastern England. In the final years of the Ice Age (10,000 years ago), ice of the Loch Lomond cold stage was confined to the western Highlands of Scotland.

North of this line the landscape shows clear signs of glaciation, but further south, and particularly in the south-western peninsula land-scapes of Somerset, Devon and Cornwall, the valleys still retain their distinctive unglaciated sharp edges and steep profiles.

Because air in the northern hemisphere circulates from west to east (the result of the earth's revolving as it orbits around the sun), most of Britain's weather systems come from the Atlantic. The air picks up water as it crosses the ocean and precipitates it over the hills of the south-west peninsula, and the mountains of Wales, Lancashire, the Lake District, Scotland and the Western Isles. By the time they have crossed the central upland spine of England and Scotland most clouds will have precipitated their rain, so the eastern part of the country tends to be far drier than the west.[1]

Although eastern Britain may be dry it can also experience greater extremes of hot and cold. From a gardening or farming perspective it is a far less forgiving climate than that further west, which is altogether gentler. Put another way, the climate of eastern Britain tends more towards the continental, whereas that of the west is more Atlantic or maritime. Climate is one of the factors that gives Britain its special character.

The weather may change from day to day, especially in the winter, when warm westerly breezes can suddenly be replaced by Arctic north-east gales, blowing in off the North Sea. Similarly, one can encounter very different conditions on either side of the Pennines: wet and windy to the west, dry and often sunny to the east. Being maritime, the climate of Britain is not simply dictated by latitude, so although Scotland may generally be colder than England, places such as the Black Isle (actually a peninsula in the Moray Firth) are bathed by the warm waters of the Gulf Stream, with the result that frosts are rarely harsh, and palm trees can survive in a manner that recalls Cornwall or southern Ireland.

Global warming has rightly become the greatest environmental issue of our time. This may have given rise to a tendency to attribute more to climate change than can actually be proved. We shall see that many of the important changes to the British landscape were caused by humans and not by climate alone. In some instances the climate may have played a contributory part, for example during the slightly wetter and colder conditions that prevailed in the centuries following 1000 BC and during the period of colder winters that characterized the Little Ice Age from AD 1300 to 1850. But with one exception, climate was never the prime mover, nor instigator of change. That single exception was the period of what has been described as 'astonishing' rapid warming, shortly after 8000 BC.[2] This led to a sharp rise in sea levels that gradually swamped the shores of Britain. The rapid increase in temperature allowed the familiar hardwood trees of Britain to spread north from the Continental mainland, but one or two were stranded by the formation of the English Channel, which is why a number of common plants, such as the green alder (*Alnus viridis*) are native to Holland and neighbouring parts of the European mainland, but not to Britain.[3]

THE LANDSCAPE OF BRITAIN IN EARLY POST-GLACIAL TIMES

The actual impact on the landscape of the bands of Palaeolithic hunters who inhabited Britain during the warmer episodes of the Ice Ages was probably very slight, so slight that almost all traces of their presence have been removed by the subsequent erosion of water and ice. So our story starts at the end of the Pleistocene period and the last of the Ice Ages, around 10,000 years ago (roughly 8000 BC).[4]

At the end of the Ice Age the great plain that underlies the southern North Sea basin was still largely dry. But water locked up in the polar, Scandinavian and central European ice caps was melting quite rapidly and sea levels were rising, as they have continued to do. In the early Mesolithic, communities along the eastern side of Britain could communicate with countries around the southern North Sea. But the journey would not have been at all straightforward and would have involved the crossing of numerous creeks, streams and marshes.

Today the marshes along the east coast and around the southern part of the North Sea basin are constantly changing. Some are very hazardous to the unwary traveller. The marshes around the southern end of the Wash, for example, have to be crossed with great care, because of quicksands and the sudden appearance of fast incoming, or 'rip', tides. The east coast of southern Britain may lack spectacular cliffs, but it more than compensates for this with extensive views and its rich and varied sources of food, such as wildfowl, samphire, fish, eels, crabs, mussels and shellfish.

It is not often acknowledged that Essex has the longest shoreline of any English county. Sometimes the marshes along the Essex coast can seem remote and even distant in time from the great capital city that lurks a few miles to the west. Terrain broadly similar to this would have continued across most of the southern North Sea basin until dry land was encountered. Then some landmark, such as the brightly coloured cliffs at Flamborough Head, Yorkshire, would have been an important signal that the long and hazardous journey was over. Around 9500 BC England from roughly the Humber to Sussex was directly linked by land to Denmark, the Low Countries and France, almost as far west as the Breton peninsula. Just thirteen centuries later (8200 BC), the last dry land bridge, roughly level with the Wash, still survived, but by 6900 BC Britain was surrounded by sea and salt marsh. It had become an island, much as we would recognize it today, by about 6000 BC.[5]

It would be a mistake to imagine that the land now flooded by the southern North Sea would have been a featureless marsh. Fens and marshes can be immensely variable. The numerous inlets, creeks and bays of the Essex coast around the Thames and Blackwater estuaries contrast with the more open country of the Wash, where high land is barely visible and where the only upstanding features are entirely modern: the earthen sea-defence banks and the tall flagpoles with their red warning flags along the NATO bombing ranges. The people who inhabited these landscapes would have been familiar with their constantly changing surroundings and would have known the current location of every creek and quicksand.

There are few, if any, surviving intact Mesolithic landscapes in Britain, but we now know a great deal about how the landscape developed in those crucially important post-glacial centuries, thanks to numerous pollen analyses and radiocarbon dates.

At the end of the last Ice Age 10,000 years ago the landscape of Britain was treeless open tundra, similar to northern Norway, Lapland and northern Siberia today, where reindeer graze the sparse vegetation of mosses, lichens and the few species of small summer plants that are able to cope with the short growing season.[6] Other animals able to survive in these conditions include the musk ox which, unlike the reindeer that migrate south to avoid the worst of the winter, stays put, protected by its massive woolly coat. Lemmings and arctic hares provided prey for wolves, arctic fox and stoat.

We know from finds of their bones and from a wealth of other indications that humans hunted reindeer in northern Europe during early, late and post-glacial times. It now seems clear that these hunters also operated in Britain and across the open plains of the North Sea.[7] We know this because of the discovery in 1882 in a gravel quarry at Earls Barton, in central Northamptonshire of a so-called Lyngby 'axe'.[8] These odd-looking implements, which resemble a perforated police-man's baton, have been well known on the Continent for some time. A stubby protrusion vaguely resembles an axe blade, which is how they acquired their name, but in actual fact they were probably multi-purpose tools used by reindeer hunters not just to club their prey, but to help with skinning and subsequent processing. The example from Earls Barton has been dated to just before 10,000 years ago. This would conveniently place it in the short final cold snap of the Ice Age, known as the Loch Lomond cold phase, when most of the North Sea would have been dry and ice sheets were confined to the highlands of north-west Scotland.

From before 8000 BC the climate became both progressively and quite rapidly warmer and soon the open, treeless plains were populated by birch and pine woodland, known as boreal forest. The equivalent of the boreal forests today is the vast areas of taiga that cover north-eastern Europe, northern Russia, Siberia and northern Canada. In Britain and northern Europe the post-glacial boreal forest phase can be dated to 7700–5500 BC or thereabouts. Its end conveniently coincides more or less with the onset of the Neolithic, although the gradual successional change from birch or pine forest to the more familiar mixed deciduous woodland was largely complete by about 6000 BC. The earliest radiocarbon dates for the first Neolithic settlements in Britain cluster around the centuries before and just after 4500 BC.

We tend to regard the North Sea as a permanent fixture that has fringed the eastern coasts of Britain for a very long time indeed. But that is not the case. We know of course that the North Sea is still encroaching on dry land, as the great barrier across the Thames at Woolwich attests. One of the more dramatic consequences of this is the almost complete disappearance of the large and prosperous medieval town of Dunwich, in Suffolk.[9] At the time of Domesday (1086) it was substantial, with a population of some 3,000, and three churches. By the thirteenth century it had eight parish churches, several friaries, town walls and two marketplaces, and rivalled Ipswich, the county's premier port. Even Domesday records that it was being eroded by the sea, but by 1300 St Leonard's church was lost and in 1328 the harbour was choked by sands after a particularly nasty storm. By 1350 more than 400 houses and other buildings had been lost. Today almost the entire town has vanished. I visit the coast near Dunwich quite often and never fail to be moved by the few surviving gravestones, leaning at strange angles in the dense undergrowth at the top of the cliffs.

Contrary to some popular ideas the marine encroachment that swamped places like Dunwich cannot be attributed entirely to global warming. Recent climate change may well be accelerating the process, but the general trend still remains a part of the widespread climatic amelioration that began in post-glacial times.[10]

'DOGGERLAND': THE LOST LANDSCAPES OF THE MESOLITHIC

Archaeologists have known that there are Mesolithic landscapes surviving on the bed of the North Sea since September 1931 when the sailing trawler *Colinda*, fishing in 19–20 fathoms of water about 40 kilometres off the Norfolk coast, between the submerged Leman and Ower sandbanks, dredged up a carved, barbed antler spearhead, of a type found on dryland sites dating to the eighth millennium BC.[11] It had been known for some time that the North Sea roughly between the north Norfolk and Yorkshire coasts is shallow; then in 1998 an imaginative and far-reaching study drew attention to its potential archaeological importance and dubbed this submerged landscape 'Doggerland' (after Dogger Bank).[12]

Today the bed of the North Sea has been surveyed and bored in the greatest detail by companies prospecting for oil and gas.[13] Using this information archaeologists are now re-creating a full reconstruction of the late glacial and Mesolithic landscapes of Doggerland.[14] The North Sea Palaeolandscapes Project shows how Britain originally extended almost as far east as Norway and how the land that is today East Anglia formed the watershed between rivers to the north, which drained into the North Sea, and south, where the Thames, Rhine and Seine all drained westwards into a large estuary that would eventually develop, shortly before 7000 BC, into the English Channel.[15] The detail the survey has revealed is truly astonishing, a submarine landscape of marshes, low hills, lakes and meandering rivers.[16]

Perhaps the most important conclusion to have arisen from the North Sea survey is that the majority of the population of north-western Europe, including Britain, would have been living on the undulating plains which are today beneath the North Sea. As sea levels began to rise after about 10,000 BC it is very likely that the population would have been subject to considerable stress, as people were forced to abandon some of their richest hunting grounds. Even as late as 8000 BC the area that was later to become the island of Britain would have been peripheral to the main settlement areas, still to be found well to the east, in Doggerland. These low-lying landscapes would have been rich in fish, shellfish, wildfowl and land mammals such as hares and deer. The generally thinner tree-cover often characteristic of salt marshes and alluvial plains would have made hunting very much simpler than in the more thickly wooded landscapes of what was later to become Britain.

Although a number of Mesolithic settlement sites have survived in Britain there are no intact or near-intact landscapes of that period, with the possible exception of parts of the Fens and the Vale of Pickering, where later peats have buried much earlier land surfaces. We can, however, still gain an impression of what the post-glacial woods might once have looked like. A large area of birch woodland, typical of the boreal forests, can clearly be seen from the comfort of the train about five minutes south of Peterborough station, on the east coast main line. These trees are growing in the peats of the Holme Fen National Nature Reserve, which includes some of the lowest-lying land in Britain, at about 2 metres below sea level.

Fig. 1.2 A view of birch woods surrounding a shallow, man-made mere in Holme Fen Nature Reserve, Cambridgeshire. The Holme Fen birch woods are among the largest in Britain and this scene would have been typical of many parts of Britain in the boreal period, following the last Ice Age, around 6500 BC.

LANDSCAPES OF INSULAR BRITAIN

Accounts of the changing landscapes of Britain traditionally begin with the Neolithic because, it was believed, Mesolithic hunter-gatherers had no reason to tamper with their surroundings, other perhaps than to make tiny clearings for their lightweight 'bender'-style houses. We know of several lightweight Mesolithic houses of this sort in both Britain and Ireland, probably fashioned from hooped hazel or willow poles and covered with hides. The evidence for them usually consists of a compacted floor area, surrounded by a ring of stake-holes.[17] So, in theory at least, it follows that the impact of Mesolithic communities on their landscapes would have been minimal. But there are a number of problems with such a perception.

The first is that even transportable Mesolithic houses were not necessarily flimsy and built to house just one or two people. Modern nomads build very weatherproof and comfortable structures that can house whole families and yet leave very slight traces in the ground.[18] Recent excavation has also revealed much more substantial, permanent-looking Mesolithic houses that might well have been inhabited for rather longer periods of time. Secondly, it seems likely that during the Mesolithic there were important changes in what one might term the perception or possession of one's landscape. During the Ice Ages many communities would have travelled widely, following reindeer and other seasonally available sources of food. So it has come to be accepted that these groups would not have owned or controlled particular tracts of landscape. They would not necessarily have regarded any specific place as 'home'; put another way, they would not have developed a communal 'sense of place'. All that was to change in post-glacial times, when the greater permanence of settlement helped to foster feelings of 'ownership' with regard to the landcape. It used to be believed that this shift of attitude did not happen until the arrival of farming in the Neolithic, but recent work in places like Star Carr in Yorkshire indicates that earlier Mesolithic communities in the mid-eighth millennium may have laid claim to their own home territories.

Fig. 1.3 A reconstruction of a Mesolithic house dating to about 7800 BC, in Northumberland. The foundations of this house were excavated at Howick, which today is a coastal site, but when it was built the house would have stood at the edge of the Great Doggerland Plain now beneath the North Sea. The dig also revealed more than 16,000 pieces of flint and bones of fox, dog or wolf, wild pig and birds.

It is difficult to exaggerate the importance of family or tribal territories in the development of the landscape. Once communities have identified a tract of country as belonging to them, they can treat it appropriately, marking out boundaries and agreeing where different families and kin groups could hunt and settle down. It is a process that can foster peace within a particular tribe but there is also the potential for conflict with other communities nearby. The laying out of tribal territories began a process of staking out and of subdivision of the landscape that has continued into the neatly partitioned suburban gardens of the present day. In the Neolithic period feelings of tribal territory and collective ownership were expressed by the construction of large ritual structures such as collective burial mounds and stone circles. The first of these monuments were constructed in the fifth millennium BC, but it now seems increasingly likely that the intellectual and social concepts that had given rise to them had already been in existence for some 3,000 years.

The third problem concerns the nature of the new permanent presence in the landscape. Was it simple, in the sense that people set up house somewhere, established the boundaries to their holding and never moved away, or was it permanent in a more flexible fashion? The latter is more probable in Britain, although in Ireland there seems to have been a greater degree of permanence in both the Mesolithic and Neolithic.[19] Anthropologists have observed communities make seasonal journeys between, say, lowland pasture in the winter and upland grazing in the summer. Such movements – known as transhumance – happened frequently, for example, in Wales during the Middle Ages, when specialized buildings were erected in the highlands to accommodate visiting shepherds.

The flexible pattern of permanent settlement probably took several forms. For a start, it did not necessarily involve the movement of the whole community, although in the earlier Mesolithic when woodland hunter-gatherers could have been organized into smaller bands, it is possible that entire family groups would have moved through the landcape, either following game, or seeking sources of raw materials. Thus the inhabitants of the early Mesolithic (c. 7500 BC) settlement at Star Carr, near Seamer in East Yorkshire, would regularly travel for a few hours east along to the Vale of Pickering to the coast near

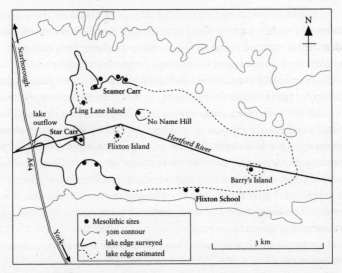

Fig. 1.4 A reconstructed map of the early post-glacial 'Lake Flixton', at the eastern end of the Vale of Pickering, North Yorkshire. The lake is surrounded by settlements and hunting camps of early Mesolithic communities (*c.* 7500 BC), including the well-known site of Star Carr. In Mesolithic times the Vale of Pickering was blocked by a glacial ridge, so the lake's outfall was to the west, belying the coast just 9 kilometres to the east. In modern times Hertford river drains the entire area and prevents it from reverting to a lake.

Flamborough Head, where high-quality flint was quarried from exposures in the cliffs.[20] Survey and excavations have shown that there were a number of settlements around 'Lake Flixton'.[21] Some were hunting camps, others more resembled home-bases. Sites were also found on the small islands within the lake. The spacing of these sites around the lake shores does not appear to be random and suggests that the various communities had agreed among themselves where they should settle. Undoubtedly there would have been numerous boundary disputes, but the overall layout seems rational and there can be little doubt that the people living in the various settlements would have regarded their part, or parts, of Lake Flixton as 'home'. It is known that the area was richly stocked with large mammals, and the inhabitants of Star Carr probably used it as a seasonal hunting camp. 'Lake Flixton' and the land immediately around it was an area of stability:

it was wooded, not prone to flooding and was protected by the nearby valley-side of the Vale of Pickering. It was therefore ideally suited for hunting and communities living there were relatively sedentary; certainly they had no need or incentive to travel long distances.

The people who lived around the edges of 'Lake Flixton' would have recognized the landscape as belonging to them, the more so that it was so richly endowed with natural resources.[22] Their regularly travelled routes to places like Flamborough Head would have formed a part of this landscape and they would have put their own mark on the place, for example preparing crossing places over streams, felling trees or clearing scrub to improve access along the way. We do know that they were perfectly capable of felling trees with flint axes.[23] Actions such as these certainly modified the landscape, but we have no idea of how extensive they might have been.

There are other reasons why Mesolithic people should have chosen to modify their landscape. Take the reed-fringed margins of the long-vanished 'Lake Flixton'. Regular summer firing of these extensive reed beds would have encouraged vigorous regrowth which would have tempted deer and other game to graze there in large numbers.[24] Similar techniques could also have been used to create clearings in and on the edges of woodlands. Again, animals would come to these spots to eat the new grass and emerging young shoots. Plants such as hazel and blackberry grow back vigorously after firing and this may help to account for the large quantities of burnt hazelnut shells found on many Mesolithic, Neolithic and early Bronze Age sites.[25] Firing could also have been used to clear areas in woodland around places where animals came to drink. In the open they would present easier targets to hunters concealed nearby.

If deliberately set fires ran out of control, they could have caused much larger problems. In certain areas where soils are thin or fragile, a serious forest or scrub fire could lead to erosion and the consequent establishment of upland moors, whose heathers and bracken are better adapted to thin soils with poor nutrients. This might help to explain the earliest stages in the formation of many British upland moors.[26]

The problem with suggesting – however plausibly – that Mesolithic communities altered their landscape lies in actually pinning down hard supportive evidence from independent sources, such as pollen analyses.

At present there seems no doubt that, in Britain (but so far not on the Continental mainland), fire had been used as a means of managing woodland and woodland-fringe resources since earlier Mesolithic times. We saw that fire could have been used deliberately in the Star Carr area and recent research along the Severn estuary and elsewhere has clearly demonstrated that the practice continued into the later Mesolithic and Neolithic, long after Britain had become separated from the mainland.[27]

One area that has produced a number of important archaeological finds over the past century or more is the generally flat and low-lying land between the Yorkshire wolds and the North Sea, north of the Humber estuary and south of Flamborough Head. This area is known as Holderness, and in Mesolithic times it must have been a paradise for hunters and fishers, very much like the landscape around Star Carr, just a short distance to the north. It has been estimated that there might have been seventy or more shallow lakes, known as meres, in Holderness in early post-glacial times, around 10,000 years ago.[28] Some of these were still in existence in medieval times, but only one, Hornsea Mere, still contains water today.

Shallow lakes could easily be fished with the technology available to Mesolithic people, and the richness and diversity of archaeological finds from the area around Hornsea Mere suggest quite a high resident population. No fewer than seventeen barbed bone-and-antler spearheads have been found in the channel of the relict stream that flowed out of the mere and into the Humber.

As sea levels continued to rise throughout the seventh to fifth millennia BC, the majority of the British population, who lived along river valleys, around the coast and its hinterland, would have lost up to half their territory to the sea. Environmental and archaeological evidence shows that the tidal marshes and mudflats were where communities spent time during the summer months, and it seems probable that the increased use of burning that is becoming evident in later Mesolithic times could also have been a social response by people who needed to place their own mark on a rapidly shrinking environment.[29] At Star Carr we discussed the early stages of landscape partition, in which groups of people identified areas of land (in that instance the shores and islands of 'Lake Flixton') as belonging to them. This may have been a process that just happened naturally, as populations grew and the rich resources of the area were able to feed the new mouths. But there could also have been an external stimulus or catalyst that hastened matters. There is only one contender, and that has to be the increasingly swift encroachment of the North Sea across some of the richest low-lying hunting and fishing grounds in northern Europe.[30] Inevitably this must have caused pressure on hunting land and the need to establish control of a rapidly diminishing resource.

We naturally tend to focus on the North Sea basin when we consider the processes whereby Britain became an island, but in many respects the changes that were happening further west were just as drastic. Take the case of the Severn estuary and the Bristol Channel. Today this area is famous for having the world's second largest tidal range, of over 13 metres. But at the close of the Ice Age it was a tranquil shallow valley with a river running along the centre. As water levels rose from about 10,000 BC the changes were increasingly dramatic and the communities living along the river which became a tidal estuary were forced to move onto higher ground. This seems to have had the effect of concentrating them together, so that today the remains of Mesolithic settlements can frequently be found along both sides of the foreshore. The discoveries on the Welsh side in the Severn Levels have been particularly exciting and have included submerged forests, settlements and perhaps most remarkable of all, the footprints of animals and of men, women and children preserved in the tidal muds. Children tend to be eclipsed from the archaeological record, but the Severn footprints show that they must have played an important part in the family economy, walking the sometimes treacherous muddy shores to gather shellfish and sea-weed, where their light weight would have helped them traverse the many quicksands.

BURIAL MOUNDS, RITUAL AND RELIGION

Historians traditionally tended to talk about a sharp break between the incoming farmers of the Neolithic and the 'native' Mesolithic hunter-gatherers. A growing body of evidence now suggests that there was some continuity between the hunter-gatherers of the Mesolithic and the first farmers of the Neolithic. The clearest examples may be seen in many areas of lowland Britain, where surface scatters of both earlier Neolithic and later Mesolithic flints occur together in precisely the same places. Very often excavation of these flint scatters reveals little or nothing in the subsoil beneath them. This might suggest that the flints represent the remains of a temporary camp or shelter which did not involve the digging of pits or holes for posts, but in most instances this apparent absence of archaeological remains can be shown to have been caused by modern ploughing, which has obliterated all shallow features, such as hearths and post-holes. In river floodplains and fens, where preservation is much better, it can now be demonstrated beyond reasonable doubt that certain areas were repeatedly selected for settlement, both before and after the introduction of farming.[31] Such a detailed and intimate knowledge of the landscape suggests it was the same people who settled there.

It seems probable that for a short period of maybe a few centuries, hunter-gatherers and farmers lived side by side. Indeed, in many instances the first farmers were probably the same people as the last hunter-gatherers. There is a tendency to think in terms of cowboys and Indians – of ranches versus forest. In reality a more open environment of secondary (that is, regrowth) woodland, or scrub, may actually have been beneficial to hunters, foragers and farmers alike. Indeed, it is quite conceivable that the early process of forest clearance may have been one of the factors that ultimately brought the two patterns of life together.

The most frequently quoted difference between hunter-gatherers and farmers is the appearance in the Neolithic period of ritual, or religion, in the form of communal burial mounds. Thousands must have been constructed. Even today, the distinctive wedge-shaped Neolithic long barrows are a feature, if not a common one, of the British landscape. It used to be believed that hunter-gatherers were too preoccupied chasing after their elusive quarry to have the time to engage with religion, and that this explained the absence of Mesolithic burials or cemeteries in Britain. Excavations of later Mesolithic cemeteries on the mainland of Europe showed clear evidence for careful and highly ritualized burials.[32] Similarly in Britain, Professor Clark's excavations at Star Carr between 1949 and 1951 had produced a number of red deer antler headdresses which are widely seen as having been used during shamanistic ceremonies, possibly associated in some way with hunting.

So the idea that hunter-gatherers were religiously backward had to be abandoned, yet the notion persisted that their religion, like other aspects of their way of life, was somehow ephemeral and of little significance. If anything, this gained in strength, as during the 1960s and 1970s archaeologists in Britain and on the Continent revealed more and better evidence for the richness of earlier Neolithic funerary and ceremonial structures. The contrast with what was believed to have happened in the Mesolithic became increasingly marked. But at about this time, too, archaeologists in Denmark revealed substantial Mesolithic cemeteries, where the dead had been buried with elaborate ceremony. Mesolithic cemeteries will probably also be found in Britain – one day. Perhaps these hunter-gatherers' cemeteries had similar roles to their Neolithic equivalents, which were both monuments to the ancestors and drew widely separated communities together for regular gatherings. Communal tombs also provided boundary markers in landscapes that were just starting the process of partition.

The first good evidence that Mesolithic and Neolithic people regarded certain key places in the landscape as being specially important for religious reasons, came as recently as 1966, when work was begun on the current car park at Stonehenge.[33] During excavations in advance of construction the pit-like post-holes for three large pine posts were discovered in a row, and twenty-two years later another, slightly off-line, was found. Normally one would expect Neolithic and Bronze Age posts in southern Britain to be of oak, but when the traces of wood were identified they were shown to be of Scots pine. The charcoal was radiocarbon-dated to around 8500–7650 BC. This would explain why pine was used, because oak had yet to recolonize this part of southern England so soon after the Ice Age. It seems inconceivable, given what we know about earlier Mesolithic houses, that these very substantial posts, which were the size of a large telegraph pole, could ever have formed part of a house. So we can only conclude that they formed part of a ceremonial or religious shrine of some sort. But what about their extraordinarily early date? Surely a gap of more than 4,000 years must

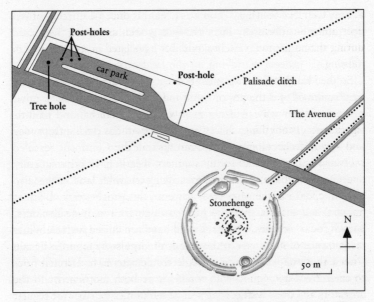

Fig. 1.5 Four holes for very large pine posts, radiocarbon-dated to the Mesolithic period (c. 8000 BC), were found in the Stonehenge car park, off the A344, about 100 metres north-east of the Stones. A possible 'tree throw pit' (the scar left in the ground when a large tree blows over) nearby may have been a fifth post-hole. The main Stonehenge site dates to about 2500 BC and a post-built palisade was erected around 2200 BC when Stonehenge was still in use.

rule out any continuity with Neolithic Stonehenge. But one cannot be certain.

It has been shown, by pollen analysis and other techniques, that in the Neolithic and Bronze Age such shrines stood in open, treeless country where they could be better appreciated; and this may well have applied earlier, too. Although there is a danger of assuming that a post-built wooden shrine had to be situated in open country, we shall see in the next chapter that earlier ideas concerning the thickly wooded post-glacial British landscape are beginning to be replaced by a rather different concept in which certain areas are thickly wooded, but others were open, covered by scrub, or lightly wooded.[34]

The first step in trying to reconstruct the landscape surrounding somewhere like Stonehenge is to reconstruct its appearance. We have already seen that Salisbury Plain was probably even more treeless than it is today, but the really big difference would have been the actual surface of the ground, which would not have been as smooth as it is today. This process of tidying up the landscape can be seen in the 'clearance cairns' of the uplands. These are large heaps of stones that were removed to the edges of fields and settlements to make farming easier. Because such cairns are mainly found in the hills we tend to forget that in rocky areas elsewhere in Britain the land surface was also very different from what we can see today.

Over the centuries farmers in southern Britain have systematically removed and broken up all large rocks lying on arable land. In the later Neolithic and early Bronze Age, however, this process was only just starting, and in areas like the Marlborough Downs, huge boulders, known today as Grey Wethers, would have strewn the surface. While the presence of hundreds of thousands of large boulders would have altered the look of the landscape, it would also have affected how people moved through it, with roads for example skirting round the biggest rocks. Grey Wethers can still be seen in one or two rare places, including a small National Trust property at Lockeridge Dene, near

Fig. 1.6 Sarsen 'Grey Wethers' in a field at Lockeridge Dene, near Marlborough, Wiltshire.

Marlborough, Wiltshire. The stones acquired the name Grey Wethers because of their supposed resemblance to sheep (a wether is a castrated male). I shall have more to say in the next two chapters about the current long-term research project into the Stonehenge landscape.[35] It has long been believed that the largest stones of Stonehenge, which are of a very hard sandstone, known as sarsen, were transported from a source some 30 kilometres away in the Marlborough Downs. But it is now apparent that at least two large sarsen boulders in the immediate vicinity of the famous Stones had always been there, just lying on the surface like the Grey Wethers of Lockeridge Dene.[36] Then in late Neolithic times they were tipped up into a freshly excavated pit and wedged in place, to stand vertical. The huge Heel Stone, close by the road (the A344) that passes directly by the Stones, is a case in point – and a very large one, at that. If it was lying on the surface around 2500 BC it must also have been there 4,000 years earlier, when it would have stood out in such a treeless landscape as a vast rock – just the sort of feature that prehistoric communities might have regarded as religiously important. It may have been the presence, just a few metres away, of the Heel Stone that led to the erection of those vast Mesolithic pine posts.

The idea that certain places were believed by ancient people to be important in and of themselves is now widely accepted.[37] As ever, the problems begin when concrete proof of the antiquity of such beliefs is required. The Stonehenge car park posts are proof of a sort, but must still be considered enigmatic. Numerous flint scatters across Britain might hint at continuity from Mesolithic to Neolithic times, but again, these are hardly conclusive. Similarly it has been observed that some of the earliest Neolithic field monuments – known as causewayed enclosures – often seem to have been deliberately positioned just off the crown of a hill, or to one side of a bend in a river, suggesting perhaps that the landscape feature was actually more important than the monument that was subsequently positioned in or on it.[38]

Burials are often a good indicator of a society's beliefs and ultimate aspirations, although they should not be studied without caution, because very often they represent what people think is right and proper rather than the world as it actually exists. One example will suffice. Take the current burial of Christian British monarchs in coffins without

Fig. 1.7 The burial of the 'Red Lady' (in fact, a young man) in Goat's Hole Cave, Paviland, on the Gower Peninsula, south Wales. It was found in the early nineteenth century when the covering of red ochre powder led to its misinterpretation as a 'scarlet woman'. The burial itself and the subsequent repeated use of the cave are good evidence that this was regarded as one of the very earliest places of special religious importance in the British landscape.

lavish grave-goods. These burials indicate that everyone is equal in the eyes of God. But the selection of a fine tomb within a great cathedral or royal chapel suggests a rather different view of their place in the real world. So far as we know, human beings have always treated their dead with respect. We have known about the Neanderthal cemetery at Mount Carmel, in Israel, since the 1930s and we also know from Continental sites of the Mesolithic and Upper Palaeolithic that prehistoric people in northern Europe had respected their dead for tens of thousands of years.[39] In Britain there is the famous example of the 'Red Lady' burial within Goat's Hole Cave, Paviland, on the Gower Peninsula, south Wales. This burial, of a modern human, *Homo sapiens* man, belongs within the Upper Palaeolithic and can be dated to about 27,000 years ago.[40] The body had been treated with reverence and the funeral rites included coating the corpse with red ochre powder which most probably symbolized blood, and thereby the life force.[41] There is other evidence from this cave that people had been respecting it as a place of special importance, most probably for centuries, and were prepared to travel for hundreds of miles just to go there. So it seems reasonable to suggest that the paucity of evidence for the construction of ritual sites in Mesolithic and earlier times does not mean they did not care about such things. It suggests that people did not think it necessary to construct great monuments. Instead they treated particular parts of the natural landscape, such as the Goat's Hole Cave, with special reverence.

Many of the caves of south Wales, like the Goat's Hole, have produced quantities of loose and disturbed human bones in addition to a handful of well-known intact burials. Some of these may prove to be the disturbed remains of Mesolithic burials.[42] This would help to explain the apparent lack of Mesolithic graves in Britain where earlier, essentially Upper Palaeolithic, rites continued in use after the retreat of the ice.[43] In places like Denmark, where there are no caves, communities developed new practices which reflected their reliance on coastal resources. In Wales, however, seasonal patterns of Mesolithic migration would also have included the uplands along the coast where many of the caves, like the Goat's Hole Cave are situated.

ISLAND LANDSCAPES

This book is about the landscapes of Britain and there is a natural tendency to concentrate attention on the mainland, if only because access to the offshore islands can so often be a problem. But the latter have landscapes, too, and these can also be of considerable interest. In many instances island communities developed settlements and landscapes that might seem idiosyncratic, when viewed from a mainland perspective, but which were the product of indigenous insular development. Just as island plant and animal species evolved in unusual ways, humans, too, often demonstrate an inventiveness and originality that might be thought of as an 'island effect'. Archaeologists have sometimes described islands as 'laboratories', where the evolution of societies can be studied without some of the complexities to be found on the mainland. I find that debatable. The organization of small communities can be just as intricate as that of a large city. It is a question of scale.

There has also been a tendency in the past to regard islands as somehow remote.[44] Indeed, the word 'insular' has acquired connotations of backwardness, impoverishment and so forth. Islands, like anywhere else, can indeed become social and cultural backwaters, but backwaters are not always impoverished. Sometimes they may develop their own unique characteristics.[45] While the communities on islands might have chosen to lead remote lives, they did not lead isolated lives; this was because in the past many islands were centres of communication. They were surrounded by water, which was more

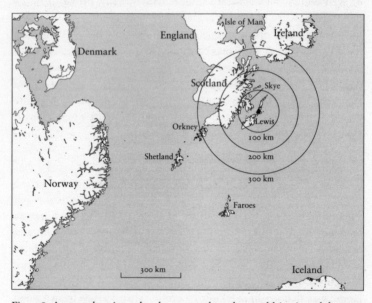

Fig. 1.8 A map showing what happens when the world is viewed from an island's perspective and the convention of placing north at the top is abandoned. This map shows the lands and waters of the northern North Sea and North Atlantic as they might have been viewed by the inhabitants of the Outer Hebrides in pre-modern times. Given the dangers of heading west into the gales of the Atlantic Ocean, Norway and Denmark would have been more readily accessible than the coast of southern England.

readily and rapidly crossed than the poor roads and trackways of dry land. This may help to explain why certain islands, such as Crete, Malta or the Orkneys, were such important centres of prehistoric culture and trade.

In the past two hundred years it has become standard in the Western world to draw maps with north at the top; at the same time – and largely for economic reasons – maps and atlases have tended to concentrate on larger land masses where the bulk of the population reside. These factors have led to the imposition of artificial perceptions on landscapes and seascapes that might have been viewed very differently in the past. Fishing communities, for example, will pay greater attention to the open sea and coastal waters than to what might be happening inland. The realization that islands were central, rather than peripheral, has led to their re-evaluation in terms of overseas contacts. Thus the Western Isles (the Outer Hebrides) are a few days' sail from Ireland, the Isle of Man, and even north-west England. The Northern Isles (Orkneys and Shetlands) are only another day or two further away from Ireland and are surprisingly close to the eastern Scottish coast. Even Norway and Denmark, which we think of today as being very distant, were part of the same maritime region. This tradition of overseas contact probably has very ancient roots. In the Neolithic the links between Orkney and the British mainland were remarkably close and reflect most aspects of life, from pottery to houses and ritual monuments, such as stone circles and collective tombs. Moreover, the exchange of ideas was by no means one-sided and there is now much evidence to suggest that new concepts originated in Orkney, just as much as the mainland.

So how would the landscape of Britain have looked in the early to mid-fifth millennium BC? The answer is not simple. The old idea of an all-enveloping dense woodland can safely be set to one side, but trees, woods and forests would have been far more evident than in the subsequent Neolithic and Bronze Age.[46] Signs of human settlement would have been most obvious around the coast, up river valleys and along the shores of lochs and lakes. In certain fragile environments, such as exposed islands, and areas which today are bog or moorland, felled or burnt trees would not grow again and in these regions permanent heathland and upland peats were starting to become established.

Far from being a trackless forest, it would have been an extraordinarily rich and diverse landscape.

The relationship of the Mesolithic to the Neolithic has important implications for the subsequent development of the British landscape. If indeed there was a slower and more gradual transition between the two periods, then it seems likely that some of the innovations hitherto attributed to Neolithic farmers, such as the opening up of forest cover and the development of trackways and ceremonial centres, may have origins one or two millennia earlier than 4200 BC, the date we currently believe that the most important landscape changes of the Neolithic period started to happen. In another fifty years' time prehistorians may see the modern era starting at the end of the Ice Age, rather than the onset of the Neolithic.

2

The First Farmers (4500–2500 BC)

We take it for granted that the world's population can be numbered in billions, yet we rarely pause to consider how this extraordinary state of affairs has been made possible. The answer ultimately lies back in the Neolithic, when mankind first mastered the arts of farming. Without these new skills human beings would never have been able to acquire the food needed to fill so many bellies.

The idea of food-production happened at various times and in different parts of the world. The origins of the types of farming that were adopted in Britain and north-western Europe lie in the Near East, around the so-called 'fertile crescent' at the head of the rivers Tigris and Euphrates, in modern Iraq. After several millennia farming started to spread into south-eastern Europe, from Iraq, by way of Anatolia (Turkey), after about 6000 BC.[1] Radiocarbon dates now show that the first farmers eventually arrived in Britain shortly after 4500 BC.

The adoption of farming was to transform the landscapes of Britain and Europe. The very first farmers to arrive crossed the Channel in seagoing vessels, bringing with them seed wheat and barley and basic breeding groups of sheep and cattle. Pig (wild boar) already existed in Britain, and dogs had been domesticated from wolves several millennia previously (dog bones have been recovered from the earlier Mesolithic site at Star Carr, in Yorkshire). Horses were to appear somewhat later, early in the Bronze Age, around 2000 BC.[2] The introduction of farming to Britain was part of a wider European phenomenon: the transition from hunter-gatherer to farmer was happening between about 3800 BC in Norway and Sweden and slightly earlier (around 4300 BC) in Denmark and north Germany.[3]

There have been various attempts to subdivide the British Neolithic.

I am opting here for a simple system of just two phases, an earlier (4500–3000 BC) and later (3000–2500 BC). The earlier period is one of transition from the hunter-gatherer way of life, but it is distinctively Neolithic from the outset. This period sees the construction of the first communal long barrows (where the mound is made up from earth) and cairns (where rocks are used instead of earth). Towards the latter part of the earlier Neolithic, around 3500 BC, the first non-funerary field monuments, the causewayed enclosures, appear in the landscape, mostly of southern Britain. These monuments were of fundamental importance.

Geneticists and others reckon that the introduction of farming involved population movement.[4] Perhaps one in four, or one in five, Neolithic Britons would have been an incomer. It was not the arrival of new people so much as new ideas that had such a profound effect. Prehistorians have talked in terms of a Neolithic 'package', which included farming, but which also contained technological improvements, such as the introduction of the first heat-based process, the making of pottery, and an entirely new way of fashioning stone tools, by grinding rather than flaking or chipping. One of the most important items in the package was entirely non-practical and had to do with the burial of the dead in collective tombs under a wedge-shaped mound, known as a long barrow, and the construction of the first ceremonial centres or meeting places, known as causewayed enclosures. I shall discuss barrows and causewayed enclosures shortly, but now I want to consider the introduction and adoption of farming. First, however, we must clear the trees, because without sunlight neither grass nor crops can flourish.

THE NEOLITHIC 'REVOLUTION'

At this point I want briefly to discuss a concept that will be a recurrent theme in this book. It concerns the idea of 'revolutions'. The best known British revolution is undoubtedly the Industrial Revolution, and we shall come to that much later (Chapters 11 and 13). The Industrial Revolution is often coupled with a near-contemporary agricultural revolution because without it the workforce needed to operate the new mills and factories would have starved. But there is a third, lesser known, revolution that became popular in academic circles in the 1950s and still resurfaces from time to time. It is known as the Neolithic revolution and has to do with momentous changes brought about by the introduction of farming.[5] It is not hard to see why this idea of a prehistoric revolution came into existence. Farmers need to settle down to weed and protect their crops both from grazing animals and raiders; they must also guard their stored grain over winter; they must assist newborn lambs and calves into this world and they must then protect them from wolves and attack from outside. People and animals must be prevented from trespassing onto growing crops. All of this means that farmers require permanent places in which to live and work. Farms need to be clearly marked out on the ground and each holding must be acknowledged by everyone in the community.

The traditional view is that farmers require the countryside be cleared of trees and parcelled up. Modern evidence suggests that in actual fact the degree of clearance that was obtained, or indeed required, would have varied from one region to another. Whatever actually happened by way of clearance, permanent markers of some sort – be they trackways, standing stones, barrows, single trees or hedges – would then be needed to fix the agreed boundaries. These are the first steps in the formation of what today we would regard as an organized landscape, and many of them probably started in the Mesolithic. The big objection concerns the initial adoption of farming. The conventional view is that a mixed farming 'package' was adopted across the board at the onset of the Neolithic in Britain. In actual fact the process was far more gradual. Mesolithic hunters, like their Upper Palaeolithic reindeer-hunting predecessors, effectively 'managed' the behaviour of their prey. We know they possessed dogs and it does not require a major leap of imagination to suppose that these could have been used both as hounds and as sheepdogs, to round up potential quarry. So most of the essential skills needed to be a livestock farmer would already have been present in late Mesolithic times. This probably explains why livestock farming alone was first taken up in areas of north-western Europe, such as Britain and Scandinavia.[6] Once the first domesticated cattle, sheep and pigs arrived, the processes of animal husbandry then developed naturally. The other components of farming (cereals, etc.) then followed a little later.

Revolutions, by definition, happen quickly. Processes happen gradually. Even when it had arrived in Britain, sometime after 4500 BC, farming in its varied forms took a full millennium to reach all corners of the island. This is hardly revolutionary progress.

So the first farmers were very much part of a wider pan-European phenomenon, but at the same time the way that farming first appeared in Britain and the north-western fringes of Atlantic Europe was rather different from how it spread across the central European plains. This may have reflected the fact that the idea or concept of farming had travelled faster and in advance of the new population of farmers, so that by the time the first farmers reached the outer fringes of Europe the local hunter-gatherer population had already modified their own way of life to accommodate them.

CLEARING THE TREES

Most accounts of the impact of Neolithic farmers on the landscape tend to concentrate on the clearance of the deciduous woodlands that had replaced the boreal forests of the earlier Mesolithic. This is usually portrayed as a simple process of felling hundreds of trees with stone axes. But experiments have shown that it would have taken groups of men with stone axes up to a day to have felled some of the massive oaks that we know were growing in the primeval woodlands. Some could have been felled slowly by pigs scuffling around their roots, by animals or people removing the bark, or by cutting through the roots and then toppling the tree over, using long ropes made from climbing plants such as honeysuckle.[7] Although this sounds improbable, many forest trees do not have a strong, carrot-like central taproot. Radiating surface roots can actually be cut through quite easily. Indeed, the large upside-down oak tree that formed the central feature of 'Seahenge', the early Bronze Age timber circle at Holme-next-the-Sea, Norfolk, had probably been uprooted in this way. A honeysuckle towing rope was found around it.[8]

There is another route to forest clearance that also avoids the necessity for wholesale tree-felling with stone axes. There is now pollen evidence to suggest that in certain parts of the English Midlands the removal of a few large trees would have breached the otherwise tight leaf canopy that formed the 'roof' of the forest. We know that trees of this sort were felled to provide the massive oak timbers of the mortuary structure beneath the long barrow at Haddenham, in Cambridgeshire (c. 3500 BC).[9] Once allowed in, rain and wind would start to erode the soft leaf compost or 'brown-earth' soil of the forest floor, no longer held in place by tree roots. The result would be the collapse of further big trees and, in time, the destruction of larger tracts of forest.[10]

Large areas of woodland would never have been suitable for clearance. We shall see that many areas with heavy clay soils were not completely cleared until very much later. Instead, people learnt to live with them and to turn the woodland to their own advantage, by extracting firewood and coppice products and by keeping pigs. Wetlands are usually thought of in terms of reeds, swamps and marshes

Fig. 2.1 A buried forest landscape brought to the surface by ploughing, at Holme Fen, near Whittlesey, Cambridgeshire. The Scots pine stumps that cover this field probably date to the Bronze Age and were growing on dry peats that had been accumulating in Holme Fen since about 2500 BC. Wet areas such as this would not have benefited from tree-clearance in prehistoric times.

but this was not always the case. In many instances peats were able to accumulate and thereby raise the land surface, giving rise at first to a very wet woodland, known as alder carr, and latterly to drier birch and pine woodland. This process happened in the Fens and the pine forests that grew there in the Neolithic are still sometimes brought to the surface by the plough.

It is also possible that trees were not only removed to make way for grass, cereals or settlements. Large areas of the countryside could have been cleared for non-practical reasons. We shall see shortly that certain types of Neolithic ceremonial sites could only be appreciated in an open landscape. But there is no reason why woodland clearance must always have been for a practical purpose. Land may sometimes have been cleared of trees for religious or ceremonial reasons – after all Neolithic people thought little about transporting huge stones from west Wales to Stonehenge for no practical purpose whatsoever.

FARMING AND THE TRANSITION FROM MESOLITHIC TO NEOLITHIC

Cranborne Chase is an area of chalk downland in northern Dorset, immediately south-west of Salisbury. It has been the subject of intensive archaeological research going right back to the nineteenth century. The work was began by General Augustus Lane-Fox, known to generations of archaeologists as Pitt-Rivers, the father of modern archaeology.[11] Pitt-Rivers owned large estates in Cranborne Chase and he developed effective methods of excavation that owed a great deal to the discipline of his military background. He was a most remarkable man: a pioneer of excavation, archaeological display, publication and communication.

Thanks to the researches of Pitt-Rivers and many others after him, Cranborne Chase is now one of the most intensively studied areas in Britain. Recent work has centred around Down Farm, where a long-term project has revealed how the region was farmed and how the environment changed through time.[12] Pollen grains require wet and acid conditions for their survival, so another indicator of past environments had to be found for the dry alkaline soils of its chalk downland. Snails, or rather their shells, have provided the answer. Many snails are very selective about the conditions in which they live.[13] Like plants, some types prefer sun, others shade; some like it wet, others dry.

The lack of information on the general environment can in part be compensated for by another, complementary analytical technique known as soil micromorphology.[14] This technique examines the development of soil structure by means of a series of thin sections which are viewed under high magnification. Using soil micromorphology we can see how the so-called 'brown-earth' soils of the early woodlands are replaced by soils that developed on ploughed and pasture fields.

The snails and micromorphology taken together have shown that many large scatters of Mesolithic flint debris across Down Farm were deposited in an essentially open, treeless environment.[15] This would explain why the region became so popular in Neolithic times, because farmers would pragmatically be drawn to landscapes that were already clear of woodland. The specialist who conducted the snail study is further convinced that other archaeologically important areas of downland, such as the region around Stonehenge, were largely treeless.[16] But open country was far from universal: Neolithic Avebury, for example, was a wooded landscape. As we shall see repeatedly throughout this book, generalizations are difficult to maintain in landscape studies, especially when a particular region is examined closely.

Once cleared, for whatever reason (including, for example, natural or induced forest fire), woodland vegetation can be slow to regenerate and as a result open clearings are not hard to find. The sandy soils of the southern Fen margins are such an area. Positioned directly alongside the natural ecological richness and diversity of the developing fen it is not surprising that they were intensively settled in both Mesolithic and early Neolithic times.[17] People living on the safe, flood-free land of the fen-edge could exploit the neighbouring wetland for fish, eels, wildfowl, reeds for thatch and wood for fuel. Often the features of sites selected for settlement were the same or closely similar.[18]

So far our examples of Mesolithic and Neolithic settlement have been taken from areas of Britain where the evidence is relatively abundant. By contrast, the heavy clay soils of the English Midland counties centring on Leicestershire and Rutland have traditionally been seen as areas of dense and impenetrable woodland whose heavy soils could not have been broken by primitive ploughs. It was believed that this was the only explanation for the extreme rarity, or absence, of any finds. So the conventional wisdom grew up that prehistoric and early post-Roman (Saxon) people had stayed clear of the region. Over the past thirty years or so detailed research has revealed overwhelming evidence for prehistoric settlement in the Midlands.[19] The finds had always been there, but it required diligent and professional searching to reveal them. Some have been spectacular, such as the recent discovery of an early Bronze Age barrow cemetery at Lockington in Leicestershire that revealed, among other items, objects of gold and copper rivaling anything produced in Wessex, the area traditionally regarded as the cultural centre for southern Britain in the Neolithic and Bronze Age.[20]

The evidence for prehistoric settlement in Leicestershire and Rutland is undeniable, but such soils are very hard to plough, especially with a rather blunt prehistoric plough (known as an ard). So what was going on? It has been suggested that occupation of the clay soils of the Midlands was some form of on-the-fringes marginal settlement, where people eked out an existence by continuing to hunt and gather. But this seems unlikely, if for no other reason than the discovery of otherwise standard Neolithic sites, such as long barrows and a large causewayed enclosure at Husband's Bosworth, in south Leicestershire. Sites of this sort invariably go with farming. As usual, too, animal bones were abundant at the causewayed enclosure and these exhibit a huge preponderance of domesticated species over wild.

Leicestershire and Rutland contain 281 parishes, of which 179 (64 per cent) have revealed finds or other evidence (for example, cropmarks on aerial photographs) of Neolithic and Bronze Age date. These parishes occur right across both counties and include all the areas of heavier clay soils. So far the evidence shows that woodland was cleared much more slowly in these east Midland counties than elsewhere in lowland Britain. So how does one explain this? The widely accepted view is that the first farmers accommodated to the woodland simply by the scale of their operations, which were small and relatively isolated.[21] Even so, by the end of the early Bronze Age clearance of woodland was starting to be significant. Elsewhere in Britain recent research has made it increasingly clear that most of the broad river valleys of the lowlands had been cleared of trees by the end of the

Neolithic, and probably somewhat earlier (say 3000 BC) in many key regions, such as the middle Thames Valley, or the Welland/Nene valleys and the plain surrounding the western Fen margins. In these areas, like the naturally open landscape of Salisbury Plain around Stonehenge, the large number of earlier Neolithic monuments (for example, causewayed enclosures and long barrows) would make no sense if they had been erected in woodland.

These early farmers of the heavy Midland soils grew crops in small clearings and made use of the woods for their animals. I should add here that pigs are not the only domesticated breed to feed in woodland. In my experience sheep, and especially primitive sheep, would much rather browse leaf fodder than graze grass, and I have seen a large flock of the most primitive British breed, the Soay, whose roots lie in the Neolithic, successfully weather a harsh winter in thick alder and willow woodland around some disused gravel pits in south Lincolnshire. They survived by eating dead reeds, scrubby grasses and bark (and the sapwood below it). By the end of winter they were in better condition than many commercial sheep.

Recent research is beginning to reveal the great variety of Neolithic farming practices across Britain. It is becoming clear, for example, that early farming on the natural 'islands' and on the drier margins of the Fens differed radically from that of the English Midlands or from that much further west, in Wales.

So far research has not revealed any bona fide Neolithic fields in Britain, but quite elaborate stone-walled fields have been found at several places in western Ireland. These fields include burial monuments, known as court cairns, together with small family farms. The latest radiocarbon dates suggest that the western Irish Céide fields had been constructed by 3700 BC and had gone out of use by 3200 BC, when they were covered by peat.[22] These astonishingly early dates reinforce the impression given by the discovery of numerous contemporary houses that the Neolithic population of Ireland was relatively much larger than that of mainland Britain.

NEOLITHIC FARMS AND FARMING

Traditionally the Neolithic and Bronze Age in Britain have been seen as periods dominated by cereal farming. This was because cereals played an important part in the ancient agriculture of those areas of the Near East, such as Iraq, where farming began. The big problem here is a simple one: the Near East is very dry, whereas Britain most certainly is not.

There is also a tendency on the part of archaeologists and historians who have never had any experience of practical farming to assume that many practices which are second nature to us today somehow took a long time to be discovered. It has taken some time, for example, for it to be accepted that coppicing must have been a regular part of Neolithic life, or that milking (and with it cheese-making) was not a later result of animal husbandry, given the high-sounding academic label, 'the Secondary Products Revolution'.[23] Far from milk being a secondary product, any farmer knows that the first thing to be done after a lamb or calf is born is to check the mother's milk. This is simply achieved by expressing a few drops of milk; this removes the natural waxy blocking material which prevents the udders from being contaminated by the bacteria that can cause mastitis. Similarly, we have tended to look at Neolithic crops through modern filters. So we see them as a rather pale reflection of the crops we grow today, mainly wheat, oats and barley. In actual fact when hazel is grown outside a wood and is not coppiced it starts to produce nuts freely after about five years and if tended well a small stand of hazel could produce a significant proportion of the oil and protein needed to feed a family. Contrary to received archaeological opinion hazelnuts can be stored and will retain their palatability right through winter and into the following spring, when many sources of food are very scarce.[24] Yet hazel never appears on a list of Neolithic crops, instead coming under the general heading of 'wild foods' or 'scavenged foods' – something one eats when desperately hungry.

For these and other reasons it can be difficult to visualize how the Neolithic landscape would have looked, because it must have been a constantly changing scene. We can be reasonably sure that earlier Neolithic landscapes would have been more thickly wooded and more lightly settled than those of the third millennium BC and the centuries leading up to the Bronze Age (around 2500 BC). At the start of the Neolithic most settlement was either in clearings within the woodland or in areas of the landscape where woodland was naturally thin, such as land liable to saltwater flooding, or certain very light sandy soils which supported a vegetation cover of pine trees, bracken, juniper and gorse, the sort of landscapes that can today be seen in the sandy regions of Surrey and Hampshire or in the Breckland around Thetford, in Norfolk. But as we have seen in Cranborne Chase and on Salisbury Plain it was not just areas with lighter subsoils that were only lightly wooded in post-glacial times.

It would probably be a mistake to see the process of woodland clearance as steady. We know from pollen evidence that some places, such as the better agricultural soils, were cleared first. We can examine the process in some detail on islands where pollen drift from neighbouring landscapes and other complicating factors can be partially discounted. In South Uist, for example, some areas were cleared of woodland early in the Neolithic, while others often close by, remained wooded until well into the Bronze Age – more than a millennium later. The situation in the Outer Hebrides as a whole, however, was rather more complex. Here recent research has revealed a large number of new Neolithic sites which include many ritual monuments such as standing stones and stone circles. We have long known about the extraordinarily elaborate complex of monuments at Callanish, on South Lewis. This site includes a stone circle, stone rows and a passage grave, and was largely covered by peat until the late nineteenth century. After it was excavated in the 1980s the land was, surprisingly, revealed to have been farmed before the construction of the first stone monument, in the early third millennium BC.[25]

MAN-MADE MONUMENTS IN THE EARLY NEOLITHIC LANDSCAPE

While modern archaeology may play down the speed of the switch from hunter-gatherer to farmer, there can be little doubt that the onset of the Neolithic brought with it some entirely new ideas. There is a more visible emphasis on communal values expressed through the celebration of shared ancestry centred around communal tombs. The commonest form of earlier Neolithic communal tomb is the long barrow. As its name suggests, a long barrow has a long mound which tapers from one end, where the burials, often within stone or timber chambers, are placed. Long barrows have strong links to the mainland of Europe, where they originated. Indeed, the shape of the long barrow is based on that of distinctive trapezoidal houses that were built in France, Germany and central Europe, but which, so far as we know, never appeared in Britain because by the time the first arrivals landed that particular shape of house had gone out of use. It only survived as a 'folk memory', in the form of long barrows.

Communal tombs were not tombs as we understand the term today. To us, tombs are places where bodies are allowed to rest in peace in perpetuity. In the earlier Neolithic many bones excavated from communal tombs at sites like Wayland's Smithy and Hazleton North, in Gloucestershire (3800–3500 BC), had not been left in peace.[26] Here bones of different skeletons were found to be muddled up. This and other evidence suggests that the bones were regularly removed from the tomb and perhaps paraded through nearby settlements during certain ceremonies to do with the ancestors. These rituals suggest that the dead – and the ancestors – played an active part in the world of the living. This went on at Hazleton for about 150 years, at the end of which the tomb was ritually sealed off and left in peace.

A number of excavations, mostly carried out since the Second World War, have drawn attention to sites known as causewayed enclosures. The more we learn about these sites the more we appreciate their importance and their complexity, but it is already apparent that their use played a significant part in the way that early farming societies adapted to their landscapes and established relationships with other communities in the region. In terms of the development of the prehistoric landscape it would be hard to overestimate their significance.

The extended name of these sites holds the clue as to how they may have been used. From the air the ditches that enclosed them are roughly circular. There may be one or more of them, but what makes them so distinctive is the way they were dug: in short lengths, separated by undug 'causeways'. There has been much debate about why they were

Fig. 2.2 The chambered long barrow at Wayland's Smithy, Oxfordshire. This view shows the forecourt and blocked entrance to the three burial chambers within the barrow mound. Behind the great stones of the forecourt is a long (52 metres), tapering mound, edged with smaller stones. Recent radiocarbon dates indicate that the tomb was built in two phases: 3520–3470 BC and 3460–3400 BC. The gap between the two periods of use was around 40–100 years. The earlier tomb held the remains of fifteen individuals; the contents of the later tomb had been disturbed, but there must have been at least eight burials.

dug like this, but there can be no doubt that it was deliberate. We know this because excavation in Britain and abroad has shown that special 'offerings' such as human skulls or upside-down pots resembling skulls were placed in the ditch butt-ends immediately alongside the causeways. These deliberately placed deposits (the skulls are upright in the ground, as in life) show that the ends of the ditches were important, as were the causeways.

The presence of so many causeways would rule out any defensive purpose for the ditch. This view is supported by excavations, which have shown that many ditches had been deliberately filled in, shortly after being dug. Again, this might seem inexplicable, except that other offerings were placed in the ground before the filling-in process began. These were clearly deliberate acts, of a ceremonial or religious sort. The scale of the ditches suggests that each segment was dug by a separate group of people. We can only guess who these groups were, but all human societies are composed of families, clans and lineages and these are likely to have been the ties that lay behind the organization of the gangs of workers.

In the 1950s and 1960s causewayed camps, as they were then called, were seen as the Neolithic equivalent of Iron Age hillforts. In other words they were strongholds, often on the tops of hills, which people could both retreat to and gather within, to hold seasonal fairs and markets. Our ideas in those days were very much rooted in practicality: whereas today anthropology has taught us that people often do things for their own sake, or because it is the right way to behave in the circumstances. Rationality need not enter into it.

Back in the 1980s I had the great good fortune to excavate a causewayed enclosure on the waterlogged outskirts of Etton, a small village near Peterborough. I decided that we must excavate it on a very large scale, if only to gain an impression of what had been happening within the area surrounded by the single oval causewayed ditch. In the end we excavated about 80 per cent of the site in a series of large open area excavations covering more than a hectare.

We decided from the outset that we would throw the archaeological rule book out of the window. This was because the first law of good field archaeology at the time was: establish chronology and sequence, above all else. We realized that we would only understand what was going on in these strange sites if we plotted everything in the ground and then tried to decide how it got there. Chronology and sequence could be sorted out later. What we revealed was a series of deliberate offerings that had been arranged in the ditch and then carefully covered in. I shall always remember the day that the patterning of the material in the ground first started to appear. I then realized that it was probably put in the ground to tell a story – maybe a family history – that would have meant something important to the spectators standing around the freshly opened ditch, while the ceremonial offerings were being made, on a special day some 5,000 years ago. It was the strangest feeling of direct communication with the remote past.

Many of the best-known ancient ceremonial or ritual landscapes, like those around Stonehenge or Avebury, seem to have origins in causewayed enclosures. They are known to occur mostly south of a line from Bristol to the Wash, but a growing number of outliers are now being found in northern England, Scotland and even Northern Ireland. They are also frequently encountered in Europe: in France, Germany and elsewhere.[27] The best-known example in Britain is at Windmill Hill, near Avebury in Wiltshire; the huge Avebury henge, constructed more than a millennium later, probably had its origins at Windmill Hill.[28]

Causewayed enclosures were placed at significant positions in the landscape. Quite often they seem to have been deliberately positioned off-centre, as if to respect a particular hilltop or bend in a river. This careful positioning emphasizes the importance of a particular natural place in the landscape to the people who then constructed the enclosure. The construction, however, was not like modern building methods. Today we are used to the idea that a building has two phases: its construction, followed by its use. In the Neolithic and Bronze Age many of the larger ceremonial sites, ranging from causewayed enclosures to henges and many barrows, were constructed and reconstructed at regular intervals, to such an extent that we now believe that in many instances their construction *was* their use.[29]

There is now evidence to suggest that major episodes of reconstruction took place with a new generation, but that regular meetings probably happened annually, most probably in the autumn, when the crops had been safely gathered in. It is also entirely likely that some causewayed enclosures may have been located along the borders of different tribal territories; these would have been seen as neutral places, where people of different communities could safely come together.[30] Some of these may have been used as markets where livestock, salt and other commodities were exchanged. Larger examples, such as Windmill Hill, were probably used as ceremonial meeting places, where different communities from a large area could come together to exchange gifts, commemorate marriages and births and remember the dead. They would be places, too, where disputes could be settled by discussion rather than conflict. Many of the larger causewayed enclosures were placed on naturally significant places such as the high hills of Hambledon Hill or Maiden Castle, both in Dorset. These sites and others continued to be revered as special places right through to the Iron Age, when they were rebuilt several times, as massive hillforts.

Some of the smaller enclosures, such as Etton, appear to have been abandoned around 3000 BC, or even before that, but the clustering of later Neolithic and Bronze Age ritual sites, such as henges and barrows, around them show that somehow their influence persisted for at least another millennium. These smaller causewayed enclosures sometimes also occur in groups. Etton, for example belongs to a group of seven or eight small, oval enclosures in the lower Welland Valley, at the point where the river enters the Fen basin.[31] The Fens had yet to form in the region at that time, so it is entirely possible that other causewayed enclosures remain to be discovered, largely intact and waterlogged, below the later peats and flood-clay alluvium of the nearby fen. The spacing of the Welland causewayed enclosures suggests that each one represented a particular community living in the rich plain of the flat valley. So here it would seem that the social purpose of these places was rather different from some of the larger examples further south. They may have been ceremonial centres for individual communities. An alternative explanation is that the Welland Valley enclosures mark the edge of an important cultural divide in earlier Neolithic Britain because it is very noticeable that while causewayed enclosures are quite common in East Anglia they simply do not occur in Lincolnshire or the east Midlands, north of the Welland.[32]

STAKING CLAIMS: CEREMONIAL MONUMENTS AND THE GROWTH OF TERRITORIES

Neolithic communities took possession of the landscape in an entirely new manner. Previously people had lived within its confines, content to accept its benefits and limitations. But the Neolithic was the period when people started to fell or clear the forest in earnest, both for practical reasons to do with farming, and most probably for other religious, or ritual, reasons too. The quantum leap in the quantity of new sites and finds is accompanied by evidence for an altogether different attitude to the landscape. This was probably a reflection of other, broader social beliefs to do with people's place and position in the world and the role of the ancestors in the practice and structure of family life. Labour was now an all-important resource, and family ties and obligations, doubtless expressed by way of myths associated with the ancestors, were the means whereby it was harnessed.

Greater attention to family structure and history would also have been important in communities where the population was rising. Many Neolithic settlements were far-flung and would have wanted to maintain close contacts. So the ties that united quite large extended families, or clans, would have been of central importance. Such factors may in part explain why barrows and burials became so prominent in the landscape. We might be witnessing something similar happening today. Society is becoming increasingly mobile and people have to move long distances in the course of their careers. At the same time there is an extraordinary increase in the number of individuals researching their family histories. As I know from my own experience, this process is not necessarily carried out by older members of the family, but it does involve a great deal of communication within the broader family network. This renewed interest in what some prehistorians have described as the Realm of the Ancestors, does undoubtedly have the effect of drawing people together.

We have seen that most of the earliest ritual monuments (mostly communal tombs) that quite suddenly spring up right across Britain and Ireland from about 4000 to 3500 BC must have been constructed in open landscapes, and there is now abundant evidence from pollen analyses at many sites to support this view. Many barrows were sited in prominent positions often along the skyline, and were frequently arranged in rows, or groups. Such locations would be pointless if the landscape around them was thickly wooded. Some monuments, by their very shape and size, could only have been erected in open country.

Cursuses are a type of monument only found in Britain and Ireland. They were named after *cursus*, the Latin word for a race. They consist of two parallel ditches and a central bank, or banks, that sometimes run across hill, valley and dale for many miles. Some were built in a single episode, others were added to over time. Most are only known as cropmarks, but some, such as the largest of them all, the Dorset Cursus, still survive as banks. The Dorset Cursus runs for 10 kilometres south-west of Martin Down in Cranborne Chase. This spectacular monument was laid out in several episodes and its alignment clearly respects the existence of earlier barrows. Like other religious or ceremonial monuments of the period it was broadly aligned on the midwinter solstice – doubtless to link it in some way with the natural order of the universe. Cursuses could only have been seen, let alone appreciated in open countryside.[33]

We shall probably never know for sure what cursuses are about, and it is probably wisest to treat each individually. Some were, however, undoubtedly used to link or tie together the different parts of the many so-called 'ritual landscapes' that started to emerge after about 3000 BC.

Archaeologists have known about ritual landscapes for some time. Anyone walking across the landscape around Stonehenge, for example, will be struck by the number of barrows. In Mainland Orkney and in the valley of the River Boyne in Ireland the modern countryside is still completely dominated by the monuments of the Neolithic and Bronze Age ritual landscapes. Although the British and Irish examples are among the best known, they also occur right across Europe, one of the finest being at Carnac in Brittany. Essentially, ritual landscapes consist of a concentration of many religious and ceremonial monuments. There can be dozens, even hundreds, of barrows of various sorts, and henges, large and small. They were usually in use from about 3000 BC until sometime around 1500 BC.

Frequently, but not always, ritual landscapes are grouped around a major central site, such as Avebury or Stonehenge in Wiltshire, or Maes Howe in Orkney, and in the past this arrangement was generally seen as their sole organizing principle. We now know that these large and impressive monuments were not the earliest and that many landscapes formed around causewayed enclosures and/or long barrows, which themselves were most probably constructed in areas that had long been seen as sacred in some way. One important development brought about by aerial photography has been the revelation of vast ritual landscapes that have been almost completely obliterated by ploughing.[34] These are found to cover huge areas of the lowland river gravels right across Britain, from the Milfield Basin in Northumberland, to the Welland Valley in Cambridgeshire, to the Thames Valley in Oxfordshire.

More recently computers and modern survey techniques have allowed us to analyse ancient 'viewsheds', the landscape features and monuments that would have been visible from a particular spot. These studies have shown that ritual landscapes were organized in a very intricate fashion with lines of sight that may have linked, for example, the barrows of the same or different families, perhaps like the arrangement of gravestones in a churchyard. Again, such complex intervisibility only makes sense if the landscape was cleared of trees.

Ritual landscapes in the uplands often took the form of cairnfields, whose structure and arrangement, at places like the upper Brenig Valley in north Wales, mirrored some of the complexities seen in the larger lowland ritual landscapes.[35] Although most of the cairns found in cairnfields across Britain are relatively small, a few giants are known to exist. A fine upland equivalent of Silbury Hill, the largest man-made mound in Britain, is the far less celebrated Gop Hill, in the Clwydian range of north-west Wales, which is second only to Silbury in size. Recently it has been suggested that many of the cairns that surrounded the Welsh megaliths probably never amounted to anything more than a low platform that set off the great stones, and probably had the effect of making them seem to hover even more effectively. The classic example of such a tomb is the so-called portal dolmen at Pentre Ifan, Pembrokeshire.

The appearance of the largest of these megaliths with their great capstones was of 'stones that float in the sky'.[36] Some of these tombs were constructed over large filled-in pits, which may have been dug to extract the capstone. Thus the stone that once lay below the ground was now hovering in the air. There is less emphasis here on sight lines and distant alignment on the horizon, as would perhaps befit communities who lived out their lives in dense woodland. Here clearings and the sky above the trees would inspire the imagination. It seems probable that these religious traditions may well owe as much to the Mesolithic as to the new ideas that were reaching Britain with the spread of farming.

Fig. 2.3 The Neolithic portal dolmen of Pentre Ifan in Pembrokeshire, south-west Wales. This is the classic example of a megalithic tomb where the massive capstone weighs many tons. Excavation has revealed that beneath the stones was a large pit. Pottery found in the excavations can be dated to about 4000 BC, towards the very beginning of the Neolithic period.

THE SITING OF MONUMENTS AND THE RISE OF 'RITUAL LANDSCAPES'

The motives that lay behind the construction of barrows, chambered tombs and cairns would have been complex and would have varied from place to place and between different communities or social groups. In the past funerary monuments were often seen to be about death alone. They were classified and studied on the basis of their shape, constructional technique and the style of pottery found within them. But their setting, and the landscape around them, were largely ignored. Today we realize that in antiquity the ancestors were thought to play an important role in regulating the affairs of the living. This belief in an active spirit world in turn affected the location of burial sites in the landscape. Anthropology has also shown that certain trees, rivers and other prominent landmarks would have been believed inhabited by the shades of ancestors.

These ideas might help to explain the way that some barrows or burial mounds are placed in the landscape. In certain areas, for example, barrows are arranged in rows along the skyline where they would be clearly visible from lower-lying settlements. This location might also be seen as being deliberately marginal, on the highest point in the landscape, the place nearest perhaps to the world of the ancestors 'up there'. In the more crowded territory of ritual landscapes, where there can be large numbers of barrows, some of the grandest, with the most prestigious burials, may also be positioned on ridges with a clear view of the central focus – if there is one. Thus the large mounds of the New King Barrows run along the western lip of the ridge that forms the eastern edge of the Stonehenge basin, for half a kilometre, from whence they look down on the Stones.

Many barrows were positioned out in the general landscape away from the great ceremonial and religious centres, such as Stonehenge. These more far-flung examples show us how spiritual forces, such as the spirits of the ancestors, helped people mark the bounds of their farms and territories. In flat land, such as the plain around the edges of the Fens, barrows were frequently distributed, either singly, or in small groups or rows, at regular intervals across the landscape. This arrangement might indicate that the barrows marked the edges of specific family holdings in a landscape where permanent field boundaries had yet to be constructed. In upland landscapes barrows may often be found at the boundary between seasonally available moorland and the more sheltered pastures of the valleys.

Other factors, such as rising or setting of the sun or moon, had an influence on the siting of ceremonial or funerary monuments. Many sites have been discovered to have had solar or, more rarely, lunar alignments. All manner of claims have been made for these observations, the most common being that they represent predictive calendars of some sort.[37] Today the consensus of opinion is that alignments were very significant and could be used to predict certain events, such as lunar eclipses, but that this was not their primary role. The main purpose of solar and lunar alignments probably had more to do with theatre, and a sort of astrology, than with science or astronomy.[38] When, for example, the midwinter sun shone along the low passage and into the chamber of the great Orcadian Neolithic tomb of Maes Howe the theatrical impact would have been magnified by ceremonies that included music, and experiments have shown that the sound would have been amplified by the special acoustics of the chamber's finely finished stone walls.[39] So whether it was Stonehenge, Maes Howe or any one of a number of other sites, the intention behind the alignment was to link the monument and the people who had constructed it with the forces that created and controlled nature.

Sites with astronomical alignments may have been used to predict the passage of the sun and moon through the year. Indeed, other predictions may have been possible too. It has been suggested that this seemingly supernatural ability to predict accurately what would have been seen as an important aspect of the future would have given the ruling élites even more control over their societies. Control and status are closely allied; so the construction of the first great field monuments – the causewayed enclosures, henges and chambered tombs – were also seen as expressions of the power and authority of an élite.

Much of the direct evidence for Neolithic settlement in England and Wales has been lost, but indirect clues can be found in the numerous Sites and Monuments Records housed in local authority offices across Britain.[40] Here single or so-called 'stray' finds, many made by enthusiastic collectors before the war, reveal the presence of many settlements that were subsequently removed by modern developments, such as new roads or quarries.

As time passed the arrangement, shape and layout of ritual sites within specific landscapes were changed to accommodate perceptions that were also changing. There are indications that these changing perceptions could have been co-ordinated across large areas of Britain, but only at a very general scale. We witness, for example, the introduction, towards the middle of the Neolithic period, of circular monuments, such as passage graves and henges, and with them a concern with such solar phenomena as the alignment of the sun at its lowest and highest points during the midsummer and midwinter solstices. Later there was a gradual switch from wooden to stone-built monuments. But these are very general trends. In the vast majority of instances, monuments within specific ritual landscapes were changed to reflect shifting interpretation and appreciation of purely local landscape features.

Studies involving computer-generated viewsheds and sight lines continue to be important, but nothing can be better than visiting a landscape and experiencing directly what it has to offer. All factors need to be taken into consideration: the way mist might creep up a valley or rain clouds shroud the higher peaks; how the rising midwinter sun could first appear on the horizon, and how the archaeological monuments that are still visible appear to respect or respond to these purely natural landscape phenomena. These approaches have been described as the phenomenology of landscape and they 'attempt to understand the way in which people experience the world they create and inhabit'.[41] Another, perhaps less pretentious definition is 'a nice long walk with your eyes open'.[42] Landscape phenomenology is an important new direction of research which draws much benefit from the experience of observant people, such as farmers, ramblers, artists and others, who have deep knowledge of a particular landscape or region.[43] It is harder to apply landscape phenomenology to landscapes that have been extensively affected by recent development, such as the lowlands of south-eastern Britain, but in places like Salisbury Plain or the higher moorlands it can provide remarkable insights.

MAN-MADE MONUMENTS IN THE LATER NEOLITHIC LANDSCAPE

In the later Neolithic the population was still growing and the process of woodland clearance continued relentlessly. After about 3000 BC there was a proliferation of new types of sites and monuments, such as the great passage graves beneath their round barrows and the first henges. Passage graves originated in Brittany around 4500 BC and were first constructed in Britain around a millennium later. In Britain and Ireland the shift in emphasis towards circularity extended not just to barrows and ceremonial sites, such as stone circles, but to domestic architecture too, with the appearance of the first roundhouses (so far the oldest known are at Knowth in the Boyne Valley, Ireland).

The tradition of constructing stone circles lasted for about a millennium, from 3000 to 2000 BC, beginning in the later Neolithic, and flourishing early in the Bronze Age.[44] Dating stone circles can be difficult as most were constructed in upland areas where acid soils can hinder the survival of bone and even pottery. Their lowland equivalents, circles of pits and posts, are generally easier to date by excavation. Some sites, such as the Sanctuary near Avebury and Stanton Drew in Somerset, began life as pits or post-holes, augmented and replaced at intervals, but 'signed off' by a permanent setting of stones at the end of their life. This may be another reflection of the idea that we shall return to when we come to examine the meaning of Stonehenge (Chapter 3), where timber might have symbolized life, whereas stone was about death and the realms of the ancestors.

There were also significant changes in the form of flint tools in the later Neolithic, where shorter, squatter flakes replaced long, thin and knife-like blades; similarly, styles of pottery changed. After about 3000 BC coarser wares were introduced, maybe better able to cope with reheating and cookery; these were usually more highly decorated than the plainer, round-based bowls and jars that characterized the earlier Neolithic. What does seem certain, however, is that many of these styles of pottery and other innovations, such as cursuses and henges, were home-grown in Britain or Ireland and did not arrive with settlers from abroad.[45]

So far I have discussed some of the individual elements that formed the Neolithic landscape and we saw how these might together have made up ritual landscapes. But these very special areas together comprised just a tiny fraction of Britain. We know, of course, that long barrows and other Neolithic monuments are almost ubiquitous, but how did they fit into the ordinary, domestic or farmed landscape? Like many practical archaeologists I am also concerned with problems of continuity: how, for example, did Neolithic evolve into Bronze Age landscapes? The only way to approach these problems is to examine a particular and carefully chosen landscape.

THE MOORS: A UNIQUELY BRITISH LANDSCAPE

The moors of south-western Britain contain some of the best-preserved prehistoric landscapes anywhere in Europe.[46] They have retained their open aspect because they have been continuously grazed by cattle and sheep ever since the first Neolithic farmers felled the tree-cover and established open pastures, around 4000 BC. This grazing has been sufficient to prevent gorse and other coarse plants from shading out the grass. But today well-intentioned regulation, based on a poor appreciation of the archaeological history of the various moors, is encouraging gorse, bracken and brambles to return. As a result, most of the prehistoric house circles, stone rows and field systems that make these moors unique in Europe have been hidden beneath dense undergrowth whose roots are already loosening stones and causing damage.

Although large areas of Bodmin Moor are now disfigured by gorse and bracken, the area around Roughtor (pronounced 'Rowtor') some 13 kilometres south-east of Camelford is still largely open and grazed by sheep or cattle, and it is still possible to appreciate there how the various elements of the prehistoric landscape related to each other.[47] The area has been surveyed in detail and shown to be remarkably rich in sites and monuments, all of which are still visible on the surface.[48] All but the very highest peaks – the tors – of Bodmin Moor would have been wooded in Mesolithic times. This woodland would have been more dense in the lower-lying areas that were less affected by the strong gales that still blow from off the Atlantic, just 11 kilometres to the north-west. Felling of the tree-cover started in the Neolithic, but once the trees had been felled, a process which pollen analysis suggests took place in the Neolithic and Bronze Age, the landscape thus opened would have been maintained as pasture both by grazing livestock and by cultivation of suitable sheltered ground.

The highest tors of Bodmin Moor and other Cornish moorlands have always been open and treeless. These peaks may well have been visited by Mesolithic groups, but there is good archaeological evidence that these open hilltops were also home to Neolithic communities who established a series of so-called 'tor enclosures' around their summits. Tor enclosures have many aspects in common with the causewayed enclosures. They were probably occupied during the milder months of summer. More importantly, they would have acted as focuses for settlement and ceremonial that continued to be significant throughout the Neolithic, into the Bronze Age and even in later prehistoric times.

Visitors to Bodmin Moor are immediately struck by the eminence of Roughtor itself, which dominates the open grassy landscape. At the bottom of the slopes are flat areas of peaty bogs. Modern plantations of spruce and larch – both non-native conifers – also detract from the appearance of the landscape, which is otherwise much as it might have appeared in prehistoric times. The north-western slopes of Roughtor are richly strewn with ancient remains.

The medieval Cornish boundaries can readily be distinguished from another set of low, partially collapsed, stone walls which are far less straight and which link and enclose a series of so-called 'house circles'. The term 'house circle' is used to describe the lower walls, and often door stones too, of long-abandoned, usually prehistoric houses. These were indeed houses rather than huts. They were usually circular or oval in plan. Some had paved stone floors, others used beaten earth; all had central hearths. A few excavated examples even had covered drains to take run-off from the roof below the floor to the downslope side of the building. Many were terraced into the hillside. The conical roof was thatched and/or turf-covered. The larger houses could comfortably have accommodated a dozen people, but most were roomy enough for a family of two parents and perhaps four to six children. A few did not appear to have had hearths and these might have been used as stores or animal byres.

Many house circles have been dated to the Bronze and Iron ages, but it is now apparent from both archaeological and environmental research that these Bronze Age settlements were merely taking possession of much earlier landscapes. Indeed, their careful siting suggests an intimate knowledge of a particular locality. It is also becoming increasingly clear that the later prehistoric communities which established the house circles, and the field systems around them, were aware of the presence nearby of barrows, cairns, standing stones and, of course, the tor enclosures that still dominated individual landscapes. They paid attention not just to features of the natural landscape, such as shelter, slope and drainage, but they also acknowledged, and most probably still respected, ancient cultural influences, too. This suggests that the Bronze and Iron Age summer visitors to the Bodmin uplands were direct descendants of the original Neolithic farmers.

Initially attention focused on the most obvious archaeological feature on the slopes of Roughtor, the bank cairn. This monument is highly unusual. It consists of a substantial, gently curving bank of stones running along a low ridge upslope towards Showery Tor, a 'cheese-ring'

Fig. 2.4 Prehistoric landscapes on Bodmin Moor. The low ridge of grass and stones, lower left, is a Neolithic bank cairn which is aligned on a geological 'cheese-ring' on top of Showery Tor on the skyline. In the middle distance the cairn turns quite sharply to the right and aligns itself on Little Roughtor (see Fig. 2.5).

on the skyline leading up to the main height of Roughtor itself. Cornwall is famous for its cheese-rings, which are found along the crests of the higher tors. In profile they resemble the two, or sometimes three, buns of a hamburger and are entirely natural features caused by the differential erosion of the harder rocks forming the upper parts of the moor. From a distance they are very striking and they must have caught the attention of prehistoric communities too, because many are either surrounded or partially covered by Neolithic or Bronze Age cairns.

Showery Tor is no exception, being surrounded by a large ring-cairn. The lower parts of the bank cairn are directly aligned on Showery Tor; then, about two-thirds of the distance upslope, the cairn gently, but quite distinctly, changes direction, this time directly towards Little Roughtor, another cheese-ring on the Roughtor ridge, but one almost completely buried beneath a huge cairn of heaped-up stones.[49] Both Showery Tor and Little Roughtor were downhill of Roughtor itself, part of which is enclosed by a bank of stones that looks remarkably like the encircling bank or ramparts of a Neolithic tor enclosure. This evidence suggests that the main hilltop of Roughtor was the original and principal focus of attention, but that details of the higher tor landscape mattered too – hence cairns around the two small peaks.[50]

The clear alignment of the bank cairn on prominent features in the middle distance is important because it demonstrates that the landscape was cleared of trees when it was constructed. It is possible of course that this clearance was selective, creating avenues through the woods, along which the cheese-rings could be seen, but there are other grounds to believe that certainly by the Bronze Age tree-felling was largely complete.

It is apparent that the bank cairn was aligned on features on the skyline, but why? What was its wider role in the landscape? Its positioning was carefully thought out: it was placed along a low ridge and it can be seen to divide the landscape into two distinct regions. To the north there are numerous cairns, many of which were probably Bronze Age or earlier burial mounds. To the south the valley sides and slopes of Roughtor are covered with well over a hundred house circles, often within stone-built enclosures and surrounded by field systems. The precise dating of the bank cairn is still to be determined, but all the excavated evidence suggests it was built in the Neolithic.

The separation of two areas, one of domestic life and farming, the other of burial (but also with extensive grazing), suggests that people drew a distinction between the realms of the living and the ancestors. The fact that the feature which separated the two areas also predated the main period when cairns and house circles were constructed further suggests that these beliefs were of some antiquity by 1500 BC, when the house circles were in use as dwellings. When one walks around the house circles one is constantly aware that the bank cairn forms the entire skyline to the north. From the settlement areas it seems to form part of a linking boundary that leads straight up to the cheese-rings, cairns and smaller tors – and ultimately of Roughtor itself. In symbolic terms, the bank cairn draws the dramatic skyline down to the level of daily life.

Clearly the skyline was of prime importance and we can only speculate on its original significance, but the presence of cairns – which in upland Britain often form mounds covering the remains of the dead – suggests a link to the afterlife. The lowest part of the bank cairn resembles a form of burial mound, known as a long cairn, and a few somewhat larger rocks resemble a collapsed burial chamber or portal stones. If this was indeed a separate and slightly earlier feature it was also aligned on Showery Tor. Excavation of the bank cairn revealed that it was far more than a mere bank of stones. The first stage of construction involved the removal of the turf in the area that was to be the cairn. This has been noted on many cairns and barrows and is usually seen as a ritual associated with the spiritual cleansing of the site. The cairn itself was constructed of two outer facing walls that were keyed into flatter horizontal stones resembling a layer of thick paving. The space between the facing walls was then filled with rubble and it is possible that the rubble was then capped with the turves removed in the initial stage of construction. The turf would have provided both a striking visual contrast with the pale stonework and a stable, smooth surface to walk on. Again, the use of turf in

Fig. 2.5 Prehistoric landscapes on Bodmin Moor: the Neolithic bank cairn when excavated. The deeper part of the trench has exposed the pre-cairn soil, from which the turf has been removed. Note the heavier stones of the facing walls on either side of the central rubble core. On the skyline the two tors of Showery Tor (*left*) and Little Roughtor (*centre, right*) can clearly be seen.

the construction of barrows, henges and other ceremonial sites is common.

The careful construction of the two facing walls, with a rubble-filled gap between them, suggests that the bank cairn was probably never a simple, rounded bank at all. More probably it would have resembled a prominently raised walkway, sufficiently wide for two or three people to walk side by side. With clear links to the realms of the ancestors provided by the cairns on the skyline directly ahead, and with a possible burial cairn behind, people walking along the raised walkway would have been aware of the presence of the afterlife all around them. The monument may have been used in an unstructured way, but more probably – as with causewayed enclosures or henges – it would have been the location for ceremonies, such as rites at death, or at puberty, when a young person crossed the threshold into adult life. Such rites of passage are symbolic journeys that can be given physical expression by, for example, a ritualized procession along a special walkway. The important point to note, however, is that the stories surrounding the rituals were probably integrated with people's perception of the landscape, and their beliefs as to how it developed. Just as Christian churches face east, towards Jerusalem, these prehistoric monuments were aligned towards their own, and rather closer, Holy Lands.

MINES AND 'SPECIAL PLACES'

As my interest in landscape history has developed I have had to turn my attention to more recent industrial archaeology and the world of work. As a prehistorian, however, I still find it difficult to think about the workplace and the household as separate areas. Indeed, in prehistoric times work, family life and religion were all closely tied together. The presence of the ancestors from the barrows around the edges of a family farm would have ensured that trespassers stayed off land where they were not wanted. We know too that animal sacrifices were frequently made, but it is uncertain whether these were to propitiate gods, ancestors, or the spirits of the animals themselves. In many tribal societies there is a belief that the meat, milk and skins provided by livestock must be paid for in some way, otherwise the milk will run dry or the lambs and calves fail to thrive.

This concept of reimbursement – of giving something back to sustain a given resource – was probably widespread. Trade in prehistory was never a matter of simple exchange: 'I want that, and you can give me this for it.' Instead, it was all about family relationships and obligations – rather like Christmas today, only more so. The obligations imposed by marriage, for example, could be 'paid off' over time by gifts of, say, livestock. By the same token the respect one owed to the tribal elders or chiefs could be honoured by the giving of valuable gifts. These gifts would have bought the donor respect and prestige. But it was far more complex than simply travelling to a market and exchanging a pen of lambs for, say, a couple of sows.

Ideas of reimbursement also applied to natural resources. During the Neolithic period flint- and stone-working became very sophisticated and people sought better and better sources of raw material, especially to make axes. The finest-grained stone for fashioning polished axes was mined from specific sources in Wales and north-western England. But these were not mines as an industrial archaeologist would understand them. They were not simply dug to obtain good source material alone, just as the Bluestones at Stonehenge were not transported from Wales because there was no suitable local stone. There were other, non-practical, reasons for using specific sources of stone. It has been plausibly suggested, for example, that the eighty-two Bluestones at Stonehenge might have been transported from west Wales because they, and the remote quarry from which they were obtained, were thought to have healing powers.[51]

A long-running research project into the identification of the sources of rock used to make polished stone axes has produced some very surprising results. If simple trade was the mechanism whereby these axes were distributed, one would expect the vast majority to be found close by the area of the quarries and a sharp fall-off at the point (maybe a day's walk) where it becomes inconvenient to fetch them.[52] Instead it was observed that axes from particular 'axe factories' were specially favoured in areas a long distance away.

Perhaps the best-known of these 'factories' is in one of the remotest spots in Britain, high on the rocks of the Pike O'Stickle, that towers

Fig. 2.6 The remote peak of Pike O'Stickle (with the waterfall, middle distance), at Langdale in the Lake District was a major 'axe factory' in the Neolithic.

above Langdale in the Lake District (see plate section). These are mysterious places that must have been treated with special respect.[53] The highest and most inaccessible parts of the Pike O'Stickle were quarried for a fine-grained greenstone which was used for polished axes.[54] Large numbers of these were transported right across Britain, where they are found in quantity in eastern England, especially in Lincolnshire and North Yorkshire, well over 100 kilometres from their source.[55] Our excavations at the causewayed enclosure at Etton (c. 3500 BC), produced many good examples of these axes, some of which showed clear signs of having been deliberately broken up before being buried in the ground, most probably during religious rituals.[56] I remember handling one axe which was about the size of a wristwatch; it had been reworked and polished so many times that it was far too small and light to have been used effectively. Others had been flaked and chipped, as if they were flint cores, yet the flakes had not been taken away and used somewhere else. It was as if these axes that had originated on the other side of Britain were being deliberately returned to the ground, perhaps to ensure that the source of supply remained sustainable. The distribution pattern of these Langdale axes suggests that in the east Midlands they were treasured items and were exchanged among tribes that shared this view of their worth. Perhaps the communities living on the plains of eastern England had a special respect for the Pike O'Stickle, just as the people who built Stonehenge had a mystical (if not a medical) regard for the Preseli Hills of Pembrokeshire.

THE PROBLEM OF NEOLITHIC HOUSES

It might be thought that houses were a sufficiently straightforward topic not to be bedevilled by issues of religion and symbolism. But this is prehistory, when people did not compartmentalize their lives as we do. To Neolithic families, reserving religious observance for a special place on Sunday would seem ludicrous. Their religion was an integral part of daily life, as it was of their world of work, and we can clearly see this in the use, positioning and layout of their houses.

It is quite unusual to discover traces of the houses occupied by the first farmers in Britain. Before the Second World War, only a handful were known, and most of these were in the Orkneys and Shetland Islands, where the adoption of stone instead of wood encouraged their survival. The Orcadian building stone is easy to find and widespread across the islands; it is also of top quality and readily cleaved into squared lintels and flat paving slabs. This is doubtless why so many prehistoric sites survive in such an extraordinarily good state of preservation. Nowhere else in Europe can one routinely expect to find Neolithic and Bronze Age houses complete with fireplaces, cupboards, beds and dressers. Since the 1970s, however, dozens of new finds of Neolithic houses have been made in Ireland and, to a somewhat lesser extent, in Scotland, too.[57] Some of the Scottish Neolithic houses have been very large rectangular structures: a recent example from Crathes Castle Estate in Aberdeenshire measured 24 × 9 metres – such a structure in earlier medieval times would certainly be described as a hall.[58]

The remains of a house, radiocarbon-dated to about 3700–2800 BC, were found just above the rocky beach of Papa Westray, the most northerly of the Orkneys, in 1929, when storms revealed an extensive midden (rubbish) deposit and traces of drystone walling. At first it was believed that the stonework was Iron Age, but further excavation in the 1970s showed that the two houses were of earlier Neolithic date and had been cut into a very slightly earlier midden. The walls still survive to a height of 1.60 metres. The main dwelling is rectangular, measuring 10 × 5 metres, with a partition wall and a hearth in the room furthest away from the sea. The outer room was paved and had a stone bench running along one wall. The doorway overlooking the sea is entered by way of a short tunnel-like corridor through the thickness of the walls. This would have provided protection against onshore winds. A doorway to the right of the main entranceway leads into another tunnel-like passage through the double wall that separates House 1 from House 2. House 2 seems to have been used as a workshop and for storage, as it includes five niche-like 'cupboards' and three recessed shelves.[59]

Neolithic houses in Orkney were generally laid out in a consistent pattern which can be seen at the Skara Brae houses and at Barnhouse, a more recently discovered settlement, also on Mainland, some 12 kilometres to the south-east. The entranceway was deliberately restricted and led into a small front hall. The arrangement of the partitions and stone furniture shows that visitors to the house then moved to the right of the hearth opposite the entrance, past a stone bed. On the back wall, opposite the doorway (and facing it), was a stone dresser. The dresser was clearly an important focal point within the house and may actually have been treated more like a small family shrine or altar. The excavators noted that the hearths were carefully positioned to respect solsticial alignments, even if the doorways of the houses faced in a different direction.

Something similar seems to have been happening at the Stones of Stenness, a late Neolithic stone circle within clear view of Barnhouse. The settlement at Barnhouse that accompanied and preceded the erection of the great stones is clearly visible from them. Slab-lined central hearths were an important feature of the Barnhouse domestic buildings and a closely similar but very much larger slab-lined hearth, accessed by a stone pathway, can be found at the centre of the Stones

Fig. 2.7   In the foreground are the reconstructed lower stone walls and internal partitions of the later Neolithic settlement at Barnhouse, Orkney. The four Stones of Stenness can be seen in the middle distance. Barnhouse was occupied and the Stones of Stenness were erected in the 300–400 years after 3300–3000 BC.

of Stenness. Excavations in the 1970s demonstrated that this hearth had been modified on several occasions, perhaps, as we shall see in Chapter 3, as part of the rites that took place within the stones.[60]

The houses at Barnhouse were arranged in two broad rings around a central open space.[61] Two houses were notably bigger and different in layout. One was a doubled-up house with two hearths and the other was a heavily constructed rectangular 'hall' set inside a high outer wall. The 'hall' was constructed with much greater care than the other buildings and was most probably used as a gathering place on special ceremonial occasions. Perhaps most significantly it faced directly towards the nearby passage grave of Maes Howe. Another link with the ritual landscape of central Orkney was provided by the Stones of Stenness, which were constructed during the three to four centuries that the Barnhouse settlement was occupied. Not only is it clearly visible, some 250 metres to the south-east, but it features at the centre of the stones an extra-large slab-lined hearth, identical in other respects to those found in the Barnhouse buildings. Excavations at both Barn-house and the Stones of Stenness revealed quantities of a distinctive and highly decorated style of later Neolithic pottery known as Grooved Ware.

Neolithic houses are very much rarer in England and Wales, where generally speaking the excavated evidence consists of an incoherent pattern of pits and post-holes, filled with varying amounts of settlement debris. Sometimes there is a hearth or two, but almost never the clear outline left by the post-holes of a building.[62] The prehistorian Julian Thomas has suggested that the meagre evidence for settlement reflects the fact that Neolithic communities in England and Wales had a more mobile lifestyle than elsewhere in Britain and Europe.[63] As they moved through the landscape they took their buildings, possibly less substan-tial, tent-like affairs, with them. This explanation fails to explain both why increasingly large areas of woodland were being cleared and why barrows, causewayed enclosures and other monuments proliferated to such an extent, especially if these ceremonial gathering places were ultimately expressions of territoriality and community cohesion. In the area around the lower Welland Valley, in eastern England, for example, we know of at least seven (and possibly as many as nine) causewayed enclosures and not one bona fide contemporary settlement that would pass as such in, say, the Iron Age.[64] It could of course be the case that the settlements were actually inside the enclosures. In many cases they may well have been, but two (Northborough and Etton) of the Welland examples have been excavated and neither produced evidence for houses or settlement. In both instances we know that this absence of evidence was not caused by ploughing as both the sites had been protected by thick accumulations of clay alluvium deposited by streams of the River Welland system.

If Thomas is right that Neolithic houses in England were probably light, skin-covered structures, resembling 'benders', it does not explain why the traces of substantial timber buildings can be sometimes found. I had the great good fortune to discover the post-holes and wall-slots of a Neolithic building at Fengate in 1972.[65] It had been a very dry summer and soil colours were bleached out by dryness, when a sudden shower dampened a freshly trowelled-over area of gravel and the clear impression of a small rectangular structure could be seen for about twenty minutes, which was enough time to mark the ground. Whatever its actual role, house or mortuary building – or indeed both – the building produced a rich assemblage of earlier Neolithic finds, including a large flake struck off a polished greenstone axe from Langdale in the Lake District. Other rectangular buildings are known from places as widely separated as Haldon, in Devon, and Lismore Fields, Derbyshire: there are just thirty-seven earlier Neolithic houses as yet discovered in the whole of England and Wales.[66] More recently, and most excitingly, the remains of at least three houses – one with an intact floor – have been found at the huge Neolithic henge site at Durrington Walls near Stonehenge.[67]

Prior to the discovery of the Barnhouse/Stones of Stenness relationship it used to be believed that ritual landscapes were just that: landscapes given over to religion and ceremonial alone. It now seems more likely that the slighter archaeological traces left by Neolithic and early Bronze Age houses might either have been missed or ploughed away by subsequent farmers. The new discoveries at Durrington Walls are actually within the largest henge monument in Britain, which in turn lies close to the heart of the Stonehenge landscape. It would be hard to find a better example of the integration of domestic and religious life in Neolithic times.

The Durrington Walls houses are oval and comparable in size to the Fengate house, and that found at Haldon in Devon, before the war. Their discoverer, Mike Parker Pearson, now has good grounds to think that there may originally have been hundreds of them within and beneath the banks of the great henge.[68] When I say 'beneath' I mean that these particular houses had been abandoned just before the banks were thrown up. If Mike is right then the great henge at Durrington Walls was also the largest late Neolithic settlement known in northern Europe. It seems probable at this early stage in the project that the Durrington houses may have been special in some way: they may have been used by people making a pilgrimage through the Stonehenge landscape, as there is much evidence of feasting (mainly on pork) on the site.

Although Neolithic houses are known in England and Wales, they are nothing like as common as in, say, Orkney; and where they are found they are 'flukes', preserved beneath thick accumulations of peat or flood-clays. This suggests that the absence of Neolithic houses from southern Britain is more apparent than real and simply reflects the devastating effects of modern intensive farming which has obliterated most traces of earlier sites and indeed of entire landscapes.[69] If this is true we shall have to radically adjust our estimates of Britain's Neolithic population. I have previously suggested that it could have been a quarter of a million by, say, 2000 BC.[70] Who knows? I could have underestimated by half.

3

The Making of the Landscape:
The Bronze Age (2500–800 BC)

During the fifteen centuries from just before 3000 BC the various communities of Britain grew in size without, so far as we can tell, any major disruptions. Ritual landscapes, like those around Stonehenge, Avebury and Maes Howe, whose origins lay towards the latter part of the earlier Neolithic, continued to develop and elaborate throughout this period. There were important developments, too, in the way that people treated the dead: communal burial beneath barrows, for example, gave way to single burial beneath barrows. These changes in burial practices undoubtedly reflected changes that were taking place within society but they did not have a significant effect on the way the landscape evolved. Pottery styles developed through time and metal-work became widespread after 2500 BC, but the general culture of Britain remained consistent, and most probably stable.

It is still generally supposed that the introduction of metal-working to Britain took place around 2500 BC, but there are now good reasons to suppose that it could have been some centuries earlier (around 2800 BC).[1] Although important to carpenters, woodsmen and those who had to quarry stone, the appearance of copper and then bronze axes was not such a transformation that it altered society by itself. Like many successful inventions, it was the right idea at the right time. People had mastered such emerging technologies as mining and the control of fire to make pottery; so the new skills of metal-working would have been a challenge, but not an insuperable one.

STONEHENGE AND THE EVOLUTION
OF RITUAL LANDSCAPES

I began my discussion of Neolithic landscapes with thoughts on farms and farming; then I moved on to religion. Here the discussion is the other way around, because I want to build on the ideas already established about ritual landscapes.

Round or circular monuments, such as passage graves, stone circles and henges became popular around 3500–3000 BC, towards the latter part of the earlier Neolithic. During the early Bronze Age they came to dominate both ritual and the wider farming landscapes where they can still be found across huge areas of upland and moor in the form of burial cairns and stone circles. Down in the fertile lowland plains and valleys they survive as tens of thousands of ring-ditches, which on excavation usually turn out to be the ploughed-out remains of round barrows and henges, the majority of which were constructed in the millennium after 2500 BC.

Not all stone circles were as grand as, for example, the settings within the great henges at Avebury in Wiltshire or the Ring of Brodgar in Orkney. In fact more than 900 are known in the British Isles.[2] Most are found in the uplands of Scotland and in north- and south-western England. In the lowlands of the south-east, circles were usually constructed from timber, but in certain instances, such as Stanton Drew in Somerset, timber circles were replaced by stone circles, generally around 2000 BC.[3]

Modern research is shedding unexpected new light on the way people used or venerated ritual monuments and how their construction was directly linked to the myths and stories that would have explained and coloured the landscape around them. A team from Manchester University, for example, has revealed quarry sites that provided stones for some of the great circles on Orkney.[4] Sources of rock were chosen for particular qualities such as colour and texture, and were then dragged for long distances through the landscape to be erected on site. The quarries were special 'natural places' that would have been spiritually important in their own right, rather like those stone-axe quarries set high on the fell in the Pike O'Stickle, at Langdale. Perhaps the most important discovery of the Manchester team was the actual site, at Vestra Fiold, in Orkney, where some of the monoliths for the Stones of Stenness were quarried. One monolith had been hewn from the layer of tabular Orkney bedrock and jacked up on stone supports ready to be levered onto the wooden sleds, which never arrived. Five huge stones from Vestra Fiold had been incorporated into the Ring of Brodgar and two into the Stones of Stenness.

It is increasingly apparent that the construction and repeated reconstruction and modification of Neolithic ritual sites was an important aspect of their use.[5] Indeed, to a great extent it *was* their 'use'. Such structures functioned as prehistoric churches, to be built, sanctified and then used for worship, maybe over centuries. Indeed there is some evidence to suggest that the builders of places like the Stones of Stenness never had any intention of 'completing' them at all. The work of building and repairing the central hearth and other features suggested to the leader of the Manchester team 'a series of projects as opposed to a unitary scheme'.[6] Excavation of the site in the 1970s revealed the sockets of twelve stones arranged in a circle, but one of these (Stone 12) could not have been erected, as the socket-hole had never been completed. Maybe their layout was complete (being a circle), in and of itself. There is also the possibility that the stones were symbols of something else again: they may even have represented individual people, living or dead – an idea that has been put forward many times for the human-sized Bluestones at Stonehenge.

Stonehenge, the Parthenon in Athens and the great Pyramids of the Nile are the most famous archaeological sites in the world. Each is blessed with a simple iconic profile – lintels, pillars or pyramid – that today appears on hundreds of corporate logos all over the world. Inevitably, as in Athens and Egypt, all attention is focused on the central icon, at the expense of its surroundings. But we must remember that the builders of all three sites saw them as a part, albeit an important part, of a much larger whole: how and why any of them were built cannot be explained without trying to understand their surroundings.

Just imagine, for example, that Big Ben was the only major public building in Westminster to survive the floods and nuclear catastrophes of the twenty-first century. Four and a half millennia from now, archaeologists might well be discussing that great Victorian clock tower in terms of a priapic cult, completely unaware that beneath layers of alluvium lay the concealed foundations of the hall with the largest roof span in the medieval world, plus one of the finest abbey churches ever built, and the various ancient and Victorian buildings of the Palace of Westminster, all grouped around Parliament Square. If they were aware of these remains their somewhat simplistic explanatory ideas would be very different. We are in a similar situation with regard to Stonehenge. The barrows and other monuments in the landscape surrounding the Stones have been known to antiquarians for at least four centuries, but only very recently have we moved beyond the idea that these were somehow attracted to the area 'because of Stonehenge'.

The key to understanding how Stonehenge might have 'worked' lies not just in the numerous modifications that took place in and around the Stones themselves, but in the changing arrangement of the barrows and other sites that surrounded them.[7] The large ritual landscapes that enfolded places like Stonehenge and Avebury were constantly being altered and modified as religious beliefs and the ceremonies that went with them evolved.

The four huge posts in the car park (p. 36) indicate that the area was already important in early post-glacial times, possibly because of the presence of the sarsen Heel Stone lying on the surface. This vast stone would have stood out starkly in a treeless environment. Earlier Neolithic times (say 3500 BC) saw the construction of a number of long barrows and the causewayed enclosure at Robin Hood's Ball, interestingly placed on the periphery of the later ritual landscape, as many enclosures of this type so often were. Towards the end of this period, around 3000 BC, the outer ditch and bank around Stonehenge appear on the scene. As yet, though, no stones have been erected. In the centuries after 3000 BC Stonehenge becomes the largest cremation cemetery yet known in Neolithic Britain. Then the earliest stones appear, a circle of eighty-two Bluestones transported to the area from Wales, sometime shortly before 2500 BC. Shortly after 2500 the main sarsens are erected and the Avenue leading down to the River Avon is constructed. There are two settings of sarsens: an external circle capped with a continuous lintel, which surrounds five so-called trilithons (two massive uprights capped by a lintel) set in an open oval, facing out onto the Avenue, which in turn is aligned on the direction of the midsummer sunrise.

The first main phase of Bronze Age barrow construction began sometime around 2400 BC and continued until about 1500 BC. A large number of round barrows of many forms (some had large mounds, others had small mounds or no mounds at all) were erected, most of them around the edges of the natural dip in the landscape – sometimes referred to as the 'bowl' or 'basin' – in which Stonehenge sits. The layout of the site suggests that the activities within Stonehenge were intended to be viewed, or more probably glimpsed, from outside the earlier bank and ditch which still encircled the Stones. Ceremonial processions would have arrived there from sites slightly further afield, such as Durrington Walls and Woodhenge, some 3 kilometres to the north-east (although almost double that distance if approached via the Avenue and River Avon).

My favourite view of the Stonehenge basin is from the King Barrow Ridge due east of the Stones, and readily accessible off the dual carriageway A303, when travelling east. These large barrows, which were probably erected around 2000 BC, were carefully placed in a dramatic row along the western edge of the ridge, where they dominate the skyline when seen from the Stones. Other substantial groups or rows of barrows were positioned around the edge of the Stonehenge basin to the north, south and west. Only a few barrows were placed close by the Stones and it is believed that these might be special in some way. The Stonehenge ritual landscape is vast, extending well beyond the basin in which the Stones sit. It is difficult to draw a hard-and-fast boundary, but the area where barrows and other sites occur with the greatest frequency measures very approximately about 6 × 7 kilometres.

It is sometimes very difficult to distinguish between the late Neolithic and the early Bronze Age. Stonehenge sits right on the bridge between the two. I discussed the houses within the great henge at Durrington Walls in the previous chapter. However, the henge at Durrington, in which they were placed, continued in use into the Bronze Age, along with the complex circular setting of posts, known as Woodhenge, alongside it. Both sites were part of the larger Stonehenge landscape and I want now to examine how that might have worked.

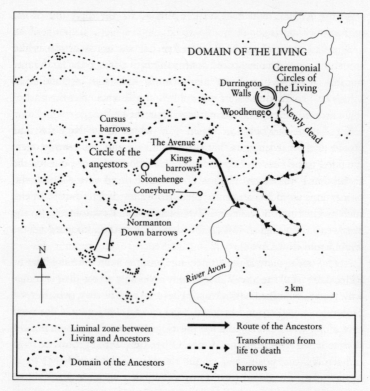

Fig. 3.1 An interpretation of how the various components of the Stonehenge ritual landscape might have operated, *c.* 2500 BC. Stonehenge sits at the centre of a landscape (the Domain of the Ancestors) given over to the celebration of death. Lines of barrows, such as the New King and Cursus barrows, differenti-ate this zone from an outer boundary zone which was probably perceived as being spiritually dangerous. Beyond this zone was the Realm of the Living where people gathered together in and around wooden henges like those at Durrington Walls and Woodhenge. The safest route through the zone was via the Stonehenge Avenue which was linked to Durrington Walls by the River Avon.

Early in the Bronze Age there was a gradual shift away from sites like Woodhenge, constructed of large timbers, towards more permanent replacements made of stone.[8] At the same time the pattern of use seems to have changed, from repeated visits to specific sites, where pits and other smaller features were excavated, sometimes seemingly at random, to fewer visits that sometimes involved major structural changes.[9] As time passed the 'use' – if that is indeed the correct term – of places like Stonehenge and Avebury could be seen to reach out into the landscape, and indeed far beyond. These later evolutionary stages of ritual landscapes can be hard to interpret with any confidence, but the earlier episodes seem somewhat more straightforward.

We shall never know for certain how people in the Neolithic and Bronze Age regarded ritual landscapes, but we can make some intelligent guesses. There does seem, for example, to have been quite a clear distinction between the Realms of the Living and of the Dead, the former expressed by timber structures, the latter by stone.[10] In the landscape around Stonehenge, for example, the Realm of the Living was around Durrington Walls and Woodhenge, some 3 kilometres west of the Stones.[11] Recent excavations have found evidence for a massive 30-metre-wide roadway leading down from the south entranceway at Durrington Walls to the Wiltshire Avon. At this point people either took boats or walked east along the riverside until they encountered the Stonehenge Avenue which led them to Stonehenge itself, the final stretch being along the summer solstice alignment of the sun. As if to emphasize the difference between the two hypothetical Realms, and the distinction between the living and the dead, archaeological excavations at Stonehenge have produced very little direct evidence for settlement, whereas Durrington Walls and the area around Woodhenge has revealed houses plus vast quantities of animal bones, pottery and other debris. The animal bones, incidentally, include many joints of pork, probably from animals killed in the winter, suggesting that here the main emphasis was on the winter solstice.

Modern views suggest that the first processional way near the Stones, the Stonehenge Cursus, was symbolic and did not link the Stones to any particular geographical or solar feature. It is now clear, however, that the Avenue was constructed sometime after the importation of the Bluestones and dates to the final phase of construction when the great stones were erected. The great stones were most likely erected closer to 2500 than 1600 BC.[12] Most of the round barrows that surround the Stonehenge basin can be dated to the centuries between 2200 and 1500 BC, which is significantly later. There can be little doubt that for a millennium after their erection the Stones were a magnet that attracted some very rich burials. After about 2000 BC Bronze Age barrows often become smaller-scale centres of importance in their own right, and are repeatedly used to receive so-called 'secondary' burials as late as 1500 BC, and occasionally even later.

The great sites of British prehistory have come to us not in their final form, but in fragments from the various periods of their use that have somehow managed to survive. Sometimes later modifications obscure what has gone before. The sight that greets the visitor to Stonehenge today would have looked very odd to a person in the early Bronze Age. For a start, more than four millennia of weathering have transformed the newly quarried pinkish sarsens, and strongly contrasting darker Bluestones, into the familiar lichen-covered greyish stones we can see today. We know from the recent work into stone circles that sometimes quite subtle differences in colour were important in prehistory.

It is only natural to concentrate on landscapes as spectacular as that around Stonehenge when they were in their prime. But a certain amount can be learnt by examining how they were treated in their decline and abandonment. The recent detailed survey that showed very few Mesolithic flint axes in the area of the Stones also mapped the outlines of late Bronze Age fields (they are shown on the general map of the Stonehenge landscape, Fig. 3.1).[13] At present we do not know for certain when these were first laid out, but parallels elsewhere in Wessex would suggest it was sometime around 1200 BC. Others were created in the Iron Age. Their distribution clearly avoids the central area we described as the Realm of the Ancestors and also most of the liminal or transitional zone around it. This could be entirely due to the effects of subsequent agriculture, because we know the area around Stonehenge was subjected to heavy ploughing in the nineteenth and twentieth centuries. But, if that were the case, we might expect to find traces of these later prehistoric fields on the periphery of the major monuments, such as around the fringes of the Stones themselves. But this does not happen. It is interesting, too, that there are known Iron Age fields directly alongside Durrington Walls, which was never within the areas reserved for the dead; quite the contrary, in fact: this henge was a focus for the living, not the dead.

So it would be very surprising if the end of the active phase of the

Fig. 3.2 Stonehenge seen from the slope of Stonehenge Down to the west. Stonehenge sits within a complex and very large 'ritual landscape' that includes hundreds of barrows and other religious Neolithic and Bronze Age monuments. This view, taken from the western side of the Stonehenge basin, shows the Stones and the ever-present visitors, who have themselves become a feature of the modern Stonehenge landscape. Behind, lit by the sun on a stormy June day, can be seen five of the seven surviving New King barrows, which overlook the Stonehenge basin from the east.

Stonehenge landscape, which happened sometime after 1500 BC, also marked the end of all interest in the site that still attracts so many visitors today. As the organization of the landscape was based essentially on ideas it seems reasonable to suggest that these persisted, as ideas will, into much later times. At first their influence was strong, but towards the Roman period they grew less persistent. In post-Roman times new myths arose to 'explain' the Stones – a process I am continuing, now.

It is by no means the case that the stone circles and other ritual sites of the late Neolithic and Bronze Age were of necessity grand, and were only to be found within long-lived ritual landscapes. There are still some 900 stone circles surviving in the British Isles, probably representing a tiny proportion – perhaps 5–10 per cent – of the number originally constructed. Even today, some five to six millennia after their erection, they still retain a remarkable presence in the landscape and demonstrate that the communities of the period lived in and exploited the British landscape, and not just the 'softer' regions of the valleys and lowlands. Some of the smaller ritual sites would have involved an enormous amount of work, from relatively thinly spread upland settlements.

Take, for instance, the stones near the village of Trellech (sometimes 'Trelleck' on modern maps) in the Welsh Marches of Monmouthshire, This was a bustling town in the earlier Middle Ages, a major centre for the production of ironwork. In Welsh, Trellech means 'the town of the stones'. Just outside the village was a group of three Neolithic or early Bronze Age standing stones which gave the place its name. They were erected on a flattened area of ground, most probably between 3000 and 2000 BC. The preparation of the ground and the transport and erection of these stones was plainly a major project, that would probably have involved dozens, if not hundreds, of people. So there was clearly a need for a focus for social gatherings and ceremonies. That place had to be made special, as it would have been important, not just to local people, but to more distant communities. The ceremonial centre would also have required communal decisions, first to choose the right place, then to prepare the ground and erect the stones; finally the community would have to arrange a regular, perhaps seasonal, cycle of events for their new centre.

The ideas that were fundamental to the use and construction of both individual sites and ritual landscapes did not remain static in the Bronze Age. It was a process of change and adaptation which has recently been closely investigated in north-eastern Scotland. One fascinating group of sites is the recumbent stone circles which were constructed in the centuries around 2500 BC.[14] They are characterized by a large (recumbent) stone lying horizontally on the ground and marked out by taller, pillar-like 'flanker' stones at each end. The three stones form part of a stone circle, and generally occur in the south-east quadrant, facing the rising sun, although this arrangement has also been linked to the moon. Perhaps more to the point, the flankers often frame a prominent landmark, such as a mountain peak. Recumbent stone circles are generally found on the most fertile land in north-east Scotland and they are often associated with cairns, which sometimes seal, or cap them off, at the end of their lives. Recent thorough excavation has shown that at least three examples are closely linked to cremation rites and it is tempting to see the framing of prominent landscape features, and the alignment on the sun and/or moon, as a means of uniting the dead with the ancestors whose realm was in the hills. The addition of solar/lunar alignment would link those beliefs with the powers of nature and the natural order of the world.

HIDDEN LANDSCAPES

The ritual landscapes discussed so far have had the great advantage of being readily visible both on the ground and from the air. This is largely an accident of their geology and subsequent history. But in many instances ancient landscapes are buried and concealed beneath alluvial flood-clay, hill-wash, wind-blown sand (often known as brickearth) or peat. In the past the only way to discover such landscapes was actively to seek them out, by using probes and augers or by looking along the sides of freshly cleaned-out drainage ditches. Recently, however, new techniques of aerial reconnaissance (such as LIDAR) have been developed that either 'see' below the ground or manage to measure the surface with such accuracy that even the slightest undulation can be digitally mapped. Often these tiny undulations conceal much larger features below ground. These techniques of aerial remote sensing are having an increasing impact on landscape survey in Britain and elsewhere. To take a famous example, the largest (260 square kilometres) temple complex in the world at Angkor Wat in Cambodia, which until very recently has mostly remained hidden from view beneath thick forest cover, has recently been fully mapped using high-resolution radar imagery obtained from the space shuttle.[15]

The best-known series of buried landscapes in Britain are those of the Fens in the counties around the Wash.[16] Here the landscape can broadly be separated into two zones, an area of marine silts closer to the coast and behind that a lower-lying region, mostly in Cambridge-shire, of freshwater peats that accumulated in shallow meres behind the silt lands.[17] Since the Second World War both landscapes have been the scene of intensive agriculture, which has involved the deep-draining of huge areas. As the peaty soils dry out they become loose and powdery, and soon blow away on windy days, especially in March when spring-grown cereals are drilled. On warm windy days in springtime 'Fen Blows' can transport huge black clouds of peaty soil for miles. As the land erodes away, in a process erroneously but widely referred to as peat 'shrinkage', pre-existing features, such as barrows that had been buried before the peat began to form, are revealed, first as low undulations which appear to grow a tiny amount each year, as the land around them erodes away.

Aside from numerous individual and smaller groups of barrows, very large barrow cemeteries below peaty soils are now known in the Cambridgeshire (formerly Huntingdonshire) Fens around Haddenham, near Ely, near Earith in the lower Great Ouse Valley and in Borough Fen, just north of Peterborough.

The problems posed by 'peat shrinkage' are not new. Engineers and farmers had known about the phenomenon ever since the first large-scale fen drainage of the seventeenth century, but technology had managed to stay ahead of potential flooding as land surfaces fell, first by the replacement of windmill pumps by steam pumps, then by oil engines and today by pumps powered by electricity. During the Second World War the national need to provide home-grown food led to the Dig for Victory campaign, where huge areas of pasture land were ploughed up. This happened on a very large scale in the Fens, but the land never reverted to grazing after the war, with the result that the area today is almost entirely arable. Such land is far more prone to erosion than permanent pasture.

INHABITING THE LANDSCAPE IN THE BRONZE AGE

During the late Bronze Age village-like settlements became an increasingly common and important feature of the British landscape. In the past, however, it was believed that there was a distinct separation between such domestic sites and the ritual sites that so often accompanied them. Today this distinction seems far less clear-cut. One example should suffice.

The previous chapter showed the Neolithic bank cairn at Roughtor, on Bodmin Moor, was aligned on prominent features on the skyline. This also served to divide the lower-lying landscape, towards the foot of the tor, into two distinct areas: one given over to open grazing and burial cairns, the other to enclosed settlements and their fields. It would appear then, that there was a clear difference between domestic, daily life and the afterlife, for want of a better term.

The project at Roughtor investigated three house circles. Each originally formed part of an enclosed village-like settlement, of probably some 200 people. At least two of the buildings reveal the unmistakable signs of deliberately constructed cairns within and across the walls of the houses. Burials were not found in these cairns, but there can be little doubt that they were the remains of rituals associated with the houses' abandonment.[18] Most probably the stones used in the cairns came from the walls that were partially demolished when the family moved out. One cannot say whether the abandonment of these buildings was an act of free will, or was imposed by others, but the tearing down of the walls and the erection of a cairn would have effectively prevented immediate reoccupation.

The full impact of the introduction of farming to Britain happened in the early Bronze Age. During the Neolithic huge areas of landscape were cleared of trees and woodland, a process that gathered pace in the early Bronze Age. But many of these were essentially open landscapes, possibly peopled by itinerant communities, or by mobile flocks and herds. It was not until the close of the third millennium BC that we begin to have evidence for the laying-out of the first field systems. These field systems seem generally to have respected territories that had come into being in Neolithic times and they can be seen as a response to a growing population, both of people and of livestock. As the farmed landscape became increasingly 'busy' it was also necessary to fence off and protect fields of growing crops. Many landscapes in less accessible upland and moorland regions were extensively farmed in the Bronze Age, and the field systems laid out survive to this day, because there has been little or no agricultural activity there since.

The moorlands of the south-west are a case in point. As we saw at Bodmin, the moors are important because they preserve features of most periods and it is possible to see relationships between barrows (or cairns) and field systems particularly well. Many of these landscapes have only been subjected to intensive farming in prehistory, the Roman period, and sometimes in medieval times, too, but these later farmers worked within limits imposed by the forces of traction at their disposal, which at best would have consisted of two oxen. In the nineteenth and twentieth centuries power farming, whether driven by steam or diesel, was much more destructive.

The creation of National Parks has protected many delicate moorland landscapes, including Exmoor and Dartmoor. Dartmoor is famous for its Bronze Age reaves, fields that run across the moor in a most remarkable fashion, regardless of the contours.[19] Reaves are low and straight stone banks, which probably formed the base for an earthen bank, on which a hedge was planted. The entire system did not appear overnight but most were first laid out in the century after 1700 BC. They continued in use for over half a millennium and began to be abandoned after 1000 BC, when conditions on the moor became wetter. The methodical way in which these fields were laid out strongly suggests that these were planned landscapes, where alignments and boundaries had been agreed between different communities long before the work began. Some of the more important boundaries actually follow earlier land divisions, as they are sometimes lined up on burial cairns that can predate the reaves by two or three centuries. The people who farmed the reaves positioned their settlements within the fields, but generally left their burial cairns outside them.

Although the moors of the south-west are superficially similar upland landscapes with a prevailing moist, Atlantic climate, they all have distinctively different prehistoric landscapes. As we have seen, unlike Dartmoor the prehistoric fields on Bodmin tend to follow the contours of the land, and house circles do not occur in loosely defined 'neighbourhoods' so much as in enclosed villages. Exmoor has revealed prehistoric field systems whose alignment follows rather different principles.[20] The orientation and layout of fields here were mostly dictated by the lie of the land, but they were also influenced by the presence of barrowfields nearby.

I have described how barrows may be positioned on the skyline, on ridges or within ritual landscapes; but frequently too they occur

Fig. 3.3 An aerial view of the Dartmoor Reaves in the Rippon Tor area of north-east Dartmoor. This view shows the layout of the reaves – long, straight, parallel banks of stone – that formed the boundaries of later Bronze Age fields. Within the fields can be seen small rings of stone. These represent the collapsed walls of roundhouses and they often occur, as here, in groups or 'neighbourhoods'. Houses were often placed within or close by reaves and are frequently found near small enclosed farmyards, where livestock and/or hay could have been kept over winter.

on their own, in small groups or out in the farmed landscape. When the land around them is excavated it is often found that their siting is far from haphazard. Sometimes they mark quite subtle places in the landscape, such as the transition from seasonally flooded to flood-free ground. Scale is important here. In a flat landscape a 'hill' of just one metre may mark the difference between land where crops could, or could not, be grown. By way of contrast, sometimes groups, rows or clusters of barrows may mark major tribal territorial boundaries, as was probably the case in Wessex around 2000 BC.[21]

It is now becoming increasingly common to find single barrows or ring-ditches located at regular intervals through late Bronze and Iron Age field systems. Excavations at Fengate, Peterborough and elsewhere around the Fen margins have shown how barrows and henges were placed at significant spots on the boundaries of different landholdings.[22] The regular spacing of these boundary barrows (and sometimes burnt mounds too) suggests that the open landscape was initially parcelled up into agreed territories, or family holdings, by barrows. Later, as land use intensified, barrows were reinforced by linear divisions, such as ditches, hedges and banks.

In certain lowland areas, such as the Trent and Welland valleys, later Bronze Age boundary markers took the form of 'pit alignments', which show up very dramatically on aerial photographs. However, the importance of many boundary-marker barrows persisted, right through to the final years of the Bronze Age. Many barrows positioned on boundaries have produced evidence for repeated use and reuse, such as the insertion of numerous secondary cremations into the mound, for several generations after initial construction.[23]

The careful positioning and repeated use of boundary barrows within a farmed landscape suggests that the presence of the ancestors mattered. They were the spiritual forces that reinforced the actual partition of the landscape and their perceived presence ensured that agreements were adhered to. In other instances there are human bodies placed in field ditches along the boundaries of different landholdings.[24] Sometimes, especially in the early Bronze Age, there are small pits carefully filled with highly decorated early Bronze Age Beaker pottery, animal bones and other evidence for feasting.[25] At the close of the last chapter we saw how recent excavation of the great henge at Durrington Walls near Stonehenge has shown that pork was an important part of such feasts in the later Neolithic and the tradition continued into the Bronze Age.[26]

I started this chapter arguing that the transition from the Neolithic to the Bronze Age was hard to detect. In certain areas, however, this was decidedly not the case. In the Western Isles, for instance, we see a marked increase in land use and settlement from the start of the Bronze Age. There is a huge increase in all sorts of archaeological evidence after about 2500 BC, by which time substantial areas of woodland had been cleared of trees.

The revelation of the extent of Bronze Age fields and farming has been one of the most important discoveries in British archaeology. Quite simply it has transformed our understanding of the landscape and of its antiquity. This new knowledge did not happen by accident. Throughout the 1950s, 1960s and 1970s thousands of sorties were flown by private light aircraft and by the RAF. Often these planes were piloted by aerial archaeologists. One can see all sorts of strange things from the air, some of which seem senseless and inexplicable, until one returns to the ground and pores over historical maps. Then what looked like a hugely elongated earthen slug turns out to be the remains of a long medieval headland (a bank of earth thrown up when the plough turns), or a group of faint parallel ditches is revealed as an extension to a long-forgotten abbey precinct. Many of the linear features (usually filled-in ditches or upstanding banks or walls) revealed on aerial photographs of this period could not be dated with any precision, but were plotted nonetheless. These new plots respected barrows and other ancient monuments, which suggested they might be prehistoric. But it took some time to show that many were important elements of long-abandoned Bronze Age field systems.

My own introduction to Bronze Age fields happened in 1971 when I began excavations at Fengate, then an area of flat farmland on the Fen margins, immediately east of Peterborough.[27] When I did a search through the huge aerial photographic archive, I was particularly intrigued by three very straight and double-ditched 'trackways' that could clearly be seen to run across the lighter gravel soils of the fen margins, down to the wetter ground of the true fen, where they vanished.[28]

Their straightness and regular spacing, approximately every 200 metres, had led people to suppose that they were probably Roman. But after studying every photograph I could lay my hands on, I realized that the three 'trackways' formed part of an altogether larger system that was actually cut through by a Roman road. So they had to be prehistoric. In our first two seasons of excavation we showed they were the main elements of a field system whose origins lay in the Bronze Age.[29] Later we discovered that the earliest parts of the system lay at

Fig. 3.4 A reconstructed Bronze Age droveway at Flag Fen, Peterborough. The evidence for this droveway was excavated at Fengate, about a kilometre from the site of its reconstruction. Droveways like this were arranged every 200 or so metres and were defined by ditches accompanied by banks with hedges; they were laid out along the margins of the western Fens from about 2500 BC. Each drove ran at right angles to the wetland and would have been used to take livestock to and from fenland pastures during the drier months of summer. The Bronze Age field systems began to be abandoned from about 1200 BC.

the very start of the Bronze Age, around 2500 BC.[30] This early date makes the Fengate fields among the earliest in Britain.

Even the largest ditches of the Fengate Bronze Age field system would not have been stock-proof. Excavation proved that the ditches were accompanied by banks, which had been placed a short distance away to prevent them from slipping straight back into it after heavy rain. I can remember looking at the ditches and their banks and wondering how they could have functioned. My theory was that they had been dug to surround fields and I was confirmed in this idea by the quantities of cattle and sheep bones we had recovered. Yet they seemed so slight and insubstantial. Then it came to me: a hedge, even quite a low one, if planted on the top of the bank would soon provide an effective barrier, especially if it was 'laid' in the manner Midland hedges are to this day. It all made sense, but there was no conclusive proof, not that is, until the summer of 2005, when I went to visit a contract excavation being run by the Cambridge University team.

The Cambridge excavation had found a deeper and wetter Bronze Age ditch where the lowest levels were waterlogged and preservation of leaves, twigs and other organic material was superb. I was acting as photographer for my wife Maisie, who was the specialist advising the team on ancient wood and woodworking. Handed a rather unprepossessing blackthorn twig she suddenly stiffened with excitement and passed it to me with a huge grin: 'That's what you've been waiting for,' she said. And it was. The twig had a side-shoot trimmed off but most importantly it had grown through a right angle in a most distinctive fashion, usually only found in trimmed hedges. Subsequently, many more right-angled pieces were found, one of which gave a radiocarbon date of 2500 BC.

Fig. 3.5 Blackthorn twig from a waterlogged deposit near a Bronze Age field boundary ditch, at Fengate, Peterborough. Note how the end of the twig to the right passes through a right angle. This pattern of growth usually results from repeated hedge-trimming. This piece of wood has been radiocarbon-dated to 2500 BC, making it probably the earliest evidence for hedging in the world.

We can only guess how the Bronze Age hedges were set but I suspect that many would have been in the form of winter hardwood cuttings.[31] These are taken from hardwood grown the previous season and are usually placed along a bank to ensure good drainage. In wet soils the cuttings can rot before they begin to sprout in the spring. So the bank was useful in two ways: as an obstacle to livestock and to keep the cuttings dry.

The double-ditched trackways were in fact ditched droveways which were used to funnel livestock being driven from the drier land of the Fen margins, and hinterland beyond, down to summer pastures in the fen. Droves or droveways were routes specially intended to be used by large flocks or herds. They were invariably well hedged and sometimes had a slightly raised surface to aid drainage. In post-Roman times some were constructed along flood-protection banks. The Bronze Age droves at Fengate were narrower than their medieval counterparts and formed the skeleton of a field system approximately a kilometre in width, but still of unknown extent. Between the major droves the landscape was subdivided into fields of various sizes. This arrangement suggests that the droveways were laid out first and formed the boundaries of individual or family holdings, which were then further partitioned.

Bronze Age field systems are recognized around many parts of the Fen margins and on the low-lying, drier 'islands' (such as the Isle of Ely) within the main area of the Fens.[32] Most seem to have been laid out for use by livestock and are characterized by double-ditched droveways that run at right angles to the wetter land. At Fengate the main settlements were on the drier, flood-free ground around the margins of the low-lying basin of Flag Fen.

The Bronze Age field system of Fengate, like those north and south, along the Welland and Ouse valleys, was primarily laid out to handle and manage large numbers of sheep and/or cattle. In many instances this pattern of farming can be linked to high-status uses of bronze, such as flesh-hooks and cauldrons, which when taken together with the evidence of animal bones suggest that feasting and the consumption of meat were important parts of social life.[33] However, when wetter conditions began to prevail in the early first millennium BC winter pastures were drowned and intensive livestock-keeping became more hazardous. One result of this was a switch to mixed arable and livestock

Fig. 3.6 The excavation (in 1974) of earlier Bronze Age field-boundary ditches at Fengate, Peterborough. Note the gravel soils of the Fenland margins into which the ditches were cut, just before 2000 BC; note also the peaty soils of Flag Fen in the middle distance and the chimneys of Whittlesey brickworks on the skyline. The two large ditches (*left and centre*) in the foreground mark the edges of a main or boundary droveway that led down to the edge of the wet fen, just beyond the field on the far side of the excavation.

farming where the majority of the community lived all year round on the higher land of the Fen margins. This would explain why the occurrence of wetter conditions actually fostered the growing of otherwise dry-loving plants, such as wheat.

The field systems of the Fen margins were laid out to take livestock returning in the autumn from the rich grazing of the open fen, during the months of summer. As Fenland water levels started to rise in October and November, the flocks and herds moved back to the drier ground and the field systems were then needed to house and manage this influx of animals, many of which had had lambs and calves during the summer. Thanks to a recent re-survey of all the available aerial photographs, we now know that the Fengate fields were laid out in a band about a kilometre wide along the Fen margins.[34] 'Inland' or westwards from the Fen, towards the drier limestone and clay soils that lie beneath modern Peterborough, the heavier clay land was not enclosed by field ditches. Presumably this open ground would have been used as pasture in the winter months as and when the better grazing in the fields along the gravel soils of the Fen margins became exhausted.[35]

Large-scale, detailed surveys of upland and moorland areas have revealed huge expanses of field systems, settlements and cairnfields. Similar long-term research in areas of Wessex has revealed what can only be described as intensive cattle ranches, dating to the late Bronze Age. But some of the biggest surprises have come from co-ordinating the results of a host of isolated commercial excavations that have taken place across large parts of south-eastern England.[36]

This research has shown that the extensive Bronze Age field systems at Fengate and around the edges of the Fens do not sit in isolation, either chronological or geographical. More recently, huge landscapes of carefully laid-out rectangular fields[37] have been revealed across most of southern and eastern England, extending from the Welland Valley in south Lincolnshire to Cornwall. Many of these new field systems were discovered during pre-development rescue excavation.[38] Small farming settlements or farmsteads are distributed through most of these field systems, which also include many examples of shallow, wattle-lined wells, dug down, usually no more than two or three metres, to reach the groundwater table. Nearly all of these systems seem, like those at Fengate, to have been laid out to handle livestock. The majority, too, had been abandoned by the start of the Iron Age, around 700 BC. These rectangular fields provide convincing evidence that most of lowland southern Britain had been cleared of trees and was being actively farmed by the middle of the second millennium BC. Many of these field systems were laid out to take advantage of the natural landscape. Around the edges of the Fens and along river floodplains, for example, the principal axis of their alignment was usually at right angles to the wetland. This arrangement allows the individual farmers to have access to all types of land: wet, flood-prone and flood-free.

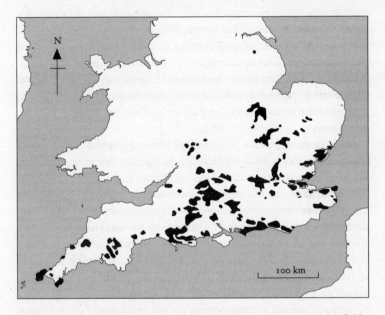

Fig. 3.7 A map showing the extent of known Bronze Age rectangular fields. These fields were mostly intended to contain and manage large numbers of livestock. They include small farmsteads, which were usually distributed throughout the fields. It is becoming increasingly apparent that the various field systems were separated by areas of open grazing where livestock could wander freely. Most date to the second half of the second millennium BC and most were abandoned by the Iron Age. The very earliest were laid out around 2500 BC.

Others were laid out on the winter or summer solstice, in the well-tried Neolithic and Bronze Age tradition.

Before the relatively recent discovery of Bronze Age rectangular fields, the best-known form of prehistoric fields were the so-called 'Celtic fields' that occur across large areas of chalk downland in southern Britain. Celtic fields are tiny by modern standards, ranging from about ½ to 1½ acres each. This size is better suited to the growing of crops than the keeping of livestock. We know that most Celtic fields were in use in the Iron Age, but there is increasing evidence that some had been laid out by the middle of the Bronze Age, say 1500 BC, and others by as much as half a millennium earlier.[39]

Although aerial photographs offer revealing traces of Bronze Age fields in upland areas right across Britain, the most easily spotted evidence for ancient farming consists of the clearance cairns, which are almost ubiquitous in upland areas.[40] One might suppose that stones were only cleared to allow the ground to be ploughed, but in actual fact simply by collecting all readily removable surface stones one greatly increases the area of available grazing and allows sunlight to reach grass leaves – and this encourages the pasture to renew itself more rapidly for that all-important 'first bite' in the spring and early summer. Heaps of stones cannot be dated of themselves, but very often they occur in areas where more formal and larger burial cairns are found. These are the upland equivalents of lowland Bronze Age barrows and come in a similar range of shapes and sizes, including small ring banks, simple heaps, heaps and banks, platforms and so on. These cairns often conceal burials or, more likely, cremations, although in most instances the acid soils have destroyed the bones themselves. What usually survives is the pot which held the cremation, or the small stone-built boxes which protected both burials and cremations.

There is evidence from upland peat bogs that the climate grew somewhat wetter from about 1200–500 BC, for the final centuries of the Bronze Age and into the Iron Age.[41] But the picture is far from straightforward. The first millennium BC saw water levels rise in the Fens, in Somerset and elsewhere, but it is not always clear whether this was the result of sea-level change or of climatic deterioration. In upland areas and in Lancashire there is evidence that peat bogs sustained by rainfall grew faster after 1200 BC. But wetter conditions did not necessarily lead to changes in the way people settled the landscape. In some upland areas, for example, there is evidence for retrenchment and the abandonment of higher fields, but in other equally exposed places, such as the Outer Hebrides, late Bronze Age settlement does not appear to falter.[42] One recurrent theme of this book is that decisions to abandon settlements are nearly always made by those on the spot and can only be understood if we also know the purely local circumstances. In the wetlands of Merseyside, for example, where one would expect a damper climate to have had potentially disastrous effects, pollen analyses indicate increasing agricultural activity in the late Bronze Age with little change or deterioration during the wetter years that followed 1000 BC.[43]

A NEW ORDER (1500–800 BC)

The world of the first half of the Bronze Age, up to about 1500 BC, was essentially a Neolithic one, with bronze tools. Then quite suddenly, halfway through the second millennium BC, we encounter an extraordinary series of changes and transformations. The old world was one of great monuments and large-scale ceremonies. The ancestors were probably regarded with the same reverence as 3,000 years earlier, when the first farmers settled in Britain. But after 1500 BC (the date that usually marked the transition from the early to the late Bronze Age) barrows ceased to be built and henges went out of use. Entire ritual landscapes were abandoned. In their stead we find an altogether different style of archaeology: everything becomes smaller in scale; the dead are cremated or buried at home or in nondescript graves in the countryside.

After the middle of the second millennium BC rituals and ceremonies cease to happen at great centres like Stonehenge and move to more mundane places, such as rivers, bogs and ponds. Monuments, as such, become less important; instead the action is what matters. And sometimes the action could involve hugely valuable objects which were often smashed and offered to the waters of a river. Thousands of late Bronze Age swords, spearheads, daggers and other items were dredged from the waters of the Thames and other rivers when these were deepened and improved in the nineteenth century. In many areas, collections of metalwork, known as hoards, were simply placed in the ground, sometimes in a pot, box or bag. We can assume that the precise spot where these things were deposited was considered to be important, but we must not suppose that the 'offering' was the entire ceremony. For example, the fine objects that once belonged to a dead person could be placed in the ground quite separately from the grave, somewhere else. It was a one-off action in a one-off place, but similar hoards were put in the ground in late Bronze Age England, Scotland, Ireland and Wales – and on many thousands of separate occasions.

The major change in attitudes which these events reflect was of the profoundest importance, and was not confined to Britain alone but happened right across Europe at approximately the same time. It marked a shift in social and symbolic emphasis from ancestors and tombs to hearths and homes.[44] When barrow burial and the old ways of commemorating and marking the dead ceased in the centuries on either side of 1500 BC, we encounter an almost complete dearth of burials of any sort. In certain parts of southern and eastern England cremation cemeteries come into existence around 1400 BC, but these are not particularly common and they cannot be said to have had a major impact on the landscape. So during the late Bronze Age and for large areas of Britain in the early Iron Age it seems probable that most corpses were disposed of by means of cremation and their ashes scattered to the four winds. Some bodies may have been exposed to the birds on platforms where they were de-fleshed, a somewhat grisly ritual, known as excarnation.[45] All we can say with any confidence is that this new approach to death and the afterlife seemed to have happened spontaneously. Doubtless it was an expression of social change, which itself was a result of growing population, improved communication and ever-larger settlements. Ultimately the changes that happened after 1500 BC would later come to be identified in Iron Age Britain, as Celtic.

The process of change from ancestors to hearths and homes was already underway at the Roughtor site on Bodmin Moor, where the earlier way of taking social and symbolic possession of the landscape took the form of the bank cairn and numerous stone rows, standing stones and burial cairns. These practices of placing monuments in the landscape were replaced around 1500 BC with an enclosed settlement and fields whose location respected the earlier sites but did not add to them or modify them in any way. In other words, the significance of the old places was acknowledged, but people now had a new view of the world, which placed emphasis on different aspects of life.

Very few sites have been found which take in this important period of change, but the settlement at Cladh Hallan on South Uist provides a fascinating exception. Fortunately for the excavators it was also unusually well preserved beneath thick accumulations of machair sands. Not only did the site provide evidence for the burial of the dead, but it also showed how that concern for the ancestors was physically and symbolically transferred from a cremation burial to the household hearth. As the excavator noted, it was a moment when the emphasis shifted from 'memorialising the dead to exalting the living'. This, surely, was the process which lay behind the great change of social and religious emphasis that happened around 1500 BC, and which had such a big impact on the shape of the countryside.[46]

The changes in burial practices coincided with the introduction of new rituals, such as the deposition of hoards of metalwork. In many instances the hoards, like the barrows and isolated graves of the early Bronze Age, were positioned at significant spots in the landscape, marking territorial boundaries or the transition from dry to wet ground.[47] This would support the idea that in certain respects hoards could be a substitute for the burial of a body, perhaps as an offering to the world of the ancestors. But in terms of the quite rapidly developing landscape, they are not of major importance. What matters now is the development of early field systems, together with the settlements that went with them. As anyone who has carried out field surveys in Britain can attest, the remains of settlements from the late Bronze Age are suddenly everywhere, whereas before that they had been rare indeed. We may be witnessing here quite a rapid 'hardening' or formalizing of the landscape in the face of growing populations of people and livestock. Whatever else they might portend, these changes certainly show that by the late Bronze Age the population was far more settled and less mobile.

Similar processes were under way in some of Britain's offshore island communities. In the late Bronze Age of the southern islands of the Outer and Inner Hebrides, for example, we see the development of permanent settlements, based on small groups of roundhouses within their garden-plot fields. This type of settlement continued until some-time around 200 BC, when the individual roundhouses were replaced by communal dwellings, which had been developing in the Northern Isles and in the north islands of the Outer Hebrides since the start of the Iron Age, in the eighth century BC.

THE INFLUENCE OF BRONZE

The influence of bronze itself in the landscape is telling. The last three decades of the twentieth century have seen the investigation of several prehistoric copper mines, principally in Wales and Ireland.[48] One might expect the earliest copper mines to have been shallow surface affairs with little evidence for large-scale production, but the mining of copper in the Bronze Age left an industrial landscape that can still be seen to this day.

Bronze is an alloy of about 90 per cent copper and 10 per cent tin. During the late Bronze Age a small amount of lead was also added to the mix to improve it. The tin used in bronze came mainly from river sources in Cornwall and was not, so far as we know, mined there in prehistory. We know from analysis of surviving metal objects that in the late Bronze Age large amounts of bronze were made from scrap metal, some of which was probably melted down and reused many times. It has been suggested that some of the larger hoards that appear in the archaeological record after 1500 BC included objects that had been chopped and cut up, as if the metal in the hoard was being accu-mulated to a certain weight. It is possible that these were specialized 'founders' hoards', or the stock-in-trade of metalsmiths. They may well have been, but some, including the largest hoard of all at Isleham in Cambridgeshire, were placed on the edges of wetlands in situations one might regard as in some way marginal.[49] Often, too, single finds may have been deliberately damaged before being offered to the waters. So it is debatable whether the founders' hoards were straight-forwardly 'industrial'. As in the case of the Neolithic flint mines and so-called 'axe factories', ritual and technology were still probably closely allied.

It used to be believed that the demand for bronze started as a trickle and only gradually became a flood. But recently discovered sites like 'Seahenge', the timber circle at Holme-next-the-Sea, Norfolk (erected in 2049 BC), can be shown by comparing the different axe-marks of the timbers to have been constructed using around fifty different axes.[50] This was most surprising, as one might have expected two or three but certainly not dozens of axes at this very early date. One reason for their rapid adoption was undoubtedly their efficiency. I have used both stone and bronze axes to fell trees and do carpentry and I can vouch for the fact that the metal tool is hugely superior in every respect. One can relax when using it, confident that a slight mis-hit will not smash the axe nor blunt it by detaching a large flake from the cutting edge. Other bronze tools and weapons were a similar improvement, the only possible exception being implements used to pierce or bore holes in tough materials like bone and antler, which continued to be made out of flint, certainly until the Iron Age, if not later.

But by far the best evidence for the extensive use of bronze comes from mining sites. The facts are these: shortly after 2000 BC the first deep copper mines were dug. The industry reached a peak between 1900 and 1500 BC.[51] Most Bronze Age mines went out of use in the Iron Age. Two of the best-known deep mines are at Mount Gabriel, in Co. Cork and Great Orme, north Wales.[52] Another major area of prehistoric mining is in mid-Wales, where five distinct areas of ore extraction have been found; here the largest and best-known mine is at Copa Hill.[53] The scale of metal-production was truly industrial by any standards: estimates based on the amount of copper ore mined and processed suggest that over their lives the Bronze Age mines at Mount Gabriel could have produced about 370 tonnes of copper and Great Orme some 175–235 tonnes. The figure from Great Orme alone is approximately ten times as much as the best previous estimate, based on surviving finds of the period, for the amount of metal in circulation in the British Bronze Age.

At Great Orme the Bronze Age mines are both opencast on the surface and penetrate deep below ground (to at least 70 metres) in a series of shafts and galleries. The less well-known opencast surface mine, which consisted of a labyrinth of roughly parallel trench-like workings, required the removal of some 40,000 cubic metres of material (probably weighing as many tonnes). The opencast workings were

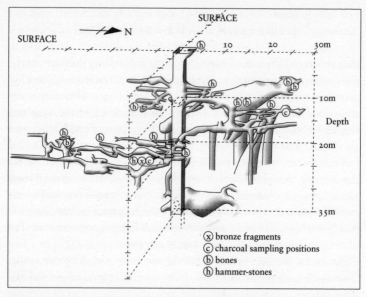

Fig. 3.8 A three-dimensional plan of the shafts and galleries of the Bronze Age copper mines at Great Orme, Llandudno, north Wales. This plan shows a small part of the original complex of Bronze Age mines, many of which were destroyed by Victorian mining operations. The mines at Great Orme flourished between 1900 and 1500 BC.

revealed in 1988 when Victorian rubble was removed during routine safety work.[54]

Recent excavation at numerous sites has produced clear evidence that most of the metal tools used in daily life were made by smiths locally, using imported metal, possibly in the form of ingots, or as scrap. Fragments of the fired-clay crucibles used to melt metal are quite often found, as are moulds, mostly of stone, but sometimes of clay too. The delicate clay moulds are difficult to spot on a dig and require careful excavation if their telltale smooth inner surfaces are to survive.[55]

CEREMONY AND FEASTING

Fengate showed how the early Bronze Age fields along the edges of the wetland were forced back by encroaching water.[56] As the fields around the edges of Flag Fen retreated, the pre-existing (Neolithic) route across the narrow strait that formed an entrance into the Flag Fen basin from the open Fen to the north began to be swamped. This strait also made the best route from the Fengate shore, with its fields and settlements, to the equally well-populated landscape at Northey, on the other side of the basin. Northey was located on the northern fringes of a large natural 'island' of clay, which today is largely covered by the medieval market town of Whittlesey. The route across the Fengate/Northey strait was elaborately rebuilt around 1300 BC in the form of a massive timber causeway. This causeway, known as the Flag Fen post alignment, was composed of thousands of posts with long pencil-like tips, which were firmly driven into the more solid ground beneath the accumulating peaty muds of Flag Fen.

The post alignment was discovered in 1982 and has been under excavation ever since, as its existence is threatened by drying out, caused by modern land drainage. The Flag Fen causeway was more than just a route, because every excavation has found dozens, sometimes hundreds, of metal objects, ranging from swords, daggers and spearheads to gold earrings, tiny pins and brooches; many of which had been deliberately broken before being offered to the waters. We now know that similar sites exist or have existed elsewhere in the Cambridgeshire Fens, in the Witham Valley near Lincoln, in south Wales, in the Trent Valley and in a drowned freshwater lake near Eastbourne. Some of these sites were also in use in the Iron Age. In one example, the causeway at Fiskerton in the Witham Valley, the posts were placed in the ground during winters when the moon had a total eclipse.[57] This shows a continuing concern for astronomical prediction; so it would seem that although many aspects of ritual and religion changed around 1500 BC, some remained constant.

A great deal has now been discovered about the prehistoric roads and trackways of Britain. The best known and earliest of these trackways was the Neolithic timber footpath in the Somerset Levels known as the Sweet Track; this has been dated by tree-ring to the winter of 3807/6 BC – at the very start of the British Neolithic.[58] So far the best evidence has come from wet areas, where the timbers of sites like Flag Fen have been preserved deep within anaerobic peats. Preserved timber can be dated by tree-rings and radiocarbon, but it is much harder to accurately date fragments of ancient trackways from dryland regions, although a number of stone-slab 'clapper' bridges from stream crossings in Dartmoor and Exmoor have been claimed quite plausibly as prehistoric.[59]

The transition from the Bronze to the Iron Age has been traditionally seen as a matter of technological change, but we now know that there was far more to it. The early centuries of the first millennium BC were a time of considerable social change, for which there is some evidence in the landscape. British society was becoming more hierarchical, both internally and between different communities. These events probably had their roots in the middle of the second millennium BC. After that, archaeological evidence becomes less stable: sites come and go with a rapidity that we would not have seen earlier. Even those most domineering sites of all, the great hillforts, have a lifespan of less than a millennium and most no more than 500 years, in comparison to the great ritual landscapes of the later Neolithic, many of which thrived for more than two millennia.

We shall see shortly how the hillforts of the Iron Age have their roots in the late Bronze Age and how we must assume that the appearance of these new sites reflected a world where society was changing. These changes probably involved a shift from more dispersed and communal settlement patterns, towards one of larger tribal groupings, under the control of a slowly emerging élite. These élites may well have travelled through their territories from one important centre to another, just as later monarchs travelled from one castle or large country house to another. It was only towards the end of the Iron Age that more permanent 'capitals', at places like Maiden Castle and Bamburgh, emerged.

A remarkable new type of site belonging to this period has recently been recognized. At first glance they have nothing to do with élites and prestige: their most diagnostic deposit is a thick accumulation of cattle manure, known as 'dark earth'. This has been built up over many centuries, but what distinguishes it from ordinary farmyard muck is the quantity of the metalwork, the evidence for metal-working and the hundreds of thousands of potsherds and animal bones founds in it. This is far too complex, rich and sophisticated to be a farmyard muck heap. Sites of this type have been found across the south-east from Wiltshire to the Thames and the Fens.[60] The best known is at Potterne, Wiltshire.[61] Most of the finds there can be closely dated to the late Bronze Age and suggest it was occupied for the five centuries from c. 1100 to 600 BC.

Potterne was excavated in the early 1980s, a time when more and more evidence was showing how the lower-lying, less spectacular landscapes of southern Britain still concealed some remarkably important sites. The more we surveyed and excavated the more convinced we became that even terms like 'site' were becoming redundant. In the uplands, for example, one can approach the ramparts of a great hillfort and be in little doubt where the site begins and ends. But at somewhere like Potterne, or Fengate, one could argue that the entire landscape is the 'site'. The gradual appreciation of the 'joined-up' nature of the emerging evidence also led to a more detailed and subtle approach to the landscape. We started to understand that very slight changes in topography – a hillock here, the bend of a river there – could have been hugely significant in the past. Even long-vanished ancient trees could once have played a part in the way the landscape was partitioned between, say, neighbouring tribes.

It is now quite clear, judging, for example, from the distribution of systems of rectangular fields right across southern Britain, that the lowlands and river valleys were becoming quite heavily populated from the middle of the second millennium BC. Perhaps the move away from places like Stonehenge and Avebury was ultimately a reflection of popular preference, just as most ordinary people in nineteenth-century London chose to visit nearby Southend or Brighton, rather than Bath or Cheltenham, which they would have visited the century before. That is probably why the evidence for ceremonial, represented by 'dark earth' sites and buried hoards, appears to shift away from places like Salisbury Plain towards landscapes that we know were heavily populated in the later Bronze and Iron ages. But that does not mean to say that the form of the landscape merely provided people with somewhere to live. In the recent past the selection of a site for a grand house, in an area where the topography is gentle, nonetheless managed to use whatever features there were to full advantage – one thinks, for example, of Greenwich Palace or Syon House in London. If the buildings are stripped away, however, the actual rise and fall of the landscape would not lead one to imagine that those particular spots would necessarily have been chosen for such grand structures. As an unashamed lowlander, I think of the late Bronze Age as the time when the British landscape came of age.

Potterne and the other 'dark earth' sites are carefully situated to overlook a particular stretch of gently undulating landscape and, although they do not dominate their surroundings like so many hillforts, their lowland setting makes this impossible anyway. It is valuable to see them first as extremely rich settlements within the most densely occupied areas of Bronze Age Britain, but also as special places, carefully positioned within a well-populated landscape. It is not hard to imagine that they were regularly visited by an emerging élite, and their retinue of attendants and hangers-on.

After 1500 BC, when barrows and great henges ceased to be built, archaeological sites can become much harder to spot, especially in the lowlands. At Potterne a modern cemetery needed to be extended; so excavations were carried out to assess what impact new graves would have on the ground beneath. The excavations revealed that the modern cemetery had been placed directly over an enormous late Bronze Age settlement, covering some 3.5 hectares and dating to 1100–600 BC. Among many other items the small dig produced some 100,000 potsherds, which together weighed a tonne.

After the momentous changes that happened around 1500 BC there was a switch from barrow burial and greater emphasis on the placing of valuable objects in the ground, usually in hoards. The objects buried in hoards mostly consist of hundreds of axes, broken-up swords, pins, bracelets and so forth. In the middle of the Bronze Age, shortly after the big change of 1500 BC, hoards often consisted of personal ornaments, such as bracelets, elaborate brooches and pins. In the late Bronze Age (1200–800 BC) the emphasis shifted towards weapons, axes and scrap metal. The change away from barrows towards hoards has usually been seen as a move away from big, centralized collective ceremonies towards more intimate rites, involving family or community.

Generally speaking, the shift is also seen as a move away from major collective decision-making, involving a number of communities spread over a large area, towards more localized leadership. This can in part be explained by the fact that around the middle of the second millennium BC there was less need to keep widely separated societies together, simply because population growth had already begun to move everybody closer. The landscape, too, was becoming better laid out and organized and communication between different communities was improving all the time.

So the Bronze Age ended more with a whimper than a bang. Nothing happened to suggest that we were about to enter a new era. No boatloads of Celts arrived, nor freighters laden with iron ore. The use of bronze for most tools continued well into the Iron Age and pottery styles also remained remarkably similar. Field systems continued to be used in both periods and the Bronze Age standard British roundhouse remained the norm throughout the Iron Age. Even hillforts, once believed to be the epitome of the Iron Age, can now be shown to have their roots firmly in the Bronze Age, as recent excavations at sites like Mam Tor, in Derbyshire, South Cadbury in Somerset and The Breiddin, in Powys have demonstrated. Nevertheless there was change and it was important. Regional identities had become more clearly defined and the landscape started to acquire a coherent pattern of distinctive regional characteristics, many of which then persisted right through the Roman period, and later. Some people see the six or seven centuries of the Iron Age as the time when the regions of Britain firmly established their distinctive character.

4

The Rise of Celtic Culture:
The Iron Age (800 BC–AD 43)

The people and communities of the Iron Age had a major effect on the development of the landscape. The change in emphasis from ancestors and tombs to hearths and homes that had begun in the late Bronze Age continued, but the Iron Age also possessed a distinctive cultural and artistic character all of its own, a character that subsequent generations have labelled Celtic. Before addressing the problem of dating the Iron Age it is worth noting how the pace of social change, as reflected by the new sites and monuments that were appearing in the landscape, is now really starting to speed up. But by the end of the Iron Age, when we are leaving prehistory, the transition into a world of recorded events and named people is not abrupt, but part of an evolutionary process.

Now to those dates. First we must define when the Iron Age started, and when it acquired its unique character. In that one respect the transition from the Bronze to the Iron Age is rather similar to that from the Neolithic to the Bronze Age, almost 2,000 years previously. The main difference between the two periods of transition is their pace. The earlier one was a prolonged seven hundred years, whereas the shift from Bronze to Iron Age took just two centuries, from 800 to 600 BC.[1]

The roots of the Iron Age lie at the middle of the Bronze Age, around 1500 BC. Without this major shift in social attitudes and beliefs, the Celts, hillforts, the Druids, Queen Boudica and the feuding tribes of the woad-painted Ancient Britons would never have been possible. The new emphasis on settlement and domestic life was also accompanied by the further adoption of early field systems, and the modification of many that were already there. The period sees the foundation of many new settlements within their Celtic fields, which today survive as banks, lynchets and cropmarks on hill- and mountain-sides all over Britain. Towards the end of the Iron Age some of the lowland settlements were becoming very large indeed. But without doubt the most iconic sites of the Iron Age are the great hillforts, whose earthen ramparts still dominate so many landscapes. In terms of straight visual impact they have never been bettered, but it would be unwise to suggest that they were necessarily centres of population. Indeed, some were never occupied at all and it is most likely that throughout the Iron Age the mass of the people still lived in the fertile valleys and plains, as they had done for countless generations.

The first iron objects appear in Britain in the early eighth century BC, when bronze implements of late Bronze Age style were still in large-scale production, and in active use. A recent discovery in West Berkshire has proved beyond doubt that there was active iron-working in the late Bronze Age. The site in question, a settlement at Hartshill Quarry, near Upper Bucklebury, has produced nearly 2,000 pieces of 'hammer-scale', the small fragments of iron that detach when the hot metal is being hammered into shape, which can reliably be dated to the tenth century BC.[2] In general, however, it would seem that iron was not commonly used in Britain for another five hundred years.[3] We assume that the new technology, with its requirement to produce sustained high temperatures, was adopted by smiths who had previously worked with bronze.

Iron ore can be smelted at just 800 °C and copper (the principal constituent of bronze) melts at 1,083 °C, so one might suppose that iron was simpler to produce. The trouble is that to make objects of wrought iron, the smelted metal must then be beaten, hot, at 1,000–1,100 °C.[4] This process requires the maintenance of consistently high temperatures and better control of the airflow. Technologically, these were important advances and the tools they produced were a great improvement on what had gone before.[5] Iron ore occurs more widely across Britain than tin or copper and from the middle of the Iron Age evidence for iron-working is found in many settlements.

Those are some of the archaeological facts, but for us the distinctive character of the period derives from its superb Celtic art and the appearance and proliferation, right across Britain, of hillforts, manned by Celtic warriors. But first a word about the Celts. The popular image is of bearded bards, dark-haired moody maidens strumming on half-sized harps and hard-drinking warriors brawling among themselves. In actual fact this vision of the Celts is largely a creation of eighteenth- and nineteenth-century scholars, antiquarians, artists and writers.[6] There is no evidence that the Celts can be equated with a distinctive ethnicity, like, say, the Basques. It used to be believed that the Celts invaded Britain from central Europe, but this idea has now been wholly discredited. Many of the religious beliefs that can be identified with the Celts, such as the deposition of valuable offerings into water, can be shown to have had origins well back in the Bronze Age, at places like Flag Fen.

The Iron Age appeals to archaeologists because the evidence for it is so good. This is particularly true in the British landscape. There are many reasons for this. After about 500 BC pottery improved in technical quality, which means that it survives much better in the soil, and that in turn allows us to identify and date abandoned settlements more readily. The population was rising in the early first millennium BC, slowly at first, but with increasing rapidity after about 500 BC. This led to a huge increase in settlements and the need for fields. Meanwhile in the uplands and in hilly parts of the south we see the proliferation of many hillforts, which have survived remarkably well because they were often positioned on the top of steep hills that are hard to plough, even with modern equipment.

The Iron Age was probably also the period when the British Isles were first circumnavigated and their existence brought to general attention in Europe, but it is doubtful whether the British would have been aware of themselves as Britons. In other words, the tribe would still have been the most important part of their individual identities. The idea of 'Britishness' probably only began to emerge later in Roman times. During the Iron Age, traders regularly plied the Channel, the southern North Sea and the western approaches via Iberia, Normandy and Brittany. An account of one particular journey, made in the fourth century BC by a merchant known as Pytheas the Greek, has survived from the Iron Age and paints a fascinating picture, not just of Britain, but of the many traders and fishermen living along the coasts regularly making sea voyages that even today we would not take for granted. He has been described as the man who discovered Britain. By the time

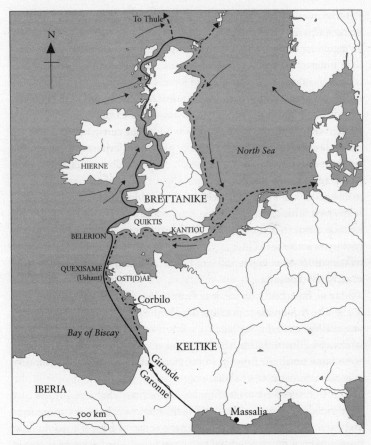

Fig. 4.1 A map showing the probable route around Britain taken by Pytheas the Greek, *c.* 310–306 BC. The names of ports and territories were those used at the time. Pytheas was a merchant from the Greek colony at Massalia (modern Marseilles) and like all ancient seafarers he would have stayed close to land and only rarely embarked on longer voyages. Pytheas wrote an account of his journey, *On the Ocean*, which has not survived, but passages from it are quoted by eighteen ancient authors, all of whom mention him by name.

Pytheas was sailing around Brittany and the western seaboard of Britain, the tin-producing areas of Cornwall and the south-west were in regular trading contact with the Mediterranean world.[7]

In the early years of archaeology, hillforts tended to dominate perceptions of the Iron Age, just as the forts themselves so often dominated the landscape. Today we realize that the landscape around the hillforts was just as important, and contains abundant evidence for the farms, fields and settlements of the people who built and occupied them. We can only ever explain the existence of hillforts if we study them in their landscape setting. Hillforts required a prosperous population to construct and then to support them – a fact that applies as much to the Iron Age as it does to the castles of the Middle Ages.[8]

No two hillforts are the same. Surveys have shown that they often form a centre – a focus – for the landscapes around them. I say 'a centre' and not 'the centre', because we can now demonstrate that the relationship of a given hillfort to its surrounding landscape was constantly changing.

Many settlements of the late Bronze Age, down valley sides and out in the floodplains, predate the local hillfort. In other instances one hillfort will be replaced by another as part of a process of landscape consolidation that was particularly well marked on the downland southern Britain. In most cases we are probably looking at a genuine process of social competition, where the people in the new 'top' hillfort are related by blood to those in the one it has just supplanted. If, as seems likely, many hillforts were centres for markets and exchange, then it would also make sense to have a consolidated system, where more potential customers could be gathered together at any one time.

Any discussion of a particular landscape in medieval or post-medieval times takes for granted that the distribution and exchange of the products of farming, and other trade, played an important part in its creation, maintenance and development. This is probably true also of prehistoric landscapes. There is little doubt that a free market economy did not exist in the Iron Age. Most authorities would also agree that such a thing did not exist in Roman, Saxon or early medieval times either.[9]

The first truly free market only began to emerge in Britain after the fourteenth century, following the first waves of plague and the consequent freeing-up of social ties and the obligations of feudalism. In earlier times most trade would have been 'socially embedded'. This means that trade, or more properly the exchange of goods, took place as part of wider social obligations, either to a lord or landlord (as in the feudal system), or to family members. The use of money is not in itself an indicator of a free market economy, as we know from numerous findspots across southern Britain that coins were used from later Iron Age times, when all trade was still firmly socially embedded. Throughout most of later prehistory leaders of society would have shown their authority by exchanging high-status gifts, which they in turn would have obtained through exchange; but it is also probable that this took place at lower levels of society too. Livestock, for example, probably changed hands as part of long-running deals that were made when a marriage contract was negotiated between two families.

Long-distance or high-status exchanges would not have precluded the possibility of many deals being made on the side, between enterprising people, but the main driving forces behind such ventures would undoubtedly have been socially embedded.[10] In essence, this was the system that drove the trading networks of prehistoric, Roman and early medieval Europe, right through to the early Middle Ages. It was the system, too, that lay behind Viking trade and that gave rise to the pan-European trading networks of the Carolingian Empire – networks that reached as far east as the early Muslim or Arab Empire during its period of rapid growth, following the Prophet Mohammed's death in AD 650. In many of these long-distance early medieval exchange networks slaves – most usually prisoners or hostages taken in warfare or raiding – were provided by the West in exchange for prestigious goods from the Arab Empire. Something very similar was happening in later Iron Age Britain, when slaves were sent to the Roman Empire in exchange for wine and other luxury items.[11] As we shall see later, by the first century BC cross-Channel trade was becoming very import-ant, but there are also good grounds to suppose that it was organized through the tribe, rather than through merchant-style 'middlemen'.

THE LANDSCAPES OF HILLFORTS

If the many barrows that still pepper the landscapes of Britain are the sites that typify the Bronze Age, then hillforts are the archetype of the Iron Age. They occur across the whole of Britain, and not just in hilly areas. There are even hillforts – at least two of them – in the Fens.

At their simplest, hillforts consist of one or more ditches dug to surround a raised but usually quite flat area of land. The earth excavated from the ditches is heaped in a continuous bank on the upslope, within the area enclosed by the ditch. Together the external ditch and internal bank form a defensive work, known as a rampart; sometimes, but not always, the rampart may originally have been strengthened with timber or stone walls.

The weakest point of any defensive structure is always the entranceway. Medieval castles defended their entrances with drawbridges and towers; the hillfort builders of the Iron Age used timber palisades and added extra ramparts to make a maze-like entrance leading up to the main gates. In some instances the interior of the fort within the ramparts was the site of a defended settlement, complete with roundhouses, outbuildings and sometimes even roads and metalled streets.[12] Other hillforts were built for different purposes, maybe for seasonal gatherings, or as secure cattle corrals. In these cases houses or any other buildings are rare, or absent.

Hillforts vary in size, ranging from less than an acre, to 19 hectares for Britain's largest, Maiden Castle in Dorset. The features, or lack of them, from within the interior provide clues as to how they may originally have been used, but although excavation of individual hillforts can provide valuable insights, by far the best way to understand how and why they were built is to look at them within their landscape setting. Only that way can one appreciate why they were constructed in the first place and what they might have meant to the people who built and used them.

Hillforts are important for several reasons. They still dominate many of the highest and most spectacular hills of the British countryside and, for reasons that are aesthetic or emotional, rather than strictly archaeological, their ramparts,[13] seen from a distance, enhance the view. Not many hillforts have been extensively excavated, but those that have have usually provided good evidence for trade or exchange – which would suggest that many of these places were either the scene of such exchanges or were used to house some of the more valuable items. Most prehistorians agree that hillforts were important symbols of power in the landscape. Some have suggested that they were sited at the centre of tribal territories; others prefer to see them as being positioned closer to the periphery, rather like the castles built along the north Welsh borders for Edward I at the turn of the thirteenth and fourteenth centuries.

It now seems that the simple polarized explanation for hillforts, of defence versus display, is missing the point. Some were for defence, others for display, many more were for both. Some were for practical purposes, such as cattle corrals, but their siting and the size of their ramparts suggests that display was also important: these seemingly 'utilitarian' hillforts may also have been about the display of wealth combined with conspicuous consumption. In many instances we also know that the role of some hillforts changed through time, just as early medieval castles were gradually converted first into fortified houses in the Middle Ages and then into country houses in post-medieval times. Perhaps something like this was happening at Maiden Castle, where the original early Iron Age hillfort was incorporated into the ramparts of the massive hillfort that still dominates the Dorset landscape. Processes like these can be followed by examining the sometimes complex relationship of hillforts to their surrounding landscapes, in which other hillforts, field systems, undefended settlements and so forth may be found.

There is much controversy surrounding the interpretation of hillforts as purely defensive structures. Were they practically and crudely defensive, like the concrete pillboxes that were built in 1940, or were they magnificently so like, say, the Tower of London? Plainly, they did serve a defensive role, but they were also very carefully placed in the landscape to be visible from far and wide.[14] When they are examined in their setting, it immediately becomes apparent that many were carefully positioned close to the centres of known tribal territories. This suggests that these particular hillforts were meant to be seen by the members of the tribe that had constructed them. The positioning of these places was more about expressing the power of the ruling élite over ordinary folk than anything else. That does not mean to say that the relationship of hillforts to ordinary people was necessarily oppressive; it is also possible that many 'tribal capital' hillforts (places like Maiden Castle in the south, and Yeavering Bell in the north) were also expressions of group pride, and that the people who constructed them shared a common tribal identity. Indeed, it seems very probable that the actual construction of many hillforts echoed the building of henges 2,000 years earlier. In other words, the digging of the ramparts was an excuse to gather people from far-flung communities together, into different working parties. We shall see later that the supposedly unfinished hillfort at Ladle Hill in Hampshire shows clear signs of having been built using gang labour. Many hillforts conspicuously crown hills,

Fig. 4.2 The Iron Age hillfort at Ivinghoe Beacon, Buckinghamshire, viewed from Ashridge. This hillfort crowns the highest hill in the area. Being on the edge of the Chalk Escarpment, Ivinghoe Beacon towers above the lower-lying landscapes of Buckinghamshire, Bedfordshire and Hertfordshire beyond. It was also located close by the ancient route known as the Icknield Way. The single rampart closely follows the contours around the hilltop and can just be seen as a low platform, marked out at the skyline by some scrubby bushes. Ivinghoe, like so many other hillforts, was placed on a landmark that had been important much earlier. An early Bronze Age barrow can be seen at the top of the hill.

and often in prominent positions, like the Chalk Escarpment, where forts such as Ivinghoe Beacon, Buckinghamshire, can plainly be seen from some 20 kilometres away.[15]

Before the Second World War most excavation of hillforts took place around the defences. In those days prehistorians were keen to spot parallels in rampart construction that might be seen to link together hillforts in, say, northern France, with those of southern Britain. However, after many excavations of numerous defences, it seems that ramparts were generally built to suit the availability of local materials, such as timber or accessible building stone, rather than any long-distance cultural 'influences'. Excavation has also moved away from the periphery towards the interior in an attempt to understand how the defended space was organized. The two most influential excavations of hillfort interiors have been at Danebury, in Hampshire and at Moel y Gaer, in the Clwydian range. Danebury showed the roundhouses and storage pits of the interior to have been arranged around clearly defined streets.[16] At Moel y Gaer the layout seems to have been rather more subtle.[17]

There seems little doubt that most hillforts, like many medieval castles, were intended to impress both outside visitors and the local inhabitants, who probably needed few reminders that they were subservient to the ruling élite. Of course, if necessary they could be used as a place of refuge, or to repel an attack, but there is remarkably little archaeological evidence to support the idea that they were the scenes of regular bloody conflict: maybe a sortie or two during the raiding season, but not a full, set-piece military siege. There are exceptions, however.

The famous, or rather infamous, 'massacre' deposit at South Cadbury, in Somerset, is one. It took place in the late first century AD and involved at least twenty-two victims, adults and children. Some of the bodies had been horribly mutilated. Ann Woodward, who wrote the report on the skeletons, noted: 'We are glimpsing the actions of people undertaken in the face of disaster, mourning, and glorification in the aftermath of internecine conflict.'[18] Such horrors could surely happen anywhere, at any time.

Although some important excavated hillforts were undoubtedly built in the late Bronze Age, the majority were probably first constructed in

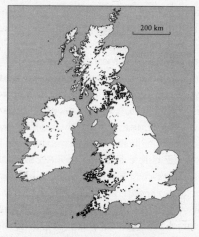

Fig. 4.3 Maps showing the distribution of (*above*) minor hillforts (under 3 acres) and (*below*) major hillforts (over 3 acres).

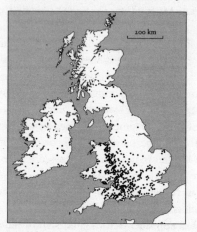

the early Iron Age, usually around 500 BC. The standard account of the British Iron Age suggests that there are about 3,300 hillforts and hillfort-like sites in Britain.[19] This accords reasonably well with two regional surveys which indicate there are about 1,400 in southern Britain and Wales and a few more, about 1,500, in northern Britain.[20] Most of the larger hillforts (over 3 acres or 1.2 hectares) are to be found in southern Britain, especially in the Welsh Marches, the west

Midlands, the West Country, along the Downs and into Devon and Cornwall. Smaller hillforts mainly occur in the Scottish Borders and Lowlands, Wales and the extreme south-west of England. I cannot possibly discuss even a representative selection of landscapes with hillforts, so I have chosen a few examples, first from the south, then from the north, where recent research has provided unexpected insights on how these fascinating places might originally have been used.

HILLFORT LANDSCAPES IN SOUTHERN BRITAIN

From the very outset the newly constructed hillforts would have been spectacular wherever they were, but in the chalkland areas of southern Britain they would have stood out as prominently as the later chalk hillside figures, with their brightly gleaming, freshly turned white chalk ramparts. The hillforts we see today have relaxed into the landscape: their ditches have lost their sharp outlines and their banks have collapsed. Even in stony regions nearly all drystone walls now lie hidden beneath rubble and any timber constructions have long since vanished beneath a carpet of topsoil, grass and vegetation. What greets our gaze is a thing of beauty that sets off the landscape and adds interesting detail to the skyline.

Accepting that the visual impact of hillforts has greatly diminished since prehistory does make it easier to think about their role within the landscape. One can best approach the problem in two ways. The first makes use of maps and it works because we can assume that not many hillforts have actually vanished entirely from the landscape without leaving any archaeological traces.

This map-based approach can best be seen in the case of the hillforts of the South Downs. Two plans suggest the simple point that the distribution of all Iron Age hillforts along the South Downs makes little sense. That is doubtless because they belong to a variety of periods. If, however, we select out just those hillforts that we know from excavation were in use in the second century BC, they can be seen to form a regularly spaced pattern, where the courses of rivers help to parcel the landscape into distinct 'territories', one for each

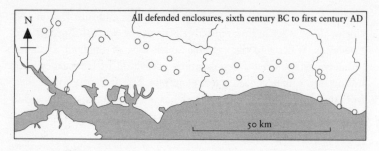

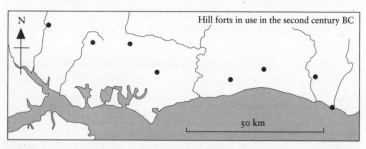

Fig. 4.4 The top map shows the distribution of all the known Iron Age hillforts of the South Downs between Southampton (*left*) and Eastbourne (*right*). The lower map shows the hillforts that excavation has shown to date to the second century BC. This was a period when many earlier hillforts had gone out of use, presumably being replaced by the later ones, shown here. These form a coherent, evenly spaced pattern where each hillfort sits at the centre of its 'territory', some of which are marked out by rivers.

hillfort. What makes this interesting is that we know from other regions that by the second century BC the landscape around many hillforts in southern Britain too was being 'rationalized': smaller hillforts were being taken over and replaced by larger hillforts, some of which at places like Maiden Castle and Hambledon Hill, both in Dorset, are exceptionally vast and have been described as 'developed hillforts'.[21]

A second approach uses maps too, but at a smaller scale. This style of analysis attempts to understand the role of individual hillforts within their own landscapes. It involves on-the-spot survey, detailed inspection of aerial photographs and limited excavation to resolve specific problems, usually to do with dating. It also requires a great deal of

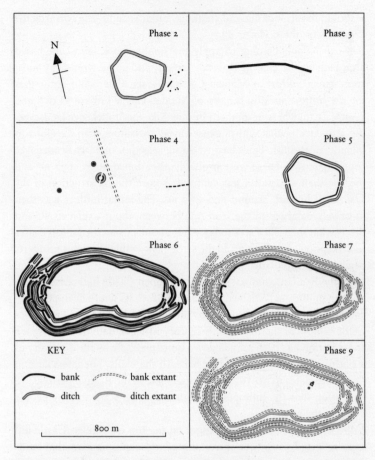

Fig. 4.5 A series of plans that illustrate the extended prehistory of Maiden Castle, Dorset. (Phase 1: (pre-3500 BC) the natural hilltop is not represented); Phase 2: (3500 BC) the causewayed enclosure; Phase 3: (3000 BC) the late Neolithic bank barrow; Phase 4 (2500–1500 BC) various Bronze Age barrows etc.; Phase 5: (600–450 BC) the early Iron Age hillfort; Phase 6: (450–150 BC) the 'developed' middle Iron Age hillfort; Phase 7: (first century BC) continued settlement; Phase 8: (AD 43–70) some early Roman occupation; Phase 9 (post-AD 367) Romano-Celtic temple.

walking about, looking and thinking, often with an eye towards the ramparts on the skyline.

It can be enlightening to apply the smaller-scale, landscape-based approach to the case of Britain's largest, and some would say most spectacular, hillfort at Maiden Castle, Dorset. One could argue that the pre-hillfort sites on the top of Maiden Castle hill are as rich and diverse as anywhere in southern Britain. Like the Stonehenge landscape, the sequence begins with a causewayed enclosure, then develops to include a Neolithic bank barrow and a selection of early Bronze Age round barrows. These were probably abandoned after 1500 BC and there is then a gap of a few centuries before the construction of the first small hillfort, around 600–450 BC. The initial hillfort was then massively enlarged in the Iron Age between about 450–150 BC and this is what the visitor sees today. After about 150 BC the hillfort ceases to be kept on such a scale and the settlement within the great ramparts begins quite rapidly to decline.

By the Roman conquest of AD 43, Maiden Castle had ceased to be both an important settlement and a major fort. Its symbolic importance continued, however, as witnessed by the construction of a small Romano-Celtic temple in the mid-fourth century AD. The date of the temple's construction has been pinned down quite precisely by the discovery of a potful of Roman coins buried beneath the walls. The latest coin in this hoard dates to AD 367, surprisingly late in the Roman period, and indicating that the hilltop still continued to be venerated by people living in the area.

We need to see how the changes on the top of Maiden Castle hill were reflected within the surrounding landscape and how that land-scape was made use of by the hillfort builders. It would be missing the point to stand in the visitors' car park at the bottom of the hill and reflect that those massive ramparts were only about protection and defence. On the contrary, recent research suggests that hillfort construction in this region of southern Britain, if not elsewhere, was actually about the aggressive seeking out and then the establishment and maintenance of power and influence. This is shown by the way that Maiden Castle and three other 'developed' hillforts, in southern Britain, at South Cadbury, Hod Hill and Hambledon Hill, grew, prospered and developed at the expense of the hillforts around them.

Traditionally, and perhaps quite reasonably, hillforts have been considered as if they were military monuments, and nothing more. However, attention has recently switched towards their political role and status which can usually be assessed by examining their changing relationship to other hillforts, fields and settlements elsewhere in the landscape. A great deal can also be achieved simply by looking and thinking about the hillfort as it sits within its landscape. So what would Iron Age people have thought about Maiden Castle as they approached it, up there, on the skyline?

A recent study of medieval castles has drawn attention to the manner in which some were approached by visitors, friendly or otherwise.[22] The route to many castles was carefully planned and sometimes passed through a structured landscape which proclaimed certain messages that the owners of the castle wanted to impart. In certain instances the journey, and the orchestrated views of the landscape along it, did not end when the visitor entered the castle grounds, or indeed the building itself. If anything, they intensified the experience.

The Iron Age equivalents of the roadside shrines, chapels-of-ease and crosses that were added to the landscape to enhance the experiences of pilgrims in the Middle Ages have mostly disappeared, even from the few remnants of prehistoric landscape that still survive in the lowlands of southern Britain. However, we can say with some assurance that sufficient barrows and large henges survived in the plain around Maiden Castle to have reminded any visitor that he was approaching somewhere special. He would certainly have been aware, too, that the hill which had become host to the hillfort had been a special place for countless generations. To return to an earlier idea, he would probably also have believed that the shades of his remote ancestors resided there. Yet from a distance Maiden Castle does not look very impressive. Of course in the Iron Age the banks would have been higher and the ditches deeper; the freshly dug chalk would have stood out like a huge white headband, but even so, when seen from across the flatter land to the north and west Maiden Castle is not so spectacular. As you approach the foot of the hill, the ramparts start to disappear as they blend together with the skyline, an effect enhanced on hazy and sunny days. You start to climb. Then quite suddenly, about 300 metres from the lowest rampart, you become aware that you are approaching something truly enormous. The ramparts suddenly cut the skyline and dominate the ground ahead as far as the eye can see. Again, these effects would have been exaggerated when the ditches and banks were first constructed.

If you approach by the less steep, western entranceway, as the visitor does today, the way ahead is blocked by a huge rampart, which has to be skirted, either to north or south, to gain access to the interior. Once you have navigated your way around the big blocking rampart you come to a series of five ramparts or hornworks past which you have to thread your way. These were revetted with drystone walls and doubtless would have been blocked by a series of gates and other obstacles. One must also imagine that the ramparts were manned by dozens of young men brandishing weapons and not necessarily in a particularly welcoming fashion. Eventually you pass through this maze of entranceworks, to be confronted by a town ringed around by the massive bank of the inner rampart which would have gradually vanished into the distance, towards the eastern entrance. Both excavation and geophysical survey have shown that the vast space of the interior was set out in streets lined with roundhouses and other outbuildings.

The arrangement of both the entranceways into Maiden Castle was clearly intended to baffle an attacker, but it would also have visibly impressed any visitor: it cannot be coincidence that the more readily approached western entrance is by far the most elaborate. This gateway was intended to frighten and impress both visitor and assailant, but it did not need to have been so complex to have been equally effective militarily. Indeed, its full labyrinthine layout can only be appreciated from the air. This might suggest that the people who constructed the western gateway had other motives, apart from defence and the creation of a quasi-theatrical experience, in mind. Perhaps they were aware that their work would have looked remarkable from the sky, where the spirits of the ancestors or other deities may have resided. Something similar may have been in the minds of the people who later created the White Horse at Uffington, in the Berkshire Downs, which is also best seen from the air. That landscape too is dominated by a major hillfort.

No modern investigation of a site like a hillfort would be complete without detailed examination of the landscape in which it sits. The

Maiden Castle survey showed that the plain between the rivers Frome and South Winterborne was covered with the cropmarks of field boundary ditches. Many of these could be seen to lie beneath, and therefore to be earlier than, the boundary ditches and ploughed strips of the Open Fields that occupied the area in the Middle Ages. A number of commercial excavations in this region have shown that many of the larger fields date to the later Bronze Age and may well have been in use when the first hillfort was constructed at Maiden Castle around 600 BC. Excavations have shown that field boundary ditches belonging to this system, and dated by pottery to the middle of the Bronze Age, actually lie beneath the ramparts of the neighbouring hillfort at Poundbury. Others belong to a second phase of landscape development in the late Iron Age and early Roman period. These include the mass of very closely spaced cropmarks that lie about a kilometre north of Maiden Castle, and extend east and north along a road or trackway. These cropmarks were part of a substantial rural settlement.

The area around Maiden Castle features a number of barrows, most of which lie on slightly higher ground towards the edge of a zone that was later to be extensively farmed and settled. If one only had the evidence of the earthworks of the barrows and hillforts, one might reasonably conclude that for the millennium following the last use of the barrows (probably around 1500 BC) and the initial construction of Maiden Castle, the landscape had been abandoned. Instead, the survey shows precisely the opposite: both Maiden Castle and Poundbury were constructed in a landscape that was in the active process of being developed. Large-scale fieldwalking has revealed quantities of prehistoric flintwork and pottery on the surface of the land between the two hillforts; this strongly suggest there was extensive settlement there.[23] So although excavation at Maiden Castle has revealed numerous roundhouses within its defences, the hillfort was not the sole location of population.

It now seems less likely that Maiden Castle was constructed just to 'protect' access to the densely farmed and settled landscape around it. It was also a symbol of the authority of the élite that had risen to power in the area. Doubtless the people who supervised the progressive enlargement of the ramparts would have claimed ancestry from the men within the Lanceborough barrows so clearly visible at the foot of the hill. We must not forget that throughout prehistory people would have possessed oral histories and genealogies that probably extended back centuries. Laying aside the obvious links, provided by its location atop a very special place of great antiquity, to a world beyond that of the living, the main 'purpose' of the hillfort might be seen as providing security to the people who lived in the area. That security was also a form of social belonging, which could have been expressed by the act of coming together to build and enlarge the great hillfort. Thus Maiden Castle was both a symbol of the unity and longevity of the tribe and a warning to others to respect that fact. This may help to explain why Maiden Castle remained such a special place long after the abandonment of the hillfort. Perhaps that was why a Romano-British temple was built there as late as the latter part of the fourth century AD.[24]

Prehistoric landscape can teach us a lot about the nature of ancient politics. Today, for example, there is much interest in the structure and application of central political power and the ways in which it can be governed, or kept under control. Traditionally, archaeologists tended to overemphasize the power possessed by members of ruling élites. This is not altogether surprising, given the magnificence of 'royal' burials, such as that within the Saxon cemetery at Sutton Hoo, in Suffolk. But the evidence in the British landscape for the way authority was actually exercised at the local level in prehistory suggests rationality and the selection of the most sensible, pragmatic options. In other words, there must have been active 'checks and balances' on the way central power was exerted in British tribal societies. The authority to make many political decisions, especially those to do with the day-to-day running of farms and settlements, was devolved to individual communities.[25] Perhaps rather unexpectedly, this even seems to have held true in the region around the great hillfort.[26]

Initially, Maiden Castle was one of three hillforts in the region.[27] Over the centuries Maiden Castle became larger and more elaborate and it is probable that the huge amount of labour needed to achieve this would have involved people from other settlements and hillforts in the region. Traditionally, autumn would have been the time of year when constructional work would have happened and this would also have coincided with the raiding season.[28]

The creation of the few massive 'developed' hillforts would have drawn upon labour and other resources from within the territory controlled by the hillforts concerned. As they became larger their territories had to expand for this to continue. This process finished by the start of the second century BC, when the ramparts were finally completed. At this time the settlement within the ramparts became better organized. These developments coincided with the introduction of well-defined regional styles of pottery whose distribution indicates that this part of Wessex and southern England was being transformed into a series of tribal confederations, known as chiefdoms.[29] These were the precursors to the initial tribal kingdoms, which only become apparent with the appearance of the first British coins, around 70 BC.

The distribution of various styles of later Iron Age pottery suggests how the societies who built the developed hillforts might have been organized. The distinctive type of pottery belonging to the Maiden Castle style is also found at South Cadbury (some 37 kilometres to the north-north-west) and Hambledon (some 29 kilometres to the north-east), which gives some idea of the chiefdom's size.[30] Both these major hillforts continued to be occupied late into the Iron Age, which would suggest that the chiefdom had three regional centres whose spheres of influence were fixed by mutual agreement.[31] The three major developed hillforts are equally spaced across the landscape controlled by the tribal kingdom that would later emerge as the Durotriges. Other smaller hillforts would have owed allegiance to one of the three main centres.

It would appear that hillforts of southern Britain lost much of their importance in the later first century BC and early first century AD. Many, including Maiden Castle, were either partially or completely deserted. These were decades of rapid change. People moved out into the un-defended settlements below the hills. They also founded new settlements in these areas. But Maiden Castle had been important for so long that the late Iron Age cemetery near the eastern entranceway, continued to be used after the hillfort had largely been abandoned.

I have considered Maiden Castle at some length because it is such a remarkable site, and can tell us so much about the way the landscape developed in the Iron Age. But the landscape around the hillfort is not typical of what was happening everywhere in Britain. I want now to shift our attention to another chalk region, further north, where hillforts

Fig. 4.6 A view from the ramparts of the Iron Age hillfort on Hambledon Hill, at the southern edge of Cranborne Chase, with the planned eighteenth- and nineteenth-century landscape of Blackmore Vale in the distance.

seem to have been organized rather differently within the landscape.

The Chalk Escarpment is the single biggest geological feature in Britain. It runs diagonally across southern England from the south coast at Dorset via Wiltshire to Oxfordshire, Buckinghamshire, Hertford-shire and southern Cambridgeshire; by the time it reaches Norfolk it is considerably less precipitous, but still manages to disprove Noel Coward's adage: 'very flat, Norfolk.' Although notably broached by the Thames and other river valleys it is more or less continuous and presents a striking series of steep hills as one approaches from the north. One of the most striking of the Chalk Escarpment hillforts, an hour or two's drive south-west, takes one to the Berkshire Downs and the picturesque landscape around the village of Uffington (transferred in 1974, by people with no historical sense of place, to Oxfordshire).[32] The area is renowned for its White Horse which was carved in the chalk about 200 metres north-east of a fine hillfort known as Uffington Castle.[33]

This, the oldest of the British carved hill figures, shows a stylized horse cantering or galloping. The style of this galloping beast (if indeed it is a horse) recalls Iron Age Celtic art, but parallels can also be found in Scandinavian Bronze Age rock art and post-Roman coinage. The shape of the figure has also been altered by centuries of 'scouring', the Victorian name for the process (often carried out annually) whereby chalk hill figures are refreshed. The antiquity of the figure has recently been proved by a detailed archaeological investigation of the horse and the area around it. Silts found *in situ* close to the belly of the horse, were dated by a scientific technique known as Optically Stimulated Luminescence to the years 1380–550 BC. The project also showed that Uffington Castle hillfort was constructed between 750 and 650 BC. These dates agree quite closely and it seems highly probable that the horse and the hillfort were constructed by the same people, at the same time.[34] The White Horse was positioned at the top edge of the Chalk Escarpment, which falls steeply away into a bowl-like dry valley known as the Manger.

A wealth of archaeological remains on the hilltops around Uffington, including several barrows, strongly suggests that White Horse Hill and the area around it had been a special place from Neolithic and Bronze Age times. But one of the most remarkable aspects of the White Horse is that it is far better viewed from the air. Where it can clearly be seen for what it is: a cantering horse. But from the ground, and certainly from the Manger below, it looks like a disjointed set of squiggles. Another remarkable aspect of the White Horse is that its very survival has depended on the action of local people, who have returned to the figure at regular intervals over the past 3,000 years, to clear away vegetation and refresh the chalk by puddling it with their feet, as part of the process of scouring.

The top of the natural chalk escarpment at Uffington is where the ancient route known as the Ridgeway is to be found. There is no telling when this long-distance road came into existence, but it seems reasonable to suppose that the origins of certain lengths, if not its entire route, may lie in the early years of the post-glacial period, some 8,000 years ago. It now seems increasingly probable that large areas of chalk hills were never cloaked with thick forest in post-glacial times, so such a long-distance route seems rather less inexplicable than might have appeared twenty years ago. Whether it was the existence of the Ridgeway or some other factor, a number of hillforts were laid out along the top of the Berkshire Downs sometime in the earlier first millennium BC.

These were probably occupied by a series of separate, but possibly related tribal groups. As time passed these groups came together to form larger and larger units, as we saw happening to the much bigger developed hillforts in Dorset.

Uffington Castle was clearly the dominant hillfort in the region and would have been the focus for regular tribal gatherings. Other hillforts contemporary with Uffington Castle probably served rather different purposes. Segsbury Camp, for example, is about twice the size of Uffington, but on excavation it revealed little evidence for housing and was probably mainly used to shelter and manage livestock, such as sheep and cattle. The much smaller fort at Alfred's Castle seems to have been the place where people actually built their houses and lived their lives.[35]

Fig. 4.7 The Iron Age hillfort of Uffington Castle, Oxfordshire, from the west. This view is taken from close by the Ridgeway and is looking towards the main eastern entranceway. Although only enclosed by a single ditch, the hillfort is located in a spectacular position. The Ridgeway is an ancient prehistoric route which may originally have passed through the main entrance to the hillfort and out through another (blocked in the Iron Age) on the opposite side of the fort. In the later Iron Age the course of the Ridgeway was diverted, probably to pass just south of the hillfort.

The larger hillforts were major feats of civil engineering and like all such projects could fail if the political situation changed. In the Iron Age the political situation was probably locally determined by the larger kin group or tribe. Further south along the Chalk Escarpment in Hampshire, we come across the famous 'unfinished' hillfort at Ladle Hill, some 8 kilometres south of Newbury.[36]

Instead of having a continuous bank rampart alongside an uninterrupted ditch, the ditch of the hillfort at Ladle Hill was dug in short lengths of about 50 metres each. The accompanying bank resembled a series of heaps, rather than a rampart. This pattern suggests gang labour where people from different communities worked on their own lengths of ditch. Soil was banked up, possibly while carpenters erected the timberwork for a box-like revetment, as has been found in excavations of Wessex hillforts of the earlier Iron Age. Ladle Hill did not survive into the later Iron Age, unlike the nearby (and clearly visible) hillfort on Beacon Hill, which continued to be occupied into the Roman period.[37] This suggests that tribal politics intervened during the latter stages of Ladle Hill's construction, and it was decided to abandon work there and instead to divert the workforce to the upgrading and improvement of Beacon Hill.

As one would expect, hillforts generally require hills, although sometimes marsh or fen can substitute for a steep hillside. A good example was recently excavated in the wetlands at Sutton Common near Doncaster and has been described as a 'marsh-fort'.[38] Broadly similar marsh-forts are known in the Fenland, which was an extremely prosperous region in the Iron Age. An example at Stonea (pronounced 'Stony') Camp, near March, was placed on a near-flat 'island' and its substantial ramparts were repeatedly enlarged.[39] Another marsh-fort is also known in the Fens at Borough Fen – also on a low 'island' – this time a few kilometres north of Peterborough. Borough Fen may have had Bronze Age origins, although limited excavations have so far only revealed Iron Age pottery.[40]

Stonea Camp (9.6 hectares) is much larger than Borough Fen (3.8 hectares) and like the hillforts around Uffington Castle the two Fenland sites appear to have served very different purposes. It would seem that Stonea was more the Uffington or Beacon Hill equivalent (that is, somewhere used for major tribal gatherings). It seems to have had hesitant beginnings in the third century BC and then went through a number of modifications involving large outer ditches. It may eventually have become a regional centre for the local Iron Age tribal kingdom of the Iceni and thus played a significant role in the Boudican revolt against Roman rule in AD 60–61.

The fort at Borough Fen was rather different.[41] For a start, the limited excavations have revealed thick dark layers of occupation debris mostly dating to the fourth and third centuries BC, but nothing much later. This would suggest that Borough Fen was a large settlement that failed to flourish in the later Iron Age – maybe because of higher water levels and the increasing risk of flooding. Few other 'hillforts' in Britain would ever have been subject to periodic inundation. Both Borough Fen and Stonea Camp would have stood out on their low, flat islands, especially during the wetter months of winter, when the reeds and glinting meres of the surrounding Fens would have contrasted with the ramparts and lush grass within the encircling ramparts.

HILLFORT LANDSCAPES IN NORTHERN BRITAIN

In the north of Britain the hillforts are generally smaller but the landscapes around them are altogether better preserved and have much to teach us about these sometimes tantalizingly enigmatic sites.

The principal hillfort in the Cheviots is probably Yeavering Bell, near Wooler, a small market town in the north-eastern part of the Northumberland National Park.[42] The landscape of the Cheviots in the Iron Age had been farmed for at least two millennia, starting in the later Neolithic, sometime in the middle of the third millennium BC. By 500 BC the original post-glacial tree-cover had long been cleared and there were areas of arable farming, maybe as large as 4–5 hectares, which often occur quite close to hillforts. There are even indications of Iron Age ridge-and-furrow arable fields in the Cheviots.[43] The rest of the landscape was essentially open grazing, with areas of scrub and woodland on the less accessible and wetter hillsides. Yeavering Bell consists of a single rampart which girdles the distinctive twin peaks of the hill. This is broached by one entranceway to the south. What makes the

Fig. 4.8 A view from the interior looking south towards the entranceway into the hillfort of Yeavering Bell, Northumberland. The stone rampart can be seen in the middle distance. The archaeologist Stewart Ainsworth, whose team surveyed the hillforts of the Northumberland National Park, is standing in the entranceway to House 2, one of a pair of large houses that was positioned back from the hillfort entrance and facing onto it. The house platform is the flat area directly to Stewart's left, at the foot of the hill-slope.

hillfort at Yeavering Bell exceptional is its size – at 5.6 hectares it is by far the largest in northern England. It is also most unusual because its interior is densely covered by about 125 houses, at least twice as many as in other hillforts in northern England, where more often one or two dozen houses are the rule. Like other forts in the Cheviots, the houses at Yeavering can still be seen, as roughly circular depressions ('house platforms') set into the hillside, with quite distinct doorways, generally aligned south and east.[44]

Yeavering, like two other large Borders hillforts, Eildon Hill North and Traprain Law, was most probably founded in the Bronze Age, perhaps around 1000 BC. That is some five hundred years before most of the Iron Age hillforts of the Cheviots had come into existence. Yeavering was certainly occupied throughout the Iron Age and may well have become the capital of the 'Votadini', the tribe named by Roman authors as controlling northern Northumberland.

The Milfield Basin, the flat plain immediately north of Yeavering Bell, is dominated by its twin peaks, and aerial photography has revealed a number of important earlier prehistoric monuments including an important ritual landscape with a substantial henge, numerous barrows and many other sites.[45] The twin peaks of Yeavering Bell are so dominant that they must have been a reason, if not the reason, why this plain became so important in Neolithic times. So it seems very likely that Yeavering Bell may have been revered as a sacred place, long before the hillfort that now crowns it had come into existence.

Today the ramparts appear to be a stone bank, but excavation has demonstrated that this is in fact rubble from a collapsed higher drystone wall. The excavations removed the fallen material and found that the base of the walls survived, largely intact, a few courses high, just below the ground surface. The twin peaks of the interior undoubtedly helped to determine the hillfort's subsequent layout. The only entranceway is in the valley between them, midway along the southern rampart. Between the two peaks there is an open area or communal space, and houses are distributed almost everywhere else, except for the very tops of the peaks themselves, which would have been bitterly exposed.

At the southern entrance are two large house platforms that dominate the route to the interior of the hillfort and were clearly intended to do just that. Both are equally distanced from the entranceway, but more importantly their doorways point directly at it. They are also significantly larger than any other houses on the hilltop. Doubtless they were for important people, but the positioning of the two large roundhouses was also clearly intended to link each to the peak into which they had been recessed. It seems likely that by the end of the Bronze Age the twin peaks had come to symbolize two groups of people – two tribes perhaps – that had united. That union was symbolized on the ground by the continuous rampart, but the layout of the houses within the hillfort and the presence of those two large buildings facing the single entranceway suggests that the two groups still retained their own identities. The hillfort therefore had a strong symbolic social role, which is probably why it seems to have played such an important part in the way that other sites in the landscape were positioned. This argument is reinforced by the miniature hillfort at Staw Hill.

Staw Hill lies some 4 kilometres to the west of Yeavering Bell. Even

Fig. 4.9 The miniature hillfort of Staw Hill, in the Cheviot Hills of Northumberland. This is by far the most impressive aspect, which would have confronted visitors as they approached the site. The scale, however, is tiny, as can be seen from the two figures behind the ramparts, and Staw Hill would never have been a defensible site, despite being a 'hillfort'; 'enhanced farmstead' might be a more apt description.

by northern standards it is tiny, roughly oval in shape and with a single entranceway which faces directly onto Yeavering Bell. The area within the ramparts measures about 45 × 30 metres and never held more than two roundhouses. Built in the Iron Age, it was occupied into the Roman Iron Age and then reoccupied in the Middle Ages. Its approach was by way of gently sloping land to the west, where first its single and then in the late Iron Age its double ramparts look the most impressive. But even if we allow for subsequent erosion and collapse, these ramparts are very slight indeed and could never have resisted attack by more than a handful of men. There is also high ground overlooking the fort, from which bowmen or men with slingshots could soon have picked off anyone foolish enough to leave the shelter of the houses. The 'ramparts' on the eastern side of the fort are barely knee-high.

We know that there were Iron Age terraced arable fields immediately north of the enclosure and in the Roman Iron Age the settlement included animal pens or shelters. This suggests that the site was in fact a lightly fortified farmstead, where the defensive works were as much to do with status and display as with anything remotely martial. In times of serious inter-tribal conflict one can imagine the inhabitants of Staw Hill removing to Yeavering Bell immediately. The close ties that must have linked the inhabitants of the two communities are clearly signalled by the alignment of Staw Hill's only entranceway, which faces directly onto Yeavering Bell.

Today most hillforts blend into the landscape and their undulating ramparts encircle hilltops and subtly enhance the skyline. In the past, however, it would have been very different. During their lives most hillforts were built and positioned to make an impact. They were, after all, places that expressed a regional identity, rather like castles and indeed churches in the Middle Ages. This can sometimes be seen in their construction. The excavations at Yeavering Bell revealed a few courses of intact walling below the ground, but some sites in the north are very much better preserved. One interesting example of this is at a site known as 'The Castles' on the easterly slopes of the north

Fig. 4.10 The south-east ramparts of 'The Castles' hillfort, near Hamsterley, Co. Durham. In the foreground the original Iron Age defensive walls survive as the lowest three to five courses of stonework; above them the stonework was reconstructed in the early twentieth century.

Pennines near Hamsterley, in Co. Durham, where the walls survive as high as a man, in places.[46]

The hillfort at 'The Castles' is roughly square, measuring 75 × 90 metres and its ramparts comprise an external ditch and a wall/bank, which today consists of a tumble of stone. Like many hillforts in the north, it is entered by a single entranceway which faces east, directly onto a small stream which feeds into the Bedburn Beck. Early in the twentieth century excavations showed that the tumble of stone concealed original Iron Age drystone walling.[47] Unfortunately, as was the practice at the time, the archaeologists then rebuilt the walls in one or two places. Recent re-excavation has showed that their efforts fell far below Iron Age standards of workmanship. The different qualities of drystone walling were particularly evident around the entranceway, where a large slab on the northern side had almost collapsed to the ground. When excavated, this slab was shown to form a pair with another on the south side. Both had been stepped back into the original Iron Age masonry, similar to the entranceway arrangements of some contemporary Scottish fortified towers, known as brochs.

The Iron Age walling employed larger blocks which were properly levelled in and fitted together snugly. Behind this facing wall the core of the rampart was filled with earth and rubble, as was the usual practice. The excavator estimated that the Iron Age walls would have stood more than 3 metres tall; more recently we estimated that over 100,000 tonnes of stone had been transported to the site in the Iron Age. This was a major undertaking, which would have had a huge impact on the landscape; what makes it even more remarkable is that 'The Castles' is by no means unique. There is also evidence of a significant post-Roman or Dark Age reoccupation of the site. Recent research on many sites elsewhere in Britain has shown that many Iron Age hillforts remained powerful symbols of local identity through the Roman period. This was particularly true in northern Britain, where Roman influence was less strong.

SETTLEMENT AND STATUS IN
IRON AGE BRITAIN

The shift in social and symbolic emphasis from ancestors and tombs to hearths and homes that happened from the middle of the second millennium BC across Britain and Europe provided a 'new' social geography far more diverse than that which had preceded it, but certain unifying factors extending across Britain suggest that most communities would have shared a common 'world view' or cosmology, which may well have been inherited from their Neolithic ancestors. After about 2500/2000 BC Britain adopted roundhouses as its principle domestic structures. Similar roundhouses are known from other lands along the Atlantic seaboard: Ireland and parts of Spain and Portugal. On the mainland of Europe rectangular or longhouses were preferred. Many dozens of roundhouses have been found from Bronze Age contexts in Britain, but they proliferated in the Iron Age, where quite literally thousands of examples are now known. In upland and moorland areas these houses remain visible on the surface as low platforms or 'house circles', but in the lowlands they are usually hidden from view and are most often only revealed by excavation.

The vast majority of Iron Age roundhouses have single entrance-ways that face south-east towards the sunrise. Where preservation is good enough it can be shown that across Iron Age Britain, from the Outer Hebrides to the chalk hills of Hampshire, these houses were all organized along broadly similar principles.[48] They share a south-easterly alignment; their central hearth was the focus of family life; meals were prepared and eaten on the southern side and beds were placed to the north. Where burials are found below the floor, they tend to be on the north side. Several principles are operating here: the daily movement of the sun, the rising and setting of the sun and the opposition of light (south) and darkness (north) can be seen as a contrast between meals (life) and sleep (death). Whatever else was happening, the similar layout of these houses suggests that the various Iron Age communities of Britain shared a common 'world view' and were in regular contact.

Single roundhouses occur in the Western and Northern Isles and in the Highlands of Scotland, where they are sometimes known as duns, but in these areas two other forms of communal building developed, that share many of the organizational principles of the British Iron Age roundhouse. These buildings are known as wheelhouses and brochs. The brochs are remarkable circular stone towers and the Broch of Mousa, on Shetland, at 13.3 metres is still the tallest surviving pre-Roman structure in northern Europe.

Brochs were defended homesteads and are found throughout the Western Isles, Orkney and Shetland and on neighbouring parts of the mainland. They were massively built, windowless, circular stone towers and their main characteristic was a strong but hollow wall, through which ran stairs. The interior of the tower was most probably roofed and the wooden supports for an upper floor, or floors, were lodged on an internal ledge, known as a scarcement. Each floor was reached by a narrow entranceway through the inner 'skin' of the wall. The cavity within the wall contained small cell-like compartments and galleries at each floor level and there was always a substantial 'guard chamber' close to the front door, at ground level. This was the sole entrance and it led into a corridor which passed straight through the wall into the interior. By far the best-preserved broch in the Outer Hebrides is the Broch of Dun Carloway, on Lewis, which still survives as an imposing tower, positioned on naturally well-defended higher land, close by the sea.

Radiocarbon dates suggest that the first true brochs were built from 400 to 200 BC and they continued to be occupied throughout the Scottish late Iron Age (AD 300–900). Brochs were developed from an existing tradition of thick-walled round buildings which were being constructed in the region from at least 800 BC. The first true brochs appear in Orkney and Shetland around 400 BC, and a couple of centuries later in the Western Isles.

It is apparent that brochs were sited and designed to impress, but they were never military buildings intended to resist a prolonged attack. Perhaps it is best to see them as regional equivalents of the much later tower houses of the Scottish Borders: local centres that may have performed many of the functions of a manor house. Their role may have been to control disputes over such matters as land and grazing. As such, they probably represent the emergence of clearly

Fig. 4.11 The Broch of Dun Carloway, on the Isle of Lewis in the Outer Hebrides. Brochs first appeared in the Northern Isles around 400 BC, but in the Western Isles from about 200 BC. They remained in use until about AD 400.

defined ranking within an otherwise classless society. The occurrence of brochs along later boundaries, and the fact that they were occupied and in use until into the first millennium AD, demonstrates that pre-Roman patterns of life played a significant role in the development of Scottish society beyond the immediate influences of the Roman Empire.

The Iron Age witnessed a contraction in the area of land settled in northern Scotland. This may have been a result of wetter climatic conditions in the earlier first millennium BC, but it may also have been a delayed and long-term effect of the earlier, and widespread, felling of woodland which caused soil degradation and allowed acidic peats to form inland in the Western Isles, away from the alkaline machair sands. Most of the brochs and duns of the Outer Hebrides cluster around the coasts away from these growing peats; wheelhouses come somewhat later, at the end of the first millennium BC, but these are mainly confined to the machair. However, the difference in settlement patterns between the Neolithic (inland) and Iron Age (coastal) in the Outer Hebrides is most pronounced and cannot be attributed to climate alone. Social and population pressures, of both livestock and people, also played an important role. Whatever else they might have been during the four and a half millennia of later prehistory, the Western Isles were never marginal, nor thinly populated. Their distinctive landscapes were not the creation of remoteness, neglect or avoidance, but of long-term, persistent and at times intensive settlement. They were highly desirable places to live.

It has generally been assumed that the Iron Age across most of Britain was the period society became hierarchical. It has also been argued that this process began early in the Bronze Age, with the emergence of, for example, the series of rich round barrow burials that appear around the rim of the Stonehenge basin, shortly after the final phase of re-building at Stonehenge itself. These barrows and other burials in the area – extending as far afield as Norfolk – contained lavish goldwork and other valuable, high-status objects. But a century or two later,

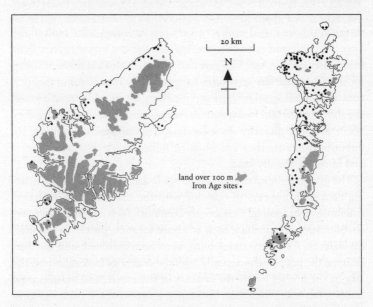

Fig. 4.12 Distribution map of Iron Age sites in the Outer Hebrides. The map is arranged with the northern islands, Lewis and Harris, to the left, and North Uist, Benbecula, South Uist and Barra to the right.

around 1500 BC, along with all other round barrows they vanish from the archaeological record, to be replaced by hoards and other deliberate offerings. This would suggest that this particular attempt to create an élite failed to take hold. Today most prehistorians would probably agree that this actually happened rather later, around 1200/1000 BC. Ultimately these new élites would give rise to the warrior-led kingdoms of Celtic Britain which the invading Roman troops had to contend with in the mid-first century AD.

We have already discussed how the brochs of the northern Scottish Iron Age can be seen as an early manifestation of an emerging élite. Something similar may have been happening further south and west, around the shores of certain lochs in Scotland. Like the brochs, these sites are rounded and difficult of access, but would perhaps have been better at resisting a longer siege. They are known by their Gaelic name 'crannogs' and consist of artificial islands, usually built from rocks and timber. They are generally, but not always, placed a short distance from the shore and in many instances there is evidence that they were joined to dryland by a raised walkway. Very few crannogs were built in the later Neolithic and earlier Bronze Age, but the vast majority were built in the later Bronze Age, Iron Age and in early historical times.[49] Today most traces of surface structures have generally vanished, but the rock core and waterlogged timbers survive. They are simple to spot around the shores of certain lochs, such as Awe, Lomond and Tay, where they occur in some quantity. As a landscape phenomenon crannogs are important because they can often be linked to specific field systems and farms on the dry land.

The growing importance of crannogs in later prehistory is fascinating because it appears to coincide with the time when water-based rituals were becoming increasingly common. So it might be an over-simplification to attribute their offshore location purely to the need for defence. Certainly status must have been involved, and one can imagine the people who actually built the crannogs looking across the lake at the houses where the families of their lords and masters now resided. But more than that, the unique location of the crannogs gave their owners a very special relationship with the watery realm of the ancestors that surrounded them. I am put in mind here of the way in which (until quite recently) in some English villages the families of the

Fig. 4.13 Spry Island, a small artificial island or crannog, at the eastern end of Loch Tay, Perth and Kinross. This crannog is first recorded on a map of 1769, but it may originally have been built in the Iron Age. In 1842 Queen Victoria visited the island during her honeymoon with Prince Albert. Keen to impress his royal visitor the Marquis of Breadalbane slightly enlarged the island with the bigger rocks towards its western (*left*) side, and planted the stand of mature trees. The Queen is reported to have found her visit very 'amusing'.

squire would enter the parish church through a door in the chancel, close to the altar, rather than through the main porch, like the rest of the congregation.

FIELDS IN IRON AGE BRITAIN

Celtic fields in southern Britain were discussed in the previous chapter, which came to the conclusion that most of the Iron Age examples in the Salisbury Plain Training Area originated somewhat earlier, in the Bronze Age. This can be said of many excavated field systems in lowland Britain. The fact remains, however, that most Celtic fields were used, and frequently modified, throughout the Iron Age and well into Roman times – whatever their actual date of origin. Thus they are still regarded as an essentially Iron Age phenomenon. Most Celtic field systems have been identified from field survey and from aerial photographic evidence. Recent attempts, however, to apply the techniques of map-regression analysis have been far more controversial. The technique works by gradually eliminating all features whose date and origin can satisfactorily be explained. First recent, then medieval, then Roman features are removed and one is then left with features that must predate Roman times. In theory, that is.[50]

Large-scale excavations across the lowland river valleys of southern Britain since the last war have revealed extensive settlements and associated field systems covering many thousands of acres, but these can only be seen as cropmarks on aerial photographs. Nothing survives on the surface. The houses were made from timber or wattle-and-daub, and the fields were bounded by ditches and hedges rather than the more archaeologically durable drystone walls found in the uplands. It is clear that these settlements were in fully developed landscapes, with roads and trackways, areas of woodland, hedges and so forth – much as one might have encountered in the Middle Ages. The population that created these landscapes must have numbered hundreds of thousands. Sadly there is virtually no evidence for them in the modern landscape, apart from a few fragments that have survived on the fringes of the main settled areas. A series of parallel ditches in the Chilterns, for example, suggest how the landscape might have been partitioned between tribal groupings.[51] This is interesting because we know that the area in question was one of the most heavily populated regions in the late Iron Age and these impressive earthwork boundaries suggest that possession of the available land needed to be well displayed.

By the final century BC some of the largest settlements in the lowlands of south-eastern Britain were being enclosed or defended by substantial ditches and banks. The best-known settlements of this type were in the most prosperous areas, at places like Colchester (Essex), Wheathampstead (Hertfordshire), Oldbury and Bigbury (Kent) and as far west as Dyke Hills at Dorchester (Oxfordshire) or Salmonsbury in Gloucestershire. These settlements are known as 'enclosed *oppida*'.[52] *Oppida* is the plural of the Latin *oppidum*, a town. So were these places towns? The evidence suggests that they were very large settlements, but not urban as we would understand the term today. A true town requires civil government and communal areas for, say, the disposal of refuse or sewage. It also implies a density of settlement where houses are constructed side by side, and, if separated at all, then by small garden plots. When excavated none of the British *oppida* has yet produced evidence of local services or the density of occupation one would associate with a true town. Some have revealed temples

Fig. 4.14 The surface traces of Bronze and Iron Age Celtic fields on Fyfield Down, Wiltshire. These prehistoric fields are marked by long banks (lynchets) which formed over centuries as ploughsoil accumulated against their boundaries. These lynchets are best seen in low angled light, in winter, or early in the morning or evening.

and cemeteries, but these also exist in other settlements and hillforts, such as Maiden Castle and Hod Hill in Dorset.[53] Many, too, have provided evidence for trade, some of it over long distances, but the fact remains that the settlement within Iron Age *oppida* never approaches the sheer density of undoubted towns, such as Roman Wroxeter or Silchester.

Many enclosed *oppida*, indeed, even the largest, such as *Camulodunum* (Colchester) included big open spaces even fields and paddocks within the enclosed area.[54] Many did possess certain urban features such as cemeteries; there were also industrial zones and good evidence for long-distance and local trade. Others show clear signs of having been regional market centres. Some contemporary *oppida* in France and Germany[55] have better claims to true urban status, but in Britain the concept of urbanism was introduced by the Romans shortly after the conquest of AD 43.

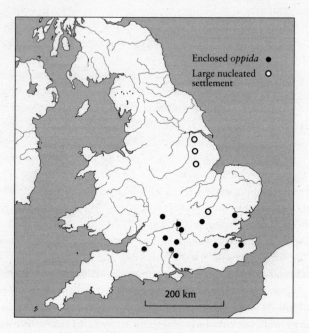

Fig. 4.15 A map showing the location of Iron Age *oppida*, at *c.* 70 BC, over a century before the Roman conquest of AD 43.

ROADS IN IRON AGE BRITAIN

It is almost impossible to say when the major prehistoric routes or trackways became established, but there are reasons to suppose that some may be very ancient indeed, possibly even reflecting pre-Neolithic patterns of long-distance and seasonal travel.[56] The course of the Ridgeway, for example, can be shown to have been respected by prehistoric field systems and its route passes close by significant prehistoric sites, such as the Neolithic chambered tomb of Wayland's Smithy and the ramparts of the Iron Age hillfort at Uffington Castle, both in Oxfordshire. Further west, however, it passes the vast ritual complex of Avebury, without deviating from its path.

Given what we know about the development of prehistoric sites and landscapes, it is almost certainly a mistake to take the idea of long-distance trackways at face value.[57] The best way forward would be to analyse the various landscapes that comprise the through routes, and closely examine the relationship of the trackway to the known and dated features it passes by, and through. It may well be that its path shifts, but it could also have been abandoned for significant periods of time. The restoration of parts of the Ridgeway in modern times should not be taken to mean that it had been open and accessible throughout its very long history.

One or two specific lengths of road can, however, be dated to the Iron Age with some precision. Invariably tracks or causeways across wet areas can be accurately dated by radiocarbon or tree-rings. During the first millennium BC conditions were becoming wetter in the Somerset Levels, where numerous trackways had been constructed since earlier Neolithic times. During the first millennium BC it seems that most trackways in the Levels were made out of hurdles or woven wattlework laid flat on the ground.[58] Between about 700 and 400 BC the Levels became too wet for trackway-building at all, and after about 300 BC the celebrated Iron Age lake villages at Meare and Glastonbury began to be built.[59] Glastonbury covered just under a hectare and would have held about fifteen roundhouses at its peak. There were two lake villages at Meare, which probably predate Glastonbury by a generation or two.[60] In effect these were vast crannogs and were probably built for

Fig. 4.16 The Ridgeway in Oxfordshire, looking towards the ramparts of the Iron Age hillfort of Uffington Castle on the skyline, to the left of the road. The Ridgeway is one of several ancient trackways that can be shown to have prehistoric origins. It is not known, however, whether these were indeed true long-distance routes, as they appear to be on modern maps, or whether they were originally a series of shorter roads that served local communities.

similar reasons, and also as centres for exchange and trade. They were discovered in the late nineteenth century at the time when the whole of Europe was spellbound by the extraordinary discoveries in the Swiss lake villages. A large post-built timber causeway over the floodplain of the River Witham was found at Fiskerton near Lincoln and another (dated by tree-rings to 76 BC) has recently come to light during a river improvement scheme near Beccles in Suffolk.[61] Both were constructed using two rows of large posts, a technique that had been developed around 1500 BC. The existence of these large, labour-intensive pre-historic trackways is important because they only make sense if they once formed part of a much larger road system.

BRITAIN AND ROME BEFORE
THE CONQUEST

Throughout my years as a student I studied the Neolithic, Bronze and Iron ages in some detail but my reading came to a grinding halt in AD 43, the year of the Roman invasion. At that point another set of students and lecturers took up the story. This split was not unusual and can still be found in many universities, where prehistory is often studied with anthropology, whereas the archaeology of ancient Greece and Rome is studied as part of a Classics course, along with the appropriate ancient languages. Quite often prehistory and Roman archaeology actually occupy completely separate university departments. In terms of the development of universities there are good reasons why this peculiar situation should have arisen, the main one being that Classical

Fig. 4.17 Excavation of an Iron Age causeway across an ancient course of the River Waveney, near Beccles, Suffolk. The plastic bags protect posts; two uncovered posts can be seen in the right foreground (with rope bands). Tree-ring dates show that the trackway was constructed around 76 BC and continued in use into Roman times. It was formed by a double line of vertical posts. Wood and brushwood was laid, and sometimes pegged into place, between the rows of posts to provide a dry surface to walk upon.

studies have their roots in the Renaissance and have been around in educated circles for very much longer than prehistory or anthropology, both of which only really got going in earnest in the 1860s and 1870s following the impact of Darwin's *Origin of Species* (1859).

One result of this artificial split in the structure of archaeology itself has been to treat the final decades of the Iron Age as a slightly irrelevant 'fag end' of prehistory. Sometimes, it can be rather difficult to decide whether a site is either Iron Age or Roman. In the south-east this is rarely a problem, because Romano-British mass-produced pottery was introduced very quickly, but many places, like Devon and Cornwall, and of course Scotland, remained almost unaffected by the Roman conquest. Life there continued in an essentially Iron Age pattern right through the Roman period and into post-Roman times.

One archaeologist whose background has allowed him to bridge the divide that separates prehistory from Rome is Sir Barry Cunliffe, who has excavated a large number of important sites of this transitional period, including Roman Bath and the palace of Fishbourne, West Sussex. More recently he has turned his attention to the brisk cross-Channel trade that began to flourish from about 100 BC. He has excavated sites on both sides of the Channel, including a remarkable trading port at Hengistbury Head, in Dorset.[62] Hengistbury Head was rather like Maiden Castle in that it was and is a very spectacular feature of the landscape; like Maiden Castle, too, it boasts a Neolithic causewayed enclosure (*c.* 3500 BC) and was later the site of an important Iron Age promontory fort (a seashore variant of a hillfort where the defences can be confined to a single access point). This promontory fort was protected from attack from the north by massive double dykes. The trading port developed two harbours on the sheltered northern side of the headland, facing over the tranquil waters of Christchurch Bay. Today Christchurch Harbour is almost fully enclosed by sands, but in the Iron Age it would have been far more open and accessible.

It is entirely possible that Hengistbury Head had been an important place for trade and exchange since the Neolithic, but sometime around 100 BC, in the late Iron Age, it acquired a more specialized role. The trading port at Hengistbury sprang up rapidly and flourished in the first half of the first century BC. Pottery found there shows its contacts extended well into Brittany and France and even reached as far afield

Fig. 4.18 Aerial view of Hengistbury Head from the south. The banks of the fort's Iron Age ramparts can be seen clearly just above the narrowest point of the promontory. Hengistbury Head was an important place as long ago as the Neolithic (*c.* 3500 BC) when it was the site of a causewayed enclosure. Later it became an important Iron Age promontory fort. In the fifty years from 100 to 50 BC a prosperous trading port with two harbours sprung up within the bay to the right of the ramparts. In those days the sands around Christchurch Harbour were still forming and although it was still sheltered, access into the bay would have been simpler than it is today.

as Italy. In Britain its contacts were also extensive, reaching to the West Country, Dartmoor and the Mendips. The trade was mostly in luxury goods. The excavation produced quantities of Breton pottery, Gaulish coins, sherds of wine amphorae and high-quality metalwork. Cunliffe reckons that the port was actually run by Breton merchants who lived at Hengistbury. After the mid-first century BC, however, trade rapidly dried up.

The immediate cause of the collapse of cross-Channel trade was probably Caesar's harsh suppression of the Breton tribes' rebellion of 56 BC, but this was only one factor. The main reason why trade moved away from Hengistbury was the rise of new trading ports further east, in Essex and Kent. Caesar had conquered Gaul from the Mediterranean to the Rhine between 58 and 51 BC, and this effectively brought the Roman Empire within sight of Britain. Then in 55 and 54 BC, in the course of his Gallic Wars, he made two military expeditions to Britain, which would have reminded some of his British neighbours, if such a thing were needed, that there was a mighty force, and a potential ally too, on the other side of the Channel.

From the mid-first century BC the tribes of south-eastern Britain were becoming increasingly dominant and from the later first century this was converted into something approaching political unity by the Catuvellauni, a tribe originally from Hertfordshire but which became far more powerful under their remarkable King Cunobelin. Cunobelin died around AD 40, having enjoyed a long reign of about thirty years. It is probably true to say that the tribal kingdoms of southern Britain were a quarrelsome bunch, and sometimes individual tribes would try to involve their powerful Roman neighbours, by forming cross-Channel alliances.

The problem with this view is that it assumes the British tribal kingdoms saw themselves as British, but it is questionable whether the idea of Britishness even existed at this period. More probably, individual tribal kingdoms, such as the Durotriges who controlled the country north and west of Hengistbury Head, would have had closer relations with groups on the other side of the Channel (who would have spoken the same language) than those in Essex and Kent. Attitudes to the Roman Empire were similarly unpredictable. In the south-east there is growing evidence to suggest that many people in the upper echelons of society in the later first century BC adopted Roman dress, to judge by the large numbers of safety-pin-style fibula brooches found there.[63] These brooches were not appropriate to tighter Celtic clothes. Many upper-class people, too, would have been familiar with Latin. An examination of the use of Latin on British Celtic coinage of this period shows close familiarity with the language, although such familiarity does not appear to extend to other inscriptions.[64] This might suggest that the adoption of Latin and Roman dress was a means whereby the literate families of the élite distanced themselves from the illiterate masses. Could this be the first archaeological evidence for the origins of that most enduring of all British traits, snobbery? Whether that was so or not, I have to say that I think it most unlikely that these people would have regarded the prospect of imminent Roman conquest with any horror at all. Indeed, many would have welcomed it.

Our story has now reached the very end of prehistoric times and all the evidence shows that the inter-relationship of the various components within individual landscapes really mattered. We saw for example how the bank cairn on Bodmin Moor was aligned on a prominent feature on the skyline, how Stonehenge was part of an elaborate ritual landscape and finally how hillforts along the Ridgeway played different roles within Iron Age society. To these elements we must add other dimensions, such as the position of the sun and moon at different times of the year. It is no exaggeration to say that for prehistoric people the landscape amounted to far more than mere scenery. It illustrated and exemplified law and religion; it helped people cope with the cycle of the seasons and linked their families to the Realms of the Ancestors, both beyond the horizon and beneath their feet. Knowledge of the landscape would have been intimately bound up with details of tribal and family history. Put briefly, in prehistoric times landscapes provided the lore of life: a child sitting at his or her grandparents' feet would have been taught the meaning and significance of different hills, streams, trees, standing stones and other features, both natural and man-made. One could even argue that landscape helped to reinforce a code of morals. In the absence of writing, it was the landscape and the complexities of its interpretation that gave prehistoric people the knowledge they needed to survive and to prosper.

5

Enter a Few Romans (AD 43–410)

To quote Monty Python, 'What did the Romans do for us?' The simple answer is that the Roman Empire gave Britain literacy. From AD 43 onwards Britain acquired a written history which affected – and still affects – the way that people saw themselves and their origins. It marked a fundamental shift away from a locally based world view, founded in the landscapes around the places where people actually lived, towards new visions whose roots lay in great cities and latterly within monarchies and the Church. None of this would have been possible without writing. One could of course argue that writing would have reached Britain anyhow. After all, it had already reached a few people in the élite classes of the south-east in the later Iron Age, as we saw at the end of the previous chapter. But few would argue that the process would have taken very much longer and the result would have been an altogether different Britain, had the Romans not invaded when they did.

So far I have discussed the adoption of writing and yet this is a book about landscapes. But in this instance I believe there is a close connection between the two. As we have seen in all the previous chapters, landscape change was rarely rapid, yet the Roman period lasted just three and a half centuries – considerably shorter, for example, than the lifespan of an average hillfort. So was that enough time for major change? Probably not, if Britain had remained in the state it had been in the Neolithic or early Bronze Age. But following the widespread innovations of the middle of the second millennium BC the rate of social change began to gather pace. By the late Iron Age, the tribes of southern Britain were on the verge of inventing towns. The Roman conquest gave British farmers, landowners, merchants and emerging industrial entrepreneurs, the extra intellectual and administrative abilities they needed both to create entirely new urban landscapes and to immeasurably improve the rural landscapes they had inherited. The new skills that came with literacy, which included everything from record-keeping to accountancy and tax collection, encouraged administrative efficiency and this in turn led to various projects being carried out with more speed.

We can better appreciate the impact of the Romans on the landscape if we know something about their attitude to Britain. The first point to note is that very few of the conquerors were actually Romans, in the sense of men and women who were born and brought up in Rome. Instead, most of the incoming soldiers and administrators had originated elsewhere in the Roman Empire, partly through the deliberate policy whereby newly conquered people were transferred to fight in distant parts of the Empire – to prevent them rebelling and causing trouble in their homelands. For example, three of the four legions of Roman citizen troops that arrived in Britain with the invasion fleet actually came from the region around the upper Rhine.

The origins of the word Britain are British not Roman. The inhabitants of the islands would probably have described themselves as *Pretani* or *Preteni*.[1] In Welsh this eventually became *Prydain*. Greek authors such as Diodorus Siculus in the first century BC talk about *Pretannia*, the term they borrowed from Pytheas, who had probably heard it first during the course of his circumnavigation two centuries previously. The 'B' spelling was first adopted by Strabo (*c.* 64 BC–*c.* AD 23) in the second volume of his monumental 17-volume *Geography*.

THE ROMAN CONQUEST

The Iron Age is conventionally taken to end with the Roman invasion of southern Britain, which happened in AD 43, somewhere in either Kent or Sussex. But the Roman troops never penetrated northern Scotland and never fully 'Romanized' large parts of northern, western or south-western Britain, either. So in these areas the Iron Age continued in spirit, if not in name, throughout the Roman period, which is why essentially Iron Age beliefs, art styles and social behaviour played an important role there, in post-Roman times.[2]

The conquest was indeed a momentous event in British history, but it needs to be put in context. When the Roman troops arrived on the south coast of Britain, either in Kent (near Richborough) or in the Solent (Chichester Harbour) they would have been familiar with the place, not just through Caesar's two earlier visits of 55 and 54 BC, but through a series of continuing contacts with British leaders. The attitude of Rome to Britain in the century between Caesar's visits and the Claudian invasion of AD 43 could be described as removed or distant. There was no ban on trade, or what today we would refer to as 'sanctions', and the result was a period of stability where the focus of wealth, power and influence shifted eastwards towards the area around London and the eastern Home Counties: Hertfordshire, Essex and Kent.

By the mid-first century AD southern Britain was occupied by a series of regional tribal groupings, sometimes referred to as kingdoms. One could argue whether or not these were indeed stable entities, but some of them did possess named leaders and issued their own coinage from their own mints. One or two leaders were exceptional. We have already encountered one of these, the powerful and aggressive ruler Cunobelin, High King of the Catuvellauni, a tribal kingdom whose origins lay in Hertfordshire. Cunobelin ruled his kingdom, from a new capital he had conquered at *Camulodunum* (Colchester).[3] After a period of ruthless expansion his domain consisted of a confederation of tribes comprising most of East Anglia south of Norfolk (home of Boudica's Iceni), together with Kent and parts of southern England. His reign lasted more than thirty years, much longer than that of any of his contemporaries. It is thought that the uncertain political situation in southern Britain that followed upon Cunobelin's death around AD 40 influenced the Roman Emperor Claudius' decision to invade, just three years later. The Romans arrived in considerable force, doubtless because they were aware of Strabo's warning that 'the whole race is war mad, high-spirited and quick to battle'.

Previous chapters have shown that by the mid-first century AD the landscape of most of Britain was fully developed. This does not mean that all woodland had been clear-felled and replaced by arable fields and pasture, because that never happened. What it does mean is that woodlands were present because communities had need of them; by the end of the Iron Age people had learnt how to exploit and manage such landscapes sustainably. Elsewhere, the landscape was parcelled up into fields or into areas of open grazing, much as it is today. As we have seen, there were no true towns, but in southern Britain some of the larger settlements were approaching the size of towns; these were usually market centres, many of which were to become true towns in Roman times. By the close of the Iron Age most rural settlements across Britain had acquired agreed boundaries which would have been marked out in some way: by large trees, ditches, banks, drystone walls or roadways. Moreover the roots of this landscape were already centuries old.

The complex man-made landscapes of Iron Age Britain would have required many people to maintain and improve them. Hoskins reckoned that the late Iron Age population was around a quarter of a million. Today estimates vary, but most authorities consider that there were as many – if not a few more – settlements in the Iron Age as in early Norman times. In 1086 the Domesday survey of England records a population of 1.5 million; so it is reasonable to assume, since we also know that there were even more Romano-British than Iron Age settlements, that the average population of Roman Britain was probably in the range 2 to 2.5 million. It could even have been closer to 3 million in the fourth century when the economy was flourishing.[4]

The military history of the Roman conquest of Britain is not the straightforward 'I came, I saw, I conquered' of Julius Caesar.[5] In actual fact the conquest was a protracted process of ebb and flow in those parts of Britain where the Iron Age population did not have close links to the Empire in the decades prior to AD 43.[6] The effects of the various military campaigns on the landscape have mainly been indirect, via roads, supply routes and depots. Many Roman towns, too, such as Colchester, were based on large military camps or fortifications. This is evident today in the neat grid-like layout of the old military areas of the towns and the fact that many names include '-chester', from the Latin *castra*, a camp. The conquest of south and east Britain was rapid, but it took longer further to the west and north. The process was also delayed by a number of tribal revolts, of which the Boudican rebellion of AD 60–61 was by far the largest. The result was that while south-eastern Britain regained a measure of stability by AD 70, it took another two decades in Wales, Anglesey and what is now northern England. And, north of Hadrian's Wall the situation remained unstable well into the second century.

ROMAN BRITAIN AFTER THE CONQUEST

The first capital of Roman Britain was at Colchester, the capital of the Catuvellauni, the largest and most powerful pre-Roman tribal kingdom in Britain. The city of *Camulodunum* (Colchester) was named *Colonia Victricensis* which roughly translates as City of Victory.[7] This position of pre-eminence lasted only briefly, because large areas of Colchester were burnt during the Boudican revolt. There were other reasons, too – mostly to do with poor communications and the lack of a good seaport – why Colchester did not meet the Roman requirements for a major provincial capital.

Fig. 5.1 View of the twin portals of the Balkerne Gate, Colchester, from inside the Roman town. This was the eastern gate through the walls for the city's main road. The wall was built in AD 65–80, following the disaster of the Boudican revolt when the city was burnt to the ground. These are the earliest city walls in Britain and they included substantial gatehouses.

The British Isles were of strong interest to the Romans. First and foremost they were known to be rich in ores and minerals, which is why areas like the lead mines of Somerset were exploited from earliest post-conquest times.[8] They were also home to the Druids, who by the early first century AD had become a powerful politico-religious influence in northern Europe. For these and other reasons Britain was a subject that interested Roman authors, but none has given such a clear account of *Britannia* as possibly the greatest Latin historian of all, Cornelius Tacitus, who also happened to be the son-in-law of Julius Agricola. Agricola was governor for seven years, during which time he completed the Roman conquest. Even though his account of his father-in-law's tenure as governor was intended as something of a eulogy, Tacitus' description of life in early Roman Britain has never been bettered. It was completed in AD 98. I find chapter 21 at first fascinating and then, at the end, quite chilling.

> The following winter was spent on schemes of social betterment. Agricola had to deal with people living in isolation and ignorance, and therefore prone to fight; and his object was to accustom them to a life of peace and quiet by the provision of amenities. He therefore gave private encouragement and official assistance to the building of temples, public squares, and good houses. He praised the energetic and scolded the slack; and competition for honour proved as effective as compulsion. Furthermore, he educated the sons of the chiefs in the liberal arts, and expressed a preference for British ability as compared with the trained skills of the Gauls. The result was that instead of loathing the Latin language they became eager to speak it effectively. In the same way, our national dress came into favour and the toga was everywhere to be seen. And so the population was gradually led into the demoralizing temptations of arcades, baths, and sumptuous banquets. The unsuspecting Britons spoke of such novelties as 'civilization', when in fact they were only a feature of their enslavement.[9]

The soldiers and administrators of the Roman Empire provided the British tribes with a new structure of regional and national government. They also introduced towns and cities. The Roman army was a well-disciplined force that imposed new forms of law and order – and of course they built a network of good quality roads, many of which are still used to this day.[10] In terms of the landscape, the network of roads, and the towns and cities they served, were probably their most enduring legacy. The new roads radiated from *Londinium*, which was to become the capital or principal city of Britain.

Initially, many of the main roads of Britain were constructed by military engineers, as part of the campaign of conquest. They tended to be straight (although this was not a universal feature) for two reasons. First, a straight road is a more efficient way of getting troops from A to B, and, secondly the Roman army did not need to take account of the ancient tribal and other territorial boundaries that existed at the time. This is why many roads built in medieval and later times seem to meander through the countryside; their routes were negotiated, rather than imposed. It used to be believed that Roman roads were either abandoned or were deliberately avoided in Saxon times, but today there seems little doubt that the vast majority continued in use and formed, as we shall see, the basis for England's later infrastructure from the Saxon period right through to post-medieval times. In short, it would be hard to overestimate the importance of the Roman road network in the history of the British landscape south of the Antonine Wall.

In rural Britain, 'the Romans' made relatively little direct impact on the landscape, simply because its inhabitants were in fact the Iron Age farmers and landowners who had always been there. It was not until the latter part of the Roman period that a distinctively new approach to the management of estates – the so-called Roman villas – arose in southern Britain. Essentially, a Roman villa was a large house in the country featuring a central building with underfloor heating, baths and sophisticated architecture in the form of stone columns and (sometimes) mosaic floors. Around the central house were barns and other buildings necessary for the smooth running of a country estate. When excavated, these villa estates are usually shown to have had roots in the Iron Age.[11] In most instances the archaeological evidence suggests that farms and rural landscapes that were already in existence continued into Roman times when in most instances they prospered and expanded. In purely economic terms, the Roman conquest was very beneficial to Britain, but those benefits were by no means evenly spread.

There was a broad divide within the province of *Britannia*, between the south and east, which was generally speaking more Romanized, and the north and west, which was less so and was sometimes (as in the case of Devon and Cornwall) almost completely unaffected by the Roman presence.[12] This NW/SE split was a direct reflection of the situation in the later Iron Age discussed in the previous chapter.

ROMAN ROADS

Formalized roads had been in existence since at least the time of the Sweet Track across the Somerset Levels, in the early fourth millennium BC. By the Iron Age the British road system would have been very sophisticated, but it was based on a network, rather than the radial system from a capital city that the Roman administration established. Some elements of the earlier system have survived, such as Peddars Way and the Icknield Way in East Anglia and the latter's south-westerly continuation along the Chalk Escarpment, the Ridgeway. The landscape would also have been criss-crossed with a network of many thousands of roads and tracks, which can sometimes be seen on aerial photographs where they are often dismissed as 'farm trackways' or 'droves'.

The Roman authorities established their road network to link towns and military centres, and most were built in the early decades following the conquest. There are two remarkable facts about the Roman roads of Britain. The first is their quality. Most were built on a low bank or *agger*, built up from the upcast out of the two side-ditches that served as drains. The *agger* was cambered to ease drainage, and the wearing surface of the road was dressed with stone, sand or gravel. We tend to forget the side-ditches, but these were essential to the success of the road and even gave their name to one of the main routes west, the Fosse Way (*fossa* in Latin means a ditch).

The other extraordinary aspect of the Roman road system is its longevity. Although some other roads were built in the Middle Ages, the fact remains that the Roman road network remained the prime means of overland travel throughout Saxon, medieval and early post-medieval times. It was only with the rise of the turnpikes in the eighteenth century that Britain was given anything better, and in very many instances (such as the first turnpike itself) these new roads

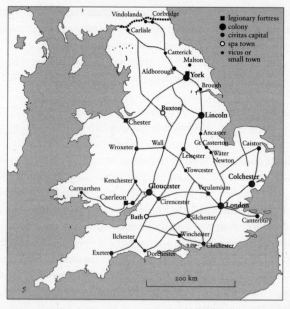

Fig. 5.2 A map showing the principal roads and the towns of Roman Britain. The various categories are discussed in the text. Legionary fortresses were the principal military centres; colonies (*colonia*) were the highest ranking Roman cities where retired soldiers settled; *civitas* capitals were the capitals of cantons (usually the size of two to three modern counties).

followed Roman alignments. Even the layout of our modern trunk road and motorway network would not have seemed at all unfamiliar to a Roman Briton.

The network of roads established by the Romans remains the fundamental structure of Britain's overland communications network today; even the main railway lines follow the general Roman pattern.[13] The network was based around the province's capital *Londinium*, from whence most roads radiate; there was also a significant north–south alignment to the west of England's central upland spine (the Roman equivalent of the modern M5 and M6 motorways). The principal roads are shown on the map of Romano-British towns (Fig. 5.2).

It used to be thought that the road network was imposed on the landscape by the newly arrived military and civil authorities with scant regard for what had gone before. In actual fact the network of military establishments (camps, forts, etc.) set up by the Roman army on its arrival reflected the nature of the opposition they encountered, which in turn would have reflected the relationships of Britain's various Iron Age tribal kingdoms to Rome.[14] Sometimes, for example in the territory of the Cantiaci of Kent, or the Iceni of East Anglia, allies of Rome before the conquest, opposition was only slight; in other areas, such as northern and western England, opposition was far more intense. Similarly, the new Roman government was pragmatic and the early civil administration made use of the pre-existing Iron Age political structure. Thus early towns were often established at Iron Age market centres and roads were built to link them together. The road network therefore reflects both the political picture of mid-first-century AD Iron Age Britain, and the Roman high command's need to supply the army efficiently.

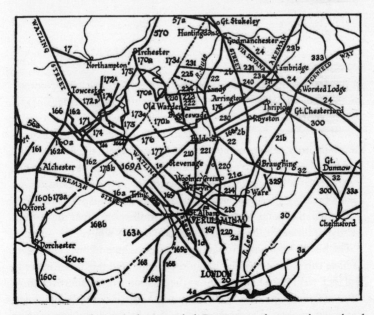

Fig. 5.3 Map showing the crowded Roman road network north of London, with Oxford in the west, Chelmsford in the east and Huntingdon in the north.

Roads also served to link the principal centres along major military installations, such as Hadrian's Wall, and across militarized landscapes, such as the territory of the Scottish Borders, north of the Wall. As they were based on many pre-existing Iron Age centres of settlement, it is also possible that the roads used to link the towns and cities of Roman Britain actually followed long-established routes. In such instances the Roman road, being far more robust and better engineered than its Iron Age predecessor, usually obliterated all traces of the earlier route.

We tend to think of the Roman road network as being one of trunk routes cutting their way straight through an open landscape, but numerous subsidiary smaller roads fed into the main system. Close study of maps and aerial photographs is still revealing new minor roads, but we know enough already to conclude that the Roman road network was comparable in every respect to that of modern Britain.[15] It was certainly appropriate for a population in the early fourth century, of some 3.7 million people.[16]

TOWNS AND URBANISM

In Europe, towns were places where people lived in close proximity and shared certain important services, such as marketplaces, water supply, rubbish collection and mutual defence, usually in the form of a wall. This concept was introduced to Britain by the first Roman administrators, who generally selected places where the British tribes had traditionally met to exchange and trade goods. These settlements were then officially declared towns. Next, the new administrators set about building the necessary infrastructure of roads, marketplaces, public buildings and houses. At first the walls were often made from earth and timber, to be subsequently replaced by stone.

The history of Roman towns in Britain was an odd one. They seem to have thrived initially, mainly in the second and third centuries AD, and then went into sharp decline at the beginning of the fourth century. After AD 300 late Romano-British towns often lack public buildings, are under-populated and generally seem to be run down. Yet the first half of the fourth century AD has been labelled the 'Golden Age' of Roman Britain.[17] It was the period when country estates flourished in southern Britain; when the Romano-British élite built themselves some truly sumptuous villa residences outside town.

The majority of Roman towns came into existence around a fort built as part of the initial conquest campaign, following the invasion of AD 43.[18] These forts were usually sited at significant places in the landscape, such as river crossings or close to Iron Age settlements. Some were founded at important road junctions, others near pre-existing Iron Age settlements, or at major pre-Roman political (for example, Colchester and *Verulamium*[19]) or religious centres (such as Bath). Roman towns served a more formal administrative purpose than their modern equivalents and the majority were laid out on a grid system, with important public buildings near the centre.

Some towns maintained a close relationship with the military: examples are Carlisle, Corbridge and *Vindolanda* on Hadrian's Wall; of these three, the town element at *Vindolanda* consisted of the informal civilian settlement, or *vicus*, outside the fort walls. Like the towns along the Wall, York (*Eboracum*) also retained close military connections.

The larger towns were formal foundations of two sorts. The *coloniae* were settlements for retired soldiers, who were all Roman citizens. These trained and disciplined men formed an important strategic reserve. British *coloniae* are known to have included Colchester, Gloucester, Lincoln, York and possibly London too. Roman Britain was divided into administrative units known as *civitates* (singular: *civitas*), which is commonly translated as canton. The *civitates* were approximately based on the territories controlled by the principal tribal kingdoms that existed at the end of the Iron Age. Each *civitas* had a capital, from whence the administration was conducted. The name of the *civitas* capital often reflected the tribal kingdom; thus Cirencester was *Corinium Dobunnorum* ('*Corinium* of the Dobunni').

The two Roman spa towns (Bath and Buxton) were based around springs which had been important in Iron Age times. With the exception of Water Newton (*Durobrivae*), which was the centre of a major pottery industry, these small towns were less formally organized and much smaller than the *coloniae* or the *civitas* capitals, some little larger than a modern village.

The decline of so many Romano-British towns at the start of the fourth century seems odd when one takes a stroll around their walls and admires the fancy mosaics. But at this late period they certainly do not seem to have thrived with anything like the vigour of their Continental equialents. Many public buildings were abandoned, never to be restored. So what was happening? One explanation is that Roman towns in Britain were more a front than a true expression of urbanity.[20] This way of looking at a Romano-British town would see it as a trading settlement within a classical façade. A more vivid metaphor is the Hollywood Wild West film set, where the street frontage is just one wall.[21]

Of course there were exceptions, where the town continued to be inhabited right through the fourth century and indeed later, but on a reduced scale. If the notion of urbanism in Britain had been an imposition from outside – an idea before its time – it helps explain what happened later. If ideas of urbanism had caught on and been taken to heart by the Romanized British population of southern Britain, then surely they would have persisted through the fifth and sixth centuries and later? But they did not. To date no undisputed towns of the sixth or seventh century are known in Britain. So far as we know, no truly urban centre could be said to be thriving at this time. It is also instructive that the first post-Roman towns, the so-called *wic*s of Middle Saxon England which came into existence from beginnings late in the seventh century, do not appear to have direct and demonstrable, Romano-British antecedents.[22] In the case of London, for example, the Middle Saxon *wic* of Lundenwic lies well outside the walled Roman city of *Londinium*. Whether or not one accepts these ideas it cannot be denied that while a few towns continued through the fourth century, very few made it into the sixth.

As a prehistorian used to dealing with rural landscapes where high-quality aerial survey has been routinely under way since the 1920s, it is easy to forget the remarkable advances that have been made in the study of urban landscapes. Aerial photography, for example, is not much use in a town, other than to show the layout of streets and garden plots – which can equally well be seen on maps and town plans. Similarly one cannot walk across a town gathering up pieces of pottery found lying on the surface, and hope to discover anything of historical importance. So the simple process of surveying, which prehistorians take for granted, is much more difficult. The only way to do it is to record all the chance finds made when people disturb the ground, whether by digging an allotment, adding a new garage or undertaking a major development.

Before the Second World War the museums of most towns in Britain were small and often run by dedicated amateurs. After the war the archaeology of some of Britain's biggest cities was transformed in the aftermath of the terrible bombing they had just suffered. Places like the City of London had always been out of bounds to archaeologists, simply because they were entirely built over. The Blitz changed all that. Bomb sites had to be cleared and this provided a unique opportunity.[23] The excavations that followed the Blitz and the early years of post-war redevelopment in the City of London were outstandingly important, but sometimes painfully slow. However, Roman London is now the most extensively excavated city of the period in Europe. The work has revealed a vast amount of new information about this, the principal city of Roman Britain.[24]

Very unusually, Roman *Londinium* was sited on an entirely new location, where no previous tribal centre had existed.[25] Its lack of history may well be the reason it was chosen as the provincial capital after the destruction of Colchester as part of the Boudican revolt of AD 60–61. London, too, was very severely damaged in that rebellion, but reconstruction was under way two years later. The city originally grew up as a planned trading and business centre on both sides of the Thames, at either end of the new bridge that was constructed around AD 50; this bridge fed the traffic of Watling Street (which served the south coast and Kent) into the radiating major roads that covered Britain north of the Thames. *Londinium* was prosperous and grew swiftly, but unlike other early Romano-British towns (Colchester, for example) it does not appear to have been defended by a fort, although the discovery of early military material in Southwark may indicate one south of the river.

Despite having no official status, the early town north of the river was still laid out on a grid pattern. South of the river the landscape consisted of several low islands, of which the most northerly one (Southwark[26]) was used as the landfall of the new Thames bridge. The landscape here made it impossible to employ a strict grid system. The layout of the walled city north of the river shows clear evidence for central planning. The main administrative building, the basilica, for example would have towered over the houses around it. Its location was intended to impress and would immediately have been seen by

any visitor travelling north from the bridge. The original basilica was massively enlarged in the second century in the Hadrianic period. This new basilica was constructed in two episodes, but the scale was enormous and it seems probable that the second Hadrianic basilica was never completed; this may have been a result of the general decline of major public building in Romano-British towns that set in after AD 300.

Excavation has revealed a number of deep, V-shaped ditches that might be parts of Roman forts or temporary defended camps, probably built during the conquest period and its aftermath, but so far the only undoubted fort was located at Cripplegate just to the north-west of the early Roman city, which still lacked permanent walls; that fort was possibly abandoned by the third century. The main city walls were built around AD 200 from Kentish ragstone with tile courses at intervals.

Fig. 5.4 Roman London: AD 60. This reconstructed view (using all the information gathered from post-WWII archaeology) shows London just before the Boudican revolt. This view is looking south-east with *Londinium* in the foreground and Southwark directly opposite on the other side of the Thames. At this time the first timber bridge had yet to be built and travellers would have crossed the Thames to the settlement at Southwark by boat and ferry. The small river running through the centre of *Londinium* is the Walbrook, that to the lower right is the Fleet river.

Fig. 5.5 Roman London: mid-fifth century AD. We now know that the area of woodland beyond the walls to the west (*left*), near modern Fleet Street, may well have been the site of a series of early Saxon settlements.

They enclosed an area of some 125 hectares and probably originally stood 6.4 metres high, with internal turrets and a parapet walkway.

London gave the province what Colchester lacked, namely, a top-quality port. A series of important waterfront excavations have revealed numerous substantial timber quays (of the first to third centuries) extending some 450 metres downstream and 600 metres upstream of the bridge. These discoveries strongly reinforce the evidence provided by numerous imported objects, that *Londinium* rapidly became a major trading port.

It is widely, and erroneously, believed that the Romans ruled through military power alone. While this may have been the case during the actual process of conquest, once new territories had been made secure, civilian government was introduced. This well-regulated system ensured that law and order prevailed and, most importantly, that taxes were levied to support the central authority in Rome, the Roman army and regional government. All this was achieved at the provincial level by way of civil authorities based in the *civitas* capitals (the principal town or city of the different cantons). The provincial authorities operated from the formal public buildings that usually stood near the centre of these towns.

Some of the most spectacular Roman structures in Britain remaining today are the oval-shaped amphitheatres, where public displays were held within the arena, sometimes for the benefit of townspeople, but otherwise for soldiers – as at Caerleon. Fine examples can still be seen at Silchester, Caerleon and at Dorchester (*Durnovaria*) where the Roman structure was placed on top of a very much earlier henge monument. The most frequently encountered remains of Roman towns are the outer defensive walls, but in many instances it is difficult, without specialized knowledge, to be certain that one is indeed looking at Roman masonry. Very often, as at York, for example, the Roman walls were extensively restored, enlarged and adapted in the Middle Ages.

Further north, the city of York, possibly because of its long-term military connections, remained important in later Roman times, so it comes as no great surprise to discover that occupation there continued into the fifth century. The archaeological evidence for this comes in the

Fig. 5.6 The military amphitheatre at Caerleon, Gwent. A permanent legionary fortress was established at Caerleon on the River Usk in the first century AD; later, during the second century, it was one of only three permanent garrisons (the others being at York and Chester). The amphitheatre was built around AD 90 and was maintained in use until the late third century. It covers an area of 56 × 41 metres. The arena was sunk into the ground and would have been surfaced with sand. It seats about 6,000 people, which was slightly more than the size of the nearby garrison. Events staged there would have included parades and games, some of which would have been brutal by modern standards.

form of coarse handmade pottery, known as calcite-gritted ware, which recent research has shown was made well into the fifth century.[27] It is found where one would expect it, close to the main crossing of the River Ouse. At both Wroxeter and York, one could suggest that the fifth-century presence was not true town life so much as life within a place that had once been a functioning town.[28]

One of the major developments of post-war archaeology has been the increasing use of geophysical prospection techniques.[29] There are currently about a dozen methods of geophysical survey. Most were originally developed by geological prospectors seeking ores or oil; but ground penetrating radar (GPR) was used by civil engineers in Japan to detect dangerous voids that would suddenly appear beneath roads in sandy districts after heavy rain. The three most popular approaches are electrical resistance, which measures the extent to which the ground resists an electrical current passed through it; magnetometry, which measures tiny fluctuations in the earth's magnetic field caused by buried archaeological remains; and GPR, which records the frequency of radio waves as they are reflected from buried remains.

Geophysical surveys have produced some extraordinary results, especially as regards Roman towns. The complete geophysical survey of Wroxeter has revealed the full complexity of this Roman city, today a peaceful scene of green fields, humps and bumps, but with one huge upstanding wall, known as the Old Work, still standing proud.[30] Wroxeter was the fourth largest town in Roman Britain and it survived for well over a century after the end (conventionally AD 410) of the Roman Empire in Britain.[31] Excavations carried out since 1966 have shown that even after the official end of the Roman presence in Britain, the inhabitants of Wroxeter lived ordered lives.

The recent projects developed excavation techniques that revealed the slight traces of timber structures not noticed when the main stone and brick public buildings of the baths basilica and its surroundings were originally excavated in the nineteenth century. The excavators showed that these central public buildings had experienced serious problems at the end of the third century, when they burnt down and were abandoned. The baths had also declined: floors were worn out, and mosaics had deteriorated. The damage was then rather crudely repaired in the late third or fourth century. Throughout this time trade

Fig. 5.7 A view of the ruins of the public buildings, or baths basilica, of the Roman city of Wroxeter (*Viroconium Cornoviarum*), Shropshire. This wall, known as the Old Work, is the largest surviving fragment of a town building from Roman Britain and owes its survival to having been used as part of a barn – hence the more modern double-door opening in the centre.

continued near the baths basilica, first with money and, after the collapse of the monetary system in the late fourth century, using barter. The post-Roman buildings of the fifth and sixth centuries were built from timber, but in Roman style, and were laid out using Roman measurements.

The centre of the city was transformed sometime between AD 530 and 580: the remains of the old basilica were demolished and the site was prepared to take a number of substantial new timber buildings. The remains of the old public *frigidarium* (the cool room of a Roman bath house) were probably converted into a church, and a new and very large timber building has been identified as a possible bishop's palace. After the Roman adoption of Christianity, bishoprics had been established by the emperors in the fourth century in every major town. Once established, they are likely to have become self-perpetuating, appointing and reappointing among themselves, since there was no other controlling authority, apart from the emperor (at that time the pope was based in Constantinople and had not yet established primacy in the Western Empire).[32] We cannot be certain, but it now seems highly probable that the survival of Wroxeter into the Dark Ages was largely thanks to the Church.

Conventional surface survey and aerial photography have produced some exciting new information on what might have been happening outside town and city walls. Surveys at Silchester, for example, have revealed extensive settlement outside the city walls.[33] Another survey, this time using aerial photographs of the small town of *Durobrivae*, near Peterborough, has also revealed the huge extent of the *vicus* or suburban and industrial sprawl outside the town walls.[34] Given what we know about places like Silchester and *Durobrivae*, some of the more successful Roman towns did indeed achieve urban status, but failed to retain it when the political and social geography changed entirely, in the late fourth and fifth centuries. It also seems clear that it was not just big cities like Wroxeter and Silchester that were able to cope with the changes brought about by the hastening collapse of the Roman economy towards the end of the fourth century. Some of the more successful small towns such as *Durobrivae* continued as regional market centres in the post-Roman era.[35]

Laying aside the question of their urban status, the towns of Roman Britain made a significant mark on the landscape, despite the fact that they only housed some 6.5 per cent of a total population of around 3.7 million.[36] Abandoned towns like Wroxeter and Silchester have left an enduring mark on the landscape. The walls of Silchester still stand high and the remains of the baths basilica building at Wroxeter are the largest surviving ruins of a Roman town building in Britain.[37] Perhaps more importantly, the routes of the roads we drive along are nearly always heading towards a Roman town. On a long and boring drive I have been known to amuse myself trying to spot the precise point where sometime later, usually in the Middle Ages, the road was diverted to skirt around an abandoned Roman town.

Fig. 5.8 The walls of the Romano-British town of Silchester (*Calleva Atrebatum*), Hampshire. Recent re-excavation of earlier Victorian excavations by a team from Reading University have shown that this walled town continued to be occupied on a large scale for some two centuries after the end of Roman rule in Britain (AD 410). Silchester then died out, never to become a town in post-Roman times.

THE NORTHERN FRONTIER OF THE ROMAN EMPIRE

The most striking Roman feature in the British landscape is undoubtedly Hadrian's Wall. Few places in Britain can be quite so evocative. The great Wall snakes its way along the highest crags in some of the wildest and most beautiful country in Britain. One glance at its setting is enough to convince anyone that the Roman military engineers knew exactly where to place such a formidable obstacle: could anywhere be more remote and inaccessible? Who on earth would wish to mount an attack across such a landscape? These are the kind of questions any casual visitor might ask, especially if he or she happened to visit in the winter. But detailed survey has shown that the superficial picture disguises the truth.

The Emperor Hadrian gave orders for the Wall to be built to define the northern limits of the province of *Britannia*, when he made a visit to Britain, in the year AD 122.[38] It was a massive undertaking involving 74 kilometres of stone walls, 43 kilometres of turf ramparts, 200 towers, 100 small forts and 20 major forts. Not surprisingly, it took some twenty years to build. The conventional view was that the Wall had been built across wooded country and was carefully positioned to take full military advantage of the lie of the land. Its location had been well thought out by first-rate military minds. But we now realize that, rather like the siting of hillforts, there was more to it than defence alone. The Wall served a dual purpose as both a boundary against the barbarian tribes of the north and by dividing, made it easier to rule them. It effectively separated the Selgovae of central southern Scotland from the Brigantes, whose main territory lay south of the wall. The

Fig. 5.9 A view of Hadrian's Wall looking east from the fort at Housesteads (*Vercovicium*), the north wall of which is visible in the right foreground. Not all the landscape along the Wall is wild and inhospitable, as we see here, where the Wall crosses lower land before returning to a higher scarp beyond the wood in the middle distance. Recent research has shown that much of the landscape on either side of Hadrian's Wall was farmed and settled at the time it was built in AD 122.

various tribes in the area had been causing the Romans major problems by forming short-lived alliances, and then launching major attacks.[39]

If the conventional picture of Hadrian's Wall was of a massive military structure thrust across a virgin landscape, recent aerial survey has demonstrated that the country on *both* sides of the Wall had already been partitioned into a series of fields and farms. This network of drystone walls formed the skeleton of what was essentially a farmed and domesticated landscape. The first fields had been laid out in the late Iron Age, and the process continued – that is, old farms were enlarged or new farms were built – as late as the mid-second century AD, when the Wall was actually being constructed. We do not know whether these farms were allowed to continue when the Wall was in use by the military, but they need not have been seen as a direct threat to the Roman army. Instead, their presence could even have been turned to advantage by providing fresh provisions for the many soldiers garrisoned along the Wall. Unlike grain, meat and milk do not travel well, and are best acquired locally. The layout of these farms followed a standard upland model, with crops grown in small fields near to the farm buildings and livestock in the larger fields, further away.[40]

The evidence provided by aerial photographs has been supplemented by studies of pollen sequences in the landscape around the Wall. These clearly show that the process of clearing the pre-existing woodland was largely completed before the construction of the Wall began. As one would expect, that construction did involve extra clearance (probably to remove trees on certain sight lines, or where they would provide cover for approaching attackers), but there can be no doubt that the large-scale tree-felling had already happened in the Iron Age.[41]

In theory, the Roman army did not permit wives and partners to be housed within forts, although we do know from the discovery of the bones of women and children within them that this rule was often disobeyed.[42] Even so, most wives and families lived just outside the forts in informal settlements known as *vici*. Recent survey of the fort on the Wall at Birdoswald, in Cumbria, has revealed two large *vici*, to the east and west of the fort walls. Again, this reinforces the impression of a populated landscape because the people living in the *vici* would have needed to feed and look after themselves. There would have been much trade with local farmers.[43]

Fig. 5.10 This aerial photograph of the shore of Greenlee Lough, Bardon Mill, Northumberland, some 2 kilometres north of Hadrian's Wall, shows the rectangular outline of the turf ramparts of a Roman army marching camp, probably dating to the late first or early second century AD. Within and outside the fort, and faintly visible lower left, are the very slight traces of late Iron Age 'cord rig', a form of prehistoric ploughing that gave rise to miniature ridge-and-furrow (which in turn can be seen in the field beyond the fort). Excavation in 1980 showed the fort was cut through the cord rig, which suggests that the landscape through which the Wall was built (in the AD 120–30s) was not an uninhabited, barren wilderness, as was previously believed.

We have known for some time that the architecture and masonry of the Wall and of the forts and fortlets along it are often of top quality and clearly intended to impress. This is not to suggest that the Wall did not serve a military purpose; clearly it did. But it does indicate that it was constructed for more than one reason: rather like the hillforts of the Iron Age, the Wall was making a political statement. This might help to explain why lengths of it were originally plastered or whitewashed.[44] A white wall would certainly have stood out from its dark background, as a strong symbolic statement of authority.[45]

Hadrian's Wall marked the southern edge of what had become by the early second century a militarized landscape. To the north of Hadrian's Wall lie the remains of the Antonine Wall, a lesser known attempt to put a northern boundary to the province of *Britannia*. Like its more southerly counterpart, the Antonine Wall has been put forward as a World Heritage Site.[46] In theory, the whole of Britain was conquered by the Romans during the reign of the Emperor Vespasian (AD 69–79), following the battle of *Mons Graupius* (*c.* AD 83/4), possibly somewhere in north-east Scotland. Very shortly afterwards, events elsewhere in the Empire led to a retreat from the north and the abandonment of all forts north of the line that was subsequently consolidated by the construction of Hadrian's Wall.

The first of the Flavian dynasty of emperors, Antoninus Pius, came to power in AD 138 and decided to reconquer Scotland. He abandoned Hadrian's Wall and moved north to the next point where there was a relatively narrow isthmus of land between two river estuaries, those of the Clyde to the west and Forth to the east. Between these he constructed what is known today as the Antonine Wall. It was made of turf on a well-constructed flat stone base, with a substantial ditch on the north side. Turf might be thought to be a soft and insubstantial building material with a short life. In actual fact, it is common to find Bronze Age barrows whose turf cores are so well preserved that one can distinguish which way up individual turves had been placed in the ground. In the damp climate of Britain turf can be thought of as a form of building stone, perhaps the north European equivalent of mud brick, which in the Near East can survive for millennia, in walls many metres high.

Fig. 5.11 The Antonine Wall is still a major feature in the landscape. This view, looking west, is of a central section between the forts at Croy and Bar Hills. The principal earth rampart and the berm or flat area which separated it from the ditch, is to the left. The more sharply defined but uneven bank to the right of the ditch is the upcast mound of material dug from it. The Antonine Wall ran between the Firths of Clyde and Forth and was in use between AD 142 and 158.

In common with its counterpart to the south, the Antonine Wall was a very substantial construction, covering about 60 kilometres of country. It was originally about 3 metres high and may well have been topped by a timber superstructure. Like Hadrian's Wall, it was additionally fortified by six major forts, each large enough to have garrisoned a regiment of soldiers, and about nineteen smaller forts. Even smaller fortlets were positioned at every Roman mile (the equivalents of the eighty mile castles along Hadrian's Wall).

At first glance the Antonine Wall appears to be an exact equivalent of Hadrian's Wall. But if one examines the details of its layout it soon becomes apparent that its constructors often took the most direct, rather than the best route from a military point of view. In situations where Hadrian's Wall would divert to follow, say, a spur of land, the Antonine Wall would cut across the spur, leaving an area of 'dead' or blind land that could not be covered by defenders on the wall. This suggests that military defence was not a primary concern of its constructors. It would appear, then, that the Antonine Wall was constructed as much to satisfy the needs of Roman power politics as to defend the northern boundary of *Britannia*.

This impression is reinforced by the behaviour of Antoninus when construction of his wall was completed in AD 142. After a small defeat of the local British by his general Lollius Urbicus he celebrated conquest of all the Britons and issued a special victory coin. He also took the title 'Conqueror', thereby turning the construction of the Wall to his political advantage. Even the most manipulative modern politician could teach Roman emperors nothing when it came to 'spin'. This was not a long-term success. The Antonine Wall was only manned for twenty years.

The two great defensive walls share something else in common. The Antonine Wall had also been built across a landscape that had already been cleared of trees in the Iron Age.[47] Aerial photographs show Iron Age and possibly Roman field systems around the Antonine Wall, perhaps similar to those around Hadrian's Wall.[48] This strongly suggests that it, too, had not been sited in a remote location, far from people and settlement. It would seem that both walls were placed where they were to be clearly visible. As statements of Roman power they needed to be seen, to be respected and to be feared.

Both walls were part of a deeply defended militarized landscape which recalls the boundary between East and West in central Europe during the Cold War. In each instance roads played a crucially important role and troops needed to be based in secure accommodation close to any potential areas of conflict. It was all about facilitating a rapid response to a new threat with the largest numbers of troops. Mobility was of key importance, as was the provision of suitable places for tactical retreat or withdrawal. Perhaps it would be better not to think of two 'lines in the sand', but of a huge militarized landscape that was given over to defence and to the proclamation of the message that the might of the Roman Empire would ultimately triumph. Of course such political messages require an audience to receive them – otherwise they are pointless. So even when the walls had been built, this landscape was not systematically depopulated.

It would be a mistake to imagine that the walls across the Scottish border country seriously inhibited trade and contact between people to the north and south. Recent research has revealed much evidence to the contrary, with numerous sites producing imported Roman and Romano-British finds up to the northern shores of the Firth of Forth and on the north-facing coast, east of the Moray Firth, around Nairn. The imposing Iron Age hillfort at Traprain Law in East Lothian, east of Edinburgh, was occupied into what was the Roman period further south and has also revealed a wealth of imported Roman objects.[49]

THE COUNTRYSIDE OF ROMAN BRITAIN

The Roman presence in Britain was relatively brief: around three and a half centuries. Furthermore, many parts of Britain were only lightly affected by Rome and some – Cornwall and most of northern Scotland – remained largely untouched, if not completely unaffected. A great deal is known about the organization of the upper levels of Romano-British society and of the Roman army and its supply chain. Surprisingly, however, there has been very little information about the rural landscapes of Roman Britain until very recently.

This persistent ignorance of the ordinary domestic, farmed landscapes of Roman Britain reflects the way that archaeologists have traditionally studied the period. In the past great emphasis was placed on all aspects of the Roman military presence. This was particularly true of Hadrian's Wall, where the names of the legions and cohorts that manned the various forts have been researched with almost obsessive zeal, whereas the farmed landscapes that provided the backdrop to all this activity were surveyed only very recently. Even today authoritative reviews of research into important regions, such as Roman Yorkshire, are forced to discuss specific sites, such as baths, roads, towns, forts and so forth, with little regard for the landscapes in which they sat.[50] At last this yawning gap in our understanding of Roman Britain has been addressed in a new review that looks at Roman sites, not as something new and imposed from abroad, but as phenomena whose roots and origins lie fairly and squarely within Britain.[51]

There has been a mass of new information produced through contract excavations. The scale of some of these projects can be truly massive. Take, for example, the excavation of a Romano-British farming settlement that showed up from the air as cropmarks along the edge of the Fens at Camp Ground, Earith, near St Ives in Cambridgeshire. The site was almost totally stripped and revealed a bewildering mass of field boundary ditches, yards, roadways, houses and outbuildings which were grouped together in a village-like settlement – and this was just one of many others ranged along the edge of the Fen in this area.

Large set-piece excavations ahead of major developments, such as a gravel quarry in the case of Camp Ground are one thing, but the vast majority of contract projects are much humbler and might involve, for example, the digging of a few trial trenches before the building of a bungalow or conservatory. But even these tiny projects produce information which today is fed into the computers of the local authority's Historic Environment Record. The result can be printed out and collated with other information to produce something approximating to an up-to-date record of Roman sites in a given area. The recent survey also carried out a number a smaller regional surveys which were intended to characterize the nature of Romano-British settlement in certain areas, and one of the largest of these, in Lincolnshire and Nottinghamshire, produced an extraordinarily dense scatter of sites which must suggest that almost the entire landscape was inhabited in Roman times.[52] It is perhaps worth bearing in mind here that the 1,639 sites mapped in the Lincolnshire/Nottinghamshire survey represent just a tiny proportion (maybe 5 per cent?) of the sites that would originally have existed in this area, in the Roman period.

There is a danger when discussing a major modern survey, of getting bogged down in detail. But certain trends were revealed which were potentially very important. The first is that they were able to identify several styles or types of field systems as being typical of certain areas. The two most important were the east Midland and chalkland types, together with a form of non-field open grazing and woodland landscape found in the south-west, the northern uplands and the Weald. The chalkland systems were based around blocks of square fields with

Fig. 5.12 The open-area excavation of a large rural Romano-British farming settlement at Camp Ground, Earith. The scale of this excavation is huge: note the three Portakabins in the bend of the quarry-haul road on the extreme left. The long dark marks show major field boundary and drainage ditches.

centralized settlements, a style of landscape often described as 'Celtic fields'. The east Midlands system was more varied, but often made use of larger rectangular fields, separated into larger parcels of land by roadways and tracks. The settlements that went with east Midland fields could either be centralized and village-like, or be smaller farmsteads dispersed through the fields.

The map (Fig. 5.13) showing the distribution of different field patterns in Roman Britain undoubtedly reflects that of the late Iron Age from which it developed and the general similarity between the Roman and the prehistoric landscapes suggests that the fundamentals that lay behind them, such as local climate and rainfall, topography, rivers and distribution networks, population centres, drainage and soil types, remained constant.

For the first time it now becomes possible to start work on a human geography of Roman Britain in which all aspects of Roman life: town, country, trade and industry, are integrated. A first step in this direction has been the identification of different rural settlement and field system forms. With the exception of the very open settlement patterns seen in upland Northumberland and Lancashire, they have a very modern look and dispel any idea that the Romano-British landscape was altogether different from that which we walk through today.

There were in effect two Roman Britains: one to the south and east, roughly from north Yorkshire to Somerset, and another to the north and west. The landscape of the south-eastern half shows clear evidence for a complex hierarchy of cities, towns, villages, hamlets and farms, all linked together by a network of roads and navigable rivers.[53] The settlement pattern here was dynamic and constantly evolving. As time passed, villas grew up in many rural regions, providing another element in the hierarchy at the same time that towns in many areas were starting to decline. With a few exceptions, like south-east Wales and the Cheshire Plain around Chester, a hierarchy of this sort never developed in the north and west, where settlement patterns remained constant, being based around enclosed farmsteads of smaller hamlets. Villas are virtually absent in these areas.

The contrast between the two parts of Roman Britain is vividly illustrated by the location of the main rural industries. These are entirely confined to the south-east where they are able to take advantage of better communications and markets, as the raw materials for each of the three principal industries, salt (seawater), iron-working (ore) and pottery and tiles (clay), occur naturally right across Britain.

I want now to turn to the ways in which we discover new sites. The simplest way is systematically to collect finds from the surface of the ground, a technique generally known as 'field-walking'. One can do rapid field-walking surveys if one wants to characterize the general nature of settlement in a previously unexplored area. On lighter sandy and chalky soils two or three good showers of rain will wash most finds clean and allow them to stand out from the earth. On the heavier soils that I am more used to, I generally allow a good two or three weeks of rainy weather, and ideally a few frosts before I set out. Usually this means for me that January and early February are the best months

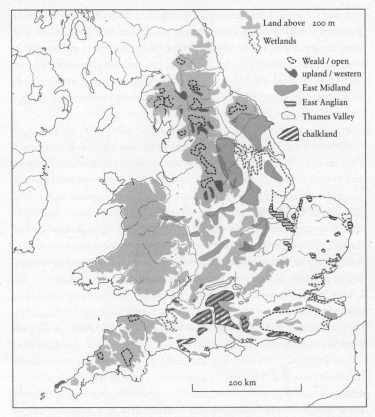

Land above 200 m
Wetlands
Weald / open upland / western
East Midland
East Anglian
Thames Valley
chalkland

200 km

Fig. 5.13 A map showing the different forms of Romano-British field systems across England.

for systematic field-walking. By March, the growing leaves of winter wheats and oilseed rape are beginning to obscure the ground.

The problem with field-walking is that it tends to favour robust finds that can stand up to ploughing, rain and frost. Most pottery, for example, includes ground-up material that that was added to the clay to make it fire better. In prehistoric times this so-called 'temper' sometimes consisted of crushed shells. These are soon dissolved away by the humic acids that naturally occur in many topsoils. This results in pottery full of small voids, which then fill up with water; in frosty weather the water freezes, the ice expands, and the pottery disintegrates. Romano-British potters rarely made use of crushed shell. They also fired their pots at higher temperatures which helped them survive in even the most acid soils. So a surface survey of a field system that had been used in both Iron Age and Roman times would probably only find Roman pottery, and fields that could have been in use since 500 BC would be labelled 'Roman'.

In the past fifteen years or so we have at last begun to acquire a better, more rounded picture of life in the Romano-British countryside. This new knowledge is largely the result of some excellent regional surveys: one of the best is on Roman period landscapes in Wessex.[54] The survey stressed the importance of the links between Iron Age and Romano-British landscapes and, rather more unexpectedly, it also made quite a strong case for continuity at the other end of the Roman period – a topic we shall return to in the next chapter. One result of the review was a map of Romano-British settlements in and around Wiltshire, where the density of settlement recalls the modern road map.

Over many parts of Britain, Romano-British settlement was far more extensive, and covered a greater topographical range, than in the medieval period.[55] This plainly reflects the fact that the Romano-British population, in southern Britain at least, was probably larger than that of medieval times. We do not understand all the reasons for this, which probably involve a number of factors such as the Black Death, climate, drainage, communication and access to markets, but it does clearly show that Romano-British society worked and that any idea of the 'native' population labouring under the yoke of a hated foreign colonial authority are wide of the mark. Many people in the higher echelons of southern Romano-British society not only wanted to adopt *Romanitas*, or Roman culture, but did so successfully and in ways that suited both the British landscape and local economies.

In some parts of Britain the arrival of the Romans signalled the beginning of the end for later Iron Age landscapes, but no instances are known of an Iron Age landscape that incoming Roman troops forced to be abandoned. In many places later Iron Age farms and fields continued to be used in the first and second centuries AD, but were abandoned shortly thereafter.[56]

It could be argued that the widespread deposition of alluvium observed in many river valleys of eastern Britain is an early indication of over-exploitation of the environment by Romano-British farmers.[57] Alluvium derives from soil erosion, and is often the result of planting winter wheat in the autumn. By the time the winter rains begin in earnest in November the young plants' roots are insufficiently developed to bind the soil together and the result is wholesale erosion. We know for a fact that the third and fourth centuries AD were periods of agricultural expansion in lowland Britain. Much of this intensification happened in the upper and middle reaches of the rivers that drained into the North Sea. The people who farmed the river floodplains in the lower-lying land closer to the coast had to pay the consequences of that success when their land was covered by huge spreads of alluvium.

The Romans introduced large-scale semi-industrial production to Britain. I can recall walking across fields in the *vici*, the informal suburbs outside the prosperous small town of *Durobrivae*, just west of Peterborough, and listening to the crunching sound of pottery breaking beneath my feet. It was impossible to take a step without breaking a few sherds, because they were everywhere. In fact, in places there was more pottery than soil, so intense and industrial had been the output of the Nene Valley pottery workshops – or perhaps factories would be a better term. The pots I was doing my bit to crush would have been the 'wasters', the misshapen and cracked vessels that had been rejected by quality control.

Such early mass-production may be one reason why we tend to think of Roman Britain as being rather boring and uniform. But the Empire did undoubtedly do much to unite the various peoples it had taken over. The Romans believed that their way of life and their political system were superior to all others. They also needed to run and administer an empire which covered most of the known world. This required efficient infrastructure, hence the roads, the same system of currency and a common language, Latin. So 2,000 years later we are left with an impression of uniformity, but out there in the real world of rural landscapes, this uniformity was, at best, skin-deep. And besides, only the upper classes would have been at all fluent in Latin. Ordinary folk would have continued to use local Celtic languages.

I have already mentioned that there were, in effect, two Roman

Britains: one to the north and west and another to the south and east, the latter being more thoroughly Romanized.

By the end of the Iron Age, most British societies in southern Britain had developed a regionalized but hierarchical social structure, capped by dominant élites. Unlike the later Normans, the incoming Roman administration did not decapitate the existing élites in favour of its own more compliant landowners. So the new system developed out of what had been there in the Iron Age. In archaeological terms we can see the development of the story in the way that late Iron Age farms and rural settlements continue in use, and there is little evidence for abandonment. The trouble is that one could demonstrate similar continuity after the Norman Conquest when many country estates were simply forced by the Crown to change owners; but this did not cause major disruption to the fabric of the properties themselves. What makes the later changes in the aristocratic administration of rural England so evident is the written records, especially Domesday Book and taxation returns. Such detailed documents do not exist for the early Roman period. So we must look for clues elsewhere.

The British villas are interesting because they were far from uniform in shape or plan, and this variation probably reflected different social traditions that ultimately had roots in the Iron Age. Both the villas, and the estates in which they sat, were part of a diverse system of landscape management. It is merely the use of the word 'villa', which presents a picture of homogeneity: of columned walkways, mosaic pavements and underfloor heating. Add a few figures wearing togas and reclining on couches (with perhaps a slave or two peeling grapes in the background) and you have villa life, as illustrated in dozens of guidebooks. I sometimes wonder to what extent such scenes are products of wishful thinking; personally, I would not wear a toga somewhere in rural Gloucestershire on a sharp February night with an easterly gale blowing about the eaves. The British have many skills, but they have never been accused of making central heating systems that actually work.

Certain landscapes, such as the Fens of East Anglia, presented special problems and opportunities for the new administration. The status of the Fenland in Roman times is still a matter of hot debate, where it has been suggested that central government (in Rome itself), was involved in the planning of the landscape.[58]

So what was happening in this undoubtedly well-to-do region? The first point to note is that the Fens include some of the best-preserved buried Roman landscapes anywhere in Europe.[59] I am also put in mind of another area where there are large areas of Romano-British fields arranged on a strictly grid-like pattern and where the landscape is also flat and low-lying. The Dengie peninsula lies in the south-east coast of Essex, between the rivers Blackwater and Crouch. The field systems there can be seen to extend a bit further south on the north shore of the Thames estuary near Thurrock, also in Essex.[60] It has been suggested that these large areas of well-surveyed rectilinear fields are evidence for a Roman imperial estate, but again the arguments to support this idea are difficult either to prove or to disprove.[61] I think we should beware of leaping to imperial conclusions. Just because landscapes are carefully arranged it does not mean that central governments are necessarily involved. A group of farmers and landowners with a common interest to manage and partition a particular tract of fertile land fairly, so that nobody is disadvantaged, are just as capable of making such decisions themselves – as we saw well over 1,000 years earlier with those beautifully laid out stone-walled fields, the reaves of Bronze Age Dartmoor.

INDUSTRIAL LANDSCAPES

The establishment of an empire usually brings with it improved trade, communications and the opening up of new markets. But it is not simply a matter of trade and commerce. Other strategic objectives, political and military, need also to be taken into account. We have seen how the imposition of Roman rule stimulated the development of both rural and urban landscapes. Changes to towns happened faster, mainly due to military and governmental pressures, because the governance of *Britannia* required them. Similar forces seem to have been at play in the rapid expansion of the lead-mining industry in the Mendip Hills of Somerset.

There is evidence for early Roman gold mining in Carmarthenshire. Copper was mined in north Wales, and iron in the Forest of Dean and the Weald, where the work was undertaken by the *classis Britannica*,

Fig. 5.14 The hills and hollows are the surface remains of Roman and medieval lead mines around Charterhouse in Mendip, Somerset. There is some evidence for pre-Roman use of lead from the Mendip Hills, but mining at Charterhouse began in earnest under military control very shortly after the Roman conquest (by at least AD 49), and continued throughout the Roman period.

the British fleet of the Roman navy. Lead was also mined in the Peak District, Flintshire and Shropshire. In all these instances the work was first undertaken by the military and only later did it come under civilian control.[62] One might suppose that the exploitation of such important natural resources would have brought great wealth to the population of the regions concerned, but this was not always the case. In the lead-mining areas of north-east Wales, for example, the population remained remarkably poor.

It would seem that the shift from military to civilian control was also what happened to the lead mined in the Mendips, where the lead-bearing ore, galena, also included significant amounts of silver. In this instance the mining was organized on a truly industrial scale: so far twenty-nine complete or fragmentary ingots have survived from the Mendip mines. All are inscribed with the emperor's name and sometimes with the abbreviated words EX ARG, meaning that the silver had been extracted from them.[63] Gold and silver were needed for their bullion value, ultimately as part of the funding of the Roman army. So imperial control of these resources had to be established from the very outset.

Charterhouse on Mendip is a most remarkable landscape, not just for the hummocks of the old mined areas, but for the survival of a major Roman settlement which has not been damaged by agriculture. The reason for this is quite simply that the ground is so polluted with lead that disturbing the topsoil is most inadvisable. Recent excavations have shown that the Roman authorities had gained control of the Mendip ore deposits by AD 49, just six years after the conquest.[64] They maintained direct control until the late second century AD and would have known about the area's potential, most probably from before the conquest, not just because lead had been mined there since at least the late Bronze Age, when it was added in small quantities to bronze to improve its casting qualities. Incidentally, a few lead objects are known from Bronze Age Britain (mostly small, pillow-like anvils used by metal-workers as a softer base-plate when doing fine, chased decoration),

Fig. 5.15 A lead ingot from the Mendip mines. This ingot carries the inscription IMP VESPASIAN AVG which translates as 'Emperor Vespasian Augustus'. It can be dated to the years AD 70–79.

but lead does not appear to have been mined in any quantity in prehistoric times.[65] We do know, however, that south-western Britain had acquired a wide reputation for high-quality tin that extended back to the fourth century BC, the time of Pytheas and his circumnavigation (pp. 120–22). It seems probable, too that the area had also become known for its silver-rich sources of lead – and the silver would have initially have been of far greater importance for its bullion value. Lead mining in Mendip continued into medieval times, and these later workings have left a far greater mark on the landscape than their smaller-scale Roman antecedents.

RITUAL LANDSCAPES

The most heavily Romanized elements within British society were the élite classes, and, to some extent too, the inhabitants of towns. Most ordinary rural people – in other words, the vast majority of society – would have continued to speak regional dialects and lead an essentially Iron Age way of life that made use of Roman and Romano-British objects when required. Thus cooking pots soon changed to the tougher, more durable mass-produced Romano-British products – such as the Nene Valley Wares. Newer household fashions would have included tableware (beakers, plates, etc.) for some of the better-off farmers and for most city dwellers. In parts of Britain, such as the West Country around the prosperous town of Cirencester, pottery had never been in plentiful supply in the later Iron Age, probably because people did not want to use it. It was then taken up in the Roman period and was used until the late fourth and fifth centuries AD, when it rapidly fell from favour. This would suggest that if these new habits did indeed represent a form of Romanization, it was probably only skin-deep.

The ancient tradition of ritual landscapes did not die out entirely in the middle of the second millennium BC when barrow-building and henges were abandoned. During the later Bronze and Iron ages the landscapes were not as large, nor as diverse, but they persisted. The ceremonial causeways at Flag Fen and Fiskerton, for example, both continued into Roman times, but in other regions too earlier traditions enjoyed something of a renaissance, albeit in a fashion that would befit an élite who saw themselves as thoroughly Romanized. As at Maiden Castle and South Cadbury, the siting of new Roman temples sometimes coincided with Iron Age hillforts. Again, this suggests a degree of continuity, if not of actual rites, then of regard for certain parts of the landscape. Sometimes, as at Maiden Castle, there was a long gap between the last Iron Age use and the construction of the Romano-British shrine. At South Cadbury the shrine appeared early in the Roman period.[66] One of the more remarkable complexes of Romano-British shrines was built on West Hill at Uley in Gloucestershire. Here there is good evidence that the particular site remained important from the Iron Age and throughout the Roman period, but substantial buildings did not appear until the fourth century.[67]

One of the most remarkable of these Iron Age to Roman religious sites was first excavated just before the Second World War. This dig exposed a well-preserved Romano-British temple near the village of Frilford, just west of Abingdon, in Oxfordshire.[68] Subsequent aerial and geophysical survey showed that the temple, within its sacred enclosure defined by an outer Temenos Wall (the equivalent of a churchyard wall) was just part of a much larger ritual landscape. Excavation has dated the temple to the late first to fourth century AD and further work has demonstrated that the roots of the temple lay firmly in the middle of the Iron Age (third century BC).[69]

There were at least two Romano-British cemetery areas within the Frilford complex, but it was only the later one which continued in use into Saxon times. There is nothing about the arrangement of graves within this cemetery to suggest that the people buried with Saxon grave-goods were invaders from outside. Besides, the fact that the late-Roman-period cemetery was the only one of the two used for post-Roman burials supports the idea that these were one and the same people.

THE END OF ROMAN BRITAIN

During the Roman era historical records are generally good, even if sometimes, like Tacitus, they have to be taken with a large pinch of salt, but towards the latter part of the fourth century the system, as regards

Britain, begins to break down and written accounts become less reliable. Historically minded archaeologists, used to working in the earlier part of the period, 'compensate' for the less reliable information by making use of historical reconstruction. The problem with this approach is that it tends to erect circular arguments that are difficult to challenge. And the post-Roman Dark Ages, as we shall see, are a period when circular arguments and white elephants alike once roamed unchallenged. That process of myth-making has its roots in the final years of the Roman presence in Britain. The myth in question is that of the sonorous, even portentous-sounding, 'Saxon Shore forts'.

The end of Roman Britain is conventionally believed to have been the result of attacks by Anglo-Saxon raiders in the late fourth century. These probably began in the third century, but developed in intensity, following the reduction of the Roman presence in Britain in the late fourth. The most frequently cited evidence for these attacks is the existence of a supposed network of Saxon Shore forts which have still left a substantial impact on the landscape. It is arguable, however, whether these forts ever formed part of a network of defences against Saxon raiders. Instead, it would seem that the main threat to the province came, as before, from tribes living in Scotland and Ireland. We shall see in the next chapter that life in Britain did not come to a grinding halt, even in the supposedly hotly contested Scottish border territories, when Roman protection was finally and officially withdrawn in AD 410.

The term first appears in an inventory of military resources and garrisons dating to *c.* AD 395 and known as the *Notitia Dignitatum* (or 'List of High Offices'). This was never intended to be an accurate historical account and it was subject to a number of alterations and additions before it reached its final version. Various military installations on both sides of the Channel were listed as being under the command of the *comes litoris Saxonici* or 'Count of the Saxon Shore'. The *Notitia* was a list made for army administrators and was never a strategic military document covering topics like rules of engagement, communication, strategy, tactics or contingency planning. In short it does not give us grounds to suppose that British 'Saxon Shore' forts on the south coast had counterparts in Gaul, which together formed part of a cross-Channel system of defence.[70] Unfortunately, historians,

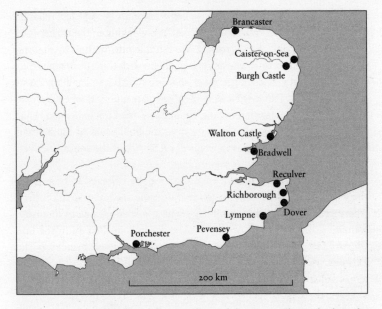

Fig. 5.16 A map of the eleven Roman forts of the 'Saxon Shore', built in the third century AD. These were most probably fortified trading or distribution stations, rather than defences or garrisons against attacking Saxon pirates, as is often assumed.

particularly between the sixteenth and nineteenth centuries, leapt at the idea.[71]

The 'Saxon Shore' forts can be very imposing. They line the south-eastern coast from Brancaster, near the Wash, to Portchester Castle, close by the Isle of Wight. Portchester is one of the most spectacular and well-preserved Roman buildings in north-western Europe. As at Pevensey, just to the east, the Roman walls of Portchester were built into a medieval castle whose tower-like keep provides a superb view of the Roman defences. The forts often feature rounded projecting towers, characteristic of later Roman military architecture and which allow archers a clear field of view of any forces attacking the main walls. They also look very imposing, when seen from the land, which gives us a clue as to how they may have been used.

Current evidence suggests that the eleven forts were constructed in

Fig. 5.17 The east wall of Portchester Castle, Hampshire. Although repaired and partially renovated in the Middle Ages, these are perhaps the finest Roman-period walls in Britain. They were probably built in the late third century AD, in the reign of Carausius, who ruled Britain and Gaul from 287 to 293. Portchester has been described as a 'Saxon Shore' fort, but there is now considerable doubt whether these forts were ever constructed to repel Saxon raiders. As this view shows, their best defences often faced inland.

two distinct episodes, with Caister-on-Sea, Reculver and Brancaster being built in the first decades of the third century. At about this time the fort of the *classis Britannica* at Dover went out of use, which means that the forts could never have been part of a defensive system that combined land and naval forces. The remaining forts were constructed between about AD 260 and 300. These dates are very much earlier than the onset of raids from overseas, which mainly happened (if indeed they did) later in the fourth century. The principal threat to Britain's integrity at this time was actually posed by other attackers from north of the Scottish border.

There are many other problems with the idea of 'Saxon Shore' forts. Portchester was the most thoroughly excavated example and its interior provided very little evidence for military activity at all.[72] Certainly soldiers, and their women and children too, were there, but this was by no means a garrison with the usual barrack blocks and granaries which occur right across the Empire. The arrangement of buildings within the interior at Portchester is best described as 'informal'. Taken together, the evidence seems to suggest that most of these forts, which were often located close to rivers, were actually used to provide secure storage for some of the surpluses (perhaps as taxes paid 'in kind') that were produced during the prosperous decades of Roman Britain's 'Golden Age', the first half of the fourth century AD.[73]

The accepted view of fourth-century Britain trembling at the prospect of imminent attack from across the sea flies in the face of the archaeological evidence, which suggests that in the south-east, if not elsewhere, there was a confident and prosperous élite, living in considerable comfort in villas outside the towns, or what little was left of them. These people had established something of a culture of their own. Later in the fourth century Britain provided considerable numbers of soldiers to serve in the imperial field armies on the Continent, but not so many as to leave the province defenceless. The archaeological evidence suggests that early in the fifth century southern Britain successfully made the transition from a money-based economy to one arranged around barter. We know that the Church had established quite a firm foothold, too, and like many archaeologists I find it hard to accept that after AD 410 Britain entered a period of social meltdown and disintegration. One reason why I find this so hard to accept is that the pragmatism of the Roman Empire had been a long-lasting influence on those Britons who did decide to adopt, to a greater or lesser extent, the idea of *Romanitas*, or Romanization.

I suspect that the Romano-British of the late fourth century were a pragmatic bunch. Their families had successfully adapted to the new circumstances at the end of the Iron Age and they were about to seek a new continental identity, which today we refer to as Anglo-Saxon. We should not forget, however, that the years around AD 410 were not completely bleak and desolate. Their time within the Roman Empire had taught the British how to cope with change and this was to stand them in good stead for the next few centuries. They also possessed a fine road system and a resilient Church, which in northern Britain would play an important part in keeping the light of literacy burning through what used to be called the Dark Ages.

The Roman interlude had also conferred another benefit on Britain, which I mentioned at the start of this chapter. It had to do not just with literacy but with the ability to manage social, and with it landscape change, far more rapidly than ever before. This new ability was the consequence of more than three centuries of social reform. The old Iron Age élite was certainly still there, but during the Roman period wealth and education had filtered down through society; towns, always engines of social change, had also had a democratizing effect. I am quite convinced that the end-result of the Roman interlude was a society, certainly in south-eastern Britain, if not everywhere else, where communities were far more adaptable and able to accommodate to the new circumstances that confronted them than had been the case at the end of the Iron Age. Too often one reads that the Dark Ages marked a return to prehistory. But human societies are composed of intelligent people who think for themselves, especially when educational standards have been improved – even very slightly. The Roman interlude had produced profound changes in Britain and the clock was not about to turn back.

6

New Light on 'Dark Age' and
Saxon Landscapes (AD 410–800)

After the withdrawal of the final Roman troops, the old history books told us, Britain slipped into the Dark Ages and the British landscape reverted to a dismal, thickly wooded wasteland. Early post-Roman history used to read like a dirge, a woeful tale of regrets. The emphasis was on what had been lost: the arts of building in stone, long-distance trade, Christianity, coinage and so forth. These were the things that made Roman Britons civilized. Sadly, although this apocalyptic view of post-Roman Britain is very outdated, it still persists.

One reason for the longevity of this vision of post-Roman Britain lies in the vivid writing of two major literary figures. The first was a British cleric, Gildas, who wrote in the mid-sixth century *On the Ruin of Britain*, the only contemporary account, in Latin, of the Anglo-Saxon settlement of what was later to become England. The title alone gives a flavour of the work's somewhat apocalyptic tone. Very much later (*c.* 731) the Venerable Bede drew heavily on Gildas when writing his *Ecclesiastical History of the English People*. Neither man was attempting to write objective history. Both had their own agendas and it suited them to portray the British as disorganized, powerless and undisciplined.

But the landscape tells a rather different story. Certainly there were changes in town and country at the end of the Roman period, but there is little evidence for the wholesale abandonment of landscapes. It is also questionable whether the Anglo-Saxon invasion was ever a complete change of population, or a true mass-migration.[1] Historical geneticists are debating the issue of ethnic change in the fifth and sixth centuries in eastern Britain, and a consensus of opinion seems currently to favour the replacement of indigenous British genes with new Anglo-Saxon bloodlines by means of some form of social apartheid in which the finding of a mate was somehow made harder for British males. But for this theory to be convincing we need independent supporting data from Dark Age and Saxon cemetery studies. So for the time being it is probably safest to regard the size, extent and speed of the Anglo-Saxon invasions as unknown. Incidentally, the speed of any migration is very important. The impact on the landscape and on society in general of, say, 5,000 boatloads of people in ten years is going to be different from 10,000 across three hundred years.

The demise of the Western Roman Empire towards the end of the fifth century (it continued, of course, in the East as Byzantium) gave way to a modified form of Roman governance which was more locally based. We may imagine the fifth-century community at Wroxeter, for example, living in this type of cultural landscape. By late Roman times the 'barbarian' world beyond the Empire was already exerting a powerful influence on many aspects of Roman life, including the army, where up to a third of the officers and men were of non-Roman origin. The result was new forms of society which were more devolved, locally based and reliant on the Church for many aspects of government. It was a form of society whose roots lay in the Roman Empire of the fourth century, but it continued and developed after the murder of the last Western emperor, Julius Nepos, in Dalmatia, in AD 480.

THE AFTERMATH OF ROME AND THE 'DARK AGES'

The picture that emerges of Britain is by no means as bleak as the traditional view would have us believe. Take population. We saw in the previous chapter that the population of Roman Britain has been estimated at around 3.7 million. We now know that there was, if anything, an increase throughout the fourth century, and a leading authority has even suggested that it may eventually have been as high as 4–6 million.[2] By contrast, the best guess in Hoskins's day was somewhere around a million.[3] This means that the population of late Roman Britain was large enough to have significantly influenced the course of history. The traditional view is that the British people in the south-east were driven westwards by invading hordes of Anglo-Saxons.

Now it may just be possible to imagine, say, 250,000–500,000 people being driven west, but much larger numbers of refugees would inevitably have caused vast disruption to the landscapes where they eventually ended up. Such turmoil ought to have left at least some archaeological trace; the Viking invasions certainly did, and they were on a much smaller scale.

The end of the Roman Empire in Britain and its aftermath was the period when the kingdoms that would ultimately form the nucleus of the larger nation of England became established and began to acquire their identities.[4] In very broad terms, it was a process that took the whole of the fifth and sixth centuries. By the close of the sixth century it was possible to sketch a map of the earliest Saxon kingdoms, and name some of their rulers. Less than a generation later, in 625, King Raedwald of Essex was buried with great splendour in a ship within an earthen barrow at a Saxon cemetery at Sutton Hoo, in Suffolk.

While there were changes to the rural economy, there is little evidence for wholesale abandonment in lowland Britain, the heartland of the Anglo-Saxons.[5] Instead, we see a shift away from cereals towards animal husbandry and grazing, and a tendency to develop a variety of regional patterns of farming that were better adapted to local conditions. These adaptations are not so much about wholesale population change, as the pragmatic responses of local communities to the changing economic conditions that followed the end of Roman administration.

In quite a few instances we actually see an expansion of land clearance between AD 400 and 800. Rather surprisingly, these are in Wales and the west, as well as the central lowlands and south-western isles of Scotland. Long-distance trade and the production of a marketable surplus were inducements that could not be offered to Saxon farmers. Areas that have produced pollen evidence for the re-establishment of woodland are in the uplands and in the regions around both of the great northern military walls. If ever a landscape has been buoyed up by artificial demand, ultimately fuelled by taxes, this is surely such a landscape.

Roman Britain enjoyed great prosperity in the fourth century, the period when villa estates reached their peak, and a leading authority has suggested that the departure of the Romans was simply an admission that they were grossly overstretched. It was also what the southern

Romano-British élite wanted – not so much to revert to a pre-Roman way of life, but to manage their own affairs as successful Romanized communities.[6] The fourth century had been a good time for them, but the years of increasing prosperity had also fostered social divisions. The result was an élite that had grown richer and more distant from the rest of the population.[7] By the second half of the fourth century they had much to lose if there was a breakdown of law and order, and they must have been aware that they had successfully established a Romano-British identity within the broader culture of the Roman Empire. The late Roman Empire was a far more diverse place than the Empire of Julius Caesar, some five centuries earlier.

There were certain practical advantages to being outside the official Empire, too. The main one was the huge burden of taxes that had been steadily growing during the fourth century. At one stroke these ended, as did the obligation to grow large acreages of cereals for the Roman army. The use of coinage quite rapidly ceased. This was not a result of financial collapse, but reflected the fact that no Roman troops were now being paid in coins. The nature of the British economy reverted to what it had been before AD 43, that is, locally organized and based around barter and forms of socially embedded exchange. Archaeology confirms that this system, which had been in operation anyhow during Roman times, functioned perfectly well. This suggests that there were no economic or wider political reasons for the fears of Asterix's chief Vitalstatistix to be realized and the skies to fall in over post-Roman Britain.

LANDSCAPES OF THE NORTH: PICTS, SCOTS AND GAELS

The post-Roman centuries were in no way a return to prehistory even in those parts of Britain that had never been conquered by Rome. The fifth century was a very different time, and the landscape a different place, from what had existed in the final years of the Iron Age. The extent of the changes that happened in the later Iron Age of northern Scotland can be seen in the Western Isles, where the first fortified brochs had been constructed from about 200 BC. These round tower buildings continued to be occupied for several centuries after the end of Roman occupation south of Hadrian's Wall.

Landscapes cannot be separated from the people who made and used them. Scotland, as we now know it, has always been an important part of the network of seafaring people around the shores of the north-west Atlantic and North Sea.[8] There would have been regular links between people living in mainland Scotland, the Northern and Western Isles, Ireland, north-west England and the Isle of Man. Further afield, across the North Sea the introduction of reliable seagoing vessels, probably from the onset of the Iron Age, meant that Scandinavia would become another component of the network. The Scandinavian contribution to the historical mix was to come a little later in the shape of the Vikings.

The Picts are possibly the best known of Scotland's early historical peoples. They are first named by the Roman writer Eumenius in AD 297 as *picti*, a Latin word that literally means 'painted people'. Eumenius described the *picti* as the enemies of the Britons, but, rather like the ancient Britons themselves, most of the accounts of the Picts are written by people who had political reasons to dislike them.

Although the Picts were not a nation as such, they may well have formed a confederation of tribes, whose roots lay firmly in the later Iron Age, until the late seventh century AD, when they were unified under a king. Archaeologically they can be identified with elaborately decorated Symbol Stones of the fifth to seventh centuries. Most are found north of the Forth/Clyde isthmus, along the eastern seaboard and in the Grampians and Highlands, away from the western seaboard, which was the province of the Dalriada (or Dál Riata), Gaels who had their tribal connections with north Antrim.[9]

In general terms, Symbol Stones mainly occur along the east coast and inland from it. Then by the late ninth century Viking settlers from Norway established themselves on the Northern and Western Isles and inland along the western seaboard as far south as Strathclyde and Galloway. Ultimately, this Viking threat united the Picts and the Dalriada Gaels and gave rise to the kingdom of Alba (a name derived from the Irish name for Britain, Albion) in the 840s. By the eleventh century Alba was more commonly known in English by the name Scotia or Scotland, but Alba remains the Gaelic name.

Pictish times saw the first developments of hierarchy in the organization of the Scottish landscape. The sites in question were positioned to dominate the landscape and were developed to extend and tighten the hold of an increasingly powerful lordly élite. Most early historic forts had origins in the sixth century and had reached their maximum expansion by the seventh or eighth. Some of the better known early historic period forts include Dundurn (Perth and Kinross) and Dunadd

Fig. 6.1 The early historic fort at Dundurn, Perth and Kinross. The first fort was placed on the top of this steep hill in the fifth or sixth century AD. Apart from its commanding position, one reason why this particular hill may have been chosen was the presence of natural terraces on its higher slopes. The upper terrace was enclosed during the late sixth/early seventh century by a strong timber wall cut into the bedrock. After its destruction by fire during a siege in 683 it was rebuilt and enlarged using masonry robbed from a nearby Roman site.

(Argyll and Bute), the leading Dalriada power centre. This extraordinary site has produced the greatest quantity of imported Mediterranean and North African pottery of any Dark Age or early Christian site in Britain.[10] Both Dunadd and Dundurn started life as citadels on the tops of hills with natural terraces; as the forts developed they took over and included the terraces. Other major early historic forts are to be found at Urquhart, by the shores of Loch Ness, and Dunollie (Argyll and Bute), by the Firth of Lorn on the western seaboard.

Forts and fortifications tend to be placed in prominent or inaccessible positions within the landscape and this often means that they will have escaped damage by farming, ancient or modern, which poses by far the biggest threat to the survival of any abandoned building or earthwork. The same can also be said of many religious sites, which often occupy similar positions within the landscape on the summits of hills or in commanding positions (such as Lincoln or Durham cathedrals). Monastic sites were located in remote places away from the temptations of daily life. This applied most particularly to the Celtic or Gaelic Church of the early historic period, which placed emphasis on meditation and self-discipline.[11] The monks lived in separate cells or huts and did not share the communal ideals of the orders that grew from the Roman Church, such as the Benedictines, who were introduced to Britain by St Augustine in 597. In contrast, the great missionaries of the Gaelic Church were famous for travelling long distances, such as St Patrick, in the fifth century, and St Aidan, who travelled from the west coast of Scotland to found the new monastery at Lindisfarne, off the Northumberland coast in 635. These missionaries helped to loosen the close links that united many Celtic monasteries with specific landscapes.

Gaelic Christianity was introduced to Scotland by St Columba, an influential man from a noble Irish family, who arrived on the tiny island of Iona, off the western tip of Mull in the year 563. Here he founded a monastery, which he used as the base for a major missionary campaign. The Gaelic Church originated in Ireland where Christianity had been introduced by St Patrick from Britain sometime in the 460s. Columba's monastery on Iona proved to be highly successful, both locally, as Iona was a fertile island, and further afield – initially this was doubtless due to Columba's personal background and leadership. The monastery on

Fig. 6.2 A view of the small island of Iona on the western tip of Mull. This was where St Columba came from Ireland in 563 to found a monastery and bring Christianity to western Scotland. Columba's church has gone and the present church is the later, medieval abbey. Note the bank and ditch in front of the church. This was the outer boundary of the original monastic site and probably makes use of an earlier, Iron Age fortification.

Iona soon became a major centre of scholarship, renowned throughout Europe and produced great works of art, such as the beautifully illuminated *Book of Kells*. During the next three centuries the Gaelic Church grew in importance in Scotland and by the mid-ninth century it had gained supremacy over the Pictish Church, whose origins ultimately lay in the immediately post-Roman period; it only fell under the strong influence of the Gaelic Church from the late seventh century. The extent of the Gaelic Church's influence in northern Britain was remarkable, ranging from the Orkneys to Lindisfarne. Many of these foundations thrived, which is probably why Lindisfarne was among the very first places in Britain to be attacked by Viking raiders in 793.

Because the focus of monasteries of the Gaelic tradition was on the individual, assembly buildings were rare, apart from the monastic church itself. The church would be surrounded by graves and significant areas in the cemetery would be marked by elaborately carved crosses, many of which show clear Pictish influences. Although the Columban Church was the most important, other Irish missionaries founded branches of the Gaelic Church in Scotland, including St Mo Luóc, and the great sailor, St Brendan.

The economy of early historic Scotland was very largely based on farming, and we know from the sensitive way that animals are treated in their art that the Picts knew and understood animals. Cattle were the mainstay of a mixed farming economy and played an important role in many social transactions, especially between lords and their clients, in much the same way that pigs and sheep were exchanged in the Anglo-Saxon world. It is probable that most cattle were kept for their milk, although of course beef would also have been prized. Sheep were the next most frequently kept animal, doubtless for their wool as much as their meat or milk. Barley and oats were the main crops, but wheat and rye were also sometimes grown and the fields were fertilized with manure, household refuse and seaweed, just as in pre-historic times.

The evidence for fields and trackways in the rural landscape of mainland Scotland is still relatively slight, but recent excavation and survey is beginning to produce exciting results. The range and diversity of known artefacts, coupled with the depictions on carved stonework, argue that the Pictish rural landscape was a developed one, with arable fields, droveways for livestock, roads, paddocks and open grazing, interspersed with the managed woodland needed to produce the wattle-work required for house and farm. The best sites have been revealed beneath peat: at Lairg in Sutherland ridge-and-furrow, field banks and clearance cairns were found beneath a layer of peat dated to the first millennium AD. Two similar sites have been found on Arran and another, this time below sand, at Freswick Links in the Highlands. Other sites have produced possible evidence that the infield-outfield system (which became so popular in Scotland in the Middle Ages) may have started to develop already.[12]

Northern Britain was not entirely populated by Picts and Gaels, however. Many of the people occupying the Scottish Borders identified themselves with what is best described as Anglo-Saxon culture. The Venerable Bede is probably the best known of these figures. In the north of England the communities of the sixth and seventh centuries are usually described as Anglian, rather than Saxon. One of the best preserved landscapes of this period is that at Yeavering in the Cheviot Hills of Northumberland. We saw in Chapter 4 that the hillfort on top of the distinctive double-crowned hill of Yeavering Bell probably had origins in the Bronze Age, but a most remarkable settlement was found by aerial photography in 1949 lying on flatter land in the valley of the River Glen, far below the great summit of the Bell, which towers above it.

It would appear that the hillfort on top of Yeavering Bell was unoccupied during the early post-Roman centuries and we can only assume that this was in fact deliberate – a sign perhaps of the hill's importance as a historical monument to the people who established the extraordinary royal settlement below it.[13] All the buildings were of timber, including several large halls and a most remarkable tiered, theatre-like 'grandstand'. Sadly, nothing remains in the landscape of the royal settlement, other than an oddly shaped field and a monument on the edge of the modern road.[14]

LANDSCAPES OF SOUTHERN BRITAIN IN THE SAXON PERIOD

Although the fertile lowlands of central and southern Britain were never abandoned in the post-Roman decades, the farming economy did nonetheless alter. One reason why direct evidence from the land-scape itself is hard to pin down is that a significant change to the agricultural regime was a switch away from arable to pasture. This was the result of a combination of factors. The army no longer needed to be supplied and the urban population, such as it was, was also in decline. The foods of pasture farming (milk, cheese and meats) are best consumed locally.

A move away from a pattern of farming that regularly involved ploughing and manuring has important archaeological implications. We saw this in the Celtic fields of Salisbury Plain, which were overlain by huge linear ditches at the end of the Bronze Age. These earthworks marked a change in farming from arable to livestock, yet when we examined the superbly preserved Romano-British villages we saw that the earlier Celtic fields were still in use, albeit modified in places. Fields provide a framework for using the landscape. They should not be thought of as archaeological artefacts that come and go. It takes a huge amount of communal effort to grub up hedges or fill in ditches. That is why, when field systems are eventually altered, the social, historical and economic implications can be huge.

The best and clearest examples of field systems that have survived from later prehistoric, Roman and Saxon times are to be found in the landscapes of drystone-walled fields of Devon and Cornwall, many of which are still in use today.[15] Although fields and field systems undoubtedly survived from Roman into post-Roman times, one of the

Fig. 6.3 The wall footing of houses at Tintagel, Cornwall. These houses date to the Dark Ages and their wall footings have been restored after excavation in the 1930s. Three groups of Dark Age houses were revealed on the east side of Tintagel in the 1930s and subsequent survey suggests that they probably all belonged to a single substantial village on the slopes above the harbour. Tintagel was a high-status site with numerous finds of pottery that had been imported from the Mediterranean in the Dark Ages.

Fig. 6.4 The promontory at Tintagel, Cornwall, with the small natural sandy harbour known as the Haven in the foreground, left. This side of the headland is protected from the prevailing winds. The walls visible to the upper left are an extension of Tintagel Castle, which was built on the mainland next to the promontory by Earl Richard of Cornwall in the thirteenth century.

most remarkable aspects of the post-Roman centuries in the west and south-west is the evidence for trade with the Mediterranean.[16]

The best-known site is undoubtedly that at Tintagel, with its legendary Arthurian connections. Excavations at Tintagel have revealed clear evidence for long-distance trade and the foundations of buildings belonging to a substantial settlement.[17] Archaeological excavation has produced many more sherds of imported Mediterranean pottery.[18] The distribution maps show a clear preference for coastal sites, which one might expect, as many of the objects traded, such as amphorae, were large and relatively delicate.

The sites where imported wares were landed were probably, like Tintagel, controlled by a powerful leader. The items themselves suggest display and feasting: wine and olive oil from the eastern Mediterranean and showy dinner wares, such as North African Slipware. In landscape terms we are witnessing the survival of ancient British élites, and there are strong echoes of Iron Age practices in such conspicuous

Fig. 6.5 A map showing the location of possible ports in western Britain where there is evidence for imported Mediterranean pottery in the fifth to seventh centuries. Many of these ports have good communications inland, often via rivers. It is generally supposed that traders from the Mediterranean would make short voyages between the ports, collecting tin, salt, copper, wool and other materials in exchange for wine, oil and fine tablewares.

consumption. Some very high-status Iron Age tombs in south-eastern England, for example, contained amphorae from the eastern Mediterranean. Tintagel itself is on a promontory and the Cornish coast contains numerous examples of Iron Age promontory forts.

The switch from arable to livestock farming with the departure of the Romans in the early fifth century causes archaeological problems. When a farmer decides, for whatever reason, to give up ploughing and let his fields revert to grass, it then becomes very difficult to establish precisely when he made the change. Without a plough to fold objects lying on the surface into the soil, it becomes notoriously hard to pin down, not just the date when a field of pasture was first laid out, but also the period of time it remained in use. Other approaches, like pollen analysis, are usually too general: they can only tell us that such-and-such a region ceased to be ploughed in, say, late Roman times.

One way through these problems is to look at detailed maps and then remove all landscape features that can be dated with any certainty. The approach has been given the rather ponderous academic name 'map regression'. A recent case study of post-Roman landscapes in Essex shows how this kind of map regression can provide fascinating insights.[19] The 'after' map showed three quite distinct patterns of landscape (see Fig. 6.6). The central area, which more or less coincides with the spread of modern Southend, consisted of irregular landscapes that resulted from the piecemeal clearance of small areas of woodland in post-Roman times – a process known as 'assarting'. Assart clearances were usually haphazard and involved the removal of trees, often in squarish 'bites' into the outside of a large wood. As the process of assarting continued it gave rise to a higgledy-piggledy patchwork of small fields.

The eastern area consisted of landscapes where the north–south boundaries of the fields seem to radiate from Shoebury. Excavation at North Shoebury has shown that these fields overlie a late Roman field system that survived into Saxon times. To the west there was a contrasting area of broadly rectangular landscapes, which have been dated to Roman times by excavations (at Wickford).

It is now becoming clear that in certain regions, such as parts of East Anglia and Essex, the layout of the Romano-British landscape continued to exert an influence on subsequent developments.[20] There does not seem to be much evidence, either, for a prolonged period of abandonment. But other landscapes were deliberately allowed to revert to woodland. Such an area is the central part of the region (now under Southend) just discussed. Here numerous Romano-British settlements were replaced by trees that were then cleared, bit by bit, in early medieval times. To the east and west, field systems either continued in use, or were replaced by new fields. It would seem that the farms and settlements around this new area of woodland required trees for their daily use, as either building material or firewood. The point is that the regrowth of woodland should not necessarily be seen as an infallible indication that an area had been abandoned.

We saw in the previous chapter that even the most Romanized parts

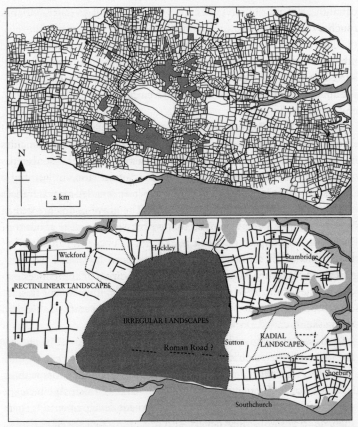

Fig. 6.6 Analysis of old maps can reveal hidden patterns. This example from south-east Essex shows the layout of fields and roads in the area now largely occupied by Southend (*above*). This information was gathered from maps made before the modern expansion of the town. In the next stage (*below*) all the fields of known date were deleted to reveal a surprisingly complex pattern of post-Roman landscape development comprising three zones. The central area (*shaded*) consisted of irregular landscapes which resulted from piecemeal woodland clearance. East of the central area the fields tend to radiate back from the shore and the tidal creeks, whereas to the west the landscape was laid out in more regular, rectangular blocks.

of south-eastern Britain retained a degree of regional diversity, both of economy and social structure. If anything this diversity increased during the fourth century.[21] In other parts of south-eastern Britain rural prosperity had begun to decline well before the final departure of Roman troops in the early fifth century. This decline is evident in, for example, areas of Hertfordshire, north Kent, Essex, south-east Suffolk and Yorkshire.[22]

The reuse of prehistoric and Romano-British barrows was a widespread practice in earlier Saxon times, when barrow burial was still important. Numerous Saxon barrow cemeteries have been discovered, of which by far the most famous is that at Sutton Hoo, in Suffolk.[23] Excavation of the largest mound in this cemetery revealed a royal burial in a chamber within a clinker-built ship. The grave-goods are quite simply breathtaking and demand that we reassess our ideas about the Dark Ages. The superb gold belt buckle, for example, which dates to the early seventh century, could not have been fashioned without generations of technical development and a tradition of apprenticeship whereby newly acquired expertise was passed on. If we accept this, it seems inconceivable that Britain could have been in a state of anarchy during the so-called Dark Ages, just a century earlier.

The reuse of barrows by pagan Saxon communities also suggests that they considered that their forebears mattered. In fact it would appear that their attitudes to death and the role of the ancestors within the landscape had much in common with earlier Bronze Age beliefs. In this much later period we have the added advantage of writing and language to flesh out their beliefs, and it is clear from the names and folklore surrounding prehistoric and later barrows that Saxon and early medieval communities often saw them as products of giants, the Devil and mythical ancestral figures.[24] We also know that at this time named barrows are often specifically referred to when boundaries are being defined. This tradition of assigning significance to pre-existing features of the landscape persisted and in certain areas, such as the Welland Valley, the headlands of earlier medieval strip field systems are sometimes aligned on prehistoric barrows.[25]

TRADE, EXCHANGE AND THE ORIGINS
OF TOWNS

The mid-Saxon period of southern Britain, between approximately AD 650 and 850, has left no direct, tangible mark on urban landscapes, as no walls and very few street surfaces of this period are still visible. The traditional view was that the seventh and eighth centuries were economically disastrous for Britain and north-west Europe.[26] This was not the case. It was a time of vigorous trade, both across the Channel and through Europe.[27] That trade required an efficient and safe network of trading stations, roads and navigable waterways, which were to link the landscapes and regions of southern Britain closely together. In the ninth and tenth centuries the network was to spread over most of the island. It was a period of fundamental importance for the development of the British landscape.

One might wonder what overseas trade has to do with the development of the British landscape, but for the next few centuries Britain's place in Europe is to become significant.[28] It would, however, be a mistake to assume that this was something completely new. Plank-built

Fig 6.7 The great gold belt buckle that probably belonged to King Raedwald of Essex, who died in AD 625 and was buried in a chamber within a longship beneath the barrow of Mound 1 at Sutton Hoo, Suffolk. This is widely regarded as artistically the finest piece of jewellery from this magnificent royal grave. The interlace consists of the stylized contorted bodies of birds and beasts and the work is most probably that of a contemporary English goldsmith.

seagoing craft have been found from several Bronze Age sites in Britain, roughly dating from 2000 BC and later.[29] There are also offshore shipwrecks of Bronze Age date in the Channel and there is abundant evidence for regular cross-Channel contacts between Britain, Gaul and Iberia throughout the Iron Age.[30] Then during the Roman period the *classis Britannica* was based at Boulogne and for a time at Dover, to protect trade along the Channel and across the southern North Sea, from the first to the fourth centuries AD.

The developments in the rural and newly created urban landscapes from about 650 to about 1050 did not happen in isolation. Similar things were happening on the continent, too. The point to emphasize here is that from well before AD 500, and during the succeeding centuries, Britain was in regular contact with the rest of Europe. These contacts were not simply about the exchange of a few high-value objects. With the objects came (and went) ideas. New styles of art, new ways of burying the dead, even of dressing, all came to Britain from across the seas. But it was also a process of give and take. Britain received influences (such as Celtic Christianity), but then adapted them and reinfluenced the Continent.[31]

The traditional portrayal of post-Roman Britain as some form of anarchic 'failed state' is quite simply erroneous. The fifth and sixth centuries were doubtless violent times, but not just in Britain. Ancient Europe could often be a very unpleasant place. Failed states, however, are different. For a start, they lose contact with the outside world, but the dazzling display of objects found in the seventh-century Saxon graves at Prittlewell (*c.* 650), Essex, and Sutton Hoo (*c.* 625) in Suffolk give abundant evidence for contacts through Europe, into North Africa and across to the eastern Mediterranean.[32] Trade, or more accurately socially embedded exchange, between Britain and the rest of Europe had been active, if not booming, from at least AD 500.[33] It is surely difficult to accept that this trade sprang up entirely from scratch. It must have been under way earlier, and from at least later Roman times.

It is widely accepted that early medieval (that is, 600–1000) trade was exchange centred on the wealth and influence of ruling élites. Recent metal-detector finds would indicate that the central élite focus of exchange stimulated a series of less high-flown exchange networks between individuals, probably of lower status, and between middlemen, or brokers, too. Ultimately ordinary British farmers of the mid-Saxon period could use the system to acquire objects, such as querns[34] made from central European volcanic lava. At this stage watermills were yet to become widespread and most households prepared their own flour using querns – two grinding stones that can be worked by a single individual. The exchange system was rooted in earlier practices and it was just beginning to develop characteristics of true market-based trade. But it was still possible for a single powerful ruler to declare that one trading centre should close, another open, because it suited his political requirements.[35] Trade had yet to acquire an independent existence in its own right, as it did in the towns of the Middle Ages.

In Saxon times trade took place at centres known in Latin as *emporia*, or in Early English[36] as *wic*s. These places, which occur in south and east Britain and on the Continent, flourished in the seventh to ninth centuries. Where known, their layout was arranged on a grid of streets, suggesting control by a central authority of some sort. Significant British *wic*s were at Bantham (in Devon), Hamwic (Southampton), Sarre (in Kent), Lundenwic (London), Ipswic (Ipswich), Northwic (Norwich)[37] and Eoforwic (York). Well-known *emporia* of the Continent included Dorestad (Holland), Emden and Hamburg (Germany) and Birka (Sweden).[38] But were these true towns or just trading posts?

The answer to that question, indeed to all questions regarding the status, role or classification of towns, lies in the individual towns themselves. Today most urban archaeologists prefer to look at each town on its own merits. Only that way can one take into account the complex history of each place and the changing network of contacts it may have developed, both locally and further afield.[39] On present evidence the *wic* at Bantham was probably more of a trading post than Lundenwic (London), Hamwic (Southampton) and Ipswich, all of which were densely settled and can surely claim urban status.[40]

It can be argued that the *wic*s of Saxon England were the first true towns in Britain. At present we do not believe they were continuously occupied from Roman times. This can be stated positively for two of the most important, Lundenwic (London) and Hamwic (Southampton), but we still lack evidence for continuity or indeed for discontinuity at York, which might otherwise be the best contender.[41]

The great antiquity of many British towns is still not widely appreciated. This is probably because most of the earliest standing buildings are the great Norman churches, castles and cathedrals. However, most pre-Norman buildings were made from wood and only survive as the faintest of archaeological traces below the ground. Second World War bomb damage led to a series of excavations in the 1950s and 1960s, when improved techniques allowed archaeologists to detect the very slight stains and soil marks left by the decayed timbers of wooden buildings. Before the war much of this material would have been ignored or discarded as the diggers headed ever deeper to reach the more obviously visible Roman remains. The discoveries, of Saxon and early medieval deposits in places like London, Southampton, Winchester, York and a host of smaller towns, have completely transformed our understanding of Britain's urban past. Until these discoveries, much of the evidence of Saxon settlement was interesting place-names – the famous London street, Aldwych (old town), for

Fig. 6.8 The area now occupied by central London in the second millennium BC, looking south-west. The prominent island in the middle distance is now the site of Westminster Abbey and Parliament. Note the Fleet river (*lower right*) and the numerous rectangular Bronze Age fields.

instance, marks the edge of the Saxon settlement of Lundenwic. Recently, however, a series of major urban surveys have placed these excavations into context and have revealed important new information about the earliest history of British towns.

Urban surveys always place great emphasis on the development of town plans. In effect, these plans are maps of developing townscapes and they clearly illustrate how the buildings and structures were positioned within the natural topography of a site. Strip away the buildings and you can see the lie of the land beneath. Topographically, large areas of London, for example, were rather like Hackney Marshes, wet and boggy underfoot.[42] The River Thames today flows in an orderly fashion through a controlled townscape. In the past it was very different; not only were its banks constantly collapsing, but the river itself was less thoroughly tamed than it is today. There were no locks or sluices further upstream and when in spate it would have been extremely difficult to control. This applied also to the many smaller rivers that flowed through the City and its suburbs.[43]

The archaeological evidence so far indicates that the mid-Saxon settlements at Norwich, which was to become England's second city in the Middle Ages, seems to have lacked the coherence of Lundenwic or Hamwic at this period. In fact it amounted to little more than a series of linked farms, rather than anything that could be termed urban.[44] Most of the roads that served these *wic*s were probably Roman in origin, which is consistent with what we know about Saxon England in general, where routes of trade and communication were all-important. Norwich lay at the heart of northern East Anglia and like all the other *wic*s was well served by road and water.

Ipswich was the dominant *wic* in East Anglia at this time and we know that the mid-Saxon focus of trade there was closer to the later Saxon and medieval town centre than at the other two major *wic*s, Lundenwic and Hamwic. These very early trading centres were placed where access to incoming vessels was most convenient. These accessible waterside locations were possible because Viking raids were not yet a problem and defences were still unnecessary. In the case of London, the later Saxon defended town, or *burh*, was positioned within the stone walls of Roman *Londinium*. At Norwich, use was made of the river and the northern settlement was defended by a great ditch.

It has generally been supposed that Roman *Londinium* was completely abandoned during the two post-Roman centuries, but a scatter of finds of the fifth and sixth centuries has been identified along the north bank of the Thames, within the walls of the Roman city.[45] Perhaps more significantly, the distribution of these finds extends further to the west, across the River Fleet into the area we know was occupied by a new settlement in Saxon times. This new settlement was Lundenwic. Taking this evidence together, it would now seem likely that the London area continued to be lived in throughout the fifth and sixth centuries, but in a much less intensive, urban manner than in Roman times.

The name Lundenwic first appears in laws that were drawn up when the kingdom of Kent had regained control of London from Mercia, in the mid-670s. Lundenwic is also mentioned in the year 604, although we should bear in mind that the Anglo-Saxon Chronicle was compiled very much later, in the reign of King Alfred.

During its most successful and prosperous period in the mid-eighth century, from about 730 to 770, Lundenwic was more than a mere

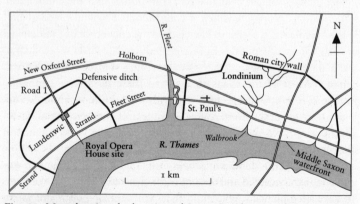

Fig. 6.9 Map showing the location of Saxon London (Lundenwic) and the abandoned walled city of Roman London (*Londinium*). The map shows the position of the Royal Opera House excavations and of a mid-Saxon main road, known as Road 1, which ran from the Strand to New Oxford Street (both Roman roads). Although the general layout of Lundenwic is still unknown we do know that a major defensive ditch was constructed in the earlier ninth century as part of defensive measures against the increasing threat posed by Viking raids.

Fig. 6.10 The walled Roman city of *Londinium* (visible here in the background, beyond the River Fleet) was abandoned for nearly two centuries at the end of the Roman period and settlement moved west, to the area around Covent Garden and the Strand. This new Saxon settlement was known as Lundenwic and made use of the river frontage for boats and ships, that brought cargoes from across Europe. The new settlement, which was not walled, had to be abandoned in 871 after a series of disastrous Viking raids.

trading post or 'proto-urban' settlement.[46] It was undoubtedly a town, and a very successful one at that.

One of the most important modern excavations in London took place over ten years, from 1989, on the site of the new Royal Opera House at Covent Garden. This project showed that the alignment of the many timber buildings remained the same throughout the middle of the Saxon period, which strongly suggests both that the site was continuously occupied and that the arrangement of the buildings seems to have been planned. Several other factors suggest a degree of urban planning and control. The many wells would have to have been kept open and free from contamination; rubbish was disposed of in specific areas reserved for temporary middens, or refuse heaps, which were then removed, probably to be spread on the fields around the settlement. The buildings were separated by open areas and there were yards in which various trades such as tanning and metal-working took place. Again we see evidence for planning, because tanning pits stank (due to the stale urine used in the process) and were placed well back from the main road and buildings around them. Some of the buildings along the main road may well have been shops. The excavations were crossed by a straight road, labelled Road 1, which probably ran from New Oxford Street, in the north-west, to the Strand. This road had been resurfaced many times and did not fall into disrepair until the settlement's final, difficult years.

Writing around 730 the Venerable Bede describes London as a major trading centre with Continental Europe. The excavations produced abundant evidence for trade with Carolingian Europe in the mid-eighth century and the discovery of a timber-revetted waterfront, dated by tree-rings to 679, confirms that the river was an important part of Lundenwic from the outset. Lundenwic would have been served by several churches, which most probably included St Martin-in-the-Fields and St Andrew's, Holborn, and possibly others.

Lundenwic began in the seventh century, flourished for most of the eighth and began to decline after about 770. A large east–west defensive ditch was dug across the northern part of the site in the early ninth century. This ditch formed a part of larger ground works that were intended to shrink the outer defences, which had become over-extended. The new, more compact and stronger defences seemed to have worked for a time. Eventually, however, they failed when attacked in strength by the Vikings, in 871. Lundenwic succumbed. Settlement then retreated back within the strengthened Roman walls of Roman *Londinium*, to the new late Saxon *burh* of Lundenburh.

The three southern *wic*s at Ipswich, London and Southampton were undoubtedly the major centres of trade, and excavation has proved this beyond doubt. But what would their impact have been on the landscape? The trading places themselves were town-like centres with domestic houses, stores and sheds along the waterfront. Thirty years ago our knowledge of England in the mid-Saxon period was largely confined to the layout and organization of the *wic*s themselves. A few rural settlements had been excavated and we knew a certain amount about the distribution of coins and of exotic imported pottery, lava querns and so forth, from finds made on these digs. The big gap in our understanding of the period was how these various components of the landscape fitted together. The answer came from a most unexpected source.

There is now overwhelming evidence that trade in this period was not confined to the *wic*s alone. There were also some thirty significant secondary trading centres in the countryside too. They were linked to the *wic*s and to smaller rural settlements by a network of communications. Most of the coins from these sites come from a restricted range of dates, between 700 and 900, which coincides pretty well with the known dates of the *wic*s.

A distribution map of the thirty-one known 'productive sites' shows them to be spread across most of eastern England.[47] When one examines the various locations in detail they can be seen to lie either close by a Roman or an ancient road (such as the Ridgeway), or by a river. In other words, they all belonged within a fully functioning distribution network – and the landscape implications of this are obvious. The

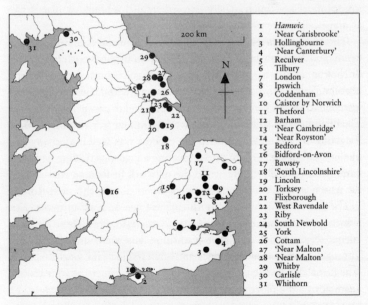

Fig. 6.11 A map showing the location of the 31 sites, mostly discovered by metal-detectorists, that have revealed large quantities of Saxon metalwork from the period 650–850. These so-called 'productive sites' form part of a network of trading centres that were linked together by rivers and roads (mostly Roman). They were also supplied with traded items from abroad via the coastal ports-of-trade known as *wic*s (in Early English) or *emporia* (in Latin).

near-ubiquity of this network across south-eastern Britain argues strongly in favour of a developed landscape with inter-linked settlements able to afford some of the more expensive items that were being traded.

It is interesting to note that the pattern of trade and distribution shown by the map of productive sites is in complete contrast to the map of imported early medieval pottery from North Africa and the Mediterranean area. This suggests that the rapidly expanding Saxon kingdoms of the eastern side of Britain were making use of new trading links, many of which would have come overland through northern Europe, and along rivers such as the Rhine and Seine, eventually entering Britain via south-eastern ports, such as Southampton, London and Ipswich. This new pattern was quite distinct from the earlier tradition of coastal trade by way of small harbours at places like Tintagel.

The four centuries that followed the end of the Roman interlude were of crucial importance to the formation of the British landscape. It took a century or so for the communities of south-eastern Britain that had been most affected by the Roman withdrawal to establish new identities, but by the later sixth and seventh centuries we see the establishment of something that was beginning to resemble modern England. By the eighth century the process was well under way and the first towns had grown up, supporting a vigorous trading network, largely based around rivers and the network of Roman roads, most of which had been steadfastly kept open during the post-Roman centuries. Away from the south-east we see increasing prosperity, which gave rise to the first fortified and monastic sites. These developments were rooted in earlier traditions, and were increasingly encouraged by the power, influence and scholarship of the Gaelic Church. The British landscape must have looked very inviting to anyone visiting from across the North Sea.

7

The Viking Age (800–1066)

The Vikings have had a very poor press. They are generally seen as bloodthirsty barbaric raiders whose single aim was rape and pillage. Mark you, this image was not helped by the Vikings themselves, choosing names like Thorfinn the Skullsplitter and Eirik Bloodaxe; and whose art frequently included weapons and warlike images.[1] But other people have also played their part. Towards the latter part of the Viking period, for example, King Alfred had strong personal and political reasons for hating them; this attitude persisted throughout medieval times. Subsequently, and as part of the same tradition of historical abuse serving nationalistic ends, Nazi propaganda drew direct parallels between glorious Aryan storm troopers and their supposed Viking ancestors.[2] In reality, the Vikings were indeed warlike and carried out many violent raids, but it was not mindless raiding for its own sake alone. There was far more to it than that; it also changed through time, so that raiding began to be replaced by settlement.

Some of the most important developments of the rural and urban landscapes of Britain took place in the two and a half centuries prior to the Norman Conquest. It was a time of unprecedented social upheaval, largely brought about first by raids and then by more concerted military conflict with soldiers and settlers from Scandinavia. The innovations of this period included the first true towns and the rationalization of rural settlement which gave rise to the Open Field system of farming, that was to be so important in the early Middle Ages.[3] Many other innovations commonly held to be Norman introductions had roots in Saxon Britain, including earthen castles and an informal form of deer park. The establishment of deer parks in particular reflected the fact that by later Saxon times Britain already possessed a substantial aristocracy. I also suspect that reform of the countryside of southern and Midland Britain would have happened anyhow, as similar changes were also taking place in Continental Europe. The rise of true towns, on the other hand, seems to have been a direct response to the threat posed by organized Viking armies on British soil. But once they were established the economic conditions of the time encouraged their growth and successful expansion.

It is one of the oddities of history that the word 'Viking' does not appear in any contemporary accounts. Instead we read of raids by 'Danes' or 'Norseman' (men from Norway). Sometimes the frightened Saxons simply referred to their hated attackers as 'heathens'. The word 'Viking' (which is Old Norse in origin) gained public acceptance in the nineteenth century with the publication of the Icelandic sagas and the heroic deeds of the semi-mythical Viking sailors and warriors that appear in them. The sagas were enormously popular and influential in Victorian Britain, and indeed across much of northern Europe. Today archaeologists tend to use 'Viking' as shorthand for 'Anglo-Scandinavian' – a mouthful, like 'Romano-British', but also the correct way of describing the Scandinavian contribution to the British way of life.

The Anglo-Saxon Chronicle contains the earliest account of a raid on a British monastery. It took place on 8 January 793 on the monastic island of Lindisfarne, just off the Northumberland coast. The raiders (described as 'heathen') sacked the buildings, killed several monks and carried away others as prisoners. While they were at it, they desecrated altars and helped themselves to valuables, which most probably including the original covers of the world-famous Lindisfarne Gospels.

Raiding was characteristic of the times. We know of many raids, especially around the Irish Sea, by British on Irish and vice versa. The Vikings were not the only people doing it. We also tend to think of northern and eastern England as the main objects of Viking attack. But in fact other parts of the British Isles also received repeated visits from Vikings, both as raiders and settlers. It was a complex picture, not the least because the Vikings were coming from often widely separated regions of Scandinavia. As a rule of thumb, it was people from Norway that raided and then colonized the north and west of Britain, and Ireland, whereas Danes came to eastern England and north-west France (Normandy).

So the raiding went on for two and a half centuries. The fact of its longevity suggests that the motives lying behind Viking raiding and later colonization changed from the original greed to something we would understand only too well today: ambition.

It has been suggested that the initial raids were based on the simple acquisition of portable wealth, like the jewelled covers of the Lindisfarne Gospels. These valuable items could then be converted into land back home in Scandinavia by way of high-status gift exchange. As time passed, however, the Scandinavian petty kingdoms became better established, with stronger ruling élites. But good-quality land was in short supply and the senior members of leading families would not

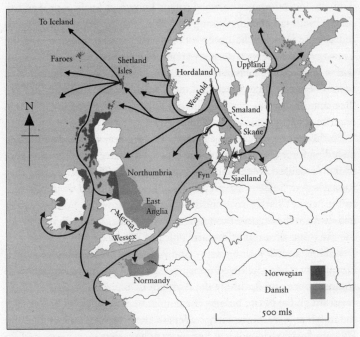

Fig. 7.1 For two centuries, starting around AD 800, raiders from Scandinavia carried out a series of often devastating raids on the coasts, and up the rivers of north-western Europe, even reaching as far afield as Greenland and Newfoundland, across the North Atlantic. Soon the raids became migrations and large areas of Britain and Ireland were occupied by Viking settlers. Orkney and Shetland belonged to Norway until 1469.

part with it. Younger people of high social rank thus had an overwhelming incentive to look elsewhere for land. Of course the single thing that made all of this possible was the Viking longship – or rather longships – which were built in a variety of shapes and sizes. These vessels gave the Vikings the means to travel huge distances and through some of the most challenging maritime conditions anywhere on earth.

The character of the Viking age in Britain changed in response to the events of European history.[4] The first phase, from 789 to 864, was marked by sporadic raids and looting. The second phase, of permanent colonization, started in 865 with the arrival of huge Danish armies in East Anglia. This phase lasted until 896 when King Alfred's defences – mostly in the form of fortified towns known as *burhs* – proved too strong for them and the Viking armies dispersed. By the early tenth century the Danelaw had been established in eastern England and the country enjoyed several decades of peaceful coexistence. The Danelaw was a large part of eastern and all northern England, where it was agreed between King Alfred and the Danish leader Guthrum (in 878) that administration would follow Viking practices; many of these practices continued into the Middle Ages.

Further problems emerged in the 980s with renewed raids, this time including forces from Sweden. The raids of the later tenth century were probably caused by the fact that strong leadership there meant that Russia was no longer easy prey, so the marauders turned their attention to the west. This led to a third phase which saw the Vikings extort tribute from the Anglo-Saxon rulers. The fourth and final phase (1013–66) was one of straightforward political conquest, when Sveinn of Denmark landed with an army and Aethelred (the Unready) fled to Normandy. There followed a series of Saxon–Viking wars that were resolved once and for all by the Norman Conquest of 1066.

Although the Norse became the dominant Scandinavian presence in the north and west, the early raiders in these areas also included the Danes, who seized Dublin in 851, only to be resoundingly defeated (in Ireland) by the Norse, two years later. Thereafter the Norse were the dominant force in the north-western approaches to Britain. In the Western Isles the Viking period is conventionally divided into two subphases: the Viking Age, from the first raids of 795 to 1000, and a late Norse period from 1000 to 1266; this was the year that the Western

Fig. 7.2 An aerial view of the settlement at Jarlshof on the southern tip of mainland Shetland. The smaller Pictish settlement is to the right and until conservation measures were taken it was being eroded by the sea. The partially excavated ninth-century Viking period longhouses are to the centre and right.

Isles were transferred from Norwegian to Scottish control at the Treaty of Perth, which followed the defeat of the Norwegians at the Battle of Largs, by King Alexander of Scotland, in 1263. Orkney and Shetland remained under Norwegian control until 1469.[5]

The northern and western isles of Scotland included a number of important Norse settlements, of which the best known is undoubtedly Jarlshof, at the southern tip of Mainland Shetland. This exposed farming hamlet is extraordinarily well preserved. The Viking settlement started in the ninth century, taking over a slightly earlier Pictish community. The Viking period longhouses are quite substantial, some being up to 20 metres long and 5 wide. One particularly tight group of two or three houses might represent an extended family.

If the general thrust of history in the ninth and tenth centuries was about conflict and competition, what was the effect of such disruption on the landscape? One might expect the late Saxon period to be one of stagnation when nobody dared to do anything for fear that it would draw the unwelcome attention of some unpleasant men wielding battleaxes. But in actual fact the two centuries before the Norman Conquest saw major and very long-lasting changes to the rural and urban landscapes of Britain. Despite the presence of Viking forces after 865, it was a time of increasing prosperity which saw the founding of many English towns and the wholesale reorganization of huge tracts of rural landscape.

The foundation and development of towns was the result of royal authority, whether exercised by the Saxon kingdoms of Wessex and Mercia (the kingdom whose heartland lay in the west Midlands) or by Viking leaders. By the same token, the rationalization of many rural landscapes that was happening in central and southern Britain at this time was also about authority. The difference was in scale. In the countryside the agents of change and improvement were the Church, together with landowners large and small. Many of these landowners were members of a new aristocracy known as *thegns* (pronounced 'thanes'). They first appear in the middle of the Saxon period but were becoming important now. The *thegns* of later Saxon England obtained their estates through grants of land from the Crown, for which they were obliged to serve the king in times of war. So by giving land away, the Crown was able to secure loyalty. It was also a measure which helped to bind society together, in somewhat lawless times.

We tend to think that the Vikings only acquired their lands in Britain by the sword. While this was certainly true in the early years, land often changed hands from Saxon to Viking (and vice versa) in the Danelaw, and elsewhere using established administrative structures. There are, for instance tenth-century charters recording the sale of land by Scandinavians in Bedfordshire, Derbyshire and (perhaps) in Lancashire.[6] There is a cluster of Viking place-names in the Wirral peninsula of Lancashire but these do not extend further west into the

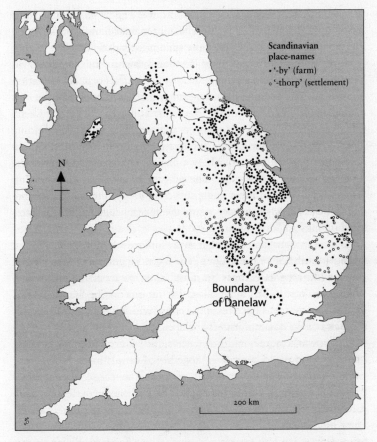

Fig. 7.3 A map showing the distribution of place-names with Scandinavian origins in England, Wales and the Isle of Man. Examples include '-by' ('farm') names, such as Whitby, Grimsby and Slingsby, and '-thorp' ('settlement') names, such as Bishopsthorpe and Towthorpe. Although most of the places with Scandinavian names were probably occupied by Vikings, the vast majority would originally have been Saxon communities and only acquired their new names when Viking settlers moved in. This distribution coincides well with the known extent of the Danelaw of the ninth and tenth centuries.

Welsh borders, where Viking settlers do not appear to have been as active as they were further north. The border lands of north-east Wales had been hotly contested for some time prior to the Viking age and were the subject of continuing disputes between the kingdoms of Mercia to the east and Powys and Gwynedd to the west. Shortly after 950 Viking raids resumed at the same time that disputes broke out among various factions within the royal house of Gwynedd. These were turbulent times in many border regions right across Britain.

The other significant force for change in both rural and urban landscapes was the Church. Many monastic estates rationalized their holdings of land at this time.[7] The process involved the gathering of dispersed settlements into a single new community, often based around one that was already in existence, and the drawing together of separated landholdings to form what in effect was a communal farm, sometimes directly administered either by a landlord (these were known as demesne lands) or by the Church. The farms of monastic estates were generally known as granges. In most other instances the farms and settlements would be administered by the lord of the manor or the local landowner through a manorial court, which would also represent the views of the community. Manorial courts sorted out disputes to do with tenure and more humdrum matters, such as crop rotation, grazing rights and so forth. The drawing together of people living in the area, and the setting up of the manorial courts and the consequent concentration of dwellings within the nucleus of a village were the principal components of the process known as nucleation, or manorialization. Once nucleation had been achieved, most (but not all) villages then farmed their land co-operatively, under the lord of the manor, the Church, or an absent landlord.

TOWN PLANNING IN SAXON TIMES

Certain mid-Saxon *wics* were already far more than just trading posts. Some possessed a grid-like layout of street plans and there is evidence for street maintenance, refuse disposal and so on. Lundenwic, Southampton (Hamwic) and Ipswich (Ipswic) were indeed true towns. The trade that was carried on from these three ports, like that of the other *wic*s of mid-Saxon England, was organized around a complex system of high-status exchange, with an important and significant 'trickle down' effect to the less exalted ranks of society. But the people at the top also had to play a role in the process, or they would soon cease to enjoy its benefits. These were the people who organized not just the trade itself, but the places where the trading took place. They, and the people close to them, would have been responsible for the layout of the various *wic*s and also for their security, which was negotiated by political agreement. There was no need to enclose these new trading settlements within walls or ramparts. One might suppose

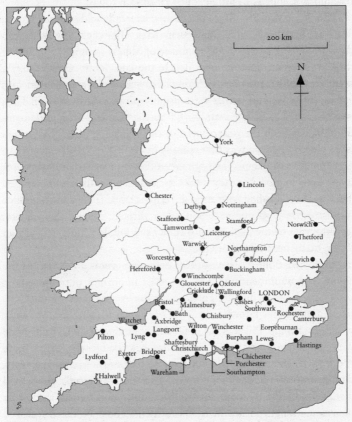

Fig. 7.4 Map of towns in later Saxon Britain (*c.* 850–1066).

that such open settlements were entirely beneficial: after all, people could expand their businesses unconstrained by shortage of space. But in terms of urban development, some degree of constraint is not always a bad thing. It can provide the stimulus for creative town-planning.

The principal Saxon response to the presence of the Vikings were the *burhs*, a series of defended new towns or reoccupied Roman walled towns. Other true towns, such as York (and Dublin), had rather different origins, but the end result was an entirely new urban landscape; this time, however, it would last. Certainly a few *burhs* failed to thrive, but the vast majority are the towns and cities that still play a significant role in the commercial life of southern Britain today.

Burhs were fortified towns established as strongholds against attack. The very first *burhs* were founded by King Offa (757–96) of Mercia. After the Viking Great Army's conquest of Mercia (around 877), half of these were retained for its own use. In the later ninth century Mercia controlled all the land north of Wessex, between Wales and the Danelaw.

The early Mercian *burhs* were usually positioned by a river. They were intended to be self-sustaining secure settlements with good communications with the other *burhs* in the system – Alfred the Great's were placed in such a way that nobody living in Wessex was more than 30 kilometres from one. Their primary aim was indeed to protect people living in the region, but they were a great deal more than mere refuges. They were established with good governance, and trade and commerce were positively encouraged. Soon they thrived, despite the political uncertainties of the age. When stability did finally return in Norman times, many became major cities.

The foundation of a network of defended towns, or *burhs*, in the eighth and ninth centuries was the most important development in early British urban history. The idea for *burhs* originated on the Continent and the best-known founder of *burhs* was King Alfred (871–99), who set up many in the 890s. The idea behind *burhs* was to provide well-planned and specially strengthened defended towns, where trade could safely be transacted. They were also centres of royal authority, administration, regional government and trade. Carefully positioned in the landscape to form a closely connected network, the *burhs* provided strength in depth. Reinforcements could be rapidly moved should the situation warrant it.

The new *burhs* gave much of the impetus for the rapid economic growth of the eighth and ninth centuries. Many (for example, Norwich and York) were founded in places which had been important in mid-Saxon times. In London there was a series of Viking raids up the river in 851, 861 and 871. The last proved too much for Lundenwic, which was moved back to the area protected by the still-standing walls of Roman *Londinium* in the 870s. It was then re-founded by King Alfred in the late ninth century, as Lunden*burh*.

The *burhs* founded by Alfred and Edward the Elder were remarkable places. One of the most important discoveries in the archaeology of English towns took place in the 1960s when it was realized that the origin of many planned towns was neither Roman nor Norman, but home-grown. These discoveries were the result of excavations preceding the post-war development of many city centres, including perhaps the most important early medieval city in southern England.

The city that might have been the capital of England, had William I not decided to be crowned elsewhere, is today a charming but essentially rural town in Hampshire. It might be supposed that Winchester's former aspirations are proclaimed by its castle and magnificent cathedral, but in actual fact the real story lies in the layout of its picturesque streets. It had been the walled Roman city of *Venta Belgarum*, and it had always been assumed that the grid-like arrangement of its streets followed the Roman layout. Up until the early 1960s nobody had thought to test the received wisdom by digging a few holes. When that happened, everything was suddenly turned upside down.

The excavators were working within the walled city around the three Brook Streets, Lower, Middle and Upper.[8] They discovered that the alignment of Middle Brook Street, a road that ran along the well-preserved foundations of medieval houses, followed the Roman alignment. That should have caused no surprise, were it not for the fact that the previous season the foundations of a Dark Age building had been found directly above the Roman street. That arrangement clearly implied that the Roman street had been abandoned shortly after the Roman period. Further excavation then revealed that the alignment of nearby Upper Brook Street differed significantly from that of the Roman road beneath it. At the same time, Lower Brook Street to the east did not appear to have had any Roman antecedents at all.

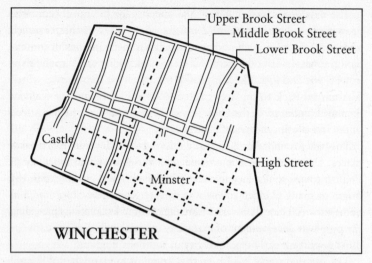

Fig. 7.5 Town plan of Winchester, Hampshire, showing the arrangement of Roman (broken line) and late Saxon streets. The main east–west street follows a straight line between two principal gateways through the defensive outer walls. This street was used as the basis for the later Saxon grid-like street plan, which ignores the layout of the long-abandoned Roman town.

The medieval street layout bore no relation to the Roman plan, apart from the High Street, which happened to run between two gateways that had remained in regular use in post-Roman times. So, although it was significantly later, the arrangement of streets in late Saxon Winchester was both regular and laid out on a grid pattern, which nearly (but not quite) coincided with the Roman layout. After major excavations, the archaeologists were able to determine that the main grid of streets was in existence by the mid-tenth century and was probably in use by about 904. This indicated that the new layout would have happened when the Roman walls were rebuilt and refurbished, at the time when Alfred (or his son Edward the Elder) founded the new *burh*, in the late ninth or early tenth century.

The regularity of the new street layout strongly indicated that the entire venture was part of a single, well-planned, operation – quite possibly with a strong military element. The excavator describes late Saxon Winchester as a town of regular streets dominated by its great minster churches, full of wooden houses and enjoying contacts with western Europe and as far afield as Byzantium.[9] The Winchester project then went on to examine other towns to set their findings in context, and they discovered the existence of a whole series of planned Saxon towns, with non-Roman grid-like streets.[10]

Some *burhs*, like Chichester and Colchester, which were re-founded by the kingdom of Wessex, have street plans where the principal streets that ran between the original gateways through the Roman walls still follow the Roman alignment, as was seen at Winchester.[11] But the side streets are either laid out completely afresh, or follow more subtly different alignments, as we saw at Winchester. Excavation has shown that some other Wessex *burhs* with grid-like street plans, such as Wareham (Dorset), Cricklade and Wallingford (Oxfordshire), were entirely new foundations without Roman origins.

The presence of Viking soldiers and settlers in England was a source of conflict and sometimes of turmoil, but it was certainly not entirely destructive. Many other towns and villages within the area subsequently called the Danelaw were stable and prosperous. Most of the *burhs* were founded by the Saxon kingdoms of Wessex and Mercia, but the Vikings themselves are known to have established at least five (the so-called Five Boroughs: Lincoln, Nottingham, Stamford, Derby and Leicester) within the Danelaw. They also encouraged the development of their most famous British city, York or Jorvík, which was brought to national attention by the five-year Coppergate excavation (known as the Viking Dig) in the period 1976–81. Large areas of the site were waterlogged and the excavations revealed the woven-wattle walls of numerous houses. Of all the many thousands of finds revealed during the excavation I am still astonished by the discovery of some twenty silk fragments, most probably imported from the Near East or Byzantium.[12] These fragments look like the offcuts of a silk-worker, who we must assume was able to earn a living making headscarves and other high-quality items of clothing. In a cold climate silk is still the warmest fabric you can wear.

The return to the renewed and rebuilt Roman walled City of *Londinium*, from the extra-mural settlement at Lundenwic, in the 870s, was a response to Viking raids. As to the area within the Roman walls, it would appear that this land remained largely unoccupied through

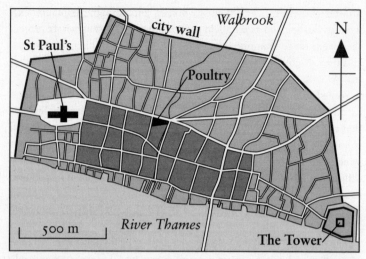

Fig. 7.6 Map showing the principal roads of the late Saxon *burh* of Lunden-burh, within the old Roman walled city. Lundenburh replaced mid-Saxon Lundenwic, which had been located outside the walls, to the west of the River Fleet. The settlement returned to the site of Roman walled city of *Londinium*, following severe Viking raids in 871. The new city was re-founded as a *burh* by King Alfred in 886, when the walls were repaired and rebuilt and a new grid of streets was laid out. The shaded area at the centre shows the size of the original *burh*, as it might have been about AD 900. Excavations at No. 1 Poultry (in black) have provided much of the new evidence on Lundenburh.

the two post-Roman centuries.[13] There was, however, some very sporadic settlement within the walls, and it seems likely that the Church maintained a presence there too. Churches were important in late Roman towns and some continued into post-Roman times, as we know also happened at Wroxeter. The continued ecclesiastical presence within the abandoned Roman walled City included the foundation of St Paul's in the year 604. It seems unlikely that this new institution would ever have amounted to the sort of urban life that was being lived in Lundenwic some distance to the west. The evidence from recent ex-cavations at No. 1 Poultry within the City suggests that the return to the walled area happened in the later to mid-ninth century. This accords well with the new *burh* of Lundenburh which was officially founded

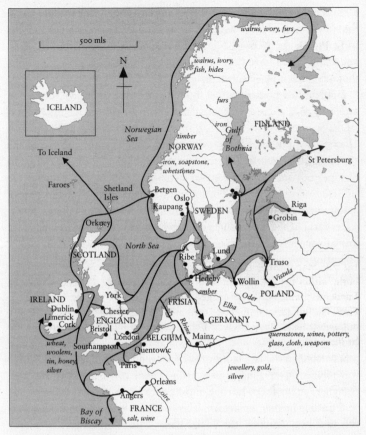

Fig. 7.7 A map showing the principal Viking trading links across north-western Europe in the eighth to eleventh centuries.

by King Alfred in 886. In common with other new *burhs* such as Winchester, Lundenburh was subject to extensive replanning, during which it acquired a new grid of streets, which did not follow the original Roman layout. A *burh* was also established south of the Thames at Southwark by the ninth or early tenth century.

There were two main areas of settlement within the City, on either side of the Walbrook, the stream which divides the walled area in half. Recent excavations at Lawrence Lane in the Guildhall have revealed a number of late Saxon timber buildings arranged side by side along the street. Some of these were probably shops.[14] By the late 1980s some sixty later Saxon or Saxo-Norman houses were known from the City, and many more have been found during the large-scale excavations that have taken place subsequently.

Lundenburh boasted a well-built timber river frontage (dating to around 970) and there was active trade with Northumbria, the Netherlands, Scandinavia and the Carolingian Empire in mainland Europe. The onset of Viking raiding from the late eighth century disrupted the commercial networks that had been established with Carolingian Europe, but the exchange never actually stopped. The presence of silk fragments in Jorvík itself argues convincingly that links were maintained with Byzantium and the Near East. The Vikings themselves established a new shipping network whose emphasis was more towards the north, which was to benefit many British and Irish ports.[15] I mention this not just because the Vikings have generally had a very bad press, but because we must help to account for the obvious prosperity of the times. That prosperity was important, because without it we would not have witnessed such a rapid growth in town life nor could there have been so many far-reaching developments in the countryside.

Sometime in the late tenth or early eleventh century London Bridge was rebuilt. Several major new bridges were constructed at this time elsewhere in northern Europe, most probably to prevent Viking raids penetrating further upstream. The southern end of the bridge was defended by a structure, the 'south work' – hence 'Southwark'. A major defensive ditch, which may well have been this 'work', was recently excavated and was dated to the early eleventh century. Late Saxon waterfronts have been excavated at Queenhithe and Billingsgate (where the late Roman quay or river frontage was deliberately removed). So far there is no evidence for warehouses, but large cellared buildings at Billingsgate and Cheapside may have been used as stores.

A NEW WAY OF ORGANIZING FARMS: OPEN FIELDS

Although the Middle Ages are rapidly slipping from the educational curriculum in Britain, some people will probably have heard of the Open Field system, a system of village-based collective farming.[16] The impression I gained at school was that Open Field farming happened right across Britain and throughout the Middle Ages. We were taught that it went hand in hand with feudalism and the manorial system. So if most readers have a similar picture of rural life in medieval times, then I am afraid I will now have to burst a few cherished bubbles.

For a start, Open Field farming did not happen everywhere in Britain. In fact, taken as a whole, most of Britain in Saxon and medieval times was farmed in the traditional way, by hundreds of thousands of small farmers and tenants with their own self-contained holdings of land. These collective farms were the product of an increasingly authoritarian society. Feudalism only functioned because certain people were in control and could call upon less well-born people to work for them. The basic principle behind Open Field farming was that the ordinary peasant farmers had to repay their landlords for the right to farm their own land, by working for so many days for him. 'He' could be a major landowner living far away, the agent of a monastic estate, or the local lord of the manor. Ultimately, it was a type of indirect social taxation or indentured labour.

We do know that large areas of central and southern Britain were farmed collectively in the early Middle Ages. These collective farms were generally organized parish by parish. The system was not introduced by the Romans, the Anglo-Saxons, or the Normans.[17] Instead it was introduced sometime in the early ninth century, as part of a series of agricultural reforms that were taking place across large areas of northern Europe at the time. It would appear that the new way of farming probably arrived in Britain as an idea, rather than in a wave of immigration.

In the later Saxon period there was a widespread movement in parts of north-eastern, central, Midland and southern England to gather together dispersed farmsteads to form larger, more concentrated, or nucleated settlements. These settlements and the Open Fields around them together formed the 'Champion'[18] landscapes so characteristic of the early Middle Ages. Incidentally, the word 'champion' derives from the Low Latin *campania* and the French *champagne*, meaning farmed countryside, as opposed to woodland. The purpose of the system was to exploit arable farmland efficiently, employing communal tools and labour, and using animals and their manure to restore the fertility of the land. It only worked because labour was increasingly plentiful in later Saxon times and in the first half of the Middle Ages.

The houses of the men who worked the fields were grouped into a village, which was surrounded by two or three large Open Fields which were worked by the inhabitants of the village. The peasant farmers of the village owned strips of land in the Open Fields which were marked out on the ground. Every strip within each Open Field had to be worked in the same way. Thus one strip could not be left fallow, and another allowed to grow a crop of, say, wheat. Much of the land was owned by the local landowner who usually resided in the manor house, where the manorial court met to decide which of the Open Fields were to be cropped and which was to be left fallow. Some of the peasant farmers paid for the use of their strips with labour. After perhaps two years of cropping, the land was left fallow (unploughed) for a year and animals were allowed to graze it. The manorial court also sorted out disputes over landholdings, tenancy agreements and matters relating to the supply of labour.

The Champion system only worked in certain areas. In wet or hilly regions, where ploughing was difficult, or in areas where the soil was simply not suitable, the older patterns of farming persisted. These regions sometimes, but not always, included large areas of woodland, which is why non-Champion farmed landscapes are often referred to as 'woodland landscapes'. Woodland landscapes are very variable. In some areas individual landholdings were small, in others they were large. Sometimes sheep dominated, other times it was cattle. Grazing, fodder-production, and of course woodland produce such as firewood and coppice products were usually important in woodland landscapes.

The contrast between Champion and woodland landscapes has been described as 'planned' versus 'ancient'. However, this twofold division is very broad indeed and is probably only useful when used to describe or define the 'planned' Champion areas of central-southern Britain with their clearly defined large villages within regularly laid out rectangular fields, isolated blocks of woodland and large farms. The woodland areas are far more diverse: some have blocks of woodland, others huge spreads of open or scrubby woodland; yet others have little woodland at all; most feature smaller farms and favour pasture over arable, but again, not always. Villages in woodland areas tend to be smaller, or less well defined; but there are of course exceptions to this rule.

You may feel that I am going too fast: that this chapter is about later Saxon Britain and yet here I am also discussing the countryside as it exists today. My reply to that important question is that for the first time in our story the action of ancient communities has had a direct effect on the *general* shape of the modern landscape. The simple fact that later Saxon farmers and villagers chose to organize themselves into communal farms has meant that subsequent land reform has been simpler. For example, the process of large-scale Parliamentary Enclosure of the eighteenth and nineteenth centuries was made far more straightforward in those areas of central and southern Britain where the lord of the manor, who ultimately controlled the operation of the Open Field system, was still both powerful and a major landowner. The areas that were farmed in common have left us a legacy of 'planned' landscapes.

By the later Saxon period the archaeology of rural England had begun to acquire a distinctly medieval feel. By this period most of the existing counties were in existence, as were many of the parishes and villages that can still be seen on the map. Just as importantly, the population was rising: without a steady supply of labour the reforms could never have taken place. The changes in rural settlement patterns that were to give rise to the Open Field system were essentially to do with rationalization and centralization; earlier settlements, which were small, dispersed and surrounded by their own fields, were replaced by a larger, centralized village with its Open Field system. These processes have been grouped together under the catch-all label of 'nucleation'. Although the early stages are not yet thoroughly understood, we do know that landholdings were drawn together, and that this process was often linked to the formation of manors (or 'manorialization'). But rather than talk in generalities two case studies from widely separated parts of lowland England will show how the process might have worked.

A detailed survey of Shapwick, in Somerset, has shown that there was quite a sudden change in the landscape sometime in the tenth century.[19] This was when the medieval village and its two large Open Fields came into being through the amalgamation of at least four farms and small settlements. This process of nucleation left the earlier church isolated from the new village, which now lay some distance to the west.

It would seem that the process of nucleation took several decades to complete. The shape and layout of the new village and its Open Fields was largely determined by what had gone before. The new village was laid out at right angles to the wetland with its east and west Open Fields arranged at each side, but on good dry arable land. The survey showed that the roads and tracks to east and west had been in existence since at least the Iron Age. Then, probably in the earlier tenth century, intermittent settlements were established along a stream which ran almost due north, from a nearby spring, towards the wetland edge of the Somerset Levels. The land closer to the spring sloped enough to allow good drainage. So this was where the house and garden (or close) plots for the new village were laid out. Interestingly, these plots were measured in multiples of 20 and 100 feet (6 and 39 metres), which strongly suggests that the layout of the new village had been planned in advance.

The new system of Open Field farming would only work if communal labour was employed and this again suggests planning and forethought. It can also be argued that the new system would only work if the people concerned were willing and wanted it to be successful. This further suggests that the entire process of nucleation must have been pushed through with the co-operation of the communities involved. In the case of Shapwick, the Church was the institution most likely to have encouraged and co-ordinated the reorganization. The Shapwick Survey established that there had been a minster church on a block of land known, rather appropriately, as 'Olde Churche' since at least the eighth century. This early church appears in Domesday (1086), along with an

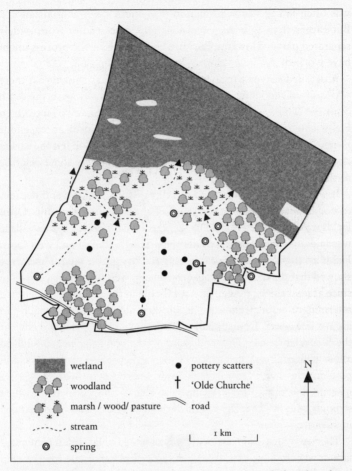

Fig. 7.8 The landscape of the parish of Shapwick, Somerset, before the reforms of the tenth century. At this time the landscape was still quite thickly wooded. A series of settlements, revealed by surface scatters of Saxon pottery, are spread along the higher ground to the south of the wetlands (part of the Somerset Levels). Some of the settlements had been occupied from Roman or even earlier times.

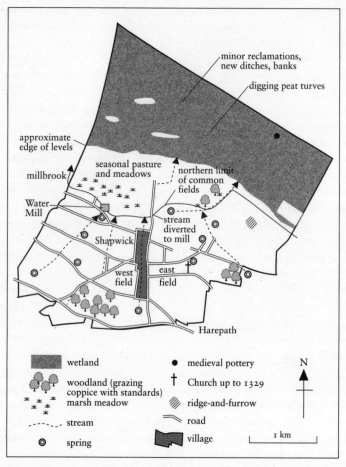

Fig. 7.9 The same landscape in the later medieval period (1100–1550), following the extensive reorganization of the tenth century. The scatter of settlements have been concentrated into a single village with two large open arable fields, the east and the west fields. Although the change at first seems very radical, many of the boundaries and alignments of this new landscape were in fact inherited from earlier periods. The new village has moved away from the parish church, which was founded prior to the tenth century.

estate large enough to sustain a small group of priests. Clearly this was a place of some importance, which we know was part of the much larger estate of the wealthy Abbey of Glastonbury, 7 kilometres to the east.

Common sense might suggest that the Open Field system developed piecemeal from the earlier Saxon landscape, as population grew and farming technology improved. But in this instance common sense would be wrong. As we saw at Shapwick, the shift from earlier settlement patterns to the new Open Field system happened quite suddenly and almost certainly with the help of a large institution, in the form of Glastonbury Abbey. Again, it is difficult to be precise about dates, but, taking central Britain as a whole, the process of nucleation would seem to have started in the ninth century and was actively under way by the early tenth century.

The new system often involved large areas of new arable land, sometimes arranged in long strips. Long fields were particularly well suited to the recently introduced mouldboard plough, which is not readily turned around and would not have been easy to use in the smaller paddock-like fields of earlier Saxon England. The mouldboard is the curved (and usually very shiny on modern steel ploughs) piece of metal that turns the sod over, thereby burying weeds and forming a true furrow. Earlier ploughs acted more like a hoe, cutting a groove through the ground, but not necessarily burying weeds. Similar developments were happening on continental landscapes within the Carolingian Empire, where in Austria and Germany, for example, long strip-like fields were being laid out in the later eighth and ninth centuries. The German examples can be dated to the period 775–850.[20] Again, these strips were set out for the efficient use of the mouldboard plough, but they also involved major landscape reorganization.

Huge strip-like Open Fields are also found in Britain. Some examples in the Yorkshire Wolds are an astonishing 2,000 metres long; other very long strip furlongs are found around the periphery of the Midlands, in south Yorkshire, around the Humber and in the silt fens around the Wash.[21] A few of these large-scale strips may have been laid out during the main life of the Open Field system, but the evidence on the ground suggests that most were arranged thus from the outset.[22]

The process of nucleation at Shapwick seems to have been pushed through by the Church and in many instances some outside institution or individual was needed to provide the incentive. The laws of economics and the economies of scale suggest that there is more incentive for a rich man to increase his income by thousands, than for a poor man to put much the same effort for a net annual reward of a few pence. A new aristocratic élite of *thegns* was starting to emerge in later Saxon times and these were just the sort of people who would have encouraged the process of nucleation on their estates. So it is time for my second case study, in Northamptonshire – deep in the heart of the Champion country of the Middle Ages.[23]

The landscape we are concerned with lies in and around the central Northamptonshire parish of Raunds. A series of major excavations in advance of the digging of some enormous gravel quarries revealed the sheer scale of late Saxon changes to the rural scene. These changes were across whole landscapes and involved a great deal of extra work and reconstruction. The land was also re-surveyed and laid out afresh, again on a massive scale, and unlike Shapwick it would seem that earlier boundaries were not treated with particular respect.

At Raunds, and probably elsewhere in the Midlands, the process of re-surveying and manorialization was well under way late in the Saxon period. It would seem that these reforms were an important symbol of the increasing power of landowners. Shapwick had been continuously occupied, but at Raunds there was a break between the farm of the eighth and ninth centuries and the first later Saxon settlement of the tenth and eleventh centuries. This consisted of four rectangular timber buildings, one of which was larger and better built that the others, and was probably a hall. These were the sort of ordinary buildings usually associated with a peasant farm at a time when this part of the county was under Danish control. The big change took place around 950–75, after the area had returned to English rule.

The first evidence that something major had happened to the land-scape was the discovery of a substantial ditch at least 230 metres long which ran right across the excavations.[24] This ditch was then shown to form one side of an enclosure of exactly an acre. The enclosure was around a substantial timber building, part of which was a large hall. Next to this enclosure was another ditched yard, probably for livestock. Further to the south there was a series of smaller enclosures, which were also linked to the big ditch; these contained timber buildings and other domestic structures. And this development did not take place in isolation. On the other side of the valley there were additional rectangular enclosures, similar to those further south, and these were probably the remains of tenant farms, belonging to the main system, because they were laid out on the same alignment and at the same time. It was all part of the same, well-coordinated and surveyed process of nucleation combined with manorialization.

THE CHURCH IN LATER SAXON TIMES

Today our knowledge of towns and villages is being enhanced by the methodical study of what has survived above ground. It began in the late nineteenth century, with general studies of the physical remains of monasteries and churches, then became increasingly specialized in the 1970s when the modern sub-discipline of church archaeology first appeared.[25] Church archaeology has become very important, because Britain's greatest archaeological and historical asset consists of the 15,000 or so ancient churches that still grace the landscape.[26] Even today, in rural Britain old churches actually outnumber petrol stations. Some may have been defaced by religious zealots in the English Civil War, or by over-restoration in the nineteenth century, but the fact remains that Britain has never had to face the horrors of all-out modern warfare across its landscapes. As a result, its churches have generally survived remarkably well.[27]

The archaeology of standing buildings is now an essential aspect of all urban studies and its subject matter reflects the diversity of modern British society, ranging from chapels to synagogues and mosques.[28] Like some other recent branches of archaeology, it relies heavily upon computers and new techniques of analysis that allow us to examine in huge detail the construction of, say, a wall. These approaches were pioneered by church archaeologists who originally did the work by hand, using tapes, planning-frames and plumb lines. They discovered that close inspection of individual bricks, stones and even the mortar used to bond them together could reveal important structural changes and the approximate date when the work was undertaken.

We tend to think that the Church only became a force in the land after the Norman Conquest and that the few pieces of pre-Norman architecture that do survive are probably representative of the Saxon Church in general. Nothing could be further from the truth. The trouble is that many Saxon buildings made extensive use of timber, and the Normans, like masons throughout the medieval period, were not averse to reusing earlier stone. The result is that nearly all traces of Saxon architecture have vanished, leaving us with a few dozen towers or parts of towers, the odd wall and other fragments. Two of the best known late Saxon towers are at Earls Barton (Northampton-shire) and Barton-upon-Humber (Lincolnshire). Both feature so-called 'long-and-short work' at the corners. This is very distinctive of Anglo-Saxon masonry and consists of long flat stones alternately placed vertically and horizontally, all the way up the corner angles of the tower walls. The conventional wisdom is that long-and-short work is mimicking woodworking, but I find that very unconvincing, simply because timber-framed buildings always use complete posts at the corners.[29] This looks more like the efforts of people unused to masonry who have worked out a decorative way of fashioning a strong corner that is securely tied into the rest of the wall by the 'short', horizontal piece at either end of the longer stone. If you want stonework that copies woodwork, then I suggest you look at the faces of the tower walls, between the corner angles.

The magnificent tower at Earls Barton was constructed during the time when the first manors were taking shape in the English Midlands. The tower itself could have held bells, and might also have served some defensive purpose, but the main reason it was built was to proclaim the importance of the Saxon noble who built it. Some of that lordly significance survives in the name of the modern village, *Earls* Barton. The 'Earl' in this instance would have been the later Norman Earl of Northampton.

Very few Saxon churches have survived intact. The fine tower at Earls Barton was probably built in the eleventh century, shortly before the Norman Conquest. But All Saints church in Brixworth is very much earlier and most remarkably has not been messed around too severely by the punching-through of larger Gothic windows and the adding of aisles, clerestories, porches, etc. Excavation has now proved that this is a building of the late eighth or early ninth century, and it is now generally considered one of the largest and finest buildings of that period in northern Europe. Its layout is that of a single large aisled hall with a semicircular apse at the east end. The origins of this distinctive

Fig. 7.10 The Saxon tower of All Saints church, Earls Barton, near Welling-borough, Northamptonshire. The tower is superbly decorated in the later Saxon style, with so-called 'long-and-short work' at the corner angles and raised bands of stone often said to imitate woodwork.

ground plan lie in the commonly occurring public building known as a basilica, which was found at the centre of most Roman towns. The word was then adopted by the early Church for its own use.

A close examination of the sources of the material used in its construction has shown that the builders of All Saints visited ruined Roman buildings over a large area of the countryside round about, and robbed them of tiles and stonework which they incorporated into their new building.[30] I still find it strange to imagine, as I stand and look up at this magnificent church, that the people who built and used it were living in a world where numerous Roman farms, villas and houses were still standing. The ruins of the nearby Roman town of Towcester would probably have resembled one of those sad towns along the Somme, where by 1918 all the buildings had lost their roofs and windows after four years of relentless shelling.

Investigations by church archaeologists have shown that the wall footings and other remains of pre-Norman churches can be identified below floor level of many standing buildings and these have proved to be surprisingly large. The pre-Norman church at Canterbury, to take one instance, was only slightly smaller than the vast Norman cathedral. We also know that a significant number of pre-Norman monastic houses had very large estates. The Benedictine abbeys at Peterborough and Glastonbury, for example, were extremely prosperous before the Conquest. So what was the Saxon Church's influence on the formation of the landscape?

We know that when Augustine and his missionaries arrived in Kent from Rome in 597, bringing with them Roman Christianity, the Gaelic Church, whose roots lay ultimately in Roman Britain, was able to welcome him with just seven British bishops, and not the entire bench.[31] This strongly suggests that Saxon southern Britain was by no means a pagan land throughout, and that the Church was a fully developed organization. The Synod of Whitby in 664, where important differences between the Gaelic and Roman churches were finally ironed out, was attended by no less a person than King Oswiu of Northumbria (642–70). By 850 the diocesan boundaries of England reflected the territories of earlier Saxon kingdoms, going back to the seventh century, when many were converted to Christianity.[32] This would imply that by this time Church and State were closely allied.

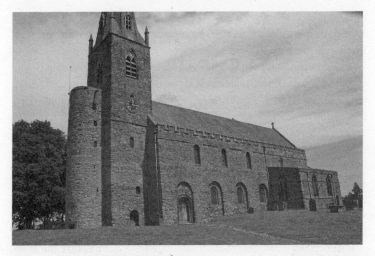

Fig. 7.11 The church of All Saints, Brixworth, just north of Northampton. This is one of the earliest complete churches in Britain. The ground plan is based on the Roman basilica, or public building. Excavation has dated its construction to the late eighth to early ninth centuries and it is still remarkably complete, the only significant alterations being the top part of the tower (fourteenth century), the addition of a two-bay south chapel (thirteenth century, *right*) and a fine Norman south doorway. The walls incorporate reused Roman building materials, presumably taken from the many structures that were still standing in the area.

The usual way of converting a pagan Saxon English kingdom to Christianity was 'top-down': first convert the king and the rest will follow. That is probably why early church boundaries so often reflect contemporary political geography. In landscape terms, elements of these boundaries will survive at many levels, from county to parish, but only documentary research will reveal the precise time and extent of such survivals.[33]

THE STABILITY OF SAXON BRITAIN

The three to four centuries prior to the Norman Conquest were crucially important to the development of Britain's communities and landscapes.

Conventional history has tended to dwell on the political and military problems of the period and this has undoubtedly affected our attitudes to it. But both those terms, 'political' and 'military', did not mean precisely the same then as they do now. For a start, the ruling élite made up a very much smaller proportion of the population than today. Secondly, most soldiers were civilians too and even the resident Viking armies were quick to set up homes and families for themselves, often forming enduring relationships with British partners. Raiding, 'rape and pillage' certainly happened, but probably not for very long. In the Norse-influenced areas of northern and western Britain, the new Scandinavian residents soon became a part of the local culture and made important and enduring contributions to it. Norse influence around the western seaways brought prosperity to these regions, leading, for example, to the construction of many new buildings, such as the numerous small churches, or keeills, on the Isle of Man. But these important influences are not of historical interest alone: it was the Norse who ultimately bequeathed Parliamentary democracy to the Isle of Man by way of the Tynwald.

I suspect that if one were, say, an elderly farm worker in later Saxon times one would not look back on one's life with horror or regret. Had one been living in the first half of the ninth century there would certainly have been tales of raids and pillage, and if one lived in a coastal area, then life could have been dangerous. But for most rural people, even in the earlier ninth century, life was getting better and the population was steadily rising. If conditions really were so tough, how on earth would people have had the time, or inclination, to think about the processes of nucleation and manorialization that were then transforming so many rural landscapes of central-southern Britain?

The rise of towns and the increases in trade – and with it of urban prosperity – are a feature of late Saxon England. Again, trade can only thrive, as any businessman, at any period of history will tell you, in stable economic conditions. Another indication of stability is the growth of the Church and of the early and very powerful Benedictine abbeys. These new institutions conferred considerable economic benefits on the region and on the people who worked on their large estates.

All these factors suggest that later Saxon Britain was actually a place of growing prosperity, where life for ordinary men and women was steadily improving, despite the undoubted political and military problems of the age. Ironically, the proof of this can be found in what is possibly the most important historical document in British history: Domesday Book. Very often Domesday is treated as a statement of the wealth of Norman England, but it was compiled from, among other sources, existing tax and other revenue records created by earlier administrations. It is a very complex document that requires careful interpretation, and its compilation, like that of most large government surveys, was far from consistent, as we shall see when we come to examine the establishment of Norman deer parks. And besides, it was completed in 1086, just twenty years after the Conquest – hardly time to transform a nation's entire economy. Domesday should rather be treated as an account of the great accumulated wealth of Saxon England. A total of some 13,000 *vills* is recorded in the five volumes of this massive report. Although the word *vill* is the origin of 'village', in Domesday it refers to an area of land rather than a settlement, which could sometimes contain several small hamlets. Even though the names of 92 per cent of the Saxon *thegns* and landowners had already been replaced by those of newly arrived Normans, the people who managed the estates and continued to do the work were folk who had created and maintained them: the native-born Saxons, British and Anglo-Scandinavians.

8

Steady Growth: Landscapes Before the Black Death (1066–1350)

On Monday, 25 September 1066, King Harold II of England defeated the army of the Norwegian King Harald Hardrada at the Battle of Stamford Bridge, in Yorkshire. Eighteen days later he and his tired foot soldiers arrived at Hastings on a less than auspicious date, Friday, 13 October. Battle was joined at nine o'clock the following morning. By the late evening the victorious Duke William of Normandy left the battlefield at Hastings and rode north towards London. He was then crowned as King William I, on Christmas Day, in Westminster Abbey. From this point on British history was to acquire dates and new names at an ever-increasing pace.

Major historical events themselves make little impression on the lives of most ordinary people. Even today, the horrors of a foreign war usually only find indirect expression at home, for example in what we pay to fill our cars with petrol. Trade may slow down, but the landscape remains untouched. It is not until a succession of wars gives rise to a global recession that we are likely to see prosperous rural commuter houses being abandoned and new prosperity returning to the fields and growing-grounds of food-producers, freed from the competition of cheap, long-distance imports. Such developments would indeed make an impression on the British landscape, but even today, in a world where change is so rapid, the luxurious houses would gradually be abandoned and the farms would only slowly improve. So the consequences of a series of events rather than any single event are what becomes archaeologically visible. That is why this book is about the processes that formed the landscape, rather than the individual incidents of history that might have triggered them. It is also wise not to attempt the linking of known historical events with archaeological observations.[1]

These rules even apply to events as monumentally important as the Norman Conquest.

Military structures are frequently linked to particular wars or battles and very often this diverts attention away from their real, long-term importance. We have already seen that Hadrian's Wall was not simply thrust across a barren landscape to defend the northern boundary of the Roman Empire against wild and woolly northern tribesmen. It was far more complex than that, and while it was undoubtedly a potent military installation, it was also a strong symbol of power and authority. The same can be said of the castles that began to appear with increasing frequency after the Norman Conquest. The best way to understand the social role of castles in the early Middle Ages is to examine their individual landscape setting with very great care; there is much we can still learn just by looking.

CASTLES IN THE LANDSCAPE

William the Conqueror was that rare combination, a ruthless military commander and a fine peacetime ruler. He did what a successful invader must often do: he replaced the existing aristocracy with his own men, on whose loyalty he could count. Domesday Book records that just twenty years after the Conquest, a mere 8 per cent of land in England was owned by people with English names. The rest belonged to Normans, the Crown or the Church, and of these the Crown had the largest single estate, amounting to about 17 per cent of the available land. This one action ensured that he and his immediate successors could govern effectively. It was ruthless, but in William's defence one could argue that without it there would have been anarchy, and besides, it did only affect a very small section of society. William and his new Norman earls built hundreds of castles.

The Normans built castles to show who was in control and it made sense to do this in places where people could see them. That is why most early Norman castles were built in towns. Initially, many would have been made from earth and timber, but soon they were replaced with stone. Most castles survive in the landscape as the earthen mounds and ditches of motte and bailey castles, where the motte was a steep

Fig. 8.1 A map showing the distribution of early Norman castles in England. The Norman policy of establishing their first castles in urban centres is apparent.

mound, on which stood a stout wooden tower or keep, and the bailey was an outer courtyard, defended with either an earthen rampart and a timber palisade, or, later, stone walls. Such castles, generally constructed in the early Middle Ages, were sometimes strengthened in the thirteenth and fourteenth centuries by the addition of a stone keep. A huge number survive to this day simply as mounds of greater or lesser size. Sometimes the earthworks of the outer bailey can also be

1. The valley of the Moffat Water looking south-west from the Mare's Tail Falls, Dumfries and Galloway, in the western Scottish borders, shows the distinctive U-shaped profile of a valley glaciated in the Ice Age.

2. Castlerigg stone circle, Cumbria. Probably built around 3000 BC, the positions of the taller stones suggest it was aligned on the equinoctial sunrise of spring and autumn, thereby linking it to the landscape and changing seasons.

3. The White Horse of Uffington, Oxfordshire. This galloping horse was carved in the first millennium BC. It was positioned to be appreciated from the air, which suggests it was created more for the ancestors than other human communities.

4. The western gateway of Maiden Castle, from the air. The interior of the hillfort is just above the top of this picture. The ramparts' complexity is so extreme that it suggests motives other than practical defence alone.

5. There are almost no 'wild' woods left. Graveley Howe, near Hitchin, Hertfordshire, first appears on a map of 1633 and was ancient then. However, it shows much evidence of management (for example coppicing) and is best seen as part of the farmed landscape.

6. The pasture field in the middle distance contains the slight earthworks of the deserted medieval village of Wharram Percy. Note how the alignment of the ditches and banks in the village bears no relationship to the existing hedge lines, which were laid out during enclosure in the late eighteenth and early nineteenth centuries.

7. The ruined rear of Old Wardour Castle (*left*) and the later (1774) Banqueting House seen from the south side of the late-eighteenth-century ornamental lake. The picturesque ruins of the castle formed an important feature of the later park.

8. Tattershall Castle, near Coningsby, Lincolnshire. One of the finest early brick buildings in Britain, this four-storey tower was built for Lord Ralph Cromwell (1393–1456), Lord Treasurer to Henry VI.

seen. A particularly fine example of a motte and bailey castle can be visited in permanent pasture in the Nottinghamshire village of Laxton, famous today for the survival of its Open Fields.

Where stone or brick castles and fortifications survive, they often tend to dominate the landscape because they are generally sited in the most unapproachable and spectacular locations. This is especially true of the many urban and rural castles constructed in the later eleventh century. These were plainly intended to remind people in no uncertain terms that there was now a new regime in control. Inevitably, we tend to think about castles like military historians, as places to be attacked. Consequently we analyse how they were defended and how they could have been taken. But there is rather more to castles than this. Like towns, each castle is different, but certain general trends have emerged.

One important role of a castle was to exert the authority of a ruling élite over the populace of a particular area or region, and in this respect they probably echo the hillforts of prehistoric times. Indeed the spectacular castle at Bamburgh in Northumberland, built on a coastal spur, was positioned on top of a much earlier Iron Age promontory fort, which was probably associated with the Votadini tribal kingdom whose rulers also constructed Yeavering Bell in the Bronze Age. Unlike Yeavering, however, Bamburgh survived into the Middle Ages, when it became an important royal castle. Bamburgh looks spectacular atop its rocky bluffs, when viewed from the beach or from sea, but most people living around it would have seen it from inland, where it also dominates the landscape (which in this instance was highly fertile agricultural land). In many respects this landward aspect could be more important than its frequently illustrated seaward approaches.

Doubtless because of their prominence and durable construction, castles have exerted a long-term influence on the landscape, but it is interesting to note that in areas like the Scottish Borders, where conflict was endemic, few great castles or town walls were ever constructed. Berwick-on-Tweed is the sole exception. In the three centuries prior to its capture by English forces in 1482 Berwick changed hands no fewer than fourteen times.[2] After that it became a potent symbol of English power in the north and money was lavished on the town defences, probably the finest examples of Tudor military architecture in Britain.

So unless they were prepared to spend vast sums of money (that they did not have), townsfolk learnt to retreat and to rebuild, as we shall see at places like Dunbar and Dumbarton, where the towns grew up close to fortified prominent rocks. Castles like Bamburgh were replaced by fortified tower houses where the public expression of authority was rather more muted. The great Edwardian castles of the Welsh Marches were only constructed when the political situation had made it relatively safe to do so.[3] Even so, their subsequent history was not always straightforward, despite their forbidding appearance and the high quality of their military architecture. Take the case of Conwy Castle, Caernarvonshire.

Conwy is one of the 'big four' (the others being Caernarvon, Harlech and Beaumaris) of Edward I's castles in Wales. Of the four, only Harlech does not have a new or colony town attached. These new towns were expected to provide income to defray some of the vast costs of Edward's hugely expensive castle-building campaign. Accordingly,

Fig. 8.2 Bamburgh Castle, Northumberland, viewed from the south across the fertile agricultural land of the coastal plain. This spectacular castle is placed on a rocky outcrop overlooking the coast and was fortified from the Iron Age and Saxon times. The earliest surviving stone building is the tall twelfth-century square keep at the centre; this is surrounded by three walled baileys.

Fig. 8.3 Conwy Castle, Caernarvonshire. The walled town and castle, founded by Edward I in 1283, as part of his Welsh campaign, overlooks and controls the best crossing place of the River Conwy. In the Middle Ages the crossing was by ferry. The first bridge, part of the western spur of Telford's great Holyhead Road, opened in 1826; this was later followed by the railway which passes the castle to the north. The northern wall of the town springs off the western castle turret (*right*); the archway for the modern road can be seen below the wall, lower left.

Edward appointed what today we would call a project manager to supervise the work. The man in question was a Frenchman from Savoy, James of St George, who served the king for more than thirty years.[4]

James saw to it that all the men were properly paid, regular hours were worked and bonuses could be earnt, where merited. Building the castles, however, was one thing. It was quite another to man and maintain them. Conwy Castle was occupied for several centuries, but only saw action on three occasions, in 1294, 1401 and during the Civil War in 1646. The attack of 1401 was extraordinary. On Good Friday (1 April) the brothers Rhys and Gwilym ap Tudor seized the castle. They achieved this with a clever subterfuge involving an undercover force and a supposed 'visiting carpenter' who killed the two men on guard duty, opened the main gates and let the undercover forces in.

After the embarrassment of having to besiege their own stronghold the English eventually had to negotiate control of Conwy from the wily ap Tudors. This incident illustrates well how even the finest, state-of-the-art military architecture could be circumvented by subtlety. It also shows that to operate properly castles had to be constantly guarded (which of course was a drain on resources), because if they did happen to fall into enemy hands, at the very least it could result in a major public relations disaster.[5]

As time passed, the need for simple military protection began to diminish. Many castles remained occupied but increasingly attention was being paid to their setting within elaborately constructed land-scapes. The approaches to a castle were considered to be particularly important and intended to impress, if not to overawe, prospective visitors. Direct access was to be avoided; instead, the visitor was taken on a circuitous route that allowed the castle to be seen from many aspects. The road leading up to Castle Acre in Norfolk provides a good (and a very early) example of the way in which views of landscape features could be manipulated to convey a number of messages that would have been fully understood by those they were intended to impress.[6] First, however, the direct route along the almost dead straight Roman road, known as Peddars Way, had to be diverted. The village of Castle Acre lies in west-central Norfolk, which was not an area afflicted by political turmoil early in the Middle Ages. Maybe this is why the early occupiers of the castle there were able to devote their efforts to matters that seem to have had more to do with competition among their peers, than siege warfare, and survival. The people at Castle Acre were the de Warenne family, who established an undefended double hall there in the 1070s, at the point where Peddars Way crossed the River Nar; both were important routes of communication.

In the later eleventh century the undefended settlement was aug-mented by a large motte and bailey Norman castle and a Cluniac priory which was established in the 1090s by William de Warenne, second Earl of Surrey. The priory took some fifty years to build and was completed in the 1140s. The baronial seat of castle and attendant priory was further augmented by the foundation of a small walled town, which never achieved the status of a borough, most probably because it was, in effect, a further outer bailey of the castle, and was not fully

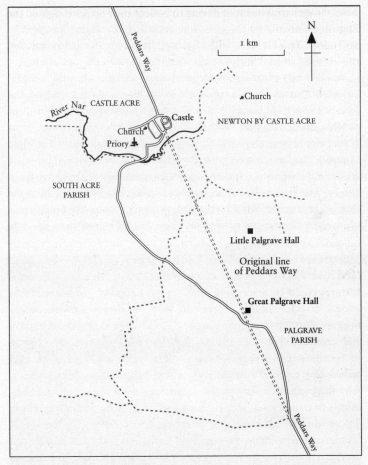

Fig. 8.4 A map showing how the straight Roman road known as Peddars Way was diverted to provide a deliberately circuitous approach to the castle at Castle Acre, Norfolk. The route was laid out in the 1140s to provide views of the newly founded Cluniac priory and the recently established Norman planned town between the priory and castle. The modern road still follows the deviated course.

independent.[7] In the 1140s this early settlement was greatly enlarged and improved. Castle Acre is often regarded as a classic example of the effect the Norman aristocracy had on the English landscape, but much of the impact was actually more subtle than defence alone.

Peddars Way provides the archaeological clue that allowed the story to be unravelled. Roman roads are by no means always straight, but Peddars Way most certainly is, and it cuts a clean swath right through central and north-west Norfolk. South of Castle Acre (where most traffic would have come from), the road was diverted from its straight course across land that we know from Domesday Book (1086) belonged to the Warenne family. It then followed a seemingly irrational route to the Priory, the new town, and thence to the castle. Coming from the north, the traveller would have had to divert around the outer castle walls and enter the new town; from there, but only from there, he could

Fig. 8.5 The straight Roman road known as Peddars Way was diverted in the 1140s to allow visitors to approach the baronial seat (or *caput*) of the Norman de Warenne family at Castle Acre, in west Norfolk. The route was designed so that the visitor's first view is of Castle Acre Priory (a Cluniac house founded by the de Warennes shortly after 1090). The sight of the priory was intended to impress visitors with the family's piety. The tower of the parish church is later (fourteenth century).

approach the castle from the south. All the evidence suggests that the diversion of the road happened as part of the extensive programme of rebuilding that we know took place in the 1140s.

If one follows the diverted road today one can still experience something of its original intention, even though the castle is now an earthwork and the field boundaries round about are very different. The intention of the de Warennes was to impress the visitor not just by the size and extent of their seat, or *caput*, and its landscape, but also with their piety. This is why the first thing one sees when approaching from the south is not the castle, but the priory. In landscape terms, this tells the visitor that the family placed God above all else. The road then dips quite sharply into a hollow, which hides the priory. Then, as we traverse the valley floor we are confronted by the Norman new town and the earthworks of the castle beyond. As the road gently begins to ascend, we are treated to the full magnificent vista of priory, town and castle. Next, the road crosses the Nar and we ascend towards the settlement, past the castle fishpond, up through the gatehouse and into the town. But by then the journey is still not complete. The daunted medieval visitor still had to negotiate the castle outer bailey gateway, cross the outer ditch, and another gatehouse before he stood before the great keep or *donjon*. Even here access was not straightforward and required him to ascend an external staircase and pass through a large entrance hall, before he was allowed to climb further stairs to meet the lord in his public apartments.

Similar circuitous routes may have been followed by people approaching certain Iron Age hillforts, such as Maiden Castle. The elaboration of the many ramparts of Maiden Castle was probably associated with the dominance of a particular tribe within an emerging tribal confederation or chiefdom. Something broadly similar might have been happening at Castle Acre where the new lordly élite introduced by the Normans were competing among themselves. Just as at Maiden Castle, the competition involved display, some of it military, but not generally speaking actual conflict. The 1130s and 1140s saw much activity of this sort in Norfolk, with the construction of the Norman new town and castles at New Buckenham and Castle Rising by the D'Albini family and the building of Castle Hedingham in Essex, by the newly created Earl of Oxford. It was probably this sort of baronial competition that encouraged the de Warennes to improve their seat at Castle Acre.

The 'revisionist' view which looks beyond simple defence to explain the social forces that may have motivated the construction and subsequent modification of castles can also be applied to town walls, and more particularly to the gateways through them.[8] Plainly some town walls were built with serious military defence in mind, from the very outset (one thinks here of the City of London, York, Caernarvon, Canterbury, Oxford, Perth, Edinburgh and Berwick-on-Tweed, to name a few obvious examples). But some, like Caernarvon, may have been built when the military situation had grown calmer and the new works were undertaken, like the first Norman castles in York and London, to make the point that a new regime was now in control.

There is one final group of seemingly fortified sites that cannot by

Fig. 8.6 The south range of Ightham Mote, Kent, one of the finest and best-preserved moated houses in England. Both house and moat were begun around 1325, and development continued throughout the Middle Ages and into the seventeenth century. The south range dates mostly to the fifteenth century. The half-timbered effect dates to the twentieth century, when the upper storey timbers were exposed. Throughout its life the moat was crossed by permanent bridges, which would suggest that its purpose was always more decorative than defensive.

any stretch of the imagination be classed as castles, yet they are widely distributed throughout the lowlands of England and Wales. In most instances they appear as a few humps and bumps in a field, or as a distinctive dark squarish ditch in cropmarks on aerial photographs. They are simply known as moated sites and consist of ditches dug around important houses, mostly between about 1150 and 1300.[9] Some of the largest moats would indeed have served as defence, but even these were intended to enhance the appearance of the houses they surrounded. The vast majority of the 5,000 or so moats that we know about were dug simply to impress, although they also served as a useful source of fish during the winter months when protein was harder to come by. As they were ultimately about status this may explain why they are often found surrounding, not just manors, but the houses of prosperous merchants and farmers, who were keen to climb the social ladder.

THE CHURCH AND THE LANDSCAPE IN THE MIDDLE AGES

While monastic foundations undoubtedly played a major role in the development of the landscape in the earlier Middle Ages, we should not forget that most non-monastic church buildings were massively modified or entirely rebuilt in Norman times. Norman rebuilding involved the extensive demolition of earlier Saxon structures, but the new places were themselves subjected to extensive modification in the thirteenth to fifteenth centuries in the Early English (1100–1290) and Decorated (1290–1335/50) styles of British Gothic architecture. With notable exceptions, such as Durham and Peterborough cathedrals, few large early Norman churches survive in anything approaching their original state, one of the finest being Southwell Minster, in Nottinghamshire. Very few other Norman churches can convey the impact that these vast buildings must have had on the people living around and beneath them.

Monastic foundations were becoming increasingly significant in later Saxon times, but they were to play a crucially important role in the development of the medieval landscape. Traditionally, the study of

Fig. 8.7 The west front of Southwell Minster, Nottinghamshire. This is one of the finest surviving early Norman minsters in Britain. With the exception of the large Decorated (fifteenth-century) west window, the towers, nave and transept are all Norman work, begun in 1108 and completed fifty years later.

monasteries has tended to focus on the buildings themselves. A number of these were destroyed shortly after the Dissolution, around 1538; but many have survived, either as fragments, or as larger ruins which can still be seen in both rural and urban areas of Britain. Less attention has generally been paid to the grange farms and other buildings of the extensive monastic estates. In England these estates are reckoned to have comprised up to a quarter of the nation's land.[10]

When confronted by the ruins of abbeys like Fountains, Rievaulx or Tintern one's mind naturally turns to thoughts of the countryside that they still adorn so perfectly. Many of the Cistercian houses like the three just mentioned were sited in steep-sided valleys, which frame and enhance the beauty of the ruins. As a consequence one tends to think of monasteries in terms of the rural landscape alone. In actual fact, however, monastic settlements played an important role in towns and cities from later Saxon times. After the Norman Conquest new orders soon became established in town and country alike. Then in the thirteenth century we see the arrival of the first friars belonging to the mendicant, or begging, orders, such as the Franciscans, Dominicans, Carmelites and Augustinians. The friars were supported by the population among whom they lived, so their communities were often located in towns and cities. The rise of friaries was rapid: in London alone thirteenth-century friaries were established near the Tower and west

Fig. 8.8 We tend to think that monastic estates were largely confined to rural areas alone. This map shows boroughs that were founded or acquired by monastic houses in England and Wales. The status of borough gave the town important tax and administrative advantages; it also assured independence from local manorial interference.

of Bishopsgate; the Carmelite or White Friars founded a house west of the River Fleet in 1241. The two largest houses belonged to the Franciscans, near Newgate within the City walls (1239) and the Dominicans, who built their settlement in the south-west corner of the City, in 1275. But even before the arrival of the friars many towns and cities had large monastic settlements which were sometimes linked to sister houses in the countryside. The great abbeys of Peterborough and Shaftesbury, for example, had many granges in the surrounding countryside.

The involvement of monastic houses in town life can be seen in their acquisition of borough status, which gave them important rights of self-government and exempted them from most manorial controls. In effect these monastic towns had sidestepped the ties of feudalism, which were far more strict in the centuries prior to the Black Death. It is generally reckoned that the Middle Ages saw the creation of some 600 boroughs in England, of which about 75 were either created or inherited by monastic houses.[11] Monastic communities also played a major role in shaping the medieval landscape in rural areas, where whole villages could be replanned and relocated, land drained, minerals mined and industries such as iron-making encouraged. Far from representing a retreat from the cares of daily life, the monasteries of the early Middle Ages were important catalysts of change and regional development.

Much Wenlock in Shropshire is a good example of a small monastic market town. It owed its very existence to the priory whose magnificent ruins can still be visited just a short walk from the town centre.[12] Like many other monastic houses, the monks and nuns of the Cluniac community at Much Wenlock Priory derived most of their wealth from farming and agriculture, although they also possessed a large private deer park, for which the first does were provided by Edward I in the 1290s.[13] By the time of the Dissolution the Priory is known to have owned coal mines at nearby Broseley and Little Wenlock.[14]

For most of the Middle Ages the fortunes of the town reflected those of the Priory, which was granted the right of an annual three-day fair in 1138, followed almost a century later by a formal weekly market, in 1224. Much Wenlock received its first charter in 1138/9, which among other provisions gave the town a court to rule on rent disputes with the Priory. By the mid-thirteenth century the town was beginning

Fig. 8.9 Some of the monastic buildings of Fountains Abbey, North Yorkshire (thirteenth century). Attention is usually paid to the great churches of Britain's monasteries, which were more respected by subsequent stone-robbers and tend to survive better than other buildings. Fountains Abbey included a large watermill from the very outset and this would have been worked by lay brothers, whose infirmary can be seen in the background. To the left is the West Guest House with the Infirmary Bridge, behind. A large monastery such as Fountains would have been the equivalent of a small town in terms of employment and its impact on the landscape.

to establish a separate identity, although many prosperous wool merchants would still have paid their rents to the Priory. Edward IV, in the new Charter of 1468, granted the town full borough status. This allowed for the setting-up of a corporation which gave the town a degree of independence from the direct authority of the Crown, as exercised by the royal sheriff. It also marked the final severing of direct ties to the Priory. The town enjoyed considerable prosperity in the late Middle Ages and early post-medieval period, when many of its fine timber-framed buildings were erected.

Each monastic house was much like a small corps of engineers or sappers and had a well-defined command structure; these were forces dedicated to improve their monastery and its estates, not for themselves, but to the glory of God. Whatever one might think of their motives they could not be accused of being self-serving, not, that is, until after the Black Death, when the labour market became less favourable to employers. This was when some of the rigidities of feudalism started to break down.

If one walks through a one-time monastic farm (usually known as a grange) there is little there in the fields to hint at its history, but if reference is made to old estate maps then very often the outer boundaries become apparent, preserved for example in a sinuous side to a rectangular Enclosure Movement field, or in the course of a stream, wall or ditch. Very rarely actual stone markers survive at significant points along the perimeter of the outer boundary. The monastic estate was an important and usually self-sufficient entity and the grain and other commodities it produced were stored in huge monastic barns. These are often referred to as tithe barns not wholly correctly; some monastic barns were indeed used by local communities to store their tithes (originally a tax in kind of 10 per cent, often of grain or livestock, intended for the support of the local church), but others were only used to store the produce of the monastic farm or estate. As a general rule, true tithe barns are much smaller as they stored the produce of a relatively small number of farms.

While monasteries and monastic settlements had a considerable influence on the development of rural landscapes in medieval England, and perhaps less so in Wales, their effect in Scotland has been described by a leading authority as a 'monastic revolution'.[15] Some of the finest monastic buildings are to be found in the Scottish Borders, where the ruins of the abbeys of Kelso, Jedburgh, Melrose and Dryburgh still dominate the landscape.[16]

Monasteries transformed large areas of the Scottish landscape, where improved methods of farming were introduced through their own farms, or granges, in a variety of forms. This variation probably results from the natural heterogeneity of the Scottish landscape and the different preferences of the monastic houses themselves. Many granges survive in the landscape and 192 can still be identified as such. Scottish monasteries also played a major role in instigating and encouraging new industries and this was something they continued to do even in late medieval times when, for example, they helped to develop the coastal salt trade, mainly around the Firth of Forth and the south-west.

Scottish monasteries encouraged the early development of lead-, silver-, gold- and iron-working. The lead mines of south Lanarkshire, for example, were gifted to Newbattle Abbey, Lothian, a Cistercian house founded in 1140, which possessed many granges in the area. A charter of David I (dated 1124–47) suggests that Dunfermline Abbey, Fife (a Benedictine house founded in 1128), was granted access to all the goldfields of West Fife, Kinross and Clackmannanshire; another charter of David I, favouring the same abbey, discusses the allocation of salt and iron.[17] The stone for the great churches that seemed to spring up almost miraculously in the early Middle Ages had to be quarried from somewhere. So by the eleventh century, if not earlier, industry was beginning to make a major, if unintended, impression on the British landscape.

INDUSTRIAL LANDSCAPES OF THE MIDDLE AGES

The dramatic increase in church-building in the early Middle Ages left some remarkable landscapes in its wake. Medieval industrial landscapes are quite rare. One remarkable survival from the early Middle Ages, however, is the extensive quarries for the high-quality Jurassic oolitic limestone (known as Barnack Rag) that outcrops near the village of Barnack at the northern tip of Cambridgeshire, not far from the picturesque limestone-built town of Stamford (Lincolnshire).

The best seams of Barnack Rag had been quarried away by 1500 and what remains are the abandoned collapsed pits and spoil heaps, known today as the Barnack 'Hills and Holes'.[18] Barnack Rag was used to build some of the finest churches in eastern England, including Peterborough and Ely cathedrals, Bury St Edmunds Abbey and the smaller Fenland abbeys at Crowland, Ramsey and Sawtry. Many of the churches built from Barnack Rag were Fenland monastic foundations that could readily be reached by water from Barnack. Some of these Benedictine houses, such as Peterborough, were very early foundations and the quarries were already being extensively exploited in later Saxon times. We know this because in a document of 1061, in which Earl Waltheof granted the nearby Abbey of Crowland rights to

Fig. 8.10 The 'Hills and Holes' of Barnack, Cambridgeshire. These are the remains of medieval quarrying, which ceased around 1500. Today the Hills and Holes are a National Nature Reserve covering some 22 hectares. Barnack church can be seen on the skyline; it features a short thirteenth-century spire atop a fine early eleventh-century Saxon tower.

obtain stone from Barnack, the quarry was already described as being 'well known'.[19]

Untouched after their abandonment, the quarries were colonized by rich and varied limestone flora, which includes eight species of orchids (such as man orchids, bee, fragrant and frog orchids). Similar ancient quarry landscapes are known elsewhere in Britain, including another large medieval limestone quarry just outside Stroud, in Gloucestershire. Here the quarrying of Cotswold limestone has left a similar undulating landscape that has recently been enhanced as a nature reserve for rare orchids and other plants of a natural limestone grassland – an increasingly scarce habitat in Britain.

Although stone quarries are among the most enduring industrial landscapes of the Middle Ages they are by no means unique – or even the largest. It is simply that other signs of industry are more difficult to discover, very often because more recent industrial activity has removed them. This is particularly true in the case of mines, where the sheer scale of Victorian and twentieth-century work destroyed the shallower workings of previous generations.[20] Recently a number of new sites have come to light, including an extraordinary and near-complete medieval iron-working landscape at Myers Wood, in Kirk-burton, Huddersfield, West Yorkshire, where all stages of the process of iron-production have been revealed.[21]

In the pre-railway age it made sense to smelt something as heavy as iron ore close to the spot where it was mined or collected. That is what happened at Myers Wood. The ore in question was sideritic ironstone, a Carboniferous sandstone, which occurs widely in the area and can still be collected on the surface. However, some substantial scoops in Myers Wood suggest that the iron-makers did rather more than just collect from the surface. The process of smelting iron from the sideritic ore first involved roasting it, and several ore-roasting hearths have been found. These, and the subsequent smelting furnaces were fuelled by charcoal, probably from nearby coppices, and at least one large charcoal-making mound was found on the site (the mound builds up below the bonfire or clamp where the charcoal is made).

Charcoal was the preferred fuel of medieval iron-makers and supplies of suitable wood remained plentiful until the sixteenth century, although recent research has suggested that even then sources of charcoal were by no means exhausted.[22] Ancient coppiced woods of the Kentish Wealden iron-working areas still contain a large number of hornbeam (*Carpinus betulus*) trees. Once established (and this can take ten years or more), hornbeam coppices well. It likes shady conditions and thrives in the wet. It also regenerates rapidly when cut down and provides excellent, fine-grained charcoal that burns evenly.

Local clay was used to make the Myers Wood furnaces, several of which were found, surrounded by huge heaps of reject iron slag. The final stage was the production of good metal following the smelting process. This was done in a blacksmiths' area where there was evidence for hammering and repeated heating, in the form of smithing hearths and quantities of 'hammerscale' – the small pieces of less pure iron that are detached by the blacksmith's hammer-blows.

The site was liberally strewn with large quantities of medieval pottery, which would suggest that many people were involved in the work there. The pottery can be readily dated and it would seem that the Myers Wood ironworks were in use during the eleventh, twelfth and later thirteenth centuries. It is estimated that during that time they produced no less than 1,000 tonnes of iron. There is also good evidence to suggest that the ironworks were probably under the control of the Cistercians. We know that the Cistercian monks at Byland and Rievaulx abbeys, North Yorkshire, had interests in iron-working at some of their granges. Another Cistercian abbey, that at Roche, near Maltby, in South Yorkshire, had a grange at Tymberwood whose land probably included Myers Wood. The Cistercians would certainly have possessed the expertise and distribution networks necessary for such a major enterprise.

Because charcoal was the fuel of industry, it used to be thought that coal was not mined in industrial quantities until post-medieval times.

Fig. 8.11 Two man-made mounds left by medieval salterns at Holbeach Bank, Lincolnshire (probably twelfth to fourteenth century). Recent research has shown that salt-extraction was a very important industry along the Lincolnshire and Essex coasts in the Middle Ages. Salt-laden mud was first air-dried and then transported further inland to salterns, where it was re-soaked and the concentrated brine evaporated off by heating. The discarded mud accumulated as high mounds which stand out prominently in an otherwise flat landscape.

Domestic supplies could either be obtained from shallow drift mines that followed surface exposures a short distance below ground, or from the simple bell pits like those around the Firth of Forth. However, the recent introduction of large-scale opencast mining has revealed the remains of medieval shaft mines. A shaft discovered in this way at Lount in Leicestershire was square-sectioned and lined with timber. Below the ground it gave access to a series of galleries. The shaft was dated to about 1450.[23]

Salt-extraction has left very substantial traces in the flat landscapes of the Fens and Essex. The earliest evidence for the industry is from the Bronze Age, where it seems to have been for local or domestic use only.[24] By the later Iron Age and in Roman times salt was being traded inland for considerable distances.[25] In the Middle Ages salt-extraction had grown in importance, but by this time the earlier practice of heating sea water to boil off the brine had been replaced or augmented by a new technique in which salt-laden tidal mud was wind-dried.[26] Next, and when much lighter, it was transported to a salt-extraction site, or saltern, further inland, beyond the reach of the highest tides. It was then re-soaked and the concentrated brine was extracted and evaporated. The spent mud accumulated on the ground around the water supply channels and settling tanks of the saltern site. Huge amounts of mud built up in this way to create small hills, which stand out prominently in an otherwise flat coastal and estuarine landscape. In Essex, salterns are known as Red Hills, because of the burnt silts and mud that still cover the surface.[27] Many of the higher saltern mounds that occur across the Fens in Norfolk, Cambridgeshire and Lincolnshire have produced pottery dating to the twelfth to fourteenth centuries.

The remnants of other industrial or quasi-industrial landscapes of the Middle Ages have survived as large bodies of water, of which by far the best known are the Norfolk Broads. Boating on the Norfolk Broads became popular in the first half of the twentieth century and today the Broads are a major source of tourist revenue for the county. So many yachts and motor cruisers ply the Broads, rivers and channels that interconnect them that in summertime it is impossible to appreciate their size and grandeur. However, one of the smaller Broads, that at Ranworth, has long been kept free of pleasure craft and is now a nature

Fig. 8.12 A view near Ranworth Broad, Norfolk. The Norfolk Broads were created when huge pits, dug to extract peat in medieval times, were flooded.

reserve of open water surrounded by large areas of reed beds and alder carr woodland.

Today the Broads look as if they have been part of the landscape as long as the Lake District, but an ambitious inter-disciplinary research project published in 1960 created a considerable stir when it proved beyond doubt that the Norfolk Broads were flooded peat-extraction pits cut in the Middle Ages, between the twelfth and sixteenth centuries.[28] This was a major local industry for which there is good documentary evidence and it has been calculated that some 26 million cubic metres of peat were extracted, most being sold through the prosperous markets of Norwich.[29]

Although direct evidence for its origins in East Anglia still elude us, it seems probable that peat-digging was introduced from abroad. Many of the largest and deepest Broads (those at Ormesby, Rollesby and Filby) are in the Flegg district, which was settled in the mid-ninth century by Viking families from Denmark, where we know that peat-cutting had been an established practice since early in the Iron Age (500 BC).[30] Most of the pits were dug to a depth of about 3 metres, possibly to reach a deposit of brushwood peat that was laid down in later prehistoric times; this peat burned hotter than the more reedy peats above it.

Peat-digging in such low-lying areas was always a dangerous business, prone to sudden and catastrophic floods, one of which, in 1287, was particularly serious. The industry declined and was abandoned from the fourteenth century, in part due to rising sea levels and the onset of wetter conditions of the Little Ice Age (from about 1300).[31] The arrival of the Black Death further damaged the market for peat and made it harder to find the labour to extract it. Demand also started to fall off as trade began to develop with the colliers plying the North Sea coast from ports around the Tyne. When peat-extraction eventually ceased, many of the internal partitions that had helped to keep water at bay were broached and isolated pits were linked together by channels. From the fifteenth century the flooded Broads became an important inland fishery. After they had been allowed to flood, reed growth rapidly obscured the angular outline of the pits – and with it the clue to their origin.

FORESTS, CHASES, PARKS AND LAWNS: THE ORIGINS OF PARKLAND

One of the glories of the British landscape is the parkland through which one drives when approaching a great country house. For a long time I laboured under the delusion that these rolling acres had been the imaginative creation of great eighteenth-century landscape designers on their own, but as I researched further I realized that these men were actually drawing on a very much older ideal of aristocratic landscape, whose origins lay in late Saxon and Norman times. Frequently, too, they made use of pre-existing medieval features, such as the ancient trees themselves. The key ingredients of the eighteenth-century country park are the open areas of mown or grazed grass, the large solitary trees, clumps of woodland and a stout perimeter wall. All of these were essential features of medieval hunting parks.

It is generally known that the Normans introduced the idea of specially designated royal hunting forests where the often rather harsh rules of forest law, mostly concerned with the preservation of the king's deer, applied.[32] There is now some evidence that the Saxon kings also had hunting forests, in areas such as the New Forest, which subsequently became the first of the Norman royal forests, but these were more informal arrangements. The fact remains that the institution of the royal hunting forest was a Norman introduction. The new forests, however, were only part of the picture.

Private hunting parks had been in existence in Saxon times, but they became very much more common after the Conquest. Great nobles were permitted by the Crown to run their own large hunting forests, known as chases, which were not allowed to be controlled by forest law, with the sole exception of the chases owned by the dukes of Lancaster. There were twenty-six chases in medieval times. Today chases are largely remembered in place-names, such as Cranborne Chase (Dorset) and Hatfield Chase (Yorkshire). Forests and chases can some-times be confusing: Hatfield Chase should not be muddled with Hatfield Forest in Essex (not Hertfordshire).[33]

It might be supposed that royal forests were only sited in places such as ancient forests, where game was naturally plentiful, but as so often happens in history such simple practical explanations fall wide of the mark. Yes, the killing of game for meat was an important part of the royal hunt, but in Norman times, as today, such social gatherings of the rich and powerful could serve important political ends. It is like a modern prime minister taking a visiting head of state for a weekend's shooting at Chequers. Accordingly, royal hunting forests were sited in places that were convenient for the king to visit as he moved between his various palaces, estates and manors. Sometimes, as in the case of Colchester, towns and villages could be located within the bounds of a royal forest. The area of royal forests could also include land owned by private individuals and it did not necessarily have to include trees at all. By 1216 only 80 of the 143 royal forests were actually wooded.[34]

Forest law existed to protect the king's deer, which remained his property even if they were hunted across other landowners' estates; it was bitterly resented by the many people, both great and lowly, affected by it. It was primarily intended to conserve deer but, although harsh, its penalties did not include mutilation, as is sometimes believed, although dogs could be mutilated to prevent them hunting, unless their owners paid a fine. Fines were an important source of income to the

Crown and to private landowners in medieval times and they were widely regarded not so much as a punishment as a form of taxation – a not very subtle 'stealth tax'. The royal forests provided the Crown with other sources of income, too. Land could be rented out to graziers in the summer and the trees could be pollarded to provide the raw material for furniture, gates and hurdles. Pollarding, where the tree is cut back about 3 to 4 metres above the ground was preferred to coppicing (where the tree is cut back at ground level) because deer are adept at eating off the young shoots in springtime. Another important source of revenue, especially in the thirteenth and fourteenth centuries, both for the Crown and private landowners, was the selling-off of small tracts of forest for farming, a practice known as assarting.

Domesday records some 25 royal forests, but that number had increased to 150 by the time of Magna Carta (1216). The area controlled by forest law could be very much larger than the actual size of the forests themselves. Thus in the thirteenth century theoretically the whole of Essex was a forest, whereas in actual fact the county contained just six, albeit substantial, royal hunting grounds, the largest of which, Waltham (which survives today as Epping Forest), covered some 24,000 hectares, but again, that was its administrative area rather than its true extent. Modern Epping Forest is a tenth the size of its medieval predecessor.[35] The royal forests became less important in Tudor times and forest law was abolished after the English Civil War of the mid-seventeenth century. With very few exceptions, such as the New Forest and Epping and Sherwood forests, the last of the many forests disappeared during the Enclosure Movement of the eighteenth and nineteenth centuries.

Although most attention has been paid to the great royal forests, there were many private deer parks in existence in later Saxon times. Domesday lists just 37 hunting parks, but this is almost certainly a gross underestimate. Another term, roughly translated as 'deer enclosure' (Latin *haia* or *haiae*) is also used, and 109 of these are recorded for Cheshire alone.[36] To complicate matters, the Domesday survey was undertaken by assessors who worked in seven circuits, from which the completed returns were received. Bearing in mind that the possession of something as grand as a deer park (*parcus*) might be seen as an asset that a landowner, especially a Saxon one, might not want the Crown to discover, it would make sense to record it as something less ostentatious. Most of the deer enclosures recorded in Domesday probably predate the Norman Conquest. There was, however, a difference between Norman deer parks and earlier deer enclosures, many of which were emparked after the Conquest. Not only did this process require permission from the Crown, but it also involved the construction of a substantial external boundary.

The form of deer parks varied widely, but the majority were oval and their boundaries rarely included sharp corners, thereby encouraging a long chase without the quarry becoming trapped. They were laid out with areas of woodland, but also with large tracts of open country, known as *launds* (later 'lawns'), where the deer could be hunted by greater numbers of people – and at greater speed than within woodland. The layout of these open runs was carefully planned and sometimes resembled that of a golf course, with lawns leading up to the green.

Traditionally, deer parks have been seen as status symbols alone and, as such, pointless in practical terms. More recently, however, a study has shown that they were of considerable importance to the national and local economy.[37] Venison was highly regarded in the Middle Ages and large quantities were eaten not just by the royal family and at state ceremonies but by nobility, gentry and other prosperous citizens. The medieval Crown, for example, received an average of 607 deer carcasses a year from royal estates. Indeed, the rush to set up new deer parks in the twelfth and thirteenth centuries was as much to do with securing supplies of venison as it was to do with courtly sport, and it could be argued that these might be seen as deer farms, and their keepers as farmers. Deer parks continued to be set up in northern England well into later medieval times and survived there rather longer than their southern and Midlands counterparts. In the post-medieval period, when deer parks fell out of fashion, the primarily arable Open Field system had become far less important and food supply chains generally were better organized, and often along regional lines.

Roe and red deer are the two native breeds. Fallow deer were introduced into Britain by the Normans, but did not become popular until the thirteenth century. Roe deer seem to have been preferred. All deer, but especially fallow, are capable of jumping over very high obstacles, which is why both private deer parks and forests were surrounded by large ditches, banks or walls, which were then crowned with a high stockade of posts. Sometimes newly established parks were given animals by the Crown, but not always, and in those cases wild deer had to be encouraged to find their way in. So park boundaries were often carefully sited in parts of the landscape that discouraged deer from jumping out, but did not hinder them jumping in. As plough-ing was discouraged in deer parks these boundaries have often survived very well in the landscape, especially around the edges of woodland.

ENGLISH FARMING LANDSCAPES IN THE EARLY MIDDLE AGES

Landscape historians have long recognized that the English landscape can be divided into two very general groups: 'planned' or 'ancient' (the latter sometimes referred to as 'woodland'). Planned landscapes consist of square or rectangular fields with straight edges, somewhat smaller but similarly shaped blocks of woodland, linked by generally straight roads and trackways. The roads are well laid out with regard to the fields and have wide verges, bounded by walls or hedges. The settle-ments found within 'planned' landscapes usually take the form of villages, often around a green, with perhaps a few substantial outlying farms. 'Ancient' landscapes on the other hand are less regular, with smaller fields and much woodland dispersed within and around them. Settlements resemble hamlets more than villages, they occur more frequently than in 'planned' landscapes. Sometimes too they are found in clusters running along valley sides, while the farms out in the countryside are often smaller and tend to be distributed right across the landscape.

The last chapter showed how 'planned' landscapes were originally reorganized into nucleated patterns of settlement in later Saxon times and were generally associated with the communal farming of Open Field or Champion systems. The next chapter examines how they coincide with the distribution of shrunken and deserted medieval villages. Here, we shall consider how they worked.

If the books of Domesday are Britain's greatest historical document, another has to be the sheets of the First Edition of the Ordnance Survey

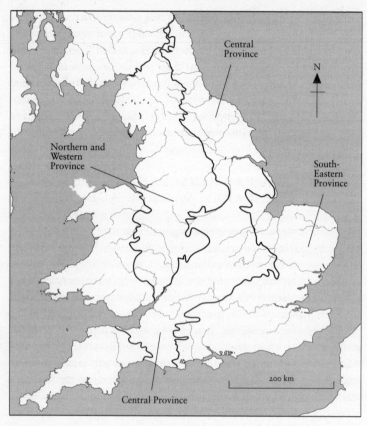

Fig. 8.13 A map showing the boundaries of the three landscape Provinces of England, as revealed in the First Edition of the Ordnance Survey 1-inch maps (published in the early nineteenth century). The Central Province is characterized by 'planned' landscapes and was mainly farmed using collective Open Field farms. The Northern/Western and South-Eastern Provinces on either side are characterized by 'ancient' or 'woodland' landscapes. In the south-west there was a mixture of 'planned' and 'ancient' landscapes.

1-inch-to-a-mile maps. The instruction was given in 1791 to the Board of Ordnance – the Defence Ministry of its day – to prepare a series of new and accurate maps as part of the preparation of defences along the south coast in case of invasion from revolutionary France. Eventually the entire country was covered, broadly working from south to north, but it took about sixty years. To give an idea of progress, Northumberland was surveyed by 1869 and everywhere south of the Humber had been mapped by 1844. Very broadly speaking the First Edition gives an accurate impression of England, especially rural England, as it had been before the full impact of the industrial expansion of the nineteenth century. In effect, these maps give an overview of the countryside that allows us to draw some rather surprising conclusions about a very much earlier period of landscape history. It all hinges upon that process of nucleation, which happened in late Saxon and Norman times, when the earlier dispersed settlement pattern was focused and centralized on a series of new or enlarged villages.

The First Edition Ordnance Survey 1-inch maps were analysed, using a series of techniques which were developed to plot the extent to which settlement patterns had either been nucleated or left dispersed. Even though the processes of nucleation had happened some nine centuries previously, their effects could still clearly be seen. As we saw at Shapwick and in rural Northamptonshire, although these events took place in later Saxon times, the map of farms and settlements has remained essentially the same ever since. The map analyses revealed three distinct zones or provinces.[38] A Central Province running from Northumberland down to the Dorset coast was flanked by a Northern and Western and a South-Eastern Province. The Central Province was characterized by nucleated settlement patterns, whereas the other two were both dispersed.

The 'planned' landscapes of England are mainly found in the Central Province.[39] This was where Open Field farming was practised in the Middle Ages. On either side of this central zone of Champion farming are two separate but distinct areas of 'ancient' or woodland landscapes. The 'ancient' or 'woodland' landscapes were generally enclosed piecemeal when the early farmers – perhaps in the Bronze Age, Iron Age or Roman times – needed land cleared of trees in which to keep livestock or grow crops.

Fig. 8.14 A view from The Tumble of the landscape north of Blaenavon, in the Brecon Beacons. This shows a typical 'ancient' landscape where fields and woods tend to be less regularly shaped. Here settlement is dispersed across the countryside; note, too, the more regular shape of the fields on the better land of the valley bottom. Very few landscapes of this sort have escaped some degree of 'rationalization' in the nineteenth or more usually in the late twentieth century when certain arable fields, such as those in the foreground, were enlarged and their sides straightened to accommodate modern farm machinery.

THE OPEN FIELD OR 'CHAMPION' LANDSCAPES OF ENGLAND

We have seen that there was a transformation of the layout of many landscapes in central and southern England in the two centuries before the arrival of the Normans. It seems to have begun in the early ninth century and was well under way in the tenth. The process involved the drawing together of far-flung farms into more centralized villages, which were often then placed under the control of a manor whose court was where disputes between different farmers could be resolved.

The new system of farming was adopted by the many new Norman aristocrats because it gave them a ready-made and efficient means of governing their new estates. So efficient was it that they extended it wherever possible and many new manors were established in Norman times. The system went on to be a considerable success, producing the food needed to feed a population that was already growing steadily in later Saxon times, and continued to increase throughout the eleventh, twelfth and thirteenth centuries.

The new system of farming was based around two to four large Open Fields in each of which individual peasant farmers held one or more strips of land. Every year the manorial courts and the farmers themselves decided what was to be grown, or not grown, throughout each of the Open Fields. Nobody could depart from these collective decisions. If they did, the manorial court would swiftly demand a hefty fine, or insist that they plough it up. These decisions were made on a rotation, to prevent the same crop being grown two years running and to restore and preserve soil fertility. There are some fields near me in south Lincolnshire where wheat has been grown continuously for ten years or more. The soil in these fields is structureless and thin. One telltale sign is the lack of molehills on such land: moles need earthworms to eat and will stay away from soil where they cannot be found. Farmers in the early Middle Ages were far too wise to behave in such a reckless fashion.

Today the best archaeological evidence for Open Field farming survives in the form of pasture fields whose undulating surface carries the distinctive traces of ridge-and-furrow. Until quite recently there were huge areas of rural counties like Leicestershire, Rutland, Buckinghamshire and Northamptonshire where the ridge-and-furrow fields of the Middle Ages still survived as prominent undulations. Usually the ridge-and-furrow was best preserved in ancient pasture that had been enclosed once the Open Fields had been abandoned (often in the sixteenth and seventeenth centuries) and then kept as sheep land.

Even as late as the 1970s, the huge scale of the Open Field landscapes could still be appreciated. Sadly, today the landscapes of ridge-and-furrow have been greatly depleted, largely thanks to the subsidy system that prevailed in the 1970s and 1980s. It seems rather odd when faced by the few surviving fragments, but those rather strange-looking areas formed part of a highly specialized and successful system, where the judicious use of livestock, fallow and crop rotation allowed some of the heaviest and most intractable soils of Midland England to be farmed profitably. By any standards, it was a major achievement, but it also had its disadvantages. In effect, most of the ordinary people in a manorial village working under the Open Field system had little or no personal freedom.

But how did the Open Field system actually operate as a farming system? Ridge-and-furrow fields were a response to heavy land and wet conditions. The ridges provided ideal growing conditions when drained by the furrows. Most ridge-and-furrow fields developed in the collective Open Field farms of the Middle Ages, but many continued to be ploughed in this way into post-medieval times. In certain upland areas with drainage problems, such as the Cheviot Hills, ridge-and-furrow was being laid out in the eighteenth century, but by then the individual strip-holdings of the old Open Fields had long been abandoned. So in this instance the ridge and the furrow were being used to provide good surface drainage on otherwise difficult arable land.

The past can survive in human behaviour just as in stone, bricks and mortar, and few places can illustrate this as well as the quiet Nottinghamshire village of Laxton. Laxton still has its Open Fields which it farms using the old system. It is the only place in Britain that operates collectively, in the way that was once standard in the medieval Champion landscapes of the Midlands; Open Fields also survive, although not in their original medieval form, in the north Devon village of Braunton.[40] Today Laxton is valued as an important historical resource and it has acquired a visitor centre and all the usual trapping of heritage celebrity. But Laxton is still a real farming village, in the sense that the voices you hear in the roads and lanes are local; the streets, even in summer, are not clogged with coaches full of tourists. So its celebrity really does just amount to one new(ish) building and a car park behind the pub.

It is now widely recognized that historic towns are best appreciated on a case-by-case basis. The same goes for rural villages.[41] Laxton was never a 'typical' medieval village because it was also the administrative centre for the royal forests of Nottinghamshire, but again, that role became far less important following the restrictions on forest law and the cutting back of forest boundaries (itself a result of the need to provide more land for a growing population) of the earlier thirteenth century.[42] Rather more typically, Laxton was part of a large pre-Conquest estate, so Domesday informs us, held by a man with a good Viking name, Tochi, son of Outi.

After its relatively brief period of administrative glory Laxton failed to develop into a town, as many other villages that had profited from the royal forests did; it even failed to acquire its own market. So in that respect it remained entirely typical of an ordinary medieval village. The village was farmed on the Open Field system throughout the Middle Ages and was partially enclosed in the 1720s and 1730s, when the East Field was taken out of the system and the meadows were enclosed.[43] However, the process was not completed, probably because local landowners could never agree among themselves. The partial enclosure helps to explain why barely a third of the parish land is actually farmed in Open Fields.

Today the three Open Fields of Laxton seem vast, but they amount to just 195 hectares, which are farmed in 164 strips held by the various farms of the village. In 1635 the Open Fields covered 767 hectares which comprised 2,280 strips.[44] Even in their diminished state the openness of the Open Fields at Laxton has to be seen to be appreciated; in wintertime these are very bleak places indeed.

Laxton is a fairly typical east Nottinghamshire parish in terms of its size and the quality of its land, which is too heavy to be considered good, but is by no means infertile if treated correctly.[45] Common land, woodland and tofts or closes (land attached to individual cottages) would have been outside the communal system, even in the Middle Ages. Today the Crown Estate is the administrative lords of the manor, but the year-to-year management is still arranged at the manorial court by the farmers themselves, who follow a three-course rotation of winter-sown wheat, followed by spring-sown crops and grass fallow.

The manorial court meets in the Dovecote Inn in late November or early December (a quiet time in the farming year) to decide on the appointment of a jury of twelve and a field foreman (now a permanent position) to inspect the fallow field in the next cycle. The field that is to remain bare (fallow) is particularly important to the running of the system. It was grazed and, while this rested the soil, livestock deposited manure which improved fertility. Abuse of the fallow was tempting in bad seasons but as it caused soil fertility to drop it had to be stopped. Today there is less livestock to graze the fallow, so hay and forage is permitted to be harvested from the fallow. The jury also checks that the field in year one (winter wheat) has had its strips correctly apportioned and marked out. The court also has the power to fine farmers who depart from what has been agreed by the court leet.

The annual court leet also meets in the Dovecote Inn a week after the manorial court and is chaired by the steward (a representative of the lord of the manor) and the bailiff. This gathering decides on the management of the Open Fields for the following season and also appoints officials and confirms the fines on individual farmers for infringements spotted during the court's tour of the Open Fields the previous week.

The best way to explore Laxton is first to visit the castle. That reminds one who was in charge, and that the entire system ultimately depended on his authority, despite the relatively democratic way that day-to-day land management decisions were made. When I first visited Laxton and walked around the castle, I fell to pondering on how landscapes so often preserve what really matters. Although we know the names of the various landowners of Laxton and only a few names of the peasant farmers who created the fields and lanes of the village, it is their work which has survived to inspire the many visitors to this very special place.

The lane that leads up to the castle branches left into Hall Lane, which runs along the back of the long, narrow fields that were the individual holdings of the cottages on the north side of the main village street. These long, thin strips of land were known as closes, and as they were outside the communal Open Field system could be farmed as the cottagers saw fit. Today some are grazed by horses, others grow vegetables and a few are down to winter wheat. Hall Lane itself is wide, and well rutted too, as it runs down to the West Field, where many farmers have their individual strips. In the Middle Ages these closes would have been used as orchards, fruit gardens and places to keep a few chickens or geese.

Even by the standards of today's intensively farmed arable landscapes these are very large fields indeed, but in the Middle Ages they would

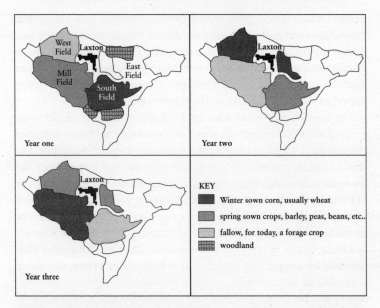

Fig. 8.15 Three maps showing the rotation of crops through the Open Fields at Laxton, Nottinghamshire. Today only the South, West and Mill Fields are part of the Open Field system (the East Field was enclosed and taken out of the system in 1903).

not have been at all unusual. Admittedly on busy days they would have been worked by many plough teams and the vast acreage would have been a scene of considerable activity. But for most of the year they would have been, quite simply the most Open Fields imaginable.

In the distance, where today modern fields reveal the gently undulating skyline, there would have been areas of grazing, scrub and rough woodland where pigs would have been turned out, and carefully managed coppice. Sometimes the rough woodland would have been temporarily enclosed and cultivated; such fields were known as brecks. Brecks were most frequently used in sandy areas where the loose, freely draining soils took many years to regain fertility. Today the sandy soils of the central Norfolk Breckland, around Thetford, raise some of the finest pigs.

The way that 'planned' and 'woodland' landscapes actually operated in the earlier Middle Ages varied from one region to another. The Champion Open Field landscapes of the English Midlands were in fact a response to both general and particular agricultural circumstances. The general circumstance was an increasing demand for agricultural produce during the times of growing prosperity from the late Saxon period up until the first half of the fourteenth century.[46]

The heavier clay landscapes of the English Midlands need to be worked with great care.[47] I know from my own experience of heavy clay-silt soils, which are not quite so sticky as those of Northampton-shire or Leicestershire, that one must be cautious. It is no good to 'seize the hour' and plough the land simply because one has the equipment or the manpower to do so. This is especially true if the land is very wet. In such conditions it is difficult to gain any traction, and if in an attempt to compensate, the plough is set high, the resulting shallow furrows quickly revert to slurry if the wet weather continues. If the wet is then followed by a sharp dry spell, as often happens in March, the entire

Fig. 8.16 This is not a view of a modern East Anglian 'grain plain' but the medieval West Open Field at Laxton, Nottinghamshire. This is what large areas of the English Midlands would have looked like in the earlier Middle Ages. The ploughed groove running away from the puddle in the foreground is the division between the holdings of two different farms.

Fig. 8.17 A view of ridge-and-furrow looking towards Billesdon church, Leicestershire. These ridges are the remnants of medieval arable strips or furlongs belonging to the Open Fields. Note the low hawthorn hedge in the foreground which was planted across the earlier ridge-and-furrow when the land was enclosed, probably in the late eighteenth or nineteenth century. In recent years huge areas of ridge-and-furrow have been destroyed by intensive agriculture, but here the heavy clay soil is better suited to the grazing of sheep.

field can develop a hard surface crust or 'pan', that germinating seeds cannot penetrate.

To be a successful arable farmer on heavy clay land, everything has to be done when the conditions are optimum. This means that sufficient labour must be brought in as soon as the land is in the right state for ploughing or seeding. On heavy land, ploughing is either done in the autumn when there is frost on the ground, or later in the spring – traditionally the best time, when some of the over-winter chill had left the soil. Winter ploughing can be disastrous if it is followed by a wet early spring. The best solution on most clay land is to plough late and fast, which in heavy soils requires very large numbers of ploughs, ploughmen and oxen. At Laxton at the time of Domesday, for example, there were no less than six plough teams available for work.[48] The Open Field system was an excellent way to achieve this sort of cooperation.

Large landowners and institutions such as the Church saw the advantages of the new system and began the process of nucleation, probably from the top down, as we saw at Shapwick, in Somerset.[49]

RURAL LANDSCAPES IN SOUTH-WEST ENGLAND

As the population continued to rise till the mid-fourteenth century, there was increasing pressure to find good arable land. In areas outside the Champion regions, where people did not have access to strips within large common fields, it was common to plough along the lower slopes of valley sides. Nobody was mad enough to plough up- or downslope, as sometimes happens today, as they knew that the result would be wholesale soil erosion, as one still may encounter in parts of East Anglia where some country lanes are regularly covered in washed-down soil after a winter storm. As time passed, the repeated ploughing gave rise to lynchets, but in the steeper slopes these were actually encouraged to form, sometimes by reinforcing the edge of the downslope. The result was a long, narrow cultivation terrace, generally known in southern Britain as a strip lynchet. These often occur in staircase-like flights, with ploughed 'treads' and unploughed steep 'risers'.[50] Strip lynchets tend to survive quite well, often in otherwise intensively farmed areas, as they occur on hills that even modern farming would tend to avoid. The most famous examples are on the slopes of Glastonbury Tor, in Somerset, but they are common elsewhere.[51]

Rural landscapes in the south-west of England are probably as diverse as any in Britain.[52] The simple distinction between 'ancient' and 'planned' fails to apply. Many of these landscapes, especially those where villages are less common, such as those in western Cornwall around Penwith, could have origins extending back to prehistoric times.[53] Others, such as the villages and fields which replaced the later prehistoric fields on Exmoor, came into existence in later Saxon times.[54] As a very general rule the 'planned' or nucleated settlement patterns, where larger villages predominate, tend to be found on flatter, lower-lying land, along river valleys and closer to the coast. A more dispersed pattern of hamlets, rather than villages, is found on hilly or upland

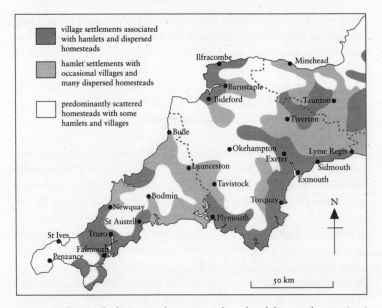

Fig. 8.18 The simple distinction between nucleated and dispersed or 'ancient' and 'planned' landscapes, evident elsewhere in Britain, fails to apply in the south-west, where an analytical technique known as 'landscape characterization' has been applied with much success. This approach has revealed a series of smaller landscapes arranged around villages, hamlets or scattered homesteads.

landscapes and a markedly separated pattern of dispersed and isolated farmsteads is found on higher and moor land.

To an easterner like myself the landscapes of the south-west seem distinctly 'foreign'. This is partly, I suppose, because the geological formations themselves, the profiles and outlines of the basic landforms, have not been softened by glacial action. But the scale of the landscape is different, too: one can be driving through a succession of small sheltered valleys and then suddenly one is on a vast open moor, as huge as anything in the Cheviots. Some aspects of the landscape seem familiar enough, but on closer inspection they are not. Take for example the 'planned' landscapes one can see around Moretonhampstead in the Dartmoor National Park. These look like standard eighteenth- or nineteenth-century Parliamentary Enclosures until one realizes that none of the field boundaries are actually straight (I shall discuss why in the next chapter). The hedges of the south-west also seem familiar until one looks at them more closely.

A visitor to Devon and Cornwall cannot fail to be impressed by the massive hedgebanks that so often confine the road into something approaching a ravine or tunnel. The hedgebanks of Devon are some-times thicker and more massive than those of Cornwall, which are often remarkably thin and tall.[55] In both counties the banks are con-structed using drystone facings and a filled rubble, or rubble and soil, core. The hedge was planted at the top and often consisted of gorse (known as furze in the region) seedlings, as this is a prickly, stock-proof plant capable of resisting periods of sustained drought. In many in-stances today the hedges have not been adequately maintained and the wall-like hedgebank survives alone. The origin, or more probably origins, of south-western hedgebanks are hard to define, but they are most probably pre-medieval, either prehistoric or early post-Roman. They continued to be constructed into the era of Parliamentary En-closure in the eighteenth and nineteenth centuries.

The purpose of a hedge – any hedge – is to retain livestock, but also (and this is often forgotten in the literature) to provide shelter. Shelter is specially needed in the spring, when wet, newly born lambs can die in a few minutes if exposed to a cold or strong wind. The stone walls below the furze hedges of the south-west would have raised the young furze seedlings out of the reach of browsing livestock and would also have provided warmth and shelter to man and beast. Few things are more pleasant than sitting against a south-facing Cornish hedgebank overlooking the sea; even on a winter's day the stones feel warm against one's back while the ever-present wind hisses angrily through the furze overhead.

Hedges, however, do more than just partition the landscape. In Britain's moist temperate climate they grow fast and thickly. If the main stem is cut down a few years after planting, numerous side-sprouts will grow up and thicken the hedge. This can also be done by deliberately 'laying' it, a process that involves half-cutting the stems low down and then bending them over. The bent-over stems are then trimmed and woven into the hedge, sometimes with the addition of short uprights; the whole structure can than be tied together with a thick 'rope' made

Fig. 8.19 Cornish hedgebanks close by the Early Christian trading settlement at Lellizzick, near Padstow, Cornwall. In this exposed location the gorse plants atop the banks have been dwarfed by persistent onshore winds. Note how two of the hedgebanks follow the curve of the turning plough, which suggests that these fields are probably medieval in date.

of twisted wattles. As time passes, hedges that have been planted with just one or two species – say hawthorn and sloe – slowly accumulate others, usually by way of birds' droppings. Elder is often the first of these colonizers.[56]

There are many regional styles of hedge-laying, but the one most commonly seen in Britain today is the Midland style, originating in parts of Leicester and Rutland, where laid hedges proved capable of standing up to a hunt in full cry. Incidentally, nobody knows when hedge-laying began, but we have already seen that a form of laying or trimming was being practised in the early Bronze Age at Fengate and I can seen no reason at all why it may not have been one of the many skills that were introduced with the arrival of farming in the fifth millennium BC. We do know that certain Neolithic long barrows were partitioned with woven wattlework – a technique that could readily be adapted to the laying of hedges.[57]

RURAL LANDSCAPES IN SCOTLAND
AND WALES

The diversity visible in the south-west of England also applies on a somewhat larger scale in Scotland. As we saw when we discussed the Reaves of Bronze Age Dartmoor, one should beware of assuming that the landscapes of upland areas were created by people living on the very edge of economic sustainability. Prehistoric communities played a crucially important role in shaping medieval landscapes. During the Iron Age and early historic period in the Western Isles, seemingly remote places often had surprisingly good communications and were able to maintain substantial and prosperous populations. Problems did occur, just as they did further south, when either disease struck or increased rainfall led to the spread of blanketing peats. But the impacts of other potentially disastrous situations could be hard to predict. For example, one advantage of living in the more thinly spread communities of the Highlands and Islands was that the effects of the successive waves of plague were less severe than in the Lowlands. This was because the vectors of plague, rats and lice, were more a phenomenon of the warmer southern towns and cities than of northern rural settlements.

The Scottish equivalent of the ridge-and-furrow of the English Open Field system was known as run-rigg (or run-ridge).[58] It was a form of infield-outfield farming that was based around a co-operative farm, usually under the control of a single landlord, as part of a multiple tenancy arrangement. This group of farms was known as a fermtoun or clachan in the islands and more westerly areas of Scotland. The term 'run-rigg' refers to the fact that individual farmers could be tenants of strips running throughout the infield. Tenancy arrangements differed from one area to another, but many were often renewed and redistributed annually. This effectively removed any incentive a tenant might have to improve his holding; this in turn might help to explain why the system was so readily abandoned during the 'Improvement' movement of the late eighteenth and nineteenth centuries.

In the run-rigg system the land nearest the settlement was more intensively farmed than the outfield beyond; in lowland areas this infield was kept in continuous arable production by the regular addition of manure. Various forms of crop rotation were employed, depending on the soil conditions of the farm, but often two crops of barley were followed by one of oats. Other crops included peas and rye. The land was ridged with a huge plough, towed by many oxen to produce a massive bank which could be up to 1.8 metres high, 9 metres broad and 800 metres long.[59] These vast ridges and the furrows beside them helped to shed heavy rainfall and guaranteed that even in the wettest of seasons crops grown along the higher parts of the ridges would survive. On lowland fermtouns the infield land would be separated from the outfield by a stony bank or 'head dyke' which often survives quite clearly. Beyond the outfield was the common grazing of the open moor.

In the very wettest and most poorly drained areas a system of ridged spade cultivation was employed, often in the inner outfield land. These narrow ridges still survive in many upland areas, where they are known as 'lazy beds'. In Scotland the climate became notably wetter, and bitter winters were common from around 1300, for the five centuries of the so-called Little Ice Age.[60] During this time complete crop failures and famine were not uncommon. In the Western Isles frequent storms led to many settlements in areas of machair having to be abandoned, due to massive sand-blows.

Fermtouns were dispersed across most of southern, central and eastern Scotland.[61] Despite their name they were not towns at all, let alone villages, which were not at all common in Scotland at this period. Fermtouns were, in effect, communal farms, often consisting of four to eight families living in individual longhouses – long rectangular thatched buildings of two to three rooms, in which livestock was housed at one end. Most lowland fermtouns would include an extra-long building for the communal grain barn; this usually featured double doors on opposite walls to create a good through-draught to separate the chaff from the grain during threshing. There would also be a number of smaller buildings, among which would be cottages to accommodate farm workers.

Recent detailed surveys of Perthshire have shown that much of the evidence for highland fermtouns is still remarkably well preserved.[62] Instead of having a head dyke surrounding the infield, fermtouns in

Fig. 8.20 A view of the valley at the Spittal of Glenshee, Perthshire. A recent survey has revealed a series of almost intact medieval and early post-medieval landscapes.

the glens of Perthshire were positioned along a linear head dyke which ran along the contour where the slope of the hill broke. One of the best preserved run-rigg landscapes revealed in the survey was at the Spittal of Glenshee, where the linear head dyke followed the 370-metre contour. The terraces, cultivation ridges and fermtouns on either side of this steep valley were created in the Middle Ages, but continued in use into the seventeenth and eighteenth centuries.

In the Western and Northern Isles there was continuity of settlement from at least the Neolithic, right through to modern times. In much of mainland Scotland, however, it is difficult to prove such a link and there is a conspicuous gap between the earliest fermtouns and the close of the late Iron Age or Pictish periods in the seventh and eighth centuries AD.

The Scottish Royal Commission survey revealed a new type of small medieval farm which they labelled 'Pitcarmick type' (after the site where they were first recognized). These were smaller than later fermtouns and were based on a single longhouse. Most significantly, Pitcarmick farms were not positioned along the glensides where the fermtouns were eventually located, but were close by groups of pre-historic house circles. This would suggest that they could have been transitional.

When I discussed the origins of ridge-and-furrow in England I was at pains to point out that what survives in the landscape today almost certainly had had medieval origins; but I also noted that the practice of ridge ploughing continued well after the Middle Ages and often into the eighteenth and nineteenth centuries. This applies with equal, if not greater force, to Scotland, where the damper climate favours a pattern of ploughing that encourages good surface drainage. Having the same cause, repeated ploughing in the same direction to heap up the soil, the ridges of Scottish run-rigg often exhibit the distinctive reversed-S shape, or aratral curve, seen in ridge-and-furrow strips further south. Because it was important to maintain high ridges in damp areas or poorly draining soils heavy mouldboard ploughs were used, often pulled by teams of oxen.

On most pre-industrial ploughs the ploughshare at the tip of the plough cuts through the soil, and the curved mouldboard behind it inverts the furrow, thereby burying weeds growing on the surface. It seems probable that heavy mouldboard ploughs were introduced to Scotland by new monastic landlords in the twelfth century.[63] Prior to the wetter conditions that set in after the thirteenth century, ridged fields were not needed on more freely draining sandy or gravel soils. Excavations in lighter lowland regions of Fife and Angus have revealed the boundary ditches of large rectangular fields, laid out on a regular system, but sealed beneath the later medieval ridge-and-furrow that was subsequently introduced to combat the wet.[64]

Not all medieval settlements in rural Scotland were in isolated landscapes. Many were located close by important royal or monastic sites. A fine example is the settlement at Springwood Park, which was positioned on good arable land about a kilometre south of the burgh and royal castle of Roxburgh, not far from Kelso and its famous abbey

Fig. 8.21 Scottish medieval farmers successfully exploited all good arable land. This aerial view of Wardhouse in Aberdeenshire shows how the whole of a small raised plateau was farmed by a small fermtoun, whose house-platforms and ditches can be seen immediately to the right of the two prominent trees in the foreground. The ridges of the run-rigg infield radiate from the settlement down to the stream bank. Prehistoric clearance cairns (grassed-over heaps of stones removed from fields and pasture) and house circles are visible on the rising land just beyond the medieval fermtoun. This poorer ground would have been outfield, or open grazing, in the Middle Ages.

in the Tweed Valley (Scottish Borders). Excavations revealed a terrace of farm cottages along a road which had formed part of a larger settlement near a bridge across the River Teviot, a southern tributary of the Tweed.[65] A rich collection of finds, including many datable coins and quantities of domestic pottery has showed it to have been occupied between the twelfth and fourteen centuries.

The settlement at Springwood Park began in the twelfth century with simple, separate cottages, later replaced by longhouses, which included animal accommodation. In the thirteenth century these longhouses were substantial structures, built using curved beams, known as crucks, which reached from the foot of the wall to the apex of the roof. Crucks were often, but not always, fashioned from the trunks of black poplar, a tree of open landscapes which grows in a natural curve to spill strong winds.[66]

It is not always a simple matter to establish from archaeological evidence alone whether people in the past owned, rented or leased their property, but at Springwood Park the excavators noted that the cottages were very orderly and regular buildings, which were comprehensively rearranged on two quite separate occasions. This suggests central planning and co-ordination, most probably from the Lords of Maxwell, on whose estate the settlement lay, or, alternatively, on instruction from the nearby Abbey of Kelso. It would also suggest that the occupants of the cottages were all tenants. The nearby burghs at Roxburgh and Peebles would have provided a ready market for surplus produce and might help to explain the settlement's prosperity.

The situation in rural Wales was very different from that in Scotland. Collective tenure and ownership only really caught on in south Wales,

Fig. 8.22 Excavations at Springwood Park, near Kelso in the Scottish Borders revealed the foundations of a series of terraced cottages built in the longhouse tradition that was popular in Scotland during the Middle Ages, and later. These houses had human accommodation at the uphill end, and a combined store and animal byre on the downslope, to facilitate drainage. Each unit measured 4 × 10 metres. This reconstruction by Alan Braby shows the terrace as it might have appeared in the thirteenth century.

where an Anglicized system was adopted, based around nucleated settlements and Open Fields with ridge-and-furrow. Elsewhere, freemen farmers, not bonded by feudal ties, lived in independent farmsteads, often, but not always, arranged in small groups or hamlets. In the north of Wales arable areas were farmed by such hamlets where local co-operation may have extended to the borrowing and lending of a plough-team. In the Middle Ages cattle were more important to the Welsh rural economy than sheep; they were hardy beasts, many of which were grazed on upland pastures.

One important obstacle to the development of the Welsh rural economy in the Middle Ages was the system of partible inheritance, in which both freehold and leasehold holdings had to be divided between all his sons when a farmer or landowner died. This system had two long-term consequences. First, it meant that landholdings became smaller and smaller, and less economically viable. Eventually even the most prosperous yeoman families were reduced to poverty. It also provided an incentive for those whose holdings had become too tiny to operate to look elsewhere and take in new land, often in the highest and most inhospitable wastes. Eventually, in 1542, partible inheritance was abolished by Act of Parliament.

THE GROWING DIVERSITY OF TOWNS IN THE EARLY MIDDLE AGES

The early Middle Ages witnessed the consolidation of the towns established in later Saxon times and the foundation of an important series of Norman new towns, sometimes known as 'plantations'. At the very start of the period the Domesday survey lists 112 boroughs in England, but this figure rapidly increased throughout the prosperous years of the eleventh, twelfth and thirteenth centuries; eventually the number of boroughs in medieval England and Wales was in excess of 700.[67] But by the end of the thirteenth century there were signs of economic decline and social tensions in the larger towns of England.[68]

The Normans were great builders and they constructed magnificent cathedrals, churches and castles that still adorn the landscape. Their buildings, with their characteristic rounded arches and thick walls, were certainly less graceful than some of the subsequent British Gothic styles, but I am sure they will prove more durable. If ever Britain were to be hit by a nuclear bomb, the finest building in Britain, in my view King's College Chapel, Cambridge, would be reduced to a pile of glass and limestone, but solid old Christ Church cathedral in Oxford, although built three hundred years earlier, would still be standing. So the Normans are rightly celebrated for their buildings, but were these their principal contributions to the landscape? Over the last forty years we have learnt much about Norman and Plantagenet foundations and these so-called 'plantation' towns that rapidly and radically altered the landscape of England and Wales.

The pace of change was equally fast in Scotland, where the remarkable King David I and his successors were also establishing a series of important new towns. David I (1124–53) had been brought up in the court of Henry I of England. Here he learnt much about the arts of Anglo-Norman government, which he applied with considerable skill to his native land. His reforms, sometimes called the 'Davidian revolution', brought Scotland into the mainstream of European political and economic life. They included the founding of the first burghs, such as Edinburgh, Dunfermline, Berwick, Perth, Stirling, Glasgow and St Andrews, some of which were established on earlier substantial but non-urban settlements.[69]

The Norman Conquest may not have altered the fundamentals of British life when it happened, but there can be little doubt that it affected the upper echelons of society in England and along the Welsh borders (the Marches). Most of the leading families of the land were replaced by William the Conqueror's friends and allies from Norman France. The Viking menace ended abruptly and the king was able to turn his undivided attention to government and the business of unifying his new realms. The office of the Crown in Norman England had more effective power than ever before and over a larger area of land. There can be little doubt either, that that power was often put to good, constructive use.

The period of gradual growth of both population and prosperity in the early Middle Ages gave rise to many new buildings in Britain's towns: churches, monasteries, guildhalls, castles and private houses. In the eleventh century many cathedrals were moved from more rural to urban sites. Exeter cathedral, for example, was moved from Crediton in 1050; Norwich from Thetford in 1094 and Chichester from Selsey, c. 1080. This was the era, too, when urban marketplaces were at their largest.[70] But almost as soon as they had been established, the merchants in the houses around them extended their frontages into the open space. Many stall-holders would leave their stalls in place between market days and as time passed these became more and more permanent, eventually ending up as buildings. The marketplace was also seen as a space where it was legitimate to erect structures for the benefit of the community, such as market halls, crosses and churches. The result was a steady encroachment on most urban marketplaces throughout the Middle Ages and into early post-medieval times. Some towns, such as Winchester, successfully combated this process in the marketplace itself, but the streets leading into it have a curious funnel-shaped plan, which suggests that these efforts were less successful as soon as one moved away from the open space. Most marketplaces today, where they survive, are usually half the size, or less, of their original medieval layout.

MARKETS

Markets were the main places where trading of all sorts took place, but to be successful they have to be secure and to occur regularly. Even in the Middle Ages that required regulation. This generally took the form of a grant of market or fair. Fairs were usually annual and lasted for around three days, and would attract people from over a much larger area than the markets, which in most smaller towns and larger villages were held weekly. Some of the more exotic items found in excavations, such as imported fine pottery, probably came from visiting traders at annual fairs. One can gain an impression of the scale of markets in the Middle Ages by looking at the figures for their grants. The English Crown made about 2,800 grants for new markets between 1200 and 1500, of which over half were in the period 1200–1275.[71] Towns were also valuable sources of revenue to the local lord, who would derive income from taxes levied at fairs and markets.

The more exotic items bought by the richer people at fairs had been obtained by the traders from the many river ports that thrived in the early Middle Ages. These included York, Lincoln, Norwich, Gloucester and Chester. Boston, on the Wash, was the principal importer of wine from the English possessions in Gascony (south-west France); wool exports from the town rivalled even those of London, which did not begin to dominate the distribution of inland trade until the twelfth century.

The roads and streets of the Middle Ages have had a very bad press. They are invariably seen as being rutted, pitted and generally useless, whereas we know that many, if not most, had good solid Roman foundations which excavation often shows below many layers of medieval rebuilding and repair. I can remember excavating a section across the Roman Fen Causeway and being delighted to come down on a firm layer of clean gravel, which I confidently announced to the local press was Roman. The following day I found a large piece of green-glazed medieval pottery. We did not reach the true Roman surface until a few days later. But if the roads have had a poor image, town streets in the Middle Ages are seen as narrow, running with sewage and with houses leaning dangerously overhead. The classic image is that of the Shambles in York. Incidentally the name Shambles refers to a slaughterhouse or butchers' row, and thus a street running with blood, but by the fourteenth century many smelly or unpleasant trades, such as tanning, butchers and fishmongers, had been confined to certain quarters within towns.

The image of narrow town streets probably arises from the fact that many of the timber-faced buildings in the old quarters of Britain's historic towns and cities are in fact sixteenth or seventeenth century in date and have often encroached on the original medieval street, which in the majority of cases was wide and spacious. We know, for example that a number of streets in Bristol in the early Middle Ages were 15 metres wide, and many were wider than 10.6 metres; when the Bishop of Worcester founded the new town of Stratford-upon-Avon he stipulated that the new streets should be 50 feet (15 metres) and the marketplace 90 feet (27 metres) wide. One of the best known historic streets in Britain is Broad Street Ludlow (see Fig. 9.18), which owes its width, not to the elegant Georgian buildings down the hill, but to the fine medieval houses at the top. The later builders were following the earlier street plan.

Most of the ordinary town buildings of the early Middle Ages were made of timber and wattle and have not survived. The few that have (for example the 'Jew's' or 'Norman' houses of Lincoln, Southampton, York and Bury St Edmunds) are of top-quality workmanship, and more importantly, are built of stone. They are far from typical.

TOWN WALLS

Like the fairs and markets, and for perhaps more obvious reasons, the construction of town walls also required permission from the Crown. The vast majority of urban defences in England and Wales were built, or begun, before 1300. A recent study has suggested there were some 640 towns or boroughs in England and 90 in Wales; of these 211 were defended in England, and about 55 in Wales (proportionally very much higher than in England).[72] It is hard to provide an accurate figure for the number of walled towns in Scotland, because many towns there have gatehouses, unaccompanied by walls, but the best estimate is that about 5 per cent were defended. If one compares that figure with the proportion in Wales (61 per cent) and England (33 per cent) it becomes immediately clear that walls and defences were not necessarily the result of military necessity alone.

Towns developed in Scotland later than in England, where as we have seen, the earliest *wics* came into existence in the later seventh century. The first towns to emerge in Scotland date to the early Middle Ages, are often on the sites of pre-existing settlements or other significant spots, such as Queensferry where early medieval ferries are known to have operated.[73] Many historic burghs were founded during the reign of David I, but also by his successors, who granted the new foundations special privileges. Perhaps the most important of these was the right to hold markets. The process continued throughout the Middle Ages and into the post-medieval period. Some of the new Scottish burghs, such as Edinburgh and Stirling, were positioned close by fortresses, but others, for example Lanark, Selkirk and Dunfermline, were built on undefended sites. By the Industrial Revolution most of the Scottish population was urban. The bald statistics are informative: 482 Scottish burghs were in existence prior to 1846, of which a minimum of 145 are medieval; these include 81 burghs granted by royalty.[74]

By 1135 the beginnings of a boundary zone of castles and fortified towns-to-be had already been established along the Welsh Marches, from Cardiff to Chester. Inevitably most attention is focused on these military-backed towns and castles, which were massively and magnificently reinforced in the 1270s, during Edward I's Welsh campaigns. These towns are particularly well preserved and provide us with some fascinating insights into how they were planned and built. But we should not forget that towns flourished in south Wales at this time, too: places like Monmouth, Cardiff, Abergavenny, Brecon, Carmarthen and Pembroke.

LONDON'S RISE TO PRE-EMINENCE

At the time of the Norman Conquest London was by far the largest city in Britain, although it only came to dominate English inland trade and distribution networks from about 1200. The roots of London's growing influence lay in its increasing political power and influence, a process that was given a huge impetus by William I's coronation in Westminster Abbey in 1066. Although Winchester, the capital of King Alfred's Wessex, remained the official capital until the twelfth century, London was by far the greatest and most prosperous city in England. Even at its zenith in the early twelfth century, Winchester was no bigger than Norwich. London's rapid expansion of pre-Conquest times continued into the Norman period despite the many physical obstacles of its floodplain setting. The river banks were unstable and there were huge areas of marshland. A number of small rivers, such as the Fleet, Tyburn and Walbrook ran through and close by the City. In winter these areas flooded with monotonous regularity. We tend to think that the marshes nearest to the centre of London were those of Hackney, but the low-lying area around Westminster was also very boggy, which added to the practical difficulties of constructing great buildings like Westminster Hall and Abbey. Other buildings, such as Whitehall Palace, were to experience similar problems. Across the river, the marshes

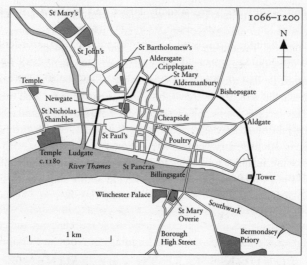

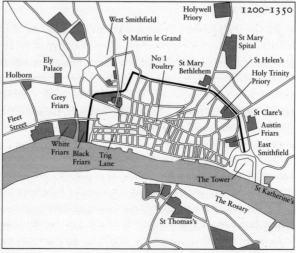

Fig. 8.23 Two maps showing the growth of London in the early Middle Ages. During the three centuries from the Norman Conquest of 1066 to the mid-fourteenth century the City of London grew and prospered. It was the City's greatest period of medieval development. During these centuries settlement spread along the riverside towards the emerging administrative and religious centre at Westminster some 3 kilometres upstream.

around Southwark were actually larger and continued to present problems for bigger stone-built buildings until recently.

The Normans introduced new continental religious orders, and monastic foundations proliferated (both within and outside the City walls) and thrived under their rule. There were also several royal palaces, including a very large one, built on low-lying reclaimed land on Thorney Island, at Westminster, 3 kilometres upstream of the City. The abbey at Westminster was also on Thorney Island and had been founded by Edward the Confessor (1005–66). The new Palace grew up around the abbey, which was consecrated in 1065, a week before Edward died. The Great Hall of the Palace was built by William II (1087–1100), who held his first court there in 1099.

After an initial battle of resistance against the invading Normans, the city prospered, like so many others, in the late eleventh and twelfth centuries.[75] The earliest domestic buildings of Norman London were closely similar to what had gone before: built from timber and wattle, they were generally positioned in areas that had already been settled. But in the eleventh century we find that increasing prosperity led to an expansion into new areas and the construction of stone churches. The first stone houses appear in the early twelfth century. Most of these, however, were only partially stone-built, the stonework being confined to the foundations and cellars. This meant that wet rot could be kept away from the wall posts. The stone had to be brought in from outside the area, so such houses were most probably built for the more successful people.

The most important innovation of Norman London was the creation of Thames Street, parallel to the river. This allowed far better access to the new docks and wharves along the Thames foreshore that were providing the trade goods that fuelled increasing prosperity. Most Londoners, however, still found their food and did their daily shopping closer to home. Many households kept pigs and poultry, and had substantial kitchen gardens. So London, like most other towns and cities of this period, still had frequent open spaces, large and small. Life in London in the early Middle Ages was by no means as cramped as is often supposed. In the Norman period markets for food and supplies had come into being and were expanding, but not on the commercial scale they were to achieve by the thirteenth century.

Southwark was London's principal suburb. Its main street was Borough High Street which linked into the road network of Kent and the south-east. It was also the site of Winchester Palace, the London base of the powerful Bishop of Winchester, in whose diocese Southwark actually lay. Southwark protected the approach to London Bridge, which was re-engineered in Norman times. This work culminated (between 1176 and 1209) in the construction, by one Peter de Cole-church, of the stone London Bridge that survived throughout the Middle Ages and into the nineteenth century.[76]

In the twelfth century London was made the capital of England.[77] No other city was equal to the task. London's population at the beginning of the century was around 20,000; a hundred years later it had doubled. After the twelfth century the pace of development in-creased. In the years 1200–1350 the rapidly rising population led to the creation of a large subsidiary network of small lanes and alleys, and by 1300 the population was around 80,000–100,000. By this time London was more than double the size of its three or four closest British rivals. The natural growth in population was aided by immigration from the countryside, towns and villages outside and around the capital. The scale of inward migration was extraordinary: throughout the twelfth and thirteenth centuries London attracted people living within a radius of about 64 kilometres of the City; by comparison, most other prosperous cities drew on a population living within about half that distance.[78]

THE FIRST GRID-BASED TOWN PLANS

Details in the layout of a townscape can reveal far more than just the minutiae of a town's history. Observant readers might have noticed that so far I have used the term 'grid-like' to describe the planned layout of streets within *wics*, *burhs* and towns. I chose the term deliberately because it described streets that were arranged more-or-less on a grid. A true, mathematically accurate grid is said to be 'orthogonal'[79] and makes use of precise right angles. Most people can eye-in an approxi-mate right angle, and the use of a long straight base-line of fixed length can aid in the layout of a grid-like street system. However, to set out an accurate right angle actually requires quite sophisticated geometry. The way that orthogonal geometry was introduced to British townscapes tells us much about the acquisition of knowledge in earlier medieval times.[80]

The knowledge behind the mathematical formulae needed to lay out true grid plans originated in the Islamic world, from whence it found its way into monasteries around the Mediterranean.[81] The concept then spread within learned circles in northern Europe; the key institution there being the cathedral at Liège, in modern Belgium, where a number of scholars and clerics were trained. Their training was wide and included geometry, astronomy, astrology and medicine. In the eleventh century some of these young men were appointed to clerical positions in England, where they spread their learning. One of the English clerics who acquired

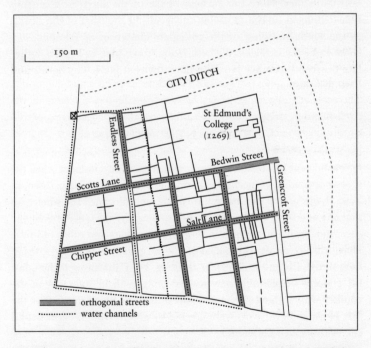

Fig. 8.24 Plan of part of the St Edmund's district of Salisbury, Wiltshire, showing layout of streets using orthogonal, or right-angled, geometry (*shaded*). The streets south-west of St Edmund's College were laid out in the 1260s.

the new knowledge was the father of Adelard of Bath, whose son was to become one of the greatest scholars of the twelfth century and responsible for the rediscovery of Euclidean geometry (without which most subsequent science would have been impossible).[82]

Initially, these specialized mathematics were only used by high-status institutions, possibly as a rather erudite symbol of their stature. One of these was the abbey at Bury St Edmunds, in Suffolk, whose library possessed many early books on mathematics. It has been suggested that it is no accident therefore that the mid-eleventh-century development of the town west of the abbey had a grid-like layout, but most significantly the arrangement of its two principal axes, Churchgate and Whiting streets, is truly orthogonal.[83]

Bury St Edmunds aside, the first orthogonal town plan in Britain is in Salisbury. Here the earliest phase of the thirteenth-century redevelopment (in the 1220s) is only grid-like, but that of the 1260s, to the south and west of the collegiate church of St Edmund, can claim to be the earliest truly orthogonal town plan in Britain. Other late-thirteenth-century Norman new towns at New Winchelsea and Flint followed suit.

NORMAN NEW TOWNS

I grew up near Stevenage and well remember the excitement when the Queen opened the Queensway shopping centre at the New Town, in 1962. I was one of the many thousands who thronged the square on that day and I was wildly excited not so much by the Queen, as by the sheer modernity of it all. Even though my parents and other old-time Hertfordshire residents moaned about the ghastly expanding town in their midst, I found it all rather thrilling. I did not know it then, but the concept of planting 'new towns' on 'greenfield' sites out in the country was nothing new and I still sometimes wonder whether the first Norman new towns were greeted by groans from older folk and cheers from their children.

Plans for the second wave of post-war New Towns emerged in the mid-1960s and the existence of a far earlier set of Norman new towns came to public attention in 1967 when they were deliberately described as such. Maybe this is why an archaeological discovery was to have such a major impact on cultural life at the time. Away went the image of ramshackle medieval urban sprawl, to be replaced by a new vision of well-planned and large-scale urban development.[84] Sadly, this new vision failed to take hold and the old view still grips the popular imagination.

A total of 172 Norman new towns are known in England, 84 in Wales and 124 in Edward I's territories in France (Gascony). Edward I (1272–1307) was the last great instigator of new towns. He was a gifted ruler and realized the importance of delegated authority. In January 1297 Edward summoned a colloquium – today we would call it a conference – in Harwich to discuss 'how best to lay out the streets, buildings and defences of a newly created medieval town, and how best to devise its form of government'.[85] By this stage Edward and his three principal town-planners had already founded many new towns, but they still felt it necessary to pool their experiences and have an open discussion. In effect, the colloquium was a parliament convened to debate the single topic of town-planning.

Although a handful of English and Welsh 'new towns' predate the Conquest, the vast majority are Norman, dating from the late eleventh to early fourteenth centuries. They were well laid out and their strategic siting was also carefully considered. Good communications were essential to supply their markets, and the design of their perimeter defences was also important. These considerations were crucial in north and central Wales, where castles and fortified towns were positioned as part of a network, in a manner reminiscent of the earlier Saxon *burhs*. Some, such as Edward's great foundations of 1283 at Harlech, Caernarvon and Conwy, were powerful symbols of royal authority.

The north Welsh 'new towns' were indeed symbols of Edward's authority, but their gridded layouts should not necessarily be used to support such interpretation. In other words, the layout was not the work of the king. If one examines the street plans of Edward's new towns in north Wales one finds that towns which are known to have been laid out at the same time do not share identical or indeed similar street layouts. On the other hand, towns laid out after long intervals have plans that are nearly identical (the plans of Conwy and Beaumaris,

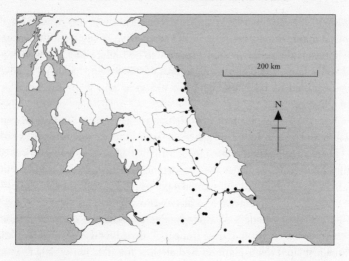

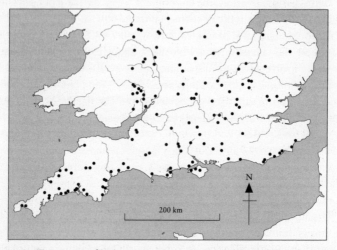

Fig. 8.25 Two maps of Norman 'new towns' in northern (*top*) and southern England (*bottom*). Note the greater concentration in the south. Large numbers (172 in England and 84 in Wales) of towns were 'planted' between the eleventh and early fourteenth centuries. These market towns were carefully planned and their locations were selected to exploit routes of communication by road and river.

for example, are almost perfect mirror images). This suggests that it was not the Crown that provided the expertise, nor indeed the day-to-day authority, but a permanent bureaucracy of planners, architects, masons and builders who were quite content to adapt old plans, if they seemed appropriate.[86]

The 'new towns' of the early Middle Ages were also carefully placed in less contentious areas, such as the Home Counties around London. There was hardly a main road leading out of the capital where a traveller in the late thirteenth century would not have passed through at least one planted town before he had gone 50 kilometres (they include Chelmsford, Buntingford, Royston, Baldock, Dunstable, Wokingham, Maidenhead and Reigate).[87] The plantation of ports was also a high priority, and eleventh-century examples include King's Lynn, Newcastle-upon-Tyne and Boston; later foundations included Portsmouth, Harwich, Falmouth and Liverpool. The urban geography of southern Britain was assuming a pattern we would recognize today.

However, a significant proportion of the planted towns of the early Middle Ages failed to prosper, and vanished from the map.[88] Examples include Newtown on the Isle of Wight, where a grid-like pattern of streets can still be seen, and Bretford (midway between Coventry and Rugby, in Warwickshire), which was planted at the spot where the old Roman road, the Fosse Way, forded the River Avon. Given such a location it ought to have succeeded, but failed, possibly in part due to the later construction of a bridge some distance away. The Black Death brought the plantation of medieval new towns to an end and few are known to have been founded after 1350.[89]

STATUS AND IDENTITY IN INDIVIDUAL TOWNS

The history of towns in the early Middle Ages can be very complex.[90] Many had stories that extended back to later Saxon times. Others were expanded by a succession of planted additions, such as Eynsham, in Oxfordshire, where a seemingly jumbled pattern of streets, might suggest unplanned, 'organic' growth. In actual fact, however, close analysis reveals a succession of small one-off developments, often

Fig. 8.26 The West Gate at Winchester, Hampshire, seen from inside the city. This view (mostly thirteenth century) is less martial than that from outside the walls, where the gate was substantially remodelled in the late fourteenth century to include machicolations (defended openings for pouring hot oil, etc. on attackers below) and gun ports. The walls have gone, as has a fine post-medieval inn, the Plume of Feathers, built next to the gate to the right, which was demolished in 1940. The small pedestrian gateway to the right of the main arch was inserted in 1791, destroying a two-storey porter's lodge. The porter's job was to collect tolls and close the gates at night. The road passed through the main arch until 1959 when it was diverted to the right.

affecting a single street at a time. These developments can be seen to have taken place in three or four periods of significant growth in the twelfth and thirteenth centuries. Other towns, such as Pembroke (Dyfed) and Montacute (Somerset), show similar patterns of successive development at this time.

Even the most functional military architecture was subject to embellishment and decoration later in the Middle Ages, when the need for actual protection became less pressing. Town and city walls were also important because they marked the limits of the borough and provided convenient places to levy taxes and tolls from travellers passing through the walls. Inns were often to be found close by gateways and many were also home to chapels which ministered to travellers' spiritual needs. In Winchester, for example, four of the five main gatehouses included provision for chapels. It is also possible that the positioning of some religious houses at the town or city limits was a statement of their marginal status; many gatehouses in the later Middle Ages were home to hermits. Winchester could boast a hermit's tower, built in the fourteenth century, and no less than four of London's mural towers are known to have been occupied by hermits in the thirteenth century.

The gateways into towns were very important in the Middle Ages. Many were clearly intended to impress from the very outset. The South Gate at King's Lynn, an important port of the Hanseatic League on the north coast of Norfolk, was built in 1520 with the clear intention of impressing any approaching visitor with its imposing architecture. In practice, however, it is far too tall to be defended under sustained attack. Often the outer faces of gateways were embellished with coats of arms and other indications of the town's protectors and benefactors. But they also served many practical purposes. Lepers, plague victims, beggars and other undesirables could be turned away, and it was not for nothing that the main gathering point for prostitutes and their clients was often just outside the town gates; this was also often the location of the town stocks and pillories. Given the importance of gateways it is not surprising that many examples occur without walls at all (for example, at Banbury, Beverley, Chesterfield, Glasgow, Oakham and Tewkesbury).[91]

Urban archaeologists and historical geographers have done a great deal of work on the analysis of medieval town plans and a number of important categories have been defined. But unlike villages, where greens, for example, usually remain open, these plans can be hard to appreciate in a modern townscape, where later buildings have filled most open spaces. Many Saxon *burhs* and earlier medieval castle towns, for example, have marketplaces and these can nearly always be demonstrated to have been later commercial developments, that followed on from the earlier more military phase of development. Many medieval marketplaces, incidentally, are accessed by way of streets that enter at the corners. This arrangement makes use of the natural funnelling effect of a corner, which would greatly assist any person faced with the task of driving large numbers of animals out of town. Similarly, fields laid out for livestock nearly always feature corner gateways.[92]

Marketplaces usually appear later than defences and this illustrates a theme that is to develop throughout the Middle Ages, where successful towns start to shake off their dependence on a feudal lord or the church. This process gave rise to a new class of free citizen, a burgess, who owed no binding allegiance to a manor, church or castle. As time passed, burgesses became both more numerous and more prosperous, especially in London after the Black Death.

Street plans often hold clues to a town's development, but there are no simple rules on how to interpret them. One type of street plan does not always indicate a particular origin or subsequent history. Take, for example, towns surrounding open triangular or irregular marketplaces. In many instances such settlements grew up around a great abbey, either before the Norman Conquest (for example, St Albans, Bury St Edmunds, Glastonbury, Peterborough and Ely) or after it. In other instances, however, similar layouts can happen for different reasons, as when towns grow up at the intersection of two or three pre-existing roads; good examples are Market Harborough (Leicestershire) and Alnwick (Northumberland). Boroughs would often grow up outside the walls of a castle and the street plan will reflect this, but in many instances these towns never grew to become great cities, largely because their original reason for existence had more to do with security than economics: places like Bere (Gwynedd), Old Dynevore (Dyfed), Skenfrith (Gwent) and Whitecastle (Gwent).

I have already mentioned grid-like plans when discussing Saxon *burhs* and Norman new towns, but by far the commonest layout for a medieval market town was a simple, undefended and linear plan; in other words, a settlement grew up along a pre-existing road.[93] The marketplace develops down the road with houses arranged on either side of it. But even these layouts are rarely simple, or straightforward, and are invariably modified by a number of subsequent changes. Marketplaces were sometimes established at some distance from the original settlement, and its church. In other instances powerful individuals and institutions would have roads diverted to pass through successful market towns. Typical towns with linear plans include Chipping Camden in Gloucestershire (the term Chipping means market), Thame in Oxfordshire, and Ashford in Kent. Many towns of this sort developed from the twelfth century, when defence considerations became rather less important. It is interesting that today many market towns actively discourage passing trade by constructing bypasses.

The archaeology of towns progressed rapidly in the 1970s when major excavations were mounted ahead of new developments in many town and city centres. In Scotland the sudden rash of new developments gave rise to a survey of the nation's historic burghs which has revealed a huge amount of new information.[94] The survey makes it clear that very little indeed has survived above ground of the houses of the poor, or of ordinary townspeople, during the early Middle Ages. Almost all information on this early period has come from excavation at places like Stirling and Perth, where preservation was comparable to Viking Jorvík. Indeed, some of the discoveries recalled the Viking Dig, including an intact thirteenth-century plank-built latrine seat from a single-room house of wattle-and-daub.[95] Some of the earlier burghs were built alongside citadels, as at Edinburgh and Stirling, others, such as Lanark, Dunfermline and Selkirk were placed on unprotected sites.[96] Although the towns' origins lie firmly in the Middle Ages the majority of the earlier domestic and public buildings in Scotland's historic burghs date to the seventeenth century, and later. Churches and ecclesiastical buildings associated with monastic settlements disprove this rule and a visit to the church will often provide a rough-and-ready guide to the earlier history of a given town. There are exceptions, however: the parish church at Kilsyth serviced the communal fermtouns that existed in the area prior to the creation of the burgh, in 1620.[97]

We tend to think that the landscape of Scotland is essentially rural, a scene of rolling hills, wide lochs, glens and tumbling highland streams. But towns and cities have played a crucially important role in the nation's history and evidence for this can still be seen in the landscape. The size and scale of Scottish urban development has, however, always been smaller than that south of the border; in the census of 1991, for example, the largest Scottish city, Glasgow, had a population of just 650,000 and approximately 80 per cent of the current population of 5 million live in towns. In England over 90 per cent of the population is urban.

Across most of Britain the early Middle Ages was a period of population growth and expansion, but by the start of the fourteenth century parts of the more crowded south were beginning to show signs of strain. The Church and the Crown had grown in both wealth and influence. Despite the political instability caused by the latest Viking wars in the eleventh century, towns had continued to expand and grow in economic importance; both the Crown and other landowners profited from taxes being levied at the growing number of fairs and markets. At the local level, landowners, monastic houses and manorial lords would never be able to exert greater influence on the men and women who worked on their estates. All of that, however, was about to change.

9

The Rise of the Individual:
The Black Death and Its Aftermath
(1350–1550)

Even though it happened some six and a half centuries ago, the impact of the Black Death, which arrived in Britain in 1348, can still be felt today.[1] It was to be followed by many other, lesser known, outbreaks of plague which continued until the mid-seventeenth century, when it came close to its end with the Great Plague of 1665; this in turn was followed, in London, by the Great Fire.

Almost nowhere in Britain escaped the depredations of bubonic plague, a disease spread by rats and fleas.[2] Consequently towns and cities, where these vectors occurred most frequently, suffered the worst. In rural regions the effects could also be devastating and few if any areas of Britain escaped completely, although the remoter parts of the Highlands and Islands of the north, where neither fleas nor rats thrived, fared the best.

A reliable early account of the disease in England is by the historian and chronicler Henry Knighton, writing some forty years after the first impact of the Black Death:

> After the aforesaid pestilence many buildings of all sizes in every city fell into total ruin for want of inhabitants. Likewise, many villages and hamlets were deserted, with no house remaining in them, because everyone who had lived there was dead, and indeed many of these villages were never inhabited again. In the following winter there was such a lack of workers in all areas of activity that it was thought that there had hardly ever been such a shortage before; for a man's farm animals and other livestock wandered about without a shepherd and all his possessions were left unguarded. And as a result all essentials were so expensive that something which had previously cost 1d was now worth 4d or 5d.[3]

The terrible and recurrent attacks of plague altered people's attitudes to death and the afterlife. Death itself, and with it decay and putre-faction, became a part of daily life. It became important to confront the realities and practicalities of death because one day and probably quite soon a man might have to bury his own children and then somehow survive and continue living. In more than one instance we know that men had to repeat this heartbreaking experience.[4] These are some of the reasons why late medieval memorials in churches up and

Fig. 9.1 The Black Death cemetery at East Smithfield, which stood on the outskirts of London when the mass grave was opened in 1348. The rows of graves can be clearly seen between the square concrete piers of later buildings. The graves are aligned east–west, as in a churchyard; in some places bodies were stacked five deep.

down the country display images of decaying corpses below the effigies of the people being commemorated.

The central image of the Black Death is of reeking plague pits, where carts back up and hooded figures toss further corpses to join the grotesquely gesticulating arms and legs that clutch rigidly at the air from the loathsome hole. It is a scene from Hell, but not one for which there is much archaeological evidence. Plague pits have been found, but despite the terrible conditions in which the bodies were interred, it seems to have been done with dignity. Two emergency mass grave pits were opened in East Smithfield on the outskirts of the City of London in 1348.[5] They have recently been excavated and together would have held an estimated 12,400 burials. These were by no means tossed in higgledy-piggledy, but were arranged in neat rows, as much as five bodies deep, aligned east–west, as in a normal churchyard. Many of the bodies were exhibiting signs of decay when they were buried, which might suggest that they had been taken to collection points after death or had remained in their houses until collected at some time *post mortem*. The excavators have suggested that the orderly arrangement of the cemetery implies that the collection and disposal of dead bodies was probably centrally organized, either by a guild, or more probably by the Crown. As we know that the cemetery was established in the initial year of the Black Death, these findings indicate that authorities were already prepared for the worst when the plague did finally reach Britain.

We can see the sometimes rather surprising effects of the Black Death in some of the churches of Britain. One might reasonably expect that church-building was halted during the years of plague and in a number of parishes ambitious rebuilding projects initiated in the years leading up to 1348 were brought to an abrupt halt by the arrival of plague. One of the best examples of this can be seen at the small church of St Andrews, Northborough, in the lower Welland Valley north of Peterborough. In the early Middle Ages the Delameres were the most powerful Norman family in the Northborough area. They had great ambitions and had completely rebuilt their magnificent manor, which still stands close to the church, between 1330 and 1340. Next they decided to turn their attention to the small Norman parish church of St Andrew and their ambitious plan was to convert it into one of the

Fig. 9.2 The parish church of St Andrew, Northborough, Cambridgeshire.

biggest in the county.[6] They had just finished the first part of this project, a magnificent south transept, when the Black Death struck, and the family along with their vaulting ambition were killed off. So the project remained frozen and their church survives to this day as a strangely unbalanced building with a south transept that rises above the diminutive Norman nave with its humble bellcote.[7]

One might expect projects like that at Northborough to have been abandoned when the plague struck, but in other instances the opposite seems to have happened. The best example of such contrary behaviour is the tower of St Botolph's church, Boston, universally known as the Stump, which has been described as 'the most prodigious of English parochial steeples'.[8] It is 83 metres high and was clearly positioned to dominate the river, the source of the port's great wealth. It is visible across the flat Fens and the waters of the Wash for well over ten kilometres, in all directions.

Boston is not recorded in Domesday, but by 1200 it was a major east coast trading port. This suggests it was a Norman 'new town' that had made good. It expanded rapidly throughout the thirteenth and into the fourteenth centuries, largely on the proceeds of the wool trade, which also benefited other eastern towns and cities, such as Norwich and Peterborough. The Stump was built throughout the fifteenth century, starting around 1425 and was completed about 1515. This was a time when the town's population was shrinking. Indeed, Boston's population continued to decline throughout the fifteenth century. Figures from tax returns suggest that between 1377 and 1563, the number of people living there had fallen by at least half.

The town would probably have recovered from the first attack of plague in 1349, had it not been for a succession of further outbreaks.

Fig. 9.3 The tower of St Botolph's church, Boston, known as the Stump.

As with London, Grimsby and many other east coast ports, the only way that Boston could survive was by attracting people from the surrounding region. Colchester only managed to survive the fifteenth century through immigration, suffering further waves of plague in 1412, 1420, 1426, 1433 and 1463.

One might suppose that in such desperate times the inhabitants of Boston would have better things to occupy their minds than the building of 'prodigious steeples' on the soft silts of the Wash shores. The matter is made more puzzling because we know that throughout the fifteenth century, trade passing through the port, like the human population, was in sharp decline. Despite this, the power of the town's commercial organizations, such as the Corpus Christi Gild had never been greater, and it was the guilds who saw to it that further storeys were added to the Stump as the century progressed. The tower became a symbol of what human organizations could achieve; it became an expression in stone of the stability and protection that such institutions could afford their loyal members. It was also a clear sign, which nobody in the landscape surrounding it could possibly miss, that people's thoughts had turned towards the Church in their pressing need to come to terms with mortality. Death now pervaded every aspect of their daily lives. Every time I visit Boston, which is quite often, I see the Stump, not, as a friend once suggested, a Fenman's finger poking rude defiance at the Almighty, but as a sign that, whatever the horrors might be, our love of life will always triumph over death.

THE PLAGUE YEARS AND THEIR LONG-TERM EFFECTS ON RURAL ENGLAND

The impact of the initial visitation of plague in 1348–9 was very severe. Society had just begun the process of hesitant recovery, when the first of many subsequent waves of plague struck again, in 1361.[9] The original Black Death of the mid-fourteenth century came at a time when, as we have seen, the population of Britain was at an all-time high and the economy in certain areas, such as Essex and Northamptonshire, was already showing signs of faltering. The population of Britain, and especially of England, had grown steadily from the eleventh to the thirteenth century, when it reached levels, just before the Black Death struck, that were not equalled again until the sixteenth century. The Black Death is thought to have caused the death of about 30–45 per cent of the population of England. It affected towns and cities, towns most seriously, but it was on rural areas that its impact was to be most long-lasting.

Directly after the first wave of the plague rural economies showed early signs of recovery. This was because the disease initially attacks the very young and the very old, leaving the strongest to survive. These people are able to cope – physically, at least – and things return to a sort of normality. But as the hitherto robust survivors in turn grew old, and became liable to infection, the later waves of plague took them, too. As further bouts of disease struck, there were fewer and fewer vigorous young people growing up to replace those that had been killed. The result of this was that the 'buyer's market' in labour that had dominated rural economies in the twelfth, thirteenth and early four-teenth centuries was replaced by a seller's market. Soon the ties and obligations of feudalism began to crack. If people had to work hard for their lord in return for the right to a small piece of land, and there was lots of good land going begging in the next village, it is not hard to imagine what most would have done. At the same time a smaller population meant reduced demand for the wheat, barley and other arable produce of the Champion Open Field landscapes. So rural production, as reflected in urban market statistics, fell sharply.

Northamptonshire, one of the principal Champion farming areas of the earlier Middle Ages, provides an excellent case study, not just of the impact of plague but of the consequent collapse in the market for arable produce and with it the onset of economic recession. The Open Field system of agriculture certainly worked well in the county, which had become increasingly prosperous until the start of the fourteenth century when population growth and agricultural intensi-fication seemed to have reached some form of 'glass ceiling'.[10] This was also the time when the first effects of the wetter and colder conditions of the Little Ice Age (roughly 1300–1850) began to be felt.[11] A series of famines are known to have affected Northamptonshire from 1315 to 1322 and the combination of bad weather and famine led to a brief, but sharp economic depression. A partial recovery was rocked by the first impact of the Black Death in 1348–9. Worse population decline happened in the second and third outbreaks of plague, in 1361 and 1368–9.

This succession of catastrophes led to the abandonment of the more marginal agricultural lands and a massive recession which caused many villages and small towns to shrink. Markets in Northampton and in other towns and larger villages were severely hit by the collapse, and there were to be no indications of recovery until just before the fifteenth century. The economic effects of the Black Death and subsequent waves of plague were to last well over a century.

These changes to the regional economy had a considerable effect on the landscape. Rural landscapes of fifteenth-century Northamptonshire were characterized by less intensive arable farming and a switch towards pastoral farming – especially of sheep – in the more marginal areas. As the century progressed, many Open Field parishes were enclosed for sheep pasture. Wool retained its value, whereas wheat prices fell. These transformations in the rural landscape were reflected in the larger villages and in market towns. Markets had been a distinctive

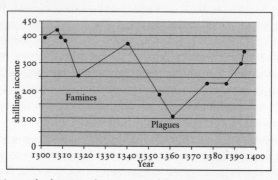

Fig. 9.4 A graph showing the income of Peterborough market between 1300 and 1400. It dropped sharply at the time of the early fourteenth-century famines, and then made a good recovery up to the mid-fourteenth century, when there was a major decline which more than doubled that of the famine years. The decline bottomed out around 1360, then recovered until 1380 to 1390, when it levelled out. In the final years of the fourteenth century it began to climb again, but not to pre-famine levels. Peterborough was a major regional centre and its market income reflects the prosperity of rural economies over a wide area of the east Midlands.

feature of larger villages in Northamptonshire prior to the Black Death, but by the fifteenth century most had closed, and trade was now concentrated in the bigger towns.

The fourteenth to sixteenth centuries saw the landscapes of the earlier Middle Ages gradually evolve into more specialized farming regions. Before the introduction of refrigeration most meat was consumed locally and, although wool continued to be traded, the mutton would probably have been consumed in the area. In other words, the gradual switch from arable to sheep and pasture also indicates the emergence of a more specialized and regionally focused economy. These emerging economies were linked to wider markets via trade in the principal market towns and cities. It was a gradual move away from the sort of socially embedded economic system of prehistoric, Roman and Saxon times, towards something that more closely resembles a free market.

Although the economic and social effects of the events of the mid-fifteenth century were most apparent in the organization of Champion landscapes, 'woodland' regions like parts of the south-west did not remain static. From the fifteenth century in many 'woodland' areas we see a process of piecemeal enclosure and rationalization of the landscape, where smaller holdings were amalgamated to form larger units. During the final centuries of the Middle Ages and into the post-medieval period this process of early, informal enclosure gathered pace.

Take the seemingly 'planned' landscape around Moretonhampstead, Devon, in the Dartmoor National Park. The fields there look at first glance like standard eighteenth- or nineteenth-century Parliamentary Enclosures, except that none of their boundaries are actually straight. In fact the landscape is not 'planned' at all. It seems logical and well laid out, but there is little by way of strategic organization, in the sense that very few fields seem to be laid off common, let alone straight boundary lines. The fields, too, are much smaller and irregular, with sinuous boundaries and roads that rarely run straight. The early enclosures were made by agreement with the manorial authorities or with neighbouring farmers. They often also involved the enclosure of common land and the piecemeal felling of areas of woodland, usually on the lower, more fertile slopes of hillsides, to form a series of bite-like fields known as 'assarts'.

Early enclosure by agreement led to the rapid abandonment of Open

Fig. 9.5 An example of an early enclosure landscape near Moretonhampstead in the Dartmoor National Park, Devon. The fields were laid out piecemeal in the later Middle Ages and in early post-medieval times. They are characteristically smaller than the later Parliamentary Enclosure fields and the hedges along their boundaries are rarely straight or parallel.

Field farming in landscapes where it was only marginally sustainable. In the west, the wetter climate of the Little Ice Age hastened the switch from arable to pasture and many of the early enclosures were by the mutual consent of larger neighbouring landowners who felled woodland and enclosed common land to provide large pastures for sheep. In the process many ordinary people lost their rights to common land and this caused much discontent, leading to peasant revolts in 1536 and 1549.[12] Writing in 1525, William Tyndale (c. 1492–1536), the translator of the Bible, expressed the common grievances: 'Let them not take in their common neither make park nor pasture, for God gave the earth unto men to inhabit and not sheep and wild deer.'[13]

The move from arable to pasture was not retrogressive; it was in part an adaptation to a wetter climate, but it was also a shift away from an earlier and rather inflexible pattern of farming not suited either to the new economic conditions or the size of the population. While some large landowners undoubtedly profited from the changes, it is equally true that many smaller one-time peasant farmers who had been held back by the rigidities of the manorial system were able to find a new economic niche to exploit. In the fifteenth century the average size of tenant farms increased and we see the rise of prosperous farmers, the 'yeoman graziers', in areas as widely separated as East Anglia and Warwickshire. This was the period when the 'woodland' sheep farmers of East Anglia provided the wealth that paid for the magnificent 'wool churches' at places like Worstead in Norfolk, or Lavenham or Long Melford in Suffolk.

Specialization in the later Middle Ages sometimes took rather bizarre turns. Most rural communities in pre-industrial Britain would have been aware that protein was harder to come by in the winter months. To help bridge this protein 'gap' the upper echelons of society hunted game, monastic communities farmed fish and many lords of the manor kept doves, sometimes very intensively. The birds in question were a domesticated form of cliff doves who liked to nest in colonies high in the cliffs. This is the habitat that the dovecotes, which were widely built right across Britain, successfully emulated. Larger dovecotes held hundreds, sometimes thousands, of doves which fed on grain left lying on the fields after harvest.

Doves also fed on seed grain and vegetable leaves, especially in the spring and winter, and were not at all popular with tenant farmers and poorer people in the parish. The indiscriminate feeding pattern could be seen as an early form of indirect local taxation. I certainly have every sympathy for the poor peasant farmer as every autumn and early winter my garden is attacked by hundreds of semi-tame pheasants and partridges, reared and released by a nearby commercial shoot. Although I am still furious, I can replace lost produce from a farm shop, but that option was not available in the Middle Ages, when winter green vegetables were all that prevented the onset of scurvy in many families.

By the end of the seventeenth century dovecotes had proliferated across Britain, some 26,000 being recorded in England alone.[14] They continued to be popular in the eighteenth and nineteenth centuries, when the droppings – the 'guano' – the birds produced was spread over the land as a very potent source of phosphate fertilizer.

Possibly the finest medieval dovecote in Britain can be found at Willington, in Bedfordshire. The village lies in the flat landscape of the Great Ouse Valley and the large dovecote was built by Sir John

Fig. 9.6 The dovecote at Willington, in the Great Ouse Valley, Bedfordshire. This two-chambered dovecot with stepped gables was constructed by John Gostwick around 1540. Dovecotes aimed to mimic the conditions preferred by the domestic doves of the time, which were related to birds that nested on cliffs.

Gostwick, a powerful man, Master of the Horse to Cardinal Wolsey, who bought the manor of Willington in 1529. Gostwick also built himself a fine house, one range of which (possibly a stable) survives nearby. Both buildings have distinctive stepped gables and were clearly intended to be a pair. Sir John died in 1545 and is buried in the village church.

A very distinctive form of specialization developed in the uplands of north-western England. Most of the higher hills of Lancashire were forested, usually for hunting, while others were rough moorland or woodland grazing. However, a surprisingly large area of upland was devoted to intensive cattle production in a series of purpose-built farms known as vaccaries (from the Latin *vacca*, a cow). The upland forests of the north-west were owned by a few large landowners who reserved their use, under forest law, for hunting. But by the thirteenth century many of the forests were grazed by other animals, including sheep and cattle. Two types of forest began to develop, 'open' forest, where access was granted to peasant farmer settlers, and 'closed' forests, dominated by specialized cattle farms which were run directly for major landlords as 'demesne' vaccaries.[15] A demesne was a farm owned and run for a particular landowner, but outside the Open Field system.

The first vaccaries were established in the thirteenth century by the Crown and by the de Lacy family and other major landowners in the uplands of east Lancashire.[16] Some monastic estates also ran their own vaccaries. The setting up of these specialized farms was carried out by their stewards, who established networks of vaccaries for each major estate. Wolves were a problem at this time in upland areas, but the casualties they inflicted were very much less than those caused by disease – which would indicate that over-stocking could have been a problem; as a general rule disease problems in livestock are made worse when animals are housed over winter. One important spin-off of the new vaccaries was the establishment of small settlements in previously unsettled upland areas. Many of the vaccaries came to be let to smaller farmers living in the settlements attached to the directly run demesne farms of the large estates.

After the Black Death the Crown and other major landowners ceased to manage their vaccaries directly, through stewards, as demesne farms, and instead leased them out at very attractive rates to anyone who would take them. Many continued to be leased or were bought out, and the population of the settlements attached to old vaccaries continued to rise into the sixteenth century, when large areas were enclosed for both grazing and arable.

DESERTED MEDIEVAL VILLAGES

It has been known for some time that many medieval villages were abandoned and never reoccupied. Their traces can still be seen in the landscape, where the most distinctive features are long-abandoned sunken lanes and the low mounds or house platforms of deserted cottages. Sometimes these are made easier to identify by clumps of stinging nettles, whose roots enjoy the phosphate-rich soils of old rubbish and manure heaps. Occasionally a church may survive on its own, surrounded by the humps and bumps of the deserted village. It has been reliably established that some 2,263 medieval English villages were abandoned and many more shrank in size. But it would be a travesty of the truth to suggest that this was directly caused by the Black Death or any other single catastrophic factor.

Many medieval villages, like Wimpole in Cambridgeshire, were abandoned in the eighteenth century when powerful local landowners decided to expand the parks around their country houses. In northern counties, like Cumbria and Northumberland, many villages had to be

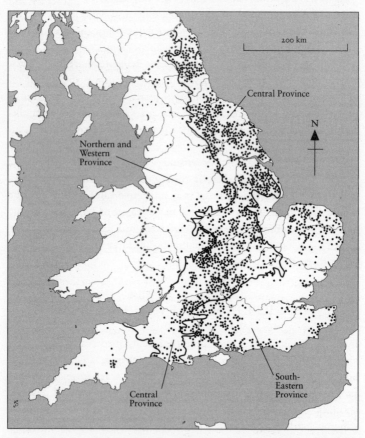

Fig. 9.7 A map showing the distribution of deserted medieval villages in England.

abandoned because of repeated raids from across the border. However, the distribution map of deserted medieval villages shows that by far the greatest numbers are found within the Central Province of England, in Champion or Open Field landscapes. Many reasons have been put forward for the abandonment or near-desertion of these villages, but it does seem likely that, being collective enterprises, they were particularly vulnerable to the devastating impacts of successive waves of plague that followed upon the Black Death in 1348.

Open Field farming was organized along feudal lines, in which the men doing most of the work were under obligations to their feudal overlords. This system, however, only functioned properly if manpower was in plentiful supply. When the labour market swung around in favour of the worker rather than the employer the sometimes harsh feudal ties became easier to break or modify. Either the disgruntled peasant farmer left the village for a borough, where such obligations no longer applied, or he negotiated with his landlord, which was the usual path. The result was that many peasant farmers quit farming altogether as they grew more prosperous, negotiating their way to larger holdings of land, albeit still within the Open Field system. Eventually these changes led to an abandonment of Open Field farming in favour of less rigid systems that were better suited to local farming conditions. The earlier process of nucleation, however, was rarely reversed. Some large farms were established outside the village core, but the original pattern of numerous small peasant farms never reappeared. Since they had already been nucleated and land-ownership rationalized, these holdings of land were also better suited to enclosure by Act of Parliament, when the time came, usually in the eighteenth and nineteenth centuries. That is why many already shrunken medieval villages received their final *coup de grace* at this time. It also helps to explain the strong coincidence of deserted medieval villages with Parliamentary Enclosures.[17]

The best-known deserted medieval village is Wharram Percy in east Yorkshire.[18] The area had been occupied since prehistoric times but the origins of the village lay in the early Saxon period, sometime in the sixth century. By late Saxon times it had become a substantial settlement. The layout of the village suggests that it was replanned in a single episode either in late Saxon times or in the early twelfth century after William the Conqueror's notorious 'harrying of the north' in 1069–70.

The decline that set in during the fourteenth century was managed and ordered. Individual peasant houses acquired larger holdings of land (or tofts) behind them and the crofts or gardens immediately surrounding the houses themselves were also enlarged in those parts of the village that did not retain earlier boundaries. By the fifteenth century the late medieval village had shrunk to half its original size and although most of its inhabitants had almost certainly had to endure personal losses through plague, the ironic fact remains that their individual prosperity and domestic circumstances had probably improved.

Wharram Percy had fallen victim to the widespread depopulation of the English Midlands of the fifteenth century. What we see is a period of population decline that ultimately led to a countryside which was better suited, not just to a somewhat smaller population, but to an economy that was developing distinctive regional identities. These were in marked contrast to the 'one-size-fits-all' approach of the Open Field or Champion landscapes. This part of Yorkshire would be known in early post-medieval times as classic 'sheep and corn' country, where sheep were run on the hills, and in areas, such as alluviated valley floors, where the otherwise light wold soils were less readily ploughed. These changes were helped by the fact that in the years after 1348 it became easier for people to move between town and country.

The houses occupied by the peasant farmers at Wharram Percy and many other villages in the north of Britain were of the longhouse type. These houses were self-contained and rather frugal. Initially they were probably intended to make use of the heat given off by the livestock that were housed next door to the farmer's family. The longhouse was a common form of rural dwelling in the north of England in the Middle Ages, but they were built elsewhere too, for example in Herefordshire and more frequently in Devon and Cornwall. They also occur in Norse areas, such as the Orkneys, where their origins probably lie in the long, boat-shaped buildings of Viking times. They can still be found in certain landscapes of northern England, where they have evolved into various regional forms, such as the combined house-and-barn so-called 'laithe' houses which can still be seen in large numbers in the Yorkshire Dales.

Some have even been incorporated into urban street frontages as towns in the eighteenth and nineteenth centuries, such as Kirkby Moorside on the edge of the North Yorkshire Moors, expanded into the farmland surrounding them.

Fig. 9.8 A drawing by Peter Dunn showing the interior of a longhouse at Wharram Percy, North Yorkshire, as it might have appeared in the Middle Ages. The roof is supported on floor-to-apex curved beams, known as crucks. The house was entered by doorways in opposite sides of the long walls, just off the centre. It was occupied by the farmer's family and their livestock. The two parts of the building would have been separated by a screen or by stout hurdles forming a cross-passage.

CASTLES IN THE LANDSCAPE OF THE LATER MIDDLE AGES

The later Middle Ages, from about 1350 to 1550, witnessed the construction of a large number of new buildings and the extensive modification of others, especially parish churches and cathedrals.[19] In terms of church architecture these were the years of the Perpendicular style of British Gothic architecture, exemplified by such magnificent buildings as St George's Chapel, Windsor, and King's College Chapel, Cambridge. The era also saw the construction of many new stone bridges and of castles which often feature extensive and quite luxurious domestic accommodation.

After the Black Death the continuing debate about the role of castles becomes harder to sustain. By this time defence had ceased to be an objective in its own right. This partly reflects the simple fact that there were fewer hungry mouths to feed, but following the political turbulence of the later fourteenth century and wars with France, the central authority of the Crown had grown and with it came a measure of stability, despite the Wars of the Roses (1455–87), when the periods of civil conflict were in actual fact very short-lived. We should not forget either that it was in the interests of the subsequent Tudor monarchs (and their historians, and playwrights such as Shakespeare) to portray the later fifteenth century as cruelly bloodstained – if only to justify their seizure of the throne. But even if defence pure and simple had slipped as a priority in its own right, many new castles and defended houses built after 1350 still retained a martial air and a number would have been perfectly capable of active defence.

One of the finest examples of these, Old Wardour Castle, is still to be seen in rural southern Wiltshire.[20] The castle's hexagonal layout around a deep central courtyard was, and is, most remarkable. It still looks splendid from its front to the north, but it is not until one passes around to its southern side that one realizes that it was demolished by gunpowder, during an attack in the English Civil War, in the year 1644 – at which point it was abandoned. So, despite the fact that the castle had large windows and sharp corners (able to be undermined), its walls were sufficiently strong to allow it to be defended – and this at a time when new fortifications were being built close to the ground and embanked with earth to resist heavy cannon shot. (We shall return to see what happened to the ruins of Old Wardour after the Civil War in the next chapter.)

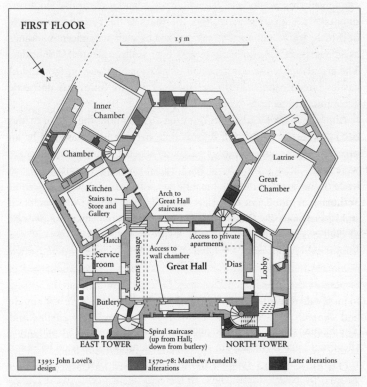

Fig. 9.9   A ground plan of Old Wardour Castle, Wiltshire, at first floor level. The hexagonal plan was intended to deflect incoming fire and the walls are remarkably thick. The windows on the other hand are large and the building clearly also had an important domestic role, which became increasingly important during the fifteenth and sixteenth centuries. Ironically, it received its first concerted attacks during the English Civil War (1642–8), when the back of the building was undermined and blown up by gunpowder (outline in dashed lines) in 1644.

Fig. 9.10 The front of Old Wardour Castle, Wiltshire, showing the East and North Towers (*left and right*). The Great Hall is behind the central recess. Built in the 1390s for the rich Lovel family, the castle was probably designed by William of Wynford, one of a select group of highly skilled mason/architects from the circle around Richard II. The court of Richard and his queen, Isabella, daughter of the French king, favoured French style, which probably provided the inspiration for this remarkably sophisticated building. Today it hosts wedding receptions.

THE EARLIEST BRICK BUILDINGS

The Romans had used bricks extensively in Britain and subsequently these had been robbed from standing structures and reused in Saxon times, for buildings such as the eighth-century basilican church at Brixworth, Northamptonshire. In the mid-twelfth century the Cistercians reintroduced the arts of brick-making to eastern England. They had pioneered the new technology in the Low Countries; it proved, however, invaluable across large parts of eastern England, where good building stone does not occur naturally, but where clays are quite common. The earliest post-Roman brick-making in Britain is probably that at St Nicholas's Chapel, Little Coggeshall Abbey, in Essex (about 1220).[21]

By the fourteenth century the manufacture of bricks had become sufficiently assured for entire monastic buildings to be built from brick. Somewhat later a specialized tradition of fine brick building arose in southern Lincolnshire and north-western East Anglia, exemplified by the superb fifteenth-century towers of Tattershall Castle and the bishops of Lincoln's palace at Buckden, in Huntingdonshire. Rather unusually, clay for the bricks used to build Tattershall came from two different sources, one 14 kilometres to the north, the other 19 kilometres to the south. Most later medieval bricks were made from clay obtained locally, often from a moat or ditch around the building itself. Herstmonceaux Castle, Sussex, is another fine example of a striking early brick building, although the walls were too thin to have resisted serious attack.[22] Between 1442 and 1452 the building of Eton College involved no less than 1.5 million bricks, probably imported from Flanders.[23] Generally speaking, imported bricks were somewhat smaller than British bricks, but after about 1400 British bricks were being added to supposedly 'imported' bricks at ports such as Hull.[24] Larger, industrial-scale brickpits did not begin to appear until the eighteenth and nineteenth centuries.

THE DISSOLUTION OF THE MONASTERIES

The Dissolution of the Monasteries of England and Wales by Henry VIII took place between 1536 and 1540 and was the largest state takeover of Church property in British history. It caused great controversy at the time, and not just in monastic circles. Most of the newly acquired land was given to powerful landowners or local gentry, through the Court of Augmentations. The monastic estates of the early Middle Ages were immense, comprising up to a quarter of the land of England. Given such an astonishingly large landholding, it is clear why the redistribution of these assets after the Dissolution was to play such a big role in early post-medieval landscape improvements, such as the draining of the Fens. Some of the richest monastic houses were located in London and their assets gave the City a welcome boost after the Dissolution. Only the great abbey church at Westminster was spared

Fig. 9.11 Fountains Hall, North Yorkshire. This Jacobean mansion (most probably by an elderly Robert Smythson) was built *c.* 1611 by Sir Stephen Proctor, the locally disliked recusant (hidden Catholic) hunter and Collector of Fines on Penal Statutes. Much of the stonework for his grand new house, which boasts the large windows characteristic of the late sixteenth and early seventeenth centuries (as exemplified by Hardwick Hall, Derbyshire), was taken from the recently dissolved Fountains Abbey, nearby. Although Proctor was undoubtedly a ruthless man, such stone 'robbing' had been a common practice throughout the medieval period. Today we would consider it recycling.

by Henry VIII, although the assets of the foundation – then the second richest in England after Glastonbury – were sold to raise the immense sum of £4,000 for the Treasury.[25]

During the fourteenth and fifteenth centuries there was a decline in the number of people in monastic orders, yet the estates on which they lived generally remained as large as before. Moreover, since they were enclosed foundations, their inhabitants, the friars, monks, nuns and lay brothers, are known to have been particularly susceptible to infection.[26] During a time of growing secularization, monastic seclusion and rumoured good living off landed estates led to a rift between the common man and the cloistered religious.[27] Many regarded the smaller houses as being particularly corrupt, and attempts were made to reform them in 1536, while most of the larger houses generally remained well governed until the end.[28] It would appear that even at the Dissolution the monastic system was not as corrupt as Henry VIII and his supporters would like us to believe.

We have lost a great deal of magnificent architecture through this, as most of the great monastic buildings were systematically robbed and demolished to reuse their building stone. Perhaps the best-known example of this practice is the fine Jacobean mansion of Fountains Hall, built in 1611 from stone robbed from the south-east part of Fountains Abbey, nearby. Despite such depredations, the remains of the great Cistercian house still give us a clear impression of the size and extent of the buildings needed to support the community from its foundation in the early thirteenth century. Much of the actual physical work in the fields and with the livestock was carried out by large numbers of lay brothers who had to be fed and accommodated. Large numbers of local people, too, would be needed to supply the great house with other goods and services. In terms of impact on the landscape and the local community, foundations like Fountains or Glastonbury could be compared with the model villages later established by enlightened industrialists such as Titus Salt (Chapter 13).

RURAL LANDSCAPES OF SCOTLAND AND WALES IN THE LATER MIDDLE AGES AND INTO EARLY MODERN TIMES

We have already seen how fleas and rats spread the plague; as a consequence the warmer towns and cities of southern Scotland suffered the worst; but that did not mean the Highlands and Islands escaped the pestilence. Taken together, it seems that about a third of the Scottish population perished during the Black Death. The overall demographic effects were broadly similar to what we have already noted in England: labour became more expensive and rents were cheaper. One consequence of this, in rural areas, was a contraction in the amount of arable land. Prior to the mid-fourteenth century, Scotland had been a prosperous place and exports flourished: by the start of the fourteenth century the wool from some 2 million sheep and the hides of around 50,000 cattle were being exported through the new burgh ports. Meanwhile the farmers themselves ate well, on cereals, dairy products (probably from milk sheep), meat, fish and kale. Lamb was probably traded to the growing urban population.

Excavations at the rural settlement at Rattray close to the north-east coast of Morayshire, near Rattray Head, some 10 kilometres north of Peterhead, have given us a fascinating glimpse of the northern Scottish landscape before and after the Black Death.[29] The settlement at Rattray was at its height during the thirteenth to fifteenth centuries and it was located in a rather special place, being a part of a coastal settlement complex that included a timber-built manorial castle.[30] Unlike most rural settlements it had been granted burgh status, but that did not prevent it from being an essentially rural community. There was nothing urban at all about Rattray. Most of the families subsisted through mixed farming of both arable and pasture. The main crops were oats and bere, a type of hardy barley, but some bread wheat and rye were also grown. These cereals were dried for storage and milling in corn-drying kilns, while flour was either prepared using small domestic querns, or in larger quantities in the lord's watermills. Bone preservation was good, which has allowed archaeologists to gain an impression of the livestock economy.

Wool and hides were exported through the burgh port. In the Middle Ages and later sheep and goats were often milked (ewe's milk makes excellent cheese, such as the fine creamy blue cheese from Roquefort). The main advantage over cows of milking sheep and goats is that they are more 'thrifty' and require less forage in the spring, when hay is getting scarce and grass has yet to start growing in earnest. The sheep bones at Rattray were nearly all from old animals, which would suggest that the ewes were being retained for their fleeces and milk, while fat lambs (today at three to five months, but then six to eight months, or even older) were probably being sent away by boat to be sold at the Aberdeen meat market.

The excavations at Rattray helped to debunk two persistent myths about the Middle Ages in Scotland. Animals were not killed in a mass-slaughter in the autumn. Instead they were over-wintered on hay, kale stalks, straw and other forage (sheep, for example, will thrive on even

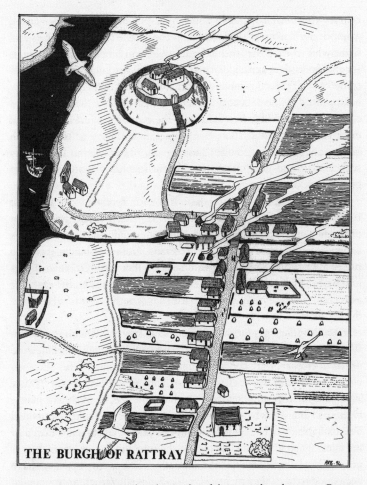

THE BURGH OF RATTRAY

Fig. 9.12 A bird's eye view by Alan Braby of the coastal settlement at Rattray, Morayshire, during the thirteenth to fifteenth centuries. Rattray had been given burgh status, but it was still essentially a rural farming settlement based around a very small port. Both the port and the settlement were protected by the presence of a timber-built manorial castle set on top of a high earthen mound, or motte. The church and graveyard can be seen in the foreground, just to the right of the main road.

coarse wheat straw), and lambing took place indoors, under cover, just as it does on most lowland farms today. The farming families and those who worked the land did not live in grinding poverty. The pigs, for example, were generally eaten young, when tender and succulent, rather than at their optimum weight. This picture of relative prosperity is supported by the many finds that the site produced. Such a standard of living would be hard to achieve if the economy was based around mere subsistence, and there is evidence from many of the Scottish burghs for a thriving money-based economy, involving cash crops such as flax and hemp, and agricultural surpluses produced during good years.

By the fourteenth century the two major foreign influences, the Gaels from the west and the Norse from the east, had produced a distinctive culture throughout the Hebrides and along the sea lochs and undulating shores of western Scotland. Not surprisingly, this gave rise to long-running tensions, leading to conflict between the medieval Lords of the Isles and the rulers of mainland Scotland to the east, but as is so often the case in such situations it was the victors who wrote the history.

In the Middle Ages most mainland Scots saw the inhabitants of the Western Isles as savages: they spoke a different language (Gaelic), wore different clothes, were constantly feuding among themselves and even went to war with the Scottish Crown. This perception found its way into Lowland lore and literature and has persisted, as a historical view, to this day. But it has had to change in the face of new evidence provided by excavations at Finlaggan, the capital of the MacDonald Lords of the Isles, who ruled the Hebrides in the fourteenth and fifteenth centuries. The walls, floors and foundations of some twenty buildings have been discovered, linked by paved roads. Finds show that far from being savages, the inhabitants consumed claret from Bordeaux and encouraged a wide variety of industry, including iron-smelting and lead extraction. It would seem that the Lords of the Isles made a conscious decision not to plant a town on Finlaggan – which they had contacts enough and knowledge to do – but instead decided to replicate the traditional style of Hebridean settlement, though more formally and on a larger scale.

The excavations in Loch Finlaggan have shown that this island

Fig. 9.13 A reconstruction of the capital of the MacDonald Lords of the Isles at Finlaggan, on the Inner Hebridean island of Islay, as it might have appeared in the fifteenth century. This site consists of two islands, Eilean Mor (the Great Island) and Eilean na Comhairle (the Council Island), both within the freshwater Loch Finlaggan. Excavations carried out since 1990 have revealed a complex of buildings linked together by paved roads and there were also buildings across the water, on the shores of the freshwater loch.

within a loch in the interior of north Islay was a remarkably sophisticated place in the fourteenth and fifteenth centuries. In actual fact, the site was located on two islands. The smaller island was man-made – and had been constructed over a period of a thousand years from origins as an Iron Age broch, many of which were constructed in or near lochs; this small island was where the Council of the Isles had its meetings. In the fifteenth century the Council Island was linked to the Great Island by a wooden causeway. Although from the air it looks small, in actual fact it was just big enough to hold three buildings, the largest of which was probably used by the Island Council. One was probably a kitchen for the Council Hall, the other a hall for the ruling MacDonald family.

Access to the Great Island was from the north, either via a causeway, or by boat and the eastern end of the island was enclosed by a stone and turf bank revetted with timber, much of which is still visible. This was quite a substantial structure and may have been for defence – and for enclosing livestock. At the east end of the island was a chapel within a graveyard. This stood at the end of a paved cobbled road lined along one side by a series of houses and stores which fronted the road, gable end on. These were substantial structures, with clear Norse ancestry, which were built using curved floor-to-roof supporting posts, known as crucks. At its west end the main road forked to pass on either side of the Great Hall, with its accompanying kitchen, and then continued west to the causeway over to the Council Island.

The settlement at Finlaggan has been described as 'proto-urban', as it was smaller than a town and more elaborate than a village. There was clear evidence that the clansmen at Finlaggan were in regular contact with places as far afield as France and Italy. In 1493 the site was systematically destroyed following the defeat of the Lords of the Isles by the ruling Stewart dynasty of Scotland. The buildings were demolished and reusable materials, such as complete roof tiles, were removed. The site reverted to agricultural use and what buildings there were in the sixteenth century were positioned without any regard for the earlier settlement. The clear intention was to erase all traces of the remarkable, but troublesome, Lords of the Isles.

The change from later medieval to early modern times in many parts of rural Scotland was a gradual transition rather than a clean break. Earlier patterns of farming based on run-rigg, around fermtouns towards the east, and clachans towards the west, often continued into the eighteenth century and later. Indeed recent research in the west Highlands and Hebrides has suggested that in many instances the clachans and run-rigg which preceded the nineteenth-century crofting townships were by no means as ancient as was once believed.[31] Instead, the new study has shown that the original, pre-clachan, landscape comprised enclosed fields and single dispersed farmsteads. These were only replaced by the communal farms of the clachan run-rigg system, starting in late medieval times. Indeed, the process of conversion was still incomplete in the eighteenth century.

In Wales, the situation at first remained much as it had been before the onset of the Black Death.[32] In the south the landscape was farmed by an Anglicized Open Field system, complete with nucleated villages and ridge-and-furrow strip fields. By the fourteenth and fifteenth centuries, however, much of the demesne land belonging to large landowners was being let out, and people who had previously been obligated by feudal ties now acquired their holdings of land as free bondsmen; they became, in effect, rent-paying tenants who set about the long business of breaking up the Open Fields into independent farmsteads. As time passed this process grew in scale and became recognizable as piecemeal enclosure, by agreement with the various parties concerned. In the north the hamlet remained the principal unit of residence, and the ideal arrangement, according to a fifteenth-century document, was a settlement of nine houses, all sharing one plough team, with one kiln, one churn, one cat, one cock and one herdsman.[33]

LIFE IN THE SCOTTISH BORDERS

The history of the Scottish Borders is usually written in terms of conflict and strife. Indeed, when one walks or drives through these landscapes today one is struck by the infrequency with which one encounters villages. The landscape is also peppered with the ruins of tower houses, which stand as stark reminders of a warlike past. But even in the Scottish Borders life had to continue, food and clothing had to be acquired and fighting was not always endemic.

One might suppose that communal farming practices, such run-rigg, which was succeeded by the development of more specialized regional economies could only have functioned properly in a secure environment. It would follow from this that regions such as the border lands between England and Scotland must have remained largely unfarmed, except for a few head of sheep and cattle that could be driven into the ground floor of a tower house when the rustlers – known locally as reivers – appeared over the horizon. But although economic life in the Borders was undoubtedly made far less pleasant by persistent feuds and lawlessness, it by no means ceased. Communities learnt to adapt and they were aided in this by the nature of the landscape itself which was not as bleak and inhospitable as it is usually portrayed. Although the highest moors can be bitterly cold in winter, the area is much influenced by warmer westerly weather systems from off the Atlantic. After all, if the area were truly bleak, the Royal Botanic Garden at Edinburgh would not be able to maintain its fine regional collections at Dawyck Arboretum in the heart of the Borders, near Peebles. The border country was also much larger than is often supposed, extending the full width of north-central Britain in a swathe over 90 kilometres across, at its wider, eastern, side.

The border country in England is wedge-shaped, far wider in the east than the west, and its southern limit is defined by Hadrian's Wall which runs east–west immediately north of Newcastle on the east coast to Carlisle on the west. Despite centuries of fighting, the border between England and Scotland has remained remarkably constant since the eleventh and twelfth centuries, except in the region around Berwick-upon-Tweed which was captured by the future Richard III in 1482. Cumberland was part of Strathclyde until conquered for England by William II in 1092; Carlisle Castle was built by the king to defend his new territories.

The northern limits of the Scottish Borders are less readily defined, but they are usually taken to be the Lammermuir Hills, to the east, and the Moorfoot Hills, towards the centre, both of which are extensions of the Scottish Southern Uplands. To the south-west the border country extends into Dumfries and Galloway, to the north shores of the Solway Firth at Dumfries.[34]

The landscape on the Scottish side of the Borders in the Middle Ages was, and still remains, surprisingly lush and luxuriant. It is also very varied, with wooded valleys and fertile river floodplains, separated by areas of upland and moor. This is decidedly not a landscape of bleak upland moors; they do indeed exist, but the transition to sheltered, fertile lowland can often be remarkably swift. Indeed the Scottish border country contains some of the richest agricultural land in Scotland, much of it within 50 kilometres of the English border. To the east, for example, the fertile cereal-producing lowlands of the Berwickshire Merse face directly across the River Tweed into Northumberland.

On the English side of the border, the mountainous moorlands of the Cheviot Hills of Northumberland, north of Hadrian's Wall, include a large area of outstanding beauty which today lies within the Northumberland National Park. Large areas of this landscape are still open and treeless, and much as they would have appeared in the time of the English–Scottish wars. The moorland Cheviot landscapes of Northumberland are more extensive than those in Scotland, where the most extensive higher uplands are to be found in Dumfries and Galloway, to the south and west.

Detailed field surveys are producing increasingly good evidence to suggest that large numbers of people lived in the Scottish Borders in prehistoric and Roman times. We saw this when we examined the landscapes around the Bronze and Iron Age hillforts of the Cheviots, but the most distinctive characteristic of the Borders area of both Scotland and England is still the rarity of small, dispersed rural settlements. This most probably reflects the region's turbulent past, but we might reasonably enquire how long this situation has existed. One way to approach this question is to work forward in time. We have already established that by the Roman period the area was well settled. During the Dark Ages and in Saxon times there is nothing to suggest wholesale desertion. Far from it, in fact: we know about the Dark Age royal palace complex at Yeavering, and northern monasteries like those at Lindisfarne, Jarrow and Monkwearmouth, where the scholarly Bede found the peace to write, were flourishing in the seventh to ninth centuries. In early medieval times we see the establishment of many important monastic communities in the Borders area at places like Kelso, Jedburgh, Melrose and Dryburgh, to name but a few. But what about ordinary people: how did they fare?

Some of the best evidence comes from the north-east of England, where a number of deserted medieval villages can be seen on aerial photographs taken in upland regions. To date we know of about fifty-nine in County Durham and (so far) thirty in southern Northumberland.[35] Many of these were abandoned as the intensity of Scottish raiding increased, following the assumption of the Scottish throne by Edward I in 1296. Next came the successive waves of Black Death, from the mid-fourteenth century onwards. So one might suppose that here, if anywhere, it would be reasonable to assume that nearly all villages were abandoned as a result of these two factors alone. A

Fig. 9.14 A reconstruction by Howard Mason of the medieval village of West Whelpington, Northumberland, during the fifteenth century. The houses are arranged around a large central village green with their tofts laid out behind them. Note the ridge-and-furrow of the fields surrounding the village.

generation ago this would have been taken for granted, but, as we saw at Wharram Percy, detailed study of a particular village often throws up a series of complicating factors. To date only one deserted medieval village has been excavated in the north-east and that is at West Whelpington, Northumberland, in the upper reaches of the Wansbeck Valley, just 8 kilometres east of the Northumberland National Park. The excavations showed that West Whelpington was flourishing by the late twelfth century, when it consisted of a series of stone-built, thatched rectangular longhouses.[36] Like many other Northumbrian communities it was devastated by Scots raids, following their victory at Bannockburn in 1314. Then gradually it recovered, and was re-founded in the late fourteenth or early fifteenth century as a rather late planned village of twenty-eight terraced longhouses and eight separate cottages, arranged around a village green. Later, a fortified house of a type known as a bastle, a hybrid between a fortification and a house, was added to the community. Some 200 bastles still survive in Northumberland. They were mainly built in the sixteenth century, more as a response to endemic cattle raiding than full-scale warfare, but a few can be dated to the early seventeenth century, which suggests that, locally, lawlessness persisted until quite late.[37] Ironically, it was not Scottish raids nor plagues that caused West Whelpington to be abandoned; that did not happen until 1720, when the village was removed as part of the complete reorganization of the old Open Field landscape, at the time of Enclosure.

We know that the monastic settlements on the Scottish side of the border generally fared well and ran prosperous farms of their own, but it is hard to obtain reliable evidence on the state of the landscape on the higher moors in the Borders. A useful way around is to avoid specific events and instead to examine what was happening to the upland vegetation over a number of years. Looking at the initial impact of the Little Ice Age in at least two different places, it is possible to draw some general conclusions.[38] The first place is in the Lammermuir Hills, north of the River Tweed towards the northern edge of the Scottish Borders. Here woodland was regenerating between 1200 and 1370; this is attributed to a series of English raids, the Black Death and the onset of the Little Ice Age. Then (rather unexpectedly) the landscape was cleared between about 1400 and the 1660s, and at the same time pollen records show the appearance of common arable weeds – which would suggest that parts at least of the landscape were under the plough.

The second set of pollen samples were taken in the Bowmont Valley in the northern Cheviot Hills. Here the pollen record shows that the hills had been grazed from Saxon times but this grazing became more intense after 1400. It seems likely that the animals involved were sheep, quite possibly from some of the monastic estates which are known in the Bowmont Valley. The pollen samples show that crops (oats/wheat and barley) were grown before about 1450 but that after that date arable farming became more intensive.

These two samples suggest that the impact of the Little Ice Age may not have been as severe as has often been supposed. Perhaps more importantly, they also demonstrate that both areas were being continuously farmed through most of the later Middle Ages and into post-medieval times. Indeed, in the earlier fifteenth century the intensity of farming actually increased. This would suggest that the usual impression of the Borders as being a barren waste laid low by constant raiding is far from the truth. Raiding happened, but so too did farming, and it is important to keep both in perspective.

STRIFE IN THE SCOTTISH BORDERS

It is impossible to understand the many fortified buildings of the Scottish Borders without having a general grasp of the historical events that led to their construction and subsequent survival in the landscape. There had been cross-border raids as early as Roman times and these most probably continued, on and off, into the Middle Ages. However the main Anglo-Scottish border wars began in the late thirteenth century and continued intermittently throughout the following three centuries until the unification of the crowns of England and Scotland in 1603.[39] By then feuding had become endemic and it probably took at least a generation for peace eventually to prevail.

The Border wars began in 1296, with Edward I's assumption of the Scottish throne. This was hugely resented by Scottish – and indeed some Northumbrian – nobles. The following year Scottish forces under William Wallace defeated an English army at the Battle of Stirling and then rampaged through Northumbria. Even after a second English defeat, at Bannockburn, Edward still laid claim to the Scottish throne. This intransigence further infuriated the Scots, who launched a series of devastating raids into England, led by a number of men, including Robert the Bruce. The raids and retaliation continued for the next two centuries, 'official' raiding being supplemented by local raiding, and a number of long-term and very bitter blood feuds developed. Sometimes even privately inspired raids could involve substantial forces. The leading English noble family, the Percies of Alnwick Castle, for example, could call upon a large private army, when one was needed.

The last of the great set-piece battles between Scots and English took place on 9 September 1513 at Flodden in north Northumberland. This was possibly the largest battle ever fought on English soil, each of the armies comprising about 20,000 men. It resulted in a comprehensive English victory, in which the Scottish King James IV and his son were killed, along with many other nobles and bishops. For the rest of the century Scotland would never be able to mount a field force sufficient to defeat the English, although cross-border raiding and feuding continued.

Throughout these extended periods of turbulence some sort of control was maintained under Marcher Law, a form of military rule introduced at the Treaty of York in 1237. The Borders on either side of the national divide were eventually arranged into three military zones, known as Marches. These were controlled by Wardens of the Marches who had the power, in theory at least, to draw upon Crown troops held in strategic garrisons. The system of Marcher Law included regular truce days, known as 'March Days' when wardens on either side of the border could meet to sort out persistent disputes. Sometimes these were occasions for rejoicing; but, given the nature of the region, disputes often moved from words to weapons. As late as 1585 Lord Francis Russell was shot dead during a 'truce' meeting between Wardens of the Middle Marches.[40]

So what does the landscape have to tell us about the way in which people coped with more than three centuries of conflict? The principal buildings in the Scottish Borders are without doubt the towers and castles, which are sometimes referred to as Peel or Pele Towers.[41] This term, incidentally, is probably best avoided unless one is using it to describe a specific type of small, barn-like stone building.[42] Tower houses were mostly built in the latter part of the unsettled times, mainly in the sixteenth and seventeenth centuries, but castles appear very much earlier, in the twelfth and thirteenth centuries. Essentially these were royal, military or administrative centres of importance. Few stone-built castles of this period survive in the Scottish Borders, although it should be borne in mind that several of the early English stone castles (including the royal castle at Berwick-upon-Tweed) were actually built by Scottish kings.

The towers were less grand than the castles in every respect and served the needs of a smaller family or community. The first tower houses in the Scottish Borders began to be built in the last two decades of the fourteenth century, but the vast majority were constructed rather later, from the mid-fifteenth. The early group includes five very substantial towers: Hermitage Castle (the largest), Cessford, Duns, Newark and Neidpath castles. Neidpath Castle (c. 1425–50) was built on the

Tweed just upstream of Peebles and was sited in a commanding position on a steep rocky bluff, above a long bend in the river.

Despite their appearance in the landscape today, most towers did not sit in splendid isolation. They were usually surrounded by a defensive enclosure wall or palisade fence known as a barmkin. This was the first line of defence against raiders. Anyone living or working in the area would retreat within the barmkin as the attackers approached. Depending on its size, the barmkin usually included buildings, which in the later examples were mainly used as accommodation for farm workers, as general stores or as livestock shelters. There is not much space for a substantial barmkin at Neidpath, which might help explain its unusual size: it had to be large enough to accommodate the people and material that would normally be housed outside.[43] The earlier towers often had lower walls that were much thicker than those built in the sixteenth century. This might either

Fig. 9.15 Dryhope Tower, with the earthworks of a large barmkin enclosure, in Ettrick Forest, near Cappercleuch, Scottish Borders. This tower house was probably built in the middle or third quarter of the sixteenth century, and was partially dismantled in 1592 on government instructions. The tower and barmkin were placed on a knoll of land which was partially protected on three sides by the stream, visible here in the foreground.

Fig. 9.16 A reconstruction by David Simon of Dryhope Tower in its defended barmkin enclosure in the late sixteenth century. The watermill (*lower left*) was powered by the stream which enclosed the tower and barmkin on three sides. Note the open woodland and scrub of Ettrick Forest in the background. The Borders Forest Trust are replanting large areas of Ettrick Forest, including 90,000 trees on Dryhope Farm alone.

suggest that labour and building materials were more plentiful in the earlier period or that, towards the latter part of the Borders unrest, raids became shorter and possibly sharper too, involving greater use of firearms, as loopholes for guns are often found in the walls of the later towers.

Even in the turbulent years of the sixteenth century rural life continued, and a good example of a tower house within an agricultural setting can be seen at Dryhope, near Cappercleuch, in the Scottish Borders.[44] This fortified farm is in an upland wooded valley, quite close to St Mary's Loch. Today the upland landscape is largely treeless and grazed by sheep, but in the sixteenth century it was within Ettrick Forest, a royal hunting forest. This was not dense forest, but rather sparse woodland, with many clearings and areas of scrub. The forest landscape included a number of small farms, known as steads, which were dotted about and each year the owners were expected to provide two bows and a spear with a horse and tackle for service in the royal army.

The barmkin at Dryhope was never intended to resist an extended siege, but it would have provided protection against raids by reivers intent on cattle rustling. The farm mill, and possibly other buildings too, were positioned outside the walls, which again would indicate that a prolonged attack would not have been expected.

THE RELATIONSHIP OF TOWN AND COUNTRY IN THE LATER MIDDLE AGES

Many of the administrative units of local government such as parishes and counties were established before the Norman Conquest. They often seem to mirror local cultural identity. This is well illustrated by the traditional rivalries between, for example, counties like Yorkshire and Lancashire. During the Middle Ages it became increasingly clear that developing patterns of trade would not necessarily reflect county-based administrative structures. Trade was increasingly about supply and demand, which could change as the economic conditions altered.

Local market centres were located in places that had access to a number of different regions, whether or not they happened to coincide with administrative boundaries.[45] The point of the trading centre was to bring buyers and sellers from a variety of different regions and local economies together. Often this would involve the positioning of market centres towards the edges of an economic area, from where neighbouring regions could be accessed more readily. This would explain, for example, why many of the largest towns and cities of the Fens, places like Cambridge, Huntingdon, Peterborough and Lincoln, are positioned at the Fen-edge, where wet meets dry, and where plain gives way to hill.[46]

Resources produced in the Fens included of course fish and eels, which were often traded live in the area, and more importantly wildfowl, which were exported to London in the seventeenth and eighteenth centuries in their tens of thousands from commercial decoys that almost resembled 'factory farms', several of which are located near Peterborough. In the Middle Ages the principal product produced on the lush fen summer pastures was wool, which gave Peterborough its medieval name of Guildenburgh, or City of Gold. But again, we must beware of treating 'the Fens' as a homogeneous entity. For a start they include parts of no less than four modern counties (six, if one includes the historic counties of the Isle of Ely and Huntingdonshire). In geographical or geological terms there were several types of fen, ranging from the spongy, often acidic peat fen of the west, to the higher, drier and more fertile so-called Marshland silts around the Wash. These terrains were as different in their economic potential as high moorland and gravel plain. They changed further, moreover, when they were drained, first in earlier medieval times and then in the seventeenth century.[47] The pattern of economic change still continues. Nowadays most of the few remaining Fenland sheep farms, myself included, sell our stock at Melton Mowbray, in Leicestershire, now that Peterborough, Norwich and many smaller markets have closed.

After the onset of the Black Death regional farming economies started to develop and economic historians have attempted to classify them as a series of 'farming regions' or *pays* (a French word meaning region, countryside or territory). Examples of *pays* one would have found in pre-Black Death times include Champion, forest, fell or moorland, fenland, marshland, heathland, downland (chalk) and wolds (limestones and sometimes clays).[48] The different *pays* became better defined and more self-aware through later medieval times and acquired much firmer identities from the sixteenth century onwards, when there was a general trend towards greater regionalization in Britain. In the Fenland example just mentioned, Peterborough was positioned at the edges of two farming *pays*: fenland and Champion, but with ready access to the wold landscapes of southern Lincolnshire. This central yet marginal location might help to explain the prosperity of the town and the large Benedictine abbey at its centre.

Self-defined regions, such as the Fens, the Thames Valley, the Scottish Borders, the Welsh Marches, acquired their identities through the frequent interaction of people going about their daily lives, usually but not always in a peaceful manner. As time passed, these identities became better defined and were maintained and perpetuated through social arrangements, such as marriage. Local society helped to maintain traditional barriers long after the original reason for those barriers or boundaries had gone. Professor Phythian-Adams quotes an example on the long-lived Leicester–Warwickshire boundary, where the actual landscape is entirely featureless, yet the border, which was acknowledged by everyone in the region, persisted for centuries.[49] The fundamental point I want to make here is important: local history has shown that farming regions will change through time, as conditions and markets also change. But human culture is far more conservative. Historical Marxists might beg to differ, but the form and shape of any landscape is ultimately determined, not by economics, but by the cultural preferences of the human societies who lived there.

The relationship between town and country only works if communications are adequate, and a myth has grown up that roads in the Middle Ages were invariably poorly maintained and inadequate. This was simply not the case, as the many surviving bridges of the period attest. Special efforts were made to traverse boggy and frequently flooded areas, such as river floodplains. A particularly well-preserved long bridge of the later fifteenth century still carries the modern road across the Great Ouse at Great Barford in Bedfordshire.[50] In upland areas

Fig. 9.17 The Devil's Bridge, Kirkby Lonsdale, Cumbria. The three arches of this fifteenth century bridge carry the road to Ingleton across the River Lune. Many upland medieval bridges have been swept away when rivers were in spate, but this fine example has survived because its piers were placed high, on solid outcrops of rock.

medieval bridges were often destroyed when rivers were in spate, but examples can still be seen, such as the fifteenth-century Devil's Bridge across the River Lune just outside Kirkby Lonsdale, in Cumbria. Whatever the other fiscal and economic reasons, simple common sense suggests that communities who were prepared to put so much effort into crossing rivers would not have allowed their roads to deteriorate so much that they became impassable.

Town and country have traditionally been seen as separate entities in many discussions of the earlier Middle Ages. This might in part reflect the fact that feudal ties and obligations were less relevant, or were less rigorously applied, in towns than in the country. In reality, however, towns and country were mutually dependent and formed part of trading networks of regional and wider importance, as we have already touched on. In the centuries following the Black Death, this interdependence, or symbiosis, would grow closer, as towns sought new sources of labour to replenish people killed by subsequent waves of disease.

There was another important trend running through the later Middle Ages. As the relationship between towns and their hinterland grew closer, so local economies began to depart from a standardized system, such as communal Champion farming. The result was increased specialization and the growth of regional economies. The traditional view of medieval towns is that they were the focus for an administrative area and provided markets for produce from the surrounding landscape. There may be truth in this, but it would be a mistake to assume that each town would necessarily have been sited at the centre of a particular region. Indeed, as already discussed, they were often positioned at the edges of farming regions, where other markets could be reached and where products from different regions could be exchanged, to the mutual profit of both – and of course of the town and its merchants, too.

URBAN LANDSCAPES OF THE LATER MIDDLE AGES

Towns in Britain enjoyed a period of general prosperity and expansion throughout the early Middle Ages until the thirteenth century, by the end of which there are strong signs of economic decline and social tension. These problems were caused by a succession of crop failures and cattle diseases which gave rise to a series of regional famines in both rural and urban areas. At the same time England was at war with Scotland and (from 1337) with France too, and these military campaigns had to be funded by taxes. Then the Black Death and the many successive waves of plague sealed the process of urban decline. Strong archaeological evidence shows that building in towns like Nottingham, Bedford, Lincoln, Hull, Warwick and York declined from the late fourteenth and early fifteenth centuries. Many of these towns had been involved with the export of wool to industrialized cloth manufacturers in Flanders, but from the late fourteenth century that trade declined and the manufacture and export of finished cloth took its place. This new trade enriched areas like the south-west and west Midlands (towns like Castle Combe, Totnes and Ludlow), East Anglia (Hadleigh and Lavenham) and the West Riding of Yorkshire (Halifax and Wakefield). The export trade also favoured ports such as Bristol, London and Boston.[51]

The archaeology of towns has to be seen as a series of individual cases set within first a regional and then a national economic setting. After the impact of the Black Death the development of most towns in Britain is directly affected by regional factors which become increasingly important. London, with its many powerful merchants and links overseas, was the principal exception to this rule. The general effects of the Black Death and subsequent waves of plague gave ordinary people more control of their own destinies. Many people moved out of manorial villages into towns and cities, both to seek their fortune and to escape feudal ties and obligations. Once in employment, and earning a living in a new trade, the rural refugee could establish an independent life in the urban environment. Dick Whittington (died 1423), was mayor of London no less than three times (in 1397, 1406 and 1419) and his life has come to symbolize the lad who escaped rustic servitude to make a fortune as a mercer in the big city. In the Middle Ages mercers were merchants who dealt in fine fabrics, such as silk. Although his background wasn't as poor as the popular fable suggests, Richard Whittington was undoubtedly a great man and none the worse for being the younger son of a Gloucestershire landowner. He also made his mark on the contemporary landscape. He had no children so when he died his large fortune was spent making improvements to St Bartholomew's Hospital, Newgate Prison and the Guildhall.

The enormous wealth of London allowed it to weather the terrible impact of the Black Death, in 1348–9. The City continued to be the pre-eminent port in Britain and although the population did not match early fourteenth-century levels until just after the medieval period its wealth had again reached and exceeded those levels by 1400 – just half a century after the plague first struck. More money and fewer people meant that average wealth was greater and some individuals were soon very much richer.[52] These people – merchants, financiers and entrepreneurs – were becoming better organized into guilds which provided institutional protection and long-term security. Markets were also developing and the cash economy continued to grow.

London was a commercial centre and goods of all sorts were traded there. Some came from overseas, but many were locally produced or, like wool and cloth, were taken to refurbished markets, like that at the Westminster 'woolstaple', from further afield in Britain. In the later Middle Ages the increasing volume, organization and sophistication of trade, mostly based around a cash economy, led to the development of new and improved market buildings, such as Leadenhall Market, established in 1493 by the Corporation of London.

Mercantile and social developments such as these gave London a series of fine new stone buildings. Meanwhile, more land was being reclaimed from the river and the city's port facilities steadily improved. Throughout the Middle Ages London continued to be a secure place in which to live.

The documentary evidence for increasing prosperity after the mid-fourteenth century is supported by archaeology. Housing was required for the new immigrant population; at the same time, increasing general prosperity was giving rise to larger houses, some of which were built in substantial plots, formed by the amalgamation of neighbouring tenements. More lanes and alleys were built in the fifteenth century, though not on the same scale as before 1300, but successive waves of plague did affect the suburbs disproportionately; in these areas late medieval development was much slower than before. Southwark, however, was an exception. Here the town continued to develop and new stone buildings appeared. Southwark had long enjoyed the privileges of an independent borough outside the rules which constricted London, which may explain why in the late sixteenth century it was the site of three theatres, the Globe, the Rose and the Swan.[53]

The fourteenth and fifteenth centuries are generally perceived as a transition between feudalism and the early modern market economy. Rural economies adapted to the changing circumstances by developing regional characteristics and the towns in which their goods were traded themselves altered to accommodate the new demands. And if anything the links between town and country grew closer; as regional economies developed, continuity and stability also became important considerations. This is why it becomes very difficult to distinguish between medieval and post-medieval in the archaeological deposits in York and so many British towns.

Some British towns went into decline in the century that followed the Black Death. Others did the opposite, especially those that benefited from the rise of the textile trade in the early fourteenth century. Ludlow, one of the most beautiful towns in Britain, was one of these. This fine Shropshire town boasts perhaps the most celebrated street in England, where the continuity between the Middle Ages and post-medieval times is striking. The houses along the gently sloping and aptly named Broad Street form a spacious and harmonious sequence of buildings that range from the late Middle Ages through to the mid-nineteenth century.[54]

Ludlow originally owed its prosperity to its magnificent castle. This was founded in Norman times and a large outer bailey was added in the twelfth century.[55] The town became an important administrative centre as the seat of the Council of the Marches of Wales. It was also a focus of the textile trade, importing wool from Wales. The successful textile businesses allowed the town to prosper to such an extent that substantial town walls were constructed between 1233 and 1270. Only

Fig. 9.18 The north-eastern range of buildings along Broad Street, Ludlow, Shropshire, with the portico of the Butter Cross (1743–4), by William Baker (*extreme left*). An arcade below the Butter Cross is continued beneath the jetty of the medieval and post-medieval buildings along the north-east of Broad Street, where the original timber posts were replaced by cast-iron columns during road improvements in 1795.

one gate through the walls, that through which Broad Street passes, still survives. The Council of the Marches ceased to operate in 1689 but by then Ludlow had begun to acquire a new lease of life as a fashionable town where in the eighteenth century local landed gentry and the newly rising professional classes built themselves fine town houses for the 'Ludlow season'. During the nineteenth century the town reverted to being a regional market town, which is why many of the older buildings have survived so well.

The varied history of Ludlow is typical of many British market towns. The main point to note is that the changes were generally gradual and rarely cataclysmic. As one trade declined another took its place, until, that is, the coming of the railways in the mid-nineteenth century, when the pace of urban development increased rapidly. The builders who created the townscapes of many older British towns often showed respect for history and ambience. The fine town of Stamford, in Lincolnshire, for example, is noted for the Georgian elegance of its many fine stone-built houses, but closer examination has revealed that very often the Georgian harmony is entirely superficial, and that behind the stone fronts are medieval buildings of considerable architectural importance. Similarly in Ludlow the finely decorated timber-framed houses at the north end of Broad Street harmonize with No. 1 Broad Street, which is an exceptionally fine three-storey shop building, dated to 1404 by tree-rings. The black-and-white buildings to the south of it are, however, mostly post-medieval in date (sixteenth and seventeenth century), with the exception of the building south of the Angel Hotel which has a large medieval range to the rear, tree-ring-dated to 1431–9.

The latter part of the Middle Ages was altogether fascinating. Architecturally it has given us buildings in the late British Gothic style which are without rival anywhere in Europe. It was also the period that saw the demise of feudalism. In landscape terms we have abundant evidence for the new yeoman farmers in the many early enclosures of the 'woodland' landscapes; townscapes too begin to acquire the strong regional characteristics that can still be seen today. Perhaps most important of all, the two centuries from 1350 to 1550 witnessed what today we would term the 'empowerment', both of a new mercantile class and of many ordinary people in town and country. If two centuries can ever be considered as brief enough to constitute a revolution, then I would vote the mid-fourteenth to mid-sixteenth centuries as a time of profound and generally non-violent social change, if not of revolution. Without the social and economic transformations that took place in these two centuries, the acknowledged 'real' political revolution represented by the success of the Parliamentary cause in the English Civil Wars of 1642–51 could never have happened.

10

Productive and Polite: Rural
Landscapes in Early Modern Times
(1550–1750)

When I took my first faltering steps into the archaeological world
outside prehistory I thought I would find things very different. I was
used to dealing with periods where individuals did not exist and where
particular events, such as battles, were almost impossible to pin down.
When we come to the post-medieval period there is a snowstorm of
documentation of every imaginable sort and thus one might expect
that the end of the Middle Ages would somehow announce itself, if
not with trumpets, then with some pretty clear signs. But alas, the
Middle Ages did not so much terminate as fizzle out. This is particularly
true in towns like York, where it is impossible to distinguish between
some of the later medieval and the early post-medieval archaeological
deposits. In the countryside it is even harder to decide whether a
particular farm or field was laid out before or after 1550, the date most
archaeologists use to mark the end of the Middle Ages. But the general
processes behind landscape change can certainly be pinned down with
some accuracy.

So what were the underlying processes that eventually gave us
modern landscapes and when did they happen? The major change at
the end of the Middle Ages was the Reformation and the Dissolution
of the Monasteries which followed directly from it. Undoubtedly these
were important historical events.[1] It could be argued, however, that
the Reformation was merely the last of a longer series of changes that
had been under way since the mid-fourteenth century. The later Middle
Ages, from 1350 to 1550, was a period of dynamic change and transition, clearly visible in both rural and urban landscapes. But it is very
hard indeed to spot many signs of what some would regard as the final
disjunction – the Reformation – in the country at large, apart, that is,

from those many estates that were once controlled by monasteries. Here the changes were rapid, often involving the expansion of neighbouring properties onto land that had originally been grange farms.

ENCLOSURE

In rural areas the process that is most characteristic of post-medieval times is enclosure. An enclosure is an area of ground surrounded by a landscape feature, such as a ditch, wall, hedge, bank or fence. Landscape historians use the term in a slightly different sense. For them enclosure is a way of partitioning the landscape to indicate that particular fields or farms are owned by certain individuals or estates, who generally possess written title to them, in the form of deeds. Enclosed land, unlike Open Fields, commons, heaths and moors, cannot be owned by several people.

In the previous two chapters I referred to a seemingly 'planned' landscape around Moretonhampstead, in the Dartmoor National Park. This landscape is by no means unique in the west and south-west, but it is particularly well preserved and is a fine example of 'enclosure by agreement' in which the various peasant farmers and landowners in an area decide to come together and rationalize their landholdings. There are many reasons why they would want to do this, but quite often it is the result of the regional economy changing from mixed livestock with arable, to a pattern of farming more heavily dependent on livestock. Speaking as a sheep-farmer, I can fully understand why the farmers around Moretonhampstead would want to graze their animals in fields close to the farm, where they could be inspected, sorted and protected without having to make unnecessarily long journeys.

Many landscapes along the western half of England and Wales and in the 'woodland' landscapes of the south-east corner (from Suffolk to Sussex) began the process of enclosure from the fifteenth century onwards. For convenience and brevity the enclosures by agreement of the fifteenth, sixteenth and seventeenth centuries are generally referred to as 'early enclosures'. The process further gathered pace in the eighteenth and nineteenth centuries during the so-called Enclosure

Movement, which comprised a new process known as Parliamentary Enclosure, which I shall discuss further later (Chapter 12).

FARMING ENGLAND IN THE EARLY MODERN PERIOD

When it comes to the history of English farming in the early modern period one has to mention the enormous contribution made by Joan Thirsk, whose work in the 1970s and 1980s began to examine landscape and economic history together.[2] She defined eight post-medieval farming regions and, most importantly, drew them on a map. The concept of the farming region, or *pays*, was then gaining popularity, but the new research nailed it down and gave it dates.

It is becoming increasingly evident that some of the early modern farming regions, as defined by Thirsk, might have come into being during the last two centuries of the Middle Ages. This was a period when the economies of both rural and urban communities were responding to the changes brought about by the Black Death and the subsequent waves of plague.

The map of early modern farming regions is remarkably complex for so small an island and it reflects the extraordinary diversity not just of southern Britain's landscape, but of its population. The social significance of farming regions should not be forgotten here, because if we do, we risk underestimating both the size and the impact of the changes that happened from the mid-eighteenth century onwards, when the map of farming regions became radically transformed.

The early modern farming regions were based on products for which markets existed. A successful economy consists of a complex system of markets, communication and exchange which in both later and post-medieval times operated at many levels, ranging from large village markets, through market towns and cities, to the major markets of London, which by the seventeenth century had become one of Europe's great cities. From henceforward the British economy, and with it the British landscape, could not be commanded by any central authority and was probably as close to a free market as any economy can be. Bankers, soldiers and politicians could, and did, affect such things as

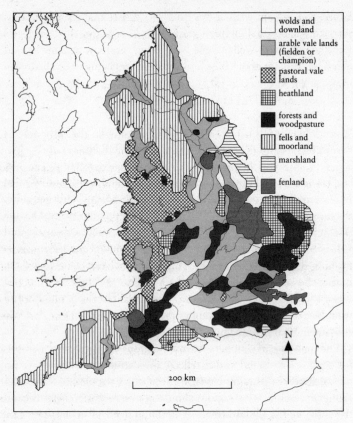

Fig. 10.1 Map of early modern (1500–1750) farming regions in England, as defined by Joan Thirsk in 1987. These regions came into being gradually from the early to mid-fourteenth century and were to last until the widespread changes brought about by the era of agricultural improvement of the eighteenth century, and earlier.

exchange rates and the ability to trade overseas, but the helmsmen who steered the economy ultimately took their instruction from the market.

Many of the processes that were in operation during the early modern period can be seen at work in what is still perhaps the largest single regional landscape transformation in British history. The drainage of the Fens is an extraordinary tale of man's continuing struggle with nature, and as I am writing this I am very aware that the continuous rain that has been falling for the past few days has swelled the levels of the nearby rivers Welland and Nene which are now running behind their high banks at about the same height as the ceiling of our bedroom on the first floor.

AN EARLY 'IMPROVEMENT': THE DRAINING OF THE FENS

The Fens occupy about 400,000 hectares of land south and west of the Wash, covering parts of south Lincolnshire, north Cambridgeshire, Norfolk and Suffolk. Fenland has two distinct zones: to the east a wide band of marine silty soils, known as Marshland, laid down by sea and storm around the Wash. Marshland towns include King's Lynn, Wisbech, Holbeach, Spalding and Boston. To the west, fringed by the dryland towns Cambridge, Huntingdon, Peterborough, Bourne and Lincoln, are the freshwater peats or Black Fens. The slightly higher and more stable silts of Marshland require less land drainage, but are susceptible to storm damage. The less stable peats of the Black Fens required deep drainage and the peaty soil 'shrank' as it dried out, thereby making drainage even more problematical.

In prehistoric times the drier land surrounding the great Fenland basin and the low natural 'islands' within it was heavily settled from Mesolithic and Neolithic times, but this never involved actual drainage.[3] In the Roman period the silts of Marshland were settled by farmers, but wetter conditions from the mid-fourth century AD led many to leave the area.[4] Again, there is no good evidence for land drainage as such. After the Roman period some of the farms around the edges of the wetter land probably continued in use into Saxon times, and there are good archaeological traces left by livestock farms on the 'Marshland silts' around the Wash. These date to the eighth and ninth centuries,[5] when substantial earthworks were erected to prevent the sea and rivers flooding Marshland. During the Middle Ages large areas of Marshland were given over to sheep-rearing; the area prospered, and some fine 'wool' churches, such as St Wendreda in March, Cambridgeshire, were built. The Marshland drainage was gradually extended westwards,

Fig. 10.2 The greatest single act of landscape transformation in modern times was the draining of the Fens in the seventeenth century. This aerial view at Welches Dam, near Welney, in the old Isle of Ely (now Cambridgeshire), is looking north-east and shows the two artificial rivers that were driven across the Fens in the mid-seventeenth century by the great drainage engineer Cornelius Vermuyden. The Old Bedford river (*left*) was dug in 1631, before the English Civil War. At the end of hostilities it was found to be inadequate on its own, leading to the cutting of New Bedford river in 1651. The land between the two Bedford rivers is designed to be flooded to ease pressure on the sluices into the Wash, at Denver, in Norfolk.

towards the huge areas of peat that occupied many hundreds of thousands of acres between the Marshland settlements around the Wash and the towns along the western Fen margins (places like Peterborough and Cambridge).[6]

So far as we know, no significant attempt was made to drain the Black Fens in the Middle Ages. In the later sixteenth century there were uncoordinated attempts to drain the edges of certain Fen 'islands', such as Thorney, many of which had been occupied by monastic houses in the Middle Ages. After 1600 there were more co-ordinated attempts at drainage, but these usually foundered through lack of capital; progress was sometimes made, but then the land would flood with catastrophic results. A fully co-ordinated approach was urgently needed.

A group of influential Fenland farmers approached the fourth Earl of Bedford, who owned some 20,000 acres around Thorney, to co-ordinate drainage work.[7] He undertook to drain the southern Black Fens in 1630, using the expertise of the Dutch engineer Cornelius Vermuyden. Vermuyden realized that the Black Fens could only be drained if in winter the swollen rivers flowing into Fenland could be taken across Cambridgeshire to the Wash by the shortest route possible. He therefore set about canalizing the Great Ouse, cutting two straight channels, the Old (1631) and New (1651) Bedford rivers, right across the Fens towards King's Lynn. The outfall of the Ouse into the Wash was complex and was not completed satisfactorily until shortly after the devastating floods of 1947. Flooding remained a constant, routine, problem in Fenland until the arrival of the first steam engines around 1820.[8] Thereafter the region became increasingly prosperous, culminating in the huge Thorney estates of the dukes of Bedford, which became one of the most successful agricultural enterprises of Victorian Britain.

TREES AND WOODLAND IN THE SEVENTEENTH AND EIGHTEENTH CENTURIES

The Open Fields of earlier medieval times were remarkably treeless and barren, as any visitor to Laxton can attest, but the land beyond the big fields would often be either wooded or scrubby; similarly, much of the land close by the village in the back lanes around the long individual tofts behind the cottages of the peasant farmers would have been hedged and set with hedgerow trees and perhaps fruit trees. If tree-cover was already thin over the Champion landscapes of central and southern England, it probably declined further through the rest of the Middle Ages and into the seventeenth century. By the eighteenth century certain areas, such as the heavy lands of the Midlands (where pasture now replaced Champion arable) and the sheep-corn landscapes of the wolds, the chalk downs and sandy heaths had all been largely treeless for centuries. This was to be reversed with the coming of large-scale enclosure in the early eighteenth century.[9]

In the eighteenth century oak was in high demand for buildings and for ships, although good-quality Baltic pine was already being imported in some quantity. Wood was still an important fuel in both town and country, although again, coal was beginning to make inroads into this trade. The point is that there were sound financial reasons for growing trees. But there were also other reasons why people decided to plant trees.

Appreciation of woods and wildlife was growing in the seventeenth and eighteenth centuries. The diarist John Evelyn published his great work *Silva*[10] in 1664. It mostly addresses the economic importance of good woodland management, but it was written for other motives too. One brief quotation will make the point. He is addressing the many landowners and potential landowners about to plant woodland. First he urges them to propagate trees by seed, or by cuttings, then he continues:

> To these my earnest and humble advice should be, that at their first coming to their estates, and as soon as they get children, they should seriously think of this work of propagation also: for I observe there is no part of husbandry, which men more commonly fail in, neglect, and have cause to repent of, than that they did not begin planting betimes, without which they can expect neither fruit, ornament, or delight from their labours. Men seldom plant trees till they begin to be wise, that is, till they grow old, and find by experience the prudence and necessity of it.[11]

These are not the words of an agronomist with an eye to the bottom line of a profit-and-loss account. Nor is this somebody who only wishes to establish woodland to impress visitors and the neighbouring gentry. Evelyn was someone who loved trees for themselves and for 'their fruit, ornament, or delight'. And he would not have been alone in this. The other major figure, although writing over a century later in 1788–9, is, of course, Gilbert White, whose great work, *The Natural History of Selborne*, is the first significant book on what today we would call ecology. White was a pioneer, but he was by no means alone in his interests. This voluminous correspondence with his friend Daines Barrington reads like the letters between two modern naturalists.[12] Given such sensibilities it seems absurd to suppose that trees were planted for economic reasons alone. There can be little doubt that tree-planting was also important for other, largely social reasons.

Perhaps the finest example of such post-medieval tree-planting is the great wooded park surrounding the late-eighteenth- and early nineteenth-century house at Ickworth, in West Suffolk. An account of 1665 describes the parish in detail and it consisted, as one might expect, of hamlets, paddocks, lanes and a small open field. In 1701 the population of the entire parish was moved elsewhere by the earls of Bristol who owned the great house. This was done to make way for their new park and thousands of trees. In the process many large medieval trees were preserved, including a huge pollarded elm that tree-ring dating shows was last pollarded around 1690, just before the new park brought such activities to a halt.[13]

Prestige was one very important, possibly even the most important, motive behind the establishment of the many plantations that appeared on newly enclosed land in the eighteenth century.[14] The presence of trees sent out an important symbolic message which became stronger as the new woodlands grew in size and area. Smallholders might plant the occasional tree in a hedgerow, where they were out of the way, but no small farmer could afford to put aside land for such purposes, especially given the fact that timber trees, such as oak, take at least two generations to mature. I can remember when I began to plant an 8-acre wood in the early 1990s an elderly man walked across the open field to where we were inserting young oak, ash and alder trees into the ground. He stood and watched us working and then remarked with Fen dryness that I would never benefit from them: 'You plant oaks for your grandchildren, boy,' then nodded wisely and headed back to the pub. He was both right and wrong, of course. Your grandchildren can indeed gain financially when the trees are eventually harvested. But the planter has the inestimable pleasures of seeing the trees grow and the wildlife change. I shall never forget the day, about twelve years after we planted those seedlings, when I first heard the rapid tap-tap-tapping of a pair of great spotted woodpeckers.

Land in many parishes in the seventeenth and eighteenth centuries was still held as part of the communal systems that had survived from medieval times. In these instances all the various landholders would never agree to tree-planting, for the simple reason that it would remove the source of immediate income. Land then and now had to be owned outright to plant trees and the appearance of new trees proclaimed this very clearly to anyone passing by. The presence of woodlands also made a clear statement about the status of the people who had planted them. Only families with large estates could afford to do such things. So someone riding through the eighteenth-century countryside, who came across a plantation, would know at once that a gentleman of substance lived nearby. But there was more to it even than that.

After the Restoration of 1660 royalist propaganda had suggested, mostly unfairly, that there had been extensive felling in the royal forests during the Commonwealth under Cromwell. One result of this misinformation was that the cutting down of trees began to be associated with ideas of republicanism. Conversely, tree-planting and the Royal Oak became a symbol of loyalty to the Crown, which is perhaps why the story of Charles II hiding up an oak tree during his escape to France, following defeat by Parliamentary forces at the Battle of Worcester in 1651, has survived for so long. The Royal Oak is still among the most popular pub names to this day. Tree-planting also showed confidence in the long-term future of the new prosperity and was also seen as a patriotic duty, because it supplied timber for the navy at a time when England was frequently at war. The navy was particularly important at home, as well as abroad. At the Restoration the navy which Charles inherited was both run down and nearly bankrupt, but it was by far the strongest asset of an otherwise precarious regime. Charles also abandoned the hated New Model Army.[15]

THE 'GREAT REBUILDING'

I strongly suspect that there was a subconscious motive behind the idea of a 'Great Rebuilding' in the later sixteenth and seventeenth centuries. The term itself originated with Hoskins, who believed he recognized a widespread rebuilding of the houses, farms and cottages of rural England.[16] It was and is still believed that the 'Great Rebuilding' was a result of many factors, but ultimately it reflected greater disposable wealth and the freedom to spend it as one might see fit. Wealth was becoming detached from many of the communal, religious and social obligations that had once been so important. In earlier times such wealth would be often be lavished, for example, on enlarging the parish church, but from the mid-sixteenth century it went towards the re-building and refurbishment of domestic structures. If it was spent on the church, it was often in the form of elaborate family memorials.

The subconscious motive I alluded to was the Restoration of the Monarchy and the return to a form of stability, law and order that required some form of physical expression. If that were so, then one would expect the process to have been 'top-down' and led by the great and the good who had the most to gain from the return of monarchy. However an analysis of the 'Great Rebuilding', which concentrated on farmhouses and cottages, recognized that for buildings of lesser status it was essentially a vernacular tradition, drawing upon later medieval concepts and skills.[17] This study also showed that the first phase, which flourished between 1575 and 1615, was essentially a response to a rapidly growing population.[18] Even Parliament recognized that something remarkable was happening and passed the Cottages Act of 1589, which insisted that each cottage must have four acres of land assigned to it – this provision was intended to prevent widespread destitution, should there be an economic downturn. Necessity aside, it would seem that the main motive behind much of the first phase of the 'Great Rebuilding' was a simple desire for greater comfort and convenience.

It was only in the second, Jacobean, phase (roughly from 1615 to 1642) that we see a change in emphasis.[19] In this instance the political and economic situation does seem to have played a large role. Certain instances, such as cloth-weaving in Suffolk, started to decline, and employment was beginning to suffer. Population growth was curbed, especially in the 1660s, by waves of plague. Enclosure was gathering pace and there was widespread disquiet, except among the most pros-perous, landowning classes of rural society. This culminated in rural revolts, such as the Midland Revolt of 1607.[20] The period ended, of course, with the Civil War of 1642–51. Wealth was increasingly un-equally distributed and this is illustrated by a proliferation of new higher-status Jacobean houses, at the expense of humbler dwellings.

Nobody can deny that there was much building and rebuilding from at least the mid-sixteenth century, and indeed rather earlier than that – say the late fifteenth century. But this was nothing new, more to the point it was the earliest *visible* episode of a series of building enhancements and renewals that had been under way for a very long time indeed. This has been demonstrated in numerous excavations in villages, towns and cities across Britain, where the alignment and arrangement of existing late-medieval and early modern buildings can be shown to have developed from a succession of earlier structures, which were often built in less durable materials.[21] At places like York the cycle of building on precisely the same plots can be traced right through the Middle Ages and back into Viking and Saxon times.

SCOTTISH RURAL LANDSCAPES IN THE SEVENTEENTH AND EIGHTEENTH CENTURIES

The century between 1650 and 1750 was one of the most troubled in Scotland's history and it left a clear impression on the landscape in the form of a large number of new barracks, specially built forts and military improvements to a few existing medieval castles, which in southern Britain would, by now, either have been abandoned or given over entirely to civilian use.[22] The conventional view is that the British soldiers were there to make the Highlands governable and to suppress two major Jacobite rebellions. Most probably today we would view the political issues in terms of freedom fighters and outside oppressors. Seen from a historical perspective, the military presence in the landscape was not altogether negative. Most certainly rural life was disrupted, by the presence of so many soldiers and their support staff, but by the end of the period many new roads had been constructed; the landscape was opened up and made safe for trade and travellers. As we shall see in Chapter 12, however, the Highland clearances of the late eighteenth century, which were a very real tragedy to both people and landscape, would not have been possible but for the political changes brought about in this earlier period.

The landscape of mainland Scotland started to become increasingly militarized following Oliver Cromwell's invasion in 1650. An English invasion was nothing new to Scotland, which the previous century had witnessed the 'rough wooing' (1544–8), when English troops under the Earl of Hertford devastated large areas of the south-east border country and parts of Edinburgh.[23] What made Cromwell's visit very different was the fact that he arrived with 16,000 men of Parliament's New Model Army, which was Britain's first truly modern army of well-disciplined and adequately paid soldiers.

The full-time soldiers of the New Model Army in Scotland were housed in purpose-built forts known as citadels at Ayr, Perth, Inverness and Leith, which were built between 1652 and 1655. The defences of these citadels were designed to resist a cannonade and they enclosed substantial barrack blocks. The carefully positioned new citadels made it possible for Cromwell to govern a country whose population did not welcome their new ruler. The presence of a full-time army did provide peace, but at a huge cost: 36,000 men were required to impose the new regime, and 10,000 garrison troops to police and maintain it. When Charles II acceded to the throne in 1660 the Treasury, if nobody else, would have welcomed the return of the soldiers to lay down their arms before the new Stuart king of both countries. So the garrisons and forts built by Cromwell in Scotland were abandoned after 1660, largely for financial reasons.

After 1660 Scotland retained a small standing army of some 2,000 men, augmented in 1678 by a militia of 5,500. It was during the later seventeenth century that the regimental system, complete with full-time officers, became thoroughly established. This small core force was augmented in times of trouble, such as the religious uprisings of 1666 and 1678, but once the troubles had been dealt with, the standing army reverted to just 2,000 men.

The attempted uprising that followed the Act of Union in 1707 worried Queen Anne's government, and work was immediately begun to improve the three main royal garrisons at Edinburgh, Stirling and Fort William. This work was completed in time for the uprising of 1715, which was defeated and led to further military works in the Highlands (despite the fact that the uprising had largely been in the Lowlands) and in the barrack towns of northern England, especially at Berwick. The military projects in the Highlands included four major

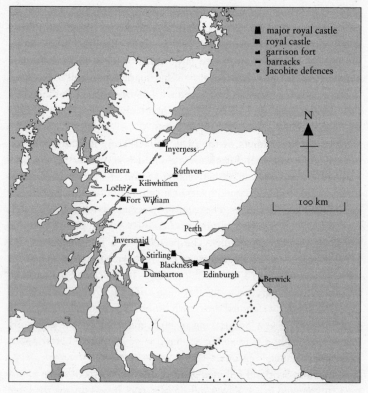

Fig. 10.3 Military map of Scotland, 1715–24.

new defended barracks accommodating between 360 and 120 'redcoats'. The siting of these new barracks, however, was not well thought out and none enjoyed a particularly long life. The strikingly positioned barracks at Ruthven, near the River Spey, just south-west of the Cairngorm National Park in the Scottish Highlands, was built in 1719 on the site of a medieval fortification, but fell to the Jacobites after a siege, in the rebellion of 1745.

In 1724 a report by Lord Lovat on the poor state of military preparedness in the Highlands led George I to appoint an Anglo-Irishman, Major-General George Wade, to the command of all forces in 'North Britain', as Scotland was then often known in official circles. Wade prepared his own report for King George, which echoed Lovat's but if anything was more gloomy. He reported that of the 22,000 men in the Highlands just 10,000 were favourable to the government, whereas the rest sided with the Jacobites. He followed this grim assessment with a list of suggested repairs, modifications and new building projects, including what was to be his greatest achievement in the Highlands, a system of roads between the various forts, garrisons and barracks. To this day these are known as Wade's roads, and they transformed access to, and communication within, the Highlands.

Wade supervised the construction of about 400 kilometres of road and some forty new bridges, most of which were constructed to a

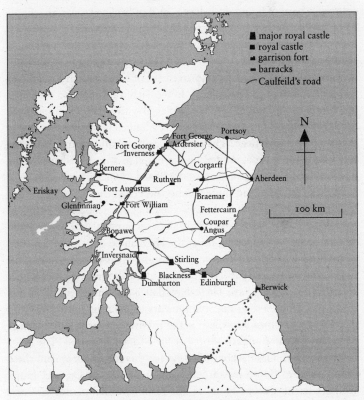

Fig. 10.4 Military map of Scotland, 1745–69.

standard, plain but very functional design. There were a very few notable exceptions, including the bridge that Wade himself regarded as his crowning achievement which was built in 1733 across the upper reaches of the Tay, at Aberfeldy (Perth and Kinross). The construction of 'Wade's roads' through the Highlands was a very remarkable feat of civil engineering and Wade was personally responsible for persuading the government in London to raise the necessary money. It is true that some roads were already in existence, but these were in very poor condition and Wade transformed them from tracks to examples of professional civil engineering, perfectly capable of accepting wheeled traffic. Wade established that his roads should be about 5 metres wide, narrowing down to 3 metres in difficult terrain, and built of three courses: a base of boulders, below a level of broken stones, the whole being capped with gravel, for good drainage. However, archaeological excavation has suggested that this rather rigid standard was not always strictly adhered to.

Wade also supervised the improvement of many military buildings, including Edinburgh Castle itself. In the early 1730s he had the entire western defences 'ironed out' and replaced with a complex zig-zagged artillery fortification capable of resisting a limited bombardment, rather than a prolonged siege. The zig-zag wall is still standing and the building work was supervised by the noted architect William Adam, who was then a master mason to the Board of Ordnance.

Wade's assistant road builder, who succeeded him after 1740, was Major William Caulfeild. He constructed about 1,600 kilometres of road and possibly as many as 800 bridges – a monumental achievement that completed the opening-up of the Highlands.

Scotland was home to some major military installations after the suppression of the last Jacobite rebellion at the Battle of Culloden, near Inverness, in April 1746. These have left an enduring mark on the landscape. One of the finest monuments of later eighteenth-century military architecture anywhere is the promontory fort, Fort George Ardersier, on the southern shores of the Moray Firth (see Plate 9 for an aerial view). Plans were drawn up for this fort in 1747 and these were described by no less a person than Lieutenant-Colonel James Wolfe (later of Quebec fame) as 'the most considerable fortress and best situated in Great Britain'.[24] It was designed by William Skinner, took twenty years to build and incorporates the very latest in late-eighteenth-century military thinking.[25]

The contrast between the landscapes of the Scottish Borders in the seventeenth and eighteenth centuries was remarkable. We saw in Chapter 9 how tower houses and their defended barmkin enclosures had been such an important feature of the rural scene during the continuing feuding of the sixteenth and earlier seventeenth centuries. Sometimes it is possible to see a reflection of the changing political climate in the buildings. At Smailholm in the Scottish Borders, for example, the sixteenth-century tower in the western courtyard was replaced after 1645 by an entirely new two-storeyed house and barmkin. This was a response to the return of more peaceful conditions in the decades following the union of the crowns of England and Scotland in 1603.

DROVES AND DROVERS

The establishment of turnpikes was to have a transforming effect on Britain's roads, but other, less formal routes remained of almost equal importance, especially to farmers. Indeed, as turnpike traffic increased, the disruption and damage caused by large numbers of animals could not be tolerated, so there was a positive incentive to retain older road systems. Of these informal routes the drovers' roads, or drifts as they are sometimes known in East Anglia, were probably the most important. Some indeed continued in use well into the twentieth century, especially in rural areas where large numbers of sheep and cattle had to be driven to market.[26] Many isolated rural pubs originated as drovers' inns and were usually provided with 'layers' or 'layerage', secure pasture for the animals overnight. My own house is located on a medieval drove-road that was last used for taking livestock off the Fen pastures to Spalding market, in the 1930s. Next door was the drovers' inn, The Gate Hangs High, which only ceased trading in the 1950s.

Drove-roads need to be wide and have good, stock-proof walls or hedges, many of which were formalized during the years of Parliamentary Enclosure. Thousands were in existence in prehistoric and Roman times. By the Middle Ages monasteries such as the great Cistercian houses of Yorkshire, had far-flung flocks and herds that needed to be moved through the countryside between different grange farms and town markets. However, it was not until post-medieval times, when regional farming economies began to flourish, that long-distance drove-roads entered their heyday. These routes were rarely direct and made extensive use of scrubland, common land and 'wastes' around the fringes of good arable land. Their use reached a peak around 1800, when some 100,000 cattle were transported from Scotland to England.

By the eighteenth century London was by far the largest city in Britain and its inhabitants had a huge appetite for meat, and especially for beef. Prior to the improvements of the early nineteenth century, the harsher climate meant that Scottish farmers were generally unable to fatten all their cattle, so they were driven south, along the substantial drove-road network of that country.[27] Some would end their journey in Yorkshire and elsewhere but many were driven to markets in Norfolk, Suffolk and Essex for sale in the autumn.[28] They would then be fattened throughout the winter and driven to Smithfield, where they would be sold to London butchers. Everyone benefited from this trade: the Scottish farmers received good prices for their tough, hardy animals capable of making the long journey south, and the East Anglian farmers were able to use their autumn surplus of straw, hay and later of root crops to fatten them up. The huge quantities of manure produced by the cattle as they were housed over winter was also a valuable by-product. The beef trade was large: in the seventeenth century, for instance, one major Scottish landowner sent 4,000 head of cattle southwards each season. In 1663, 18,574 beasts were passing through Carlisle alone. Scottish drovers would usually accompany their beasts all the way to Suffolk, averaging 19–24 kilometres a day (the graves of two who died in the 1680s may still be seen in the churchyard at Thrandeston).

It would be a great mistake to assume that the droves and drovers of Britain were irregular or haphazard in some way. Too much depended on them to allow the safety of the animals to be placed at risk. There was a well-established system of droves. The complexity of this system is remarkable and by the later eighteenth century the drovers who took the fat beasts to Smithfield were certainly the equivalent in social standing of the butchers with whom they traded. It took skill to ensure that the beasts arrived in London still with a good covering of fat on them.

Fig. 10.5 Lower Old Hodder Bridge, with its daring central span, is one of the finest packhorse bridges in Britain. It crosses the River Hodder, near Clitheroe, in Lancashire and was probably built by Sir Richard Shireburn in the late 1580s. These bridges were built with increasing frequency from the sixteenth century onwards, and were essential to the growing industrial economy of south Lancashire. The packhorses carried side-panniers which could reach quite close to the ground, which is why many packhorse bridges have low, or in this instance, no retaining walls. The roadway looks precarious from the side, but viewed end-on it is somewhat less daunting (*below*).

The increasing number of toll roads and restrictions caused by numerous new parish enclosures from the late eighteenth century added to the problems faced by drovers. But it nevertheless continued to be a lucrative trade which is no doubt why the early railway companies were quick to build cattle wagons. Although local droves leading to regional markets and railway centres continued for much longer, the new railways had finished off the long-distance drovers by the early 1850s.

Some of the most inaccessible parts of upland Britain were served by packhorse roads. These were areas where steep gradients and narrow paths made it difficult to use carts or wheeled vehicles. Many pack-horse roads still survive and they probably have origins extending back perhaps even to prehistoric times. By the sixteenth century regional workshops and traders were growing in importance and needed to take their goods to market. The result of this increasing prosperity and greater traffic was that packhorse roads were substantially improved. Particularly difficult places were crossed by distinctive packhorse bridges, hundreds of which still survive in Cumbria, the Pennines and elsewhere.[29] These bridges were built for sure-footed ponies and make little allowance for other road-users.

'A PROSPECT OF . . .': EARLY TOPOGRAPHICAL PRINTS AND DRAWINGS

By the eighteenth century a growing number of people were able to express the pride they felt in the towns where they lived or grew up. This sense of pride of place provided a ready market for publishers of accurately drawn views of various towns and cities, where prominent individual buildings were clearly portrayed. Print publishers would announce a new panoramic view, generally known as a 'Prospect', in the area where it was to be sold. Potential subscribers were then persuaded to pay their subscriptions, which covered the artist's fees and other production expenses.

Prints are simpler to reproduce and often show small details of particular towns or buildings, usually on specified dates.[30] Some of the finest and most useful topographical prints of Britain were produced in the first half of the eighteenth century by the brothers Samuel and Nathaniel Buck, whose detailed prints and drawings were to have a lasting effect on later topographical artists.[31] Their work included more than four hundred illustrations of antiquities, many of which have subsequently been damaged or destroyed, and a unique series of more than eighty detailed panoramic views of England's principal towns and cities, all sketched and published in the years leading up to the industrial era.

POLITE LANDSCAPES: EARLY PARKS AND GARDENS

The great landscape parks that still surround Britain's many surviving country houses are enduring symbols of their creators' wealth and an expression of their fine artistic tastes. The greatest period of the British landscape park was undoubtedly the eighteenth century, when world-renowned landscape designers such as Humphry Repton and Lancelot 'Capability' Brown were at the peak of their powers. More than two centuries later we can appreciate that they were part of a still continuing succession of landscape designers whose roots ultimately lay in the elaborately arranged paths and beds to be seen in wall paintings at Pompeii or indeed in those gardens expertly excavated, and later replanted, at the first-century AD Roman palace at Fishbourne in West Sussex.

While the gardening tradition was essentially domestic or monastic, the eighteenth-century country house was also surrounded by parkland, and this had its origins very much earlier in the medieval tradition of the deer park and royal hunting forest. As we saw in Chapter 8, these parks contained many of the features found in later land-scape parks, such as single trees, 'lawns' of grass, boundary walls and areas of woodland. They also contained the delicate, spotted fallow deer that even today are the commonest parkland deer. It cannot be denied that each of the components of a park is attractive in its own right and that when combined the effect can be superb, but there was more to it than that. Such landscapes could only be created by immensely rich and powerful men. Permission, too, was required from the Crown. So in the seventeenth and eighteenth centuries parkland was already a very long-established symbol of status and prestige.

During the Middle Ages the arts of gardening thrived in many monastic settlements and aristocratic great houses. By the end of the Middle Ages this long tradition had culminated in garden designs that were very geometrical and contained. It is as if their designers were doing their best to depart as far as possible from the natural landscape – not that there was much left of it in lowland Britain by the later

Middle Ages. A few parks and gardens of the sixteenth century have survived, or have been carefully restored.

One of the best is the garden of Lyveden New Bield ('Build'), near Corby, Northamptonshire. Lyveden was built by Sir Thomas Tresham, a complex character who also built the well-known Triangular Lodge, nearby at Rushton (1594–7).[32] The ground plan of Lyveden is cruciform and the entire building is steeped in religious symbolism. The house was never completed and Tresham, a well-known Catholic with links to the Gunpowder Plot,[33] supervised most of the work, in great detail, from his prison cell. We tend to think that Elizabethan gardens were necessarily stiff, geometric and formal, but the grounds at Lyveden show that not always to have been the case, especially away from the house itself. The earliest surviving practical garden manual, *The Gardener's Labyrinth*, by Thomas Hill (*c.* 1577) shows that Elizabethan gardens were intended to be productive and great emphasis was placed on good plants, healthy soil and appropriate cultivation.[34]

STOWE AND THE EVOLUTION OF 'POLITE LANDSCAPES' IN THE LATE SEVENTEENTH AND EIGHTEENTH CENTURIES

Britain has made at least two major contributions to world art. The first was the insular development of Celtic Art in the last two centuries of the Iron Age and the second was the country house with its land-scaped parks and gardens. During the last two decades of the seventeenth century ideas on landscape design changed. This evolution gave rise to its greatest flowering, widely known as the English style.

The late seventeenth and eighteenth centuries saw a new perception of the British countryside. It was a shift away from a workaday place, where crops were harvested and game hunted, to somewhere altogether more special, where the mind could rise to higher things. In terms of the 'polite landscapes' – the landscape parks – that this gave rise to, we see a movement away from formality and geometrical design, towards a new, increasingly naturalistic, albeit often highly stylized, tradition. This most probably reflected contemporary philosophy, but it has also been seen as an opposite reaction to the wholesale 'taming' of the rural landscape that followed upon ever-more intensive farming and the growing pace of enclosure.[35]

The shift from a utilitarian to a romantic perception of the rural landscape owed much to the writings of the French philosopher Jean-Jacques Rousseau (1712–78). Rousseau lived an itinerant life and had seen all sides of French society, from servant to aristocrat. He strongly disliked the fashionable salons and intricate rules of social behaviour that had to be observed within them, and wrote extensively about the benefits of a simple existence. When still a youth he had lived in the mountains around Lake Neuchâtel where he had acquired a strong attachment to simple rural life. He very much admired what he perceived as its dignity and self-sufficiency – so much so that his contemporary Denis Diderot described it as his 'Swiss rusticity'.[36]

In the seventeenth and eighteenth centuries the urban population was growing with increasing rapidity, and the period also saw the emergence of a well-educated middle class. Many of these people lived in towns and suburbs, and from the eighteenth century the idea of the rural idyll grew in popularity. These ideas were exemplified in Britain by the paintings of Thomas Gainsborough and John Constable. A central component of the rustic idyll was the concept of the view, which is still with us today, except that in the twenty-first century we do not have to find our own views, but are guided to officially designated Areas of Outstanding Natural Beauty where we may marvel at the scenes before us from the safety of designated viewpoints, dutifully mapped by the Ordnance Survey. It is almost as if the landscape between the views did not exist (which for many motorists using Sat Nav is probably true). But is this obsession with views entirely modern?

In the eighteenth century it was believed that most rural landscapes could provide fine views, with a little manipulation. Britain's most famous landscape designer would explain to a potential client that his land had great 'capability' for improvement, provided, of course that he, Capability Brown, was paid a fortune to dam the stream to make the lake and plant the trees, where necessary. Similarly, Humphry Repton would provide his clients with a Red Book, in which he drew the best views of the landscapes he had improved for them. Again, it was all about looking at the (improved) landscape from fixed positions.

As we shall see in Chapter 12, this tradition of landscape appreciation through fixed 'views' was to gather pace and become even more important in the nineteenth century.

Most of the great estates were never reserved for the sole and exclusive use of the owner. They were built to be seen and enjoyed and many were open all year round.[37] Some of the more senior domestic servants in these great houses would often benefit from tips received from grateful visitors, after conducted tours.[38] Members of the gentry when travelling would often visit great houses as part of the journey and some kept records of their various trips. One of the best and most prolific of these was Celia Fiennes, who wrote between 1682 and 1712.[39] She was the daughter of a Cromwellian colonel, and her travels took her to most parts of England, where she recorded what appears to have been everything she saw, and in remarkable detail, ranging from coal mines, to Oxbridge colleges, to individual rooms in country houses.

The first phase of eighteenth-century landscape garden design actually began earlier, about 1680. Throughout the seventeenth century fashionable English gardens had been heavily influenced by the grand French designs such as those by André Le Nôtre (1613–1700), creator of such royal gardens as the famous parterres at the Tuileries. A truly stand-alone English style of garden design only emerged around the turn of the century. Happily, two of the finest examples have survived in remarkably good condition at Stourhead, in Wiltshire, and at Studley Royal, in North Yorkshire.

The gardens at Studley Royal were created by John Aislaby, who inherited the estate in 1693. He was an ambitious man: a Member of Parliament, and by 1718 Chancellor of the Exchequer. This was the year when he began to improve his estate and decided to create a garden in the wildest part of the park in the Skell Valley, at some distance from his house, which was another very unusual feature of so early a garden. Two years later disaster struck. He had been a major investor in the infamous South Sea Bubble and was forced to resign from office in 1721, whereupon he decided to devote his energies to his gardens, in a retreat from public humiliation. He died in 1742 and was succeeded by his son William, who continued work on the gardens. The father's creations belong within the earlier eighteenth-century geometrical tradition, whereas the son preferred a more natural style of landscaping, but he had the good sense, or possibly lacked the money, to tamper with the earlier work.

Although inspired by French masters like Le Nôtre, the Studley Royal water gardens are altogether different; for a start they are far simpler and less fussy than anything of the period in France and owe much to John Aislaby's appreciation of a landscape with which he was deeply familiar. The sheer size of the great Canal, which forms the spine of the gardens and approximates to the natural course of the River Skell, and of the formal ponds around it, allow the waters to reflect the buildings and the scenery around them. This effect is enhanced by the fact that the gardens and the ponds are sheltered from the wind, and their mirror-like surfaces reflect both the sky and the trees of the steep wooded valley. There are also a few buildings which were added after the main framework of the garden, the water features, had been completed. They were placed with great care, either to highlight a vista or to take advantage of their reflection in the waters. A few well-positioned statues were added in the 1730s.

Fig. 10.6 Studley Royal water gardens, North Yorkshire, looking south-east across the Small Half Moon Pond and the Canal. In the trees across the valley of the River Skell is the gothic Octagon Tower (c. 1740–50).

One of the best-known aspects of Studley Royal is the 'borrowing' of the ruins of Fountains Abbey. The formality of the Half Moon Pond suddenly gives way to a more naturalistic landscape where the romantic ruins of the abbey can be seen in the distance, carefully framed by planting on either side of the steep valley of the River Skell, which once supplied the abbey with water and today feeds the Studley Royal water gardens. The Skell Valley is naturally steep-sided at this point, but the northern side, nearer to Fountains Abbey a short distance upstream, was made even steeper when stone for the abbey and its buildings was quarried in the twelfth and thirteenth centuries. Judicious tree-planting along the valley sides frames the ruins.

I sometimes wonder why I find the famous landscape gardens at Stowe, in Buckinghamshire, so appealing. Perhaps it is because they were in a fairly run-down state when I first visited, and I had to use my imagination to recreate what textbooks on landscape history had told me was there. Since then a vast amount of work has taken place

Fig. 10.7 Landscape as theatre: the view of the misty ruins of Fountains Abbey, as seen from the Half Moon Pond in the water gardens at Studley Royal, North Yorkshire. The planting, originally by William Aislaby in the mid-eighteenth century, has been carefully arranged to heighten the drama of the valley through which flows the River Skell.

and the garden, doubtless as a result, has become much more popular. The guidebooks are better and the various phases of design are now less muddled up than they once were. All in all, I suppose it is a great improvement, but sometimes I wonder whether such otherwise admirable restoration, which is becoming increasingly popular at many other important houses and gardens, is not also removing some of the charm of imperfection.

So what were these gardens really about? Certainly they expressed and displayed for all to see aristocratic good taste and, in the case of Stowe, a critique of current national politics. They also reflected the rise and fall of different styles, such as Classical Allegory or Neo-Gothic. Bearing in mind that many such gardens were always open to the public, we can see that they are also vehicles for demonstrating wealth, power and influence. However, I wonder whether there were other, perhaps, unconscious motives behind them. It is widely accepted that such places were an experience that was intended to convey something much deeper than pleasure. Moving through a structured landscape where legend, myth, religion and fantasy are artfully contrived reminds me of the stage-managed approach to a medieval castle or indeed the complexities of a prehistoric ritual landscape. I suspect that much of what motivated people to create these extraordinary places, which still have the power to affect us profoundly today, will always remain beyond mere analysis – or indeed restoration.

The gardens at Stowe are hugely important because they contain examples of all three periods of English eighteenth-century landscape design. Most of the garden that survives today belongs to the final, naturalistic, phase and during this final re-creation some elements of earlier designs were removed, but enough remains for us to appreciate the three main movements in the development of the English style of landscape gardening: starting with the formal phase of the royal gardener Charles Bridgeman, followed by the earlier mid-eighteenth-century phase of classical allusion, epitomized at Stowe by the work of William Kent and James Gibbs. The final, idealized naturalistic phase, was initiated by Capability Brown and Lord Cobham himself, but the full flowering of the naturalistic style was actually achieved by Lord Temple, the third owner, who showed a close interest in the grounds and gardens, in the second half of the eighteenth century.

Sir Richard Temple demolished the Tudor house he had inherited and rebuilt on a larger scale and higher up the hill. The new building commanded the view to the south where he also laid out three formal garden compartments. The second owner, Viscount Cobham, laid out a massive new garden, surrounded by a continuous ha-ha. A ha-ha consisted of a ditch where one side had been cut vertical and strengthened with a revetment wall. The other side sloped down to the wall very gradually. The vertical face prevented deer and livestock from entering the garden from the park beyond, yet the view of the landscape from the great house was not obscured by unsightly walls or fences. It was another clever, but expensive way to impress one's guests and visitors.

Temple's garden unified the three compartments of the earlier garden at Stowe. The new garden was more naturalistic than anything that had gone before, but it still retained the strong formal elements that

Fig. 10.8 This plan of Stowe was published in 1739 by the widow of its principal designer, Charles Bridgeman. It shows the first and more formal phase of the gardens of c. 1714–35. The landscape gardens around the house were enclosed and defined by a five-sided ha-ha, with military-like bastions at the corners. Within the gardens were a series of sight-lines, straight paths and avenues which were arranged to provide carefully selected views. A series of more naturalistic subsidiary gardens developed inside Bridgeman's original framework.

Fig. 10.9 Stowe, Buckinghamshire. This view shows the Temple of Concord and Victory (1748), with the Grecian Valley beyond. The Grecian Valley looks entirely natural, but is actually the result of much earth-moving, carried out under the supervision of Capability Brown, head gardener in the 1740s.

have provided the basic structure for subsequent developments. This first phase in which the main garden design was by Charles Bridgeman, lasted from about 1714 to 1720. During this phase Vanbrugh, who collaborated with Bridgeman on the buildings, also created the first of the many temples that would become a defining feature of Stowe. After 1726 Bridgeman doubled the size of the gardens, extending them to the west. At this stage he also introduced the first informal or semi-natural features within the geometric master design of the first, formal phase of the garden.

The second phase, of Classical Allegory, began around 1735 with William Kent's creation of the watery valley known as the Elysian Fields, which includes possibly Stowe's best-known monument, the highly political Temple of British Worthies, an altar to party political favour. These new projects were made possible by the moving of the entrance road to the west of the gardens. Kent designed his own buildings and probably their landscaping too, but his work was largely confined to the centre and west of the gardens. Cobham was still keen to expand the gardens and soon after 1740 began work in a new area to the east (in Hawkwell Field) and around the Octagon Lake, where the buildings were designed by James Gibbs. These buildings included the Queen's Temple and the Gothic Temple. It is assumed that Cobham himself supervised the landscaping here, although he was probably assisted by 'Capability' Brown who joined the staff at Stowe as head gardener in 1741. The last stage of the central garden's evolution was Brown's creation of the Grecian Valley, where work began in 1746. Sadly, Brown's plan to flood the valley failed and the result although nominally Grecian owes more to the Home Counties than the Aegean.

The final phase took place under Lord Temple, who inherited Stowe in 1749 and worked tirelessly on the gardens until his death in 1779. The gardens that survive today are a tribute to this remarkable 'hands-on' owner. He transformed the straight lines and geometric

Fig. 10.10 The scale of the landscape gardens at Stowe, Buckinghamshire. This view northwards, is across the Octagon Lake, up the south vista, towards the south front of the house, which was rebuilt by Lord Temple in 1774 (*left*). The central trees hide the earlier Elysian Fields, laid out by William Kent around 1735. To the right, in Hawkwell Field, is the Gothic Temple by James Gibbs, built between 1744 and 1748, during Stowe's second phase of expansion under Lord Cobham.

layout of the earlier layouts into more naturalistic sweeping curves that harmonized with the Grecian Valley. He also constructed a number of vistas looking towards monuments he had positioned well outside Bridgeman's ha-ha, thereby 'borrowing' elements of the surrounding landscape to give the whole garden a more naturalistic air. The scale of these new monuments ensured that the estate retained its princely character, but today some of the more far-flung look rather odd, standing as they do in a modern farming landscape. Lord Temple's greatest achievement was the south vista down to the Octagon Lake, which involved the felling of an existing avenue, the moving of two Vanbrugh pavilions and the construction (in 1765) of a magnificent Corinthian arch as the focus of the vista, well beyond the outer ha-ha. To match the magnificence of the vista, Lord Temple also had the house substantially rebuilt (1774) with the help of architects who included Robert Adam.

The Gothic Temple was built to contrast with the many classical temples around it. Its interior was adorned, after his death, by painted coats-of-arms belonging to entirely fictitious Anglo-Saxon ancestors of Lord Cobham and around the walls were arranged seven marble statues of Saxons. These have been removed, but the juxtaposition of the Saxons and the Gothic, which sets an archaeologist's teeth on edge, was perfectly acceptable in the eighteenth century, when both were metaphors for perceived English values, such as freedom, Magna Carta and trial by jury – all of which, so Whigs believed, were saved from Catholic Stuart absolute monarchy by Cromwell's Commonwealth and by the Glorious Revolution of 1688.

The Gothic Temple was built to celebrate the English values of liberty, enlightenment and democracy that were then an important component of Whiggish ideals. However, like so many political ideals, they were to prove awkward when actually put to the test. Much later, in the 1820s, the Whigs being major landowners with their own vested interests, opposed Parliamentary reform when they were first approached by radical reformers such as William Cobbett.[40] Thanks to their prolonged resistance the Great Reform Bill was not passed until 1832.

THE ROMANCE OF RUINS

Eighteenth-century gardeners were adept at using ruins for dramatic effect, the more so as they could also be portrayed as crumbling romantic places possessed of the dark secrets that were slightly later to become popular in the horror film equivalents of the time, the Gothic novels whose creepy-sounding titles such as *Nightmare Abbey* and *Crotchet Castle* actually conceal some fine satirical writing.[41] While the academic study of antiquity was becoming established with the well-illustrated and accurately surveyed books of men like William Stukeley (1687–1765), the popular imagination also saw ancient monuments, such as Neolithic stone circles, as the creations of Druids, Danes and mythical Celtic heroes, who provided a welcome contrast to the sometimes rather austere ideals offered by Classical Allegory.[42]

In fashionable rather than academic circles, the growing interest in the remote past had much to do with the supposed 'horrors' of pre-history, such as human sacrifice by the Druids. Ancient-looking grottoes and other features became an important part of many landscape gardens, where they provided a dark emotional contrast to the tranquillity of mirror lakes and reflected Grecian statuary. Ancient monuments like Stonehenge, Avebury and the Rollright Stones in Oxfordshire, started to become significant visitor attractions at about this time. Even an academically inclined observer such as the antiquarian William Stukeley described the Rollrights as 'the greatest Antiquity we have yet seen . . . corroded like wormeaten wood by the harsh Jaws of Time'.[43] But of course they were always capable of 'improvement'. We know for a fact, for example, that a significant proportion of the Rollright Stones were erected or re-erected at this time.[44]

If an ancient monument could not be 'borrowed' from the landscape near one's fashionable Romantic landscape garden, then the next best thing to do was to dig one up and transport it to where it could be better appreciated. This is what happened in the new Romantic gardens being laid out around Old Wardour Castle in the 1790s. We saw in the previous chapter (pp. 350–51) that the back of the castle had been destroyed in 1644. The old castle was then abandoned by its occupiers, the Arundell family, who built themselves a new house nearby before

Fig. 10.11 The Gothic Temple of Liberty at Stowe, Buckinghamshire. Stowe is the largest and finest eighteenth-century landscape garden in Britain. Today it contains some thirty-two classically inspired temples, shrines and grottoes, most of which are built from a pale, creamy oolitic limestone. The Gothic Temple was intended to contrast with these, being constructed from a dark honey-coloured ironstone. The gardens at Stowe were constructed by rich Whig landowners to proclaim, among other virtues, Whig values.

Fig. 10.12 In the later eighteenth century ruins like those of Old Wardour Castle were 'improved' by the addition of Romantic features, such as this twin rustic alcove, set alongside two of the surviving stones of a reconstructed Neolithic stone circle (*right*). The Romantic garden was commissioned in 1792 and the contractor was told to use fragments from the old castle, whose south side had been demolished during the English Civil War.

moving into the current New Wardour House, a fine stately home completed in 1776. The eighth Lord Arundell realized the potential of the ruined castle as he took possession of New Wardour House and he employed various leading landscape architects, including 'Capability' Brown and Richard Woods, to improve the setting of Old Wardour Castle. These improvements included a new lake and the construction of a fine Gothic banqueting house in 1773–4. Somewhat later the historical theme of the grounds around the ruined castle was continued with the construction of a large grotto, two rustic alcoves and a re-erected prehistoric stone circle reputedly removed from an ancient site at Tisbury, a few miles away.[45]

Some landowners in the seventeenth and eighteenth centuries, not content with fashioning ancient-looking grottoes in their parks and gardens, created ancient-looking carved figures on chalk hillsides. The 'horror' of prehistoric times was vividly conveyed, especially to ladies of gentle birth, by the vast size of the figures' priapic manhood. Two of the best known examples are the Long Man of Wilmington (probably eighteenth century) and the Cerne Abbas Giant (probably seventeenth century). Both are located close by genuine prehistoric monuments, just like the only proven ancient hill figure, the White Horse of Uffington.[46]

Doubtless their deliberate positioning near genuine archaeological sites was done to emphasize their 'antiquity'. The Cerne Abbas Giant is first mentioned in a history of Dorset, published in 1744, but was almost certainly constructed earlier. He has achieved a degree of notoriety by virtue of his aggressively priapic nakedness – which was doubtless intended to convey barbarous antiquity, an intention further enhanced by his positioning close by an Iron Age hillfort.

The sudden rash of hill figures that appeared in counties like Dorset

Fig. 10.13 The Long Man of Wilmington, East Sussex. This is one of the most strikingly positioned hill figures, visible from many points in the Weald. The figure has become elongated over the years and his two sticks have grown in length. At first glance he seems ancient, but in actual fact he does not occur in any literature until 1779, by when he was in poor condition. A date in the late seventeenth or eighteenth century seems most probable.

and Wiltshire was a strong sign that local landowners were not afraid to express themselves and also that there was healthy competition among them. The same messages can also be found in the caves and grottoes of the landcape parks and gardens that were being created with increasing regularity right across Britain. The early modern period, almost more than any other, witnessed the liberation of ordinary people not just from the last remnants of feudal authority but from the ecclesiastical authorities. But it would also be true to say that the freedom enjoyed was far more constrained by social obligations in the many villages of Britain than was the case in towns and cities, where the pace of change was much quicker.

So far we have tended to view town and country as being clearly separated, but many rural households in areas of western Britain in the post-medieval period ran a dual economy with primary production (say, wool or milk) and secondary production (say, cloth or cheese) combined. As time passed the secondary production often became more important and the original mainstay of the household was dropped. We shall see in the next chapter that part of this process, in the eighteenth and nineteenth centuries, was the development of rural workshops, which became an important part of many regional economies. These privately owned and run establishments were often linked, sometimes via merchants and other middlemen, to markets and manufacturers within the commercial centres of large cities. In this way the old distinction between town and country that had been so important since the Middle Ages, began to break down, a process that has continued with gathering speed to the present day.

II

From Plague to Prosperity:
Townscapes in Early Modern Times
(1550–1800)

The massive growth and development of British towns and cities during the post-medieval period was the most important process in the entire history of the British landscape. It is, moreover, still continuing. Most towns in Britain suffered a severe decline through the later Middle Ages, but from the mid-sixteenth century this was reversed. The figures speak for themselves. In 1550 just 3.5 per cent of the population of England and Wales lived in towns of more than 10,000 people. Fifty years later the figure had risen to 5.8 per cent, by 1700 it was 13.3 per cent and by 1800 it was over 20 per cent. In Scotland, although the starting figure at the end of the Middle Ages was lower, by 1800 it had almost caught up with England.[1]

Certain general trends emerge, but again, as with the story of the countryside, most of these had already started to appear by later medieval times. The regionalization of farming was reflected in the towns of rural Britain where merchants and markets became better adapted to serve the requirements of agriculture and of the growing population. But during this period we also see the expansion of new types of urban centres which owed their existence, not directly to agriculture, but to the emergence of service industries that looked after the needs of a growing population of industrial workers and management. These people included a new class of city-based merchants and financiers who, together with the more astute gentry, were capital-rich and enjoyed the profits of Britain's growing industrial base. This growing and remarkably diverse middle class spent time at a variety of spas and resorts. These places were rather more important than is often supposed.

Perhaps it is the fault of Georgian literature, in which gossip, love and marriage are the dominant themes at places like fashionable London, Brighton and Bath, that we see resorts as little more than elegant playgrounds. But in actual fact these were places where people from all over Britain met and where they made the deals that allowed their businesses to grow. I find it inconceivable that the growth of so many resorts was entirely a matter of pleasure. This thought struck me when I first entered the elegant Pump Room at Bath, because it was not what I had expected. Despite having seen numerous photographs and engravings, I reacted to that space as though I had just walked into a conference centre. In today's jargon, it was structured to facilitate networking.

As the resorts had to cater to their customers' requirements they developed their own character, and I shall spend some time discussing them, as they seem to illustrate well the growing diversity of Britain, which is so characteristic of early modern times. It was in London and in growing regional centres such as Birmingham, Bristol and Manchester that the all-important financial arrangements were made that enabled the rapid expansion of the early industrial era. That expansion was served, but was not made possible by, a growing infrastructure of canals and turnpikes. The single most important factor that allowed Britain's rapid industrial expansion was the diverse social systems that existed at the end of the Middle Ages. These were sufficiently flexible to accommodate the emergence of new industry and, most importantly, that growing middle class of managers and financiers. We shall follow the development of these processes in the textile trades of East Anglia and the north-west together with the rise of heavy industry, at places like Coalbrookdale. But first I want to examine the extraordinary case of London, which by the end of the Middle Ages was by far the largest city in Britain.

LONDON: GROWTH AND EXPANSION, THROUGH PLAGUE AND FIRE

I have discussed the impact of the Black Death and the subsequent waves of plague. Although it happened more than three hundred years after the Black Death, the effect of the Great Plague on London in 1665 was almost as horrific. The impact of plague was vast on population and rural society, but it had long-term effects on life in towns and cities as well. Immigration from south-east England and abroad helped to sustain the population of London, which more than doubled in the period 1550–1650. The nation's capital embarked on a period of sustained growth from the sixteenth to eighteenth centuries.[2] Expansion was certainly aided by the closing-down of many monastic houses following the Dissolution. Some of these sites, such as St John Clerkenwell, already included secular streets within their layout and these became a part of the general city street plan. Many of the smaller monastic houses were torn down and were incorporated into the city. Some of the grander ones were given to nobles, such as the dukes of Norfolk and Newcastle, who built themselves large houses at places like Charterhouse and St Mary, Clerkenwell. One unpleasant knock-on effect of the Dissolution in London was the closing down of the great monastic hospitals by Henry's Secretary and Chancellor Thomas Cromwell, who refused the pleas to hand them over to the city by the Lord Mayor, Sir Richard Gresham. St Thomas's and St Bartholomew's reopened a few years later as secular institutions because of the enormous hardship their closure had caused.[3] Growth continued, despite a series of plagues in 1603, 1625, 1636 and culminating in the worst outbreak of 1665, when 100,000 people are believed to have perished. During the plague years the population of London was maintained by drawing new people in from the small towns and villages of the Home Counties.

London's growth in early modern times was a result of its economic success and the fact that it was both the largest port and capital of the nation. Thanks to the expansion of London, eighteenth-century England was one of the most urbanized states in Europe. In the mid-eighteenth century London was the largest city in western Europe. Estimates suggest that in 1550 its population was around 120,000. Fifty years later it had risen to 200,000 and by 1650 to 375,000. In 1700 it was half a million and a century later, in the first census of 1801, it was just under a million (959,000).[4] So by the start of the nineteenth century the population of London had grown some eight times from the level it had been at the end of the Middle Ages.[5]

Inevitably the history of post-medieval London is dominated by the

Fig. 11.1 London before the Great Fire of 1666. A view from Southwark around 1650. This painting was made shortly before the Great Fire of September 1666 which destroyed most of the buildings in the city in just six days. The old St Paul's Cathedral dominates the north side of the river to the left of London Bridge.

Great Fire of 1666. Before the fire London looked like a late medieval city, with numerous timber-framed buildings and crowded narrow streets. In the century after the fire London had been transformed into something that generally resembled the capital city of the early twentieth century. The natural emphasis placed on an event so cataclysmic should not draw attention away from the very real achievements of Londoners during the previous century or so. As we have seen, the population more than doubled during that time, and it had probably recovered its pre-Black Death level by 1550. This is considerably earlier than most other towns in Britain. The economic success of pre-Great Fire London was fuelled by immigration from south-east England, but also from abroad, via the port of London. London's prosperity also had a beneficial effect on other regions of England. The collieries of the north-east, for example, were entirely sustained, in the centuries prior to the development of the canal and railway network, by trade with merchants in London, mostly via Newcastle.

Recent excavations in the City of London have thrown new light on the extent and impact of the Great Fire. It is now clear that the fire destroyed about five-sixths or 176 hectares of the buildings within the City walls and almost a quarter of a mile of the extra-mural city, as far as Fetter Lane. One reason that the fire got so out of control was the Lord Mayor's unwillingness to tear down some of the expensive stone buildings that had been built in the previous century or so. The rebuilding of the City was something of an English compromise and grand schemes, such as that proposed by Sir Christopher Wren were rejected in favour of a more piecemeal approach. In part, this decision was forced upon the City fathers by the costs of reimbursing so many property-owners had one of the grand new schemes been put into effect. In the event, the rebuilding of the City benefited from the lessons of the past, and although the medieval layout was largely retained, the rebuilt streets were generally wider, to prevent fire from jumping across, and all new buildings were now made of brick or stone.

In all, the Great Fire destroyed some 13,200 houses, but only 8,000 had been rebuilt by 1673. This deliberate attempt to reduce overcrowding is reflected in the population figures for the City, which fell by at least 10,000 to 190,000 in 1690, by which time the City only accounted for a quarter of London's population. During the seventeenth century the economic and administrative geography of the capital had become firmly established. It was a case of success fuelling success: the administrative heart of England was also its largest port and the centre of both trade and commerce. Government and administration were centred around Westminster, which also became the cultural centre. Docks and industry were tending to concentrate just downstream of the City, to the east, in the area later to be called Docklands.

In terms of town planning the most important development of the early modern period took place in 1630, when the architect Inigo Jones, a follower of Palladio's simple classical style, introduced the Italian idea of a piazza: an open urban square. His first piazza, built at Covent Garden, has been almost completely demolished, except for the Palladian church of St Paul, which was rebuilt in 1795 to precisely the same design as the original. Jones subsequently carried out further structured developments, of which the layout of Great Queen Street is the best known. It was Inigo Jones's work that provided the inspiration for the massive West End developments at Bloomsbury and Belgravia in the late eighteenth century.[6]

SMALLER TOWNS AFTER THE
MIDDLE AGES

While London managed to remain steady and even grow during the later Middle Ages, most other British towns and cities reeled from the effects of successive waves of plague. But during the sixteenth and seventeenth centuries these depredations generally ceased and urban populations expanded rapidly, though in many instances without affecting the overall size of the town.[7] So the growing population of many towns and cities became increasingly cramped. This applied most particularly to areas of working-class housing, where the plots of ground within town and city centres were continuously divided and subdivided in the earlier nineteenth century, forming some of the appalling slums of Georgian and early Victorian Britain.

We have seen how the Reformation and Dissolution affected London, with its many hospitals and friaries, but other towns, such as Gloucester, where about 16 per cent of the urban area consisted of monastic buildings, were also affected; here, the monastic sites were replaced by new housing. Many of the new houses built in British towns were like their contemporaries of the 'Great Rebuilding' in rural areas, built from more durable and fire-resistant materials such as brick and stone.

The increasing diversity of early modern town plans makes it very hard to generalize, but during Tudor times the eastern side of Britain with cities such as York and Norwich continued to be economically more powerful than the west. This, however, was to change in the seventeenth century, when both York and Norwich began to lose ground to cities such as Bristol, which had become Britain's third city by 1700. The process accelerated in the eighteenth and nineteenth centuries with the rise of the industrial areas of the north-west.

The Reformation saw much money that would once have gone to the Church being diverted to the state and the result was a spate of new civic buildings such as schools and almshouses. In the second half of the seventeenth century the two universities at Oxford and Cambridge saw the construction of many fine buildings in the classical manner, such as the Wren Library and Nevile's Court at Trinity College, Cambridge, and the Sheldonian Theatre, Oxford. Less visible, but just as important, private money was also devoted to the improvement of sewers and water supplies, such as Lamb's Conduit Street in London, which commemorates William Lambe's benefaction of 1577, and Hobson's Conduit in Cambridge (1614).

Most town defences became redundant in post-medieval times, with the notable exception of Berwick-upon-Tweed, which possesses the finest Tudor artillery defences, erected on the medieval walls of Edward I by Henry VIII. Elsewhere defences of the English Civil Wars survive at Worcester, Pontefract and Newark on Trent. Among naval dockyards, Portsmouth still retains fine examples of Henrician fortifications, including parts of Hurst Castle on the Isle of Wight which guards the western approaches to the Solent (see Fig. 13.26).

Although the markets of most country towns were established during the Middle Ages, the commercial expansion of the rural economy in the early seventeenth century led to the establishment of a number of new markets, including Blackburn and Stevenage, and, in Cumbria, Hawkshead, Ambleside and Shap.

I mentioned at the start of this chapter that urban development from the sixteenth to the nineteenth century was very rapid in Scotland. This is certainly evident in Edinburgh, where in the seventeenth century most of the wooden Tudor and late medieval buildings were replaced in stone. Many of these survive to this day. Edinburgh was a capital city, port and financial centre and it would be a mistake to see it as typical of what was happening in Scotland generally. Rebuilding did indeed happen in many of the historic burghs, but sometimes not until the later eighteenth and nineteenth centuries. At all events it is rare to come across surviving medieval or sixteenth-century buildings in Scottish towns.

We know of the one-time existence of these earlier buildings from maps and excavations, but little survives above ground today, apart, that is, from churches and abbeys. The earliest surviving houses and public buildings still standing usually date to the seventeenth century. This survival represents the introduction of better building techniques and more durable building materials, which led to the construction of buildings that were intended to last for several generations. The granting of royal charters to hold markets was an important component of most Scottish burghs in the Middle Ages and gave many of the towns a focus for the development of their and the surrounding region's economy. This is reflected in the history of its smaller towns, which prospered and declined at different times in the sixteenth to eighteenth centuries. Three examples taken across the central Lowlands, moving from east to west, should illustrate this.

In the fifteenth and sixteenth centuries Dunbar on the southern shore of the Firth of Forth had developed its fish trade but this began to fail by 1700, by which time the town was very impoverished.[8] Then English raids twice razed the town to the ground. It was not to revive until the seventeenth century, when the herring fishery returned to profitability. By this point the burgesses of the town had turned their attention inland towards farming and agriculture for their income. Excavation has shown that the medieval town was arranged along the north–south High Street, probably starting close by the castle gateway at the north end, where protection would have been the greatest. The long, thin burgage plots (the land that accompanied town houses) behind the dwellings that lined the High Street are still preserved in property boundaries, although the medieval buildings themselves have not survived (in part thanks to the 'rough wooing' of Henry VIII and to later wars). The tollbooth was built towards the southern end of the original medieval High Street in the late sixteenth century.[9] This was where the burghal courts met and where taxes and market dues were paid. It also served as a lock-up for temporary prisoners, such as the unfortunate suspects of witch hunts in the early seventeenth century.

Dunbar revived in the seventeenth century and new, formally laid out burgage plots were arranged on either side of the High Street towards the south, possibly on former monastic lands released after the Reformation. The town was also defended, most unusually in Scotland, by the construction of a stone wall, perhaps early in the seventeenth century; we know that it was in a battered and ruinous state by 1669, following the Cromwellian wars, and little of it survives today. The new tollbooth played an important part in the growing market which took place close by. Towards the latter part of the seventeenth century new stone buildings along the High Street were a sign of increasing prosperity, brought about by the considerable success of the herring fishery, which thrived in the sixteenth and for much of the seventeenth century; but by 1660 this was in sharp decline, due to a lack of fish. In 1692 tax returns indicate that for three years the port had done almost no trade at all.

Some Scottish historic burghs manage to hide their earlier history quite effectively. Take Forfar, in Angus. This town was a residence of early Scottish kings and was probably given burgh status by King David I (1124–53). During the Middle Ages it remained a small market town and in early post-medieval times markets continued to be of importance; these were often marked with elaborate market crosses, and the stone base of Forfar's seventeenth-century cross still survives.[10] The cross was erected at the expense of the British Crown in 1684 and was just one of a number of later seventeenth-century improvements to the town, many of which – for example improved flood-water drainage – were hidden below ground. Despite these various measures Forfar did not prosper in the early eighteenth century and a visitor in 1743 described it as having just two public buildings, the church and a tolbooth. The big changes to the town happened in the later eighteenth and nineteenth centuries with the growth of the local linen industry, which brought the region considerable prosperity and with it a fine new church and numerous houses and workshops.

The later post-medieval prosperity of Forfar is not repeated when we move further west to the town of Dumbarton on the north side of the Clyde, downstream from Glasgow.[11] But there were problems. The sixteenth and seventeenth centuries were turbulent times in this area and the political hazards were made worse by frequent flooding, especially in the spring when the (tidal) River Leven was in spate with meltwater running off the southern Highlands – a problem that was not to be solved until 1859. There were numerous disputes, too, with neighbouring burghs Renfrew and Glasgow over the control of shipping along the Clyde. These continued even after 1611 when Glasgow received the Charter of a Royal Burgh from James VI (1567–1625).

Like Dunbar on the east coast, Dumbarton was also actively involved with internal trade in salmon and herring, coarse cloth, hides and livestock, the latter driven across the Leven at low tide. Despite efforts to have one built in the seventeenth century, it was not until 1765 that the town acquired a bridge, which was positioned near the line of the old ford. By the late seventeenth century Dumbarton's economy was in trouble: exports had shrunk to a trickle and even local trade had sunk to the redistribution of a few goods and commodities out of Glasgow. In 1643 the population was a mere 600 or 700; even by the end of the century it was still less than 1,000. For comparison, the population of Glasgow in 1610 was around 7,600 and had doubled again by 1660.

I have to admit that when I examined the history of the smaller Scottish burghs I found it hard to avoid the conclusion that a great deal – perhaps too much – rested on the shoulders of the leading inhabitants of the various towns. Sometimes I found it quite depressing – why did they receive so little outside help? Certainly matters were made no simpler by repeated English raiding, and later by the Jacobite uprising of 1745. Nevertheless the extent to which individual Scottish burghs prospered in the three post-medieval centuries did seem to rely too much on local drive and initiative, rather than co-operation with neighbouring towns and cities. In the smaller burghs, finance appeared hard to come by, but this was to change in the later eighteenth century with improved communications and the increased capitalization of mercantile centres such as Edinburgh, and with it the growth of industries such as ship-building and textiles – as we saw with the later linen industries in Forfar. As a result of these improvements Scotland, and particularly Glasgow, was to play a significant role in the trade that developed with the rest of Britain and the Empire in the nineteenth century.

While the majority of British towns and cities grew organically in the seventeenth and eighteenth centuries, there were exceptions, including the spas and resorts which competed with each other for what today we would call the leisure market. These places had to look impressive, while at the same time operating smoothly as well supplied and serviced social centres. This took planning.

SPAS AND RESORTS IN THE EIGHTEENTH CENTURY

I noted at the start of this chapter that resorts and spa towns played an important part in the development of Britain as an industrial and mercantile centre. They were not just about leisure, any more than the Lord Mayor's annual banquet in the Guildhall is about food. They were important social centres that helped to keep the wheels of commerce turning, but they were also major regional employers. In landscape terms these towns are some of the most elegant in Britain, which is why many of them still continue to attract visitors.

As with other towns of the post-medieval period, it is impossible to generalize about spas and resorts because each has its own story to tell, but some of the common themes that emerge are the wish to retain health and youth, the need to meet and socialize with other people and the importance of maintaining social position.[12] Most resorts and spas started life by catering for their patients but it was soon realized that those who stayed to take the waters had friends and families, whose needs also had to be taken into consideration. That is why the most successful spas developed areas of housing – whether in terraces or villas – that could accommodate the many visitors who accompanied those seeking treatment. As time passed the number of spas increased and competition intensified, whereupon many decided to move into different markets within the developing leisure sector. These tendencies became more marked from the mid-nineteenth century, with the arrival of the railways.

Bath has always been the principal spa town in England and its origins go back to the Iron Age, when its springs are known to have been popular. In Roman times fine classical buildings were erected around the springs of what became *Aquae Sulis*, the shrine to the goddess Sulis Minerva. This popularity continued into medieval times, but Bath only became a spa town, as we would understand the term today, in the sixteenth century. Bathing in its warm waters was believed by doctors to have a curative effect on many disorders, ranging from skin diseases and gout to lead poisoning. Physicians took up permanent residence near the springs and it was plainly in their interest to encourage patients to visit them. Further visitors or patients arrived when the drinking of spa water became popular as a cure for internal problems, from the seventeenth century onwards. Spa water was not a 'rapid fix', whether taken in a bath, or internally, and patients were encouraged to take up residence near the springs, together with their family and friends, for a protracted stay. Soon the increasing numbers had to be accommodated by the building of new pump rooms in the early eighteenth century.

Fig. 11.2 The Royal Crescent, overlooking the Royal Victoria Park, Bath. This magnificent Palladian design by John Wood the younger was the first crescent to be built in Britain; it took several years to finish, from 1767 to about 1775. By the time of its completion the plain, undecorated exterior would have appeared somewhat old-fashioned when compared with the decorated buildings then being built in London by the Adam brothers. Number 1 was the 'show house' and the first to be built; in 1968 it was given to the Bath Preservation Trust and is open to the public with a restored eighteenth-century interior.

The interest in spa water was not confined to Bath alone. By way of contrast, the iron-rich and saline springs at Cheltenham provided treatment for conditions different from those at Bath and it is interesting that the 'season', when it was believed that the treatments were most effective, just overlapped, meaning that some people could visit both spas: Bath between April and June, Cheltenham from May to October.[13] The hot springs at Hotwells on the Avon Gorge were thought to be effective against diabetes, kidney disease and, later, tuberculosis. The way that the different seasons were arranged and structured suggests that the different spa authorities must have collaborated to some extent in order to avoid conflict, and would also suggest that quite soon it had become apparent to those 'in the know' that the market was not bottomless and would require care to exploit efficiently.

As time passed the patients and their families who visited Bath and Cheltenham became increasingly prosperous and there was also a change in the social mix. Towards the latter part of the eighteenth century the landed gentry and aristocracy began to be augmented and then replaced by members of the emerging professional classes, such as merchants, bankers, lawyers and clergy. These energetic people demanded higher standards of accommodation and entertainment and it was at this time that many of the great buildings of Bath, such as The Circus and the Royal Crescent were built.[14] The change in clientele when these new buildings were erected supports the idea that they served more than a social role and must have helped middle-class, professional people meet new clients and colleagues. Bath thrived throughout the eighteenth century but suffered the inevitable fate of the extremely fashionable in the early decades of the nineteenth: it fell from fashion. At this point it reverted to its 'core business' and continued as a health spa throughout that century, only this time to a more diverse and less exclusive clientele.

Prosperity came slightly later to Cheltenham, where the lighter Regency architecture is very different, featuring brick and stucco rather than imposing dressed stonework. Unlike Bath, the Cheltenham springs were dispersed through the fields that surround the town and the new estates sprang up around them.[15] The villas of the partially finished estate in the Pittville area of the town are set well back and like others at Cheltenham have an airy, spacious feeling to them – quite different from Bath. This style of accommodation suggests that many of the groups who arrived in Cheltenham to share a villa had actually met up in advance, perhaps before they arrived.

The emphasis at Cheltenham Spa was on respectable Victorian family gatherings rather than the more freewheeling Georgian society found earlier at Bath. This is not to say, of course, that 'networking' to do with business did not take place; far from it, in fact, as many successful Victorian businesses were organized along family lines. From the mid-nineteenth century the non-terrace style of housing adopted in later developments at Cheltenham found favour with elderly and retired people, when the town began to decline as a spa. This led to a revival of its fortunes which has ensured that most of the fine older buildings have survived to this day.

The principal rival to Bath in the late seventeenth and early eighteenth centuries was Tunbridge Wells, which earned its full name Royal Tunbridge Wells from frequent visits and longer periods spent there by members of King Charles's court, after the Restoration of 1660. While exiled abroad, many courtiers of the Stuart court had acquired a taste for spa life at Spa itself, in Belgium. After the mid-eighteenth century, however, Bath far outstripped Tunbridge Wells in popularity. Even after the coming of the turnpikes, travelling to Bath was never an easy matter and consequently several important spas grew up much closer to London at, for example, Sadler's Well and Clerken Well in

Fig. 11.3 The Pittville Pump Room (*right*) and two villas in Cheltenham Spa, Gloucestershire. Cheltenham Spa was built in a series of developments from the late eighteenth century on open country north and south of the original medieval town on the Gloucester–Broadway road. Pittville (named after the developer John Pitt) was begun in the second quarter of the nineteenth century as a planned development centred on the Pump Room and the fine park in which it sits. Only 200 of the proposed 600 houses were actually finished when the developer died, heavily in debt, in 1842; by this time the spa was in decline.

London itself, and at Dulwich, Sydenham, Streatham or Epsom Wells, just outside. The need to escape crowded London was often pressing, even in the eighteenth century, and fashionable society would repair to resort towns that did not possess springs, such as Richmond-upon-Thames. Time for successful people was becoming increasingly precious and, in a foretaste of today's world, short visits to places like Dulwich or Epsom Wells were often at 'the end of the week'.[16] (The word 'weekend' did not become current until very much later, in 1878.[17])

Buxton in Derbyshire is one of the better-known and more successful of the regional spa towns. Today Buxton is less crowded than its grander southern counterparts and although it is smaller, in many respects its atmosphere is as well, or better, preserved. Its failure to thrive might be due to the fact that it remained largely in private hands and a degree of restraint (if not of stuffiness) was maintained. This might also account for its longevity. It was never so exclusively fashionable that the public could react against it. We can see something similar happening at privately owned coastal resorts, such as Skegness before the takeover of its beach by the local council in the 1920s, and at Hunstanton, in Norfolk, where the heirs to the medieval Le Strange family still own the beach to just beyond the low-tide level.[18]

Like Bath, Buxton (*Aquae Arnemetiae*) was a Roman spa that continued throughout the Middle Ages.[19] It became very fashionable in Tudor times, being visited by the highest in the land, including the earls of Leicester, Warwick and Shrewsbury – the latter accompanying Mary, Queen of Scots. In the eighteenth and nineteenth centuries the present spa was developed near the springs in the valley below old Buxton, which incidentally is the highest market town in England. The development of the fashionable spa was due to the dukes of Devonshire. The project began around 1779 when the fifth Duke commissioned the architect John Carr of York to build the fine Crescent, close by St Anne's Well, then on a desolate hillside. The Duke's intention was to make Buxton a rival to Bath, and the Buxton Crescent was a direct response to Woods's slightly earlier Royal Crescent.

The fifth and sixth dukes continued the development, with a number of elegant Georgian terrace streets and squares. Cheltenham slipped from public favour in the 1840s, but Buxton if anything became more popular. Building continued and Wyatville, the sixth Duke's architect at his great house Chatsworth, laid out the gardens facing the Crescent. Somewhat later Sir Joseph Paxton, following the success of his Birkenhead Park (see below p. 565), made initial designs for Buxton Park, but only a few features of his original plans actually appeared on the ground. Thermal and natural baths appeared in 1853 and the building of apartments and hotels continued. Then in 1863 the railway arrived and Buxton's development increased in pace, at the same time somehow managing to remain upmarket, if not a bit snooty. More churches were built, together with a Pavilion, accompanied by fine Pavilion Gardens, and a Concert Hall. Buxton was now a well-established and relentlessly respectable Victorian resort. Development even continued into the twentieth century with the building for which the town is probably best known, the Opera House, built alongside the Pavilion in 1903 by Frank Matcham.

Spas were never as successful in Scotland as they were in England and Wales. Instead, hydrotherapy was popular.[20] These hydropathical centres, otherwise known as hydros, sprang up in many Scottish towns from the 1840s, sometimes in existing large buildings, sometimes in purpose-built hydros, which by the later nineteenth century were often built on the outer fringes of town. They were sometimes huge buildings, to accommodate friends and family as well as patients. During the 1870s 'hydro mania' gripped Scotland and large numbers were built. Inevitably there was a reaction, and in the following decade many of the companies that had thrived in the boom went bust. There was, however, an underlying steady public demand which was not confined to Scotland. Malvern, in Worcestershire, is an English example.

Many in the medical profession regarded hydrotherapy as quackery, but this view was not shared by everyone. Charles Darwin was an enthusiastic advocate and wrote of the 'wondrous Water Cure', after making repeated visits to Great Malvern.[21] Hydrotherapy was a medical procedure which was believed to be able to cure conditions as varied as rheumatism, gout and nervous disorder. It was not always very pleasant: 'Here I am in a state of perpetual thaw, ceaseless moisture, always under a wet blanket and constantly in danger of kicking the bucket . . . I have been stewed like a goose, beat on like a drum, battered like a pancake, rubbed like corned beef, dried like Finnan haddock and wrapped up like a mummy in wet sheets.'[22]

Although the hydros contributed their large buildings to townscapes and certainly brought prosperity and employment in their wake, they did not affect the layout and arrangement of towns in quite the same way as spas had done previously, or as seaside resorts, with their esplanades, piers and great hotels, were increasingly doing. In Scotland, hydros remained popular and well attended until the First World War. Health farms, their modern equivalents, are, however, currently thriving right across Britain, and are helping many otherwise redundant Victorian country houses to survive into the twenty-first century.

In 1753 a paper by a Dr Richard Russell suggested that sea water could have a beneficial effect on diseases 'of the glands', and from the mid-eighteenth century drinking sea water and sea-bathing were believed to ease or cure many ailments, including asthma, ruptures, madness, deafness, skin and glandular diseases.[23] Bathing in hot sea water was thought to help in the treatment of rheumatism and gout – the latter no doubt encouraged by the high meat content of the upper classes' diet in the eighteenth century. The leading West Country seaside resort was Weymouth in Dorset, which early in its development rivalled even Brighton. Much building took place there in the later eighteenth century under the influence of the Bath entrepreneur Ralph Allen, who visited the resort regularly between 1750 and 1764. Allen introduced the resort to the dukes of York and Gloucester and to George III, who came there with his family and took his first dip in 1789. George and his family continued to visit until 1805. The presence of the Royal Family and of nobility encouraged the town's development, and large numbers of new lodging houses were built around the bay. At this time bathing machines were regarded as essential to modesty and in 1800 no fewer than thirty were in operation. During the winter season visitors bathed in indoor baths. During the second half of the eighteenth century the improvements brought about by the new turnpike trusts allowed other seaside towns in the West Country such as Sidmouth and Lyme Regis to develop themselves as resorts.

TOWNS AND THE INDUSTRIAL ERA

Industrial archaeology has gone a long way towards transforming our ideas about the industrial era.[24] The subject may have begun as a movement to preserve old machines and buildings, but it has developed into a more rounded view of the post-medieval past, in which industry was just one among many different aspects of human experience. Recently industrial archaeologists have become more concerned with the wider relationship between factories, housing and workshops; the effect has been to look at industries within the landscape: how and why they arose in a particular area and the influences they had on a given region's population and economy.[25]

The concept of landscape is particularly significant within industrial archaeology, because it can be used to decide why certain sources of power were originally selected – coal and water are obvious examples. Landscapes can also help to explain why workers' housing, for example, was located in certain areas, but they can never be divorced from purely social considerations. For example, the switch from waterwheels to steam power often necessitated 24-hour shift working to cover the additional costs of coal. This in turn meant that housing had to be positioned close by the factory or mill, whether or not the terrain was actually suited to such a change.

Sometimes social motives were less functional. The great mill-owners frequently aspired to join the landed gentry (which they often achieved with notable success) and to do this they built and positioned their own dwellings to resemble the great country houses of the nobility, far from the mills and back-to-back housing that actually generated the wealth. So industrial archaeology can often reveal the complex relationship between the form of the physical landscape, and the lives of the people who inhabited it, with remarkable clarity.

Examining the local economies and landscapes which gave rise to the industrial era, it is very difficult to pin down with any precision precisely when the Industrial Revolution, which supposedly gave birth to it, began. We do know that the British economy started a hundred years of extremely rapid growth sometime in the mid-eighteenth century and this is generally taken as the nominal start of the Industrial

Revolution. But in most instances these 'new' industries were nothing of the sort: cotton, for example, was imported and processed in the north-west of England in areas where woollen textiles had long been important; one fibre-based industry was simply replacing another. It is also becoming increasingly apparent that the Industrial Revolution in Britain cannot be said to have had a single source. Like the beginning of farming, the previous world-changing human development, the roots of Britain's industrial expansion lie in different places at different times.

The diversity of industrial origins is clearly illustrated by the case of Birmingham, England's so-called 'second city'. This great Midlands conurbation has long been a symbol of the Industrial Revolution.[26] Recently an intensive series of excavations have demonstrated that industry did not suddenly appear there in the eighteenth century. Instead, most of the industries that thrived had been there since the twelfth century and had made use of the city's abundance of water, both as a source of power and as a resource in its own right (flax and leather require much water to process the raw materials).

The industries which were present in Birmingham during the Middle Ages included leather-working, metal-working, pottery and textiles. Metal-working, for which Birmingham is still best known, was already taking place in the Middle Ages, probably using coal imported from the Black Country; the industry then seems to have taken off from about 1550. This period of expansion continued until the late eighteenth century, when many metal-working mills were established along the River Rea and its tributaries. Although the river itself was not navigable, the city had had excellent communications for some time, via a system of long-distance drove-roads. The droveways had kept the butchers and leather-workers supplied with meat and hides since at least the twelfth century, when close links with the Black Country were first established; these were firmly cemented in 1769 with the arrival of the first canal.

The question really is, why were early industrialists able to develop and expand in Britain, rather than elsewhere? As I hinted at the start of this chapter, the answer has to do with the social and political culture of Britain in the late seventeenth and eighteenth centuries. Hard work, too, was seen as a positive virtue by many Nonconformist denominations, such as the Quakers. It would be tempting to see the success of Britain's early industrialists as a by-product of the Reformation, but this would be misleading, because at least one significant family of early industrialists, who developed local industry and the Cumbrian port of Whitehaven, are known to have been Roman Catholic.[27] There was also tolerance and a degree of military fatigue after England's Civil War and the peaceful change to constitutional monarchy that followed from the Glorious Revolution of 1688. For these and many other reasons, Britain was the principal birthplace of the modern industrial world. But even this is an oversimplification. Important elements of the industrial process – motive power and farm and factory machinery – did indeed make their appearance in mid-eighteenth-century Britain, but that is not to say that the rest of the world was doing nothing; the proof of this is that within a few decades industrialization had become a worldwide phenomenon.

This leads me to the use of the term 'revolution'.[28] We saw in the previous chapter that the agricultural 'revolution' was far more extended than was believed fifty years ago. So we ought, in theory, to be careful about using the term 'revolution' with regard to the more rapid growth of industry. This is for essentially the same reasons, because many of the industries that became so important in the late eighteenth and nineteenth centuries actually had strong local roots going back hundreds of years.

The dual economies that had developed in early post-modern times in the pastoral landscapes of western England encouraged the growth of home workshops, which then formed the basis of the earliest mills or factories.[29] In other areas, such as south Wales and north-eastern England, mining, which had been under way since earlier medieval or even Roman times, became industrialized as part of a seamless and not very revolutionary process. The structure of certain regional societies whose origins lay in the Middle Ages was naturally well adapted to accept the processes of industrialization. Again, the changes were evolutionary rather than revolutionary. Despite all these arguments to the contrary, the Industrial Revolution is a concept that has become deeply entrenched. So for ease of reading, if nothing else, I will henceforward use this term.

The process of wholesale industrialization started to become evident in Britain from at least the mid-eighteenth century. The half century that followed was an astonishing period of technological, managerial and financial development, not, of course, without its exploitative side, too. The result was that Britain did indeed become 'the Workshop of the World' and London its financial capital. The Industrial Revolution made a major impact on the urban and rural landscapes of Britain, and although much has been destroyed by even more recent industrial and service sector developments, many of the key places have survived – and have much to teach us. In the following pages we shall examine how early industrialization affected the pre-industrial landscape, but first we must consider the impact of the first significant prime mover of the Industrial Revolution: water.

WATER POWER AND THE INDUSTRIAL LANDSCAPE

It is well known that water provided the power for the first part of the Industrial Revolution, but it was by no means a new source of energy. Watermills have a long history in Britain, since at least Roman times.[30] As a general rule the mills of Roman, Saxon and medieval times were positioned in the landscape at points where roads and trackways provided ready access.[31] Although individual sites can provide many fascinating insights, the use of water power is best examined across the landscape in a particular region. One area where water played an important part was around and within the modern city of Sheffield.[32] Sheffield was the centre of the cutlery trade, and initially the workshops and factories of that industry were powered by water. The edge-tool industry was based on the workshops of smiths and cutlers and became established in the Sheffield area for a number of reasons, principal among which was the availability of flowing water from the five rivers that passed through the city. By the 1760s these rivers were almost fully exploited by no fewer than 115 known water-powered mills and workshops.

There were other reasons why the Sheffield area became an important early centre of industry. These included plentiful fuel first from local coppice woodland and then from the local coal measures. High-quality iron ore was also available. The coal measures supplied refractory sandstone and clay for smithy hearths and furnaces and abrasive rock

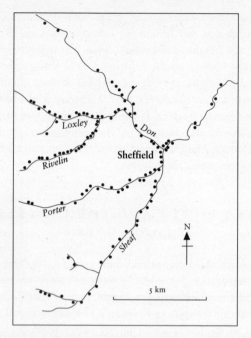

Fig. 11.4 A map showing the distribution of known mills and workshops along the five rivers that flow through Sheffield (the direction of flow is left to right). Most of these sites belonged to the edge-tool and cutlery business. The use of water power reached a peak by 1794; thereafter steam began to take over.

for whetstones and blade-grinding. Outcrops of harder rock on river-beds provided a natural base for the angled dams that diverted water into the 'head goits', the channels or tail-races feeding the millponds, which were known locally as dams. There was also a good supply of labour in a region where secondary employment had become a feature of family farms in post-medieval times. For these reasons the area had become a focus for industry long before the Industrial Revolution. Watermills (for grinding corn) were known in the region from the later Middle Ages. The earliest reference to powered grinding, a lease for a mill on the River Sheaf, dates to 1496. By the mid-sixteenth century many powered grinding wheels were being constructed. By this time, too, the courts of the local manorial system were unable to cope with

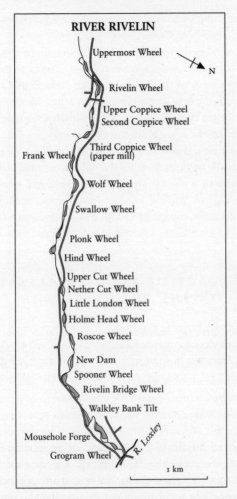

Fig. 11.5 A map showing the distribution of water-powered mills and work-shops along the River Rivelin in the Sheffield area of South Yorkshire. A significant proportion were established in the sixteenth and seventeenth centuries, prior to the Industrial Revolution. Waterwheels were not run directly from the river, but from individual ponds, known locally as dams, which ensured a steady flow of water. This map shows how by the mid-eighteenth century the banks of the River Rivelin could not readily have accommodated any more mills.

regulating the rapidly growing industry. This led directly to the formation of the Company of Cutlers, in 1624.

The most rapid period of growth was from 1720 to 1790, when all the available places on rivers were developed, leading to the construction of multiple mills on the best rivers, such as the Don. Construction also moved into the less accessible upper reaches. By 1794 the use of water power began to decline, as steam gradually took over. There was a small revival on the River Loxley in the second half of the nineteenth century, following a disastrous flood in 1864 when a large reservoir upstream burst through its dam; several mill-owners decided to rebuild, using their insurance money. Two of these rebuilt mill wheels, at Low Matlock and Olive Wheels, Loxley, have survived. Elsewhere the remains of old mills, especially the footings of diversionary dams or weirs and pond revetments, can still clearly be seen in the landscape.

THE IMPACT OF INDUSTRIALIZATION ON THE TEXTILE TRADE

The processes that lay behind the adoption and development of particular industries are best examined at a local and regional level. The idea that industrialization was unwillingly adopted by reluctant and oppressed seventeenth- and eighteenth-century rural communities has been widely accepted, but is very much open to question. Oppression and exploitation certainly happened, but in most cases considerably later.

The climate of Britain is uncertain and its population has always required good, warm clothing. There is evidence for the spinning and weaving of cloth since at least the Bronze Age, in the centuries following 2000 BC. Throughout prehistory and into post-Roman times the production of fabric was a domestic craft. Then in early Saxon times certain areas, such as the upper Thames Valley, began to emerge as centres of the wool trade. By the Middle Ages wool was a vitally important component of the British economy, especially in areas such as Lincolnshire and East Anglia, where the magnificent fourteenth- and fifteenth-century 'wool churches' still dominate the landscape. The south Pennine area of Yorkshire and Lancashire was another such region. Often spinning and weaving was done out of doors, to take advantage of natural light, but in the wetter north-west many small-scale fabric workshops were placed upstairs, in gallery rooms with long windows for maximum light.

The early impact of industrialization on the landscape and the lives

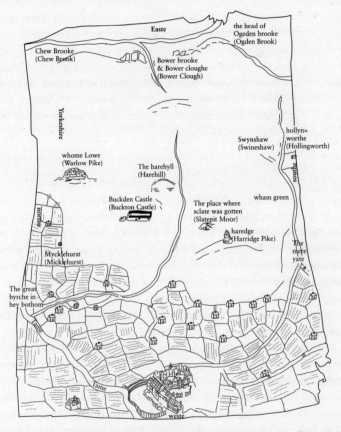

Fig. 11.6 A simplified drawing of a late-sixteenth-century map of the Staley area in Tameside, Greater Manchester, after Barker and Cranstone. This shows a typical pre-industrial landscape consisting of a major hall, lower centre, and isolated farmhouses within enclosed fields, many of which show evidence for ridge and furrow. The higher open moorland beyond the arable zone was used for rough pasture and slate quarrying.

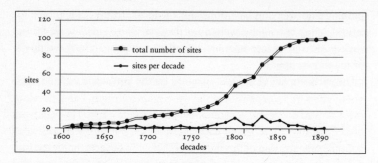

Fig. 11.7 A cumulative graph showing the introduction of new types of archaeological sites in Tameside, Greater Manchester. Most new types of site are associated with the industrialization of the textile industry. The graph shows an initial adaptive phase of slower growth, followed by an expansionary phase of rapid growth and a final consolidatory phase. The smooth S-shaped profile is what one would expect of a naturally growing population; it does not suggest that industrialization was resisted, or rapidly imposed from outside.

of the people living there have been examined as part of a recent study of the Manchester district of Tameside.[33] This area, which lies in the eastern part of Greater Manchester, is on the borders of Derbyshire and the old West Riding of Yorkshire. It is a pleasant and varied landscape with lowland clay plains to the west and steep-sided valleys to the east, but the soil is generally poor and the rainfall high. From around 1350 to 1650 the landscape was entirely rural, with scattered manors or major halls, together with isolated farms surrounded by enclosed fields. It was an area where upland pasture was important, but arable fields were also cultivated, using ridge-and-furrow, which persisted into early modern times as in other regions of upland Britain, because it was an efficient way of improving surface drainage.

While major elements of the earlier landscape were essentially prod-ucts of the later Middle Ages, so was the social system that gave rise to it. The manorial lords were the leading, and by far the richest, members of society. Below them were the freeholders, who owned their own houses and land, and the tenants who rented theirs from the lords. Industrialization began to make an impact on the landscape from the late seventeenth century. The Tameside survey constructed a graph showing the introduction of new types of sites, which were plotted against the total number of sites.[34] These new sites covered a huge range including ice houses, hatting shops, pumping-engine sheds and canals. The three most common were terraced workers' houses, textile sites and farmsteads.

The process began with a phase of slower growth, followed from about 1770 by an expansionary phase of rapid growth. Later, development slowed down and consolidated from around 1840. The new types of site fell into three broad categories, which more-or-less coincided with the organization of pre-industrial society in the area. Some twenty-eight of the new sites could be linked to manorial lords. These included manorial halls and town halls. Forty-eight new sites were identified with middle-ranking people, freeholders and yeomen; these included country houses and textile workshops. Twenty-four new sites, such as weavers' cottages and farmsteads, could be tied to tenants.

The Tameside survey has shown that the rural landscape of the area in the sixteenth century was something of a backwater. The land itself was poor and much of the moorland was of only marginal economic use. One result of this was that landlords tended not to become closely involved with the day-to-day management of the farms under their control; many indeed were absent. The social hierarchy that developed in their absence was short and relatively simple, being based upon landholdings. As time passed it developed into a remarkably open society that was keen to exploit new opportunities to make money. There was also a substantial 'land bank' of free and available land in the river valley bottoms. Perhaps as importantly, there were families who traditionally worked as a single economic unit on their isolated farms. Both were backed up by a good transport system, and a local tradition of Puritanism that placed a high value on hard work. It was a traditional society, but one that would not discourage 'upward mobility' and as such it was ideally suited for the adoption of the new industrial way of life. The landlords continued as landowners and then as significant local politicians, but many of the freeholders and tenants did very well indeed, for both themselves and their families.

TOWN TO COUNTRY: THE VERNACULAR WORKSHOP TRADITION

The onset of the industrial era tends to be linked to towns and large cities. The great mills and factories built in the mid-eighteenth century have left an enduring mark on the landscapes of Britain, although huge numbers were destroyed in the mid-twentieth century. It could be argued, however, that small-scale workshops made an equally import-ant contribution to the industrialization of Britain. These workshops are also important because they were often the means whereby industry took hold in a given area.[35] We saw this in the Tameside area of Greater Manchester and it applies elsewhere too, but it was a process that certainly took time. At Tameside we were looking at two or three centuries, but if we take workshops as a whole then we must think about their growth and development over a very long period indeed. A recent study, for example, considered the half-millennium from 1400 to 1900.[36]

Workshops survived into modern times because they were popular with the craftsmen and craftswomen who worked in them. I work at home and I know exactly why they felt as they did: in a nutshell, they could set and maintain their own pace of production. In a factory they would have had to adapt to the pace set by the mill-owner and the machines of the mill. Certain industries never developed large mills and factories, at least not until very recently. The boot-and-shoe trade of Northamptonshire, for example, was mainly organized around smaller factories and workshops well into the late nineteenth and early twentieth century. These were usually humble, built cheaply and without much regard for contemporary style or fashion; often too, their huge windows gave them a rather ungainly, even bizarre appearance.

Some of the earliest surviving vernacular workshops are to be found in Suffolk and Essex, where they have generally been described as shops.[37] A recent survey has shown that in actual fact they were workshops which were used more for the production than the retailing of goods. This can clearly be seen in the arrangement of the doors and windows of an early sixteenth-century 'shop' in Lavenham, Suffolk. If the workshop explanation for buildings with large windows

Fig. 11.8 An early sixteenth-century 'shop' building at 26 Market Place, Lavenham, Suffolk (*foreground*). Large ground-floor windows occur in many medieval and Tudor buildings in the area and have usually been interpreted as shop windows. However, many like these have high sills, and the doorway next to them is too narrow to allow easy access for shoppers. The wider doorway of No. 26 (with the dark hinges, to the right) opens onto a cross-passage and would have been used for goods, such as bales of cloth. The retail shop is therefore best seen as a workshop.

fronting onto streets is accepted, then the relatively narrow width of many external doorways can also be explained, together with the often rather high sills of many of the windows. A window set high in the wall illuminates the interior of the room much better. Anyone with a workshop/garage or garden shed will know that direct access to the exterior can cause many problems in breezy weather, and access which requires doors to remain open for any length of time is better provided from within. That is why many East Anglian textile workshops are also entered from a cross-passage, via a series of wide doors.

The modern clear-cut distinction between shop and workshop did not apply in medieval and early modern times, where workshops often had a smaller retail side, in any case. In the Middle Ages most general trade took place in markets. Specialist shops were essentially a post-medieval urban phenomenon, often developing from permanent market stalls in the early sixteenth century.[38]

Some later medieval and Tudor wool trade workshops in East Anglia were built into the courtyards of the large houses of cloth merchants. Others were grouped together, much as we saw in the textile trade of north-west England. It is probable that in both these instances the houses-cum-workshops were provided by wealthy merchants as 'renters' or tied cottages for their tenant weavers and other craftsmen. These workshops were often lit by large 'shop windows' on the ground floor, but there was no direct access from the street; instead, visitors and tradesmen had to enter via the cross-passages that separated the individual properties. The wool trade made fortunes for many East Anglian merchants, whose fine houses can still be seen in several places, especially in Lavenham.

The hosiery industry moved from London to the east Midlands in the late seventeenth century. Indeed, there was something of a general migration of industry from town to country from the sixteenth century. This was a time of increasing prosperity and the shift from urban to rural might have been a response to increasing demand for such goods as fine knitwear and hosiery, which the urban guild-controlled manufacturers were unable to provide. But whatever the reasons – and they are probably far more complex than this – from the late seventeenth century we see pre-existing timber-framed houses in Leicestershire starting to be converted to workshops. Elsewhere in Britain the textile industry adopted water- and steam-powered factories, but this was resisted in the east Midlands, where hand-operated frame-knitting machines continued to be used till the late nineteenth century. The first frame-knitting machine had been introduced somewhat earlier, around 1598. In the east Midlands the early phase of building conversion was followed in the late eighteenth and early nineteenth centuries by purpose-built weavers' houses, where the workshops were combined with domestic accommodation. In the nineteenth century non-powered but wider knitting frames were grouped together into collective workshops. These were generally located near to, but separate from, the weavers' houses.

The tradition of vernacular workshops continued in many other industries, such as the nearby frame-knitting and lace-making areas of

Nottinghamshire, the jewellery quarter of Birmingham and the gold-and silversmiths of the City of London. Even in areas of heavy industry, such as Sheffield, where large factory buildings were erected in the nineteenth century, many master cutlers and other craftsmen continued to ply their trade in independent smaller workshops.

William Blake's famous characterization of industrial England as a place of 'dark Satanic mills' in contrast to the idyllic rural, 'green and pleasant land' will doubtless remain the popular – if exaggeratedly bipolar – image of the early industrial era. The landscape in between these two poles, that of urban and rural workshops, where industry happened without Satanic smoke or soulless regimentation, is unlikely to fire the popular imagination. But it existed, and it was the means whereby the mills and factories were able to come into being. Without these workshops the early entrepreneurs would have had nobody to organize. This tradition of independent 'outworkers' did not cease with the main growth period of the industrial era, in the first half of the nineteenth century. In this period workshops continued to provide employment for more people than did factories. Two examples should make the point. In 1833 there were two and a half workshop 'out-workers' for every 1,000 employees of the textile mills in the Trow-bridge area of Wiltshire; in the early 1880s Karl Marx estimated that, twenty years previously, Tillie's shirt factory in Londonderry had employed 1,000 operatives but nine times that in the community outside the main works.[39] We shall see shortly that workshops and independent, self-sufficient craftsmen even played a major role in the capital-intensive world of the early iron industry of the Coalbrookdale colliery in Shropshire. For a few decades in the late eighteenth century this was the most productive iron-producing area in Britain.

THE IMPACT OF HEAVY INDUSTRY ON THE LANDSCAPE: IRON

While recent perceptions in the world of industrial archaeology have tended to stress the continuing and growing importance of crafts and light industry, it cannot be denied that many of the machines that drove the early industrial era, the mills and factories that housed them and

Fig. 11.9 The ultimate icon of the early industrial era: the great iron bridge across the River Severn at Ironbridge, Shropshire. The bridge was designed by Thomas Farnolls Pritchard and the ironwork was produced by Abraham Darby III (1750–89) at Coalbrookdale. The main span was built between 1777 and 1781, the smaller iron land arches on either side replaced wooden originals in 1821–3. The main span ironwork was actually erected in the year 1779. The inscription reads: THE BRIDGE WAS CAST AT COALBROOKDALE . . . AND ERECTED IN THE YEAR MDCCLXXIX (1779).

the aqueducts, bridges and railways that linked them, were made, or were held together, by frames constructed from iron fashioned in the foundries of the great iron-masters.

The extraction of ores and metal from the ground has left us a huge legacy of industrial landscapes – some would say of dereliction. But as we saw earlier, when discussing quarries of the Middle Ages, even the most disturbed ground can heal. Modern industry is a complex business and its archaeology is similarly complicated. Even the medieval extraction of iron from ore involved several processes, as we saw at Myers Wood (Chapter 8), and these have left behind a complex set of archaeological remains. To complicate matters further, the early industrial era is quite well documented, since by the eighteenth century all of the larger commercial transactions required appropriate paperwork.

At school we were taught that one reason why the Industrial Revolution happened in Britain was that coal and iron coincided in the same places there. Coal and iron, however, occur in the same places right across the world. It was not a geological coincidence that allowed industry to develop in Britain, but a combination of inventive people and a society able to adapt to the new conditions of an emerging industrial economy. Technological change was important, but quite often the significant changes were relatively minor, acting more like catalysts. Indeed, when one examines the evidence more closely it is difficult to avoid the conclusion that the development of modern

Fig. 11.10 The underside of the bridge. This view clearly shows bubbles and dimples that formed on the surface of the iron at the time of casting. The furnaces that produced the iron were most probably at Abraham Darby III's Upper Furnace complex at Coalbrookdale, a short distance from the bridge. Many of the joints used to fix the various components of the bridge recall techniques of carpentry, such as the use of wedges and dovetail and shouldered joints. The bridge uses some 800 castings, of just twelve different types, weighing a total of just over 384 tonnes. The largest ribs are 21.6 metres long and weigh over 5 tonnes each. Castings of this size would have been at the very limit of later eighteenth-century iron-working technology.

industry was indeed a long-drawn-out, gradual process, that began to speed up rapidly in the latter part of the eighteenth century. It is sometimes supposed that blast furnaces, for example, were invented during the early industrial era, but actually they were first introduced to Britain in the fifteenth century. Similarly, iron-working at Coalbrookdale did not begin with Abraham Darby I in the eighteenth century, as there is evidence of simple furnaces, known as 'bloomeries', operating there from at least 1546.

The key development, which happened at Coalbrookdale in 1709 under Abraham Darby I, was the use of coke (roasted coal) rather than charcoal as fuel in the smelting process (which did not involve the use of blast furnaces until 1755). Smelting is the process by which ore is converted to metal. One possible stimulus may have been the fact that by the late seventeenth century supplies of good-quality charcoal were supposedly becoming increasingly scarce and prices were rising, and of course there was an abundant alternative supply of carbon in the Coalbrookdale coalfield. The Darbys and their workforce set about improving the process, so that by the mid-eighteenth century coke-blast iron was fully competitive with the more conventional charcoal-produced iron.

The Darbys, father and son, were great iron-masters and like the industrial textile pioneer Richard Arkwright they provided their work-force with good, if not model housing in a series of terraced 'rows' in Coalbrookdale. But these 'rows' could never possibly have accommodated the entire Darby workforce. The vast majority were living somewhere else. In the past four decades a substantial body of research has shown that the great achievements of the Coalbrookdale iron-masters took place against a backdrop of informal squatter and tenant settlement, involving large numbers of self-employed craftsmen without whom the iron foundry could never have functioned.[40]

In the eighteenth century the settlement pattern in the Coalbrookdale colliery was varied and informal and there is little evidence for the controlling influence of a major landowner or industrialist. Settlements began by people moving onto common land, or tenants buying their holdings from compliant landowners. In the early nineteenth century some of the larger landowners became more assertive and took better control of their estates. By then, however, the settlement pattern had

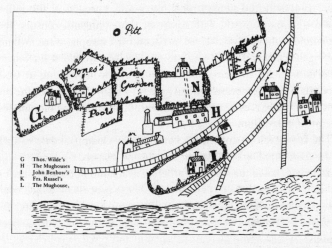

G Thos. Wilde's
H The Mughouses
I John Benbow's
K Frs. Russel's
L The Mughouse,

Fig. 11.11 A mid-eighteenth-century picture map (redrawn from the Broseley Estate Book, after Barrie Trinder) of an informal settlement at the Calcutts in the Ironbridge Gorge, Shropshire. Settlements of this sort grew up as a result of squatters moving onto commons, or tenants buying small parcels of land from landowners who were not particularly interested in the running of these parts of their estates, which were generally of poor agricultural quality. The Mughouse is an inn or alehouse.

become established. The occupants of the informal settlements were usually self-sufficient. They occupied plots of land large enough to keep a house-cow and a few pigs or to grow patches of flax, hemp or grain. Flax and hemp were processed into yarn by the households, where the man of the house was either a coal miner, an iron-worker, a bargeman or a craftsman.[41] This 'dual economy' was also used extensively by the early iron-working companies; these needed the services of craftsmen such as carpenters, tallow chandlers, ropemakers and hauliers who kept their own packhorses.

The course of Britain's industrial history has been well charted by economic and other historians. Our task is rather different. We are seeking traces in the landscape for what has gone before and that evidence is often idiosyncratic. Sometimes it may reflect historical reality, as we saw at Coalbrookdale, but in most cases it does not. Take the case of the Dowlais works at Merthyr Tydfil, in south Wales. In the late eighteenth and nineteenth century this was one of the largest ironworks in the world with no fewer than eighteen working blast furnaces. None of these has survived, and the only standing building is an unrepresentative brick-built engine house, dating to the late nineteenth century. By contrast, a short-lived failed enterprise in Leicestershire has provided us with some of the best evidence for early nineteenth-century iron-production and the climate of enterprise that prevailed at the time.

The Moira furnace was part of a regional industrial development by Francis Rawdon-Hastings, second Earl of Moira, who inherited the large estate, which includes the town of Loughborough and much of Ashby-de-la-Zouche, in 1789.[42] There had been a successful if small-scale coalfield in the area since the thirteenth century. The previous Earl had been a recluse and the second Earl set about making major changes. These included enclosing rural land and constructing the Ashby Canal, which opened in 1804.

A blast furnace has to be run continuously and may be fuelled by charcoal or, latterly, coke. The blast of air needed to reach the high temperatures necessary to smelt pig iron from ore can be provided by bellows or fans; the latter may be powered by waterwheels or steam engines. Pig iron is then further refined into usable (that is, malleable) metal in a finery, using first charcoal then coke as a fuel. The basic processes of iron-production require a well-trained and available workforce, and ready supplies of both iron ore and fuel. Good communications are also needed to export the finished products, which, being iron, are usually heavy. The Moira ironworks of Leicestershire were built in 1803 and are among the best and most complete surviving early ironworks in Britain.[43] The reason they have survived is quite simply that nobody wanted to rebuild them. They had experienced a technical failure and had to be abandoned when the chimney collapsed into the furnace below, sometime around 1811.

The opening of the Ashby Canal allowed the coalfield to expand, but throughout its short history the enterprise was held back by lack of cash. The iron-making operation seems to have been doomed from the outset: both the coal and the iron ore were of poor quality and recent excavation of the furnace buildings has revealed a number of quite serious design flaws. It would, however, be a mistake to conclude that the Moira furnace was a fiasco. It did manage to work for several years and it should also be recalled that such early coke blast furnaces were at the forefront of metallurgical technology: at that period there was no such thing as a 'standard' design.

THE TURNPIKES: THE FIRST MODERN ROADS

The story of Britain's infrastructure began in the Mesolithic, when people moved from one area to another, following game and other seasonal resources. Their routes, like those along the sides of the Vale of Pickering in Yorkshire, skirted ancient wetlands and are still preserved in the modern road pattern. By the arrival of the Romans all the settlements of Britain were linked by a network of roads and tracks. Generally speaking, these were local routes that joined different settlements. So far as we know, there were few arterial, or long-distance roads, exceptions being the Ridgeway from Dorset to Wiltshire, Icknield Way in Hertfordshire, Peddars Way in Norfolk and a few others. We do not know whether these longer distance roadways were always kept open along their entire routes, but the fact remains that prehistoric people shared many ideas in common, ranging from the way they laid out their roundhouses, to the decoration and shape of their pottery; this suggests not only that routes of communication existed but that they were used regularly, and probably routinely. It was never a case of hacking one's way through impenetrable forests with a flint or bronze machete.

Perhaps Rome's greatest physical legacy to Britain was a radiating road system based around arterial routes. This system was laid out across the landscape, often with little regard for what had gone before. The reasons for this vary from one place to another, but in many instances it reflects the fact that Roman roads were often surveyed-in by military engineers whose main concern was to build a good, direct road, regardless of local opinion. Many (but not all) of the new roads were straight, just as the Iron Age Peddars Way is straight, or indeed Neolithic cursus monuments are straight – after all, a perfectly straight road can readily be surveyed by one person with three canes.

The Roman road system was not abandoned in the post-Roman and Saxon periods. Indeed, many continue in use right up to the present. But as time passed the informal road networks that fed into the arterial – and essentially Roman – system developed lives of their own. Many regional route systems had ancient origins and they were all adapted to the requirements of particular landscapes. The drovers' and packhorse roads that flourished in the eighteenth and early nineteenth centuries were an important development in this tradition. The result of this long evolutionary history was that local people in individual parishes controlled and maintained their own roads. But as the population, industrial activity and traffic all began to increase it soon became evident that certain important roads could not be treated in this piecemeal fashion. The result was the rise of the turnpikes.[44] A turnpike, incidentally, was originally a spiked defensive barrier at a castle gate, but the name was retained for any toll barrier. It was tolls that paid for the turnpikes.

The conventional view is that the development of Britain as an industrial nation began in the eighteenth century with the construction of a canal network, which was later enhanced and then replaced by the railways. These were the great civil engineering contracts, but they tell only part of the story. Early roads have generally received less attention, perhaps because their construction was seen as straightforward: a few new toll houses, the odd bend straightened out, but not much heavy-duty earthmoving. This impression is, however, very misleading. The turnpikes were every bit as important as the canals and often required major projects of civil engineering, including some of the finest bridges, built, moreover, with new techniques that are still in regular use. It is worth recalling that the world's first iron bridge at Coalbrookdale was built not for a canal, nor for a railway, but for a turnpike, whose tariff can still be seen on the bridge toll house.

The first turnpike trust was established in 1663, when a section of Ermine Street in Huntingdonshire, Cambridgeshire and Hertfordshire fell into disrepair and suitable replacement materials could not readily be found by local authorities in the parishes it passed through. The route in question, originally a Roman road, is now generally known as the Old North Road. It had become the principal easterly route northwards out of London in the Middle Ages. During the Middle Ages

Fig. 11.12 The octagonal Butterow toll house at Rodborough on the outskirts of Stroud, Gloucestershire. This attractive building of local Cotswold limestone was built around 1825 for the new turnpike that linked Bowbridge (on the Thames and Severn Canal) to Stroud, an important centre of the West Country textile trade, which was flourishing at the time. Many turnpike toll houses are polygonal to give a clear view up and down the road. Some, like this, still display their original tariff boards, showing the rates of toll charges.

settlement in the villages along its route tended to gravitate towards the roadside.[45]

The first turnpike trust was supervised by county justices, who already supervised the repair of bridges in the county (but not in corporate boroughs). Three toll bars were set up to provide income for the road's repair and maintenance, from the people who used it. The route of the first turnpike is particularly well preserved where it passes through the villages of Kneesworth, Arrington, Caxton and Papworth Everard in Cambridgeshire.[46] Caxton is locally well known for its roadside gibbet, the original of which was erected to display the corpse of a notorious highwayman, showing that there were rich pickings to be had from the many people who used this road – the authorities were showing other potential criminals that *they* were the only people who were going to benefit. The first turnpike, like those

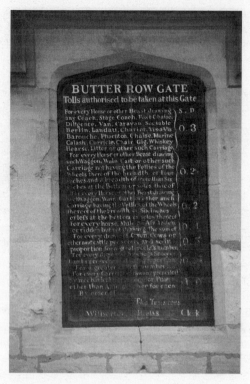

Fig. 11.13 The tariff of tolls levied at the Butterow turnpike toll gate.

that followed it, was well laid out, with wide grassy verges. The administrative arrangements of the first turnpike worked well and seven more trusts had been established in England, by 1700.

The early decades of the eighteenth century saw the establishment, by Acts of Parliament, of many more in England. These were usually set up to run for a period of twenty-one years, or sometimes less. Some 870 individual Acts were passed by Parliament in the years 1751–71. By 1830 there were 1,100 trusts, which together managed some 35,000 kilometres of roads; despite this progress, in the later eighteenth century some 168,000 kilometres were still in the care of parishes. It could, however, be quite a cumbersome system. Many of the early trusts controlled short stretches of road – often as little as 30 kilometres – and major through-routes could take a long time to establish. The London to Bath road west of Newbury (Berkshire), for instance, took fifty years to turnpike completely, and was controlled by no fewer than six individual trusts. Despite these problems, turnpike roads transformed travel times. Take the journey by coach from Edinburgh to London: in 1754 it took ten days; in 1776, four days, and just forty hours in 1840, on the eve of the railway age.[47]

In Scotland the first Turnpike Act was passed in 1714 for Midlothian, a Lowland county, but the new way of organizing roads did not become popular until the latter part of the eighteenth century. Previously, as we have seen, many Highland roads had been built by General Wade and his successor, but these were originally intended for military traffic, especially for marching men, and often had steep inclines that could not be used by heavy commercial traffic. In Wales, the first turnpike trusts were also for counties, the first being for Glamorganshire in 1764. But the situation in Wales went wrong and turnpike trustees abused their rights. A result of this was that prices rose and toll houses proliferated, a situation that led to public unrest and sparked the chartist Rebecca Riots of 1838–44, in west Wales. The chartist riots were of course about more than tolls alone, but they were nonetheless a significant factor. Troops were employed to suppress the rioters, but eventually the situation could only be resolved by the passing of an Act of Parliament, which fixed the level of tolls. The control of roads first passed from turnpike trusts to county (council) boards in south Wales, but this reform was resisted elsewhere by the vested interests of turnpike trusts, and only became widespread in the 1870s.

Much of the direct evidence in the landscape for the turnpikes has inevitably been destroyed by road improvement schemes. A few toll houses do of course survive, as do mile-posts and some bridges. Indirect evidence, such as the thousands of roadside inns that were built during the 'turnpike explosion' of the second half of the eighteenth century, often survives well in some of the smaller towns along the route. In upland areas difficult stretches of country were often bypassed by later improvements, leaving the original road in place. In this way stretches of the Wakefield to Austerlands turnpike can still be seen in moorland near Oldham. This turnpike was built by the famous road engineer,

Blind Jack Metcalf of Knaresborough, in 1759. Although valuable in their own right, such fragments do not constitute turnpike 'landscapes'. Far and away the finest example of such a landscape is to be found in Snowdonia.

The route in question is the Welsh section of Thomas Telford's (1757–1834) great Holyhead–Shrewsbury road.[48] We tend to think of major early civil engineering achievements in terms of railways or canals, but some of the turnpikes were equally ambitious and Telford's Holyhead road is a fine example, because unlike most other turnpikes it has not been obliterated by too many insensitive improvements. Today it comprises the A55 in Anglesey and the A5 in Wales and England. It is particularly well preserved as it passes through the mountains of Snowdonia. Much is original here: revetment walls, embankment facings, mile-posts, weighbridge buildings, toll houses and the fine 'sunburst' iron gates that anticipate the less elegant creations of Art Deco. Telford, also a Scotsman, succeeded John Rennie (1761–1821) as Britain's greatest civil engineer. Telford was a pioneer of the suspension bridge, and he built two superb and internationally renowned examples for his Holyhead–Shrewsbury road: the Menai Straits and Conwy bridges. The more conventional cast-iron Waterloo arch bridge across the River Dee at Betws-y-Coed has a span that was huge for a single-arched bridge of the time, and, most unusually for Telford, it is highly decorated. It would seem that this bridge, which would have been more expensive to maintain than a more conventional double-arched stone structure, was erected as part of a high-profile political and PR campaign to secure funding for the road, which was planned by Telford and ably supported by the famous Irish politician and patriot, Sir Henry Parnell (1770–1842).[49] The first contract was awarded in 1815, and the Welsh sections of the road were completed when the Menai Straits bridge was opened in 1826.

The success of the railways signalled the end of the turnpikes, which could not compete and were often bought out by the more successful railway companies. Thousands of toll houses and booths became redundant and most were torn down. The last toll gates, on the Anglesey section of Telford's great Holyhead road, were removed in 1894.[50] In the late nineteenth century responsibility for the road network was passed to the local, usually district and county, authorities.

CANALS AND PORTS

Canals actually appeared relatively late in the industrial era. In the sixteenth, seventeenth and early eighteenth centuries most inland transport of goods and people was either by road or by navigable river. The first were built in the 1740s, and they were still being constructed at the height of the 'turnpike explosion' of the 1750s. Water transport was the only available means of moving heavy goods, before the development of railways in the mid-nineteenth century. Before canals, existing rivers were improved and made more navigable, a process that often involved straightening and canalization; many of these early river navigations are still in use today.

Some of the schemes undertaken to improve river navigation were very early and involved substantial civil engineering, comparable in many respects with later canal construction.[51] New techniques learnt from Dutch drainage engineers who had helped drain the Fens and Somerset Levels were often employed. These included the use of locks, plus extensive dredging and bypassing of shoals and shallows. Special arrangements of locks were often needed to get around the weirs raised to divert water through existing mills. A major early river improvement was to the River Exe, in Devon, in the 1560s. This sophisticated project involved the bypassing of difficult bends by constructing a new cut of 4.8 kilometres, which was reached by a flight of locks. The work was accompanied by the construction of new buildings such as a Customs House and warehouses in Exeter. Somewhat later, the 24-kilometre-long Wey Navigation, in Surrey, linked the Thames at Weybridge to Guildford. It was opened in 1653 and its construction involved locks, weirs, bridges and an 11-kilometre artificial channel. There were many other examples, not always so large, and work was gathering pace in the early eighteenth century. Indeed, it was often the river navigation companies who opposed the setting up of new turnpike trusts, as they feared losing traffic to them. Certainly they provided stiff competition to the turnpikes when it came to the bulk carriage of heavy materials, such as coal.

Canals played an important part in developing the complex project-management structures that were needed if projects were to be completed on time and to budget. Civil engineering and the construction industry have always been pioneers in this field. Although project management must have played a role in earlier times, when for example great cathedrals were being built, it only became an explicit requirement when work was spread across the landscape and was delegated to a number of different subcontractors. It was then that the engineer and his financial backers – often referred to as 'adventurers' because they 'adventured' the necessary capital – stood to lose money if work was not carried out to cost and to deadline. Prior to the canals the previous major civil engineering project had been the draining of wetlands, especially the Fens, and it has recently become apparent that the first large-scale drainage work there in the early seventeenth century did not benefit from careful project management, and many expensive mistakes were made.[52] After the English Civil War the great Dutch engineer Cornelius Vermuyden improved the situation, but the overall drainage of the Fens was never actually perfected, until the later 1950s – and today it again looks at risk, as sea levels continue to rise. Techniques introduced to Britain from Holland helped in the draining of the Fens and also played a significant part, as we have seen, in improving river navigation. These techniques became essential when it came to the construction of canals, and the many locks required to traverse gradients.

Good communication and control are essential to the successful completion of a project that involves water. If levels, for example, go awry then water will not behave in a predictable manner. A mistake of a couple of metres can prove disastrous. Perhaps this was why the early canal builders took so much personal responsibility. James Brindley, the builder of Britain's first major canal, the Bridgewater Canal, not only prepared all the drawings for the canal and its bridges himself, but he also designed the boats, negotiated with landowners, supervised the work, paid the men and personally surveyed the land. Telford did much the same when he built the Ellesmere Canal in 1793, although he was criticized at the time for taking too much on.

Canals had a constant depth and were an excellent way of moving heavy loads.[53] Fifty tonnes could be towed by a single horse along a canal towpath, whereas laden river barges weighed considerably less – around 30 tonnes. By way of contrast, just 2 tonnes could be hauled by a single horse on a road. The early canals allowed landlocked coalfields to get their products to new markets. The coalfields of the north-east had to compete for the London trade with those of Nottinghamshire and Derbyshire that were now linked to the outside world via a canal to the River Trent. In the later eighteenth century the coalfields of south Wales expanded by way of narrow-gauge canals that could cope with the many locks and gradients, and take barges down to ports along the Bristol Channel. Certain landscapes, however, were not suited for canals, such as hilly parts of the County Durham coalfields, or the porous ground of the limestone-mining areas of Leicestershire and south Derbyshire; waggonways proliferated in these regions.

Most canals only made sense when they formed part of a network with other canals and navigable rivers. The famous Forth and Clyde Canal, for example, was originally conceived as a means of joining the North Sea, or German Ocean, to the Atlantic. Construction began in 1768 and was halted a decade later when money ran out. Eventually further funds were raised from a number of sources, including the forfeited estates of Jacobite supporters, and the canal was completed and opened in July 1790. It is 56 kilometres long and passes across the Kelvin Aqueduct (designed by Robert Whitworth), one of the great engineering achievements of the late eighteenth century. The Forth and Clyde Canal was remarkable because it could accommodate seagoing vessels and all road crossings were via bascule bridges – a counterweighted lifting bridge, many examples of which can still be seen across canals in Holland. The canal had an important effect on the economies of the towns it passed by, but it was soon linked with the Monkland and the Union canals, which together formed a lowland canal network that was sufficiently prosperous and cost-effective to be taken over by the Caledonian Railway in 1867. The railway company operated the Forth and Clyde Canal until the nationalization of inland waterways in 1948.

The early canals were usually constructed to serve a specific industry, such as iron-making in the west Midlands or south Wales. Coal was moved on James Brindley's famous Bridgewater Canal, the initial length of which ran from Worsley (today in Greater Manchester) to Manchester; work began in 1759, and finished in 1765.[54] Remarkably, this canal included underground lengths dug directly to coalfaces at Worsley

Delph.[55] Brindley (1716–72) was a far-sighted engineer who appreciated that if canals could be joined together into wider networks they would have an economic impact on more than a single industry. His scheme was arranged in the shape of a diagonal cross, with Birmingham and the Black Country at the centre, and with branches radiating out towards the Mersey, the Humber, the Severn and the Thames.

By the 1820s Britain's canal network had reached its peak and canal companies enjoyed several very prosperous decades. During the early nineteenth century some of the finest examples of canal architecture were created, including the famous Pontcysyllte aqueduct on the Llangollen branch of the Shrewsbury Canal, which carries the canal across the River Dee in an iron aqueduct atop elegant, tapering stone piers.

The coming of railways in the 1840s hit the canals hard and eventually led to their almost complete demise as a commercial network. Prices began to fall from the late 1830s. Some canals folded; other were taken

Fig. 11.14 The Grand Union Canal at Stoke Bruerne, Northamptonshire, showing the parallel locks. The original (1805) lock is to the left (today it is blocked off and used as a dry dock). The new parallel lock is to the right and is still in active use; it was added in 1835–40 to speed traffic in an ultimately unsuccessful attempt to compete with the emerging railways.

over by railway companies and either operated in concert with a railway, or were emptied of water so that the level canal bed could be adopted for a new permanent way. Yet others improved their systems and for a short time were able to compete with the railways by spending money on straightening out bends and in duplicating locks to speed through-traffic. Duplicated locks can still be seen at Hillmorton, War-wickshire, on the Oxford Canal or at Stoke Bruerne, Northampton-shire, on the Grand Junction (later Grand Union) Canal. Certain areas coped better with competition from the railways than did others. For example, canals continued to thrive in the Birmingham region throughout the nineteenth century. By 1906 the Birmingham Canal Navigations operated 255 kilometres of canal, with 216 locks. The secret of this success doubtless lay in the twenty-six railway–canal interchange basins that were built after 1850.

During the nineteenth century a number of much larger ship canals were built and these faced less competition from the railways. Often they were routed to miss hazardous estuaries. The first, which opened in 1808, was constructed near Loch Fyne to avoid a long haul around the Mull of Kintyre; it took sixteen years to dig, and suffered from the labour shortages that were such a widespread problem in Britain during the Napoleonic Wars. A more successful project was the Gloucester and Sharpness Canal which was built in 1827 to bypass the tortuous lower reaches of the River Severn. It was 25 kilometres long, 27 metres wide and was capable of taking vessels of up to 750 tons. However, far and away the most famous ship canal was the Manchester Ship Canal, which finally opened, after prolonged construction, in 1894. This was the first canal project to use steam shovels and mechanical excavators and a labour force of no fewer than 17,000 men. It is capable of taking 600-foot seagoing vessels.

As inland communications prospered and improved, so did Britain's ports and harbours.[56] The earliest official port facilities of post-medieval times were those of the Royal Navy. The first of the royal dockyards was established at Portsmouth by Henry VII in 1496. Others followed at Woolwich (1512) and Deptford (1513) on the Thames and Chatham (1570) on the Medway. The Anglo-Dutch Wars of the mid-seventeenth century gave rise to new royal dockyards at Harwich (Essex) and Sheerness (Kent). Plymouth was founded soon after, in 1691.[57] These facilities were composed of fine buildings when they were established but they were regularly added to and improved over time, a good example being Rennie's Royal William Victualling Yard at Plymouth, completed in 1823. This consists of a square ship basin surrounded by 5 hectares of fine early nineteenth-century industrial buildings.

Extensive new civil port facilities were built at Southampton in Tudor times when it was a major outport to London.[58] In the seventeenth century, as the economy began a period of expansion, ports like Falmouth were built by developers, such as Sir Peter Killigrew; the church which he partially paid for is still there and was founded in 1665. Whitehaven in Cumbria was another successful private venture, with a population of 2,000 by 1690 when it rivalled the northern ports of Liverpool and Newcastle. In 1668 a large plot of land was purchased on the south side of the Clyde, 32 kilometres downstream, by the Provost of the City of Glasgow. In the eighteenth century this was to become Port Glasgow, an outstandingly successful development carried out in this instance by the city authorities. But by the end of the century the prosperity of Port Glasgow had declined, largely as a result of the dredging of the Clyde, which allowed seagoing vessels to sail much closer to the city itself.

In the final analysis, industrialization is about producing more things at less cost. This requires that fuel, raw materials and the finished goods themselves be transported in large quantities. During the half century or so that followed the opening of the Bridgewater Canal in 1763 the growing network was able to cope with the movement of fuel and raw materials. Some of the heavier finished products (such as iron and pottery) could also be distributed by water, but many items still went by road. Such, however, was the pace of Britain's growing industrial development that within just two generations new means of efficient bulk transport would be needed urgently.

12

Rural Rides: The Countryside in
Modern Times (1750–1900)

In the early modern period we saw the emergence of distinct farming regions, but as time passed and communications improved these too began to lose their distinctiveness. The construction of the railway network during the 1840s, combined with rapid progress in agricultural technology, led to a massive rationalization of the landscape into the two broad regions that we have today: a more arable and intensively farmed south and east and a largely pastoral north and west. The south and east have a drier climate than the north and west, where growing conditions can be described as more maritime. In farming terms, grass and livestock prefer the maritime climate, whereas cereal crops grow better in the more Continental conditions of the south and east, where the drier summers assist harvesting and the cold winters deter the development of fungal and other crop infections. There is also an east–west split in the quality of farmland, with heavier, often acidic and more moisture-retentive soils in the Midlands and west, and generally lighter loamy soils to the east. The lighter soils require less energy to cultivate and tend to be better at absorbing fertilizers.

A map of the two farming regions of England was originally published in 1852 by James Caird.[1] It shows England divided into two zones, with one to the east and one to the west. The landscapes to the east, in Caird's words were the 'chief corn districts of England', whereas those to the west was given over to grazing and dairying. Of course Caird's map is something of an over-simplification, especially as regards the eastern zone, where it ignores the large-scale sheep and cattle pastures of the Yorkshire and Lincolnshire Wolds, the sheep lands of the chalk downs and the (then) rich pastures of Fenland meadows,

Fig. 12.1 James Caird's map of the two farming regions of England in the mid-nineteenth century, east and west of the central heavy line (counties are shown in light outline). This map would be essentially the same today, but the boundary south of the Humber has probably moved west by up to two counties.

which put the flesh on many of the heavy horses that were used on farms across south-eastern England.

The main change between both the earlier medieval and the early modern maps was in the Midlands, where the intensively ploughed Open Field systems had been converted from arable to pasture. In areas outside the Central Province of medieval England, the process of enclosure started in the sixteenth century, but on the heavy clay soils of the Midlands the process was far more complex because it involved the drawing together of widely separated strips and other landholdings, and the sorting out of some complex tenancy contracts. When enclosure did eventually happen in these areas it was late; gaining momentum in the late seventeenth and eighteenth centuries. It was also a traumatic process that involved the depopulation of many villages.[2]

PARLIAMENTARY ENCLOSURE

The increasing trend to enclose land had developed by the beginning of the eighteenth century into a distinctive phenomenon. Most of these enclosures were arrived at by agreement, and in England they were to do with the conversion of ordinary mixed and arable farms on heavy clay soils, to pasture. This process continued throughout the first half of the eighteenth century, when population growth fell and agricultural prices slumped. In the Midlands the process even accelerated in the mid- and later eighteenth century, when farm prices improved.

The first enclosure agreements had been entered into by the sixteenth century, when landowners needed more pasture to graze sheep, but they were not approved of, by either the government or the Church. After 1750 it was found that the problems associated with complex enclosures, especially on the heavy Champion landscapes of the Midlands, could best be overcome, or circumvented, by individual Parliamentary Acts of Enclosure, the first of which had been passed in 1604. In the eighteenth century these rapidly became the most usual means of enclosure and some 4,000 individual Acts were passed between 1750 and 1830 in England; this amounted to about a fifth of the country's surface area.[3] In Scotland, most enclosure in the Lowlands took place in the 1760s and 1770s and in the Highlands at the end of the century, but these did not require Parliamentary legislation.

Individual Acts of Enclosure would apply to named parishes and townships and were intended to speed up and formalize the existing system of enclosure by agreement. A group of landowners would petition for a Parliamentary Act, and this would be followed by survey and award, the whole process being supervised by a commissioner who had the task of ensuring that small landowners were not penalized. He also had to see that roads linked up with others in the area and that the boundaries of individual landholdings were indeed proportional to the pre-enclosure situation. Most areas of common land were also redistributed among the individual landowners of a parish, under the supervision of the Parliamentary commissioners. This was not always popular with everyone in the parish.

Although the first Enclosure Act was passed in 1604, the movement did not gain a hold until the first half of the eighteenth century when some 200 Acts were passed. After the passing of the General Enclosure Act of 1836 a scheme could be carried through, even if the majority of landowners in a parish opposed it. It was not about numbers of people, but the size of their holdings: so if one or two landowners who happened to own most of the land in a parish (usually this meant three-quarters, by value) wanted enclosure, then their wishes prevailed, even if numerous smallholders objected.[4]

Much of the cost of Parliamentary Enclosure was met by the landowners themselves and this seems to have had a rather ruthless 'rationalizing' effect, as men with the smallest holdings, which of course had proportionately longer boundaries to fence and hedge, found the process of fencing and hedging too expensive and sold out to their larger neighbours. The taxpayer, too, helped defray the costs of this wholesale reorganization of the landscape, which proved to be very expensive. It has been estimated that the cost to the Exchequer of Parliamentary Enclosure amounted to about £29 million, about £9 million more than the cost of the canals, but far less than the increase of £500 million in the National Debt, which arose from the Napoleonic Wars.[5]

The landscapes of the Enclosure Movement are the classic 'planned' landscapes that still dominate most of eastern and central-southern England. They are characterized by straight-sided rectangular fields, usually bounded by hawthorn hedges and straightish roads with wide verges, marked off from the surrounding fields by hawthorn hedgerows and with trees – often oak or ash – at regular intervals. These may indeed be planned landscapes, but they are never predictable and they possess a charm all of their own. Unlike today, when seedlings for new hedges are often imported from commercial growers in Holland, the winter hardwood cuttings used to propagate Enclosure Movement hedges were taken from the fringes of local woods, so the natural botanical diversity of the region was successfully replicated.

While the motives for enclosure were relatively straightforward in areas where people wanted to convert from arable or mixed farming to pasture, the same cannot be said for areas of eastern and southern Britain, where arable farming was still viable and profitable. There was no real point in enclosing land that needed to be ploughed, especially as people had already been rationalizing widely separated holdings throughout the later Middle Ages and in early post-medieval times. As modern farmers know, hedges can get in the way of successful agriculture, their roots can be hungry and their shade can cause uneven germination and ripening in crops grown alongside them.

The introduction of new crops, the elimination of cyclical fallow land and the changes in crop rotation brought about in the early to mid-eighteenth century did not require enclosure to be put into effect, but they may have helped, especially if some of the farmers working land in a communal system were unwilling or unable to adapt to the new regime. Communal farming systems only work by agreement and once people started to follow altogether different philosophies of farming, then enclosure, and with it separation, became a necessity. These were the motives behind the enclosure of the good arable soils of regions like the Lincolnshire or Yorkshire Wolds and the heathlands of north-west Norfolk that gathered pace throughout the eighteenth century, reaching a climax of activity during the Napoleonic Wars.

Major alterations to the landscape have to be carried out by people. It is a process that requires labour, co-ordination and supervision. We saw how the landscape reorganization of later Saxon times was supervised by the Church, by powerful aristocratic landlords, who in turn were influenced by royal authority, and by smaller landowners working in co-operation with village communities. Although they were not inspired by such socially motivated factors, the changes of the eighteenth and nineteenth centuries were instigated by more or less the same landowning classes, only this time, of course, the monasteries had long since been dissolved, and the Church played a minimal role. Royal authority, too, was of little or no significance, except in those few areas where the Crown still owned estates.

A cynic might argue that the changes to the British landscape of the eighteenth and nineteenth centuries were fuelled only by the wish to make money. That view, however, ignores the different intellectual and moral climate of opinion that prevailed in the Georgian and Victorian periods. Religion and a sense of civic duty were still very important in most people's lives and rural communities were close-knit. Many people felt strong social obligations, too. Indeed, prior to the Poor Law Amendment Act of 1834, which established the widely hated workhouse system, rural parishes in England and Wales looked after their own social welfare, as laid out in the original Elizabethan Poor Law Act of 1601.[6] So there were strong traditions of communal interdependence in rural communities, albeit combined with equally strong, class-based social barriers. Even so, the ultimate motive lying behind the great landscape changes of the eighteenth and nineteenth centuries was the pursuit of prosperity by landowning families, large and small. Allied to this was the need to display this newly acquired wealth. Whatever their motives – and they varied from one individual to another – these were the people with the labour and the money to make the changes happen.[7]

Today the concept of land-*ownership* is straightforward enough, but in the past it was less so. In the early Middle Ages, for example, ownership, as we would now understand it, did not exist. The lords of the manor theoretically owned their lands, but existing tenants also had absolute rights and could pass their holdings on to their children. Similarly, men higher up the feudal tree than a mere lord of the manor had certain rights over manorial land, as indeed did the Crown. This was to change, however, in the fourteenth and fifteenth centuries, along with so much else, when legal definitions evolved. Meanwhile earlier lees and tenancy agreements persisted in a complex geography of land-ownership.[8]

The general trend in the law relating to later medieval and post-medieval land-ownership was in favour of larger landowners, at the expense of smaller peasant farmers. In the sixteenth and early seventeenth centuries both local gentry and great landowners expanded their holdings, largely at the expense of small farms. After the Restoration it was the great landowners who were to profit, once again at the expense of small farms, which suffered most severely in times of agricultural recession, such as the early eighteenth century.

Large estates are not distributed evenly across the British landscape and there are several reasons for this.[9] Contrasting patterns of land-ownership developed in the eighteenth and nineteenth centuries on different types of earlier post-medieval landholdings. For example, bigger farms and estates tended to grow up in those farming regions where arable farming predominated. Conversely, in pastoral farming regions, earlier patterns of landholding persisted from the seventeenth to the nineteenth centuries; these took the form of smaller family farms, set in landscapes where there were many more minor gentry than large landowners. As a general rule, these pastoral areas provided a greater degree of prosperity to farmers as a whole than was the case in the arable regions, which may also help to explain why smaller arable farmers were more willing to sell up.

There was another important aspect to life in pastoral areas which was to play a significant role in the early industrial era. Pastoral farming produces what some archaeologists have described as 'secondary products': wool and milk, which need to be distributed and sometimes to be further processed, for example, into cheese or cloth. In the mid-eighteenth century new crops such as flax became widely available.[10] Flax likes to grow in wetter conditions, and part of its processing into fibres, known as retting, also involves soaking and rotting in water. For these reasons the growing and weaving of flax was an ideal supplement for a pastoral farm in the wetter regions of Britain.

This gave rise to a dual economy, where farmers and their families were also wool- or flax-weavers, cheese-makers and in many instances miners, too. Many sources of coal in the seventeenth and eighteenth centuries were still quite close to the surface and miners were also part-time farmers (as a few are still today in the Forest of Dean in Gloucestershire). It is not hard to see how the success of this thriving dual economy could provide the basis for industrial expansion. At first the majority continued in the traditional dual way, but some decided to follow the 'value added' route and gave up farming in favour of industry, based on secondary processing of various commodities.

The farms and landscapes of Improvement, such as those around the seat of the famous agricultural 'Improver', Coke (pronounced 'Cook') of Norfolk, at Holkham Hall near the north Norfolk coast, did not appear without a struggle. About 30 per cent of the land in north-west Norfolk was enclosed by Parliamentary Enclosure. Another 35 per cent had been enclosed prior to 1660, by agreement. This means that another 35 per cent must have been enclosed in the period after 1660, by various means and methods.[11] This is hardly simple, quick or straightforward and, again, people, or rather the intricacies of their land tenure arrangements, lay at the root of the problems.

The changes in post-medieval land tenure and ownership resulted in a diverse settlement pattern in the nineteenth century that was composed of 'closed' and 'open' parishes. Open parishes were bustling places with a growing population, many landowners, tenants and a diverse economy. Closed parishes were owned by one or a few landowners, who did not welcome incomers. These places tended to be under-populated, with slow or stagnant economies. One might suppose that the larger land-owners would want to stimulate the economies of the areas they controlled, to make them more 'open' than 'closed'. But in reality the opposite happened.

In the eighteenth century enclosure was easier to achieve when fewer people were involved; so many of the richer landowners set about the task of 'engrossment', or buying out potential opposition before any Act of Enclosure was undertaken. Engrossment was often an aggressive process, not carried out for economic reasons alone. Social factors could also play an important role. Estates had to impress neighbours and passing travellers, so landowners did not just attempt to build large estates, but to create continuous and compact ones. This allowed them to make their own mark on the landscape: not just on fields, but on woods, roads, lanes and housing.[12]

Given such attitudes, it is hardly surprising that landowners did not want 'open' villages at their doorsteps with large and rowdy populations and many alehouses – the haunts, it was believed, of poor labourers, ruffians and political dissenters. There were other reasons, too. In the seventeenth and eighteenth centuries claimants for relief were ultimately paid by the landowners of the parish, so it was in nobody's interests to own land in open parishes, where the numerous population would have had its share of the old, the sick and pregnant mothers – all of whom were at liberty to claim relief. Instead, landowners tried to acquire land close by such settlements, where they could take advantage of the large workforce, without incurring the financial obligations of relief.

From a large landowner's perspective, the ideal solution to these problems was sole ownership of all land in a parish. In the seventeenth and eighteenth centuries, whenever the opportunity to acquire such land arose it was often taken – sometimes regardless of cost. It was not in the landowner's interests to encourage growth in the population of the villages he had obtained majority control over. So many of these villages were subsequently (and this could be much later) closed down and incorporated within a country house park – an operation known as emparkation.

It is sometimes believed that the mid-eighteenth-century process of buying out villages, closing them down and incorporating them into parks happened quickly, but if the records of the individual villages are consulted they often showed signs of marked decline several generations prior to their emparkation. For example, the village of Everingham in the Wolds of east Yorkshire was owned by Sir Marmaduke Constable, who wrote to his steward in 1730 and 1740 that he would rather have fewer houses there, but better ones.[13] Like that of the villages around it, the population of Everingham fell sharply in the late seventeenth and early eighteenth centuries: there were fifty-seven households in 1672, but only twenty-seven in 1743.

THE AGRICULTURAL 'REVOLUTION'

The main reason why the idea of an agricultural revolution has taken such firm hold is that common sense seems to demand that it happened. We know that the rapid expansion of industry from the mid-eighteenth century led to a population explosion in the new industrial cities, and these people, it was argued, had to be fed somehow. Such a rapid rise in population demands a revolution on the part of the farmers who provided the food. A little additional thought would then suggest that the food must have been in place before the population began its rapid increase. So it followed that the agricultural revolution must precede the Industrial Revolution.

Just like the Darby dynasty of Coalbrookdale, the heroes of the agricultural revolution were colourful and highly motivated 'Improvers', such as the first Earl of Leicester, Thomas William Coke (1754–1842), of Holkham Hall, Norfolk, one of the most important pioneers of the agricultural revolution. Others included larger-than-life figures such as the Whig Cabinet Minister Charles 'Turnip' Townshend (1674–1738), who devoted his retirement to the improvement of his estate where he helped to develop the famous Norfolk four-crop rotation. My own particular hero, as a sheep-farmer, is the remarkable creator of the New Leicester breed, Robert Bakewell (1725–95) of Dishley Grange, Leicestershire.[14] Even today, many of the large commercial flocks seen in pastures right across lowland Britain comprise 'Mules', a cross-bred ewe, sired by one of Bakewell's improved Leicesters.

Another reason for the persistence of the agricultural revolution, as an idea, is the logical link it makes with the Industrial Revolution, which as we have seen was part of an extended process that in many instances could be traced back to medieval times. The conventional

Fig. 12.2 Holkham Hall, Norfolk, from the south. This great Palladian country house was built between 1744 and 1762, probably to drawings by William Kent, who is known to have designed the interior. The well-managed estate at Holkham became home to 'Coke of Norfolk' perhaps the best-known agricultural 'Improver', and has come to symbolize the progress made in the agricultural revolution.

wisdom would also have it that the agricultural revolution was vitally important, because it successfully fed the rapidly expanding populations of the great industrial cities. But this never actually happened.

The traditional, rather narrow, historical view is that the agricultural revolution took place in the seventy or so years between 1760 and 1830. If one takes a broader view (1700–1850), the main events of the revolution can be seen to have taken place in three stages, none of which would have been possible without the widespread reorganization of the landscape brought about by the Enclosure Movement, which as we have seen was under way well before the eighteenth century.[15]

The first stage was completed sometime around 1750–70 and saw the introduction of new crops, especially roots such as turnips. Roots were grown between cereal crops in the famous Norfolk four-crop rotation cycle of wheat, turnips, barley, clover and/or grasses.[16] The Norfolk four-crop rotation required the land to lie fallow for less time (if the land became too depleted the final clover/grass ley could be extended for an additional season).[17] This cycle produced more grazing and fodder in the form of turnips, which in turn resulted in more and fatter livestock and, perhaps just as important, more manure to be spread on the fields. With better crops and knowledge of soil fertility went improvements in tools and machinery, of which the mechanical seed-planting machine, or drill, publicized but not invented by Jethro Tull, was perhaps the most important.[18]

The improvements both in crops and in the productivity of labour, achieved in the first stage, were matched in the second half of the eighteenth century and in the early nineteenth by improvements in livestock. While all of this was going on, Parliamentary Enclosure was gathering pace and the improvements of agricultural productivity extended further and further across the country. The third phase started around 1830 and was a period of great prosperity. It saw the flourishing of large estate farms and the construction of some remarkable buildings, many of which still survive.

The traditional view of the agricultural revolution is of an essentially East Anglian movement, with famous pioneering Improvers blazing a trail which others, often reluctantly, followed. Today the agricultural changes of the eighteenth and nineteenth centuries are not seen as the end-product of a process, in which the ideas and inventions of educated landowners percolated down to the broad mass of British farmers. Instead, the changes are now viewed as being more general, 'involving the widespread adoption of new techniques by farmers of all kinds'.[19]

Economic history and a close study of the landscape support this conclusion. Many of the improvements that were once believed to have been introduced in the mid-eighteenth century were in fact made very much earlier.[20] Some of the supposedly eighteenth-century innovations such as new crops, crop rotations and deliberately flooded water meadows in fact originated up to two centuries earlier. It would be more sensible to view agricultural improvements as a continuum, where there were periods of more and less rapid change, which were largely governed by market forces and political events at home and abroad.[21] For example, the sharp rise in the English population in the sixteenth century stimulated the production of grain, but the slump in grain prices between 1570 and 1750 shifted farmers' interests towards other, newer crops. There were further changes that encouraged the production of livestock, a return to grain and so forth, until the great agricultural depression of the 1870s and the meagre decades that followed.

However, influential people outside Britain were well aware that something altogether remarkable was happening there. For example, the young aristocratic La Rochefoucauld brothers, François and Alexandre (and their extraordinary tutor M. de Lazowski), made tours of England in 1774–5, during which they kept copious notes on everything from Bakewell's new breeds of livestock, to crop rotation and details of cotton-mill machinery. The translator of their journals, Norman Scarfe, is convinced that there was more than a hint of industrial espionage involved, possibly motivated from within the highest political circles.[22] Incidentally, after the French Revolution of 1789 the younger of the two brothers set up his own cotton mill in France, based on English examples.

So far we have merely noted that Parliamentary Enclosure was well under way in the mid-eighteenth century. However, contrary to popular perception, it was a complex and quite extended process. Moreover, many of the changes attributed to it actually happened in advance of the passing of a particular Act. Some have seen the Parliamentary Enclosure landscapes of the English Midlands as 'markedly monotonous'.[23] For me, the lanes, fields, woods and hedgerows of counties like Northamptonshire, Leicestershire and Nottinghamshire are some of the most tranquil and typically English of all. I love their modest charm; in fact, I get quite cross when self-appointed aesthetes, who ought to know better, sneer at them.

The new farms produced by Acts of Enclosure were laid out according to the best current farming practices. That is no more than one would expect from people who were not being led by the great Improvers, but were carrying out their own improvements, when local circumstances allowed. This surely is evidence for the 'widespread adoption of new techniques by farmers of all kinds' that we have just discussed.

Parliamentary Enclosure did not force the landscape into a preconceived, standardized shape, or pattern. The diversity of field sizes in Midland enclosure landscapes reflected the size of farms. So we find fields of 2–4 hectares on small farms and 20–24 hectares on much larger ones. The layout of the squarish fields was supervised by the Parliamentary commissioners who attended the enclosure of each parish, and who generally seemed to prefer fields of rectilinear shape, and roads with wide verges. They certainly did not favour the narrow winding lanes that are such a distinctive feature of 'ancient' landscapes. They have been criticized for this,[24] but I cannot see what else they could have done. To have added picturesque touches here and there would have been expensive, incongruous and absurd – the sort of thing a modern local authority might attempt to do badly, through some local arts initiative.

Some of the practices that were widely accepted by eighteenth-century Improvers were actually rather dubious. Pioneer graziers such as Robert Bakewell were right when they said that parcels of grazing should be no larger than about 10 acres (4 hectares). However, I am less convinced by his contention that the grass should be grazed down so close that 'you could whip a mouse across it', before moving the animals on. For what it is worth, this may have been the received wisdom of the time, but it is not good farming practice. If land is over-grazed there will be problems of clostridial (soil-borne) diseases when cows and sheep accidentally lick the bare earth. Also, by massively depleting the leaf area of both grass and clover, the process of photosynthesis becomes less efficient, and recovery of the grazing is far slower.

Archaeological evidence for a rapid and wholesale enclosure 'revolution' is also hard to find. Certainly we have maps of Parliamentary Enclosure which provide the broader picture, but the reality on the ground is not always so clear-cut. Even in Norfolk, the supposed epicentre of any possible revolution, there is little evidence to support the idea of rapid change.[25] Even something as seemingly clear-cut as enclosure turns out to be uncomfortably messy in practice. For example, a detailed examination of the documentary evidence relating to the famous 'Improvement' estate at Holkham Hall has shown that it was not always simple to distinguish between enclosed and unenclosed land. In one case a map clearly shows strips, but a contemporary note attached to it says that these strips were only put there for legal reasons and that that piece of land had actually been enclosed for some time.

We have seen that enclosure by Act of Parliament required the agreement of the owners of the majority of the land in a parish to begin the process. In reality this meant that in cases where a large landowner owned most of a parish he would be able to drive the process of enclosure forward, even though he was in the minority. As enclosure also included common land, there was a considerable inducement for him to enclose, because he would benefit from this in proportion to the size of his original holding. We can see this process at Holkham, where two villages on the estate were completely relaid in the early nineteenth century and two areas of common land, one very substantial, were incorporated into the new rationalized field system.

The increasing rate of adoption of Parliamentary Acts of Enclosure from the mid-eighteenth century is usually taken to indicate the extent and progress of enclosure through time. While this might be true for Britain as a whole, the situation on the ground seems to have been rather different. It has been demonstrated that many fields were enclosed by mutual agreement or unilateral action long before the entire parish was enclosed by an Act. In other words, the Act was essentially a process of tidying up loose ends or completing a job that was already half-done.[26]

The pattern of enclosure in England was uneven, with marked regional disparities that usually reflected the different histories of the

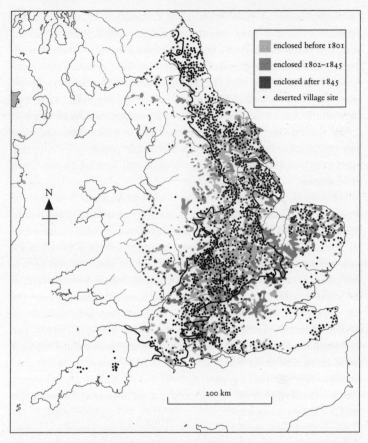

Fig. 12.3 A map showing the distribution and date of Parliamentary Enclosure plotted against the three provinces of medieval England and sites of deserted medieval villages.

pre-existing farming districts and earlier, medieval, patterns of land use.[27] For example, most of the enclosures in counties along the Welsh borders, the south-east and the south-west – all 'ancient' landscapes – were by mutual agreement and did not require Parliamentary Acts. Much of the Midland heavy soils were enclosed early (that is, before 1800) in the Parliamentary process, together with the lighter clay lands of Lincolnshire and east Yorkshire.[28] More than half the farms in

Northamptonshire, Cambridgeshire and Oxfordshire had been enclosed between 1760 and 1815 and the period of peak activity coincided with the Napoleonic Wars. Forty-three per cent of all Acts date to these years and they included not just the three counties just mentioned, but the lighter land of East Anglia and large areas of marginal ground in the Pennines and Lake District and the heaths of Dorset and Hampshire. After 1815 the pace of enclosure decreased and by 1850 it had slowed considerably. By the end of the nineteenth century it was complete, except of course for that single parish of Laxton (see pp. 298–9), in Nottinghamshire, which is still farmed on the Open Field system.

The scale of work involved in the Enclosure Movement in England was quite extraordinary. For a start, accurate maps and plans had to be prepared and this involved a detailed parish-by-parish survey of large areas of England. If we assume that all the work itemized in the Acts happened at the same time (which we have seen was not always the case), then nearly 322,000 kilometres of hedges were planted in the century after 1750. This was as much as was planted over the preceding half-millennium. One significant improvement brought about by Parliamentary Enclosure was to the roads within a parish. The Parliamentary Enclosure commissioners of the eighteenth and nineteenth centuries would insist that roads should be of adequate width, and would usually stipulate 40, 50 or 60 feet (12.19, 15.24 or 18.29 metres). This width allowed horse-drawn carts to steer around and avoid fallen trees, or major potholes.[29]

While enclosure itself had a huge impact on the landscape, many technological improvements of the eighteenth and early nineteenth centuries had little direct effect on the form or shape of the countryside, apart from a few marl (clay) pits. Marling, incidentally, involved the addition of clay to the topsoil, thereby lowering its acidity.[30] The principal alteration to the landscape came in the form of some fine new farm buildings. One technological development did, however, leave clear traces that can still be seen in many pastoral regions of central and western Britain.

In the seventeenth and eighteenth centuries many farmers in traditional 'sheep-corn' areas on lighter, chalk and wold soils moved into sheep in a very big way. Huge fields were put aside for them, but the light soils proved problematical in drier seasons, during later winter and early spring, when good fodder became scarce. This was because grass grown on non-moisture-retentive soils is slow to 'get away' in a dry spring, which is when lactating ewes and the older lambs need good, nutritious grass. It is a crucial time, and in my experience if 'the first bite' of springtime grass is poor when the lamb is young, it will never catch up satisfactorily.[31]

WATER MEADOWS

One way around the problem of early season grazing was the introduction of irrigated water meadows.[32] Water meadows are artificial irrigation projects and should not be confused with floodplain meadows, where flooding happens naturally when the river is in spate. Sometimes, indeed quite often, an irrigated true water meadow will be an extension of a natural river floodplain, where the flooding will be carefully managed to benefit the grass.

The first water meadows were developed in the sixteenth century, but they came into widespread use in the seventeenth and eighteenth centuries. While the principles behind water meadows are relatively simple, their actual layout and operation could be very complex and required considerable skill and experience to operate successfully. The usual form consists of a series of artificial channels, or leats, that

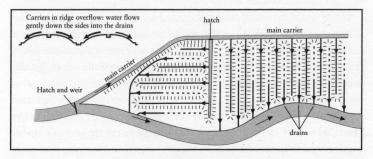

Fig. 12.4 A diagram showing how a water meadow worked. The water was taken off the river via a hatch or sluice and was taken by the main carrier channel to the area to be flooded.

were dug along the sides of a shallow valley and were fed from a pool behind a dammed stream. These leats were often connected by a header channel from which water was dispensed via a system of hatches or sluices. The leats that took the water to the meadows were known as carriers, channels cut along the tops of a series of parallel ridges which joined the main carrier at right angles. The water spilled out of the carrier channel and ran down the banks into a second set of channels within the 'furrows' between the banks. These channels were known as drains. The drains either emptied directly into the river or fed into a main drain. There were numerous variations on this basic theme, some of which were remarkably complex, but the idea was to flood the land late in the winter. This had two purposes. First, it irrigated the soil, so the grass was able to grow on warmer days. Secondly, the water also contained fine silty particles which precipitated out as the flow along the leat decreased.[33] This thin layer of nutrient-rich alluvium helped to rejuvenate land that was probably being over-grazed.

Water meadows became an essential feature of large-scale sheep landscapes of the chalk downs, where they were located along the river floodplains below the hills. They were crucial to the prosperity of farming in these regions until the agricultural depression of the late nineteenth century, although a few persisted in use just into the twentieth century. One reason why they were so important was that the greater population of sheep led to the production of more manure, which was an essential part of the mixed sheep-corn economy.

In the arable areas of eastern England a practice known as warping allowed ploughed land to be flooded with water enriched with alluvium to regenerate the soil. Warping was extensively employed in the Isle of Axholme and the lower Trent Valley of north Lincolnshire. It differed from the flooding of water meadows in that the aim was to enclose an area of flat land and then flood it with heavily charged water that deposited a layer of highly fertile alluvium from 15 to 40 centimetres thick. This was then tilled for several seasons, with or without the addition of manure. Large areas were treated in this way and were capable of massive yields: by the 1850s warped land near Hull was producing 10 tons of potatoes to the acre.[34] With the major changes brought about by drainage, warping and other improvements that took

Fig. 12.5 A remarkable photo of the parallel channels, or leats, of abandoned water meadows revealed by floodwater along the shores of the River Avon in Hampshire.

place on the flat landscapes of the county, the agricultural revolution in Lincolnshire appears to have lived up to its name.

RURAL LANDSCAPES IN SCOTLAND AND WALES IN MODERN TIMES

The agricultural improvements in Scotland and Wales differed from those in England in certain important respects. The Improvers of the eighteenth century did not sweep away all traces of traditional farming. Some fermtouns continued to prosper and many of their houses and barns were rebuilt in the eighteenth and nineteenth centuries. Only one, at Auchindrain township, Kilmichael Glassary, Argyll, survived into the twentieth century with its communal tenancy still intact.[35]

We currently believe that the era of agricultural improvement was somewhat extended in England, but the same cannot be said for Scotland, where it was both fast and comprehensive. The countryside of Scotland had been largely open prior to 1745, and in the following fifty years most of it had been enclosed. Those simple facts, taken at face value, do indeed sound revolutionary.

Prior to 1745 the process of agricultural change had certainly been 'top-down', led by two societies for agricultural improvement, founded in the 1720s, which numbered important landowners among their members. The improvements included the spreading of lime over acid land and some of the larger estates beginning to enclose. The real changes, however, happened after the suppression of the final Jacobite rebellion, following the Battle of Culloden in 1746.

The end of the '45 uprising meant the exile of traditional Jacobite lairds and their replacement by more businesslike men who included many Improvers. Again, these moves were imposed from above, led by organizations such as the Board of Agriculture and the Board of Management of Annexed Estates, set up after the rebellion. Under this new regime, the thirteen very large annexed Jacobite estates were re-surveyed and were laid out as single tenancies. At the same time trees were planted, fisheries developed and new rural industries, such as linen, were introduced.[36]

Although potatoes and turnips had been introduced to Scotland at about the time of the rebellion, new strains of oats and rye were added to the list of crops which were eagerly adopted by farmers on single-tenancy farms. Once the land reforms had been introduced, and the majority of the old collective-style fermtouns that lay at the core of the old run-rigg system had largely been replaced – and this happened by the end of the eighteenth century – agricultural reforms could really take hold and soil drainage, marling and other practices that had been developed south of the border were soon introduced. The rapid agricultural improvements in Scotland included the reclamation of much marginal land; indeed, some of the higher moors could not be sustained and were abandoned in the late eighteenth century, but lowland moors fared better, with the result that the total area of farmed land in Scotland rose between 1750 and 1825, by some 40 per cent. At the same time productivity doubled.

There was a steep human price to pay for these improvements. The new single tenant was usually the strongest member of the original fermtoun community, and the rest, who were no longer needed, moved to the growing industrial towns, or emigrated, often to Canada. One example is the parish of Kilmarnock, where the population halved between 1765 and 1790, falling from just over 800 to 400.[37] Perhaps the most infamous area for these clearances was Sutherland in northern Scotland where from 1805 the great Sutherland estate, with much financial help from well-capitalized interests in England, cleared thousands of people to make way for sheep. The main breed introduced into the cleared Highlands in the last quarter of the eighteenth century was the so-called 'Great Sheep', or Cheviot, which had been developed in the border country of Northumberland. It was a hardy, large and well-meated ewe with good wool, having been crossed with a Merino late in its development. But in fairness to the Improvers of the Sutherland estate, considerable trouble was taken to find employment for the displaced population, either in new smallholdings along the coast, or in projects which today would be seen as diversification, such as a new town and harbour at Helmsdale and a new whisky distillery at Clynelish.[38]

It is debatable whether the undoubted human cost of the clearances, which is still much resented locally, was rewarded by a suitable financial return, because many of the schemes were poorly thought out and were more the result of enthusiasm for 'improvement' than good business sense.

The reorganization of the new Scottish single-tenancy farms, and the estates on which they occurred, also witnessed the construction of some remarkable new farm buildings whose size mirrored the extent of the lands they served. Most of these farms hit very hard times in the lean years of the 1870s, when many were reduced in size or closed altogether. Even if we lay aside the entirely negative effect on rural Highland society produced by the clearances, the figures do not always add up. For instance, during the period of expansion in the first two decades of the nineteenth century the income of the Sutherland estate tripled between 1803 and 1817, but expenditure had risen nine times. Prior to 1812 income had exceeded expenditure by up to £1,900, whereas between 1812 and 1817 the estate spent £29,427 more than it received in rents.[39] So it would seem that the motives behind both the clearances and the associated 'improvements' may also have involved competition with other landowners, the need for prestige and a reforming zeal for its own sake that was also characteristic of earlier agricultural Improvers in England.

The social effects of the Highland clearances were appalling. One direct consequence was the collapse of the traditional clan system that had provided coherence and identity to sometimes widely dispersed rural communities. The Highlanders who had survived the clearances no longer found themselves living in the traditional house clusters, or clachans, that had been the pre-Improvement equivalent of fermtouns in the western Highlands and Islands. These unfortunate people found themselves eking out a frugal subsistence in small crofts which were mostly distributed around the coast, where small-scale farming could be augmented by fishing, weaving and kelp-burning.[40] (Kelp is a seaweed which was burnt and used as fertilizer, as an ingredient of gunpowder and in the glass-manufacturing industry.) Many were further exploited by ruthless landowners and some even had their smallholding removed. Discontent among the crofters ultimately led to the 'Crofters War' and the formation of the Highland Land League in 1882 to press for tenancy reform. In 1886 the Crofters Act was passed which granted crofters security of tenure via the Crofters Commission, in Edinburgh. After the First World War land administered by the Crofting Commission was transferred to state ownership, in order to facilitate the settlement of ex-servicemen on the land.

The changes made to Scottish rural landscape between 1750 and 1840 were undoubtedly huge, but their impact was by no means confined to the mainland. The traditional landscape of the Isle of Eigg in the Inner Hebrides is a case in point.[41] The island belonged to the Clan Ranald estate, who commissioned accurate surveys of their holdings by the surveyor William Bald. Bald's map of Eigg in 1806 shows a confused pattern of run-rigg fields, through which were dispersed traditional settlement clusters, or clachans. Shortly after this survey the Eigg estate was reorganized. The earlier, probably medieval, landscape was entirely ignored and buildings were demolished. The 'improved' landscape consisted of seventeen new crofts laid out within severely rectilinear walled fields, which ran up the hills behind the houses. Each croft was sufficiently large to allow the grazing of three

Fig. 12.6 A view of a crofting landscape on the Isle of Skye. Each 'white house' is a croft in its holding of two to eight small rectangular fields, with small barns and workshops. The crofters would also have had limited and prescribed rights to graze common land. Sometimes crofts were arranged in clusters, with their fields radiating around them. These crofts are dispersed across the landscape.

to five cows and there was also an area of common pasture, where individual crofters were allowed to graze a horse. Initially the system worked quite well, and the kelp industry prospered rapidly because of the high demand for gunpowder during the Napoleonic Wars. But the kelp 'bubble' burst after Napoleon's defeat at Waterloo (1815), and the crofters lost their main form of secondary income. As the population increased, so did poverty, until disaster finally struck with the potato famine of the mid-1840s.

In the decades after 1815 many island landowners were forced to sell up. The clearances and the power of Scottish landowners to improve their farms meant that the rural Scottish landscape was transformed between 1750 and 1840, with the creation of new farmsteads, new roads and regularly shaped fields which have removed most traces of earlier farming practices. As sheep-farming became less profitable, from the latter part of the nineteenth century, many of the larger and more extensive sheep farms in the Highlands were instead given over to deer-stalking and grouse-shooting.

The situation in the Scottish Lowlands was altogether different. Here a rapid move towards new crops and machines during the latter part of the eighteenth century was stimulated both by the sudden increase in single tenancies (and with it enclosure) and improved market prices brought about by the urbanization of places like Glasgow and Edinburgh. Lowland farmers were quick to adapt to these changes, which may help to explain why there was no equivalent here of the Highland clearances. The changes in the Scottish Lowlands during the last quarter of the century included not only new crops and equipment but the widespread use of liming, marling, leys and improvements in the productivity of labour. In a few decades Scottish Lowland farmers were able to catch up with their counterparts in England in terms of yields and income. This prosperity was to continue into the era of Victorian High Farming (see below, pp. 492–ff.). Construction of new farm buildings gathered pace between 1780 and 1820; many were built on a larger scale than in England, but often in the same Italianate styles, and with all the flair and confidence of their southern counterparts. The intensive rearing of beef cattle, often making use of turnips as a winter feed, was very much a feature of these decades.

The situation in Wales was altogether different from that in Scotland.[42]

As we saw in Chapter 8, the practice of collective farming – run-rigg in Scotland, Open Field in England – had never really caught on, except in a few lower-lying valleys that were penetrated by the Normans. Elsewhere holdings were scattered and far-flung. A scattered pattern could even be found in the Vale of Glamorgan, but here enclosure began in the seventeenth century and resulted in small farms of 10–28 hectares. Cattle were the main animal on lowland farms, while sheep were kept in the mountains, where oats were the only cereal grown. With a run of upland grazing to draw upon, an enclosed farm of 6 hectares was considered sufficient to support a family.

In highland areas of Wales seasonal or transhumant movements were the best way to farm in such a harsh environment. People and animals moved between a protected lower-lying winter base-farm or 'hendre' and higher summer sheep pastures. The higher land was occupied between May and October and the household moved into upland summer farmhouses, or 'hafods'. This medieval transhumant system was in decline by the eighteenth century, when land around both summer and winter farms began to be enclosed. Along with this went piecemeal enclosure around the edges of common land. Such enclosure had actually been under way for some time: about 800 hectares were enclosed in Cyfeilig, Montgomeryshire, between 1561 and 1573. But the pace of enclosure changed rapidly after 1795.

The enclosure of commons brought the already declining trans-humant system to an abrupt halt. The scale of the enclosure was vast: between 1793 and 1815 more than 81,000 hectares of Welsh common land were enclosed, but strangely enough this did not give rise to new farms. Instead the existing, mostly very small, holdings, were enlarged to make them economically viable.

In parts of upland northern Britain, seasonal transhumance from sheltered lowland pastures up onto highland grazing had become more important in early post-medieval times. Certain members of the com-munity – mainly the more vigorous – moved, together with their livestock, into upland huts – the Scottish equivalent of hafods – often known as shielings, for the summer months.[43] These shielings usually occur in groups or clusters and are recorded in Northumberland from the early seventeenth century. Although more of a post-medieval phenomenon across northern Britain as a whole, the earliest shielings

Fig. 12.7 The ruins of a shieling on the Isle of Lewis in the Outer Hebrides.

are recorded in documents from the Forest of Lowes, north of the central sector of Hadrian's Wall, in 1171.[44] Other medieval examples, from both sides of the wall, have been dated to the fourteenth to sixteenth centuries. In the Scottish Highlands shielings continued in widespread use in the seventeenth century and some were converted to permanent dwellings in the seventeenth and eighteenth centuries, as the rural population continued to grow. Most shielings were abandoned with the introduction of commercial sheep-farming in the early nineteenth century, although in areas where the climate was too wet to keep sheep on a commercial scale, such as the Isle of Lewis in the Outer Hebrides, shielings continued into the twentieth century.[45] Today they survive on Lewis as standing structures rather than the more usual grass-covered foundations, that occur so widely in upland areas.

RURAL LANDSCAPES AND THE FEEDING OF THE URBAN POPULATIONS

The fact remained that the population of urban Britain was growing rapidly and those extra mouths needed to be fed. This story is of fundamental importance, not just to Britain but to the rest of the industrialized world, and like all important narratives the widely accepted version has taken on a life of its own and come to bear little resemblance to what actually may have happened. We saw this previously with the Open Fields of the English Midlands which came to represent the totality of rural life in the British Middle Ages. The same can be said for the era of agricultural improvement and its gentleman farmer pioneers. Not only was this a more gradual process than we once believed, and its pioneers were merely significant individuals working in a climate of general change and innovation, but it is now apparent that the burden of feeding the new and growing urban populations of the late eighteenth and early nineteenth centuries was not met by the large estates and farms of the lighter arable, so-called 'sheep-corn' lands (principally the wolds and downlands), where the pioneers of 'Improvement' had introduced new regimes of marling, four-crop rotation and improved technology. No, it would seem that the real business of producing food in bulk happened elsewhere.

By 1750 agricultural improvements had made their mark. Farmers across Britain could appreciate the advantages of greater yields and productivity and they were perfectly capable of 'catching up' very rapidly, as we saw in the Scottish Lowlands. At the same time the growing population of the great cities was providing markets for their produce. The sheer scale of population increase can be hard to grasp, especially today when population growth is almost at a standstill. In England and Wales the rapid growth started in the earlier sixteenth century when the population stood at about 2.4 million, which was approximately the same as, or slightly less than, Iron Age levels. By 1760, some 220 years later, it had more than doubled, to 6 million. But in the following period of just six decades, from 1760 to 1820, it doubled again, from 6 million to 12 million (in 1821). The next doubling also took six decades, between 1821 (12 million) and 1881 (26 million).[46] Feeding these extra mouths was a major challenge.

In the second half of the eighteenth century the improvements of the previous hundred years or more were put into effect outside the lighter sheep-corn lands of the wolds and downs. This was the period when the twofold pattern of farming, with arable to the east and pasture to the west, came into being. Light soils, such as those of the wolds and downs, have the great advantage of being easily tilled. But they do not retain moisture very well; they also require frequent manuring, because the effects of one application may be washed away quite rapidly in a wet season. It is difficult, too, to build up the fertility of these soils with any degree of permanence. Any competent vegetable gardener knows that heavy clay land may be progressively improved by the addition, over the years, of grit and manure and in time it can become much more fertile and productive than lighter soils. That is precisely what happened in the late eighteenth and early nineteenth centuries.

The new urban populations were fed by bringing the heavier soils of eastern England into cultivation – soils like those of the Marshland Fens around the Wash, and the heavier clay lands of Essex, Suffolk and Norfolk. The improvement of this heavier land involved major drainage schemes in the Fens and large areas of soil under-draining in the clays of East Anglia, where huge drainage dykes did not need to be dug.[47] The under-draining of the heavier soils of eastern England was a major, and largely unacknowledged, engineering achievement, comparable in its way with the construction of the canals and turnpikes. It ensured that by the 1850s large areas had become fully arable and highly productive.

By contrast, many of the improvements introduced by the pioneering aristocratic farmers and landowners to the lighter soils of eastern England failed to produce the dramatic and long-term changes in productivity that had originally been hoped for – especially when compared with the slightly later improvements made to heavier soils. Perhaps the most celebrated example of a light-land improvement that went wrong was the attempted introduction of irrigated water meadows to Norfolk. Water meadows were far less suited to the lighter wold soils of Lincolnshire and parts of Norfolk, but by the eighteenth century they had become identified with Improvement. Keen to be seen as progressive, some of the most successful Norfolk-based Improvers introduced them at considerable cost, but relatively late: after 1790. By 1900 all had been abandoned except for the system at Castle Acre in Norfolk, whose remains can still be seen on the river floodplain, below the castle earthworks.[48]

It is still commonly held that the era of agricultural improvement and the subsequent period of Victorian High Farming did indeed provide all the food needed by the growing population of industrial

Britain. On examining the statistics for food production in Britain and setting them against the known growth of population, we can see that the supply of food fails to match the demand.[49]

Between about 1730 and 1780 yields from selected English counties remained fairly constant at around 21.5 bushels per acre, but in the following forty years (up to 1820), instead of rising – as one might expect given the impact of the Improvers – they actually fell. This was most probably due to poor weather and a succession of bad harvests; the result was that despite undoubted improvements to farming methods, yields fell by an average of 1.5 bushels. In 1821 the weather improved and the consequence, taken together with the improvements which were now widespread across the arable areas of the country, was an average yield in the decade of the 1820s of 23.6 bushels. In the first decade of High Farming yields rose steadily – thanks to new fertilizers and more manure resulting from cattle cake feeds – and levelled off at around 28.5 bushels from the 1840s to the 1880s. These figures may indeed be remarkable, but the fact remains that the absolute quantity of food produced would have been insufficient to have fed Britain's rapidly growing urban population.

The relationship between production and demand was not straightforward. Between 1830 and 1870 the population of England and Wales rose by 64 per cent. Given such a dramatic increase, one would expect wheat prices to have risen sharply too; but they did not. In fact, they fell steeply after the end of the Napoleonic Wars. Yields continued to rise until about 1840, at which point they stubbornly levelled out. These statistics are not what one would expect of a buyer's market, where yields and prices should both continue to rise, until, that is, the demand was satisfied. So how was Britain's growing urban population fed?

The repeal of the Corn Laws in 1846 ended protectionism and led to an increase in grain imports, which accounted for about 8 per cent of grain consumed in the 1840s. By the 1860s this figure had increased to 40 per cent. Even these figures fail to account for the feeding of all the extra mouths. If we take the earlier part of the era of agricultural improvement as conventionally understood (say, 1750–1830), the population rose from 6 to 14 million, yet wheat yields increased by just 10-15 per cent, which would have been far below what was actually required. It is possible that the growing gap between hungry mouths and available food was met by the expansion of arable acreage, but it has been calculated that this only amounted to about 22 per cent (by area), at a time when demand must have more than doubled. In short, the figures cannot be reconciled, but we do know the population must have fed themselves somehow. It is clear, however, that the era of High Farming had been successful, if not in quite the way we had been taught at school. Wheat production, for example, in 1871, just before the years of depression, was not to be equalled again until 1944.[50] The only explanation has to be that grain was imported in greater quantities than we once thought. But it will need to be demonstrated.

THE ERA OF VICTORIAN HIGH FARMING (1830–70)

Perhaps it is because the stories are better that archaeologists and historians tend to concentrate on periods of change and pay rather less attention to times of stability. But the great era of stability known as Victorian High Farming was very important because it grew from the reforms of the previous two centuries and led to the all-important production of food for the rapidly expanding populations of urban Britain. In broad terms the period of High Farming lasted from about 1830 until the agricultural depression of the 1870s. Many medieval churches still standing in country parishes today owe their survival to the profits made during High Farming, when the large incomes from rural estates allowed village squires up and down the country to pay out large sums towards the repair of their often rather dilapidated chapels. It is fashionable to sneer at Victorian over-restoration, but without those much-needed repairs many of the country's fine parish churches would have collapsed. As it happens, quite a few did fall down, especially in areas like the Fens, where the ground is unstable; but many were saved.[51]

The era of High Farming saw the introduction of fertilizers, such as nightsoil and bonemeal, acquired from non-farm sources.[52] From the 1830s guano[53] imported from South America was used extensively to enrich the light soils of East Anglia. Land drainage also became increasingly important and was adopted widely. High Farming saw the improvement of many animal breeds and the development of new high-energy feeds from the mid-century, such as oilcake (which initially used imported ingredients). The roast beef so often eaten in Victorian novels was the result of an increasingly important cattle industry. The rapid fattening of cattle benefited greatly from the new feeds and the beasts themselves were accommodated in the new spacious farm buildings that are such a feature of High Farming. During this era farm buildings were regarded increasingly as factories for the production of food. Writing in 1863 the author and agricultural engineer J. B. Denton noted that to farm successfully with defective and ill-arranged buildings was no more practical than to manufacture profitably in scattered, inconvenient workshops.[54]

With these improvements in farming went improvements in roads, communications and marketing, which all helped to maintain commodity prices. High Farming witnessed the construction of some remarkable farm and estate buildings, many of which are constructed in an Italianate style. The style had its origins in the late eighteenth century, and some farm buildings were constructed by architects who specialized in such structures. The mid-nineteenth-century buildings of the model farm at Holkham Hall, for example, are very reminiscent of much contemporary railway architecture – especially the rather severely Italianate buildings of King's Cross station in London (1852).

These attractive buildings were not confined to the prosperous estates of Norfolk. Top-quality farm buildings are to be found over most of Britain.[55] Some are particularly fine. Demesne Farm, Doddington, in central Cheshire, was built in the 1780s and was designed by Samuel Wyatt (who was also involved with Holkham).[56] The main two-storey barn is built in the Italianate manner and forms the centre point for radiating single-storey stables and dairy cowsheds (known locally as shippons). The entire complex is extremely well designed and integrated within yards where animals could be kept out of the wind, from whichever direction it was blowing. The two-storey farmhouse formed the third side of the shippon yard. This arrangement was convenient for the farmer's wife and milkmaids who would process the milk, cheese and whey in a dairy within, or attached to, the house. It was an ideal set-up.

I mentioned earlier that Victorian squires often paid for the restoration of their parish churches and were great builders of farms, houses and cottages. Like other Victorians they had a remarkable confidence, both in themselves and what they were doing. My own great-grandfather owned and successfully ran a large estate in Hertfordshire and many of the buildings he had erected are still in use. But he was also an academic geologist of some standing and fellow of a Cambridge college. He was by no means unique. Many Victorian landowners had similarly wide interests. Take, for example, the greatest pioneer of modern archaeology, General Pitt-Rivers, who was a major landowner and a soldier, too.[57]

The General's most significant archaeological researches took place on his estates in Cranborne Chase, in the 1880s, just after the era of High Farming. While many of the large estates did much to soften the economic impact of the agricultural depression on the lives of their employees, Pitt-Rivers was a passionate believer in Darwin and in the importance of bringing the results of his archaeological researches to a wider public, through many large reports and some highly original museum displays, including what is arguably the earliest (1880) educational theme park, the Larmer Grounds, at his home in Cranborne Chase. Despite being in the depths of the countryside on the Dorset–Wiltshire borders, and moreover operating in the pre-motor car age, the Larmer Grounds attracted no fewer than 44,417 visitors in 1899.[58] Men like Pitt-Rivers, for all the faults of the rigid hierarchical social system in which they operated, brought a vision to the running of their estates that we lack in rural Britain today. They also encouraged a form of admittedly paternalistic social care for the families of the people who worked for their estates. I also believe that many of them cared deeply about the look of the countryside and their estate villages, a number of which have survived remarkably intact.

It is worth noting here, amidst much talk of prosperity in High Farming England, that all was not well elsewhere. Highland Scotland was still experiencing the effects of landscape clearance, but, even worse than that, in Ireland people had to face the horrors brought about by the first potato blight, which struck in 1846. Potatoes had provided the staple diet for Irish rural and poorer urban families, and the famine of the 1840s and 1850s led to wholesale immigration and terrible hardship. Many of the navvies who arrived in Britain to build railways and drain the land were refugees from the famines.

Taken as a whole, the era of High Farming did much to improve the look of rural Britain, if only because the changes it brought about were motivated by more than just the need to make bigger profits. Admittedly, today profits are held in check by the imposition of increasingly demanding environmental constraints, but this system of carrot-and-stick will never work until the farmers and landowners of rural Britain are allowed the personal freedom to express their undoubted affection for their landscapes in practical ways.

High Farming produced some remarkable buildings and made fortunes for many people. But it was not suited to all areas, even in England. For example, regions where grazing and milk-production were traditional were less affected by the drive to increase cereal production, although, as we have seen, intensive beef-rearing continued to be important throughout the Victorian period. High Farming also witnessed some quite extraordinary technological achievements in the rural landscape, many of which had origins somewhat earlier. One of the most remarkable of these took place in the estate of the dukes of Bedford around the drier 'island' of Thorney in the central Fens, just east of Peterborough. In the Middle Ages Thorney Abbey had been a prosperous Benedictine house and an aisle of the original large abbey is still being used as the parish church. After the Dissolution the lands belonging to the abbey were granted by Henry VIII to the earls, later dukes, of Bedford.

By the 1880s most of the estate was under arable (12,000 acres) but over half (7,000 acres) had still to be retained as pasture, because grass is far less severely affected by flooding than crops. Although many of the original Bedford estate farms have recently collapsed as the peaty ground beneath them has contracted (because of drainage), the central estate buildings on the firmer land of Thorney 'island' still survive in good condition. The estate built a series of fine detached and terrace houses for its employees during the mid-nineteenth century which still make the village of Thorney one of the most pleasing in the area. Chief among the estate buildings is the great water tower, built in 1855, which formed the focus of the main estate workshops and yard at the very centre of the village. Today, as in Victorian times, the water tower

Fig. 12.8 Like a cathedral to the wealth generated by Victorian High Farming, the estate water tower soars above the Duke of Bedford's workshops at Thorney, in the Cambridgeshire Fens. The tower was built, in the Jacobean style, in 1855 and features a higher polygonal stair-turret.

dominates what is left of the original medieval abbey just across the Peterborough road, a short distance to the south. The long, straight drove-roads, usually lined by the wet-loving lime trees that were so important in the seventeenth and eighteenth centuries when the first reclaimed land was used almost exclusively for pasture, are a feature of the area, which still manages to retain its distinctive character, despite some of the most intensive farming in Britain.

It would be a mistake to see the Fens as a homogeneous landscape, where huge agricultural estates were the norm. Large farms predominated – and still dominate – much of the so-called 'Black' or peat fenlands well inland from the Wash, but the slightly higher marine-deposited silts of Marshland in north-west Norfolk and north Cambridgeshire were drained and developed much earlier. These areas evolved their own distinctive patterns of farming which included cherry and Bramley apple orchards and soft fruit, from the mid-nineteenth century. Today Marshland silts around Spalding grow vegetables and the largest crop of daffodils anywhere in Europe.

Although the vast majority of Victorian estates of the middle order (up to, say, 2,000 hectares) were owned and run by landowners with an active interest in country sports and farming, a proportion were bought by successful merchants and industrialists. Sometimes these people showed greater imagination in the design and layout of their estate buildings and of their villages. Too often the estate villages of traditional landowners are characterized by a uniform and at times rather lacklustre style of architecture where the tenants' houses are marked by large date-stones carrying the landlord's initials and coat-of-arms. In such villages nobody could be in any doubt who was the benefactor. But there are exceptions, such as the small, but very fine Arts and Crafts village of Fortingall in Perth and Kinross. The origins of this village are ancient, but it was transformed in the 1890s by the addition of new houses and the rebuilding of the church, whose stunning barrel-vaulted interior is entirely made from local oak. Outside in the churchyard is the famous Fortingall Yew which could be as old as 5,000 years – making it a good contender for the oldest living thing on earth.

For ordinary farmers the depression of the 1870s would have been almost as bad as the great stock market crash of 1929 and Depression of the 1930s, but it lasted very much longer than the latter, only ending with the outbreak of war in 1914. The roots of the problem lay ultimately in the much earlier repeal of the Corn Laws. The Corn Laws were a protectionist measure originally passed in 1815, when British farmers feared that the artificially high prices of corn that were sustained during the Napoleonic Wars would come crashing down. By the 1840s it was clear that the high price of corn was having a very detrimental effect on the growing population of Britain's industrial towns, and the Prime Minister, Robert Peel, despite fierce resistance from his Tory colleagues, had them repealed in 1846, using the Irish potato famine as an excuse. Despite dire predictions, prices failed to tumble and it was not until 1870 that the full effect was felt when cereal farmers from across the Atlantic began to export large quantities of grain to Britain, at very low prices. The result was the great British farming depression which brought the prosperity of Victorian High Farming to an abrupt end.

LANDSCAPES OF PLEASURE: HUNTIN', SHOOTIN' AND FISHIN'

I wrote in rather rosy terms about intellectual diversity of many Victorian rural squires, but the truth must be admitted that they also enjoyed slaughtering game in quantities that verged on the industrial. There was nothing new in this; rural men had long enjoyed what in the Middle Ages were known as the pleasures of the chase. Even men as enlightened as the social reformer William Cobbett, and the late-eighteenth-century country vicar and diarist Parson Woodforde, took part in what some today would call blood sports, others field sports. During the late eighteenth and nineteenth centuries the leisure time enjoyed, not just by great landowners, but by ordinary yeoman farmers, increased, and so did popular demand for good hunting, shooting and fishing. Hunting and shooting became a major part of the winter social season at many country houses, both large and small, right across Britain. In Highland Scotland and in some regions of northern England grouse-shooting became a highly important component of the rural economy from the mid-nineteenth century and has left an enduring mark on the landscape, not just in the form of huge tracts of managed moorland, but in numerous lodges and inns built for the shooters themselves, and in the housing required for ghillies, gamekeepers and their families.

The fashion for grouse-shooting seems to have its origins in the late eighteenth century. By the 1790s organized shooting parties were a feature of moor-owning families in north-western England and in 1797 the Duke of Devonshire devoted several of his moors around Settle to grouse-shooting; the aim was to produce a monoculture of heather to provide the fledgling birds with the tender shoots they need when young. This was generally achieved by a programme of controlled burning, which gives the grouse moors of the Pennines a distinctive patchwork pattern, as the burnt-off areas of heather flower at different times.

In lowland areas the popularity of pheasant- and partridge-shooting in the nineteenth and twentieth centuries resulted in the planting of 'shelter belts', where young birds may be reared. Shoots are well-organized affairs, with separate groups of shooters (generally known as 'guns') who stand at points that have been pre-selected by the head gamekeeper. Birds are driven towards the guns by beaters, who walk through the grass or bracken shouting and generally making a din. As the birds fly towards the guns, the gamekeepers will often have arranged the 'drive', as each individual set piece of the shoot is known, in such a way that a previously planted belt of trees will force the birds to fly higher. As they cross these shelter belts, flying high and fast, they will be met by the guns. Shot birds will then be collected, either by the gundogs of the guns themselves, or by dedicated pickers-up. Shelter belts for shooting are a common feature of lowland landscapes in East Anglia and the Home Counties. They may also be seen on the large estates in many parts of lowland Scotland.

Another sporting pastime which became something of an obsession in the nineteenth century was fox-hunting. Fox-hunting requires small woods or coverts where foxes may breed and jumpable hedges, which are maintained low and free from hedgerow trees. This sort of landscape was created on the heavy clay pastures of Leicestershire and Rutland, arguably the finest fox-hunting country, during the Enclosure Movement of the late eighteenth and nineteenth centuries.[59] Today these hunting landscapes still survive, although many of the hedges have grown up and have acquired trees since the war. Often designated jumping places (guaranteed free from hidden barbed wire) are clearly marked by painted signs.

We tend to think of rivers as being largely unaffected by the hand of man, but in actual fact most lowland streams have been 'tamed' or managed in some way. We know, for example, that rivers such as the Thames flowed in a series of complex, braided stream channels in the Bronze Age. Over the ages they have been taken in hand. Most of this work was carried out for purely practical purposes: to prevent flooding or to harness tail-races for mills. But some chalk streams were particularly prized for their sport fishing and this has directly affected, not just their flow, but the character of the vegetation along their length. One of the most prized chalk streams for trout fishing is the River Test in Hampshire, which has been managed for fishing since the nineteenth century. Following the demise of water meadows after the First World War, fishing became the principal management objective of many chalk-stream owners.[60]

CREATING A RURAL IDYLL: THE LAKE DISTRICT

Shooting has always been a primarily masculine pastime, but during the nineteenth century there was increasing emphasis on the ideals of family life. Holidays, which were taken *en famille* became increasingly popular among the growing numbers of educated people. The poets and painters of the late-eighteenth- and early nineteenth-century Picturesque movement, rather than landscape designers, were among the first to draw attention to the beauties of the natural, unadorned landscape. Poets like Wordsworth, Keats and Coleridge and artists like Turner, Constable and later Samuel Palmer were less concerned with improved landscapes – a cynic might say because they could, and did, improve them with their art – preferring instead to portray the natural scene.

It is hard to avoid the impression that the beauties of what was later to be dubbed the Lake District remained unappreciated until the Wordsworths, brother and sister, famously moved back there (they were both born in Cockermouth, Cumbria) in 1799. Thereafter Wordsworth, most ably supplied with ideas by Dorothy, produced a series of works in prose and poetry describing the picturesque wonders of the Lakes. He even coined the term Lake District in his *Guide to the Lakes* (1810), which is still in print.[61] These publications had a huge impact on the nation at large and have left a dubious, if lasting, legacy in the form of hundreds of thousands of annual visitors to the region's many beauty spots.

In actual fact, however, the residents of the area had long appreciated the strong character of its landscapes. An anonymous poet of *c.* 1600, for example, wrote of the fells as 'stately beings, rearing their haughty heads to the skies'.[62] Many of the hills have been given personalities, such as Coniston Old Man and Knock Old Man and numerous folk rhymes about the weather show a local pride in their surroundings, which often included conflicting claims that such-and-such a hill was the highest in the country.

The elevation of the Lake District into an icon of the Picturesque began in 1754 with a celebrated poem by Dr John Dalton describing

Fig. 12.9 Grasmere, Cumbria from the south. In 1799 William Wordsworth and his sister Dorothy moved back to the Lake District from Dorset, after William's turbulent time as a revolutionary in France. They set up home in Dove Cottage, near the small town of Grasmere. He describes this crag above Grasmere in Poem III of *Poems on the Naming of Places* (1800):

> And, when at evening we pursue our walk
> Along the public way, the Cliff, so high
> Above us, and so distant in its height,
> Is visible, and often seems to send
> Its own deep quiet to restore our hearts.

the Derwentwater Valley; in 1766 another doctor of divinity, Dr John Brown, described Derwentwater in terms of the delicate sunshine of the cultivated dales contrasting with the horrors of the rugged cliffs and foaming waterfalls. Such visions, whose roots probably lay in the paintings of Lorraine and Poussin a century earlier, inspired many people to visit the region and by the end of the 1770s tours of the Lakes had become popular with middle-class people. The Lakeland tour gained formality with the publication in 1778 of Thomas West's *Guide to the Lakes*. In this early practical guidebook, visitors were conducted to the best viewpoints to appreciate picturesque views. The tourism boom of the late eighteenth century led, as so often happens, to housing development a few years later: from 1780 to 1830 the shores of the more accessible lakes, such as Ullswater, Windermere and Derwentwater, were liberally peppered with villas, often set back from the water, but with lawns and meadows to frame the view. This meant, of course, that they were clearly visible from some distance away.

During the mid-nineteenth century there was a strong reaction against the eighteenth-century idea that landscapes could be improved by the judicious placing of a lake here, a grotto or temple there and so forth. The man who did more than anyone else to change this aesthetic was yet another Lake District resident, John Ruskin (1819–1900). Ruskin has been described as an outstanding critic who was able to determine the direction in which the visual arts of the Victorian age should go. In his *Modern Painters* (1843–60) he called for the meticulous observation of nature and re-established the then fading reputation of J. M. W. Turner, whom he admired for his ability to penetrate the inner forces of nature.[63] His work also stressed the importance of current art and the need to look at the world as it was at the time. Not surprisingly, he reacted against and disliked previous generations' efforts to 'improve' the landscape.

Internationally well-known views, such as those in 'Constable Country' around Dedham Vale and the River Stour in Suffolk, have led to the acquisition of visitor centres and the other trappings of modern tourism. But the celebration of fine views is nothing new. Indeed, famous views sometimes seem to acquire an independent life of their own. In his *Guide to the Lakes* Wordsworth praised a particular view of the River Lune, at Kirkby Lonsdale, in Cumbria. Eight years later Turner painted it in a moody, if not a particularly well-known picture. The same view became nationally celebrated in 1875 when Ruskin described it in extravagant terms: 'The valley of the Lune at Kirkby is one of the loveliest scenes in England – therefore in the world. Whatever moorland hill, and sweet river, and English forest foliage can be at their best, is gathered there.'[64] Thereafter the view from Kirkby Lonsdale Churchyard has been known as 'Ruskin's View'.

I had heard about 'Ruskin's View' and was determined to explore it for this book, and for myself. So we rented a small cottage that had been built around 1830 by the local parson, who admired the famous view and wanted somewhere tranquil to write his sermons. I have to say it was unusual to enter one's temporary home through a churchyard and I am sure the knowledge that we both had to negotiate a passage home through dozens of gravestones moderated our behaviour when we visited some of the excellent pubs in the little town beyond the churchyard wall. I tried to take a photograph that replicated Turner's picture precisely, but a large stand of trees made that impossible. Turner had also increased the height of the hills that form the backdrop of the view, presumably for dramatic effect. Similarly, as I thought at the time, he had added swirling mists to add a fashionable air of 'horror' to the scene.

On the last of our four days' stay it had rained heavily overnight, the clouds finally passing over an hour or so before dawn. Like most livestock farmers I am used to getting up early. At about six in the morning I went to the window to see what the driving conditions would be like for our long journey home. To my astonishment I was looking down on 'Ruskin's View' during a classic temperature inversion, where cold air from above was retaining mists that were rising off the warm waters of the River Lune. (See Plates 15 and 16 to compare the two views.) This was precisely what Turner had painted and one must assume that he, too, had been up early one morning after heavy rain. Just fifteen minutes later the mists had completely dissipated and after breakfast we drove home in bright sunshine.

Another new focus for landscape appreciation was the Highlands of Scotland. The Highland clearances had effectively emptied vast tracts of the northern Scottish landscape and when sheep became less profitable many of the higher moors were given over to grouse-shooting. During the reign of Queen Victoria, too, what one might term 'Scottishness' became very fashionable. The Royal Family built their Aberdeenshire house at Balmoral in 1853–6, replacing a Jacobean house. Balmoral was built in the rather extravagant style of Scott's 'Scottish Baronial', influenced by contributions from Prince Albert, no less.

The royal interest in Scotland took place at a time when richer members of the English upper classes were taking to grouse-shooting and fly-fishing in Highland streams. Of course the very wealthiest owned their own estates, but many, especially the fishers, came north as tourists, staying in hotels. The opening up of northern Scotland by the railways in the second half of the nineteenth century led to a growing popular interest in the enjoyment of Highland scenery, which the railway companies were keen to exploit. Even as late as the mid-1920s railway companies such as the London and North-Eastern Railway found it worth their while to publish posters in England advertising the pleasures of salmon-fishing and grouse-shooting in Scotland.

In the second half of the nineteenth century the English discovered the pleasures of golf, and in the early twentieth century the game had become the major tourist 'draw' in those parts of Lowland Scotland that lacked stirring scenery and grouse moors. Golf is known to have been played in Scotland as early as the fifteenth century and the first official club was founded in 1744 (later known as the Honourable Company of Edinburgh Golfers). The railway companies saw at once that here was a means to get people to travel to some of the farthest reaches of their lines. Not only that, but hotels could be built to accommodate their stay on the links. Most of these golf-tourism ventures were successful and are still prospering today.

The Romantic ideals so popular in garden design in the late eighteenth century were not killed off by the unpleasant realities of the Napoleonic Wars. When hostilities ceased in 1815, Switzerland had become part of the itinerary of wealthy tourists keen to experience more than just the classical landscapes of Italy. Swiss cottages (such as the eponymous example in north London) and chalets became picturesque symbols of rustic simplicity. Many country houses acquired 'Swiss' chalets in which estate workers were housed, and these were often set against planting of dark, brooding pines. At Hawkstone Park, Shropshire, there is a series of rocky clefts, known since the late eighteenth century as 'A Scene in Switzerland', which lies to one side of the Swiss Bridge, a somewhat perilous rustic wooden bridge over a vertically sided gorge. Some places went even further: at Alton Towers, Staffordshire, a retired Welsh harpist could be heard from a chalet on a hill in the park. However, by far the best and most extensive example of the style is still to be seen at Old Warden, today the seat of the Shuttleworth family, near Biggleswade in Bedfordshire.[65] This is not where one might expect to find such a picturesque idyll, being flat land, surrounded by malodorous fields of commercially grown Brussels sprouts and within sound of the A1. The Swiss chalet and Swiss Garden at Old Warden were built in the 1820s for Lord Ongley and the garden was progressively enlarged and imaginatively improved by the Shuttleworth family into the late Victorian period.[66]

ARTIFICE IN HIGH VICTORIAN GARDENS

The great British landscape gardens of Georgian and Regency Britain continue to delight modern eyes, which may marvel at the detail of elaborate parterres, but prefer to enjoy a well-composed sweep of woodland and lake. By Victorian times tastes were rather different; the design of British gardens became more artificial. Greenhouses had been around since the late sixteenth century, but only became popular in

Fig. 12.10 The Palm House, at Kew Gardens, Richmond, Surrey. This is the finest surviving Victorian glass and iron building. It was designed by Decimus Burton and built by Richard Turner. The flower beds in front are bedded out each summer season with non-hardy plants. Such bedding-out, often in very bright colours, was a distinctive feature of High Victorian gardening and would have been impossible without the use of heated greenhouses over winter.

the eighteenth and early nineteenth, at a time when travelling botanists and plant-hunters were returning from foreign parts with new specimens. Many of these can still be seen in the great botanical gardens which have become such an important feature of many British urban and suburban landscapes.

Many examples of the large pines, such as the Douglas fir and the Sitka spruce, that are still such an important presence in many parts of the British landscape were brought to Britain from North America by the famous Scottish botanist David Douglas (1798–1834). The great botanical garden at Dawyck Arboretum, in hilly country on the northern fringes of the Scottish Borders, contains some of Douglas's original seedlings, planted in the 1830s. Incidentally, plant-hunting could be dangerous. Douglas died in Hawaii, aged just 36, when he fell into a pit-trap that already held a wild bull.

As technology and building materials improved, the size of glasshouses and conservatories increased. One of the first of these glass monsters, the Great Conservatory, was built by Joseph Paxton at Chatsworth House, Derbyshire, between 1836 and 1840. At the time the architecturally minded Paxton was head gardener for the Duke of Devonshire. The Chatsworth conservatory was so vast that Queen Victoria and Prince Albert were driven through it in a carriage. Sadly, it was demolished in the 1920s. The great Palm House at Kew Gardens, near London, is one of the finest of the High Victorian stove-houses and still, remarkably, contains a few of the original plants. It was designed by Decimus Burton and built between 1844 and 1848. The taller central area can be viewed from an overhead gallery, rather in the manner of the Crystal Palace, which was built for the Great Exhibition of 1851 by Paxton – by this time Sir Joseph – more architect than head gardener.

The repeal of the Glass Tax in 1845 led to an increase in smaller, domestic conservatories. Heated greenhouses, or stove-houses, grew in popularity because they allowed tender plants to be grown over winter. Labour was relatively cheap and many of the large private and municipal gardens employed huge numbers of gardeners and undergardeners. When the danger of late frosts was past these men would be sent into the garden with barrowfuls of tender herbaceous plants – and sometimes even of woody plants like palms and tree-ferns – that were then planted out in brightly coloured bedding schemes. With hindsight it is easy to poke fun at many Victorian bedding schemes, which today would be seen as an unsympathetic, and certainly unsophisticated, 'riot of colour'. But Victorian towns and cities could be dour, grim places and the bright flowers in the annual bedding schemes in municipal parks up and down the country would have lifted everyone's spirits after the dark days of winter.

One important development in modern garden design was the subdividing of large gardens into smaller subsidiary 'rooms', usually within tall hedges. This style of gardening has proved enduring because it can also be employed to good effect in the smaller gardens of modern suburban houses. It is still generally supposed that 'rooms' made their first appearance in the large gardens of Hidcote, Gloucestershire, and Sissinghurst Castle, in Kent, which was laid out by Vita Sackville-West and Harold Nicolson. Hidcote was created by Lawrence Johnston in the first half of the twentieth century, using ideas derived from his travels in France and Italy. However, the earliest example of 'rooms' in a British garden is actually to be found in the grounds of Biddulph Grange, in Staffordshire, whose innovative gardens were created by James Bateman in the mid-nineteenth century.

ARMCHAIR LANDSCAPES

I have always preferred to experience the landscape at first hand, by being there, on the spot. For me, a gallery of paintings would never replace that experience of looking out of our bedroom window at 'Ruskin's View', shrouded in the dawn mists. No sooner had I taken the photograph than I had pulled on whatever clothes were lying on the floor, and was outside breathing it all in. The emotions evoked by the experience of the muted sounds of the first people going about their daily business, together with the soft light of the early morning, the damp, the scent of decaying leaves and the sharp chill of the still air permanently fixed the experience in my memory. It was worth countless words, or pictures. But if everyone had felt like this, the great artists and poets who have celebrated the British landscape would have eked out a pretty miserable existence.

In the eighteenth century the concept of the rural idyll was shared by most people of the landowning and educated classes, as the numerous grand portraits in country houses throughout Britain, of squires, their ladies, families and pets, by the likes of Gainsborough, Romney and so many others, attest. These are frequently set against a background of sun-drenched parkland, real or imagined. As time passed, the appreciation and enjoyment of the landscape was to become more widely spread through society and this involved a return to the very roots of the landscape ideal – the painterly view. From the late eighteenth and nineteenth and much of the twentieth centuries the portrayal of the countryside by amateur and self-taught artists working in watercolours became something of a national pastime. In addition to the great names, there were a host of perfectly competent though less widely known artists such as Peter De Wint (1784–1849), John Varley (1778–1842), John Sell Cotman (1782–1842) and the wonderfully named Anthony Vandyke Copley Fielding (1785–1855).

The Royal Watercolour Society, the first of its type in the world, was founded in 1804 by artists such as John Varley who were annoyed that the Royal Academy, which had only been established thirty years previously, would not exhibit paintings in watercolours. So popular was the new society that its first exhibition in 1805 drew large crowds and the paintings sold briskly. Watercolour artists primarily painted landscapes and sold their pictures in the salerooms of London and provincial towns, but they were also paid to stay in country houses, where they gave tutorials to the wives and daughters of the landed gentry.[67] Huge numbers of perfectly competent amateur watercolours were produced by masters and pupils during the century leading up to the First World War; indeed so many pictures were painted that even today saleroom prices are still remarkably flat for all but the very best.

Many British poets have extolled the beauties of the landscape. But only a few had hands-on experience and knowledge of the countryside, including Scotland's national poet, Robert Burns (1759–96), who was the son of an Ayrshire tenant farmer and even tried his hand at farming, but failed. His knowledge and love of the country flavours much of his work. Slightly later the poet and novelist Sir Walter Scott (1771–1832) helped to create a pseudo-antique style of rural Scots landscape and architecture that has come to be known as Scottish Baronial; the style is exemplified by his rambling house on the Scottish Borders at Abbotsford. Other poets of the eighteenth and early nineteenth centuries, such as Wordsworth, Keats and Shelley, following Rousseau, extolled untamed nature, rather than the landscape as such. Perhaps the best-known poem about the English landscape, Thomas Gray's 'Elegy Written in a Country Churchyard' (1751), is remarkable because throughout it acknowledges the efforts of ordinary working men to maintain the countryside in its idyllic state:

> Let not Ambition mock their useful toil,
> Their homely joys, and destiny obscure;
> Nor Grandeur hear with a disdainful smile
> The short and simple annals of the poor.

But of all the poets of this period who wrote about the landscape none did so with greater knowledge and awareness than John Clare (1793–1864) of Helpston, Peterborough (originally in Northamptonshire). He knew and understood the landscape around the Fen-edge village intimately and even today it is possible to find some of the streams, paths, marshes and woodlands he writes about. Clare had the humility to confine his attention to a single parish, and his verses have given us what the poet Ronald Blythe has described as 'the most authentic view which we possess of rural England at large as it existed before mechanised farming'.[68]

THE LANDSCAPE AS FOOD FOR THOUGHT

While men of power and influence were creating their own landscapes others were content to record what they would have regarded as God's landscape, the natural world. Quiet observers, such as Gilbert White, the curate of Selborne (Hampshire), who wrote an account of the natural history of the parish which has become the fourth most published book in the English language. White wrote in an epistolary style, but others kept more straightforward diaries, in which day-to-day events are mixed with observations on the countryside. Of these, perhaps the diaries of parson Woodforde are among the best. Woodforde's diaries give a remarkably vivid picture of the Norfolk countryside in the second half of the eighteenth century. The detailed accounts of the various, and often huge, meals he devoured give his diaries a special flavour. I would not have liked to have been his horse.

Neither Gilbert White nor Parson Woodforde was a remotely political figure, but this certainly cannot be said for perhaps the best-known recorder of British rural (and also urban) landscapes, William Cobbett, whose colourful career included a spell in the army, serving time in jail for criminal libel, and two trips to America.[69] He was a prolific journalist, he loathed hypocrisy and he worked tirelessly for social reform. Apart from numerous political pamphlets and articles he also wrote on gardening, farming and the Cottage Economy (a Regency term for what we would call self-sufficiency). But by far his best-known work is his discursive *Rural Rides*, of 1821–32, which not only describes lanes, roads, fields, farms, market towns and the countryside, but also comments in detail on the lives of the people who inhabited the various landscapes he passed through. He uses these essays to ride his many hobby horses, which he does with some of the most colourful and endearingly bombastic writing in the English language. Nobody could bring the landscape better to life than Cobbett. He injected a radical anger into his reading of the countryside and what was happening within it. I think of him as an archetype curmudgeon. A radical, a countryman, but above all else an Englishman. Yet in his *Cottage Economy* (1821–2), which is still a Bible of self-sufficiency, containing in its numbered paragraphs a wealth of sound practical advice on everything from cows and cabbages to the brewing of good beer, we still find he is unable to resist sounding off about something which irritates him – and remember, this from an Englishman: '33. But is it in the power of any man, any good labourer who has attained the age of fifty, to look back upon the last thirty years of his life, without cursing the day in which tea was introduced into England? Where is there such a man, who cannot trace to this cause a very considerable part of all the mortifications and sufferings of his life?'[70]

The Victorians were not perfect. Some, myself included, see their architecture as heavy and not always very subtle. The materials they used in many of their country houses, too, were harder than those of the eighteenth century and have weathered with less grace, though doubtless they will outlast many houses currently being built. The Victorians were not always as quick to tear down earlier buildings as is sometimes supposed, and they were at great pains to restore and repair Britain's many thousands of medieval churches, introducing the first legislation to protect Historical Monuments, in 1874. It is time that we acknowledged what the Victorians did for rural landscapes, if only to prevent their wholesale destruction in the name of 'productivity', 'efficiency' and 'progress'.[71] It seems to me that the Victorians of rural Britain can teach us something today, because one of their greatest achievements was massively to increase agricultural productivity, while at the same time enhancing and not diminishing the look of the countryside.

13

Dark Satanic Mills? Townscapes in
Modern Times (1750–1900)

A principal theme of this book has been the extraordinary diversity of the British landscape. Britain has a high rocky spine and rivers flow east and west into the North Sea and Atlantic, but the principal routes of communication run north and south, so they have to contend with numerous and often steep-sided river valleys. This varied and sometimes precipitous terrain has provided some major challenges for the engineers who built Britain's roads, canals and railways. Few managed to escape having to confront the underlying form of the landscape.

In the late eighteenth and nineteenth centuries the increasing demands of industry meant that good communications were of fundamental importance. Without the ability to transport people and things, towns simply failed to prosper. A classic example is Stamford, in southern Lincolnshire, which did well in the Middle Ages because it was on the crossing of the North Road over the River Welland.[1] In the post-medieval centuries the town continued to grow, gathering pace, if anything, in the eighteenth century, as its market increased in importance. In the mid-nineteenth century, however, the fate of Stamford was largely sealed by the earls of Exeter, whose magnificent seat, Burghley House, lies on the town's southern boundary. In 1846 Lord Exeter refused to have the Great Northern railway line routed across his land, a decision, incidentally, that had wide local support. So instead, the contractor Thomas Brassey shifted the route further east, through a part of Earl Fitzwilliam's Milton Park estate, in Peterborough.[2] The result was that Stamford remained a pleasing market town, whereas Peterborough developed into a major railway centre and industrial city.

Water always finds its own level, so canals cannot cope with slopes, except through flights of locks, which slow down traffic and are costly both to build and to maintain. Valleys can be crossed on embankments and aqueducts, but again the forces of gravity come into play and small seepages and leaks rapidly develop into major losses of water. Roads are quite good at coping with slopes, but the larger the incline the smaller the load that can be pulled by horse-power alone. So it was in the interests of the turnpike trusts to level out their roads as much as possible both to attract traffic and to allow greater tolls to be charged for heavier vehicles. And when it comes to the negotiation of inclines, railways fall somewhere between canals and roads. In the early days it was not uncommon for locomotives to be unhitched and the train hauled up a sharp incline by a large stationary steam engine positioned at the top of a steep hill. The geography of Britain played a major role in the opening of the earlier main lines, especially those that headed north out of London.

THE AGE OF THE TRAIN

Take the railway routes from southern England to Scotland. The west coast route is well known for its bends and inclines, such as that up to Shap Fell, in Cumbria, but even the gentler, lower-lying east coast route has to enter a tunnel directly outside King's Cross station, then fifteen minutes later the train is soaring high above the Mimram Valley, near Welwyn in Hertfordshire, on Lewis Cubitt's famous Digswell Viaduct.[3] It is entirely possible, of course, that, far from daunting them, these physical challenges have inspired the engineers of the past three centuries – and indeed of our own time.

The horse-drawn railways are sometimes dismissed as primitive and not very effective. These early railways are generally referred to as 'waggonways' which is an unfortunate word, conjuring up the creak of aged timbers straining under a heavy load. But nothing could be further from the truth. It was principally the movement of coal that led to the construction of many wooden railways. By and large the early horse-drawn waggonways have not left a significant mark on the modern landscape, except where they involved the construction of bridges. This is often because later waggonways used cuttings and

Fig. 13.1 The Digswell Viaduct, near Welwyn, Hertfordshire. This viaduct carries two tracks of the Great Northern railway over the steep-sided valley of the River Mimran. It has forty-nine brick arches, each with a span of 9.1 metres, and was built between 1848 and 1850. The engineer was Lewis Cubitt (1811–72), and the construction was the work of Thomas Brassey (1805–70), who built about a third of Britain's early railways with great efficiency – usually to budget and to time.

bridges that were subsequently incorporated into railways or roads. A recent discovery, during restoration work, of an intact wooden railway, probably dating to the 1750s, at the Bersham Ironworks, near Wrexham in north Wales, shows that these waggonways could be remarkably sophisticated, even employing points to switch between different tracks.[4]

The conventional view is that the arrival of the railways caused the transformation of British industry, opening up fresh markets and creating all sorts of new opportunities. This ignores the fact that British regional industries had already found ways of moving their goods in sufficient bulk to meet market demands. Take the horse-drawn waggonways. Yes, they were somewhat crude when compared with the sophistication and complexity of the steam railways, but they were extremely effective and remarkably cost-efficient. Above all else, they *worked* and enabled certain regional industries, such as the coal mines of the north-east to prosper and proliferate.

The key to a successful horse-drawn waggonway was to keep distances to a minimum and to flatten out inclines. Given suitable conditions, a horse could pull several four-wheeled chaldrons and the wooden rails would rapidly be worn through. Maintenance needed to be constant. One of the first recorded waggonways was built around 1600 by Lord Middleton to bring coal from his mines at Strelley to be sold in Nottingham.

Waggonways had a transforming

Fig. 13.2 The Causey Arch, crossing the Causey Burn at Tanfield, near Stanley in Co. Durham. This is the oldest surviving waggonway bridge, constructed between 1725–6, and at the time the longest single-span in Britain. It formed part of a wooden railway to transport coal from the Durham coalfield across the East Durham plateau to the River Tyne, where it could be transported south by sea. In the 1727 the line saw the movement of 930 chaldron-loads of coal a day. Chaldrons (*above*) were high-sided wagons with four wheels that carried 2.70 tonnes.

effect on the coalfields of north-east England, where the first one opened in 1669. Like so many others in the region it brought coal from an upland colliery (at Ravensworth, Co. Durham), down to the Tyne (at Dunston). Already by 1700 there were 59 kilometres of wooden rails on Tyneside; by 1800 that figure had risen to 146. One of the best preserved of these later waggonways is that which brought coal from the Tanfield and Causey collieries down to Dunston, during which journey the steep-sided Causey Burn had to be crossed with the famous stone-built Causey Arch. The sheer size of this single-span bridge gives some idea of the economic importance of waggonways.

The first iron rails were cast in short lengths at Coalbrookdale in 1767 and the first flanged wheels (standard on all railways today) were introduced in the late 1790s in the waggonways of the north-eastern coalfields. The digging of the early canals provided an incentive to construct further waggonways to the canal head. Many were constructed, for example, in south Wales where products from coal mines, limestone quarries and ironworks were linked to canals, often by very steep inclines.

The first glimmerings of the dawn of the railway age came in 1801 with the passing of an Act of Parliament for the construction of the Surrey Iron Railway between Frying Pan Creek on the Thames to Croydon, then a separate town about 16 kilometres south of London (Battersea).[5] This railway was the first public line that was not owned by a canal company. The first of many new iron railway companies to carry passengers opened in 1804 near Swansea. It ended its life as an electric tramway and finally closed in 1960.

The era of horse-drawn waggonways came to an end with the passing of the Act for the Stockton to Darlington railway of 1823, which authorized both steam locomotives and horses to pull wagons. As every schoolboy used to know, the most famous engine of all, George Stephenson's *Rocket*, was built for that line.

At first steam power was only used for mineral traffic, and horses hauled passengers, but after 1833 steam locomotives took over both duties. The small station at Heighington, Co. Durham, which was probably built in 1835, like others along the line without a platform, is probably the best surviving building on this important railway. George Stephenson (1781–1848) was engineer to the first inter-city mainline, the Liverpool and Manchester railway, which opened in 1830. It was a major engineering achievement that involved the crossing of Chat Moss, which Stephenson engineered with a combination of drains and wattlework brushwood 'rafts' which floated the line on the peats. His son Robert (1803–59), as great an engineer as his self-taught father, adopted a similar strategy when twenty years later he took the Great Northern railway across Holme Fen, near Whittlesey, Cambridgeshire (see Fig. 2.1).

The coming of the railways had a major effect on the British landscape. In the country, the railways engineers cut through and ignored pre-existing field boundaries, woods, tracks and lanes. Many country roads crossed railways on bridges that were placed at right angles to the tracks, to keep construction costs to a minimum. This forced roads to go through double bends to accommodate the new bridges. Railways did not, however, encourage ribbon development into rural areas, although of course they did bring prosperity to the destinations along the route, which often led to a local building boom. In the late nineteenth and twentieth centuries urban railways actively encouraged the development of suburbs, such as Hendon, in north London. At first these suburbs were relatively compact, although not overcrowded, because the commuters who lived in them had to reach the station on foot or by bicycle.

The principal impact of railways on rural landscapes was caused by the need to flatten gradients. Initially this could not always be achieved successfully, so the steam-driven stationary winch systems that had been a common feature on horse-drawn waggonways continued to be employed on certain steep inclines. As time passed, however, the great civil engineers of the railway age, such as Brunel and Robert Stephenson, bridged ravines and tunnelled their way through mountains. These are still the most spectacular monuments to the railways in the landscape, although, in point of fact, cuttings and embankments, being far less costly to create, outnumber them many times over. Few rural landscapes in Britain are without a railway earthwork, either still in use, or more often abandoned, following the 'rationalization' of Dr Beeching in the early 1960s.

We tend to take railway cuttings and embankments for granted, forgetting that prior to the mid-1870s all the main and branch lines

Fig. 13.3 Navvies digging the Tring (Hertfordshire) cutting on the London and Birmingham railway, June 1837. Note the steep, planked barrow runs. Sometimes barrows would be emptied into waiting wagons if the spoil was to be taken to an embankment.

of Britain were created by gangs of men working with the simplest tools – usually just a pickaxe and shovel.[6] Sometimes the loose earth was taken from a cutting to an embankment by rail, but before that happened it had to be barrowed up the cutting sides on perilously dangerous planked barrow runs. Whenever laden barrows broke free, which happened quite often, any men in its path as it hurtled back down to the bottom were either killed or severely injured. Explosives were used in rocky areas, but the huge rocks and rubble left by each detonation had then to be removed by hand. Mechanical diggers were first used on a major project with the building of the last main line in Britain (prior to the recent Channel Tunnel Rail Link), the Great Central railway through the Midlands in the 1890s. Even there, the majority of the work was still done by hand.

The era of railway building began in earnest with the Liverpool and Manchester Railway of 1830 and then gathered pace. It would be difficult to exaggerate the speed and extent of the railway building that took place during the so-called 'railway boom' of the 1840s: in 1830 there were less than 160 kilometres of railway lines in Britain and by 1853 that had risen to some 10,000 kilometres.[7] At this point, and after just two decades of work, Britain's railway network was largely in place. No wonder that the pace of railway building in Victorian times has been described as 'heroic' and fired by 'daemonic energy'.[8] More moderate terms, such as 'revolutionary', almost seem too tame.

So far in this book I have tried to stress the long-term processes that gave rise to change. But when one is confronted by something as dramatic and sudden as the railway boom of the 1840s it is worth pausing to examine what was happening rather more closely. The

Fig. 13.4 The railway network in 1845. This map also shows a number of projected lines that were either never built or had not been completed by this date, such as the line west of Exeter or the line through central Wales.

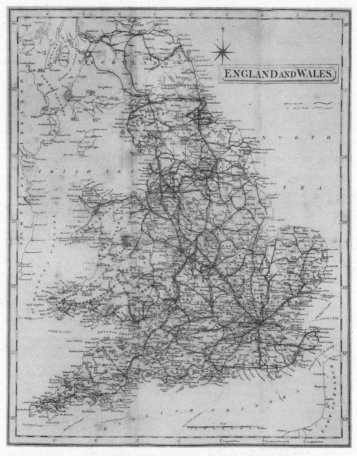

Fig. 13.5 H. G. Collins's map of the railway network in 1852, after a decade of intensive railway building. The network shown on this map is essentially that of Britain today.

general context seems relatively clear: the tradition of railway building already existed and the development of iron-working made it technically possible; furthermore, great engineers like Brindley, Telford and Rennie, and almost as importantly their bankers, had established the management and financial structures needed for such projects. The economic climate was right, too, and the markets existed for the new services.

More importantly, perhaps, success fed success: industry and commerce prospered, fuelling the demand for yet more railways. That is perhaps why the railway period saw no less than three investment booms: in 1824–5, 1836–7 and 1845–7; of these the last was far and away the largest.[9] The step-change that happened as a result of the last of the three periods of major capital investment is best illustrated by contemporary maps, which show that by 1845 a rudimentary network had indeed come into existence, but by 1852 the situation had been completely transformed. It was a revolution within a revolution and even today it seems almost impossible to comprehend.

One might suppose that the greatest engineering achievements of the railway age were dictated by commercial considerations alone, but in human affairs such rationality is rare, as we saw in the Highland clearances. Sometimes deeply felt rivalries could force hard-headed directors of large companies, like the Midland Railway, into seemingly irrational and very expensive decisions. One of the strangest was the proposal to build the Settle and Carlisle railway right through and across the axis of the Pennines. This was to be the last of the main railway routes to be built by navvy labour alone. The purpose of this line was to provide the Midland Railway with their own route northwards to Scotland.[10] The new line would mean that they would not have to make use of the north-western main line, which was operated by their arch-rivals, the London and North Western Railway. The crowning achievement of the Settle and Carlisle railway, which opened in 1876, was undoubtedly the great Ribblehead Viaduct.

This extraordinary engineering achievement was built at a terrible human cost: the settlements of the navvies and their families were horribly squalid and some 200 people – men, women, children and babies – died in the seven years it took to drive the line across Ribblesdale, from 1870 to 1877, when waves of disease ravaged the navvy camps. Most were buried in unmarked graves in the graveyard of the little church of Chapel-le-Dale, nearby.[11] The churchyard north and west of the church had to be enlarged to take the unmarked graves. Today low humps and bumps are all that is left of the camps on Blea Moor Common, which are now Scheduled Ancient Monuments. The camps' names recall the Bible and the Crimean War: Jericho, Jerusalem, Sebastopol and Inkerman. (The camp called Belgravia was either a case

Fig. 13.6 The Ribblehead Viaduct, North Yorkshire. This viaduct crosses a bleak stretch of Ribblesdale, high in the Yorkshire Dales National Park. It was built as part of the Midland Railway's Settle and Carlisle railway, which opened in 1876. The line, the last of the great hand-built main lines, is probably the most ambitious and challenging ever constructed in Britain and includes no fewer than sixteen major viaducts and ten substantial tunnels. It was a hugely expensive project, in cost and in human lives, and its financial justification is still questionable.

of wishful thinking, or irony.) The census of 1871 shows that there were nearly 1,000 men, women and children living in these settlements on Blea Moor Common.

While the coming of the railways affected rural landscapes, it transformed those of towns, especially their outskirts and fringes, where land was still relatively cheap. This was where the great London termini were built. They were grandiose structures, intended to impress travellers ('cathedrals of the railway age'); they were potent symbols, too, of the railway companies that built them. So they were designed, not just to look spectacular, but also to suggest such solid virtues as reliability, safety and corporate security. It is not for nothing that some of the Gothic windows of St Pancras look distinctly ecclesiastical. Today's large airport terminals are meant to address similar themes, but not always so successfully.

The great London railway termini now lie well within the heart of town. Sadly, they have not all fared well at the hands of local authorities. The greatest symbol of the railway age, the Euston Arch, was torn down in 1962 and the remainder of the old station was destroyed when the current building was erected. Liverpool Street has been modernized more recently, with greater sensitivity. Of the main stations that serve the south, Victoria is better preserved than Waterloo, which has been subject to many twentieth-century modifications.

King's Cross is probably the finest and most intact station of the great railway age in London. Its restrained, Italianate architecture, gives a modern 'feel' to the double-arched train shed, built by Thomas Cubitt in 1852. By way of contrast, alongside Cubitt's restraint we find Sir George Gilbert Scott's over-the-top Gothic exuberance: the vast red brick baronial Midland Grand Hotel (built 1868–74) that fronts the single-arch train shed of St Pancras, built in 1868 by William Barlow for the Midland Railway. At the time it was the largest single-span roof in the world; it has since reopened as the London terminus for Eurostar.

Of all the great stations in London, the most atmospheric is still Brunel's Paddington, built for the Great Western Railway and opened in 1854.[12] Paddington has a grace and spaciousness all of its own.[13] This is partly accidental, however, as the station was originally built for the broad-gauge trains that Brunel favoured (7 feet; 2.13 metres), and was only converted to the narrower standard gauge (4ft 8 1/2 inches; 1.44 metres) that Stephenson preferred, quite late in its life. For a time both gauges were run together, but eventually in 1892 broad gauge was abandoned. Arguments still continue as to the merit of the two track widths, but the narrower one made long tunnels and deep cuttings much more feasible. Indeed, if Brunel had won the argument, the railway network of western Britain, where the landscape is more precipitous, would be very much smaller than it is today. Most probably too the Settle and Carlisle railway would have been impossible.

The effect of railways on rural landscapes has been superficial rather than profound. Even in their much reduced modern state they seem ubiquitous, but they have weathered well and their visual impact is generally slight; it may even be beneficial – as at Ribblehead. In towns, the situation was altogether different. In the past, cities were often adversely affected by large marshalling yards, and tar from the smoke of hundreds of locomotives had a corrosive effect on the ancient stonework of churches and cathedrals. The railway companies employed large numbers of people and often the housing they provided for them was good.[14] The companies now possessed the means to bring in new and cheaper building materials that sometimes contrasted unsympathetically with more traditional local stone and brick. Railway stations and marshalling yards are often to be found in parts of town characterized by row after row of rather unimaginative Victorian terrace housing. This is often blamed on the railway companies, but in actual fact the vast majority of such housing was built by speculative builders taking advantage of the increased employment and general prosperity brought about by the arrival of the railways.

I mentioned that the railway companies often built very good accommodation for their workforce. The Midland Railway, for example provided large-scale housing, together with a railwayman's clubhouse and lodging house, in Derby, when it opened its locomotive works there in 1840. Other significant railway centres of the nineteenth and early twentieth centuries were Crewe, Doncaster and York, but the most important planned town of the railway age has to be Swindon, where most of the buildings were either built by, or for, the Great Western Railway.[15]

Swindon is also important because it has survived far better than any other railway town and its future as a railway heritage centre seems assured. The overall planning and layout of the railway town, known as New Swindon, took place between 1841 and 1849 and was the work of the Great Western's chief engineer, I. K. Brunel. By the mid-twentieth century the railways, junctions, marshalling yards and their associated buildings completely dominated the landscape of Swindon.

So far we have considered the railways' impact on the landscape in terms of settlement and engineering, but as the popularity of mass travel increased the railway companies diversified their interests. Soon they had moved into the leisure market.[16] At the top end of the social scale grand hotels were built by railway companies, such as the Zetland Hotel at Saltburn, on the north Yorkshire coast. This grand building

9. An aerial view of Fort George Ardersier, on the Moray Firth, east of Inverness. This massive fort was built after the 1745 Jacobite Rebellion. Virtually intact, it is one of the finest examples of eighteenth-century military architecture anywhere.

10. Great bridges are seen as a legacy of the railway age. But the Menai Straits suspension bridge (1826), links the Anglesey and mainland sections of Thomas Telford's great Holyhead–Shrewsbury turnpike road (now the A5).

11. A grouse moor south of Yeavering Bell, in the Cheviot Hills of Northumberland. Rotational burning, to provide tender shoots for the young birds, leaves a distinctive patchwork of purple when the heather is in flower.

12. Fields produced by parliamentary enclosure in the Vale of Evesham, Worcestershire. These landscapes were created in the eighteenth and nineteenth centuries. Note how roads follow field boundaries, whereas streams take their natural course.

(*above*) 13. The scale
of the Victorian leisure
industry is illustrated
by the Grand Hotel,
Scarborough, North
Yorkshire. Built by
Cuthbert Brodrick in
1863–7, it dominates
the restrained Georgian
architecture of this early
seaside resort.

(*left*) 14. The railway
came to Saltburn-by-the-
Sea in 1861, and a cliff
lift was built to connect
the station and town at
the top with the beach
at the bottom. In 1884
the first lift was replaced
by the present water-
powered tramway.

15. 'Ruskin's View' from Kirkby Lonsdale Churchyard, Cumbria, by J. M. W. Turner (1818). This view was praised by Wordsworth, in 1810. The octagonal late-eighteenth- or early nineteenth-century gazebo (*left*) is still standing.

16. The same view from nearby Church Brow Cottage, which was built to admire the scene. This photograph was taken just after dawn and shows the low-lying mists of a temperature inversion, following rain. Turner must have seen something similar.

17. The City of London today, with Sir Norman Foster's huge 'Gherkin' office tower in the foreground. The plot of land in which the Gherkin sits was first laid out in Roman times; it was then re-surveyed as part of King Alfred's new burh of Lundenburh and finally replanned, following the medieval street plan, after the Great Fire of 1666. From the seventeenth to nineteenth centuries Sir Christopher Wren's St Paul's Cathedral dominated the skyline; in this view it can just be seen in the middle distance, left of centre.

18. 'Do-it-yourself' landscape change. The white branches of black poplar (*Populus nigra*)
stand out against the dark clouds of a springtime thunderstorm. Black poplar is a British
native tree, but it is under threat because it readily cross-hybridizes with non-native poplars.
The author planted these trees as cuttings of a proven 'pure' specimen from the Thames
Valley, in 1994. When planted, the cuttings could be carried in one hand. Just fifteen years
later they are already making a significant impact on the landscape.

was the nucleus of a new seaside resort and was built with its back door actually on the platform of a new station of the Stockton and Darlington railway, which opened in 1861. Some well-established upmarket resorts such as Brighton became very much more popular with the arrival of the railways and began to appeal to a far broader cross section of the public. By the late nineteenth century this once-exclusive Regency resort lived up to its popular name 'London-on-Sea'. We shall see in the next chapter that resorts such as Skegness on the Lincolnshire coast owed their very existence to the second railway boom of the 1870s.

From the late nineteenth century all major commercial ports leant heavily on the railways. Some ports, such as Barry and Fishguard, in south Wales, and Immingham, in Lincolnshire, were developed as ports in which the railway companies also operated the ferry and shipping lines. By 1913 railway companies controlled about fifty ports in England and Wales.

PORTS AND HARBOURS IN VICTORIAN TIMES

Britain has always been a trading nation and it would be possible to write several books on the development of ports in the post-medieval period. Each town and city has its own unique history which sometimes, but not always, reflected the state of the national economy. While farmers languished during the great agricultural depression of the 1870s, many ports prospered as imported food flowed into the country. London continued to be the principal port in the land, as indeed it had been throughout medieval times, but some aspects of its dockland development actually happened remarkably late.

During the Middle Ages vessels trading out of London had relatively shallow draught and were light enough to be beached on low tides: this meant they could sail right into the heart of the City and exchange cargoes at well-constructed docks that we know about from excavations carried out in the 1970s.[17] As seagoing ships increased in size it became necessary to stand at anchor out in the Thames and transfer cargo into lighters that would then travel upstream into the City docks. The first proper dock, the Howland Dock, was built between 1697 and 1700 at Rotherhithe. It covered 4 hectares and was specifically intended for empty craft, rather than for unloading cargo. The first true cargo docks were planned for London in the 1790s. Both were closed docks, surrounded by walls: the West India Dock, off Blackwall, covered 22 hectares and opened in 1802; the London Dock at Wapping was smaller (8 hectares) and opened in 1805, for the North American and European trade. Other smaller docks followed and a canal was cut through the Isle of Dogs. In 1855 the vast, 40-hectare Victoria Dock opened. It had no warehouses and all goods were transferred by railway to the City, 7 kilometres upstream. In the late nineteenth century ocean-going vessels became enormous and required docks in deep water, so in 1886 a 180-hectare dock estate was constructed at Tilbury, in Essex, 42 kilometres downstream of London. Even today Tilbury often acts as a secondary or redistribution port for the gigantic Europort at Rotterdam, in Holland. The late-Victorian and twentieth-century dock and harbour developments have transformed the landscapes of the Thames estuary.

London aside, the three principal ports of post-medieval Britain were Bristol, Liverpool and Glasgow. At their height in the late eighteenth century Bristol and Liverpool together threatened the domination of London. Both made their fortunes on re-exports, of which the most controversial, and for a time the most important, was the trade in African slaves to North America. Bristol was the oldest and originally the most prosperous of the three major ports. Like London, its location was not well suited to the introduction of the ever-larger ocean-going vessels of the nineteenth century. The port of Bristol was on the junction of the rivers Frome and Avon, which were subject to tidal fluctuations. During the late eighteenth century it prospered, and became very congested. This was the period when the fine Georgian squares and terraces of what was then the suburb of Clifton were built on the higher land that overlooks the city from the west. These later buildings were added to the earlier terraces that had been erected when Clifton had been the residential area of the nearby Hotwells spa, which overlooked the Avon Gorge from the north.

The continued growth of the port of Bristol in the nineteenth century was made possible by an ambitious scheme to bypass the sinuous course

Fig. 13.7 An aerial view of central Bristol looking upstream, with the New Cut (1804–9) to the right (south). The Cumberland Basin is at the centre with its locks. Note the length of the locks, which were designed to hold seagoing vessels. Beyond the Cumberland Basin is the main Floating Harbour, which was entered via the Cumberland Basin. The entire scheme was completed in 1809.

of the River Avon with a New Cut. The old river then became the Floating Harbour, where tidal fluctuations could be removed by the construction of large locks at the western end, which retained the high 'floating' water level in the Floating Harbour and allowed vessels to enter and leave at high tide. William Jessop's Floating Harbour was deepened and developed in the dry when a temporary dam across the river diverted its course down the New Cut. The project took five years to complete and opened for business in 1809. Various teething problems, including silting, which were dealt with by Brunel when he was engineer to the Floating Harbour (1830–31).

Many of the nineteenth-century buildings around the Floating Harbour were subsequently demolished, but some fine examples have survived between Princes and Bristol bridges. The Bush tea warehouse (1834) near Princes Bridge is a distinctive landmark. The three huge brick-built warehouses that dominate the west of the harbour were bonded tobacco warehouses, built in the first decade of the twentieth century. Towards the end of the nineteenth century ships became too large even to use the improved Floating Harbour and a new dock complex was built 11 kilometres downstream, at Avonmouth on the Bristol Channel. Today drivers crossing the high bridge of the M5 at the mouth of the Avon can look down on a industrial landscape of fuel redistribution depots, power lines and vast car parks, packed with rank upon rank of new vehicles for import or export.

The modern development of Britain's docks often follows a consistent pattern, largely dictated by the need to accommodate bigger and bigger ships. Liverpool was no exception and its docks were required to accommodate larger, long-distance vessels, many of which had made major trans-Atlantic voyages. The origin of the port of Liverpool lay in the late Middle Ages, when it traded actively with marchants in Scotland and Ireland, and by the sixteenth century its trading links extended to the Atlantic coasts of France, Spain and Portugal. In the eighteenth century the so-called 'Atlantic triangle' pattern of trade developed in which traders from Britain took trinkets and other manufactured goods to Africa in exchange for slaves, which were taken across the Atlantic to the Caribbean and North American plantations. Ships then returned to Britain with cargoes of rum, sugar and cotton. The port of Bristol competed with Liverpool for this business in the eighteenth century, but early in the nineteenth Liverpool became ascendant (more than 4,000 movements in 1800). Commerce from Liverpool was largely unaffected by the abolition of the slave trade in 1807, as alternative links had been established with India, China and South America (by 1871 there were more than 19,000).[18]

At first ships at Liverpool had to be beached along the shallow foreshore of the River Mersey, but in 1716 Britain's first dock that combined commercial and legal (that is, customs) quays was opened. This dock covered just 1.61 hectares. Jesse Hartley was appointed engineer to the Port Authority in 1824 and he provided a series of docks with walls that projected out into the Mersey estuary, as shoreline space was restricted. The Clarence Dock was built for steamships and this was followed by the Brunswick Dock (1832). His trademark dock was a square basin enclosed and surrounded by warehouses and other buildings.[19] Hartley built five of these between 1834 and 1836, culminating in the construction of the Albert Dock, which opened in 1845. The square enclosed docks were too restricted to cope with larger vessels, and were superseded by branched docks that opened out from a central basin. These narrow docks allowed ships to be unloaded from both sides; there were no warehouses and goods were removed by road or rail. The Langton (1879) and Alexandra (1880) docks were the first of this type to open in Liverpool.

Fig. 13.8 The world's first purpose-built commercial wet dock at Liverpool. This dock was alongside a tidal inlet of the Mersey, known as the Pool. The project was commissioned by Liverpool Corporation and work by the constructor Thomas Steers began in 1710. It opened just five years later. Vessels entered and departed from the enclosed dock (10) at high tide and the watertight lock-gates were closed when the tide began to go out, thereby retaining the water within the dock at the high tide level.

Fig. 13.9 The Albert Dock, Liverpool. These dock buildings are among the finest in Britain. The dock (1845) was the first in the city to include bonded warehouses. Ships were loaded and unloaded directly, through wide doors and with cranes located at the first floor of the warehouses.

TEXTILES AND THE IMPACT OF THE EARLY INDUSTRIAL ERA IN THE NORTH-WEST OF ENGLAND

In Chapter 11, we saw how the dual economy in places such as Tameside, in Manchester, first gave rise to small textile workshops attached to the weavers' cottages and how these developed into communal workshops and latterly into mills. This evolutionary process was only made possible by the social structure of local communities in which freemen farmers, and importantly their families, were able to concentrate their efforts on what had traditionally been seen as a 'secondary' source of income.

Manchester and the area around it was the focus of the north-western textile industry. We have already discussed the industry's origins in the small-scale domestic workshops of the Middle Ages, which continued into the early modern period; this was a time that saw the rise of yeoman clothiers, who might have been wealthy farmers keen to diversify. Essentially they were middlemen who would both supply yarn and buy in spun cloth from hand-weavers. In today's terms they also 'added value' by converting fabric into clothing. Post-medieval examples of the workshops of both weavers and clothiers, with their distinctive gallery-like first-floor windows, can still be seen on the moors and uplands around the city, especially in the Saddleworth area of Greater Manchester.[20]

The invention of power looms and carding machines[21] in the mid-eighteenth century led to the introduction of larger water-powered mills, which began to replace the smaller hand workshops. The hand-weavers, the original 'Luddites', who feared for their livelihoods, put up a vigorous struggle, but were eventually forced to give in. This helps to explain why water-powered mills did not become a common sight in Britain until around 1770–90, when many were built. However, this

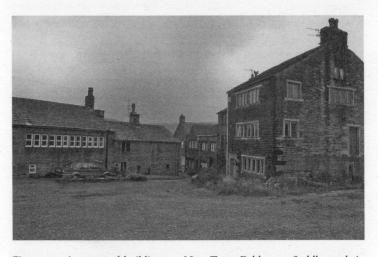

Fig. 13.10 A group of buildings at New Tame Fold, near Saddleworth in Greater Manchester. These workshops are grouped around a farmhouse belonging to a yeoman clothier who supervised the conversion of cloth to clothing. Note the long windows to admit the maximum daylight and the first-floor taking-in door in the gable-end wall of the building to the right; this was where cloth and yarn were brought into the workshops, from hand-weavers in the region.

simple picture of noble hand-weavers struggling with grasping mill-owners is only part of the picture. In Saddleworth and elsewhere, especially on Tameside, the transition from domestic workshop to mill was somewhat less stressful. In Saddleworth, the cottage weavers and the merchants and master clothiers reached amicable agreements that limited the size of workshops, so that the first factories were not introduced until well into the nineteenth century. From the 1830s steam power began to replace waterwheels in most of the mills around Manchester.

The foundations of the first steam-powered textile mill in Manchester were excavated in 2005 at Shude Hill, near the centre of the modern city. This was the famous entrepreneur Richard Arkwright's last mill, and the excavations showed that, although the mill had been positioned close by a gradient with a suitable supply of water, Arkwright's original, optimistic, intention in 1781 had been to power the mill machinery by a rotative steam engine. The early steam engines, however, still worked on the atmospheric principle and lacked the power of the later engines, which used steam pressure to return the piston in the cylinder. It took another five years for the first successful steam-powered cotton mill to begin operation, at Papplewick, in Nottinghamshire.[22]

The first atmospheric engine at Shude Hill lacked the power to drive the looms and other equipment in the mill, but was adapted instead to raise water from the lower level, back to the tail-race, which drove a waterwheel, which now had enough power to do the job. Textile mills, especially those that spun cotton, were very prone to fires, and the Shude Hill mill was seriously damaged in 1854. Rather surprisingly, the excavations revealed that most of the original eighteenth-century walls managed to survive the blaze. As a fire precaution many Victorian textile mills featured water tanks that fed an internal sprinkler system; these tanks were built above the roof-line and were often disguised as turrets, which became a characteristic feature of the skyline of many industrial mill towns.

The textile mills could never have existed on their own. They required transport systems for raw materials inwards and finished cloth or clothes outwards. Once steam became the usual motive power, they also required a regular supply of coal. The early Manchester mills were serviced by the Huddersfield Narrow Canal, which opened in 1811, and by the Huddersfield and Manchester railway (which followed the same route), opened in 1844. In the Middle Ages the buying and selling and the exchanging of commodities necessary to keep a great industry working took place at town and city markets, but the first purpose-built Yorkshire cloth hall was built at Heptonstall in 1545. This would have taken products from the domestic workshops of places like Saddleworth. Others soon followed, including the Halifax Piece Hall (1779), which today includes a museum of the woollen industry, and the later, highly ornate Gothic Wool Exchange (1867) in Bradford.

The story of the textile industry is of technological and social developments, many of which have left an enduring mark on the landscape. But it was by no means a tale of continuous 'improvement', certainly when viewed from a mill-worker's perspective. While the Shude Hill mill was being investigated it also proved possible to excavate the lower levels of a demolished contemporary terraced house that fronted onto Angel Street, immediately north of the mill. The original late-eighteenth-century accommodation included a cellar room, a ground floor and first floor, each consisting of one reasonably sized room, accessed from the rear via a stairway. Originally, this small house would have been occupied by a single family. As time passed however, the house was divided and subdivided, so that by the mid-nineteenth century it accommodated three tenant families; one of these had the misfortune to inhabit just the cellar room, which was lit by a tiny window close to the ceiling and was literally running with damp when the excavations were taking place in late summer. In winter it must have been squalid in the extreme.

By the mid-nineteenth century economic conditions had changed. Competition with and for foreign markets had increased, the population had grown hugely and in the vast industrial conurbations many of the social structures and safeguards that had been inherited from earlier centuries had broken down. The scale of the changes during the industrial era are most simply illustrated by figures for the population of Manchester. In the first census of 1801[23] it was a large town of 90,000 people; by 1831 it had grown to 237,000 and in 1861 to 400,000.[24] This late phase of growth is astonishingly rapid.

Although most attention is usually paid to the very much larger textile industry of Manchester and the north-west, there was also a very significant industry in the south-west. The roots of this industry go back to the twelfth and thirteenth centuries when fulling mills developed, centred on towns like Exeter, Salisbury, Bristol, Gloucester and Malmesbury. These mills were built to beat and tease the cloth, to thicken it up and cleanse it. They show that by the early Middle Ages

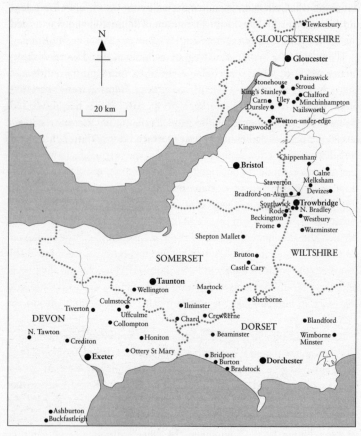

Fig. 13.11 A map showing the location of the principal towns and villages involved in the textile industry of the south-west. The industry has its roots in the twelfth and thirteenth centuries and continued to prosper through to the late nineteenth century when competition from the larger industry in the north-west became too strong.

the production of cloth had moved beyond domestic production. The first water-powered fulling mill is recorded on the estate of Winchcombe Abbey, around 1200.[25] The industry continued to survive and develop throughout the Middle Ages, and its profits contributed to the construction of several grand churches, as in East Anglia. One example should suffice. The fine Perpendicular south aisle of Steeple Aston church, in Wiltshire, was built with money donated by the clothier Walter Lucas and his wife in the late fifteenth century. The north aisle was added by a rival clothier, Robert Long, a little later.[26] The industry continued to prosper into post-medieval times around places like Stroud, in Gloucestershire, where several fine early nineteenth-century textile mill buildings can still be seen.[27] By 1850, when competition from the north-west proved too intense, some of the fabric mills had converted to manufacture the elegant walking sticks that many Victorian gentlemen liked to flourish, when strolling through the park after church on Sundays.

Fig. 13.12 Many of the towns in the area around Stroud, in Gloucestershire, still preserve textile mills and workers' housing built in the early nineteenth century. The Bliss Tweed Mill on the outskirts of Chipping Norton is a particularly fine example; the building shown was constructed after a fire in 1872. The mill produced vast quantities of khaki cloth for the Great War.

THE IMPACT OF HEAVY INDUSTRY
ON THE LANDSCAPE: TIN, LEAD
AND COAL

Iron-working was by no means the only heavy industry of the early industrial era. Others had also been in existence for a very long time indeed. Lead had been extracted in industrial quantities since at least Roman times, in Somerset and north-east Wales, and copper ore was being deep-mined in thousands of tonnes, in the Bronze Age at Great Orme, near Llandudno, in north Wales. Interestingly, coal had mainly been of local importance until the eighteenth century, after which it became the fuel that powered industry.

Lead mining was an important industry in the north Pennines, centred around the towns of Alston, Cumbria, and Stanhope, Co. Durham, and comprising much of Weardale, Teesdale, and the Nent Valley.[28] The mines were sited to follow veins of lead ore (the mineral galena), which has to be smelted in furnaces to produce metallic lead. In the nineteenth century much of the power used to drive machinery in the mines was provided by water and although the mines themselves were probably safer than a coal mine, as explosive gases were generally rare within them, lead poisoning was a major problem, especially around the smelting furnaces. Long stone-lined flues were constructed to take the fumes up to tall chimneys on the skyline, many of which can still be seen in the area today. But sometimes they failed to work and concentrated fumes could be blown back down the hill to the smelting mills and the people within them.

Today the north Pennine lead-mining landscape has lost much of its Victorian industrial brutality. The many spoil or 'dead' heaps are now covered with moss and grass while trees and shrubs have regrown along the streams at the valley bottoms. In the higher moors, however, old mine buildings can still be seen, together with the narrow arched entrances into the horizontal galleries of the mines themselves. Lower down the hillside are the crushing mills and washing floors where the ore was concentrated ready for smelting. These areas are still marked by long flat-topped spoil heaps where the waste rock was tipped from horse-drawn railway wagons. In the late nineteenth century the north

Pennine mines produced about a quarter of the lead needed by British industry, but the ore sources themselves were rarely very rich or prolific and a great deal of effort was required to separate the ore from the rock in which it occurred. The north Pennine industry flourished in the 1870s and into the 1880s, and then began a period of steady decline, finally ending around 1930. Today there are no lead mines in Britain.

The landscape of Cornwall in particular has been much affected by the mining of tin. In the remote historic past, and in prehistory, tin was probably extracted by panning in streams.[29] So far as we know, there were no opencast or deep tin mines similar to the examples of copper mines we now know existed in Ireland and in central to north Wales, of which the most famous is that at Great Orme, near Llandudno (see pp. 111–12). The processing of both tin and copper ore involved a series of procedures that took place on the surface, either in the open or within buildings. First, the ore had to be crushed and dressed, a process whereby impurities were removed. It was then washed in buddles, where even more impurities were removed. In the past manual labour performed many of these tasks, but from the late eighteenth and nineteenth centuries first water then steam power took over.

The surviving evidence in the landscape is complex and must be interpreted with care. It is easy to jump to false conclusions and it is essential that fieldwork is fully backed up by documentary research. Take for example a detailed study of a complex of tin mines in south-west Cornwall, near Redruth.[30] The documentary evidence clearly demonstrated that the Basset mines had been most profitable in the mid-nineteenth century. By the late nineteenth century, however, huge capital investment led to the construction of numerous new buildings, such as engine houses, which have largely obliterated all earlier evidence in the field. Ironically, company accounts show that, despite the influx of new money, the late-nineteenth-century mines were never as profit-able as those they superseded. This is not the impression one gains from the rich assemblage of late-nineteenth-century structures that have survived on the surface.

The ore-treatment processes made use of the hilly terrain and gravity. So the ore-crushing and dressing areas were placed above the buddle houses, where the ore was finally washed. Many nineteenth-century Cornish mine managers were concerned by the activities of freelance panners who worked the streams coming out of the buddle houses. Despite the best efforts of the mining companies these streams were still rich in tin ore and the freelance panners were able to help themselves to tidy sums of money, which reduced mine profits.

Close scrutiny of the Basset mines revealed the sometimes extraordinarily rapid pace of technological change. The mines were in

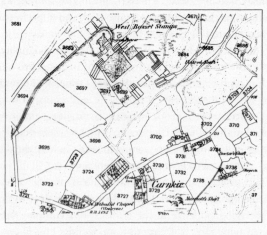

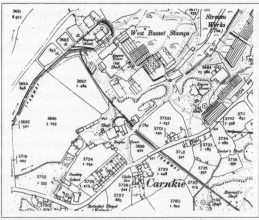

Fig. 13.13 Two maps showing the rapid growth of the Basset tin mine landscape, near Redruth, Cornwall, between 1878 (*upper*) and 1906 (*lower*).

existence when two editions of the Ordnance Survey 25-inch maps were published, in 1880 and 1906. These clearly show the extent to which the landscape had changed in less than three decades. The appearance of two tramways (private mine railways) is an obvious feature of the later map. The earlier map was actually surveyed in 1878, but field and documentary evidence shows that it had already become significantly outdated when it was published just two years later.

It was not always easy to attract labour to the tin mines of Cornwall. In the early nineteenth century Francis Basset offered up to 2.4 hectares of land to families who would work in his mines. This encouraged independent smallholdings and gave rise to a successful secondary economy. The ten-yearly censuses of 1841 to 1881 showed that the local population had grown sharply, but began a rapid decline in the 1880s – at precisely the same time that large sums of money began to be invested in the mines. This would suggest that the people who later worked the mines were part of a more mobile population who followed the work as and when it became available.

The landscape of Cornwall is of course best known for its tin mines, but it actually reached the height of its industrial development during the copper boom of the mid-nineteenth century, when no fewer than 600 steam engines were in operation and scores of foundries came into existence to manufacture the large engines needed to pump out the deeper mines. The British copper industry had been revolutionized a century earlier with the rediscovery of the vast copper ore deposits that made up Parys Mountain in Anglesey. Today the hill still carries some scars of its industrial life, but viewed from a distance it has reverted to rural tranquillity. It seems hard to imagine that most of the interior of the hill has been replaced by a honeycomb consisting of thousands of shafts and galleries. So productive were they that in the 1780s the output from Parys Mountain was greater than any other mine in Europe (over 3,000 tonnes a year). The shafts and galleries were dispensed with in the late eighteenth century when the entire top of the mountain became a vast opencast pit, some 21 metres deep, which was drained by a five-sailed windmill, the tower of which still survives on the skyline.

Large areas of Cornwall are still being disfigured by china clay mining, although the glaring white waste heaps are now being land-scaped rather more sympathetically than was the case in Hoskins's day.[31] The scale of individual mines is, however, rather larger, as are the settling lakes. In the mid-1990s the output of china clay from Cornwall was 2.5 million tonnes – much of it destined for the paper industry in Germany and Scandinavia, where it is used for producing high-quality glossy finishes.

No discussion of the landscape of the industrial era could be complete without coal mining.[32] From at least the sixteenth century coal was the prime fuel for industry, and by the late eighteenth century was being mined in large quantities. Coal occurs in continuous and predictable seams, whereas ores are found in veins which are difficult to predict and can cease without any warning. As we saw in the case of the tin mines of Cornwall, this unpredictability gave rise in the late nineteenth century to a highly mobile and specialized workforce. Coal mines, on the other hand, were more permanent and have been a lasting influence on the landscape – although not always as one might expect. Take the mines themselves.

The most striking feature of a coal mine, often visible from miles away, used to be the huge slag heaps that dominated mining landscapes. These were frequently located close by the mining villages that grew up around the pits. The disaster near Merthyr Tydfil, in South Wales, was to change the landscape of coal mining in Britain profoundly. During a very wet period in 1966 part of a slag heap slipped over the adjacent village of Aberfan, engulfing several houses and the village school. Mining waste suffocated 144 people, including 116 children. Anyone alive at the time must vividly recall the horror of the occasion. After Aberfan, slag heaps were physically removed from village outskirts and were landscaped and structured to prevent slippage.

During the twentieth century most of the evidence for earlier coal mining was either destroyed by new mines, mine buildings or slag heaps. Almost anything that escaped was subsequently obliterated when mining landscapes were 'reinstated' for amenity purposes. Some mines have remained open as museums, but, these and a few machines aside, most traces of pre-twentieth-century mining have been removed from view. So the lasting influence on the landscape has not been the physical remains of the mines themselves, but the houses of the miners and their families. Being more permanent than other forms of mining, the settlements associated with coal mines have left their mark on the townscapes of mining areas in south Wales, northern and Midland England and south-western Scotland.

The landscape evidence for early mines survives and should be mentioned, but the traces left are usually slight. The earliest mines were drifts that followed surface exposures of coal seams a short distance into the ground, either as horizontal passages into the side of hills, or as sloping shafts. Such drift mines are still operated by the free miners of the Forest of Dean, in Gloucestershire. Another form of early mining was the bell pit, in which a shaft was sunk to a known coal seam and the coal removed in the area around the bottom of the shaft. This continued until the mine became unstable, at which point it was abandoned, and collapsed. The surface remains of old bell pits are very distinctive, with an outer ring of coal waste and a deep depression where the shaft caved in. Sometimes this floods, to make a circular pond. Abandoned bell pits can still be seen in areas of ancient mining, such as Strelley in Nottinghamshire, Nostell in West Yorkshire and Lount in Leicestershire, where recent opencast working revealed the remains of fifteenth-century mining (p. 287).

Coal began to be used in the lime-burning, malting, baking and glass-making industries in the sixteenth century. It was also used as a domestic fuel in houses with built chimneys, which in early post-medieval times were mostly those of more prosperous people. The output of coal rose from some 210,000 tonnes in 1560 to nearly 3 million tonnes by 1700, but then it levelled off as mine-owners tried to deal with problems of flooding at greater depths. Various means were employed, such as sough (tunnel) drains and horse-powered windlass draining, using buckets, but these were barely able to cope, and the national output of coal remained level.

The first steam pump was introduced in a colliery in the Black Country, in 1712. These early atmospheric engines were expensive to install, but by 1733 there were around fifty of them. By 1778, shortly before the introduction of the Watt engine, there were at least 140 engines working in the Newcastle coalfield, alone. By this time the output of coal was rising rapidly.

Although the early coal-mining landscapes themselves have been removed, we do know from paintings and other sources that huge slag heaps did not appear until much later, in the nineteenth century. In the late eighteenth century mines were still working the better seams, with cleaner coal and little waste. Even as late as 1850 the surface structures of these early mines consisted of an engine house and little more. In the second half of the nineteenth century the buildings around the mine-head became ever more elaborate, with buildings to house screens, where coal was separated from waste mechanically, and picking belts, where the work was done by people (usually women). Other buildings included washing plants and stores. The tall headgear that was such a familiar sight to anyone passing through a mining area in the 1950s and 1960s had only been in existence since the late nineteenth century, when cages were introduced to allow faster and safer access to the deeper pits. The huge wheels mounted on top of low towers winched the cages up and down the pit shafts. Today such headgear can only be seen in preserved mines, such as Chatterley Whitfield in Nottingham-shire or Big Pit in Blaenavon, south Wales (see Fig. 14.9).

Like the early textile weavers in the north-west, early modern miners were often part of a dual economy with pastoral farming. The settlement pattern reflects this, with their houses dispersed across the landscape, rather like those of the Coalbrookdale coalfield in the mid-eighteenth and nineteenth centuries still visible in the area today. Even in the nineteenth century miners in certain areas, such as Leicestershire and Nottinghamshire, had smallholdings, whereas allotments were often an important feature of more formal mining villages elsewhere. By the early nineteenth century, however, mine output was rising rapidly and mine-owners needed to provide their miners with accommodation. This could of course be densely packed and of poor quality and has given mine-owners a very bad image. Most if not all of such sub-standard housing has been demolished, but not all early mine-owners were necessarily exploitative. One example should suffice to make the point.

The Earl Fitzwilliam had large estates near Wentworth on the South Yorkshire coalfield and in 1795 he opened the New Colliery at Elsecar, near his vast country house at Wentworth Woodhouse. Initially the miners lived in scattered settlements but very rapidly a 'model' village grew up with some of the houses designed by John Carr who had worked on Wentworth Woodhouse itself.

Much of the housing provided for miners that has survived, like that at Elsecar, tends to be of the better sort; often, too, it was built later, when building regulations had come into effect. Mining companies regarded the housing of miners and their families as their responsibility, and treated house-building as part of their capital set-up costs for a new mine or an addition to an existing one. Incidentally, the miners were nearly always tied tenants, which meant that they could be evicted when and if they went on strike. Standards of housing could vary, especially in the way that settlements were planned and arranged.

Coal is heavy and is usually needed in quantity. In the Middle Ages it was mostly distributed in panniers on packhorses, or by horse and cart, whence it was taken to local markets. Certain coalfields became established early in the post-medieval period because they had good links by water to centres of population. The North Sea, for example, provided the link for colliers plying between London and the coalfields of the north-east, out of Newcastle. The movement of coal in bulk often provided the incentive for the development of the earliest improved river navigations, canals and later, of course, steam-drawn railways. Without improvements to the infrastructure of Britain, the rapid growth of industry that happened in the hundred years from 1750 would have been impossible.

HOUSING THE WORKFORCE

Most of the eighteenth- and nineteenth-century workers' housing that became overcrowded and reverted to appalling slums has been demolished and is no longer visible in the landscape. This distorts our view of the past, as the surviving buildings of the industrial era tend to be those of the great industrialists, the upper classes, or the more prosperous and rapidly growing middle class.

Industrialists and entrepreneurs in the late eighteenth and nineteenth centuries have had a bad press – much of it well deserved. Vast fortunes were made and grinding poverty was commonplace. It was also a time of major change when new social structures were being developed to cope with the requirements of an ever-changing working environment. Even employers like Richard Arkwright in Lanarkshire who generally treated their workforce well were strangely manipulative. For example, the entrance to Arkwright's first cotton mill at Cromford, Derbyshire, built in 1771, was from the mill yard only.[33] The yard was enclosed by a tall perimeter wall and none of the ground-floor windows overlooked the mill road. The layout of the mill yard allowed the workforce to be closely supervised, yet nobody from outside could look in and spy on the machines within. Industrial espionage was a very real consideration. Within the buildings the workforce operated in tight spaces that were made easier to control and supervise by the arrangement of the machines. In the large mills that appeared as the nineteenth century progressed, the significant developments were not just technological. Human beings had to adapt their patterns of behaviour and their social structure to take account of their new working environment. It would be difficult to overestimate the importance and long-term effects of these social developments, which later find expression in the model villages created by enlightened industrialists.

The most enlightened industrialists were often Quakers, such as the brothers George (1839–1922) and Richard (1835–99) Cadbury, who

Fig. 13.14 The confident, imposing Italianate architecture of Salts Mill, Saltaire, near Bradford, West Yorkshire. The philanthropist and industrialist Sir Titus Salt closed his cotton mill in central Bradford and opened a new one in a model village on the outskirts of the city, in 1853, on his fiftieth birthday.

inherited their father's cocoa business. In 1879 they established the model village of Bournville, in the west Midlands, for the benefit of the workers in their Birmingham factories. Bournville has provided much of the inspiration behind modern town planning. In 2006 attempts to sell alcohol there by a supermarket were rejected following demonstrations by the local community. It would seem that the Nonconformist spirit of the brothers is still alive and well.

Somewhat earlier than Bournville, Sir Titus Salt (1803–76) moved his mill from central Bradford and created the model community of Saltaire, then on the rural north-western fringes of the city, between 1851 and 1876. The mill still dominates the model village, as well it might, given its prodigious output.[34] It was powered by fourteen boilers that ran 1,200 looms, capable of producing 30,000 metres of cloth a day. Sadly, Salts Mill was hit by recession and closed in 1892. Saltaire was, and is, a substantial settlement, which has survived largely intact.[35] It consisted of 22 streets, some 775 houses and 45 almshouses arranged on 10 hectares of land. The model village is well built and laid out and the houses reflect the status of their occupiers in their size and in the details of their construction. The street layout was intended to provide ready access to Salts Mill, but the scale is generous and the general atmosphere of the place is spacious. As one might expect, Sir Titus provided his workforce with a large and well-appointed Congregational church.

Even despite the laudable efforts of people like Salt and the Cadbury brothers, the vast majority of workers' accommodation in the nineteenth century was provided by speculative builders who first bought or leased land and then rented the houses. It was plainly in their interests to fit as many dwellings as possible onto a given plot, which is why most developments of this sort featured terraced housing. Some industries, like certain textiles and the boot and shoe trade, were organized around smaller factories or collective workshops and it was often in the interests of the speculative developer to provide such facilities within the new housing estates.

While most industrial housing was provided by independent builders, certain industries in the nineteenth century required a large workforce within easy reach of the workplace. Railway companies, for example, would often provide housing for their staff, which can still be seen in towns, such as Crewe, Swindon and Peterborough. In other instances, the Cumbrian ports of Maryport, Whitehaven and Workington were created by wealthy landowners eager to export their coal to Ireland.

The builders who constructed the industrial towns of Victorian Britain were constrained by their ability to find land – just like their modern equivalents. Very often individual fields were bought and then developed, piecemeal, often by their owners – as happens today, too. In the nineteenth century, however, there were few effective planning constraints and individual developers worked without regard for what was happening around them. This process led to the 'fossilization' of pre-urban field boundaries, roads, tracks and footpaths in the layout of the developing town, which Hoskins memorably illustrated with a map of a part of Victorian Nottingham, where the layout of the streets and lanes strongly resembled what it had developed from: an Open Field parish of the Middle Ages.[36] Meanwhile the mill-owners and entrepreneurs who had supervised the growth and expansion of industry were able to build themselves large villas on the fringes of the great

Fig. 13.15 An aerial view of Newquay, Cornwall, looking north-west. In the foreground the distinctive strip fields which resulted from early post-medieval enclosure by agreement have become fossilized in the layout of the town, whose outer suburbs were developed one field at a time.

cities, safely insulated from the places where the actual wealth creation was taking place. Life on the boundary between town and country was made simpler for servants and support staff, if not for the families themselves, by the introduction of horse-drawn trams.

Another good example, where even individual strip fields can still be seen, is the layout of house-lined streets in Newquay, Cornwall.[37] After the Middle Ages the Open Fields of the villages surrounding the small town were enclosed piecemeal, by agreement, an arrangement which in Devon and Cornwall often led to the preservation of the medieval strips that had been owned, or assembled, by individual farmers. As land was required for housing on the fringes of the expanding town, the already fossilized strip fields were developed one at a time, causing the earlier landscape to become locked into the town plan. This can most clearly be seen from the air.

FOUL DRAINS AND CLEAN WATER

One might suppose that, prior to the introduction of building controls in the mid-nineteenth century, all earlier development had been unfettered and at the whim of developers, but that was not the case. Large cities cannot function without governance of some sort and in medieval London, for example, from 1212 thatch was banned as a roofing material because it posed a fire hazard; furthermore, after 1245 it was specifically stipulated that roof tiles or shingles should be employed instead. London also possessed some remarkable stone-built conduits, built in 1236–45 at Cheapside in the City, which were linked to a network of lead pipes to provide a good supply of clean water.[38] We have seen how the Reformation freed private money from going to the Church and some of it went towards clean water supplies. But the extraordinary rapidity of development in the late eighteenth and early nineteenth centuries subjected the somewhat ad hoc infrastructure of Britain's rapidly expanding industrial cities to the most extreme pressure, and it began to creak. After fire, disease was the principal problem.

Cholera is an Asiatic disease that first appeared in Sunderland in October 1831 and swiftly spread to Newcastle, Edinburgh and

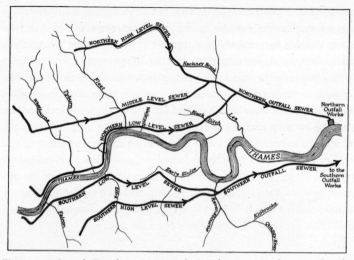

Fig. 13.16 Joseph Bazalgette's 1858 design for an entirely new plan for London's sewers. This was one of the greatest civil engineering projects of the mid-nineteenth century.

London.[39] It is caused by a different pathogen to typhoid fever, but both are spread through contaminated water. Cholera usually kills within 24–48 hours unless treated; typhoid fever is less deadly but is harder to eradicate, as those who recover then become carriers. That first outbreak killed some 31,000 people in England and Scotland. A second outbreak in 1848 was even worse, killing 65,000 in Britain. The last two outbreaks in Britain, in 1853–4 and 1866, were less severe, in the latter instance because of urgent measures adopted by national and local government to improve the provision of clean water and adequate sewerage, following 'The Great Stink' of 1858 when the smell from the Thames was so intense that the windows of the Houses of Parliament had to be draped with curtains soaked in chloride of lime to kill the odour. The death of Prince Albert in 1861 from typhoid fever at the early age of 42 proved a final incentive for both government and local authorities across Britain to take practical measures to improve urban sewerage and water supplies.

Sir Joseph Bazalgette (1819–91) was largely responsible for the improvements to both the water supply and sewers for London, which he designed and pushed through.[40] In 1856 the Metropolitan Board of Works was formed, with Bazalgette as its chief engineer. The system of sewers, which had developed piecemeal from Roman times and made use of the natural river catchment, was not up to the task. His new master plan cut across the existing rivers and was based on two converging systems of main sewers arranged on three levels north of the Thames and two to the south. Both had outfalls well downstream of what was then the built-up area of London. That arrangement is still in use to this day, but enhanced by huge additional sewage treatment works.

Fig. 13.17 A fine polychromatic brick water tower at Shooters Hill, south-east London, built in 1910.

London was not alone in having health problems in the late nineteenth century and local authorities everywhere took measures to ensure a good clean supply of water. The large numbers of new houses that were being built in the towns and large suburbs of Victorian Britain required mains water, and hundreds of new water towers were constructed to give the mains the head pressure needed for a reliable supply to so many homes. These towers became symbols of civic pride in their own right and many were built in slightly outlandish styles reminiscent of castles or churches. Multi-coloured brickwork was very much a feature of the towers built at the turn of the century. There is a very fine example on the crest of Shooters Hill, south-east London. This prominent position would have guaranteed good water pressure, but just as important it gave the tower's builders a chance to show off their bricklaying and roofing skills.

SPAS AND RESORTS IN THE NINETEENTH CENTURY

The railways transformed many seaside towns, bringing goods and visitors to them in hitherto unimaginable quantities. We saw how the post-medieval ports of Britain fared in the industrial age, but some of the longer-established resorts also had to change their ways, or lose their market share. Some were to be more successful than others.

Seaside resorts in the West Country expanded rapidly with the coming of the railways. Weston-super-Mare to the north was linked to the Great Western railway in 1841 and Weymouth in 1857. Weymouth could also be reached from London (Waterloo) in less than four hours via the Southern railway. This was the period when British holiday towns acquired, piers, bandstands and esplanades – the necessary trappings of a High Victorian seaside resort.

Many early seaside resorts, such as Weymouth, Scarborough, Brighton, Southampton, Hastings and Margate, initially marketed themselves as spa towns because these already had a long record of success. Southampton and Brighton, for example, possessed iron-rich springs that were sampled by nobility and even royalty, but after about 1750 they became better known as upmarket and highly fashionable seaside towns.

Brighton was soon to become the leading seaside resort in Britain, the coastal equivalent of Bath.[41] The author of the paper that had started it all in 1753, Dr Richard Russell (p. 437), took up residence there and attracted many eminent people to the town. Soon houses began to be built over the Open Field strips, known as leynes, a name which today survives in the well-known Lanes district of the town.

It would be difficult to overestimate the importance of resorts in eighteenth- and nineteenth-century Britain. In the first census of 1801 Brighton had a population of 7,000; by 1831 there were 41,000 and it had become the twentieth largest town in England; during the decade between the censuses of 1811 and 1821 it was also the fastest-growing town in England. This extraordinary growth took place during the industrial era yet it owed little directly to industrialization, although of course industry ultimately created the wealth that was spent there. During the 1830s the large numbers of fashionable people visiting

Fig. 13.18 The complexity of a modern seaside resort townscape is well illustrated by this view of Brighton, taken from the Eastern Pier. The white stuccoed Regency houses of Georgian Brighton still dominate the townscape. Above the Regency houses are tower blocks built in the late twentieth century and below is the reinforced sea front, of earlier twentieth-century date.

Brighton were accommodated and entertained in a variety of hotels, lodging houses, theatres, baths, shops and libraries, built along the coast in the elegant Regency style for which the town is still so renowned; the development was in two main areas: Kemp Town to the east and Brunswick Town to the west.

The railway came to Brighton in 1841, further boosting its popularity, but as visitor numbers increased, proportionately there were fewer who stayed overnight. By 1851 its population had overtaken that of Bath. Then during the 1850s 'day trippers' from London had become the overall majority. Queen Victoria stopped visiting and, mercifully for posterity, sold the Pavilion to the town corporation, for a song. By the late nineteenth century Brighton had become 'London by the sea', with huge crowds on festivals and bank holidays. The fine Regency buildings still stretched, as they do today, along a unique sea front of 2 kilometres, but behind this façade were the buildings of the permanent residents of the town, whose shoddy and hastily built brickwork was crumbling in the salty air. Soon slums developed and these became notorious in the early twentieth century and were not repaired until after – well after, in some instances – the Second World War.

There is, of course, more to the south coast than Brighton, just as there were other spas besides Bath. We have already mentioned Weymouth, but other major Victorian resorts included Bournemouth, Eastbourne, Bognor, Southsea, Margate, Ramsgate, Folkestone and many more. Most were local versions of Brighton, and some, such as Bournemouth, Folkestone, Eastbourne and Bognor, made efforts to retain their more fashionable visitors after the coming of the railways. Resorts around the Solent were given a royal boost when Queen Victoria and Prince Albert took up residence at their magnificent summer mansion at Osborne House on the Isle of Wight. Not all resorts catered to the upper and middle classes alone. Some, especially those with good railway links to London, developed a broader social appeal. Good examples of the more brash and popular resort may still be seen at Southend-on-Sea, in Essex, and Margate, in Kent. Herne Bay, also in Kent, began life as a planned resort, laid out on a grid pattern near the village of Herne, but from the early twentieth century its boarding houses became commuter homes, because of its proximity to the capital.

Two outstanding resorts that were sufficiently far removed from London not to have felt its effects were Llandudno and Scarborough. Llandudno, in north Wales, is one of the best preserved Victorian resorts. It lies beneath the massive rocky headland of Great Orme which was mined for its veins of copper ore from the Bronze Age until the mid-nineteenth century when they gave out. When that happened a local landowner and entrepreneur, Lord Edward Mostyn, and a group of local businessmen began to develop Llandudno into a seaside resort. Happily for them the railway arrived in 1858. With its fine Marine Parade[42] Llandudno is typical of a successful Victorian resort. Few resorts have retained their charm so well and for so long.

Scarborough in the East Riding of Yorkshire is sometimes cited as the first seaside resort and had been a fashionable spa from the seventeenth century. It flourished as a resort when therapeutic sea-bathing became more common in the mid-eighteenth century,[43] and grew in popularity throughout the eighteenth century, as shown by Sheridan's play *A Trip to Scarborough* (1777). The three piers were built between about 1730 and 1817. Scarborough continued to expand throughout the nineteenth century and a number of notable features were added to the town, including the fine stone-built Crescent (1835–40), which echoes Bath and Buxton, numerous churches and Non-conformist chapels, a spa building (1877–80) and a magnificent museum (1829–9) in The Valley, which forms the heart of classical Scarborough. Then in 1863–7 came the Grand Hotel. This vast edifice towers above the beach and is to elegant Scarborough what St Pancras is to King's Cross. It is built, not in stone, but in yellow and red brick in a style described by Pevsner as 'Mixed Renaissance'. It would be hard to find a more exuberant statement of Victorian overconfidence.

Seaside resorts were never a major feature of eighteenth- and nineteenth-century Scotland. There were a large number of small resorts which remained what they were, seaside towns, and mostly catered for local visitors.[44] Analysis of visitors to the Marine and Royal hotels at Dunoon, Argyll and Bute, for example, showed that between 1885 and 1900 most of their visitors were from Scotland, of whom 50 per cent were from Glasgow and a mere 15 per cent or so from England and Wales. Closer to the big cities, the growth of resorts was hampered by strict laws on Sunday observance and less tolerant attitudes to bathing that persisted far longer north of the border. In the late nineteenth and early twentieth centuries golf proved to be the great attraction of inland and coastal resorts right across Scotland. The many new golf courses attracted both locals and visitors from England alike, in ever-increasing numbers.

As the middle-class population of Britain's towns became increasingly prosperous, people wanted places where they could relax without having to travel to a resort. So many provincial towns and cities acquired parks and promenades, such as the New Walk along the River Ouse in York, where it was possible to take a stroll, *en famille*, with everyone wearing their Sunday best.

MODERN PLANNED TOWNS

Much urban expansion in Victorian times was completely unplanned and housing was built when and where it was required. 'New towns' have been a recurrent feature of the British landscape since at least Norman times, but some of the finest were created in the eighteenth and nineteenth centuries. One of the very best was James Craig's scheme for Edinburgh New Town, of 1767.[45] Despite the fact that Craig's original intentions were not followed through as he would have wished, his simple, elegant plan has given us an early masterpiece of Georgian town planning. One reason for its success is that it respects the landscape and does not attempt to dominate or change it. It also makes use of vistas, with subtlety and to great effect.

Craig's New Town was arranged on a grid pattern that more or less follows the crest of a ridge running ENE–WSW. George Street, the central axial road, runs parallel with two other streets, Queen Street to the north and Princes Street to the south. Craig planned that both Queen and Princes streets should be built up on one side only, to allow views across the Forth Valley to the north and the castle and the medieval city to the south. Today Queen Street and Princes Street Gardens ensure that a large part of Craig's original vistas remain intact. The architecture along the central axial thoroughfare may lack unity, but the street's width and the presence of statues (the likes of William Pitt and George IV) give George Street an air of spacious grandeur. Like that along George Street, the architecture of the cross-streets

Fig. 13.19 A view north along Charlotte Street at the west end of James Craig's New Town, in Edinburgh. This view taken from Charlotte Square, which was designed by Robert Adam in the 1790s shows a less formal arrangement of buildings beyond the square and a glimpse of the Forth Valley in the distance. Craig's plans were accepted by the city authorities in 1767. Despite being laid out on a strict grid, Craig's New Town is notable for the way it makes use of the landscape. The main thoroughfare, George Street, follows the crest of a ridge. Queen and Princes streets which bound the New Town are built up on one side only, giving fine views of the Forth, to the north, and the medieval city, to the south.

reflects the chequered developmental history of Craig's New Town, but the contrasting views of the landscape to north and south still remain breathtaking.

The early history of Craig's New Town could be the story of urban development anywhere. Craig made rules and the city fathers tried to implement them. Unfortunately, however, developers nearly always try to build what they can get away with. Despite its carefully considered layout, the developing reality of the New Town fell short of Craig's original intentions and eventually, in the 1790s, the city authorities were shamed into taking more assertive action; so piecemeal development was abandoned when it came to the building of Craig's western square, originally to be known as St George's Square, but actually built as Charlotte Square, off the most westerly cross-street of the grid, Charlotte Street. Charlotte Square was designed by Robert Adam as a unitary whole and it remains one of the greatest masterpieces of Georgian urban architecture.

Non-industrial towns and cities, places such as Bath, Buxton, Edinburgh and Brighton, were the centres of large-scale, 'enlightened' and controlled town planning, whereas the great cities of the north of England grew up piecemeal, when funds for development became available. The result was fine – indeed over-elaborate – civic buildings, surrounded by mills and back-to-back housing. However, although industry was never far distant, most of the England's northern industrial cities can boast some very fine architecture.

Like other medieval walled towns and cities, the streets and lanes

Fig. 13.20 A view along Grainger Street towards the Grey Monument, the focus of Grainger Town, Newcastle.

confined within the walls of Newcastle had become extremely cramped and congested. During the seventeenth and eighteenth centuries, the city grew very much more prosperous through coal mining and industry, and it became clear that something had to be done. The first successful redevelopments took place in the 1770s, but some of the finest and until recently most neglected Regency and early Victorian planned development took place there, in a central area that has recently been renamed Grainger Town, after the man who did so much to create it.[46]

Richard Grainger (1797–1861) was the son of a labourer and a soldier's daughter, born in a poor quarter of Newcastle. After a rudimentary education he set up a small building firm with his brother George, who died early in 1817. A few successful years later, and after the wholesale redevelopment of the city centre, he undertook the transformation of the area now known as Grainger Town, between 1834 and 1842. The style adopted for Grainger Town was Greek Revival (locally known as 'Tyneside Classical') and the central area was based around two main streets, Grainger Street and Grey Street, which converged on a circus, in which a monument was erected to Earl Grey, commemorating his administration's passing of the Great Reform Bill in 1832. Richard Grainger decided not to use a more conventional grid layout and instead based Grainger Town around a triangle of streets in which commercial and residential buildings were successfully mixed together. The only comparable development in early Victorian England was Nash's work in Regent Street, London, but there many of the humbler buildings were swept away. In Newcastle, most have been retained and this gives a fine impression of the totality of urban life at the time.

COPING WITH GROWTH: LONDON IN THE LATE EIGHTEENTH AND NINETEENTH CENTURIES

During the nineteenth century the new manufacturing and service industries, such as the railways, attracted many new residents to what was developing into Greater London. The huge London market also encouraged regional economies to specialize: in Bedfordshire, for example, 'nightsoil' – the contents of privies – was removed to the fields around Sandy and Biggleswade where it manured the land for the growing of green vegetables which could be taken to London markets overnight by train. Strawberries were grown on the silt Fens for the London trade and fruit in large quantities was grown in Kent, 'the garden of England', but more appropriately 'the garden for London'.

Much has been written about the rebuilding of London following the Great Fire of 1666, but it is important to keep it in perspective.[47] Considerably less than half the conurbation was destroyed and many areas, including most of the West End, escaped altogether, as did the somewhat smaller East End. The administrative centre at Westminster also escaped and it was from here that the post-Fire plans for rebuilding were made. The geometric grand designs of men like Wren and John

Fig. 13.21 An extract from sheet 7 of the Ordnance Survey 1-inch ('Old Series') map, published in 1822. This remarkably accurate and detailed map shows the extent of London immediately prior to the industrial age. The two principal straight roads into London are Maida Vale/Edgeware Road, running NW–SE (the A5) and Bishopsgate/Kingsland Road, running N–S (the Old North Road or A10). Both have Roman origins. Regent's Park lay on the fringes of the conurbation and the main northern railway stations (Marylebone, Euston, St Pancras and King's Cross) were all later built on the north side of the Marylebone/Euston/Pentonville Road which passes along the south side of Regent's Park and defined the northern limit of Georgian London.

Evelyn were rejected for pragmatic reasons. The finance for such schemes was not assured and the reconstruction which followed the Acts for Rebuilding of 1667 and 1670 generally followed the old, Roman and medieval street plan. The Acts for Rebuilding, however, stipulated that buildings had to follow certain rules to avoid a recurrence of disaster. These were, in effect, the first building regulations and were subsequently drawn together in the Building Act of 1774.

A major development in the sixteenth century had been the uniting of the City and Westminster by extending the Strand, an ancient road set back from the Thames, but running parallel to it. In the seventeenth and eighteenth centuries this road became a fashionable area in its own right and was fringed with noblemen's London residences, such as Somerset and Northumberland houses. Fashionable coffee houses sprang up along it, as did theatres (Drury Lane in the 1790s) and gentlemen's clubs (for example the Athenaeum). More bridges were built across the Thames: Westminster (1750), Blackfriars (1769), Vauxhall (1816), and John Rennie's two fine bridges, Waterloo (1817) and Southwark (1819), both of which, sadly, have been demolished. These bridges encouraged London to expand southwards.

After the Great Fire rebuilding in the City and along the Strand was nearing completion in the 1680s. This was the period when speculative builders developed the idea of the London square, a major British contribution to urban architecture, many examples of which continued to be built until the 1880s. St James's Square was built around 1668, followed by Golden and Soho squares. Cavendish and Hanover squares were finished by 1717. Away from the river in the West End there were major episodes of residential building which saw the development of some of the great private London estates, like those of the Duke of Westminster (Belgravia) and the Bedford estates (Bloomsbury), where Bedford Square is the best preserved example of an open and airy London square.

During the early nineteenth century squares were supplanted by terraces and crescents, as exemplified by Nash's developments around Regent's Park (Cumberland Terrace and Park Crescent). Laying aside his extension and redesign of Buckingham Palace (1825–30), perhaps Nash's greatest contribution to modern London was the development of Regent Street (1810–30), which provided part of a new axis that

connected the various centres of the West End. The new thoroughfares linked Regent's Park to St James's where the park was entirely
remodelled and Trafalgar Square laid out.

This was the period when London south of the river started a phase
of rapid expansion. Southwark had long benefited from being outside
City legislation, which is one reason why theatres such as the Rose (1587)
and Globe (1599) had been built there. By 1678 Southwark's population
was at least 26,000, and being separated from the main concentration
of housing by the width of the Thames the area became the centre of
the leather-working industry. Tanning involved the use of stale urine and
the process (and the area) was infamous for its stench.[48]

London was the only capital city in Europe that was also a great port.
The early nineteenth century saw the construction of extensive new
docks to the east of the City. London remained by far the largest port
of Britain in Stuart and Georgian times and from the mid-seventeenth

Fig. 13.22 A view of Bedford Square, London, in the Bloomsbury estate of
the dukes of Bedford. The square was built between 1778 and 1783 and is
one of the best preserved of the original London squares. This view shows the
south (*right*) and east ranges, looking towards Bloomsbury Street. The centre
of the square was open when first built and the London plane trees (*left*) were
added in Victorian times.

century the import of sugar in large quantities from the West Indies grew in importance. It is sometimes believed that the slave trade was only carried out from ports like Bristol, Liverpool and Hull, but in 1755 there were 147 registered slave traders in London.[49]

One general trend of some importance began to emerge in the seventeenth and eighteenth centuries, when richer people started to purchase properties on the edges of the conurbation to escape the overcrowding and atmospheric pollution closer to the centre. This gave rise to a centrifugal tendency, where outlying areas, for example in the north, places like Kilburn, Hampstead Heath, Stoke Newington, Muswell and Highgate, became residential areas for the families of well-off bankers and businessmen who could still manage to commute to the City on horseback.[50] The centrifugal tendency was to gather pace in the nineteenth and twentieth centuries.

It is probably only a small exaggeration to call late-Victorian London the capital of the world.[51] In landscape terms the Houses of Parliament and Big Ben were the new symbols of British Imperial success.[52] The fact that they were new, like so many other great structures of the nineteenth century, gave that symbolism added force. London was transformed in Victorian times. There were of course major developments in the public sphere, such as the construction of the new railway termini and covered market buildings, like Covent Garden (1830), but perhaps the largest single development was the growth of the huge suburbs north and south of the river, where new patterns of social life began to emerge that are gently parodied by what is perhaps my favourite book, the brothers George and Weedon Grossmith's *Diary of a Nobody* (1892).[53] Meanwhile, at opposite ends of the social spectrum, the rich moved to new villas in the country or on the outskirts of town, and slums developed in what had once been smart areas in places like Spitalfields and Whitechapel in the East End. Victorian London was a place of contrasts.

The impact of the early industrial era was comparatively slow to affect London. In the later Middle Ages and in early modern to Georgian times, most crafts and industries were located around the north, eastern and southern fringes of the conurbation. During the period from the seventeenth to the nineteenth centuries industries such as paper-making, calico-printing, gun- and gunpowder-making, foundries, leather trades and malt distilleries moved into the dockland area of the City.

The landscape around London is not rich in natural resources. There are no coal measures or outcrops of iron ore nearer than the Weald. Similarly, reliable supplies of timber for fuel had been depleted by the sixteenth century – hence the brisk trade that began around then in coal from the north-east. This might help to explain why the industrial era took hold relatively late; but when it came it was remarkably diverse, reflecting the variety of trades and industries that were already there. As well as being the nation's capital, centre of commerce and leading port, London was also the main centre of manufacturing well into Victorian times. London became a regional centre for the brewing of ale and beer from at least the late seventeenth century.[54] The census of 1861 showed that in Britain more than one worker in six employed in manufacturing industry was based in London. In the late eighteenth century London was home to a greater concentration of steam engines than anywhere else in the country, where they were to be found in numbers comparable with heavily industrialized areas such as the Midlands and Cornwall.[55]

While new manufacturing and service industries drew people into London in ever-increasing numbers, the rise of the City as a centre for commerce was having an altogether different effect. In the half-century after 1850 the population of the City fell from about 130,000 to less than 30,000, as residents, many of them living in poor, overcrowded accommodation, moved out to make way for new roads, railways, shops and offices.[56]

The depopulated City now separated the increasingly different West and East End. The construction of building projects, both public and private, in the West End had caused large numbers of people to be displaced and they clustered in increasing numbers in a zone around the fringes of the City. This area was described by contemporaries as 'the abyss', 'darkest London' or 'town swamps'. In the Cripplegate area in 1856, for example, 9,500 were living in 1,178 houses, where cholera was described as 'rife'. Other appalling slums grew up around areas of employment, such as King's Cross and St Pancras and the docklands of Wapping, the Isle of Dogs and Rotherhithe. On the south side of the river closer to the City, at Southwark, the slums of Jacob's Island were notorious and provided the setting for Fagin's den in *Oliver Twist*.

Elsewhere, in Bermondsey and Lambeth, river trades and the food-processing industry required ready access to the workforce and produced huge slums with open sewers, described by the social campaigner Henry Mayhew (in 1849) as a 'Venice of Drains'.[57]

It would be impossible to separate townscapes from the social problems that both caused and were caused by them. Usually these came in the form of cramped housing, poor drains, inadequate water supplies and a lack of readily accessible open spaces. The early nineteenth century saw crowding increase in working-class areas, often becoming very much worse than in the late eighteenth century, as we saw at Arkwright's Mill, in Manchester. By the mid-nineteenth century the slums of Britain's industrial cities were starting to cause concern in the world of politics. It would be misleading, however, to suggest that the vivid accounts of men like Dickens and Henry Mayhew were lone voices. This was the era when the methodical study of poverty and its causes had its roots. These studies were based on field surveys in which existing housing was classified and categorized by men like Charles Booth in London and Seebohm Rowntree in York, both of whom based their conclusions on detailed maps, where different degrees of poverty were plotted, house by house.[58] Booth was one of the first to realize that a prime cause of poverty was the need to support older members of the family when age forced them to retire, and he is widely acknowledged as a major figure in the introduction of the Old Age Pensions Act of 1908.

A more genteel suburban London began to grow rapidly with the coming of the railways, from the 1840s. These brick-built houses with Welsh slate roofs occurred in terraces, but more usually in pairs, as semi-detached. Early examples include Clapham Park (begun in 1825), Battersea Fields and Highbury New Park (1860s). From the 1860s railway-based suburbia extended to outlying villages, such as Catford, Eltham, Wimbledon, Leytonstone, West Ham and Plaistow, or further out still, to Bromley, Barking and Ilford.

THE RISE OF MUNICIPAL PARKS
AND GARDENS

From the second half of the eighteenth century open spaces had become a natural focus for the more prosperous and increasingly numerous professional and middle classes, many of whom would have spent time visiting the great landscape parks at places like Stowe, where they would have acquired a taste for space and open landscape and where buildings can be appreciated from more than just the front. That is probably why open spaces such as Hampstead Heath and Blackheath, in north and south London respectively, are still fringed with substantial individual houses and villas dating to the late eighteenth and early nineteenth centuries.[59] We shall see shortly that this move by the well-to-do towards open spaces, where their houses could be viewed to better advantage, was also seen half a century later around the fringes of many of the newly established Victorian city parks, for example, in Birkenhead and Liverpool.

Before the nineteenth century little concerted attention was paid to the recreation of ordinary people. Towns like Bath and Brighton were initially laid out for the benefit of fashionable society. In London from the late seventeenth and early eighteenth centuries there were a number of private pleasure gardens attached to great houses, such as Burlington House and Buckingham House (later Palace). There were also one or two notable public examples, of which the best known are Vauxhall, near Lambeth Palace, and Ranelagh Gardens, next to the Royal Hospital, Chelsea. These places remained fashionable into the early nineteenth century, but were never intended for the use of ordinary people, any more than country houses, whose many visitors were invariably from the upper classes.

The municipal parks and gardens that are such an important feature of British towns and cities came into being in many ways. Some were given to the municipality by successful and philanthropic industrialists. Some were based around common land; others were royal possessions; many more were purchased by Victorian municipal authorities for the benefit of the town or city. Their subsequent growth and development, however, became part of a broader movement which began in Preston,

Fig. 13.23 The scene by the side of the lake, with the Boathouse in the
background, on the opening day of Birkenhead Park, 10 April 1847.

in Lancashire, in 1833. The most influential of the early parks was
undoubtedly that at Birkenhead, on Merseyside, which was swiftly
followed by others in Derby and Southampton.

Birkenhead Park was laid out in 1843. It lies in the heart of the city,
not far from the docks, in William Laird's new planned town, which
came into existence in the 1830s.[60] The men behind Birkenhead new
town were acutely aware of the terrible problems of overcrowding in
the working-class areas of Liverpool, across the Mersey, where the city
had expanded piecemeal, and without planning. They were determined
not to repeat those mistakes in their town. So in 1833 Parliament passed
an Act that established the Birkenhead Improvement Commission,
many of whose members were prosperous Liverpool merchants who
were only too aware of their city's housing problems.[61]

In the same year that the Birkenhead Commission was set up, the
Parliamentary Select Committee on Public Works published a report
which stated:

> With a rapidly increasing Population, lodged, for the most part in narrow
> courts and confined streets, the means of occasional exercise and

recreation in the fresh air are every day lessened, as inclosures take place
and buildings spread themselves on every side . . . It cannot be necessary
to point out how requisite some Public Walks or Open Space in the
neighbourhood of large towns must be . . . confined as they are during
the weekdays as Mechanics or Manufacturers, and often shut up in
heated Factories: it must be evident that it is of the first importance to
their health on their day of rest to enjoy the fresh air, and to be able
(exempt from the dust and dirt of the public thoroughfares) to walk out
in decent comfort with their families; if deprived of any such resource,
it is probable that their only escape from the narrow courts and alleys
(in which so many of the humble classes reside) will be the drinking
shops, where, in short-lived excitement they may forget their toil, but
where they waste the means of their families, and too often destroy their
health.[62]

That extract strikes me as humane, realistic and unpatronizing. We
should also bear in mind its very early date: just a year after the Great
Reform Bill and four years before the reign of Queen Victoria (1837–
1901). Although this report was not followed up by any government
action, it did arouse public opinion and the Birkenhead Commission
were the first civic authority to attempt something practical. They knew
they had a potential problem on their hands. Birkenhead had been a
success and the population was growing extremely fast: the census of
1841 showed it to have risen to 8,529 – an astonishing threefold
increase on 1831. In 1843 the Commission established a body, known
as the Improvement Committee, who were given the task of overseeing
the new park, whose overall concept and design they delegated to Sir
Joseph Paxton in the same year.

The new parks were designed from the outset as large open spaces
which were intended to accommodate the crowds that gathered in
them on Sundays and public holidays. Early examples reflected
country house parks of a previous generation, with temples and
gazebos reminiscent of Stowe. By the 1860s, however, park design
had developed its own vocabulary, which was altogether better suited
to the urban environment. Prominent among the usual park buildings
are public lavatories, bandstands and tea shops, although civic pride
could sometimes be magnificently expressed in the construction of

special buildings such as the elegant Palm House (1896) in Liverpool's Sefton Park.

The heyday of the Victorian municipal park was the second half of the nineteenth century, when many were established right across Britain. This process was helped by two Acts of Parliament in the 1850s which stimulated the donation of land to local authorities. The laying out of parks also provided employment at a time when the 'cotton famine' was putting many people out of work.

The Public Health Act of 1875 allowed local authorities to keep land for recreation, and, just as importantly, to raise funds to do so. This was all part of the later Victorian movement to do something about improving public health, and, as we saw previously, it went hand in hand with better sewers and clean water supplies. Today it is widely recognized by planners that open spaces need to be no more than five minutes away from housing, if they are to be visited regularly by local people. So while big parks are of course excellent, they serve only a proportion of the populace. The Open Spaces and Disused Burial Grounds Acts of 1881 and 1884 respectively have helped provide many of the much-used smaller recreational areas in Britain's towns and cities.

'PALMERSTON'S FOLLIES': DEFENSIVE LANDSCAPES IN THE MID-NINETEENTH CENTURY

It seems strange today, but in the mid-nineteenth century, at the height of Britain's economic and imperial power, there were widespread public fears of invasion from France. Naval ports and dockyards were seen to be particularly vulnerable and a series of massive fortifications were constructed, sometimes generically referred to as 'Palmerston Forts'.[63] Lord Palmerston became Prime Minister in June 1859 and in August he had set up a Royal Commission to look into certain key areas that might be attacked by France. These included the naval dockyards and certain other vulnerable places. With admirable promptness the Commission produced a report which was passed by Parliament in 1860.

The Commission's survey stipulated many improvements to existing forts (including some ancient ones, such as Portchester Castle, the Romano-British 'Saxon Shore' fort) and the building of a series of altogether new ones, still known as Palmerston Forts (at the time cynics referred to them as 'Palmerston's Follies'). Many, being so massive, still survive almost intact in the landscape. In some instances, like the fort built in 1865 on the cliffs above the port of Newhaven, in East Sussex, the new forts were built on their own, but most were constructed as integral parts of much larger schemes, particularly in areas that the Commission regarded as weak. The many Palmerston Forts that surround Plymouth and Portsmouth are still an extraordinary varied and vivid expression of Britain's power in the nineteenth century. But

Fig. 13.24 Some of the most massive of the so-called 'Palmerston Forts' were built to defend the northern approaches to the naval base at Portsmouth from attack overland. Although brick shatters on impact, the earthen roof could absorb serious punishment. Work began on the five forts on Portsdown Hill in 1863. This view is of the south-western face of Fort Purbrook, which features a massive brick-lined defensive ditch along its eastern, northern and western sides (in the foreground). At the time these were the most modern and impressive forts in the world, but they also included some architectural touches, such as the fine round-arched Romanesque gateway, just visible halfway along the main wall.

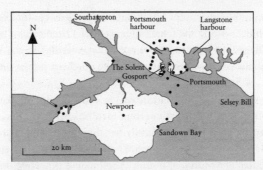

Fig. 13.25 Map showing the location of forts around Portsmouth and the Isle of Wight. This map shows the situation in 1860 when the fortifications were hugely improved to ward off potential attack from France. The cost of upgrading existing forts and building new ones was about £2 million. The scheme made use of pre-existing forts but also built many new ones, especially at three points of potential weakness: the eastern approach into the Solent, via the Needles; the entrance into Portsmouth Harbour, at Gosport; and the approach from inland, which was protected by an arc of forts to the north. Many of these forts can still be seen.

it is important to note that they were not constructed in isolation, but form part of two carefully thought-out schemes of strategic defence which made excellent use of the entire landscape. Some of the Palmerston Forts, such as Fort Nelson and Fort Purbrook, on the hills overlooking Portsmouth, feature steep walls and plunging brick-faced artificial cliffs (somehow 'ditches' or 'ramparts' seem inadequate descriptions). They both appear, and were, very expensive. William Gladstone, then Chancellor of the Exchequer, threatened to resign when he first learnt of their cost. As one might expect, many were built facing out to sea, but there was also fear of a large-scale landing away from the defended shoreline, followed by an attack from inland. Both Portsmouth and Plymouth have curved lines of forts around their northern approaches to deter a major overland attack.[64] The forts arranged in an arc along the top of Portsdown Hill on the northern approaches to Portsmouth are still extremely impressive, as too are the smaller forts placed far out in the Solent, such as Spitbank Fort. The entrances to the Solent and the approaches to the Isle of Wight itself were also heavily protected and some of the Palmerston Forts actually made use of the first serious attempts to provide strategic defences for Portsmouth and the Solent, during the reign of Henry VIII. Often the well-designed and heavily built Henrician forts are incorporated into the Victorian forts, as at Hurst Castle which protects the northern side of the western access to the Solent.

Newhaven Fort was remarkable for the first use of concrete in large quantities as a general building material. Slightly later, concrete would also be used very specifically for the aprons and surrounds of gun-emplacements. Hitherto granite had been used in such situations, but tests had showed that although a shell would penetrate deeper into concrete than granite it produced far fewer lethal fragments of stone shrapnel and the concrete remained generally more stable, as even large masonry blocks would shift and loosen when hit by heavy artillery. Concrete was used for the gun-emplacements of the new forts around

Fig. 13.26 A view from Fort Victoria on the Isle of Wight across the western access into the Solent basin, looking towards Hurst Castle. Hurst Castle was positioned at the end of a long pebble spit and was built during the reign of Henry VIII, when the rounded gun-emplacement (*extreme left*) and the taller octagonal keep were constructed. These were later incorporated into the much larger and lower Palmerston Fort, which was built from granite and features gun positions whose square openings are clearly visible. The enlarged fort proved slow to construct. It was begun shortly after 1860 and was not completed until 1885 when it housed just twelve of a planned battery of sixty-one guns.

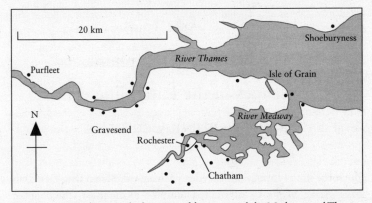

Fig. 13.27 Map showing the location of forts around the Medway and Thames estuary in the late nineteenth century. A Royal Commission appointed by Lord Palmerston suggested in 1860 that the defences of the Thames estuary urgently required attention, given a perceived threat from France. Many were upgraded and a number of new ones were built, especially around the approaches to the naval base at Chatham. These massive fortifications proved useful in 1940 when several were adapted for military and civil defence.

Chatham, and by the end of the century it became widely used on the Continent.

The size and scale of the mid-nineteenth-century fortifications around the Thames estuary reflect the fact that this was still the principal route into the nation's capital and required major defences. As with the fortifications around Portsmouth and Plymouth, those to the south and east of London involved massive expenditure. The naval base at Chatham was given special protection. Chatham's defences included the last five large forts to be built in Britain. In 1860 their cost was estimated at £1.6 million and a light railway was needed for their construction. In time of war they would have been home to 417 guns and 4,650 men. It was quite an undertaking, given the rather nebulous nature of the supposed threat. Perhaps someone in government circles had heard well-founded intelligence reports about weapons of mass destruction that lay concealed across the Channel. Not surprisingly, many of the nineteenth-century defended positions around London were so sturdily built that they were readily modified when a very real threat to the capital emerged, in the summer of 1940.

14

The Planner Triumphant:
Landscapes in the Late Nineteenth
and Twentieth Centuries

For some time I toyed with the idea of using the Bonzo Dog Doo Dah Band's song 'My Pink Half of the Drainpipe' as the title to this chapter, since the suburbs are such an important aspect of late-nineteenth- and twentieth-century landscapes. The song[1] poked fun, of course, at those dual-painted downpipes that divide suburban terraced and semi-detached houses of the 1950s and 1960s. The strangely painted pipes were emblematic of the fact that many British people did not want to share their terraced or semi-detached house with another family; they wanted somewhere entirely of their own. One result of this has been the proliferation since the middle of the twentieth century of bungalows and detached houses.

Although residential suburbs were very much a feature of the *vici* that arose outside the walls of Romano-British towns, they only really came into their own in late Victorian times. Many would consider them *the* defining feature of the twentieth century. We shall discuss the history of suburban growth later in the chapter, but it is necessary to draw attention to the suburbs at the very outset, simply because they *are* an everyday aspect of life in modern Britain and are therefore taken for granted. Many people mistakenly regard suburbs as unimportant and not worth cherishing, largely because of their very ubiquity.

The twentieth century undoubtedly produced its share of eyesores. Ribbon development was a big problem in the 1930s and some of the tower blocks of flats built in the 1960s were loathed by their residents and demolished in the 1980s and 1990s. But despite the fact that recent suburbs are indeed vast, they are nevertheless tiny when compared with the areas of farmed land, upland, forest, lake and moor that are still so characteristic of Britain. Even though nearly everyone lives or works in a town or city, somehow Britain has managed to retain its uncluttered rural areas. We take these for granted, but I consider them a huge achievement. I never thought I would one day be singing the praises of unassuming bureaucrats in town halls up and down the country, but it is almost entirely down to planning. Town and country planning, which arose and developed in the twentieth century, is now the single most important factor affecting the look of Britain. And we meddle with it at our peril!

RURAL LANDSCAPES IN THE LATE NINETEENTH AND TWENTIETH CENTURIES

In this chapter I want to move out of rural Britain and into the inner cities, by way of the suburbs. But our journey must start in the countryside, which at the beginning of the century was still feeling the effects of the agricultural depression of the 1870s. This had proved, and was still proving, a disaster for many farmers. To give an example of its impact: wheat and wool prices halved between the 1860s and 1890s.[2] Farmers responded, just as they are doing today, by diversifying and by seeking niche markets closer to home. The large structures built during High Farming for the intensive rearing of beef cattle were instead given over to the production of fresh milk, providing, that is, there was a suitable market available nearby. Wherever possible, farmers moved into commodities such as milk, fruit, vegetables or flowers, where freshness was essential because such items could not be imported, given the lack of refrigeration and the speed of transport at the time. It was also an advantage if there was a large urban population reasonably close by, to provide a ready market for perishable produce. Such changes to the farming economy were made somewhat simpler by the introduction of better roads and of course, from the mid-nineteenth century, by the coming of the railways.

The sharp increase in dairy production in farms around towns and cities in the late nineteenth and early twentieth centuries led to the demise of the urban dairies that had been a feature of town life for a very long time. The process was considerably speeded up by a cattle plague in 1865. Most urban dairies had gone by the First World War but one or two bravely soldiered on. In certain rural areas the switch into fresh milk led to the widespread conversion of arable into pasture. Many farms, especially in the Home Counties, within easy reach of the capital, had dairy herds. Some of the smaller farms were exclusively dairy, but most were mixed. The seven principal farms in the village of Weston in north Hertfordshire where I grew up all had dairy herds as part of their farming mix, in the 1950s and 1960s. None do so now.

The late nineteenth and early twentieth centuries saw the rise of industrial-scale production of other perishable goods, such as fruit and vegetables, for home consumption. The silt soils of south Lincolnshire are ideally suited to potatoes, largely because they are moisture-retentive, loose and easily tilled, and sufficiently coarse-grained to deter slugs. The large farmers of the region, either individually or together in co-operatives, constructed narrow-gauge railways to bring this heavy commodity to the railheads.[3] The Wisbech and Upwell tramway, which also carried passenger traffic, was constructed to link the fruit and strawberry growers of the Norfolk Fens to the railway at Wisbech.[4] Similar light railways were constructed by growers in Suffolk.[5] Sometimes this trade in perishables could be over long distances, if the rail links were sufficiently rapid and reliable. For example, the Great Western Railway in 1889 carried 300 tonnes of strawberries, 4,500 tonnes of potatoes and 8,000 tonnes of broccoli[6] from Devon and Cornwall, mostly to London and other urban markets.[7]

Arable farmers were hard hit by cheap imported grain; so if they decided to stay in cereals at all they often switched from wheat to barley, which was used mainly as animal feed but also by brewers and maltsters. Barley became the favoured livestock feed in preference to roots. There was also a sharp decline in sheep numbers after 1880, when wool prices fell in the face of competition from Australia. By this time, too, sheep had long since ceased to be a significant part in the crop rotation cycle, having been replaced by manure from housed cattle and by imported fertilizers such as guano. However, despite this general scaling down, better quality British beef and lamb continued to be an important part of the national diet and the farming economy.

Many of the changes that followed the era of High Farming did not affect the structure of the rural landscape significantly. New fields of pasture were accommodated within the boundaries of old arable fields. As farming had become a less profitable activity, most farmers were not prepared to invest in expensive capital projects, such as new farm buildings, even on larger estates. Most surviving substantial Victorian farm buildings date to the era of High Farming. If the decades that followed High Farming were hard for many farmers, the disarray eventually gave rise to a well-integrated system that was generally

Fig. 14.1 Detailed map of arable land (the dark areas) in England drawn up by the Land Utilization Survey during the 1930s, towards the end of the Depression. Arable areas are shaded. This map compares quite closely with that of Caird (Fig. 12.1), published almost a century earlier. Both show the long-term persistence of a general east–west, arable–pasture distinction, which continues to this day.

sustainable and supplied the day-to-day requirements of most towns and cities without much long-distance trade.

The changes brought about to the rural landscape of England in the decades between 1870 and 1930 are most apparent on the map of arable land in England compiled during the 1930s and published in 1940 by the Land Utilization Survey. This map compares quite closely with that of Caird, published almost a century earlier. Caird's map was drawn to show general trends in farming and does not show the concentration of arable farming around Liverpool and Manchester in the Cheshire Plain. Many of these farms had their origins in the years of High Farming, but continued to prosper after 1870, serving the needs of the great cities nearby.

Since 1914 there have been two major changes in British farming. The first, which happened in the middle of the century, is readily explained as the result of technological innovation meeting the demand of market forces. The second, which happened after Britain's entry into the European Economic Community in 1973, is harder to explain in simple economic terms.

In the twentieth century one of the biggest influences on the arrangement of farms and fields was the employment of mechanical equipment. Almost any machine will perform better and more efficiently if it can operate in straight lines, without too many corners. This tends to favour the formation of huge 'grain plain' fields of more than 50 acres that are today such a feature of the landscape of the eastern side of Britain, from Caithness to Kent. Machinery and hedges do not go well together. Tall hedges and hedges with trees can impede sprayers; their roots can tangle ploughs, and crops grown along their northern sides will often germinate poorly and be flattened in wet or windy weather. For these and other reasons, so-called 'conventional' (that is, chemical) farmers and those who favour wildlife and biodiversity are often at variance.

The first mechanical improvements to agriculture happened in the eighteenth century with men like Jethro Tull and the first seed drills. In 1829 a Lincolnshire landowner, Henry Handley, offered a prize of 100 guineas for a satisfactory method of ploughing by steam power.[8] Much of the pioneering work took place on the flat lands and lighter soils of Lincolnshire, where many traction engines were manufactured. John Fowler, the first agricultural engineer of the steam age able to produce traction engines in commercial quantities, co-operated closely with Lincolnshire engineers before building his factory in Leeds. Many Fowler engines can still be seen at rallies to this day. The result of the technological development was a system that employed two self-powered engines standing at opposite ends of a field and hauling a reversible plough between them by way of steel cables and a drum or winch. Steam ploughing was quite widely adopted. For example, Lord Willoughby de Eresby, of Grimsthorpe Castle, near Bourne in Lincolnshire, was a pioneer of steam traction engines and possessed no fewer than four in the early 1850s.[9] Steam ploughs could give rise to distinctive straight ridges that are easily distinguished from the reversed-S curve of much earlier ridge-and-furrow. Sometimes steam furrows ran up and down hills, thereby adding greatly to soil erosion.

The 1920s saw the appearance of the first tractors powered by internal combustion engines. At first these were manufactured by a few local firms, but from the 1930s larger motor manufacturers and mass-production agricultural engineers were assembling tractors and other farm equipment in high volumes, and at low cost. Initially, tractors were mechanical replacements for horses: they could pull heavy loads but were capable of little else other than driving a looped belt, which rotated stationary equipment such as threshing machines. By 1940 the first tractors with hydraulic lift systems and independent power take-off shafts were in production and these allowed farmers to attach heavier, powered equipment to their machines.[10] But by this time the world was in turmoil and a change was about to happen to the British rural landscape that I believe was truly revolutionary, both in the speed with which it happened and the longevity of its after-effects. As is so often the case, it took a war to change things profoundly.

LANDSCAPES OF DEFENCE: THE SECOND WORLD WAR

Given the stability, even the monotony, of much of Britain's landscape today, it is sometimes hard to appreciate that twice in the last century the nation lived under the very real threat of invasion from abroad. Today the landscape still contains some remarkably substantial monuments to the defence of Britain in both world wars. It could be argued that, in their stark and utilitarian fashion, they are just as historically important as the finest of Edward I's great castles.

The land defences dating to the two world wars still respected features in the landscape. High ground around cities, for example, was either fortified, or was the site of anti-aircraft batteries and barrage balloons. The concept of a stop line was important to Britain's defence in 1940. It consisted of a natural feature, such as a stream, which could be reinforced with mines, barbed wire and pillboxes to form an obstacle capable of delaying an armoured advance. Stop lines followed rivers, canals, dykes and railways, all natural tank barriers. Steep valleys were incorporated as other natural tank traps. Use of such naturally defended features in the landscape meant that efforts could be concentrated on defending flat land and other vulnerable areas. We shall see shortly that when the concept of stop lines was replaced by the idea of strengthened 'nodal points' from 1941, geography and the lie of the land became even more significant, which is why it is instructive to understand the detailed planning that went into their fortification. When we examine these measures it soon becomes apparent that the military forward planning must also have involved local farmers, gamekeepers and others who had a detailed knowledge of particular landscapes.

During the early twentieth century defensive work was most concentrated around naval bases, like Portsmouth and Plymouth, where Palmerston Forts and other huge fortifications were improved and modernized. Many defensive sites of the First World War were subsequently reused in the Second and it is not generally appreciated now how seriously the threats posed by Zeppelin airships and heavy Gotha bombers were taken. By the end of the First World War some 400 anti-aircraft guns were in use, and not just in defence of London; by 1917 Tees and Tyne AA Command, for example, had anti-aircraft guns in forty-two different locations. Air defence was also provided by fighters, and by counter-attack with bombers, from no fewer than 400 airfields, by November 1918. These airfields had grass runways and they mainly survive in the landscape today as barrack buildings and hangars.

The reaction to the horrors of the the First World War saw a sudden and dramatic fall in the number of military airfields in Britain, so that by the early 1920s there were just twenty-seven. After 1938 grassed airfields began to be replaced by concrete runways for heavier aircraft. In the 1930s some fifty new military airfields were constructed, in the face of the growing threat posed by Hitler and the Third Reich.

Very early in the Second World War the British army had been driven out of mainland Europe, losing almost all of its equipment in the process. Thanks to a heroic rearguard action at Dunkirk, in May 1940, some 200,000 fighting troops were evacuated from France and these would subsequently help to form central mobile forces to defend Britain. The first wartime defence of Britain strategy was produced by the appropriately named general in command of Britain's land defences at the time, General Sir Edmund Ironside.

British strategists had seen how Nazi troops had simply bypassed the massively fortified Maginot Line as they entered France, and they determined not to repeat the mistake. So in May 1940 Ironside came up with a system of defence-in-depth which was only intended to delay the enemy for two to three weeks, long enough for the Royal Navy, still by far the largest fleet in Europe, to sail south from its base in Scapa Flow in the Orkneys and cut off the invader's supply chain. The delay would also allow the two remaining forces of regular soldiers with tanks, trucks and artillery that had been held in reserve (and not sent with the British Expeditionary Force to France) to be deployed at the right time and place. Two other factors would have been in Britain's favour: first, the initial invasion forces could not have been accompanied by heavy tanks or artillery and, secondly, it had been assumed by both German and British strategists that the invading forces would have had air superiority, which they had been denied following the Battle of Britain in the summer and autumn of 1940.

The most astonishing aspect of the defensive works that were undertaken on the ground, while the Battle of Britain was being waged overhead, was the speed and scale of the operation. The main defensive lines were finished by the end of 1940 and the entire system was substantially complete by the spring of 1941.[11] It has been estimated that during the war some 28,000 pillboxes were constructed, of which some 5,000 survive to this day.[12] These were intended to provide cover for a heavy machine gun, anti-tank gun or light field artillery. They

Fig. 14.2 The universal symbol of the Home Front during the Second World War was the polygonal pillbox. This eight-sided example was built near Kirkwall on Mainland Orkney and is most unusual in being made from concrete-filled sacks. This rough exterior would not have deflected incoming shells or bullets very effectively. Note the earth heaped on the roof to provide camouflage against aerial reconnaissance.

were often sited behind an existing or enlarged ditch or bank, which acted as the primary tank barrier that slowed or stopped the potential target.[13] At the start of the war there were about thirty airfields in Britain, and by 1945 almost 750. Perhaps the most remarkable statistic of all has huge implications for the landscape: by 1944 some 20 per cent of Britain's land surface was under some form of military control.[14]

Ironside's first line of defence was the so-called 'coastal crust' which was begun in May 1940. The coastal crust made extensive use of pre-existing First World War and Victorian defences, augmented with additional armaments, including a number of reused pre-war naval guns. The coastal crust also required the construction of many thousands of concrete anti-tank cubes, seaward-facing pillboxes, artillery emplacements, barbed-wire entanglements, minefields and a forest of scaffolding and other impediments to impede access across beaches.

Certain key areas, such as Spurn Head in East Yorkshire, were seen to be crucially important. The artillery and fortifications on Spurn Head controlled all shipping into the Humber, which had been used in Viking times to gain access to the Trent, and thence into the heart of the Midlands. Today Spurn Head boasts one of the finest collection of wartime and earlier defences in Britain. They include numerous pillboxes, a number of road blocks, two major forts and many anti-tank cubes.

Inland, Ironside's defences consisted of a series of stop lines, whose purpose was to stall the enemy, usually by making use of pre-existing

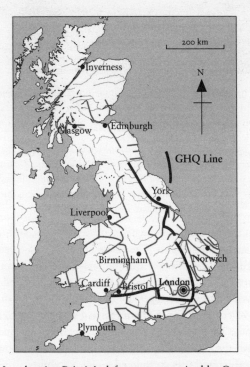

Fig. 14.3 Map showing Britain's defences as organized by General Edmund Ironside in the summer of 1940. The coast was protected by a 'coastal crust' (not shown here), with a series of 'stop lines' inland. Both coastal crust and stop lines were intended to be a system of defence-in-depth to delay, rather than halt, any invading forces.

Fig. 14.4 Following the retreat from Dunkirk in May 1940, most of Britain's coastline was defended as part of General Ironside's 'coastal crust'. This view shows an ex-naval gun mounted in a new emplacement built on the cliff top directly over the 1865 'Palmerston Fort', which protected access into Newhaven (East Sussex) harbour, from the English Channel.

features in the landscape, strengthened by pillboxes, anti-tank cubes, barbed wire and minefields. The most important of these defensive lines was the GHQ (General Headquarters) Line which ran from near Bristol eastwards, around London to the south and east and then north through Essex and Cambridgeshire to Lincolnshire and the Humber. It passed west of York and more or less in a straight line to Edinburgh and beyond. One interesting feature is a series of stop lines that ran north–south through Wales; this was because an invasion launched from neutral Ireland was considered a real possibility.

By the end of July 1940 Ironside was promoted and his replacement was General Brooke (later Lord Alanbrooke), who had served with the British Expeditionary Force in France, where he had learnt some painful lessons about the mobility of modern warfare. His assessment of

Ironside's defensive measures was not favourable. He realized that many of the fixed defences, such as the stop lines and particularly the numerous rows of anti-tank cubes, would actually impair his defending forces. Also by this time British factories had gone a long way towards replacing most of the armoured cars, tanks and trucks that had been abandoned in France. With the men rescued from Dunkirk, the two existing armoured forces, and the new equipment that was rapidly becoming available, he now possessed a highly capable and most importantly a mobile defensive army. This was supported by the formation of the Local Defence Volunteers, better known later as the Home Guard, in May 1940. These men included numerous veterans of the First World War and although poorly armed at first they would have been a formidable fighting force. It was they who manned numerous local defensive installations along the coast and inland. Their orders were to delay the advance of the enemy for as long as possible.[15] By 1943 the Home Guard consisted of some 2 million men.

Brooke's new strategy, which came into full effect in 1941, was immediately to abandon further work on the inland stop lines, especially in southern Britain. He had little faith in static structures and opted instead for a network of strengthened nodal points which could be held with relatively few men and protected by lighter defences. Very often the Home Guard was employed at these nodal points which were placed in strategically important locations, such as bridges over rivers. The idea was to provide continuous resistance to an advancing enemy and thereby buy time to employ defending forces in overwhelming numbers and at places chosen by the defenders, rather than the attackers – one of the principal objections to the stop-line strategy. These defensive measures have left less striking traces on the landscape, but many can still be seen in rural areas, especially in Wales.

Protecting cities, railways, airfields and ports against aerial bombardment was almost as important as counter-invasion defence. Various measures were employed, including decoy airfields and even fake cities, but these have left little impact on the ground. Airfield perimeter defences have left a bigger mark. The guns and machine guns were mounted in pillboxes and all were controlled and co-ordinated from a battle headquarters, usually positioned on the airfield perimeter. What makes most airfield defences remarkable is that the guns were trained on, and not away from, the airfield. This was because the biggest threat was believed to be from paratroops who would take the airfield and then use it to land further troops. This is what happened in the invasion of Norway, where troops landed at captured airfields then advanced to take a nearby port, to establish a bridgehead for the landing of further troops and supplies.

The need to remove any landmark that might be obvious from the air led to some strange incidents. For instance, there was a fear that the Cerne Abbas Giant and the Uffington White Horse Hill figures could have been used as navigation aids by German bomber pilots, so both were concealed beneath a camouflage of turf, hedge trimmings and box plants, all held down by wire netting, for the duration of the war. The camouflage of the Uffington Horse was so effective that it suffered slight damage when it was driven over by a tank on military manoeuvres in 1943!

Fig. 14.5 Heavy anti-aircraft battery at St Margaret's-at-Cliffe, near Dover, Kent. The anti-aircraft gun would have been mounted at the centre of this circular arrangement of slab-built concrete ammunition lockers. In the background is the battery command and communication centre. Heavy anti-aircraft batteries were established along the south coast to protect London from bombers and later from V1 flying bombs launched in Holland and France.

Anti-aircraft batteries (usually 3.7-inch calibre) have left substantial traces in the landscape, as each gun required a thick concrete base, protected ammunition dumps and substantial semi-subterranean command buildings. The heavy anti-aircraft batteries were initially mainly sited along the southern approaches to London, but many more were moved, during Operation Diver, both south and east into Essex and Kent, between June 1944 and March 1945, to combat the threat posed by V1 flying bombs. Most of these new heavy anti-aircraft gun emplacements were on permanent sites, like some examples which still survive around Dover, but a few were able to use newly introduced mobile heavy anti-aircraft artillery.

LANDSCAPES OF DEFENCE: THE COLD WAR

The defences of Britain in the Second World War were the last manifestation of the type of conventional military planning whose roots lay ultimately in the hillforts of the Iron Age. From the late 1940s onwards Britain entered another era, where detailed planning of this sort was unnecessary. In the Cold War the concept of Mutually Assured Destruction meant that stop lines, the lie of the land and 'nodal points' were irrelevant; instead, all thought was about retaliation – and the survival of civil governance. Seen from a military perspective landscape had largely become irrelevant.

The onset of the Cold War saw the arrival of a new era of 'total' nuclear warfare. Some excellent studies of the period have recently become available and they list in great detail the new buildings, massively strengthened bunkers and other improvements to pre-existing Second World War airfields that were needed to bring them into the nuclear age.[16] Civilian measures included the construction of regional centres of government and a network of Royal Observer Corps underground observation posts. By and large, however, these measures have not had a major impact on the day-to-day landscape, largely because many of the new structures were either below ground or semi-subterranean. There was one major exception to this rule, which emerged when it was realized that nuclear explosions caused a massive

Fig. 14.6 A microwave relay station tower at Newton, in the flat landscape of the Cambridgeshire Fens, near Wisbech. This tower is unusual because two of its original (early 1960s) horn-shaped aerials are still in place. One of these large aerials can be seen close to the top of the tower; the later aerials are mostly circular, dish-shaped. Horn-shaped aerials were considered unsightly and were difficult to mount on the outside of a tower, so the early relay towers were built in a stepped pattern, to allow the aerials to be fixed in the steps. This tower has two sloping steps, but only has horn-shaped aerials on the upper step.

Electromagnetic Pulse, or EMP.[17] EMP had the same effect as a direct lightning hit, destroying all telecommunications. Experiments showed that the optimum EMP could be achieved by an air-burst nuclear explosion of one megaton, at 30,000 metres over the North Sea. This one bomb could effectively destroy all above-ground telecommunications systems of northern Europe.

Various measures were employed to combat the threat posed by EMP, including the burial of important telephone lines deep below ground, but these still had vulnerable points, especially when they came to the surface. It was the continuing vulnerability of the telecommunication system, even after large parts had been buried, that led to the development of a network of less vulnerable microwave communications, known initially as Backbone. The basic technology for microwave broadcast had been developed at Birmingham University in the early 1950s. The microwave tower transmitters and receivers of the Backbone network had to be within sight of each other, which is why they were located in extremely prominent places and have made such a big impact on the landscape. Most are still in use for civilian purposes and include some notable structures, the best known of which is undoubtedly the Post Office Tower in central London, built to designs by Eric Bedford, Chief Architect of the Ministry of Works, in 1961.[18] By the 1980s the original Backbone network had grown to cover all of Britain. There are, of course, many other relics of the Cold War, some of which, like the tall strategic grain silos, are still in use, often now festooned with the dish aerials of mobile phone networks.[19]

THE FRONT LINE OF FREEDOM

On 14 October 1940, in a speech to the National Farmers' Union, Winston Churchill declared that 'today the farms of Britain are the front line of freedom'.[20] It was fighting talk, but, given the threat posed to food imports by the growing success of German U-boats in the Atlantic, it would have had more than a ring of truth for his audience. Today we seem to have forgotten just how important the war years were to the development of modern farming in Britain. Farm output grew more rapidly between 1945 and 1965 than in any other period

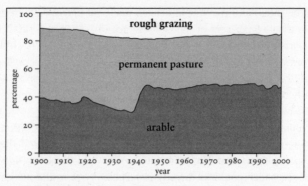

Fig. 14.7 Graph showing the changing proportion of rough grazing, permanent pasture and arable in Britain during the twentieth century. Note the sudden steep rise in arable land during the Second World War and the fact that the graph remains high thereafter, which would indicate that this had been a permanent and significant change in land use.

of the twentieth century; this was a direct result of the changes that were made in the war years. Indeed, I would argue that Britain's only 'real' agricultural revolution took place in the Second World War.[21]

During the war the switch from pasture to arable was strongly encouraged by central government, working through a network of local committees and advisory bodies, but unlike previous major changes in British agriculture there was no reorganization of land tenure, nor were there significant changes in crops grown or livestock breeds.[22] Even so the transformation was quite extraordinary. During the First World War there had been a concerted drive to increase farm output, which had achieved a fair measure of success, but, as with the Napoleonic Wars, this was followed by a long period of economic stagnation and decline. So there was still a long way to go if Britain was actually to feed itself after the start of hostilities in 1939. During this first year of the war there were actually 200,000 fewer hectares of arable land than in 1914; pasture was also in a far worse state, and there were about 25 per cent fewer farm workers on the land.

The bare facts speak for themselves. Between 1939 and 1945 the arable area increased by 63 per cent in England and Wales (land to wheat by 82 per cent, barley 89 per cent and potatoes 116 per cent). These changes took place against some stiff competition for resources from the forces and the War Office. To make matters worse, by 1944 no less than 20 per cent of the land surface of Britain was given over to the armed forces and much of the flatter land used to site airfields, for example, was of the best quality. Levels of output were boosted by the use of artificial fertilizers and large numbers of tractors, which actually trebled between 1939 and 1942, largely thanks to lend-lease arrangements with America.

One unfortunate outcome of the wartime agricultural revolution was a different attitude to food production, which disregarded the environment almost completely. Farming was seen as a business and one, moreover, which could be directly influenced by central government. During the war the income of farmers rose, but the real changes happened in the early years of peace, when world food shortages ensured that commodity prices rose steadily. The result was that farmers' incomes more than doubled between 1953 and 1973.

The practical effects of this prosperity on the countryside came in the form of a rather brutal 'rationalization', whereby solitary trees and small copses vanished, streams were straightened and hedges disappeared at an extraordinary rate. From an aesthetic point of view matters were only made worse by the introduction of the large grants that were made available by the Common Agricultural Policy, following Britain's entry into the European Community in 1973. I recall carrying out archaeological surveys in the Fens in the early 1980s. At the time huge areas of potentially waterlogged archaeological sites were under threat from wholesale land drainage, as it was the stated aim of the Ministry of Agriculture to produce arable land that had the soil drainage characteristics of chalk downland. So at less than 2 metres above sea level, the rapidly drying peats of Fenland were transected by many deep land drains – doubtless inserted with the help of some profitable drainage contracts. With hindsight, the 1970s and 1980s will be seen as an era of Low rather than High Farming.

FARMING IN THE POST-WAR DECADES

Farmers soon discovered that the newer and larger machines that became available during and after the war worked better in big fields, where fewer turns had to be made at the end of each row. The introduction of ever-larger crop sprayers in the post-war decades gave farmers an incentive to regularize the internal organization of their farms: wedge-shaped fields, for example, were difficult to spray without leaving bare patches. The first concrete farm roads and yards began to appear in the 1960s. Increasingly, trees and shrubs were cut down within the turning circle of the sprayer's arms. From the 1950s improvements in arable techniques, such as the introduction of 'tram line' spraying added further impetus to such landscape changes and also hastened the process of soil degradation through compaction.

The transformation of farm productivity brought about through mechanical improvements, pesticides and ever-increasing levels of artificial fertilizer application has meant that even the largest buildings constructed during the years of High Farming have proved inadequate to house the cereals and some of the new crops (such as rape, maize and linseed), grown by modern European farmers. Many fine Victorian buildings now stand idle, or are used as occasional stores for fuel or equipment; they are dwarfed by their vast steel-clad replacements, mostly built in the 1980s and 1990s, when planning permission for new, and often rather garish, farm buildings was easy to obtain.

Towards the latter part of the twentieth century the increasing use of contractors made many larger barns and other farm buildings redundant. If these were attractive brick or stone-built buildings, and lay within commutable distance of cities, they could be converted into homes, offices and workshops for light industry. Many farmers and landowners found such conversion a profitable source of income, independent of government or the fluctuations of commodity markets. Smaller farmers in the largely pastoral counties of the north and west, however, found it much harder to adapt their redundant buildings and many in the early years of the twenty-first century have been forced to sell up, as the livestock industry faced successive crises from waves of disease and the fluctuating price of animal feeds. The result, as any traveller through rural areas of counties like Shropshire and Worcestershire can see today, is small farm after small farm where attractive brick-built stockyards are deserted and collapsing.

Although modern, steel-clad farm buildings and vegetable-packing houses can be very intrusive in undulating and small-scale landscapes, they do have a certain grandeur in the flat, treeless, agri-business countryside of Lincolnshire and parts of East Anglia. Like the Italianate buildings of Victorian High Farming, they proclaim confidence and prosperity. Many in Britain have learnt to appreciate wartime aircraft hangars, and one day the industrial agricultural buildings of the late twentieth century may be seen for what they were: a brave attempt to keep Britain farming in the face of massive competition from abroad. The net result of these changes is that in 2007 some 80 per cent of the landscape of England was given over to farming, yet just 2 per cent of the population worked on the land.[23]

Taken together, these various factors can be seen to have caused a genuine post-industrial agricultural revolution in the landscape of Britain and most especially that of eastern Britain. In Suffolk, for example, the dairying industry of the claylands has largely vanished, replaced by arable. The speed of the transformation has been truly revolutionary, especially after 1973. The changes have undoubtedly had some adverse effects, of which by far the most important has been the reduction, verging on the elimination, of regional distinctiveness. Many lowland arable landscapes of the early twenty-first century have a horrible homogeneity. The damage to biodiversity is now widely acknowledged, but this should hardly be surprising if one bears in mind that some 400,000 kilometres of hedgerow have been destroyed since 1950. This is massively more than in the era of Victorian High Farming, the other period of agricultural industrial expansion, when some 112,000 kilometres of field boundaries (often hedges) were removed.[24]

ACCESS TO THE COUNTRYSIDE

Apart from farming, rural landscapes in Britain have witnessed some important developments, such as the construction of motorways and bypasses and the development of housing and industry that has followed in their wake. Huge areas of the lowlands have been mined away for sand and gravel. One might be forgiven for thinking that these have all been changes for the worse, but it is not that simple. Take, for example, the case of reservoirs.

It is generally supposed that the creation of these huge artificial lakes was one of the few positive developments in the landscape of the twentieth century.[25] In some respects they have been beneficial to the appearance of the landscape (because water, any water, is usually attractive), even though in many instances their initial creation has given rise to lasting ill-feeling in the locality. As the great industrial towns and cities of Victorian Britain grew, so did their demands for water, both for drinking and for industry itself. Initially the demand was met locally, by whatever means, but by the late nineteenth century it was apparent that an assured and clean supply of water was needed. In 1879 an Act of Parliament was passed which specified that a proposed reservoir at Thirlmere in the Lake District should be the principal source of water for Manchester. Construction started at the beginning of the twentieth century and involved the construction of a 34.8-metre-high dam and involved the swamping of three small lakes and the village of Wyborn. The eventual reservoir was 5.6 kilometres long.

Most of the reservoirs were located in north Wales and along the western side of upland Britain, where the rainfall was heaviest and suitable steep-sided valleys occurred. In some instances reservoir construction went too far, transforming the landscape. A classic example is in the remote Dark Peak area, sometimes known as the 'Peakland Lake District', in the upper valley of the Derwent, in Yorkshire. A series of three large reservoirs were constructed early in the twentieth century, following the establishment of the Derwent Valley Water Board, specifically to supply Derby, Nottingham, Sheffield and Leicester. The first of these large reservoirs included Howden Reservoir (1912) and Derwent Reservoir (1916), and these involved the flooding of valleys and several small villages, hamlets and isolated farmsteads. The last of the three, Ladybower Reservoir, was completed in 1945 after ten years of construction that involved the exhumation of the graveyards of the village churches of Ashopton and Derwent, both of which were to be flooded; the bodies were reburied in a special extension to Bamford churchyard.

Some reservoirs involved the further flooding of pre-existing lakes, such as Haweswater in Cumbria, which was drowned when a new dam was built to provide even more water for Manchester in 1929. This involved flooding the village of Mardale, with its school, inn, church and four farms. Many of these early reservoirs were then planted

Fig. 14.8 Part of Kielder Reservoir, Northumberland. This is the largest man-made body of freshwater in western Europe, supplying Northumberland, Tyne and Wear, and Durham. It was completed in 1982 and its construction involved the flooding of large areas of good farmland in the upper North Tyne.

with intensive woodland of spruce and larch, but more recent examples, such as the largest reservoir in western Europe at Kielder, in Northumberland, originally constructed to supply a steelworks that was never built, were laid out with recreation in mind from the very outset. The size of Kielder Reservoir is staggering: it covers 595 square kilometres and has a shoreline extending for almost 48 kilometres.

I was personally involved in archaeological work associated with the creation of Rutland Water, near Oakham, which opened in 1977 and today is the largest reservoir in the east Midlands. Our task was to find ancient wells, because once the area had been flooded the sheer pressure of overlying water would cause the wells to act in reverse and drain water back into the underlying aquifers. So they had to be found and then filled and capped off. When viewed today it seems permanent and it is hard to imagine that the vast expanse of water is both recent and entirely man-made, with all its 124,000,000 cubic metres of water pumped in from the nearby River Nene. As climate change begins to gather pace and water shortages become more frequent we are likely to see many more large reservoirs created in the British landscape.

The spectacular landscapes of the hills and fells around the major industrial cities of northern England provided working people with a welcome retreat from the often cramped and overcrowded conditions in which they had to live. These landscapes were important because they gave people a chance to expand their horizons and breathe freely. Ultimately, it was a matter of liberation of mind and body; it was about far more than mere aesthetics and enjoyment of the picturesque. That is why the movement to obtain the freedom of the hills was so essential to so many people; it also explains why this particular freedom fight was prosecuted with such vigour.[26]

The enjoyment of the hills began with rock climbing, the origin of which is sometimes credited to the poet Coleridge's famous ascent of Broad Strand on Scafell, Cumbria, in 1802. It soon became a popular pastime of both of locals and visitors to the region. Soon informal rock-climbing clubs emerged and through time these grew. Eventually, in 1906, this led to the foundation of the Fell and Rock Climbing Club whose well-to-do members purchased the summit of Great Gable and some 1,200 hectares of mountain moorland around it. This was given to the National Trust in 1923, as a tribute to club members who had died in the First World War. While some climbed, others dived deep into the ground following the underground caves that are such a feature of the limestone uplands of the old West Riding of Yorkshire.

Potholing, as it was known, first became popular in the 1840s when caves around Settle and Chapel-le-Dale in the Yorkshire Dales were explored by local men; this was a grim landscape in winter, later to become notorious during the construction of the Settle to Carlisle railway (pp. 521–2). The sport grew in popularity and in 1892 the Yorkshire Ramblers Club (which in those days was largely given over to potholing) was founded. Other clubs then came into existence, but the sport grew rapidly in popularity only from about 1930. Meanwhile throughout the nineteenth century Lancashire mill-workers had relaxed in the local upland landscapes in a less formal or structured fashion. Generally speaking, such 'rambles' were enjoyed by groups of people who organized themselves into clubs for the purpose. Often these organizations were motivated by ideas of socialism and/or Nonconformist Christianity, and many of the rambles also included educational elements, such as botany and natural history.

Much of the uplands and moors around the great industrial cities of the north-west had been given over to grouse-shooting since the mid-nineteenth century (p. 498). These moors were guarded by gamekeepers anxious to provide their employers with plentiful game, if only to retain their jobs at a time of relatively high rural unemployment. There was also a clash of wills between the landowners and the urban workforce who were becoming increasingly politically aware thanks to better education and the increasing popularity of the socialist movement. The result was a series of prolonged clashes and arguments over access to the Pennines and Lakeland fells.

One of the earliest disputes began in 1878, when five men were prosecuted for trespass over moorland behind Darwen, near Blackburn, in Lancashire. The row was not finally resolved until 1896, when the corporation took over the land and granted open access. There were numerous relatively polite disputes in Lakeland prior to the First World War; but after it popular politics became more militant. The result was a rapid increase in the 1920s and early 1930s of politically inspired rambles, as people sought the freedom to take walks in the open countryside around the great cities where they worked.

The Youth Hostel Association grew from the organized rambling tradition and played an important part in opening up the hills to a wider public: in 1931 there were 71 YHA hostels; five years later there were 260. The newly energized rambling movement culminated in the famous Kinder Scout 'mass trespass' of 1932, when a large group of Manchester ramblers confronted gamekeepers. It was a highly politicized occasion: Mancunian ramblers affiliated to the British Workers' Sports Federation, under their leader Benny Rothman, sang 'The Red Flag' and the 'Internationale', as they walked towards a group of gamekeepers and temporary wardens in the moor.[27] 'The pushing and shoving that followed saw only a few open fights; and then they left.'[28] When they returned to the nearby village of Hayfield five supposed ringleaders were arrested and were later given sentences ranging from two to six months. This and other actions led directly to the foundation of the Ramblers Association in 1935. Today the hill of Kinder Scout is a part of the Peak District National Park and access to it is unlimited.[29]

By the late eighteenth century the creation of idyllic rural parks and landscapes had become a thriving art form in Britain. The continuance of an essentially aesthetic tradition of landscape appreciation was greatly enhanced at the turn of the twentieth century by the growing realization that certain landscapes were also important for their wildlife value, as writers like Gilbert White and later Charles Darwin himself had made so clear. Such a convergence of art and science ultimately led to the foundation, in 1895, of the National Trust for Places of Historic Interest and Natural Beauty, a body which perhaps still reflects its worthy middle-class origins, but which (with nearly 3.5 million members) has undoubtedly done more to preserve Britain's landscape than any other single organization.

We have seen (pp. 500ff.) that the natural beauty of the Lake District, initially celebrated by the circle surrounding Wordsworth, was at first enjoyed and appreciated mainly by middle-class, educated people. But its appeal was soon to transcend social boundaries. With the opening up of the landscape brought about by the railways, from the 1850s and the rise of coach or charabanc tours in the early twentieth century, the Lake District became accessible to the growing populations of cities like Manchester and Liverpool. In the twentieth century the principal railway company serving the area, the London Midland and Scottish Railway, described the delights of the Lakes in leaflets aimed at visitors from the United States and Canada:

Here you are on the edge of a country – a famous and beautiful country – which has given a school of poetry to England and to which crowds of visitors come every year, where Wordsworth lived and died and where all at one time Southey, Coleridge, De Quincey, Arnold of Rugby, his son Matthew Arnold, and Miss Martineau lived and worked, drawing their inspiration from the quiet beauty of the mountains and the buildings that England has not let die.[30]

Today this leaflet would probably be well over the heads of many students of English literature, let alone casual tourists from the other side of the Atlantic.

From the 1930s discussions were taking place about the creation of a Lake District National Park, but these were delayed by numerous disputes over its precise boundaries. Then the war intervened and it was not until 1951 that the National Park Authority actually came into existence. A major part of the Lake District is undoubtedly the large National Trust estate which came into being due to the efforts of the celebrated children's author and conservationist, Beatrix Potter.[31] Thanks to her generosity, large areas of the Lakes were saved for the National Trust and the region became the first to demonstrate the economic benefits of what today we would call sustainable tourism.

GARDENS IN THE
TWENTIETH CENTURY

It was only in the post-war decades that planning became an accepted part of daily life for most people. Certain groups, farmers for example, could still get away with aesthetic murder erecting vast asbestos-clad buildings, dwarfing the brick-built yards of their High Farming estates, but ordinary people needed planning permission to erect a garage for the new car, or even a porch over the front door. Some of these restrictions were undoubtedly heavy-handed, but as prosperity increased some control needed to be exercised over the appearance of Britain's towns and villages, especially around their historic cores where the installation of early double glazing, for example, sometimes ruined the appearance of fine Georgian houses. One area where the hand of the planner did not extend was into people's gardens. So these became the new arena where people could express their individuality. Gardening rapidly became immensely popular.

After the war a gardener's requirements were met by numerous small nurseries, and plants came from a restricted range that had changed little since the 1920s and 1930s. One seemingly minor innovation was to change all that and have a considerable effect on the landscape, in the form of garden centres. In the early 1960s the appearance of plastic flowerpots made it possible to sell container-grown plants all year round.[32] Nurseries where large numbers of container-grown plants were sold were soon transformed into garden centres and rapidly proliferated across almost every city, town and village in Britain. But there were subtle changes afoot. In the early twentieth century, for example, one could readily buy specimens of giant pampas grasses, large bamboos and plants for herbaceous borders that grew to great heights (one of my favourites is the relative of the sunflower *Helianthus salicifolius*). After the war the new garden centres offered rather different plants for sale. Many of their labels included the Latin word *compacta* or *nana*, referring to compact or dwarf forms. This reflected the fact that gardens were proliferating and becoming smaller; gardening was no longer a pastime of the more wealthy middle classes alone; it had become democratized and to an extent classless.

The gardens of Britain in the late twentieth century played an important role in maintaining biodiversity. Out in the countryside intensive farming was destroying habitats, so many species of birds and insects found refuge in the flourishing gardens of suburbia. At the start of the century, innovative garden design was still confined to the larger city parks and the gardens of the wealthy. In the late nineteenth century there had been a reaction to the labour-intensive High Victorian style of gardening, in which exotic plants were moved from large heated greenhouses to formal bedded borders where they made a magnificent display for a few months.

Gertrude Jekyll, perhaps the greatest British gardener of the twentieth century, began life as an artist, and she put her sense of colour to good use when she took up gardening. The gardens designed by Jekyll use principles of informality and simplicity.[33] She had a high regard for traditional cottage gardens and used many of their themes in her own designs. She paid close attention to detail, not just in her gardens, but in the hard landscaping – for example, the gates, furniture, walls, even the bricks and tiles – that accompanied it. She is best known for her collaborative work with the principal architect of the time, Sir Edwin Lutyens (1869–1944). After the First World War Lutyens became imperial architect to the War Graves Commission and the planting he specified around many cemeteries and war memorials shows the clear influence of Gertrude Jekyll.

Since the war there has been an explosion in the number of different gardening styles. Most reflect the two facts that British gardens are becoming smaller and British gardeners have less time in which to garden. There is also a tendency to keep modern gardens too tidy, with the result that the peace of late summer and autumn weekends is shattered by the incessant din of entirely unnecessary high-powered leaf-blowers. Scythes and sickles, too, have been forsaken in favour of strimmers, whose rapidly revolving nylon lines, powered by screaming two-stroke engines, effectively remove the bark from young trees and shrubs – a form of damage, leading to lingering death, now widely acknowledged as 'Strimmer Blight'. Despite such irritations, contemporary British gardens, both rural and urban, continue to delight. I regard them as quite simply the finest in the world. A walk down any suburban street in springtime, for example, will reveal a superb display of magnolias unmatched even in China, one of the plant's native habitats.

NEW TYPES OF INDUSTRIAL LANDSCAPES

Britain in the twenty-first century is a service economy. Apart from a scattering of oil refineries, chemical works and car assembly plants, there are remarkably few large factories when compared to the first half of the last century. The second half saw the demolition of thousands of factories and the rise of new industrial landscapes in which massive opencast pits were excavated to extract various raw materials, such as coal, brick- and china-clay, iron ore and gravel. It is debatable whether extractive industries caused more destruction to the landscape in the nineteenth or the twentieth century. During the nineteenth the scale of mining was very much smaller, but few efforts were made to reinstate the land or to conceal the ever-growing heaps of slag and waste which disfigured the countryside. On the whole, I incline to favour the twentieth century, simply because the scale of extraction was so vast. So vast, in fact, that the extent of these scars in the landscape is best appreciated from the air. So many old gravel pits have become (usually through neglect, but increasingly by design) seemingly natural ponds and lakes; while clay pits are either flooded, or are filled with millions of tonnes of household waste in the form of 'landfill'. When I see the flickering blue flames of methane collected from deep within newly capped landfill sites I still find them somehow symbolic of our times. But whether those flames signify Hope for the Future, or the Fires of Hell, I would not like to say.

Given the damp climate, it is not surprising that people in Britain have always been able to find uses for gravel. Excavating the floors of Iron Age roundhouses at Fengate, in Peterborough, we found they had regularly been dusted with thin spreads of clean gravel. Rather later we found more sand and gravel scattered across the slippery planks of wood that formed the Bronze Age walkway at Flag Fen, and in 1973 we came across a large pit filled with rubbish tipped in from the side. The pit had been dug in the later Bronze Age and, to prove that people had climbed in and out of it at regular intervals – presumably whenever they needed a bucket of gravel – we found the notched-log ladder that they used, still upright on the bottom. That was then Britain's earliest ladder; subsequently my wife Maisie, who specializes in ancient wood-working, tells me she has seen nearly two dozen more, most of them from prehistoric wells or gravel holes.

Like my Bronze Age pit, gravel was generally extracted from hand-dug holes near where it was needed. Indeed, most medieval sites in London have produced evidence for gravel-digging.[34] After the First World War the pace of gravel extraction increased rapidly and this was largely due to the need for ballast used in road- and house-building. From late Victorian times concrete had been becoming a more important building material and by the 1930s it was to be seen everywhere. In fact it became something of a symbol of 'modernity' featuring prominently in Hitler's new autobahn system. By now, hand-digging had of course given way to mechanical extraction.

Most of the lowland river valleys of Britain contain deposits of gravel, usually laid down during the Ice Ages. By no means all of them are worth the time and expense of digging, but there are, nonetheless, some substantial deposits. The trouble is that these are also the areas where people have settled and built towns, partly due to the fact that, away from the actual floodplains, the land is very well drained. The sheer density of past human settlement on the gravel terraces only became fully apparent in 1960 when a complete survey of the English gravels was reported under the appropriate title of *A Matter of Time*. This showed that by far and away the largest reserves of gravel in England were to be found in the Thames Valley, mostly upstream of London. The survey's authors reckoned that the Thames gravels stretched for about 200 kilometres, at an average width of 8 kilometres; the next largest river deposits were those of the Trent (105 × 5 kilometres) and Severn (98 × 3 kilometres).

Gravel-digging along the Thames has taken place on a truly vast scale. Having spent much of my life working on ancient sites in gravel quarries I have made many visits to the Thames gravels and every time I go there I am amazed by their sheer scale. But nothing prepares one for the vast expanses of water that today cover the 8 kilometres between Heathrow and the Thames, to the south. They are best seen from an aeroplane, but when they are mapped it is clear that by no means all were originally intended as gravel quarries. Certainly some were, but many were dug as reservoirs, largely because the landowners had no hope of selling off their land for building, given the noise from the nearby airport. The result has been described as a 'no-man's-land of water, motorways and industrial estates'.[35]

Today sources of gravel are being used that would never have been touched forty years ago. Some are getting very close to historic monuments, such as the Thornborough Rings, a group of Bronze Age henges in Yorkshire, and other sensitive areas such as the natural Fen 'island' of Thorney in Cambridgeshire with its fine abbey and monastic remains. As the sources of gravel become more scarce they also become thinner in the ground and the pits dug to extract them proportionately larger. From about the 1970s planning requirements stipulated that disused gravel pits could not just be abandoned with plant and machinery rusting within their waters. Old workings now have to be landscaped and reinstated, either as recreational lakes, or as nature reserves; sometimes they are reinstated at a lower level and then farmed, but one has to wonder whether this practice will ultimately prove sustainable since in most low-lying areas large pumps have to be run continuously, even in the driest of summers, to prevent these sunken fields from flooding instantly.

Gravel was of course not the only material to be extracted from the ground for industry. We saw in the last chapter that china clay continues to be extracted in large quantities in Cornwall, although today it is used more in the paper industry, as a finishing material, than for making china. A very different type of clay has also had to be extracted in industrial quantities to make the bricks from which London and most of the cities in south-eastern Britain are built. These brickworks made use of a special carbon-rich source of clay which catches fire when heated in a kiln. It is a process that has left behind some vast and (unlike gravel) very deep pits in Bedfordshire and around Peterborough where they are known locally as 'knot-holes'. A knot-hole near Fletton was reputedly the largest man-made hole in Europe.

POWERING BRITAIN IN THE TWENTIETH CENTURY

For the first half of the twentieth century coal still provided the main driving force for British industry, whether used directly to fuel boilers in factories or to fire the power stations that provided the nation with its electricity. Vast tonnages of coal were also used to run the steam locomotives that the railways depended on until the 1960s. The coaling towers that fed the locomotives' tenders were a characteristic feature of the skylines of most railway towns and cities.

During the course of the twentieth century the role of coal changed profoundly, but little remains in the landscape to remind us of Britain's coal-mining past, apart from one or two preserved mines and remod-elled slag heaps. During the 1970s large numbers of coal mines were being closed down, a process which eventually precipitated the national miners' strike of 1984–5. After the defeat of the strike, mine closures continued apace and today coal is mined in huge opencast pits; the landscape is then reinstated, afterwards. The last deep mine in south Wales, the Tower Colliery, ceased operations in January 2008.

One of the best-preserved nineteenth- and twentieth-century indus-trial landscapes is that around the town of Blaenavon, in the south Wales coalfield. The coal measures at Blaenavon are interspersed with ironstone, which was worked in medieval times. The hills surrounding the town are extraordinarily rich in industrial remains which is why

Fig. 14.9 Two rows of terraced workers' cottages near Blaenavon, Torfaen, south Wales. These cottages, probably built in the late nineteenth or early twentieth century are directly downslope of some large colliery spoil heaps, with further pit workings in the background.

the area was designated a UNESCO World Heritage Site in 2000. Special efforts are being made to preserve the landscape without, for example, bulldozing spoil heaps which instead are planted to encourage a restraining 'crust' of roots, soil and vegetation to develop. Any visitor to the area is at once struck by the ubiquity of the spoil heaps throughout the landscape. Indeed in certain places they *are* the landscape. Many were positioned close by housing.

As a general rule the arrangement of late Victorian and Edwardian miners' housing improved through time. But not always. The Bolsover Company, for example, built many tied houses. One of its earlier estates was built close to Bolsover Castle in 1890 and consisted of 190 houses arranged around a three-sided square with good access to a central park, allotment gardens and playing fields. Today these houses are still used, although of course adapted to modern standards. Fifteen years later, in 1905, the housing the Bolsover Company built for its miners at the new Crown Farm colliery near Mansfield crammed 324 houses into nine rows of eighteen, arranged around a narrow central access;

admittedly there were allotments and recreation grounds nearby, but the housing itself must have been depressing in the extreme.

Coal still provides fuel for many British power stations which are close by the few surviving pits. Many are in the Trent Valley of Nottinghamshire, where their huge, convex-sided condensing towers still dominate the landscape for miles around. Until recent measures were taken to clean up emissions from their chimneys, these power stations were responsible for much of the acid rain which destroyed so many square kilometres of Scandinavian woodland. The problem can be said to have begun with the Electricity Supply Act of 1919, which established a national grid and led very quickly to a rash of pylons, often positioned in the most inappropriate places. The earlier

Fig. 14.10 Sutton Bridge gas-fired power station (*right*), viewed from across the River Nene, in Lincolnshire, on a strong ebb-tide. In the late twentieth century the 'dash for gas' led to the construction of many new power stations along the east coast of England and Scotland. The two gas turbines of this power station, completed in May 1999 at a cost of £337 million, are capable of generating 790 megawatts of power. This is approximately 2 per cent of the total electricity needed in England and Wales. The course of the River Nene in the foreground is entirely artificial; it was opened in 1832 and was based on designs by Rennie and Telford for the Nene outfall east of Wisbech.

pylons were much smaller than those of today, and there were many more of them, but whether their visual intrusion has lessened is another question altogether: in the 1970s it was fashionable for newspapers to run articles on 'Birdcage Britain', and since then public opposition seems to be rather less vocal, although I find the suggestion that pylons have served to liven up and add interest to the dreary grain plains of eastern England rather hard to accept.[36]

In the latter part of the twentieth century alternative sources of energy to coal and hydroelectric power became available. Of these, North Sea gas has probably had the greatest impact on the landscape. There are still relatively few nuclear power stations, but the east coast of England and Scotland is now peppered with gas-powered stations at regular intervals, usually close by the landfall of undersea pipelines: from my house near the Wash, I can see the vapour columns of four (Sutton Bridge, King's Lynn, Spalding and Peterborough). Although some people find them obtrusive, others, like myself, find that, like windfarms, they can fit quite well into a visually robust and open landscape. Most have been constructed with a designed life of less than fifty years, so they are unlikely to be a lasting influence on skylines in the later twenty-first century.

Atomic energy has recently returned to favour as a low-carbon method of generating electricity. The original nuclear power stations were erected in the later 1950s, following a government decision in 1955.[37] The first to be built was at Calder Hall, in Cumbria, alongside the first nuclear reactor at Windscale, which had played a major part in the development of Britain's atomic bombs. Following a disastrous, and nearly catastrophic fire, in 1957 the air-cooled reactor pile was closed down and permanently quarantined. One might suppose that high-tech facilities such as nuclear power stations would have been located on greenfield sites miles from anywhere. But as so often happens in the landscape, history played its part too. Sellafield, as Calder Hall and Windscale later became rebranded, had originally been a TNT factory during the war and, although it was placed in a remote spot, like many of the wartime and Cold War ammunition dumps around it, it was quite well served by road and rail. Today Sellafield is a vast industrial complex which sits rather incongruously in the west Cumbrian coastal plain.

Fig. 14.11 The Sellafield nuclear industrial complex. This vast centre of nuclear technology, which includes a power station and waste reprocessing plant began life as a wartime TNT factory, hence its remote location on the Cumbrian coast. It has good road and rail links and is by far the largest installation of its type in Britain.

LIVING IN A CROWDED ISLAND: THE ROLE OF TOWN AND COUNTRY PLANNING

At the start of this chapter I stated that planning controls were the main reason that the cities, towns and suburbs had not completely covered the landscape of Britain. I should also have added that it is planning that allows people to live in comfort at some distance from their place of work, free from atmospheric and noise pollution. It was realized in the later nineteenth century that building and planning controls were needed in towns, but the rural landscape had not yet become so crowded that it was felt to be under threat. That was to happen very much later, in the inter-war years, when the countryside around London became covered with uncontrolled residential developments. This was also the time that the construction of the first new arterial roads gave rise to the phenomenon of ribbon development, which was quite promptly dealt with by the Restriction of Ribbon Development Act (1935). The end-result of a steadily expanding economy has been a battery of planning laws and Guidance Notes and the rise of an entirely new profession, the Town and Country Planner.

I have no intention of attempting a history of town planning in a few paragraphs, as my work takes me to many local authority Planning Departments and nobody likes to be an object of ridicule. With that proviso, I must offer an outline. I was struck as I looked into it by the number of new Planning Acts and amendments that have passed through Parliament. If anything does, this surely shows how important MPs and their voters, too, consider the subject. Indeed, as I write, the government are in the process of producing a major reform of planning law. I do hope they get it right.

The first Planning Act was the Town Planning Act (1909), which allowed local authorities to prepare town-planning schemes.[38] Birmingham was one of the first to take advantage of this, with the creation in 1913 of the Quinton, Harborne and Edgbaston scheme which joined the suburb of Edgbaston to two of its outlying villages with a series of new roads; it created new parks and open spaces and stipulated that housing density should be no more than twenty an acre (0.4 hectare). The explosion of new 'bungalow towns' that had taken place in the 1920s was dealt with by another Town Planning Act, in 1923, which allowed rural district councils to prepare planning schemes which preserved 'natural beauty' – by limiting the building of bungalows.

There have been a series of Town and Country Planning Acts. The first, in 1932, was rather toothless and failed to control the biggest planning problem at the time: the uncontrolled building of factories, a problem, however, that was soon addressed by the impact of the Depression. These failures did result in a form of inner-city blight which caused many people to move away from the industrial centre out into the suburbs; it also caused a general drift of population away from the declining cities of the industrial north, to the south and east.

The Act of 1947 addressed the problems likely to be caused by post-war expansion. This time the Act had sharper teeth and was more successful. Like the first Town Planning Act it encouraged local authorities to draw up plans, which many places did. Most of these plans had elements in common, such as ring roads to protect town centres and the first pedestrianized shopping areas. By this time, too, local authorities were aware of the problems caused by ribbon development, and the new plans confined housing more closely to the area of the town, rather than the countryside around it. Another post-war problem had been the wholesale demolition – some 450 had been destroyed by 1974 – of manor houses, often to make way for housing and golf courses. The long-overdue Act of 1968 required owners of listed houses to seek permission before alteration or demolition. It seems incredible now, but prior to the 1968 Act they only had a duty to inform local authorities and the then Ministry of Works, which supposedly controlled historic buildings, of their intentions. So, having sketched a selection of planning laws, let us now turn our attention to the results of planning, as seen in the landscape. I start with an example familiar to everyone.

It is still widely accepted by planners that an unprepossessing development, be it in town or country, can somehow be 'screened' out of sight. As a consequence of this mistaken belief, huge conifer 'screening' hedges have become one of the least attractive features of late-twentieth- and early twenty-first-century urban and rural landscapes. If, as usually happens, they are left uncontrolled, they soon form tall, inky dark scars across the landscape. The hedging plants are usually the ultra fast-growing hybrid cypress, known as the Leyland cypress, which comes in two forms: dark green or bright yellowy gold.[39] The latter is slightly slower-growing than the former. There are signs that planners are beginning to realize that to many the non-native Leyland cypress is a blot on the landscape in its own right, especially in winter, when its dark foliage contrasts so markedly with the otherwise delicate silhouettes of deciduous trees, such as oak and ash, and the warm reddish tinge of the berries on hawthorn hedges.

Besides, I am not sure that I agree with the philosophy behind 'screening'. I would much rather look at something necessary, if utilitarian and rather unsightly, out in the countryside, such as a canning factory, or electricity sub-station, than be confronted by a vast conifer hedge – at which point my curiosity is immediately aroused and I have to see what lies behind it.

We tend to view the spread of suburban 'sprawl' – itself an emotive

Fig. 14.12 A huge evergreen hedge on the A436 near Stow-on-the-Wold, Gloucestershire. In the second half of the twentieth century fast growing evergreen trees such as the Leyland cypress were increasingly being planted, both in gardens and to screen various new developments. If clipped regularly (like the yellow *Leylandii* hedge on the extreme right of the picture) they do not intrude on the landscape, but if they remain untended they soon form huge dark walls of vegetation that can be seen for miles around.

word – as wholly bad, and it can be, if it happens at the expense of top-quality rural landscapes. But if it destroys the usual hedgeless and treeless arable 'grain plains' that now surround many of Britain's great cities, such value judgements become less straightforward. Numerous studies have also shown that suburbs encourage biodiversity much better than intensive arable farming. So the growth of suburbs since the late nineteenth century has not been an entirely gloomy picture. First and most importantly, millions of British citizens enjoy their lives in the suburbs, which can often indeed be leafy and are generally free from serious crime. From a social perspective, some of the older suburban landscapes have been around long enough to have developed strong local identities and loyalties.

In his BBC film *Metroland*, John Betjeman eulogized the suburban landscapes that grew up in the early twentieth century, following the extension of the Metropolitan railway from London into the Buckinghamshire countryside. It does not matter whether one shares his love for these places or not, because it cannot be denied that they have a character all of their own and one, moreover, that is alive and constantly developing. I am delighted that planning authorities have also had the good sense to approve the construction of many mosques and Sikh temples in otherwise residential areas; these reflect very different cultures but they are becoming more common and their arrival adds a welcome air of the exotic to what can sometimes seem like the bland, over-planned appearance of urban British landscapes.[40] Many of the areas settled by Asian communities in Midland towns of England were originally developed in the latter part of the nineteenth century as part of the commercial and industrial expansion that was stimulated by the arrival of the railways. These streets are characterized by rather drab terrace housing which is greatly enlivened by the appearance of a new brightly coloured mosque or temple. Urban open spaces, too, are also

Fig. 14.13 A view of the Faizan-e-Madina mosque in the Gladstone Street district of Peterborough. The mosque was completed in 2006 and provides welcome colour and contrast in this part of the city, which was developed in the early 1870s during the prosperity which followed the opening of the railway to London, in August 1850.

enjoying something of a renaissance and many Victorian parks in town centres are being restored to their former glory, thanks in large part to Lottery funding and enlightened local authorities.

But are suburban landscapes significantly different from any other townscape? At first glance they are, but when you look more closely, as with so many other aspects of the landscape, it is not quite as simple. Some later Victorian suburbs of English cities in the Midlands and north, for example, have in the last forty to fifty years become part of so-called 'inner-city' areas, often with large ethnic minority populations. Again, the term 'inner city' is not a simple geographical description, either. For better or for worse it has become synonymous with the older, politically incorrect 'ghetto' and today is just another way of describing a place where middle-class people would not voluntarily choose to live. The urban spectrum has 'inner city' at one pole and 'suburb' at the other. In reality, of course, the real world of towns, where people actually live their lives, lies somewhere in between.

MODEL TOWNS AND GARDEN CITIES

It cannot be denied that the cities of Victorian Britain were often grim places. Many social reformers tried to put this right by combining the benefits of urban and rural living. We have seen how enlightened industrialists like Sir Titus Salt went about creating model settlements, and the process was to continue into the twentieth century, notably at Port Sunlight, Cheshire.

The houses of Port Sunlight were built in a variety of styles. There were many open spaces, trees and wide boulevard-style roads. The houses themselves were airy and spacious, with a kitchen, scullery, parlour and three to four bedrooms. By 1899 the first of two schools provided by the Lever brothers held 500 pupils and there was also a library, a cottage hospital and a museum. The brothers insisted that the pub was to be alcohol-free, as they were both teetotal themselves, but when the villagers were asked for their opinion, they rejected the idea and the brothers gave way. By 1909 there were 700 houses in Port Sunlight and a population of 3,600. By this time the town also had its own fire brigade, a municipal swimming pool and gymnasium.

Fig. 14.14 A view of Port Sunlight, the model town built by the Lever brothers on The Wirral, Cheshire. These houses in Park Road, quite close to the factory were built in 1891–2, during the early expansion phase of the development. They are examples of the project's principal architect William Owen's four-bedroom Parlour Cottage type. The building on the left (designed by T. Raffles Davison, 1891), and now a tea room, was first the general store, then the Post Office.

Port Sunlight has been criticized, but one could also argue that without the enlightened paternalism seen at places like Port Sunlight and Saltaire progress in housing and urban planning would not have been so rapid.[41] After the First World War the Unilever businesses continued to expand and eventually Port Sunlight became part of the same conurbation as Birkenhead. But the area still retains its character to this day.

Ebenezer Howard (1850–1928) was a leading pioneer of a new way of thinking about town planning, which he developed in his ideas for Garden Cities.[42] Leading intellectuals such as Bernard Shaw were won round to his suggestions, which soon gathered many influential supporters in the increasingly popular socialist movement. Howard had lived through the agricultural depression of the late nineteenth century and he was keen to see that town and country should cease to grow apart; each should exist for the benefit of the other. Brought up in inner London, he was only too aware of the shortcomings of traditional cities, with their atmospheric pollution, crowded housing and lack of public and private spaces – of parks and gardens. His proposed Garden Cities would avoid these problems, through planning and public ownership. His towns would have entertainment, shopping and administration at their centres. Around the core would be parks and housing, along wide, tree-lined streets. All the housing would be within walking distance, both of the town centre and of the fringes of the town, where industry and railways would be concentrated. The fact that the core and the periphery had to be within walking distance limited the size of the Garden Cities.

Following a successful first meeting of the Garden City Association in Bournville, it was proposed to build the initial Garden City at Letchworth, in Hertfordshire. In 1903 the Garden City Association

Fig. 14.15 Letchworth Garden City, Hertfordshire. Letchworth was the first of Ebenezer Howard's Garden Cities. The first buildings appeared in 1904. This view is from Norton Way South, looking towards the Howard Garden Social Centre (thatched roof, on the right). The photo captures the spacious feel of the place, with wide tree-lined, boulevard-like streets, and extensive parks and open spaces. The houses are set well back, behind neat front gardens and are rarely accompanied by garages.

bought 10,120 hectares to build its city near the village of Letchworth, which then had a population of just 508 people.[43] True to Howard's principles, the plan of the new city included low-density housing well separated from industry and many open spaces. Even today, when the original Garden City has become a part of a north Hertfordshire conurbation that includes Hitchin and Baldock, Letchworth has retained a very distinctive and spacious character. Nowadays most of the tree-lined streets are also lined with parked cars, as Howard was just too early to provide his houses with garages.

The town was actually laid out by the architects Raymond Unwin and Barry Parker and one of their major contributions was the stipulation that an acre (0.4 hectare) should not hold more than nine houses, if overcrowding was to be avoided (compare this with the twenty stipulated by Birmingham in 1913). This ratio was adopted in the Housing Act of 1919 and it remained the guideline figure for the rest of the century. Letchworth was planned around individual estates where the houses were designed by different architects; their various designs are held together by the influence of the Arts and Crafts movement. Each estate had its own parish church, of which there were nineteen by 1930 when the population stood at 14,500. By 1971 the population had doubled. Somewhat idealistically, a proportion of the earlier houses were based around communal kitchens and dining rooms, of which Howard strongly approved, moving into one himself in 1913. The idea did not, however, last for long, nor did its alcohol-free inn. Locally, Letchworth is still famous, or infamous, depending on one's viewpoint, for having more churches than pubs.

In 1919 Howard bought 1,688 acres (689 hectares) from the Cowper estate in order to establish Welwyn Garden City, also in Hertfordshire, but on the east coast main line further south. The town was developed by Welwyn Garden City Limited and the first house was built in 1920. By 1951 Welwyn's population was more than 18,000, but by then it had been handed over to a New Town Development Corporation. Today Welwyn retains some of its Garden City atmosphere, although it contrasts with Letchworth, being more open in layout and with a classically inspired rather than Olde English town centre.

A somewhat less bold, but no less successful approach to the problems posed by city living in the early twentieth century was the Garden

Suburb, of which the best known example is in north London. Like other Garden Suburbs, that at Hampstead was laid out according to Garden City principles, with wide streets and low-density housing. The scale, however, was much reduced. Work began in 1906 and followed the extension of the Underground northwards. The new Hampstead Garden Suburb was mostly middle class, but it did attract some working-class residents to work on the Underground and in local shops. Many of its inhabitants did indeed commute to work via the Underground, but a significant proportion worked in the area, and still do. Today Hampstead Garden Suburb is rightly regarded as a triumph of modern town planning. Its houses quite strongly recall Letchworth and many are influenced by Arts and Crafts ideas. Although the streets do not seem quite as spacious as Letchworth, the houses are set back from the road and many front gardens are surrounded by neatly clipped privet hedges.

The Garden Cities were a response to the constantly growing population, but elsewhere towns and cities continued to expand outwards in an altogether less planned fashion. By the 1920s, too, London was growing faster than anywhere else and its rapidly increasing population required housing. This led to a major boom in speculative building in the Home Counties in the two decades prior to the Second World War. Eventually something had to be done to manage the situation and the legislation that gave birth to the Green Belt appeared in 1938.

THE LONDON GREEN BELT AND NEW TOWNS

The expansion beyond London's core urban area began in the 1860s, continued into the twentieth century and rapidly gathered pace in the inter-war years. The process was initially encouraged by numerous offers of cheap fares by railway companies and this led to the development of large new estates, such as the White Hart estate in Tottenham, in 1904. London County Council offered cheap tram tickets and after 1890 started to provide public housing. An early popular development was the LCC Totterdown estate at Tooting, which began in 1903 and achieved a population of 4,500 at the end of the First World War; the

LCC also began to build 'out county' estates, the first being at Norbury, Surrey (1906–10).

Much of the outward expansion of London was only made possible by the extension of the Underground network. By 1907 tunnels penetrated the Hampstead hills to reach Golders Green, which boasted 3,600 new houses by 1914. After the First World War the Bakerloo, Northern and Piccadilly lines were extended and the famous suburbs of 'Metroland' came into existence along the lines of the Metropolitan railway in once-rural Buckinghamshire. The highest growth in England's population from 1921 to 1951 was in the suburban parts of the Home Counties.

The census of 1901 showed London's population to be 4.4 million and that of Greater London 6.6 million.[44] The growth of London reached a peak in the mid-twentieth century and the census of 1951 showed the population of Greater London to be almost 8.2 million, which was approximately 14 per cent of that of England and Wales.

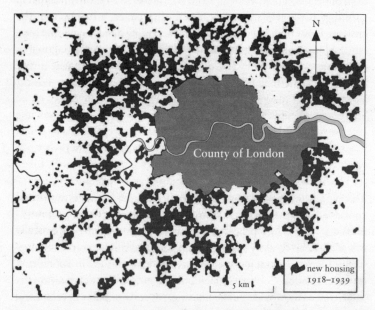

Fig. 14.16 A map showing the extent of new housing built in the landscape around the County of London in the inter-war years.

That same census also revealed there were only 5,000 permanent residents within the City itself. Fifty years later the population of the City has risen slightly to 7,200, largely thanks to new residential developments, such as the Barbican. But the population of Greater London in 2001 had dropped to 7,172,000 (or 13.8 per cent of the total population of England and Wales).

The inter-war years witnessed massive expansion of housing into previously rural landscapes around London. After the war the government reacted by tightening up Green Belt legislation and by proposing a series of New Towns to take London's 'overspill' population. But all this activity around the fringes of London did not mean that development within the centre slowed down. Many of the new buildings, such as the department stores Selfridges (1909) and Debenham and Freebody (1906) in Oxford and Regent streets and the new BBC's headquarters at Broadcasting House (1926) were made from Portland stone rather than brick or stucco, and by the 1930s access for cars, taxis and lorries along most of central London's main streets had been greatly improved.

Although the largest concentration of population has been in the south-east, around London, other areas have had to manage the consequences of rapid population growth. In the south-east, increasing prosperity and shortage of land has led to the demolition of earlier mass-housing in the course of its replacement and improvement. The result is a mixture of urban and suburban housing that can be homogeneous and rather characterless, with notable exceptions like Letchworth and Hampstead Garden Suburb proving the rule. Other, generally less prosperous areas have been less cavalier with their stock of older housing and have managed to retain a sense of history where the earlier buildings can still be seen in their original context.

In his *English Journey* written in the 1930s, J. B. Priestley dismissed Gateshead, across the Tyne from Newcastle, as 'a huge dingy dormitory'. A recent survey, however, has shown that this large city successfully and imaginatively developed housing for the vast workforce required to run the developing industries of Tyneside from the mid-nineteenth century onwards.[45] Taken as a whole, remarkably little was actually destroyed as the city grew, leaving us today with a series of urban and suburban landscapes that beautifully illustrate the history of mass-housing, starting with fine terrace housing built by a local iron-master between 1819 and 1824. The then suburbs of Bensham and Shipcote were used to house huge numbers of workers keen to move away from the increasingly unsanitary conditions of the main city nearer the Tyne river front. In the mid-1850s Bensham was still largely rural, but by the First World War it had been completely blanketed with terrace housing, most of which was divided up into flats, which dominated housing there from the 1860s to 1914. The characteristic Tyneside flat, being designed as such from the outset and not a later conversion, was a well thought out, compact but far from cramped place in which to live. Some of the first-floor flats also had two additional heated rooms in the roof-space. The secret of their success lay in the depth of the houses, which extended well back from the street frontage.

Between the wars mass-housing was provided by Gateshead Council in a series of well-planned estates, mostly of semi-detached houses.

Fig. 14.17 Eastbourne Avenue, Gateshead. This attractive street of characteristic Tyneside flats was built in the late nineteenth and early twentieth centuries.

Fig. 14.18 The first phase of the Carr Hill housing estate, Gateshead. This estate was begun in 1922 and the houses laid out with spacious gardens at front and back. There are also plenty of good open spaces nearby, such as Hodgkin Park, named after the first Chairman of the Housing Committee, to the right in this view.

Although they were built as fast as the rather ponderous planning and funding procedures of the day would allow, they never fully sorted out the housing shortage. By 1936 the council had torn down large areas of slums and had provided no fewer than 2,360 houses, all of which, by today's standards, were affordable. It was no mean achievement. All these developments meld with and complement each other in a most successful way.

THE POST-WAR NEW TOWNS

The massive expansion of London into the surrounding countryside during the inter-war years was a major cause for concern. Slums were probably a more serious post-war problem than bomb damage. The Labour government realized that post-war reconstruction and development in Britain could not be left to private enterprise alone and would have to be planned with care. Louis Silkin was appointed Minister for Town and Country Planning in 1945 and his proposals were to have an enduring effect on the development of the landscape through the remainder of the century.

Perhaps the most important of the new Minister's decisions was the New Towns Act, which was passed in 1946. Stevenage was designated the first New Town and was created (in 1947), like others, with its own largely independent Development Corporation. The Chief Architect for Stevenage was Leonard Vincent and his confident designs for the shopping areas at the centre of the New Town have generally weathered quite well, although the original parts of the New Town are now in need of refreshment.[46] This is particularly evident in the winter, when bright summer bedding schemes die back and rain brings out the stains on concrete walls.

Eight other New Towns were designated in southern Britain and an additional six in the north. Most of the southerly New Towns of the first wave were in a ring around the outer edges of London's Green Belt.[47] These towns were intended to take London's 'overspill' population, following bomb damage and slum clearance. From the outset they were to be medium sized (50,000–80,000 inhabitants) and surrounded by their own individual green belts. Other New Towns of the first phase were intended to house workers at major manufacturing centres, such as the steel towns of Corby, in Northamptonshire, and Cwmbran in south Wales. Peterlee was to be a town for the scattered mining communities of the Durham Coalfield. Today places like Hemel Hempstead are far more than mere receptacles for 'overspill' and have become important centres for regional employment, both in the service industry and in banking, finance and insurance. In the 1990s the population of

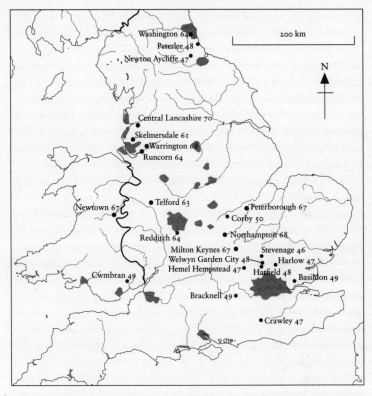

Fig. 14.19 Map showing the New Towns of post-war England and Wales and the dates they were begun. The first wave of New Towns (1946–9) was intended to take 'overspill' population from London and other industrial cities where housing had become overcrowded. The second generation (1961–70) took some overspill but were mainly intended to be regional centres in their own right.

Hemel Hempstead was about 80,000, of whom about 50,000 were employed locally.

The second wave of fifteen New Towns and three New Cities were created between 1961 and 1970. By this stage town-planning philosophy had moved on from the Garden City movement. The emphasis was now on employment, access and regional distinctiveness. There had also been a public reaction against the destruction of so many greenfield sites in the first wave of New Towns and it was decided that the second wave should be centred around pre-existing regional centres, such as Peterborough (1967) and Northampton (1968). The advertising put out by these later New Towns accentuated their individuality. Like other second-generation development corporations, such as Northampton and Milton Keynes, the Peterborough Development Corporation gave substantial grants to the excavation of archaeological sites in its area of development.[48] This work provided good publicity material and helped to bolster the New Towns' regional distinctiveness.

Three second-generation New Towns were singled out to become major regional centres. All had excellent communications and were situated in landscapes where expansion was possible without destroying too many green fields. These New Cities were Milton Keynes, in Buckinghamshire, Telford, in Shropshire, and the Central Lancashire New Town.[49] The population of the towns and villages that now comprise Milton Keynes, for example, was 40,000 in 1967 when the area was designated as a New Town. The layout of Milton Keynes differs from other cities in the east Midlands by not being so centralized and a deliberate planning decision was taken to foster the development of smaller communities within the new city.[50] Only time will tell whether is has been successful. By 1992, when the Development Corporation was finally wound up, the population had risen to 148,000. Some New Towns have far exceeded their original population estimates. For instance, it was not anticipated in 1967 that the huge brickpits to the south of Peterborough could be filled with power-station fly-ash and then built over. The new settlement that is being constructed there is known as Hampton, currently one of the largest private housing developments in Europe.

TOWNSCAPES AFTER THE SECOND WORLD WAR

This book has been about the landscape as it survives in the present, and I have naturally tended to stress the new developments and changes that history saw fit to bequeath us. This has meant that we have paid rather less attention to what history in its wisdom decided to remove from the record. But as we come closer to our own time we should pause and consider what we have done to the landscape in the name of 'progress'. Today many historic industrial buildings, such as warehouses, are being imaginatively redeveloped, but this would not have happened in the 1960s and 1970s when England, in particular, witnessed the wholesale redevelopment of most of its historic town centres. The historic towns of Scotland largely escaped this orgy of senseless and ill-thought-out destruction.[51] But in England it was different.

Even acknowledged jewels, such as the Hanseatic League port King's Lynn, in Norfolk, have been blighted by insensitive development: in 1962 Pevsner wrote that 'the scale of the streets is . . . intimate everywhere, and very little has been disturbed by later 19th and 20th century interference'.[52] He must have been aware that the previous year the town had been declared an official 'overspill' town, and that great efforts were being made to record and excavate ahead of the inevitable destruction that was to ensue.[53] King's Lynn is my local town, but I still find it hard to walk along Norfolk Street and the streets alongside, which were wholly redeveloped by a large insurance company a few years after Pevsner wrote those words. Until very recently the drab concrete shops of this redevelopment were either empty or stood forlorn. Strangely, there were no 'For Sale' signs evident, as the insurance company had already seen a good return on its investments and by the early twenty-first century had lost all interest in the place. The borough council then stepped in and commissioned a second re-redevelopment which has certainly been an improvement, but no substitute for what had been there in 1962. Elsewhere the town's many surviving historic buildings and streets continue to attract large numbers of visitors from outside the region. What has survived of this historic town makes me determined that such stupidity must never be allowed to happen again.[54] Landscapes have the power to preserve mistakes as well as successes and anyone interested in their history must be prepared for anger as much as pleasure.

After the Second World War overcrowded housing was again a problem in Gateshead, with 5,620 people known to be living in substandard houses in 1942. Directly after the war the Council set to work and had completed two estates by 1948. Two years later it had finished the much larger Beacon Lough Estate of 347 houses, which was recognized by the then Minister for Health as one of the best laid out in the country.[55]

By the mid-1950s there was a growing shortage both of housing and building materials all over Britain. This led to the construction of system-built concrete houses and then of high-rise blocks of flats, which were able to rehouse the large numbers of people displaced as the result of slum clearance close to the industrial areas of the city. These blocks of flats could be huge, but they were well designed and positioned in attractive parkland. Compared to similar blocks in, for example, south and east London, they have stood the passage of time well. Of course there were many teething problems, not the least being the failure of high-rise residents to develop a sense of community. In retrospect it is easy to criticize the growth of tower blocks, but something had to be done: there was a real crisis in the early 1960s. In 1965, for example, the Borough of Gateshead successfully built 1,000 new homes. From 1965 the Council returned to the construction of low-rise houses, including additions to the remarkable estate at Beacon Lough East, which won the government's award for 'Good Design in Housing 1968'. This estate featured an interesting mix of various house types, including four twelve-storey high-rise blocks, containing forty-eight flats each and set within parkland, a group of patio bungalows for older people, brick-built terrace houses, and concrete 'gunnel' houses: these were semi-detached houses arranged along a common passageway, which ran through them.

One unique development which falls broadly within the Garden City or idealistic tradition of urban residential development is that inspired by the current Prince of Wales on Duchy of Cornwall land, on the outskirts of Dorchester, in Dorset. The development is known as Poundbury and it is currently nearing completion of its second major phase of development. The architectural styles of Poundbury might be described as neo-archaic and in this it recalls the Arts-and-Crafts-inspired houses of places like Letchworth. There are fewer green spaces, however, and the atmosphere of the place is more urban than suburban. Employment, in the form of offices rather than factories, has not been relegated to the fringes. The large classical building in Beechwood

Fig. 14.20 New buildings in Beechwood Square, Poundbury, Dorset. Poundbury has the air of a film set; apart from the circular building, the mix of styles in this view is mostly Georgian with hints of something earlier in the background. The large colonnaded building, which is the focus of the square and resembles an eighteenth-century town hall, is given over to offices.

Square, for instance, was occupied by offices, whereas the other two sides (the fourth is still open) were for houses. Only time will tell whether the Poundbury experiment has successfully attracted a variety of people – rather than the office-working middle class alone – to reside there.

Each time we have approached the topic of urban landscapes we have begun with an observation about the uniqueness of every individual town and the problems inherent in attempting to categorize them. This was probably true of British towns up to and including the early twentieth century, but after the Second World War changes occurred that were as profound and far-reaching as anything that had gone before. In many instances towns lost their traditional industries, as manufacturing itself moved out of Britain. Towns like Northampton ceased to be the centre of the boot and shoe trade, cutlery became a relatively minor contributor to the economy of Sheffield and great ships ceased routinely to be built on the Tyne and Clyde. Manufacturing was replaced by new service industries that could operate from offices and industrial estates anywhere, so long as ground rents were cheap.

While Britain was losing its manufacturing base, houses were being built at an increasing rate: in 1951 there were 13.8 million houses and by the year 2000 the figure had risen to 24.6 million – an increase of 78 per cent. Nearly two in five of all British houses were built after 1965, the year when for the first time the number of houses exceeded the number of households. As post-war prosperity increased, so did house-ownership: in the second half of the twentieth century the number of people who owned their own homes rose from a third to over two-thirds.[56] The townscapes of the late twentieth century have rightly been criticized for being homogeneous 'clones', with similar houses and the same chains of stores located in identical out-of-town plazas and malls. It should, however, be remembered that these plazas and malls with their vast car parks were concepts that were developed in America, where land is both plentiful and cheap. It is highly questionable whether they were ever appropriate in land-starved Britain.

There is always a danger when writing a general overview of concentrating on the unusual and spectacular, while ignoring the places where many people live their lives. While it is certainly true to say that late-twentieth-century Britain became increasingly city-based, small towns still continued to play an important role in the life of the nation.

LONDON

London's varied townscapes were much affected by the events of the war, most notably, of course, by the two bombing campaigns of the Blitz, followed by the V1 and V2 flying bombs. This bombing had caused serious damage to large areas of the East End and to other significant parts of London, especially around railway termini, such as Euston and Paddington. Post-war reconstruction generally followed the two Abercrombie plans of 1943 and 1944, the latter of which was the first to suggest the construction of New Towns to draw population away from central London. This went hand in hand with a major programme of slum clearance in the East End. Some of the displaced population was rehoused within huge new estates in central London, such as the Keir Hardie Estate in Canning Town. Others were dispatched to New Towns and new estates outside London. Many people from Balham, for example, moved to Cove in Hampshire, and St Neots in Cambridgeshire received people from Deptford and Greenwich.

The extraordinary post-war growth of the City as a centre of global commerce has led to the construction of a number of iconic buildings, and the new Docklands cityscape where the skyscrapers are capped by the huge Canary Wharf Tower. This development is intended to form the western end to a vast planned development, the Thames Gateway regeneration scheme, which will include the new 'legacy' facilities being built for the London Olympics of 2012. One might question, of course, whether it is altogether wise to build huge areas of housing on the low-lying land of the Thames estuary, given predicted sea-level increases.

THE IMPOSITION OF HEATHROW

The story of Heathrow and its consistent ability to dodge around planning laws might be cited as the exception that proves the greater rule. I can well remember when I first took any notice of the name Heathrow. It was in a lecture at Cambridge on the Iron Age and the lecturer was discussing Romano-Celtic temples. In those days many people still referred to Heathrow as London Airport and, being a penniless student, I was not often in a position to fly around much. The square Heathrow temple had been revealed by Professor W. F. Grimes when carrying out excavations in advance of the construction of the first concrete runways during the Second World War.[57] Little did I or Professor Grimes know then that his excavations should not have taken place, as the airfield that was then constructed was never used. It is all part of a rather murky episode in the story of London's landscape that throws an unflattering light on the way that central government made important decisions that have had a direct effect on the lives of many thousands of ordinary people in what was once west Middlesex.

Today Heathrow is a landscape of frantic activity, entirely appropriate

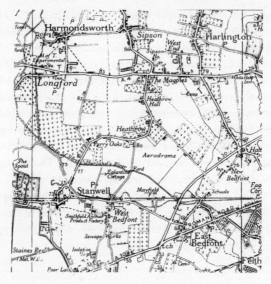

Fig. 14.21 An early twentieth-century Ordnance Survey 1-inch map of
Heathrow, then a small Middlesex hamlet with an 'aerodrome' attached.

to the century that created it. But it was not always thus. Writing in
1935 G. Maxwell described the scene like this: 'If you turn down from
the Bath Road by the Three Magpies you will come upon a road
that is as rural as anywhere in England. It is not, perhaps, scenically
wonderful but for detachment from London or any urban interests it
would be hard to find its equal; there is a calmness and serenity about
it that is soothing in a mad rushing world.'[58] The pub Maxwell mentions
actually appears on the Ordnance Survey map of the area (see
Fig. 14.21). The first aerodrome at Heathrow was built by the Fairey
Aviation Company, of Hayes, Middlesex, in 1929.[59] It was mainly used
by the company for test flights, having been evicted by the Air Ministry
from their previous airfield at Northolt, which also became a civilian
airfield after the Second World War. Between 1929 and 1943 Faireys
bought more of the strip-like market garden fields that surrounded the
airfield, amounting in all to 179 acres (72.4 hectares). Then in the early
years of the war they bought another 48 acres (19.4 hectares). Soon the
company decided to move its premises out of Hayes and into Heathrow

and by 1943 they owned about 240 acres (about 97 hectares) in all.

Even before the war, Fairey's aerodrome at Heathrow attracted large numbers of visitors and by 1937 there were suggestions that it might one day make a suitable airport for London. Then politics intervened in a fairly big way. The airport-to-be was commandeered by the government for wartime duties. That seems straightforward enough, but it was not given concrete runways until 1944, when it was supposedly intended for use by the American Air Force to house heavy bombers. In the event neither the RAF nor USAF ever used it, although the Air Ministry spent some £350,000 (at 1946 prices) having concrete runways added, laid out in the standard pattern developed by the RAF. It would seem that all of this had been an elaborate ruse to allow the government to acquire the site using wartime emergency powers. Had they done it the 'correct' way they would have had to have borne the immense costs of a post-war public inquiry.

It had been a 'win-win' situation for both government and taxpayer,

Fig. 14.22 A view of Heathrow in 1932. In the foreground are arable fields and market garden strips. The main aircraft hangar is clearly visible, with the grass airfield beyond.

but not for Sir Richard Fairey. On learning in 1944 that the Air Ministry had requisitioned the airfield he had so carefully, and expensively, built up over the years, he sent a despairing cable to his co-chairman, Sir Clive Baillieu: 'Decision so utterly calamitous, suggest liquidation only practical prospect.' A later communication makes his view of the government's reasoning quite clear: 'And why the haste? I cannot escape the thought that the hurry is not uninspired by the fact that a post-war government might not be armed with the power or even be willing to take action that is now being rushed through at the expense of the war effort . . . '[60] He was not to receive compensation for another twenty years.

So Heathrow happened. And ruthlessly too. Not content with just the Fairey aerodrome, the 1944 requisition order also grabbed an additional 1,300 acres (526.3 hectares) of agricultural land. This was about 15 per cent of the farmed land of west Middlesex. After the war the area of the great airfield became even larger and it effectively and rapidly destroyed the very prosperous pre-war west Middlesex market garden industry, which had become established in the region because of its freely draining soils and proximity to the vast London market.

The original wartime airfield was never used by military or civilian aircraft. Instead, an entirely new airfield was constructed when Heathrow was handed over by the Air Ministry to the Ministry of Civil Aviation in January 1946. The first three runways were completed in 1947; a further three were also begun, to give the Star of David ground plan so familiar today. In 1950 work began on the central terminals and BEA (British European Airways) and BOAC (British Overseas Airways Corporation) built their engineering complexes on the east side of the airfield. In 1974 the plan to build a third London Airport at Foulness was cancelled and a pressure grew for a fourth Heathrow terminal to be built on the south side of the airfield, outside the southern perimeter. This time a public inquiry could not be avoided and the inspector's report, published in 1979, concluded that 'present levels of noise around Heathrow are unacceptable in a civilised society'; despite this he then went on to recommend in favour of Terminal 4, provided that 'Secretaries of State should reiterate that it is the Government's policy that there will be neither a fifth terminal nor any other major expansion of Heathrow'.[61] That had no effect on the eventual building of Terminal 5.

Fig. 14.23 A corner of Heathrow Airport today. The Middlesex village of Heathrow has long since been obliterated by London's largest airport. Most people are aware of the five main public terminals, but the airport also includes large numbers of cargo facilities, most distributed around the perimeter.

I have discussed the local effects on the landscape of what one might call 'Heathrow Blight', but in addition to man-made bodies of water, a huge array of new roads have been built to service the monster in their midst. The old Bath Road has been upgraded to dual carriageway. Most drivers today use the nearby M4 and M25 and Terminal 5 is now served by a new spur off the M25. In addition, the Piccadilly Line has been specially extended and there is a rapid rail link to Brunel's Paddington. I suspect the great man would have rather approved.

TOWN AND CITY CENTRES IN THE LATE TWENTIETH CENTURY

For much of the twentieth century the centres of many of Britain's larger towns and cities were often unpleasant. Recently, local authorities have made a conscious effort to improve them and generally speaking they have succeeded. But there are problems, and sometimes quite serious ones. For example, many towns close to large cities have become mere dormitories. When the New Towns were built in the 1960s and 1970s the various development corporations made efforts to provide pubs and clubs to serve the inhabitants of the new estates. But subsequently this has only rarely happened and most of the huge estates that today surround the towns and cities, especially of south-east England, are given over to housing alone. So on Friday and Saturday nights there is a ritual exodus of young people travelling from the suburbs to the city centre for their evening's entertainment.

Increasingly, too, pressure on land means that the new housing estates are dispensing with gardens. The result is that rainfall runs straight off roofs, paved forecourts and roads into the sewers where it adds to the

Fig. 14.24 Tyneside at the end of the twentieth century. This view is looking upstream from the southern (Gateshead) side of the river towards Newcastle-upon-Tyne.

ever-increasing problem of flash flooding. Often, too, archaeologists have noted how frequently their pre-development excavations have encountered thick layers of clay alluvium right across many proposed new housing estates and it comes as no surprise to subsequently learn of catastrophic floods.[62] We ignore the landscape around us at our peril.[63]

City centres have either declined or have developed a lively new cultural life, often centred around converted industrial buildings, such as Tate Modern, a converted power station on the South Bank of the Thames at Battersea, or the 1950s warehouse, the Baltic Flour Mills, at Gateshead, which is also now an important arts centre. In the final years of the twentieth century many larger cities also acquired entirely new iconic structures of considerable architectural merit. Tyneside, for example, has the graceful arch of the Millennium Bridge across the Tyne and London can boast the vast Ferris wheel of the London Eye (1999) on the Thames Embankment and the much derided, (although to my eye a masterpiece) Millennium Dome, at Greenwich. Despite all this prosperity, it is worth bearing in mind that at the end of the twentieth century much poverty still existed within Britain's townscapes. In the year 2000 London, for example, possessed twenty of the most deprived boroughs in the country.[64]

The towns that lost out in the changes of the later twentieth century were middle-sized: large enough to attract new housing, but too small to foster cultural development, good or cosmopolitan restaurants, pubs or cafés. Like most people I can only speak from my own experience, but some of the towns near my home are in a pretty sorry state: places like Holbeach, Long Sutton, Grantham and Wisbech. In some respects the structure of social life, especially for young people, has broken down in these places, and it is hard to avoid the conclusion that some of the actual townscapes of late-twentieth-century Britain were having an adverse effect on the lives, health and happiness of their residents.

FUN AT HOME

The twentieth century was the first time since the onset of the industrial era that working people had been given anything approaching adequate time for themselves and their families. In the nineteenth century and earlier, when working people stopped work their wages stopped too. But from the 1930s we see the introduction of paid holidays for factory workers. This one measure was to transform resort towns and the leisure industry in general, closer to where people actually lived. Far-sighted men like Titus Salt had been worried about the health of their workforce in the past, but had been prevented by the economic necessities of life from doing much about it. It was only with increasing prosperity and the immense social changes that resulted from the First World War that working people were able to demand more leisure time, as a right. This time away from work was spent on holiday and at home. We shall consider holiday resorts shortly, but we should not forget that most British towns and cities in the twentieth century made efforts to provide their residents with opportunities to relax and unwind.

Pubs have always been important in urban life, but the growth of motoring and increased leisure led to the appearance of large, purpose-built roadhouses on the outskirts of many towns and cities.[65] These are often characterized by substantial car parks. We saw how local authorities had established city parks in the mid-nineteenth century. After the First World War, in the 1920s and 1930s, ordinary people felt more relaxed about appearing in bathing costumes and this was when many municipalities built public bathing pools and lidos.[66] Some of these became miniature landscapes of sport and recreation, and were often surrounded by playing fields and open spaces, many of which have sadly (and short-sightedly) been developed for shops and housing.

The main form of mass-entertainment in British towns of the late nineteenth and twentieth centuries was football. Following the disastrous failure to control crowds on the terraces of the Sheffield Hillsborough Stadium, in which ninety-six people died, the Taylor Report suggested that all major stadiums should be all-seater by 1995.[67] This led to a large programme of rebuilding and reconstruction. In the first half of the twentieth century fans travelled to football grounds on foot or bicycle and special trains serviced away matches. Consequently most stadiums were located near the centre of town, within easy reach of the station. Although some, like the celebrated Stadium of Light

(1995) at Middlesbrough, were located on old industrial sites, many of the new stadiums that followed Hillsborough were built on the outskirts of town. The Kassam Stadium, new home of Oxford United, is typical of many of these. It is located alongside a large low-cost hotel on the southern fringes of the city near the Science Park, and is surrounded by its own huge car parks.

Many of our older industrial cities, and most especially Birmingham, were surrounded by numerous canals, many of which were disused and were slowly filling up with rubbish. Rather unexpectedly they acquired a new lease of life in the 1960s, when pleasure-craft took over from commercial narrowboats as the dominant canal traffic. The result is that today many disused waterways have been restored to working order and attract thousands of visitors in summer. Canal-side buildings such as warehouses have benefited from their improved surroundings and their survival into the twenty-first century has been assured by their redevelopment as flats and apartments.[68]

FUN BY THE SEA

The popularity of bathing in the sea, which had begun in the mid-eighteenth century, increased in the twentieth century. If it were not for a growing fear of skin cancer it would probably still be increasing today. A few resorts owed their very existence to the railways. Skegness on the Lincolnshire coast might be thought to have little going for it. Sand has to be dredged out at sea and the beach 'refreshed' every season. There are no cliffs and a bitterly cold north-east wind can howl its way off the North Sea. Yet the railway companies, aided by an inspired advertising campaign, which began in 1908 and was centred around a skipping fisherman and the famous slogan: 'Skegness Is So Bracing!', attracted trainloads of visitors to the resort every summer.[69] Thousands of factory workers from the industrial cities of the east Midlands would spend a week there every summer. Nottingham formed a particularly close relationship and even today it is possible to buy copies of Nottingham daily papers there during the summer season. Soon Skegness had become the east coast equivalent of the very much larger Blackpool, which grew rapidly thanks to

Fig. 14.25 This is perhaps the most famous of all British railway posters. Rail links played an important role in the development of Skegness as a seaside resort. The original poster (by John Hassall) appeared in 1908 and has been drawn and redrawn many times. This version, by Frank Newbould (1933), proved very popular.

packed trains and cheap tickets from Manchester and Liverpool. Skegness was laid out around the railway station upon which it depended.[70] In the early nineteenth century it had been a lightly frequented but quite select watering place, but when the railway arrived in 1873 it was given a new lease of life. Three years later the decision was made to build a new town on a grid pattern between the station and the sea, and plots were sold off to developers. The entire project was controlled by the Earl of Scarbrough, who kept development restrained until 1921, when he sold the foreshore to the Town Council who were much less reticent about such things. Today Skegness is popular and brash, far more reliant on car and caravan than the train.

In the previous chapter I discussed the impact of the early railways on the larger seaside towns of the West Country. Later the railway network was expanded to reach smaller resorts such as Swanage (1885) and Lyme Regis (1903).[71] The arrival of the railway in 1871 at

Minehead, on the Somerset coast, had a major effect on the development of the resort. To the south, when the railway came to Bridport Harbour the local authorities renamed the new resort at the mouth of the River Brit, West Bay, as a rebranding exercise to make it sound more inviting than a harbour. The railways played a big part in the marketing of resorts along their routes, as it was very much in their interests to do so. The Great Western Railway, for example, proclaimed that it was 'The Nation's Holiday Line'. From the 1930s paid holiday time allowed many working families to visit the seaside for the first time, and factory workers from South Wales and the Midlands took holiday trains to Weston-super-Mare in huge numbers. In July 1930 some 5,000 Great Western Railway workers and their families took trains to Weymouth from their works in Swindon during 'Swindon Fortnight'.

The first holiday camps were established by Sir Billy Butlin's company at Skegness and Clacton, in Essex, where an attempt was made to establish an enclosed escapist world, structured around the Hollywood imagery that was popular in the 1930s.[72] The opening of the first two Butlins camps coincided with the giving of holiday pay to factory workers in 1938. By the following year 15 million people were receiving holiday pay and Butlins advertisements reflected this: 'Holidays with pay: Holidays with play: A week's holiday for a week's wage.' After the war many more coastal holiday camps were built and other firms such as Pontins entered the field. Some of the post-war camps, such as Minehead, were truly massive. But fashions in the world of twentieth-century leisure could change very swiftly. In 1983 the Butlins camps at Filey and Clacton closed. Others have been given a major makeover: the camp at Skegness is now 'Funcoast World'; many more have had to ape inland theme parks and include roller-coasters and other 'white knuckle' rides. The main difference in terms of the landscape is that coastal areas are usually lower-lying and more undulating than other parts of Britain and the visual impact of the many new seaside theme parks can be very severe.

One of the biggest intrusions into the landscape of seaside resorts must surely be the modern marina, full of hundreds of yachts, whose ropes make such a distinctive sound as they slap against aluminium masts. Vast marinas have been built in resorts along the south coast in particular, since the 1970s. They are a vivid symbol of post-war prosperity and depend entirely on their boat-owners' ability to drive down to them on weekends. Many have been placed in old docks and in new purpose-built harbours, where they are often surrounded by car parks, chandlers' stores and multi-storey holiday flats. There are, however, some major disadvantages to marinas. They are visually intrusive – or at least the hundreds of bright yachts within them are – and they can often mar the appearance of a seafront or old harbour. Blackrock Marina, Brighton, is a case in point. This was one of the first of the huge south coast marinas. It opened in 1972 and is still the United Kingdom's largest, with some 1,600 berths.

Brighton successfully made the transition from an élite resort to one with broader appeal; other places, as we saw in the previous chapter, resisted this. Some such as Blackpool, in Lancashire, perhaps the most successful popular resort of the twentieth century did not need to make the change. Despite some problems in the latter part of the twentieth century, and continuing challenges from cheap holidays abroad, Blackpool has remained popular.

The roots of modern Blackpool lie in Victorian times, when it became the preferred resort of workers in the great cities of the north-west, such as Manchester and Liverpool. In later Victorian times it outstripped its local rivals in its size and ambition and extended its appeal from the north-west, right across Britain. This was made possible, of course, by the network of railways which covered the entire country. In the twentieth century Blackpool was to be well served by motorways such as the M6, running north–south and M62, east–west. In the early 1880s more than a million visitors were visiting Blackpool each year. By the 1890s that figure had doubled and by 1900, tripled. Just before 1914 it stood at 4 million and by the 1930s, 7 million. In the 1970s and early 1980s the visitor numbers peaked at 17 million, but in the past two decades they have fallen back to 10 million, largely as a result of people taking their holidays abroad. After the initial impact of the 'credit crunch', I suspect Blackpool will soon be fighting back.

Blackpool's three huge piers were built in the nineteenth century, as were the other principal attractions for which the resort is so renowned: the Tower (1894) and Winter Gardens (1870s). The front and its illuminations date to the late nineteenth century. Blackpool was a pioneer of electric street lighting (1879) and built the world's first electric tramway, in 1885. At the turn of the century the Pleasure Beach began to take shape along the south promenade. This was the world's first permanent seaside amusement park. By the 1890s most visitors were already staying for over a week and their housing was provided by speculative builders who built row upon row of distinctive bright red-brick boarding houses along roads that either radiated out from the railway stations or ran back from the promenade, at right angles.

Unlike nearby resorts such as Lytham St Annes, Blackpool was never the property of a single owner who might have been able to exercise restraint in town planning. Up to seven principal landowners controlled development there.[73] The result is that Lytham is a charming low-key resort of gentle architectural distinction and Blackpool is what you see today: a mix of largely unplanned Victorian residential developments and a sea front explicitly planned to extract as much money as possible from its millions of visitors.

Blackpool is a unique place that has pioneered some major architectural and technological achievements and has rightly, if belatedly, been suggested as a World Heritage Site.[74] By 1900 Blackpool was completely dedicated to mass-entertainment on a colossal scale. There was nowhere else like it anywhere in the world, but such expansion was only made possible by the foundations that were laid in Victorian times. The major late-Victorian reforms ultimately resulted from the town's incorporation as a borough in 1876. The new borough council determined to promote tourism, which the town's subsequent history demonstrates they did with spectacular success.

As prosperity increased in the second half of the twentieth century many attractive rural landscapes became the weekend destination for individuals and families with homes and jobs in towns. From the 1970s it became widely possible to own two homes and the era of 'second homers' was born. There were even tax advantages to obtaining a second home. The result was that rural housing soon became unaffordable to local people unless they possessed a large middle-class income. Today second homes are a feature of many coastal towns and villages from Cornwall to Norfolk to North Yorkshire. Second homes and holiday cottages can now be found in most rural areas of southern England and in regions popular with tourists, such as the Lake District and Yorkshire Moors. In the summertime these are cheerful places full of happy people, but from October the roads back to town are choked with cars whose roof racks are piled with suitcases wrapped in plastic that flaps and rattles in the wind as they drive along. This sound of modern migration can again be heard after Easter when the visitors return. In our more prosperous times we engage in seasonal trans-humance in the pursuit of leisure rather than survival. During the months of winter the empty villages of 'second homers' can be depress-ing places, with depopulated shops and pubs, unlit windows, and everywhere the telltale net curtains that announce to the world that these houses are empty.

THE AGE OF THE MOTOR CAR

In the late twentieth century politicians and planners realized that the various ways in which the nation was physically held together – the roads, drains, power lines, railways, canals etc. – mattered economically, and the term infrastructure was born.[75] Today the word has expanded to embrace all aspects of the built environment, to include shops, housing and places of work. If anything the increasing tendency in the 1980s and 1990s to favour the expanding privatized sector that emerged after the Thatcher years caused greater fragmentation in the infrastructure, whether it was in the railways, the roads or the network of power lines.

The term 'infrastructure' has managed to remain unloaded, unlike that demon of the environmental movement, the motorway. There is no doubt that the construction of motorways had severe impacts on particular natural and historic environments, but we should also pause to think about the benefits they have conferred on British society, especially to those who lack some of the advantages of the prosperous middle classes. It was road transport that ultimately enabled Britain to recover from the war. Without good roads both the New Towns and the prosperity that Britain enjoys today would have been impossible. Despite what some might have us believe, Britain has not been covered by tarmac, any more than it was blanketed by impenetrable forests in the Mesolithic.

The absence of anything approximating to an integrated transport policy has become something of a British national characteristic, with a remarkable history in the twentieth century. Let us first take the case of the railways, once Britain's greatest infrastructural asset.[76] We have seen how the railways continued to expand throughout the nineteenth century; the result was that by 1901 England alone had 18,000 miles (29,000 kilometres) of tracks that reached to almost every corner of the country. The first car was registered in London in 1895 and motoring became an increasingly popular activity, following the repeal (in the following year) of the legislation that required a red flag to be carried by a man walking in front of a motor vehicle. Motor buses became increasingly available from about 1910 and the growth of railway passengers was outstripped by the numbers of people using the roads, in the years leading up to the First World War. Rail transport did, however, expand between London and its outlying suburbs, many of which were served by the electrified Southern Railway. The Southern was the only financially successful railway company when the other 'Big Four' companies (the London, Midland and Scottish Railway, the London and North-Eastern Railway and the Great Western Railway) were compulsorily created in 1923 (from 120 smaller firms).

The railway network had been overworked and was rundown at the end of the Second World War, prior to its nationalization in 1948 as British Railways. The railway modernization plan saw the replacement of steam by diesel and electric locomotives and the west coast main line was electrified between 1959 and 1974. The Beeching Report of 1963 disregarded the railways' social role altogether, treating them as an economic asset alone. Many 'uneconomic' branch lines were torn up and the land sold to neighbouring landowners, or for housing. Sometimes the land was used for other specific purposes; Whitemoor Prison in March, Cambridgeshire, for example, was built on the huge Whitemoor marshalling yards which had been one of the first mechanized and containerized freight-handling yards in post-war Britain. By selling the land off in this way, the British Transport Commission effectively prevented most of the lines from ever reopening. In the 1980s closures ceased and the national railway network stabilized at around 11,000 miles (16,000 kilometres), around half the mileage of the peak that had been attained in the pre-war years. In the final decades of the century there was an increase in rail travel, but even so a mere 1.5 per cent of all journeys in Britain were by train. These low figures are readily understandable, given high fares and the poor reputation for reliability that rail travel currently enjoys in Britain. Those great pioneers of the railway age, the Stephensons, Brunel, Cubitt and Brassey, must be turning in their graves.

Today almost without exception British roads are well made and well maintained; they are also generally safe, with cambered surfaces that shed rainfall readily. At the turn of the nineteenth century, however, it was all very different.[77] Traffic congestion in central London was as bad as it is today, but the jams were caused by horses that deposited thousands of tons of dung, which every day had to be removed; it was spread over horticultural land in the Lea Valley of Hertfordshire, and elsewhere too. But by 1915 horse-drawn vehicles were in sharp decline, and in London had ceased to be used for public transport.

The speed with which Britain adopted the motor car was astonishing. As we have noted, the first car was registered in 1895. As so often happens in Britain, the cachet of royal approval was needed to start the avalanche, which happened in 1900 when the dashing (and rather 'fast') Prince of Wales bought a Daimler. By 1905 there were 15,800 cars and by 1914 the figure had risen to 132,000. By the time the Second World War began there were some 2 million vehicles on Britain's roads.

Early motorists often complained about the state of the roads, even though the national speed limit had been set at just 20 m.p.h. in 1903 (it was abolished along with all speed limits in 1930). Solid-rubber car tyres damaged the road surface, especially when wet, and in dry conditions the early motorists were accompanied by huge clouds of white dust, against which they protected themselves with hats, veils, goggles and huge scarves. The roads within central London had been paved by the mid-nineteenth century and several other larger city centres had metalled roads by 1900. Outside these few places, the roads of early twentieth century Britain were unmetalled. Then in 1902 the County Surveyor of Nottinghamshire patented a method whereby bitumen and stone were combined to form a material that sealed the road surface. He named it tarmac and established a company to exploit it. Initially the response to the new product was slow, but in 1913 the entire length of the Bath Road in Berkshire had been covered with tarmac and it proved so successful that others quickly followed. By 1930 the majority of trunk roads had been metalled in this way and only minor rural roads remained 'white'.

During the processes of enclosure in the eighteenth and nineteenth centuries the Parliamentary commissioners generally stipulated that the widths of new roads should be either 40, 50 or 60 feet (12, 15 or 18 metres). The new tarmac roads did not need to be so wide, as cars were narrower than carts and cavernous potholes were a thing of the past. So most rural roads were constructed to the statutory minimum width of 12 feet (3.6 metres), which left wide and attractive grass verges on either side, when old enclosure roads were metalled. The usually positive impact of improved roads in the countryside, could prove negative. The declining village of Faxton, in prosperous Northamptonshire, for example, was abandoned at the end of the Second World War when the local authority decided not to improve the roads leading to it.[78]

Fig. 14.26 Prior to the widespread application of metalled tarmac surfaces to most British roads in the 1930s, roads in the countryside would have been unmetalled and 'white', like this example that crosses the ancient Ridgeway near Uffington, in Oxfordshire. Even this remote route has the well-set-back hedges and wide verges that are so characteristic of many eighteenth- and nineteenth-century Parliamentary Enclosure roads.

The road situation at the start of the twentieth century recalled that at the beginning of the turnpike movement in the early eighteenth, but instead of parishes the roads were the responsibility of larger local authorities. The Great North Road (the A1), for instance, passed through seventy-two local authorities, of which just forty-six took responsibility for its upkeep. Public pressure led to the setting up of a Road Fund with money levied from a tax on engine horsepower and petrol duty. This fund was administered by the Road Board for England and Wales and was responsible for the 23,500 miles (38,000 kilometres) that were in the care of county councils (95,000 miles or 15,300 kilometres remained the responsibility of rural districts). The board ceased to function when war was declared in 1914, having had little or no effect on the state of the roads in its care.

The Ministry of Transport was created in 1919. From 1920 central government funds were used both to maintain and to build new roads, the first since the era of turnpikes. An important early development was the Trunk Roads Programme of 1929, which was also intended to help unemployment in the Depression. The 1920s and 1930s saw the prolonged planning and construction of new arterial roads, such as the East Lancashire Road from Liverpool to Manchester. Planning for this road began in 1923 and the road was finally opened by King George V in July 1934. These roads were usually routed through agricultural land, for which compensation was paid; generally speaking they skirted around towns and cities, to keep traffic flowing. It was all, however, belated and very much slower than what was happening in Germany and Italy: between 1899 and 1936 the total road network in England grew by just 4 per cent.

The impact of motoring on the landscape of the twentieth century was very considerable and it was not just caused by roads and cars on their own. Car-ownership was increasing fast and the people who owned or had use of cars were now a significant proportion of the electorate. Many people who may not have been drivers themselves were reliant on road transport, either for goods and services, or for public transport. Between 1924 and 1936 car prices halved, while their production increased by 500 per cent. By 1938 there were half a million trucks and lorries, nearly 2 million cars and 53,000 coaches and buses. The speed and scale of the growth of road transport was indeed revolutionary and like all revolutions it proved almost impossible to control in its early stages.

One feature of the new arterial roads built in the 1930s was the appearance of large signs advertising plots of land in the greenfield sites along the road. Soon these were sold to speculative builders, who were able to take advantage of the road (and the services running along it) to build new bungalows and houses very cheaply. The result was a rash of one-house-deep ribbon development, particularly on the fringes of towns and cities. The Restriction of Ribbon Development Act (1935) put an end to the practice and was to prove an important influence on both town and country planning and road design.

Cars and people both require fuel for their journeys. The first filling station was opened by the Automobile Association at Aldermaston in Berkshire in 1919, and soon petrol companies were building their own in large numbers. Most of these have been removed as garages and forecourts have developed over time, but a handful have survived more or less intact, usually when the original garage moved away to better premises elsewhere.

Ribbon development and roadside buildings were obvious impacts on the landscape, but the huge popularity of the car and of motoring has had more lasting effects on Britain's towns and suburbs. The car gave people the independence they demanded, but it came at a price that we shall continue to pay for many years to come. The growth of traffic has always outrun the provision of roads and of parking. Vast multi-storey car parks disfigure the centres of most towns and cities; the appearance of new commuter 'rat runs' can make life in the suburbs and rural areas close to cities very hazardous indeed at either end of the working day.

Many of the cars that clog Britain's roads, and can become stationary features in the landscape themselves, are and were made in Britain. Today new factories have been constructed on the outskirts of large cities in the north-east of England and in Wales – in places where car-building was not traditional. This is because modern car assembly is like many other industrial processes and does not require special skills or experience. In the early twentieth century Daimler set up a factory in an old cotton mill in Coventry. They were attracted to the Black Country because its factories had not been given over to heavy engineering and already manufactured a range of small metal items, such as bicycles and gas engines, and could readily be adapted to the car industry. In 1900 just 151 people were employed in the motor trade in Coventry; by 1905 there were twenty different motor manufacturers in the Hillfields area of the city alone. The first British car, the Wolseley, was made in Birmingham from 1895. Birmingham then became the second centre of motor manufacture and a main source of components. By 1914 the auto industry in Britain employed 53,000 workers and had spread to other towns, notably to Oxford, where in 1912 William Richard Morris began production of the highly successful 'bull-nosed' Morris (thus named for the rounded shape of its radiator), using local bodywork and components manufactured in the Midlands.

Morris was financially astute and weathered the worst of the Depression, when many other firms became bankrupt. He employed large numbers of out-of-work Welsh miners in his Oxford factories. The city prospered as a result: during the inter-war years 10,000 new houses were built and the population rose by 30,000; by 1936 Oxford, Coventry and Luton (home of Vauxhall Motors) were the three most prosperous towns in Britain, after London.

Even the rapid growth of road travel before the last war seems insignificant when compared with later figures. There were, for example, 12.2 million cars in 1970, but this figure had more than doubled to over 25 million by 2001, when on average 93 per cent of the miles travelled in Britain were by road. In order to cope with this extraordinary increase in traffic successive governments embarked on a massive programme of trunk-road improvement and motorway construction. This work has had a huge effect on Britain's rural and urban landscape. In the decades after the Second World War cities such as Birmingham had their centres effectively removed and replaced with roads and cars. If anything, the impact on the rural landscape was even more drastic and it was not long before the road-building programme drew protests from groups concerned with the natural and historical environment. The Newbury bypass, mostly in Berkshire, caused great dissent, both when it was planned and then built, in the 1990s.

Today the internal combustion engine is seen as an important agent of climate change and pollution generally. Roads, especially those like

Fig. 14.27 The A34 Newbury bypass, West Berkshire. This view taken at the southern end near Tot Hill Services, Burghclere (Hampshire), shows the road cutting through Great Pen Woods on Tot Hill. The planning process and eventual construction of this road in the 1990s caused a storm of protest, as many Sites of Special Scientific Importance were cut through. After Newbury, the benefits and disadvantages of a new bypass had to be defined far more rigorously before any construction could begin.

motorways intended for motor vehicles alone, are seen as eyesores that cut through and destroy the environment. It is probably too early to know whether these perceptions will survive the test of time. I firmly believe that one day motorways will come to be viewed like the surviving railways of the nineteenth century, as magnificent engineering achievements that enhance, rather than diminish the landscape. In their day the construction of the early railways was vigorously resisted by huge numbers of people, ranging from landowners to politicians and poets.[79] For over a century the steam locomotives that ran along them belched out huge quantities of soot and smoke. Anyone alive in the 1950s and 1960s will remember the grimy buildings of the great railway cities and how they were transformed when they were cleaned after the departure of the last steam locomotives from about 1965. Today it would be unthinkable to destroy the Ribblehead Viaduct, but many people would be overjoyed if the multi-tiered motorway bridges of Spaghetti Junction were to be blown up overnight. Why is this?

The answer might be that we are losing sight of the true polluter: it is not the road that emits fumes and carbon dioxide, just as it was not the railway lines that belched coal smoke in the days of steam. Modern railways are remarkably environmentally friendly and motorways could be so too, if we all used vehicles that ran on electricity or hydrogen – or sunlight. This surely is where we should focus our attention. Eco-warriors should come out of the trees and instead picket the filling stations and car factories that are the real cause of the problems. The construction of the modern road network did undoubtedly cause damage, but now that it is here surely we should look after it. Any attempt to 'do' a Dr Beeching to the motorways would be similarly short-sighted. In their favour it can also be argued that the motorways have witnessed the planting of many thousands of trees and miles of hedges, and the rough grassland of their large verges and intersections provide a welcome haven for wildlife.

The building of the motorways was the biggest infrastructural project since the era of turnpikes and railways. Like them, and the earlier Roman roads, their construction was all about connecting distant places in the landscape in the shortest possible time. They served no other purpose. They did not mark the edge of a parish, nor a county boundary. They did not need to skirt around the estate of a difficult or hostile landowner, so they cut across field boundaries and earlier roads regardless. It all began rather hesitantly in 1956 when construction started on the first motorway project, the Preston bypass in Lancashire. This road led to Blackpool as part of the M6 and was the busiest holiday route in England. The Preston bypass was designed by John Cox, who had previously been involved with the rapid construction of several new wartime airfields, and it was opened by the Prime Minister, Harold Macmillan, in December 1958. Soon the motorway system began to take shape. The M6 later acquired the most notorious, and to many the most beautiful, too, of the motorway junctions. Junction 6, a short distance north-east of Birmingham city centre is officially known as the Gravelly Hill intersection, but to the rest of Britain it is simply known as Spaghetti Junction.[80] It can be daunting to drive through, especially if one misses one's exit, but it looks magnificent from the air.

The central section of the M1, from Watford just north of London, to the junction with the A5 near Crick in Northamptonshire, was opened in 1959 after a difficult but short period of construction that involved the building of 130 bridges. This can now be seen as something of a golden period for the motorways, which were still being welcomed by the public. I can remember being taken for a spin along the M1 shortly after its opening in my father's pre-war Lancia in which we managed (just) to top 100 m.p.h. It was an exciting – even dangerous – journey, as British drivers had yet to learn to keep a sharp eye on their mirrors and we had to swerve wildly once or twice as unsuspecting

Fig. 14.28 The Gravelly Hill intersection, otherwise known as Spaghetti Junction. This famous, or infamous, interchange is where the M6 (running left to right) meets the separated lanes of the A38(M) (rising from lower right). These major through-routes also join up with local roads, giving access to the nearby city centre. Note also the railway line and the Tame Valley Canal.

slower motorists wombled across our path. Drivers in Germany and Italy had acquired their motorway driving experience a full generation previously and the design of bridges beneath roads like the M1 still captured a flavour of these pre-war styles. These were, of course, the first modern roads to be fully designed from the very outset and recalled the great years of Telford's Holyhead Road, almost a century and a half earlier.

The design of the first motorways took time and certain routes were dictated by the lie of the land. That is why the M1 takes the same route through the Jurassic ridge as does Robert Stephenson's much earlier (1833–8) London and Birmingham railway (now the west coast main line out of Euston).[81] The railway in turn followed the route of the Roman Ermine Street, or A5, but encountered enormous problems when it came to driving the deep and regularly flooded Kilsby Tunnel for more than 2 kilometres through the Watford Gap. Although the M1 passes through the Watford Gap in a cutting, elsewhere it makes effective use of natural features in the landscape. It showed more respect for natural topography and the lie of the land than later motorways, which were often more brutal in the way they were engineered. Modern roads tend to be regarded as uniformly boring, but the observant traveller can always spot interesting features, such as the change in design of the M1 extension north of the Crick/A5 interchange or the interesting single black arch footbridge across the A1(M) at Baldock in Hertfordshire. The original intention had been to build all the bridges along this section of road in a similar style; sadly, the plan had to be abandoned for budgetary reasons, but at least one managed to get built.

In the later twentieth century the motorway system expanded to cover most of the populous areas of Britain. The M62 was driven across the Pennines, joining Leeds to Manchester and the M4 and M5 provided alternative routes to the West Country and the longest route of all, the M40/M6 linked London to north-western England and ultimately to Glasgow. Latterly the M11 has joined London to East Anglia. But of all these routes the busiest and most controversial is undoubtedly the M25. This, the London Orbital Motorway, soon became the busiest road in Europe; efforts were made to improve traffic flow but these merely caused additional delays to what soon became known as 'London's orbital car park'. One important purpose of the M25 was to link London's two busiest airports, at Heathrow and Gatwick, and also to provide better access to the smaller ones at Luton and Stansted. One noticeable feature of ring roads and orbital motorways is that planning authorities regard them as an outer limit for urban expansion; this can be seen as another way of encouraging development within the area enclosed by the road. So by the final decades of the twentieth century traffic engineers were effectively defining towns.

Like the turnpikes, railways and pre-war arterial roads, the motorways encouraged development along certain key or 'corridor' landscapes. Perhaps the best known of these is Britain's 'Silicon Valley' along the M4 corridor west of London, which includes towns like Wokingham, Reading, Newbury, Swindon and Bristol and over the Severn into south Wales. This region also benefits from the railway links originally established by Brunel and from good north–south trunk roads, such as the A34 to Winchester. This area is actually best appreciated from the train, where the new high-tech office blocks can be seen reflected in the lakes that so often accompany them. The lakes in turn are the landscaped remnants of Thames Valley gravel pits. Many of these were first dug in the inter-war years and subsequently enlarged to provide aggregates for wartime airfield runways, as well as the post-war construction boom that saw the enlargement of Bracknell New Town (from 1949) and the building of the M4 itself.

CONSERVING LATE-TWENTIETH-CENTURY LANDSCAPES

The closer one gets to one's own time, the more critical one becomes. For me, nothing is more ugly than the concrete multi-storey car parks that were built in the 1970s to serve city centre shopping precincts. Yet their ultimate purpose – to save city centre areas of commerce – was entirely laudable. One day we shall probably see these eyesores being listed (by statute) for preservation. Perhaps this is why it is so much easier to be generous about the natural world than the modern built environment.

Ever since the 1960s, which witnessed the rise of popular environmentalism, diverse natural habitats have been given special protection. Pioneer conservationists, such as Sir Peter Scott who founded the Wildfowl and Wetlands Trust in 1946, were aware of the problems that lay ahead and made individual efforts to protect some of the most important areas for wildlife. The process of general site selection began to be placed on a secure scientific footing from 1965 with the start of a detailed research project into the biological sites of Britain, carried out by staff of the then Nature Conservancy Council of Britain. Today the NCC has been divided up between England, Scotland and Wales, so that such a comprehensive assessment would no longer be possible.

The results of the NCC survey were published in two volumes edited by their chief scientist, Dr Derek Ratcliffe.[82] In this most remarkable study every important habitat in Britain was recorded in some detail, location by location. It was to provide the factual basis for subsequent landscape legal designations, such as Sites of Special Scientific Interest (SSSIs). There are about 4,000 SSSIs in England, more than 1,000 in Wales and about 1,450 in Scotland. Today these designated areas, together with others developed through the European Union and similar organizations, are proclaimed by politicians as important, but many will be harmed by prospective developments, such as the controversial Thames Gateway housing project. It should also be emphasized that site selection is a continuing process and new areas are constantly being added to the various lists.

Nature reserves and other protected and environmentally sensitive landscapes cannot, however, remain static. Our surroundings are constantly altering as the climate itself changes. As I write this, I have just returned from a quick walk to check my in-lamb ewes and on my way back to the house I saw a little egret sheltering from the chilly northeasterly wind in a dyke at the end of the drive. A bird-watching friend of mine says that both great and cattle egrets have been repeatedly sighted in Sussex. Such sightings would have been unheard of twenty years ago. Today it is becoming routine. It follows that if we are to adapt successfully to the new circumstances, then our most sensitive and best-preserved regions must change as well. Indeed, as we shall see in Chapter 15, nature reserves should not just react; instead they should play an active part in attracting new species in order to help ecosystems adapt to global warming.

Landscapes in more or less the sense used in this book are currently being analysed using map-based techniques such as Landscape Characterization. Landscape Characterization is essentially a process that was developed in Cornwall, a county that possesses a series of very distinctive types of landscape.[83] It has evolved into a sophisticated analytical tool and many, myself included, who were sceptical at first have subsequently been won round – largely because it seems to work. Essentially, it is based on the long-observed fact that some landscapes appear to be planned, or organized, and others seem more random, piecemeal and 'ancient'. Other factors such as detailed analyses of geology and geography, drainage and patterns of industry are used to create detailed maps that categorize the landscape in a way that seems to be objective.[84]

These techniques have proved to be effective when drawing up policies for conservation and forward planning. I find it hard to be altogether rational when faced by 'monstrosities' such as concrete multistorey car parks, but somehow we must escape from such prejudices when we consider what is likely to prove significant about the late twentieth century, in, say, fifty or a hundred years' time. There is a pressing need for us to characterize in some detail what we now have, before we can address the problems posed by its conservation.[85]

From a rural perspective, it may be questioned to what extent we do want to preserve for posterity the semi-industrialized arable landscapes of 'prairies and tin sheds' bequeathed to us by the final decades of the twentieth century. The same question might well have been posed by a traditional farmer in the 1860s, when confronted with one of the huge new cattle enterprises of Victorian High Farming. In both instances one could question whether it was possible to turn the clock back and reinstate old lanes, field boundaries and so forth. Surely it would be better to attempt something new by way of rebuilding or re-creating biodiversity: new lakes and woodlands, for example, with improved public access. One could also argue that it is somehow more honest to admit that we have destroyed an important part of our agricultural heritage, but are attempting something innovative to put matters right, albeit in a small way.

A large proportion of Britain's annual carbon 'footprint' comes from farming and it is likely that attempts to lower this will result in some innovative new projects, which may well prove suitable for conservation in the future. There does, however, seem to be a general consensus that the rural and urban landscapes of today will best be appreciated in the future if they are conserved entire, rather than as individual sites or buildings. To this end, the English Heritage Conservation team have been looking at various categories of landscape (seaside, industrial, defence, etc.) to see where might be the best potential candidates for ultimate conservation. The task is made more urgent by the fact that many modern buildings are erected with a finite and usually quite short lifespan in mind.

In the retail sector it is often the site, rather than the buildings on it, which will retain its value into the future. So when the time comes, even developments that now seem so massive, like the Bluewater Shopping Centre in Kent, may be pulled down and replaced by something else, possibly bigger, possibly smaller, but certainly unpredictable. The actual

Fig. 14.29 The Bluewater Shopping Centre, Kent, opened at the very end of the twentieth century on 16 March 1999. 'Retail therapy' had became an abiding theme of life at the time and a series of huge out-of-town shopping centres grew up to satisfy the demand. By 2007 this theme had begun to turn unpleasantly sour.

demolition will have been a process that will already have been considered, if not actually planned – and it will be quick. So we need to be aware which are the modern buildings and landscapes that we want to preserve. Then we must act rapidly. At first glance this might seem an impossibly ambitious attempt to second-guess posterity, but we must make it.

15

Sat Nav Britain: What Future for
the Landscape?

The landscape is where people live out their lives. And of course there are landscapes within landscapes. A child will view the landscape very differently from an adult, just as a man will see it differently from a woman, or a priest from a farmer. I suspect that William Wordsworth saw the Lake District very differently from the men who ran their flocks across its Fells. From a geographer's analytical perspective, both poet and shepherd inhabited the same tract of countryside. But did they?

What I am saying here is that the landscapes that we define, discuss and inhabit exist within our minds and imagination. But that does not diminish their reality: they are still there, because we know they are and we have experienced them. Wordsworth appreciated the Lake District's sense of place and his poems added a further dimension to its identity, without altering the landscape itself. This gave the imagination of visitors to the region, or indeed to readers of his verses, or Wainwright's famous *Guides*, more fuel for the imagination, from which they could create their own Lake Districts. We should not, however, assume that these well-known interpretations of landscape are somehow 'correct', because they will only continue to exist for as long as the public at large is prepared to accept them – and the places themselves remain unspoiled.

Artists and scholars like Wordsworth, Hoskins and Wainwright have enhanced and defined regional character in a manner that is absolutely necessary. The development and recognition of regional distinctiveness will be the key to the long-term survival of the British landscape.

Throughout this book I have used examples of landscape taken from the Salisbury Plain Training Area (SPTA), which owes its survival to the army. The SPTA has been a battlefield training area since the late nineteenth century and has been traversed by huge tanks and bombarded with live ammunition by artillery, helicopters and bombers. Despite this continuing frontal assault the delicate chalkland soils and traces of long-lost landscapes have fared far better here than in the surrounding arable country. What tanks, bombs and guns could not destroy, modern farming has effectively obliterated elsewhere in just four decades. The main concern raised by this is that, if destruction continues at the rate established in the latter half of the twentieth century, future archaeological discoveries will only be made in areas that are not suited to modern farming or plantation forestry (which can be even more destructive than so-called 'conventional' agriculture). If huge areas become in effect archaeologically barren, I cannot see how we can ever hope to write a balanced story of Britain's past. It would also become impossible to make a sound case for regional distinctiveness. Indeed, one could argue that the process of regional identity-loss is already well under way over large areas of south-east England, where the survival of the landscape must be considered in real jeopardy. While the scale of destruction is undoubtedly huge, certain fragile landscapes have always been particularly vulnerable.

The true extent of the destruction of the last few remains of ancient landscapes on the lighter gravel soils of Britain has only become apparent since the late 1950s. The problem posed by the gravel-extraction industry is made worse for archaeology because, once excavated, instead of being abandoned and partially filled with derelict machinery or other rubbish, as happened until very recently, they are landscaped and reborn as wetland nature reserves. But the destruction of irreplaceable ancient remains has happened, and this should not be forgotten. You can always replant a hedge, but you can never replace a barrow.

Turning to the destruction of archaeological and other features in the arable landscape, the post-war decades have seen the pace of damage or destruction increase rapidly. By the start of the twenty-first century the only areas that can be considered reasonably safe are the poorest soils classified as Grade 5 (Grade 1 being the best) by soil scientists.[1] These are mainly very thin, wet or poorly drained, high upland soils. Admittedly, archaeological remains are often very well preserved in these areas, but with the best will in the world they cannot be considered as representative of the countryside as a whole. In all other areas the situation is bleak.

At the very end of the twentieth century there was a widespread switch by most British farmers away from smaller machinery owned by individual farmers, to massive tractors used by contractors. This was a result of the sharp decline in the profitability of British farming following the withdrawal of direct production subsidies from the European Union Common Agricultural Policy. There have been other problems, too. Certain crops require the soil to be de-stoned and ridged up, which can cause great damage to any underlying remains. Intensive farming of row-crops such as potatoes in areas like the Vale of Pickering in east Yorkshire, or daffodils around Spalding in Lincolnshire, leads to the development of viral and other diseases that can only be controlled if the crop is moved onto land that has not grown potatoes or bulbs previously.[2] This practice means that it is becoming increasingly hard to confine the crops and the problems they pose to certain restricted areas.

When it comes to the destruction wrought by modern farming on the landscape, it is difficult to think of a solution which has any hope of long-term success. I am in little doubt that in fifty years' time it will be much harder to write detailed landscape history, whether urban or rural, from evidence gleaned from our surroundings. The tendency of the twentieth century was towards greater homogeneity. This is in direct opposition to regional distinctiveness, quirkiness and character. The accusation of homogeneity and blandness can also be levelled at some of the measures we are adopting to preserve regional character, such as Landscape Characterization. What worries me about such well-intentioned and well-executed efforts is that they are essentially top-down and are therefore, almost by definition, patronizing. They assume that the specialists in landscape analysis know what is best for the people out there in the landscape, living real lives in a real world.

Although legislation on the preservation of the historic environment has subsequently been tightened up, the fact remains that the future of the landscape actually lies in the hands of the people who own it, whether they be directors of supermarkets, farmers, the Prince of Wales or ordinary individuals in their pubs, shops, flats, houses, gardens or allotments. As in 2001, when the Ministry of Agriculture tried to slam the stable door shut after the administrative fiasco that attended the outbreak of foot-and-mouth disease, no amount of red tape can ultimately stop people from doing what they have to do. This is the only source that I can see of any hope. It takes individuals, not authorities, to defeat blandness and uniformity – but how they will eventually achieve this is entirely up to them.

In his excellent book on the twentieth-century landscape, Trevor Rowley writes about theme-park England, in which idealized versions of lost landscapes are offered to visitors as a painless, pre-packaged 'experience' (which of course it is not). Increasingly, people are feeling distanced from their surroundings. It is one thing to visit a place, but quite another to live there and to be part of it. Many people are discovering that one way to establish oneself in a new area is quite literally to put down roots and fashion one's own slice of landscape, be it ever so tiny.

Today politicians and retailers boast about 'choice', but when it comes to that essential fuel of life, food, it is a choice that never alters: a huge range of largely taste-free ingredients that are available all year round in supermarkets. I would much prefer to return to the situation before the war, when food was both more nutritious and tasty and when the admittedly more limited choices varied from year to year and from season to season.

DO-IT-YOURSELF LANDSCAPE IMPROVEMENT

If, like me, you regard good food as an essential part of a full life, then the only option is to grow it yourself. Many town allotment associations have folded in the face of recent 'brownfield' development, but some have survived, and increasingly people are setting out their own vegetable gardens. In a world where the essentials of life are so often provided by somebody else, the simple act of cutting one's own lettuce becomes disproportionately pleasurable. I don't even begrudge slugs a nibble if they want one. In 2006 the Royal Horticultural Society reported that seed companies had announced that, for the first time, vegetable seeds had out-sold flowers.[3]

Fig. 15.1 Controlling your own landscapes: part of my vegetable garden in summer. To the left are potatoes (four varieties), then two rows of peas, grown on hazel pea sticks cut in the winter from the wood, visible in the middle distance, behind the hornbeam hedge. To the right of the peas are rows of garlic, onions and shallots, then a row of broad beans and, beneath the dark mesh cloche, next winter's Brussels sprouts. Sweet peas and runner beans are growing on the hazel and cane 'wigwams', upper right.

Gardening has become immensely popular and garden centres are now a major part of the retail sector. Some people, presumably not gardeners themselves, have seen the growth of gardening as a form of escape from the modern rat-race. Like others, I garden because I *have* to. Many people find gardening a creative and profoundly satisfying pursuit that has the important additional benefit of physical exertion with some purpose to it (which exercise in a gymnasium lacks). I find that my garden allows me to create and control my own mini-landscape.

It is still widely held that changes to the landscape must, almost by definition, be slow: I can well recall having discussions about the future of Stonehenge when the revival of the chalkland landscape around it was considered in terms of generations.[4] This may indeed be true for certain plant communities in extreme upland landscapes, in sandy heaths and chalklands, where delicate species of orchids prevail; it is also true of the many bluebell woods that are such an important feature of ancient woodlands in southern Britain. But it does not apply across the board and people should not feel daunted by the prospect of doing something themselves. Modern techniques of propagation, involving, for example, the insertion of plugs of ancient floristically rich meadowland, can expedite the processes of recovery or restoration enormously. So my advice would always be to go for it.

I have been astonished to discover just how quickly you can transform your surroundings, provided that you reintroduce species that are appropriate for the existing conditions. Until very recently the native British black poplar (*Populus nigra*) was dying out and its very existence was threatened. But in the last two decades a number of people have set about methodically replanting these majestic trees. I myself have planted more than sixty and have passed hundreds of cuttings on to friends and neighbours (see Plate 18). Botanists have subsequently discovered that black poplars naturally reproduce in this way – through rooting their lower branches, or by rooting when blown over. They grow very fast and support large numbers of insects, including poplar hawk moths.

When we planted our wood and garden we were fully expecting to

Fig. 15.2 Private landscapes: the view from my sitting-room window.

wait for a very long time indeed before we saw any changes to the rather mundane wildlife that inhabited our intensively farmed stretch of Fenland. But a year after planting the wood, when the young saplings were just poking out of their growing tubes, we were regularly visited by barn and short-eared owls hunting for mice and voles living in the thick weeds and vegetation in the land around the tubes. The hedgehog population, feeding on slugs and snails, expanded rapidly, too. After about ten years we had resident green and great spotted woodpeckers. Last winter we decided to thin out the trees in the centre of the wood as they were beginning to become leggy, and were advised they would probably collapse in a severe gale. The thinning let in more light and encouraged the few primroses that we had planted there fifteen years previously to burst into extravagant growth. Next year they will probably have produced an abundance of seedlings.

We have been astonished by the speed with which nature grasps opportunities. I have spoken to others who have done similar projects and they too confirm that the changes have been far more rapid than they had been led to expect. The good news is spreading and I wonder to what extent do-it-yourself landscape improvers, ultimately motivated by the need to do something about both their surroundings and bio-diversity, will start to transform the British landscape in this century. I just hope the process can be allowed to happen without too much interference from those who believe they know better.

PLANNING THE NATURAL LANDSCAPE AND OTHER 'HISTORIC ASSETS'

Traditionally, the British landscape has been protected by a variety of planning control and Ancient Monuments Acts, the first of which passed into law in October 1882, the last in 1979.[5] Today there are also other designations above and beyond scheduling (for ancient monuments) and listing (for historic buildings) under the Ancient Monuments Acts. There are also Areas of Outstanding Natural Beauty (AONBs) and Sites of Special Scientific Interest (SSSIs), and, in towns and villages, conservation areas, not to mention National Parks. The complexity of the legislation and planning controls surrounding the various elements of the historic environment is becoming quite bewildering and reform is urgently needed.

As a response to this unsatisfactory situation, on 8 March 2007 the government published a White Paper, *Heritage Protection for the 21st Century*, which sets out proposals for new, unified and simpler legislation.[6] The new proposals are for a single category of 'historic asset' which will include ancient monuments, ruins, historic buildings, parks, gardens, battlefields and – most importantly – landscapes. They will all be subject to essentially the same protection, which will be administered, it is hoped, in a less bureaucratic but more open way. There will be greater public involvement in the designation and scrutiny of individual historic assets, which will come as a great relief to anyone who has crossed the sometimes unimaginative bureaucrats who can lurk in the depths of the various institutions that protect our national heritage. Landscapes will benefit from the expected removal of the current Class Consent system which allows activities, such as ploughing, to continue, even through it is recognized that great damage is being caused to specific landscapes. Sadly, these much-needed proposals were not be given Parliamentary time in the 2009 session, thanks to the current economic crisis.

Britain has also signed up to the Valletta (1992) and World Heritage Conventions (1972).[7] The former is an initiative of the European Council and the latter of UNESCO. Both aim to ensure that national governments protect and effectively manage the most important sites and landscapes within their borders. In essence, both work through the power of public opinion, at both a European and global level.

The test case for the effectiveness of the World Heritage Convention in Britain will undoubtedly be the Stonehenge landscape. The present visitor arrangements at Stonehenge have been described as 'a national disgrace'. Any visitor to the monument has to contend with the roar of traffic from the nearby A303, not to mention the A344, which passes close by the Stones. The A303 is the most direct route from London to the south-west. Because the Stones sit in isolation, completely removed from their landscape, the visitor cannot get a feeling for their original importance, as the spiritual focus of a gigantic and constantly changing ritual landscape. There is a pressing need for the A303 to be buried in a long tunnel and for the minor road to be closed and torn up. The current hideous visitor centre and car park also should be moved. When those three things happen the Avenue and the wider landscape will be reunited with the Stones and we will be able to appreciate why the best-known prehistoric monument in the world was carefully positioned within a vast ritual landscape all of its own.

Of course legislative protection is one thing; it is quite another actually to safeguard what is there. Today much damage to the landscape, both rural and urban, is a result of innumerable acts of vandalism or insensitivity. In 2007 Bill Bryson, the new President of the Council to Protect Rural England, complained about litter and fly-tipping which are fast becoming major problems. As a very small landowner myself, in the first five years of this century I have had to see off a local builder dumping a trailer-full of rubble into a dyke and on various occasions I have found refrigerators, a demolished caravan, numerous mattresses, tyres and tons of rubble thrown into ditches. The ultimate cause of fly-tipping is the charges levied at landfill sites. Lying behind those charges is the mistaken belief that problems can be sorted out by passing unenforceable legislation, which the unscrupulous are more than happy to ignore. It is tempting to see fly-tipping as just one symptom of a society where people are more concerned with their rights than their obligations.

Large parts of the British landscape are undeniably under actual threat of destruction. Indeed, the very survival of the physical evidence for the past in particular regions, such as wetlands and arable lands, is at stake, largely due to modern intensive farming, peat- or gravel-extraction.[8] The damage caused by modern farming has long had archaeologists wringing their hands; many (myself included) believe that the worst damage has already taken place, mostly in the 1970s and 1980s. These concerns are fuelled by field surveys that show increasing concentrations of finds on the surface of arable fields, which would suggest that archaeological features below the topsoil are being damaged by ever-deeper ploughing. But we still lack good, objective, empirical evidence, which ought soon to be provided by two practical experiments being carried out under the auspices of English Heritage and DEFRA (the government department currently responsible for agriculture).[9]

Rather unexpectedly, archaeological remains in less intensively farmed areas, such as south-western moors of Dartmoor and Bodmin, are threatened by the otherwise laudable intentions of nature conservation interests. In these regions large tracts of prehistoric and ancient landscape have been protected by the grazing of sheep since pre-Roman times. Recently, however, sheep numbers have been drastically reduced, supposedly in the interests of biodiversity, and the consequent under-grazing is allowing invasive scrub regeneration (mostly gorse and thorn) which is both obscuring and damaging fragile ancient features.

There is not a great deal that individuals can do about these problems, other than to avoid spreading thick layers of washed gravel on driveways (this encourages gravel-extraction elsewhere), to avoid peat-based garden composts or to question the need for yet more roads. I suppose one could also argue that matters are under a sort of wobbly control, with a loose confederation of concerned individuals and institutions becoming increasingly aware of the situation. There is moreover an important sign of hope that portends well for the longer-term future. During the 1980s and 1990s the material remains of the past, what archaeologists today refer to as the 'historic environment', came to be recognized as an important component of the surviving natural environment.[10] There are many reasons for this change, but one was the realization that few, if any, parts of Britain are indeed truly natural.

In 2007 the householders of Hampstead Garden Suburb celebrated its centenary. Hampstead Garden Suburb is widely acknowledged to be a special place and great efforts have been made to retain its ambience.[11] Other historic inner suburbs have been less fortunate. These areas are under threat because the housing they offer is less in demand (often due to inadequate parking), and local authorities are keen to increase housing density both to meet their targets and to take pressure off their 'greenfield' sites.[12] The result of these and other pressures is that the original character of much suburban housing, not just in London, but right across Britain, is being destroyed. The London Assembly has estimated that two-thirds of London's front gardens have been modified to accommodate car parking.[13] This usually involves the paving over of front lawns and flower beds. Low boundary hedges are also disappearing fast. Taken together these modifications, relatively minor in themselves, are having a detrimental effect on biodiversity.

They also lead to rapid surface run-off and ultimately increase the chances of flash flooding.[14]

Britain is heavily populated and the need for planning controls is more pressing now than even the last century. Every development of any importance is subject to scrutiny by many groups and committees of the various stakeholder organizations who are likely to be involved. Increasingly, too, following the adoption of the Freedom of Information Act, local government is subject to closer public scrutiny and there is now far greater transparency. These entirely laudable developments might also become a means whereby the quirky, the odd and the peculiar are eliminated from new landscapes in the future. Local authorities are risk-averse at the best of times, but increased levels of public scrutiny could make them even more conservative. It would be sad if better planning procedures and financial control were to deprive us of such gems as the Greenwich Dome or, on a somewhat smaller scale, my own personal favourite, the great yew topiary avenue at Clipsham, Rutland, which I have illustrated here.

Fig. 15.3 In 1870 Amos Alexander, the head forester of the Clipsham estate, Rutland, started clipping the yews outside his home in the gatehouse cottage of Clipsham Hall, visible here in the background. The squire of Clipsham Hall was so impressed that he asked him to clip all the yew trees along the avenue leading up to the Hall.

When I first came across Clipsham I could not believe my eyes. A small lodge near the road was positively dwarfed by the dozens of tall clipped yew trees that surrounded it. I pulled off into a small car park and then found myself on the great Yew Avenue, which led towards a not very large house sitting within parkland. It made no sense whatsoever: it was clearly not part of a grand design by a Repton or a Capability Brown, as it seemed to draw one's attention more to the lodge than the big house. And besides, many of the topiary figures carried clear references to recent historical events, such as Neil Armstrong's moonwalk. I later learnt that the first topiary had been done, as a hobby, by the estate's head forester, who lived in the lodge, and his boss, who lived in the big house had approved, and encouraged him to extend the topiary along the Avenue.

Then in 1955 the estate was taken over by the Forestry Commission, who also encouraged change within the spirit of the original idea. My point is that the Clipsham yews were one man's whim, encouraged by an imaginative employer. As histories go it is unplanned, unscripted and idiosyncratic. You could call it eccentric or inspired, it matters not, but it is there, nonetheless. I simply do not believe that it could have appeared, like, say, *The Angel of the North*, through a decision made by a committee of the Arts Council or a local authority. Instead it happened via another route entirely – certainly less travelled, but none the worse for that. By definition that route cannot be predicted, pinned down or defined.

THE LANDSCAPE AND CLIMATE CHANGE

There can be very few people who do not by now accept the overwhelming evidence for global climate change.[15] Predictions for the rate of change and its consequences always vary. Similarly, it can be hazardous to suggest that specific events, such as the Great Storm that devastated southern England in 1987, are or were a direct consequence of it. It boils down to a question of scale: how does one argue convincingly that a one-off event is necessarily part of a long-term process? Perhaps in fifty or a hundred years' time we shall be able to demonstrate statistically that such events, along with many others that have not yet happened, were the result of global warming, but we cannot say that at this stage. I merely suggest that even though I experienced the Great Storm well to the north of its centre, I have never seen anything like it before or since. I had driven to Flag Fen early in the morning following the impact of the main storm, as I was convinced that the outside displays might be damaged. It was still extremely windy as I drove my Land-Rover across the Fens and I was lucky not to have been blown into a dyke. When I arrived, I went straight across to our reconstructed Bronze Age roundhouse, just as the gales increased in ferocity. I had to stoop almost double to avoid being blown over and reached the roundhouse with some relief.

Once inside I was astonished by the peace and tranquillity of the place. Nothing was moving and the entire structure was stable. Its conical roof and round walls were spilling the gale and I recall standing at the door sipping a mug of warm tea from my flask and watching as steel sheets of wall cladding blew down the Bronze Age droveway from the nearby industrial estate, like so many vast and luridly coloured autumn leaves. This made me think that all of our much-vaunted 'progress' of late has actually been in the wrong direction, if we are ever to cope with the sort of rapid climate change that our ancestors had to face at the close of the last Ice Age. The trouble is, we have come too far to turn back.

In the previous chapters we discussed gravel pits, mining and reservoirs, which have made their impact on the landscape either by drowning, or by digging down into it. In the 1980s and 1990s, and increasingly in the twenty-first century, we have seen the construction of windfarms, whose impact on the landscape is above ground.[16] It could be argued that these majestic turbines have a minimal 'footprint' on the ground, can readily be removed and produce renewable energy. Surely, therefore, they are to be welcomed? There are, of course, reasonable objections from people like ornithologists who rightly protest if turbines are sited on migration routes; but, such problems aside, surely most sensible people would conclude that they are to be welcomed? Not so, it would seem, even in areas that are under severe threat from rising sea levels due to climate change, such as the Fens. Proposals to erect wind turbines near the village

Fig. 15.4 A windfarm near Amlwch, Anglesey. Note the buildings of the Wylfa nuclear power station in the background, on the skyline. The Wylfa power station is in the process of being decommissioned. Wind turbines in the more windy parts of western Britain are erected on shorter masts than their eastern counterparts, where wind speeds are lower.

of Gedney Hill, in Lincolnshire, for example have stalled because of strong local opposition. Most of the land in the area around Gedney Hill is about 2 to 3 metres above sea level. (Incidentally, the word 'hill' in the Fens either refers to a corner (a 'heel') in the arrangement of drainage dykes, or to a low rise of a metre or two on the ground surface.)

The arguments that surround windfarms are of special interest because they centre around perceptions of the landscape, which takes us straight back to the origin of the term itself – a painter's view of the world. Today it is just as valid to discuss proposals to build windfarms in language that addresses the appearance and beauty of the landscape, as on the basis of more practical concerns, such as noise, traffic or damage to wildlife. It can seem ironic that the issues to do with the possible impact of windfarms are addressed not with paintings or artists' reconstructions, but with high-tech, computer-generated animated reconstructions, where the viewer is taken on a dramatic fly-by, fly-through and fly-over visit. Some see the turbines as visually intrusive, others worry about noise or vibration and the consequent effect on house prices in the region. It is very much a question of landscape aesthetics. Relatively rarely, it seems, is the central issue of global warming raised in local inquiries into new windfarms. Speaking entirely from a personal perspective, I see wind turbines as starkly beautiful and as a symbolic reminder of the fact that if we value the British landscape above personal wealth we must do something – anything – to resist climate change.[17]

This is not the place, nor am I the person, to suggest likely climate change scenarios, but informed predictions make it quite clear that the British landscape is about to undergo some major changes.[18] The scale and impact of these changes will largely depend on the extent to which carbon emissions can be curtailed in the near future. Much damage has already been done, starting in the late eighteenth century, and even if all emissions are stopped – an impossibility – sea levels will continue to rise, as a response to the warming that has already taken place.[19] During the twentieth century average temperatures increased by 0.6 °C, of which 0.4 °C happened after 1970. The 1990s were the warmest decade since records began in the 1660s, and 1998 and 2006 were in turn the warmest years on record. If carbon emissions can be moderated, then temperatures by the 2080s may rise between 2 and 3.5 °C in Britain. If emissions continue to grow unchecked, then south-eastern Britain may be 5 °C warmer by the same time. By the 2080s sea levels around the shores of south-eastern Britain will be between 26 and 86 centimetres higher than they are today.[20] We should note, however, that sea levels are linked to climate, but not always directly, and this can make prediction difficult.[21] Winter storms will be more severe and it is hard to see how low-lying areas, such as the Fens, can escape periodic severe marine inundation – if not permanent abandonment.[22] There seems little point in extending this catalogue of gloom, but one has to question the sanity of the DEFRA decision to cut its spending on coastal defences for 2006/7.[23] Doubtless the banks around the Wash look less insubstantial when viewed from an office in Whitehall.

Some changes to the landscape are easily predictable. Warmth-loving (thermophilous) trees, such as the lime, will be found in northern Scotland. Heavier rainfall will cause major problems in historic buildings whose gutters cannot cope with increased winter rain and major storms. Lawns and mown grass, currently the single most characteristic feature of 'classic' British parks and gardens, will cease to be either viable or attractive, given hotter, drier summers. As any gardener knows, mixed herbaceous borders require large amounts of water, especially in July and August, and are likely therefore to prove unsustainable. A huge variety of new pests and diseases are likely to spread northwards from warmer regions closer to the equator. These will probably make the attack of Dutch elm disease in the 1960s and 1970s seem relatively trivial. As I write, fatal new diseases are reported to be attacking horse chestnuts, English oak and the common alder. Box hedges – another important feature of British formal gardens – are everywhere being attacked by a new strain of fungal disease known as box blight. The catalogue of woes, many of which can probably be linked to global warming or at best to the poorly policed globalization of trade, seems endless.

One factor that might hold some hope is Britain's position on the globe. By and large the British Isles do not have as many low-lying areas as, say, the Netherlands or Bangladesh. Northern Europe is also far from the equator where the very worst effects are likely to be felt. But Britain is a very crowded island with a huge urban population and its lowland areas are being farmed with increasingly intensity. Prairie fields and huge housing estates can only respond to climate change in very limited ways. As conditions become more harsh, such places are likely to become barriers to the new species of plants and animals that will need to move in, if biodiversity is to be maintained. Apart from anything else, the new plants will help absorb carbon dioxide and thereby ameliorate the effects of climate change. Fresh species of insects and other animals will be required, for example, to pollinate the new plants. We all know the disadvantages of importing a single species, such as the grey squirrel, into a new environment, without also bringing with it its natural predators. In other words, change should be encouraged to happen in nature's way, without forcing the pace.

It is therefore essential that we should start organizing the existing landscape in a manner that will allow the natural environment to respond to warmer conditions.[24] In Chapter 14 I mentioned seeing a little egret in a dyke. I saw my first one two years ago and it caused quite a stir when I mentioned it in the pub at lunchtime. Today, while not common, they are not an unusual sight in the Fens. There must be half a dozen in the fields around our village. Egrets can fly long distances, and happily – for they are very attractive – they are not fussy eaters and can find food in our area, which is far less intensively farmed than other parts of the Fens. Other species, however, are less mobile and are far more picky about what they eat. They require more diverse environments than streets and arable fields. Those environments already exist in the form of nature reserves and other protected habitats, but these are nearly always isolated places, deliberately cut off from centres of population and other likely sources of disturbance. Somehow we must find the means to join these refuges together, because if we do not they will fail to adapt to climate change and will eventually lose the biodiversity they exist to protect. Narrow wildlife 'corridors', such as hedgerows and stream banks, have traditionally been sufficient to tie isolated habitats together. But they will not be adequate in the near future; just as medieval roads were replaced by turnpikes, these corridors will have to be supplanted by much wider wildlife 'highways'.

This view of Britain's landscape in the twenty-first century would be good for wildlife and for people too. Instead of the sudden jump from suburb to a bare and intensive arable landscape, towns and cities would be surrounded by buffer zones and other semi-natural areas which would absorb pollution and also act as wildlife highways. They would be accessible and would help to reconnect urban people with the rural landscapes around them. But will it happen? Ultimately it simply depends on whether national and local government, developers and conservationists can come together and co-operate. If they can, it will; if they cannot, it will not.

Britain is blessed with a maritime climate and, even if one of the secondary effects of climate change were to be the death, or diversion, of the Gulf Stream, the British Isles would always be a more favourable area for the growing of crops than, say, inland parts of continental Asia, Africa or North America. Future crops could include olives, almonds, or indeed grapes – which were first grown in Britain during Roman times.[25] At present the British climate is only just suitable for the growing of vines, and vineyards are still something of a rarity, although growing quite fast in popularity. Most are in the southernmost

Fig. 15.5 Planning for climate change. The landscape of the twenty-first century will provide the best means of adapting to climate change. But it will need drastic modification. Instead of a sharp transition from cities to intensively farmed arable – neither of which favours biodiversity – we shall have to establish broad wildlife 'highways' (dotted lines here) which will provide semi-wild buffer zones around towns and cities and link existing areas of high biodiversity together. As the climate grows warmer, plants and animals will constantly need to move to more suitable habitats. The nature reserves that exist will need to change and conserve rather than preserve.

counties of England, although recently I spent a very pleasant weekend visiting Wroxeter Roman Town in Shropshire. Near here vines are grown on a truly commercial scale. By the middle of the twenty-first century vineyards will probably be a common sight in Scotland. Perhaps milking parlours will be stripped out and converted into bottling stores. If the production of wine is not of itself a reason to be cheerful, it does at least provide us with a proven means of escaping gloomy prognostications.

Certain groups, mostly in the United States, are keen to deny or discount the changes likely to be brought about by global warming. I have also encountered a view which suggests that the warming we are going to experience this century will not be as rapid as that which took

Fig. 15.6 A common sight in the British landscape of the twenty-first century? Vines growing in the Wroxeter Roman Vineyard, Shropshire. The Roman city of *Viroconium Cornoviarum* lies behind the trees at the far end of the field.

place at the end of the last Ice Age. That is indeed the case, but other factors must also be taken into account. This mistaken view suggests that global warming can be discounted because communities in the early Mesolithic period were able successfully to adapt to a very much warmer climate. If people back in the Stone Age were able to make the necessary changes, then surely we, with all our technological know-how, will be even better equipped to cope? There are at least three good reasons why this is an entirely fallacious argument.

Firstly, we are not in the Stone Age. We cannot simply retreat uphill as the North Sea rushes towards us, because the globe is now so heavily populated that such migrations would cause massive social and political disturbance. We are also not in the final throes of an Ice Age, when environmental warming could be seen as positive. Barren, treeless tundra landscapes were replaced first by pine and birch and eventually by deciduous oak forests; this was accompanied by an increase of game and other resources, such as fish and shellfish. Perhaps most important of all, however, the warming of the climate that followed the end of the last Ice Age levelled off within a very short time (roughly half a century) and then temperatures became much as they are today. The best scenarios for modern global warming, however, show only evidence for increase, not decrease, unless, that is, carbon emissions can be massively curtailed, and eventually reversed; this, of course, is unlikely to happen if the very fact of climate change is denied.

LANDSCAPES AND PEOPLE

The story of the British landscape up until the middle of the twentieth century was essentially a tale of ordinary people living their lives, largely untouched by the great events of history. I am not saying that people lived in ignorance of, say, the Battle of Waterloo, because we know that was not the case, but even the final defeat of Napoleon did not affect most folk directly. They continued to live their lives and farm their farms. Economic conditions might change, but the landscape continued, and humans still inhabited it. Of course there were very bad times that led to population decline – such as the plague years of the fourteenth to seventeenth centuries, the farming recession of the 1870s or the Highland clearances of the eighteenth century, but still the landscape continued and life went on. Archaeology can detect the effects of these changes on the ground and provides a witness to the continuing efforts of ordinary people to live honest, dignified lives despite their historical circumstances.

The archaeology and history of landscape is the story of day-to-day decisions made by ordinary people. They may well have been organized by Church authorities, powerful landowners or industrialists, but it was they who did the actual work of hedge-making, ditch-digging, house-building and so forth. And when one excavates, or carries out a detailed field survey, one has to get into the minds of the people who worked on the land, if one is to understand why they adopted particular solutions to the day-to-day problems that confronted them. I remember excavating the site of a late-eighteenth-century cotton mill in Manchester. The mill had been built by the great industrialist Richard Arkwright, but the brick floors were worn down by the feet of countless mill-workers and we were able to record details of those minor alterations – a new doorway here, a blocked window there – that happened during the long life of the mill until it burnt down around 1850. It was rebuilt and then was finally destroyed by the Nazis in the Manchester Blitz. As we worked through the two destruction levels, my thoughts were not with Arkwright, but with the poor people who had survived the two fires.

I believe that for too long the story of Britain has concentrated on a version of history that both concerns, and is relevant to, a minority at the upper, usually better educated, end of society. Most conventional accounts are about those important, some would say defining events, such as the battles of Hastings, Waterloo or Britain. They are about a succession of prime ministers, kings and queens, but while these things were happening, life continued in the towns and villages of Britain. Even during the Civil War of the seventeenth century a few houses were built, the landscape was maintained and millions of people fed themselves. It is high time these stories emerged into the light, not as a sub-text, but as narratives in their own right.

I sometimes think that in the past the landscape developed *despite* the events of history. But before we dismiss that thought out of hand, we should just pause to reflect on the situation nowadays, because there really has been a major change, a transformation indeed, in the way we do things. If I were to suggest that the landscapes of both rural and urban Britain in the twenty-first century were disconnected from political events, there would be howls of derision, because politicians and civil servants intervene at every level. As I write, huge areas of good nineteenth-century terrace housing are about to be destroyed by the Pathfinder Project across northern England – seemingly at the whim of planners and their political bosses.[26] Further south and east, the so-called Thames Gateway project will eradicate large areas of low-lying landscape around the Thames estuary.[27] To my mind both projects are verging on the insane, in their planning and execution. I hate to think what they will look like in fifty years' time.

Thirty years ago farmers were paid large sums to grub up hedges. So hedges vanished across huge areas of Britain, regardless of their individual regional contexts. Today farmers are paid rather less by environmental grant schemes to put them back, in the half-informed belief that they can replant the original, lost, biodiversity. The hedge-makers of the Enclosure Movement had the good sense to take their cuttings from local woods and thereby preserve the existing regional pool of botanical genetic diversity. Fifteen years ago I took part in one of these environmental schemes. My contract insisted that I had to obtain my saplings from the cheapest suppliers, who I now realize almost certainly used non-British stock plants (to judge from the early date when my young hawthorns come into flower each year). Such meddling may be annoying and does little for the self-respect of those who want to maintain the landscape. It further exacerbates the growing town–country divide because urban people, with some justice, resent their taxes being spent on supposedly 'well-heeled' farmers. But it is the system, it is politically embedded, and it will continue to exist for some time.

The study of landscape history is becoming better recognized and more popular. This applies equally to the general public and to academic researchers, as the large numbers of popular books and scholarly papers on the subject attest. Medieval landscapes have always played a major part in landscape history and they will certainly continue to do so, but even in this branch of our subject I detect signs that the idea of landscapes as self-defining and self-evident entities may be on the retreat.

The way the study of historic landscapes is developing, map-based regions, largely defined using criteria provided by economic historians working at the local level, will replace those self-defined and self-evident landscapes we discussed at the start of this book. That will not mean, of course, that the landscapes will disappear. But it might mean that those of us who enjoy landscapes and who like to appreciate what they are walking through when out and about, find that the new knowledge and exciting insights provided by research are only discussed in academic publications and never appear in more general books on the topic.

What worries me about these recent trends towards greater compartmentalization is that, for many who are either unable or unwilling to spend the time needed to grasp the new complexity, the appreciation of the British landscape will return to where it began, as a rather unstructured painter's view of the countryside. Such an approach is centred on the viewer and his or her emotional response to what he or she sees. There is no imperative to get out into the real world and work out why it changed, using the clues that survive in the landscape itself. The important thing is to look, learn and not merely to admire.

This final chapter is called Sat Nav Britain: I chose the title because road atlases, and increasingly satellite navigation systems are efficient ways of guiding people to their destination but without regard to what they can see along the way. True, mass-market hamburger chains are usually marked on road atlases, as are Travelodge hotels, speed cameras and certain visitor attractions, such as National Trust houses. But even the leaflets produced by visitor attractions rarely tell one much about the landscape. They refer to the road and to travel along it: *Why not break your journey at Ghastly Grange, just ½ mile of the A45, 3 miles south-west of junction 17 on the M99. Thrill to its Tudor charms and enjoy light meals in the licensed cafeteria (closed Mondays from October to March). Coaches and children welcome.* Today it is entirely acceptable for historical places to be detached from their landscape, and in the process they lose most of their true worth. When it comes to the Last Judgement, tourism consultants will have much to answer for.

The landscape is a resource that has the potential to enrich our lives at many levels. At Flag Fen we welcome many school parties to look round the exhibits in the museum and then wander outside and see how Bronze Age people might have lived. We have a small flock of brown Soay sheep and visitors can enter reconstructions of Bronze and Iron Age roundhouses. But in recent years our staff have been upset by a number of quite grown-up children who have stung themselves on stinging nettles, unaware of what the plants were. Some of the children cannot recognize sheep, let alone primitive ones.

THE LANDSCAPE AND REGIONAL IDENTITIES

In a world where perception and the virtual can matter more than reality, our mental images of the landscape may prove to be the key to its survival. Such images are usually based on history, often in a very loose sense, and frequently they include many recent accretions of dubious historical validity. However, this does not matter. Whether or

Fig. 15.7 Regional expressions of identity can sometimes take unexpected forms in the landscape. This seemingly straightforward 'Neolithic' stone circle in the grounds of Tredegar House, Newport, Gwent, was actually constructed as part of the arrangements for the Gorsedd ceremonies of the 1897 Eisteddfod.

not Robin Hood and his Merry Men ever hunted in Sherwood Forest, it is likely that the Hollywood depiction of their antics is likely to play an important part in the future of rural landscapes in Nottinghamshire, whose official signs remind us that it is 'Robin Hood's County'. Names that perpetuate historical clichés are now being attached to regions at a laughable rate. Norfolk is 'Nelson's County'. The part of north Hertfordshire where I grew up is now 'Forster Country'.

Sometimes regional identities find subtle expression in the landscape. The hedges that managed to survive the depredations of the late twentieth century are generally 'maintained' by flail cutters that promote a bushy top growth and leggy stems. These hedges are almost useless as livestock barriers, but as most of lowland Britain is increasingly being given over to arable, this probably does not matter. At least a flailed hedge is better than no hedge. In a few areas traditional hedge-'laying' is still practised. In the east Midlands, for example, hedge-laying became a fine art – or rather a skilled craft. In theory it should be done at least every ten to twenty years, and the purpose of the exercise is to create a dense, livestock-proof barrier. This is done by partially cutting through the tallest mature stems, known as 'pleachers', and then bending them over; the pleachers and their side-branches are held in place by vertical stakes which are then woven into the top of the hedge by a 'heathering' or rope-like binding, usually of hazel or willow. The stakes and heathering will hold the hedge in place and be stock-proof for about two years, after which growth from the laid pleachers will have taken over. Today one can see many more examples of top-quality east Midland-style laid hedges than was possible, even in the 1970s.

The landscape can still provide a focus for entirely new expressions of regional identity, and often in a way that acknowledges traditional values, even if some of the traditions are quite recent, or invented. In the urban context we are witnessing the use of townscapes as settings for new rituals, many of them introduced from overseas. Diwali, or the Festival of Lights, is now an important occasion in cities such as Leicester. The Notting Hill Carnival owes much of its character to the streets of the area and would soon lose its special 'magic' if transferred to somewhere with better Health and Safety features, such as a football stadium.

In rural Britain we are witnessing a revival of cheese-making, a process which gains its special character from an area's soils, air and pasture. One might see cheeses as symbolic expressions of the landscape and this is certainly reflected in their names. One of the most popular high-quality cheeses in Britain, Shropshire Blue, was created after the last war. Counties such as Lincolnshire, where farmhouse cheeses had been swept aside in the race to grow more wheat and sugar beet, now boasts entirely new, but at the same time very traditional cheeses, such as Lincolnshire Poacher, Tennyson, and Dambuster – all names that reflect the local landscape and the people and events that made it famous.

The twenty-first century will probably be a time when people have more leisure in which to express their identity. Some will choose to do this in ways that have no links to the landscape. Others, such as folk musicians and traditional performers, for example mummers and morris dancers, will take old customs as the basis for modern ceremonies that are appropriate for our times. It might be supposed that the imposition of a New Town on the landscape would effectively smother

Fig. 15.8 'Goth' molly dancers at the Whittlesey Straw Bear Festival, January 2005. The local custom, revived in 1980, takes place every January. Molly dancers of the Fens belong to the broader morris tradition and are often distinguished by white-painted faces.

local communities and customs under a blanket of bricks and tarmac. However, in the one case familiar to me it seems that the opposite actually happened. I was involved with the archaeological problems caused by the development of Peterborough New Town. The project began with an assessment of archaeological sites threatened by development, then large-scale excavation on several sites took place throughout the 1970s and into the 1980s.[28] By 1990 the New Town was substantially complete. In the late 1960s the city had about 80,000 inhabitants. Today it has closer to 200,000.

During this time of continuous development and upheaval a number of previously forgotten folk traditions were revived. Initially this may have been a response by local people keen to assert their identity in the face of an influx of new inhabitants from outside. Whether or not this was the case, the new arrivals, and their children, soon adopted the revived customs, which then played an important part in binding the enlarged communities together. Three traditions were involved.

The best known is probably the Whittlesey Straw Bear, a molly ceremony that had died out since just before 1914,[29] and was revived in 1980. Whittlesey is a small market town on the fringes of Peterborough New Town and molly dancing is the Fenland variant of morris dancing, a tradition of English folk dancing whose roots lie further west, in the Cotswolds. Some of the participants, such as the very striking goth morris side I saw there in 2005, were clearly reflecting entirely modern traditions. Today the Straw Bear has become important to the local economy and attracts folk musicians from across Britain, and crowds of thousands.

The tradition of cheese-rolling in Stilton, a village where the famous blue cheese was sold (but not made) to travellers along the Great North Road since the eighteenth century, was reinvented once the Great North Road, or A1, had been removed to bypass the village. This happened in the 1970s as part of the general infrastructure improvements to the Peterborough region. The archetypically British 'World Conker Championships' is another case in point. It takes place every autumn in Ashton, a charming estate village of the Rothschild family near Oundle, Northamptonshire, which like Stilton and Whittlesey, is just a short drive outside the New Town. The Conker Championship is now well known throughout the country but it was invented from scratch, in the 1970s.

It is difficult to predict how far the new regionalization will go. At present it seems probable that it will splinter into a variety of separate entities: cheese-making, might be one, morris dancing another. On their own they are unlikely to affect British society at large, but if the landscape of a particular region was to come under threat they have the potential to unite and provide the core of more sustained resistance. We saw something of the sort happen in the previously rather sleepy world of fox-hunting, where the network of mostly Victorian hunts came together to form the Countryside Alliance which in turn drew attention to the rapidly growing split between town and country. It is entirely debatable, of course, whether that split has been made better or worse by the Alliance's existence.

WHAT NEXT? THE LANDSCAPE IN THE FUTURE

There are two landscapes. The first and most important is the actual physical landscape out there in the real world. The second, which can seem just as real, is the landscape of the mind. In a truly rational world I should now offer a few words on the importance of keeping the two strictly separate, just as my 1960s university lecturers would tell us that we must always make our reports unbiased and 'objective'. In those days people believed that such things were possible; today we are less naive and recognize that although it helps the credibility of your research to state any possible objections, true objectivity can never be achieved, because no two people could ever agree on what it (objectivity) is, or was. In other words, our thoughts are a product of our upbringing, reading and research and in these things we tend to follow our instincts or inclinations. All of this means that even the 'real' physical landscape is already being altered in our minds as soon as we look at it, let alone when we write about it, or study it closely.

Throughout history and probably going back to the causewayed enclosures of prehistoric times, the landscape has been a symbol of identity. During the Second World War, for example, people sang about 'bluebirds over the white cliffs of Dover'. At that time those cliffs came to symbolize British resistance to Nazi aggression. After the war there was surprisingly little exultancy, perhaps because by then most people were dog-tired and lacked the time and money to spend on such things. But my parents' generation did allow themselves a few expressions of victory and these too used landscape themes as their metaphors.

Britain's naval and maritime past still influences the development of modern townscapes. Take Portsmouth, the Royal Navy's principal base. Today the well-preserved remains of earlier defences still ring the Harbour, the Solent and the Isle of Wight, and it is still possible to appreciate the complexities of the military landscape when standing on Portsdown Hill, whose massive Palmerston Forts once defended the Harbour's northern approaches. But after the 1950s, when Britain's naval power began to decline, Portsmouth became a rather sad shadow of its former self, with many parts of the town run down and decayed.

That was to change towards the end of the twentieth century when the importance of the area's maritime heritage became better known, largely due to the raising and display of Henry VIII's great flagship, the *Mary Rose*. The revival of the city's fortunes was symbolized by the construction of the huge steel and concrete Spinnaker Tower, the crowning achievement of the city's Millennium Renaissance Project. Although less well known than the Greenwich Dome, and completed several years late, I reckon this is by far the most remarkable of all Britain's high-profile Millennium projects.

I have tried to make clear in the course of this book that physical landscapes can be seen and understood in various ways by different people. So it could be said that their interpretations of what they see amount to a second set of landscapes, albeit mental images rather than grass, trees, bricks and mortar. Increasingly, too, the 'real', physical landscape is being supplanted in many people's minds, not so much by a virtual, computer-generated cyber version – although that will doubtless happen soon – but by an idealized, romanticized and 'safe' version dished up by glossy magazines and on television.

These versions of the landscape in the media perpetuate many of the myths I have tried to debunk in these pages and they succeed because they are upmarket and nearly always well crafted. By that I mean the magazine pieces feature mellifluous prose and fine photography, and the television versions have popular and very professional presenters (seldom experts in the landscape, incidentally) and breathtaking cinematography. But they very rarely, if ever, address a coherent, let alone a controversial, theme. At best the idea they centre around can be vague: the landscape as seen through painters' eyes, or the British coastal fringe (as exemplified by the various series of the BBC's *Coast*, to take just one popular and long-lived example). Doubtless in the future a grateful public will be offered equally bland televised glossy magazine series on *Lakes*, *Mountains* or *Lovely Views*.

Glossy picture books and television programmes present the landscape as wallpaper. Britain is portrayed as either beautiful, or once ravaged by industry, but it is a vision of such profound blandness that it is difficult or impossible to challenge. It is a case of take it or leave it, and many millions of people, eager to watch or read something to relieve the stresses of modern life, simply take it. And in a way one cannot blame them. Indeed, I have watched some of these programmes myself after a particularly hard day, strong gin and tonic in one hand. As wallpaper goes they were certainly not William Morris, but neither were they particularly unpleasant. Having said that, I could not remember what on earth it was that I had watched when I thought about it the next morning. It had all flowed over me and left not a trace in its wake. Hoskins' books, on the other hand, stimulated fierce debate that continues to this day.[30] He may have written beautifully and taken some fine photographs, but he was never bland.

It is easy to poke fun at victories of style over content, but it seems part of a longer-term trend which began in the late twentieth century, when the coffee table grew mightier than the scholar's desk. If the British landscape really does become nothing more than a vehicle for rosy retrospection, then we shall have lost one of the best mirrors we possess for looking at ourselves and our society, both as we were, as we are – and as we might be. Of course, we shall never understand the landscape in its entirety, but we must continue to try to do so, in an honest, disciplined and imaginative manner.

Artists like Antony Gormley use the landscape as more than just a tranquil setting for their installations. His vast *Angel of the North* (1998), for example, would never sit comfortably within an eighteenth-century country house park. Gormley's more recent work *Another Place* is a further case in point. It consists of 100 cast-iron statues based on the artist's own body. These face out to sea between the high and low tide lines and were spread out over a 3-kilometre stretch of the beach at Crosby, near Liverpool, in 2005. The figures have become a part of the landscape, and it of them; whether one likes it or not, one cannot avoid being drawn into the mysterious and constantly changing scene. It can be exciting – and disconcerting at the same time. The clichéd photo is of the figures staring out to sea, as if waiting for something, or someone, to arrive. I rather prefer to relate them to the real world of the wind turbine and watchtower. So too does the artist.[31] Landscapes can reduce us all to a human size.

I want now to think about the future, or futures, of the 'real' physical landscape of rural Britain. As more assiduous readers may have gathered by this point, I am a prehistorian, but also a sheep-farmer and for

Fig. 15.9 Two of the 100 cast-iron statues of himself by the artist Antony Gormley from his installation *Another Place*. Each statue is 1.89 metres tall and weighs 650 kilos.

nearly two decades I have been a member of the National Farmers' Union. As a matter of habit I always listen to *Farming Today* on Radio 4 every morning, as a break from my early spell of writing. In recent months the talk has been about the growing of bio-fuels, which in Britain means straw and biomass coppice willow for power stations, or wheat, or an oilseed such as rape, for bio-ethanol. This is seen by many arable farmers as something of a lifeline, because recently the price of some feed wheats[32] has dipped below £60 a tonne – a price that is about the same or slightly lower than the cost of production.

The livestock sector on the other hand has received little good news. In the first half-dozen years of this century lamb prices dropped by a third, thanks to supermarkets buying in cheap supplies from New Zealand. Beef and pork prices continue to be low and everyone has also become aware that animals produce methane and carbon dioxide which contribute to the greenhouse effect. This has been happening, of course, for some 6,000 years, whereas industrial carbon has only been produced in large amounts since the late eighteenth century, when all these problems first became detectable. It seems somewhat unnecessary to 'blame' farmers for something they did not create, although everyone today must do what they can about CO_2 emissions, and that includes cows. The result of the recent economic trends is that the western side of Britain, where livestock farmers still predominate, and where the historic landscape has not been ploughed up, now looks more threatened than ever. Similarly the eastern, arable, side looks as if it is about to become even more intensively farmed – with obvious implications for what little is left there of the physical remains of the past.

Britain now exists within a global economy. It would undoubtedly be a mistake to assume that even in the distant past changes to the British landscape were all self-generated. To take just three examples at random: the departure of the Roman army caused farmers in south-east Britain to move away from cereals; the Scottish kelp industry ended with the Napoleonic Wars (when the demand for gunpowder ceased) and the era of Victorian High Farming finished with the agricultural depression of the 1870s and the bulk importation of cheap food. But today the picture is very different. Not only are most forms of protectionism on their way out (the EU itself being the last significant buffer between Europe and the outside world), but the internet now makes the buying and selling of commodities so much faster and simpler. Large countries with huge populations, such as China, India and Brazil, have rapidly expanding economies which demand cheap food, and they quite rightly want their voices to be heard in the context of global politics.

Other countries, like Bangladesh, are going quite literally to be swamped if climate change continues unabated. Large parts of Africa, on the other hand, will revert to desert. So nobody can afford to ignore the causes of climate change. The issue will continue to grow in political importance as its first effects become manifest. It is now widely accepted, for example, that the recurrent droughts in Australia that have had catastrophic effects on farming communities there are caused by global warming.

The production of maize for bio-ethanol has been greeted by politicians in the United States with some enthusiasm. But this makes little sense, although it is true that the growing crop does absorb carbon dioxide and the resulting bio-ethanol lessens America's reliance on places like the Middle East. American farmers are happy because corn prices have improved. But in Mexico there have been food riots, because of the cost of imported American maize.

It seems likely that food prices around the world will increase significantly.[33] Scenes like the food riots in Mexico may become commonplace. This is partly because food prices can fluctuate from day to day and longer-term contracts for bio-fuels are giving farmers a more reliable outlet for their products. It also reflects an even more profound change in the world: the move from the country to the town. In Britain this happened in the nineteenth century and it began a worldwide demographic shift. In 2007, for the first time ever, there were more people worldwide living in towns and cities than in the countryside.

From 2008 the developed world began to feel the impact of the credit crisis, brought about by a greed-driven banking 'bubble', for which there are many historical precedents. Already this is having a small effect on the rural landscape, with less housing development and far fewer horses and equine centres. The grass in some small horse paddocks is already overgrown and soon we shall see them colonized by sloe, hawthorn and birch seedlings, which is undoubtedly an environmental plus. As I have just noted, British farmers will still have to provide food, and the British public (with or without government support) will probably be able to afford to buy it. But it is predicted that Africa and the developing world will feel the economic downturn far more severely and the outlook there looks, frankly, grim.

The move from rural to urban areas has led to the wholesale abandonment of farms in places like China and India. Largely uncontrolled urban sprawl is covering huge areas of good arable land in the fertile plains around many of the developing world's great cities. What makes this such a serious problem is that urban sprawl is almost impossible, and certainly very costly, to reverse. Another factor is the growing distrust in the Western world for 'conventionally' (that is, chemically) grown food. Prices for conventionally farmed produce remain stubbornly low and many of the larger vegetable growers are in danger of going out of business.[34] Increasingly, people are demanding organically produced food and, moreover, they seem prepared to pay for it. Many farmers like it too, for a variety of reasons. This, again, is fine, when viewed from an ecological perspective, but seen globally, it presents long-term problems. Organic crops are vastly less productive than those grown with chemical fertilizers and pesticides – let alone those produced through genetic modification. The result is that the best organized farming areas of the developed world will be producing bio-fuel and some food, much of it organic – but marketed in the First World. The cost of food around the globe is bound to rise steeply.

At this stage we cannot predict what the direct effects of these economic trends will be on the British landscape. Maybe another devastating influenza pandemic will wipe out 50–80 million people, as the World Health Organization believes might happen. But even death on such a terrible scale is unlikely to have a long-term effect on the overall problem of expensive food. The need to ensure a regional and global food supply does, however, suggest that rural landscapes of Britain do indeed have a long-term future, and that planners and politicians have an even stronger motive to restrict urban sprawl. If there is something positive that planners in Britain and the European Community can do to help agriculture in the twenty-first century, it will be to work on regional development plans. During the latter decades of the previous century we saw how EU-wide agricultural policies could be both unfair and hopelessly cumbersome, often having a bad effect on both biodiversity and rural scenery. At present some form of regional planning seems the most sensible way to avoid further muddle in the future.[35]

An afterthought. I can remember driving through the outer suburbs of north London with my father sometime in the mid-1950s. Bungalows were being built everywhere. My father shook his head sagely and prophesied that in a few years' time they would be banned. I asked him why. He explained that single-storey houses used a huge amount of ground to accommodate a handful of people, and that land in south-east England was in very short supply. I could see it made plenty of sense, even then. Half a century later, I have just returned from a shopping trip to our local town and drove through a posh housing estate, built on what was until recently a green field. It was jam-packed with brand new bungalows. There are still far too many loopholes in our planning laws.

I suspect that the land at the edges of Britain's towns and cities will be where we shall see the greatest change in the next half-century. Industrial and commercial buildings became progressively larger from the 1970s, when the first metal-clad industrial structures began to appear in Britain. These new buildings made use of a laminate consisting of a layer of insulation foam faced with ridged and painted metal on at least one face. Sheets of this metal-and-foam sandwich were then bolted to a steel frame. The new materials often favoured the use of rounded corners, where the walling material was crimped to give an effect of 'crinkly tin'. These techniques, first developed in the western United States, allowed vast steel-framed buildings to be built both quickly and cheaply and have been extensively employed in, for example, huge new redistribution centres for supermarkets and other large multiple stores. They often feature a relatively small office space and an enormous warehouse area with docking doors for articulated trucks along at least one side. Security around the perimeter is another recurrent and somewhat unwelcoming feature of these buildings, which are usually located in industrial parks on the outskirts of many towns

Fig. 15.10 Buildings of the future? A huge steel-clad redistribution centre off the A45 on the outskirts of Wellingborough, Northamptonshire. It is probably questionable whether they will still be used in the second half of the twenty-first century.

and cities where large plots of land can still be acquired at relatively low cost.

It is hard to decide what attitude to adopt to the aesthetics of such colossal structures. Usually they are extremely dull, if somewhat stark and brutal in appearance. They are, however, essential to commerce and to ban them would cause great unemployment. It could also be argued that their size and bright colours are a bold statement of twenty-first-century confidence, comparable in their way with, say, St Pancras station. At all events, I can see little sense in being angry about them, despite the fact that they sit very unhappily within the small scale of the British landscape. It may well happen that the economies of scale that are currently such an important feature of the global economy, and which favour the creation of ever-vaster warehouses, will one day be replaced by a different economic order – perhaps when petrochemical prices do eventually begin to rise steeply.[36] When and if that happens, these vast buildings may vanish as rapidly as they appeared; whereupon archaeologists like myself will doubtless describe the early twenty-first century as 'the golden age of redistribution centres' and plead for a few examples to be preserved for posterity.

WHY DOES THE HISTORIC LANDSCAPE MATTER?

I must now attempt to address a final, and, for me at least, crucially important question. Why should the landscape matter to us as individuals? True to the spirit of this book I shall try to answer it with a case study, but first we must assume that certain beautiful places like Snowdonia, the Derbyshire Peaks, the Lake District and the Cairngorms will continue to exist and to be visited. So, setting worries about tourism and the income it generates to one side, some financially minded people might reasonably argue that life in the modern world is about achieving more and more each day. It is about the bottom line: time and motion. Productivity is the watchword. In the Middle Ages it was lords and priests and in Victorian times entrepreneurs and industrialists who set the pace of life. Today accountants dominate the world and increasingly we are forced to obey their laws, which lie behind a form of economic

Darwinism that urges the survival of the fattest. It is easy to scoff, but the fact remains that if enterprise is to flourish and to create wealth for the wider community as well, then productivity *does* matter, and the organization of the landscapes where we work, together with the infrastructure that links us all together, are now crucial to everyone's prosperity.

Roads and airports are regularly being improved to get us from A to B swiftly, without having to negotiate our way through the bottle-necks created by towns and villages along the way. Bypasses continue to proliferate and in most instances everybody rejoices: locals regain the use of their streets and travellers do not get held up interminably. But the other day I was driving home and had just passed through the small Cambridgeshire town of March, when it suddenly struck me that I had not seen the Guyhirn Chapel-of-Ease for many years. It is a small, unassuming building I am particularly fond of. So I pulled off the main road and drove into the village where the houses cluster beneath the vast earthen banks of the River Nene, whose silty waters flow by at roof level.

Everyone in the area was delighted when the A47 Guyhirn bypass was opened in 1994, a major project which involved the construction of a brand new bridge across the river. The Guyhirn river crossing had been a problem for decades and on bank holiday weekends the queues of traffic could extend for miles. The new road brought this congestion to an end and although a few traders in the village suffered, the general feeling locally was one of relief. But what about the Chapel-of-Ease, I thought, as I walked past the leaning gravestones towards the tiny church. It had been built during the Commonwealth with money left in 1651 and is a rare example of what was actually happening in the landscape while the country at large was occupied with the momentous political and military events that attended the close of the English Civil War. John Betjeman loved this place, with its austere and beautifully preserved Nonconformist interior.

In the greater scheme of things, it probably does not matter that a tiny fragment of British history has been marginalized by a new road, although I am worried by the cumulative effect of thousands of similar decisions on our collective consciousness. Anyhow, it was a fine day and I enjoyed a leisurely stroll around the little chapel. But as I walked

Fig. 15.11 Guyhirn Chapel-of-Ease, Cambridge-shire. The Fens were strongly supportive of Cromwell and this small chapel was built in the 1650s, during the Commonwealth, by Puritans. It was completed in 1660 when a date-stone was carved over the door (*right*). After the Restoration it was adopted by the Anglican Church, although it seems never to have been consecrated. The pews and other furnishings of its interior are still largely of seventeenth-century date.

back to the car, I found I was beginning to feel a sense of loss and not a little anger – doubtless born of frustration.

I realized that the new road had deprived my daily life of something valuable, but also of something I had foolishly taken for granted. Through the low boundary fence around the churchyard, motorists passing by used to be able to see the changing of the seasons, with aconites and snowdrops among the gravestones in February, daffodils in April and roses in June. On warm autumn evenings, when their windows were wound down, drivers could hear the chimes of the thin Gothic bell-cote, and the calling of jackdaws as they scattered into the sky. Occasionally, too, the rich brown soil surrounding a newly dug grave would remind all who drove past of their own mortality. But now the road flies over the river on its smart new bridge, and that familiar glimpse of a once-proud Puritan world has gone from our daily lives – and we are all the poorer for it.

Such changes to the landscape can affect our moods and our lives in ways that might seem irrational to outsiders. These changes, however, do not always have to be negative. I certainly do not share Hoskins' extreme gloom about the post-war landscape. In certain respects he was right: some fine country houses were destroyed, but many also survived and a high proportion of these are now open to the public, which only rarely happened before the war. And I would also argue that country houses only tell a small part of the story. They represent, too, the world of what a prehistorian would describe as the 'controlling élite'. I believe that if we take the time to investigate our physical surroundings, then landscapes can teach us far more. Most importantly, we can learn about ourselves, through the activities of earlier generations and we shall discover they were remarkably like us. Only a very few people possess the talents and fiery ambition to become political leaders. The rest of us are generally content to lead our lives away from the public eye. And in the past, as today, these lives routinely involved such difficult but mundane things as running a business, building a house, or raising a family. We should not forget that the survival of old houses owes as much to the people who lived in them as to their builders.

The new communications media are empowering ordinary people, whose views must now be noted by all politicians. Thanks to technology, too, individuals can discover how they themselves can do something to ameliorate climate change and other contemporary problems, such as racism or religious fundamentalism. These developments represent, in effect, a new, global individualism. But for most of us such empowerment only extends to the here-and-now. The past remains loftily immune. Even recent history is still served up the old way, as a top-down process where policy is decided at one level and is implemented by the population at large. I believe that political history has grown out of step with the modern world because it's largely about 'them', not 'us'.[37]

By contrast, any study of the landscape must acknowledge the many achievements of ordinary people. I concede that great men and women did indeed affect our surroundings by creating mansions, parks, 'model' villages, suburbs and even towns, but the majority of the landscape arose through an infinity of small actions by individual householders, farmers, factory managers, planners and workers. It is not enough to preserve the landscape for its own sake. We have to do more than that; after all, it is *our* story, as told by ourselves. That, surely, is why we must love and cherish it.

Notes

For abbreviations used in the notes, see List of References (pp. 750–62).

PREFACE

1. I write this having just watched Bill Bryson, President of the Council to Protect Rural England on television last night. His impassioned plea to politicians to clear up the mess (*Panorama*, Monday, 11 August 2008: 'Notes on a Dirty Island') will probably fall on deaf ears, but maybe it won't, if the voters make it clear that they are not prepared to tolerate living their daily lives surrounded by garbage. His campaign is 'Stop the Drop'.

2. By geomorphology I refer to the geological processes that have given rise to the landscape today. These include the action of glaciers and rivers, changing sea levels and so forth.

3. Garry Campion, 'Outworking Dynamism and Stasis: Nottinghamshire's 19th Century Machine-Made Lace and Framework Knitting Industries', in Barnwell, Palmer and Airs (eds.), (2004), pp. 101–21.

4. In this book I use the word prehistory to refer to human society in Britain prior to the arrival of the Romans in AD 43.

5. For an excellent critique of such books see Johnson (2007), p. 118.

6. I have discussed my own research in two general books: Pryor (2001b) and Pryor (2005).

7. I have discussed the practicalities of prehistoric farming and animal husbandry in Pryor (2006b).

8. David Hall, *The Fenland Project, Number 10: Cambridgeshire Survey, Isle of Ely and Wisbech*, East Anglian Archaeology, 79, p. 182 (Cambridgeshire County Council, 1996).

9. Sir Harry Godwin, *Fenland: Its Ancient Past and Uncertain Future*, p. 1 (Cambridge University Press, 1978).

INTRODUCTION

1. Rowley (2006), p. 4.

2. The term 'countryside' will be used as a rural equivalent of 'townscape', to connote a specifically rural tract of landscape.

3. The *Shorter Oxford English Dictionary* records 'landskip' in 1598, which was probably derived from the Middle Dutch word *lantscap*, a painter's term for a view. 'Landscape' was in common English usage from the first half of the seventeenth century.

4. Cyril Fox, *The Personality of Britain: Its Influence on Inhabitant and Invader in Prehistoric and Early Historic Times* (National Museum of Wales, Cardiff, 1932).

5. For example, N. Woodcock and R. Strachan (eds.), *Geological History of Britain and Ireland* (Blackwell Publishing, Oxford, 2000).

6. Bogs are essentially low-nutrient, acid habitats, dominated by sphagnum moss. Fens and marshes have a higher nutrient status and are more alkaline. Fens occur inland and are fed by freshwater and their dominant plants are reeds and willows; marshes are closer to the sea and feature salt-tolerant plants such as certain fibrous grasses and samphire (glasswort).

7. For an excellent recent discussion of soil formation, alluviation and archaeology, see Charles French, *Geoarchaeology in Action: Studies in Soil Micromorphology and Landscape Evolution* (Routledge, London, 2003).

8. One book, no longer in print, which very successfully linked geology and scenery was A. E. Trueman's *Geology and Scenery in England and Wales* (1949, revised 1971). The fully revised edition (revisions by J. B. Whittow and J. R. Hardy) was published by Penguin Books (Harmondsworth, 1971).

9. E. G. Bowen, *Britain and the Western Seaways* (Thames and Hudson, London, 1972).

10. Cunliffe (2001).

11. Such as the 3,500-year-old Dover Boat. See Peter Clark (ed.), *The Dover Bronze Age Boat* (English Heritage, Swindon, 2004).

12. L. Dudley Stamp, *The Land of Britain and How It Is Used*, p. 3 (Longmans Green, London, 1946).

13. The fiftieth anniversary of *The Making* stimulated at least two conferences, which have resulted in a number of publications. Perhaps the most enduring will be the three collections of essays (Prehistoric, Medieval and Post-Medieval) published by Windgather Press in late 2007 and early 2008, under the collective title *Landscape History After Hoskins*. Unfortunately they appeared too late to be considered in this book.

14. Johnson (2007), p. 52.

15. Hoskins is such a major figure that we tend to forget about the contributions of others. For a balanced critique see Matthew Johnson, 'Intricate Themes and Magic Harmonies', *British Archaeology*, May/June 2005, pp. 16–19.

16. Bob Bewley, 'Understanding England's Historic Landscapes: An Aerial Perspective', *Landscapes*, 1, 2001, pp. 74–84.

17. Perhaps the most significant recent development in aerial remote sensing has been the appearance of satellite images and their widespread availability through the internet. Initially images were mostly provided by the earth resources technology of the LANDSAT satellites, but today a variety of satellites and technologies can be brought to bear on almost any tract of landscape. In the past such images were used to define and resolve large-scale problems, such as the distribution of wet peatlands in otherwise dry landscapes, or the location of lost roads or drainage dykes, but today satellite images provided by Google Earth and other agencies can be brought to bear on individual sites, such as barrows or deserted villages.

18. The most concise and up-to-date account of aerial remote sensing is in the standard archaeological textbook, Renfrew and Bahn (2004), pp. 89–91.

CHAPTER I. BRITAIN AFTER THE AGES OF ICE (10,000–4500 BC)

1. Nobody has discussed the British climate in a more readable manner than Professor Gordon Manley: *Climate and the British Scene* (Collins, London, 1952). There are many good books about weather and climate, but the one I generally have with me when I travel is the *Collins Guide to the Weather* by Gunter D. Roth (Collins, London, 1981). This well-illustrated book explains the principal types of cloud, what to look for in an anticyclone and so on.

2. Mithen (2003), p. 4.

3. I am grateful to Maisie Taylor for suggesting this example.

4. For a thorough yet readable discussion of what happened after the Ice Ages, and the influence of these events on the development of world civilizations, see Mithen (2003).

5. See Pryor (2003), maps, pp. 108–9.

6. For natural tundra and taiga landscapes, see Adrian Friday and David S. Ingram (eds.), *The Cambridge Encyclopaedia of Life Sciences,* pp. 195–7 (Cambridge University Press, 1985).

7. For a map of these hypothetical migration routes, see Nicholas Barton, *Stone Age Britain*, p. 134 (English Heritage and Batsford Books, London, 1997).

8. Jill Cook and Roger Jacobi, 'A Reindeer Antler or "Lyngby" Axe from Northamptonshire and Its Context in the British Late Glacial', *Proceedings of the Prehistoric Society*, 60, 1994, pp. 75–84.

9. Williamson (2006), p. 115.

10. We use the term '*post*-glacial' routinely, but in fact we have no solid evidence for it. The current warm spell could equally well be another *inter*-glacial warm period, within a larger Ice Age.

11. J. G. D. Clark and H. Godwin, 'A Maglemosian Site at Brandesburton, Holderness, Yorkshire', *Proceedings of the Prehistoric Society*, 22, 1956, pp. 6–22.

12. B. J. Coles, 'Doggerland: A Speculative Survey', *Proceedings of the Prehistoric Society*, 64, 1998, pp. 45–82; Gaffney (2007).

13. N. C. Flemming (ed.), *Submarine Prehistoric Archaeology of the North Sea: Research Priorities and Collaboration with Industry*, Council for British Archaeology Research Report, 141 (York, 2004).

14. Gaffney (2007).

15. I have summarized the state of knowledge prior to the recent survey in Pryor (2003), pp. 107–15.

16. Vincent Gaffney, Kenneth Thomson and Simon Fitch (eds.), *Mapping Doggerland: The Mesolithic Landscapes of the Southern North Sea* (Archaeopress, Oxford, 2007).

17. As yet unpublished recent excavations are providing further examples, but the area around what was probably quite a substantial house at Thatcham, Berkshire, which was strewn with a mass of flint and other settlement debris indicates a degree of permanence. See Pryor (2003), p. 93; for a more typical 'bender', see p. 98.

18. Andrew J. Lawson, 'The Nomads of Ancient Wessex', *British Archaeology*, 93, March/April 2007, pp. 28–34.

19. Richard Bradley, *The Prehistoric Settlement of Britain*, p. 55 (Routledge and Kegan Paul, London, 1978).

20. Star Carr has been under almost continuous excavation since Professor Grahame Clark and his team from Cambridge University revealed a brushwood platform on the edge of a now peat-filled post-glacial lake, 'Lake Flixton'. The site, which was discovered in 1947, is most remarkable for its early date (around 7500 BC) and the fine preservation of wood, bone and antler recovered from the excavations. Some of the wood (mostly poplar) appears to have been worked, which would make Star Carr the earliest known site in northern Europe to have produced evidence for carpentry. There was abundant evidence for the making and use of flint, antler and bone tools which are similar to examples found on the bed of the North Sea and in

Holland and Denmark. For more information, see Taylor (1998). For axes and adzes see Clark (1971), p. 111.

21. Mellars and Dark (1998), p. 13.

22. R. T. Schadla-Hall, pers. comm., August 2006.

23. Taylor (1998). For axes and adzes see Clark (1971), p. 111.

24. Carol Law, 'The Uses and Fire-Ecology of Reedswamp Vegetation', in Mellars and Dark (1998), pp. 197–208.

25. A. Brown, M. Bell, S. Timpany and N. Nayling, 'Mesolithic to Neolithic and Medieval Coastal Environmental Change: Intertidal Survey at Woolaston, Gloucester', Archaeology in the Severn Estuary, 16, 2005, pp. 85–97.

26. Christopher Smith, Late Stone Age Hunters of the British Isles, p. 135 (Routledge, London, 1992).

27. See papers on Goldcliff by M. Bell and others in Archaeology in the Severn Estuary, vols. 12–14 (2001–4).

28. Robert Van de Noort and Stephen Ellis (eds.), Wetland Heritage of Holderness: An Archaeological Survey (Humber Wetland Project, University of Hull, 1995); D. D. Gilbertson, Late Quaternary Environments and Man in Holderness, British Archaeological Reports, 134 (Oxford, 1984). For a recent overview, see Robert Van de Noort, The Humber Wetlands: The Archaeology of a Dynamic Landscape (Windgather Press, Macclesfield, 2004).

29. I am most grateful to Martin Bell for useful discussions of his work along the Severn estuary.

30. Knight and Howard (2004), p. 41.

31. See for example French and Pryor (1993). For an excellent introduction to modern approaches to archaeological soil science, see Charles French, Geoarchaeology in Action: Studies in Soil Micromorphology and Landscape Evolution (Routledge, London, 2003).

32. Although they do occur frequently on the continent, especially in Denmark. Some, such as the Mesolithic 'boat burials' in dug-out canoes, could be quite elaborate. See, for example, Ole Grøn and Jørgen Skaarup, 'Møllegabet II–A Submerged Mesolithic Site and a "Boat Burial" from Ærø', Journal of Danish Archaeology, 10, 1991, pp. 38–50.

33. See Pryor (2003), pp. 174–6 (with references).

34. Richards (1990), p. 16.

35. Parker Pearson et al. (2007).

36. The second stone is the Cuckoo Stone, a short distance south-west of Durrington Walls.

37. The concept is fully explored in Bradley (2000).

38. Pryor (1998), p. 372.

39. Erik Trinkaus and Pat Shipman, *The Neandertals: Changing the Image of Mankind*, pp. 246–9 (Jonathan Cape, London, 1993).

40. Stephen Aldhouse-Green (ed.), *Paviland Cave and the 'Red Lady': A Definitive Account* (Western Academic and Specialist Press Ltd., Westbury-on-Trym, Bristol, 2000).

41. Pryor (2003), p. 52.

42. I am grateful to Martin Bell for this suggestion.

43. This idea is developed more fully by Chantal Conneller, 'Death', in Conneller and Graeme Warren (eds.), *Mesolithic Britain and Ireland: New Approaches* (Tempus Books, Stroud, 2006).

44. Parker Pearson *et al.* (2004).

45. Andrew Fleming, 'Dangerous Islands: Fate, Faith and Cosmology', *Landscapes*, 2/1, spring 2001, pp. 4–21.

46. I. G. Simmons, 'Ecology and Landscape: Some English Moorlands in the Later Mesolithic', *Landscapes*, 2/1, 2001, pp. 42–55.

CHAPTER 2. THE FIRST FARMERS (4500–2500 BC)

1. For a succinct summary see Renfrew and Bahn (2004), p. 482; for good collections of essays, see T. Douglas Price (ed.), *Europe's First Farmers* (Cambridge University Press, 2000), and Ammerman and Biagi (2003).

2. Juliet Clutton-Brock, *A Natural History of Domesticated Mammals*, p. 84 (British Museum, London, and Cambridge University Press, 1987).

3. T. Douglas Price, 'The Arrival of Agriculture in Europe as Seen from the North', in Ammerman and Biagi (2003), pp. 273–94.

4. Bryan Sykes, *The Seven Daughters of Eve*, pp. 169–84 (Bantam Press, London, 2001); Martin Jones, *The Molecule Hunt: Archaeology and the Search for Ancient DNA*, pp. 156–63 (Penguin, London, 2001).

5. See, for example, Sonia Cole, *The Neolithic Revolution* (British Museum of Natural History, London, 1954). This little book was standard reading for all students in the later 1950s and 1960s.

6. I discuss the adoption of farming in Pryor (2003), pp. 105–33.

7. I am grateful to Maisie Taylor for this idea.

8. Brennand and Taylor (2003).

9. Christopher Evans and Ian Hodder, *A Woodland Archaeology: Neolithic Sites at Haddenham*, McDonald Institute Monograph (Cambridge, 2006).

10. Knight and Howard (2004), p. 51.

11. M. W. Thompson, *General Pitt-Rivers: Evolution and Archaeology in the Nineteenth Century* (Moonraker Press, Bradford-on-Avon, 1977).

12. Martin Green has written a very readable account of the Down Farm

story: *A Landscape Revealed: 10,000 Years on a Chalkland Farm* (Tempus Books, Stroud, 2000).

13. John G. Evans, *Land Snails in Archaeology* (Seminar Press, London, 1972).

14. Charles French, *Geoarchaeology in Action* (Duckworth, London, 2005).

15. Charles French, Helen Lewis, Michael. J. Allen, Robert G. Scaife and Martin Green, 'Archaeological and Palaeo-environmental Investigations of the Upper Allen Valley, Cranborne Chase, Dorset (1998–2000): A New Model of Holocene Landscape Development', *Proceedings of the Prehistoric Society*, 69, 2003, pp. 201–34. Michael J. Allen, 'The Chalkland Landscape of Cranborne Chase: A Prehistoric Human Ecology', *Landscapes*, 3/2, 2002, pp. 55–69.

16. I am indebted to Mike Allen for this information.

17. The pioneering study of the Fens is by Sir Cyril Fox, *The Archaeology of the Cambridge Region* (Cambridge University Press, 1922). For another example in the northern Fenland see Crowtree Farm Northborough, in French and Pryor (1993), pp. 31–51.

18. Hall and Coles (1994), p. 46.

19. Two recent examples of detailed research in the Midlands: Knight and Howard (2004); Bowman and Liddle (2004).

20. An excellent and well-illustrated report was produced with admirable promptness by Gwilym Hughes, *The Lockington Gold Hoard: An Early Bronze Age Cemetery at Lockington, Leicestershire* (Oxbow Books, Oxford, 2000).

21. Matthew Beamish, 'The First Farming Communities: "Out of the Unknown" – But Still Not Out of the Woods', in Bowman and Liddle (2004) pp. 30–39.

22. I discuss Céide fields in Pryor (2003), pp. 135–7; for dates see Bradley (2007), p. 43 (with references).

23. The term was first coined by the distinguished prehistorian, the late Andrew Sherratt, in 1981.

24. The author is currently carrying out practical research into the yields and storage of hazelnuts.

25. Patrick Ashmore, *Calanais: The Standing Stones* (Urras nan Tursachan, Stornoway, 1995).

26. Alasdair Whittle, Alex Bayliss and Michael Wysocki, 'Once in a Lifetime: The Date of Wayland's Smithy Long Barrow', in Bayliss and Whittle (2007), pp. 103–21. Alan Saville, *Hazleton North: The Excavation of a Neolithic Long Cairn of the Cotswold-Severn group*, p. 179, English Heritage Archaeological Report, 13 (London, 1990).

27. Gillian Varndell and Peter Topping (eds.), *Enclosures in Neolithic Europe* (Oxbow Books, Oxford, 2002).

28. Joshua Pollard and Andrew Reynolds, *Avebury: The Biography of a Landscape* (Tempus Books, Stroud, 2002).

29. Francis Pryor, 'Abandonment and the Role of Ritual Sites in the Landscape', *Scottish Archaeological Review*, 9/10, 1995, pp. 96–109.

30. Oswald, Dyer and Barber (2001), p. 33.

31. Ibid., p. 110.

32. Francis Pryor, 'The Welland Valley as a Cultural Boundary Zone: An Example of Long-Term History', in Lane and Coles (2002), pp. 18–32.

33. Alistair Barclay and Jan Harding (eds.), *Pathways and Ceremonies: The Cursus Monuments of Britain and Ireland*, Neolithic Studies Group Seminar Papers, 4 (Oxbow Books, Oxford, 1999).

34. *A Matter of Time* (HMSO, 1960).

35. Pryor (2003), pp. 257–62.

36. V. Cummings and A. Whittle, 'Stones that Float in the Sky: Seeing Place, Myth and History', in Cummings and Whittle (eds.), *Places of Special Virtue: Megaliths in the Neolithic Landscapes of Wales*, pp. 69–91 (Oxbow Books, Oxford, 2004).

37. Gerald S. Hawkins, *Stonehenge Decoded* (Doubleday and Co., New York) caused an immense furore when it appeared in 1965. For a rejoinder see *Antiquity*, 40, pp. 212–16.

38. For a balanced and comprehensive review of alignments see C. L. N. Ruggles and A. W. R. Whittle, *Astronomy and Society in Britain During the Period 4000–1500 BC*, British Archaeological Reports, British Series, 88 (Oxford, 1981).

39. Aaron Watson, 'The Sounds of Transformation: Acoustics, Monuments and Ritual in the British Neolithic', in Neil Price, *The Archaeology of Shamanism*, p. 185 (Routledge, London, 2001).

40. Now more generally known as HERs (Historic Environment Records).

41. Timothy Darvill, *The Concise Oxford Dictionary of Archaeology* (Oxford University Press, 2002).

42. Miles Russell, 'The Dangers of Archaeo-doublespeak', *Current Archaeology*, 212, November 2007, p. 31.

43. The approach was pioneered by Chris Tilley, *A Phenomenology of Landscape: Places, Paths and Monuments* (Berg, Oxford, 1994).

44. Burl (1976); Parker Pearson (2005), pp. 58–60.

45. It used to be thought that henges were unique to Britain and Ireland. A few examples are now known on the continental mainland, especially in Germany.

46. For an excellent overview of south-western moorlands, see Rippon (2006).

47. Even on Roughtor the grazing regime has been reduced and the first (autumn 2006) flowering shoots of gorse have appeared.

48. N. Johnson and P. Rose, *Bodmin Moor: An Archaeological Survey, volume 1: The Human Landscape to c. 1800* (English Heritage, London, 1994).

49. The bank cairn actually aligned on three skyline cairns, but one has been removed by post-medieval stone quarrying.

50. This account is based on conversations with Peter Herring. See also P. Herring and P. Rose, *Bodmin Moor's Archaeological Heritage* (Cornwall Archaeological Unit, Truro, 2001). Peter Herring has also kindly shown me versions of a paper currently in preparation: 'Commons, Fields and Communities in Prehistoric Cornwall'.

51. Christopher Catling, 'Message in the Stones', *Current Archaeology*, 212, November 2007, pp. 12–19.

52. This pattern of distribution is known as 'down the line exchange'. See Colin Renfrew, 'Alternative Models for Exchange and Spatial Distribution', pp. 77–80, in Timothy K. Earle and Jonathon E. Ericson, *Exchange Systems in Prehistory*, pp. 71–90 (Academic Press, London, 1977).

53. Bradley (2000).

54. Mark Edmonds, *The Langdales: Landscape and Prehistory in a Lakeland Valley* (Tempus Books, Stroud, 2004).

55. T. H. McK. Clough and W. A. Cummins (eds.), *Stone Axe Studies*, vol. 2, Council for British Archaeology Research Report, 67, map 6, p. 270 (London, 1988).

56. Mark Edmonds, in Pryor (1998), pp. 260–68.

57. Eoin Grogan, 'Neolithic Houses in Ireland', in Darvill and Thomas (1996), pp. 27–40; see also G. J. Barclay, 'Neolithic Buildings in Scotland', in Darvill and Thomas (1996), pp. 61–76.

58. Hilary Murray, Charles Murray and Shannon Fraser, 'A Prehistoric Complex in the Dee Valley, Aberdeenshire: Further Work Reveals More Surprises', *Past: The Newsletter of the Prehistoric Society*, 54, 2006, pp. 3–4.

59. Anna Ritchie, 'The First Settlers', in Colin Renfrew (ed.), *The Prehistory of Orkney*, pp. 36–53 (Edinburgh University Press, 1985).

60. Richards (2005a).

61. Ibid.

62. See, for example, the scatter of pits and post-holes at Fengate, which comprised the best evidence for a later Neolithic settlement there. Francis Pryor, *Excavation at Fengate, Peterborough, England: The Second Report*, pp. 11–68, Archaeology Monograph, 5 (Royal Ontario Museum, Toronto, 1978).

63. J. S. Thomas (1991); Julian Thomas, *Time, Culture and Identity* (Routledge, London, 1996).

64. Francis Pryor, 'The Welland Valley as a Cultural Boundary Zone: An Example of Long-term History', in Lane and Coles (2002), pp. 18–32.

65. Pryor (1974), pp. 6–14.

66. Timothy Darvill, 'Neolithic Buildings in England, Wales and the Isle of Man', in Darvill and Thomas (1996), pp. 77–112; J. G. D. Clark, 'A Neolithic House at Haldon, Devon', *Proceedings of the Prehistoric Society of East Anglia*, 4, 1938, pp. 222–3. Daryl Garton, 'Buxton', *Current Archaeology*, 103, 1987, pp. 250–53.

67. I am grateful to Mike Parker Pearson for this information. The three houses were revealed in the 2005 excavations.

68. Professor Mike Parker Pearson (pers. comm., 2007).

69. Professor Mike Parker Pearson (pers. comm., 2006).

70. Pryor (2003), p. 269.

CHAPTER 3. THE MAKING OF THE LANDSCAPE: THE BRONZE AGE (2500–800 BC)

1. Professor Mike Parker Pearson (pers. comm., 2007) has told me that he has found the possible impression of a copper axe in chalk dating to the later Neolithic at Durrington Walls; more importantly the site has revealed almost no evidence for the use of stone axes, despite the discovery of numerous large post-built structures. It should also be recalled that the so-called 'Iceman' was found with a copper axe and we know from the discovery of the Amesbury Archer that there were links between Salisbury Plain and the Alps in the third millennium BC, so there is no good reason why Britain too may not have enjoyed several centuries of a Copper/ Stone Age (or Chalcolithic) prior to the introduction of bronze around 2500 BC.

2. Burl (1976); Aubrey Burl, *Prehistoric Stone Circles* (Shire Archaeology, Princes Risborough, 1979); Parker Pearson (2005), pp. 58–60.

3. Mike Pitts, *Hengeworld*, pp. 15–22 (Arrow Books, London, 2001).

4. Richards (2005b).

5. Francis Pryor, 'Personalities of Britain: Two Examples of Long-Term Regional Contrast', *Scottish Archaeological Review*, 3, 1984, pp. 8–15.

6. Colin Richards (ed.), *Dwelling Among the Monuments: The Neolithic Village of Barnhouse, Maeshowe Passage Grave and Surrounding Monuments at Stenness, Orkney*, p. 222, McDonald Institute Monographs (Cambridge, 2005).

7. Lakes of ink have been spilled on Stonehenge. The standard account is Cleal, Walker and Montague (1995), although the chronology advanced there is currently being challenged by Parker Pearson *et al.* (2007). My favourite accounts are *Stonehenge Complete*, by Christopher Chippindale (Thames

and Hudson, London, 1983), and Richards (1991); the latter is based on Richards (1990), a superb survey of the area.

8. For a clear recent interpretation of this idea see Joshua Pollard and Andrew Reynolds, *Avebury: Biography of a Landscape*, pp. 105–10 (Tempus Books, Stroud, 2002).

9. I have discussed some of the complex issues surrounding the changes in ritual landscapes in Pryor (2003), pp. 234–51.

10. This idea was first suggested by M. Parker Pearson and Ramilisonina, 'Stonehenge for the Ancestors: The Stones Pass on the Message', *Antiquity*, 72, 1998, pp. 203–14.

11. For a discussion of Stonehenge ritual landscapes see Pryor (2003), pp. 234–41.

12. Parker Pearson *et al.* (2007).

13. Richards (1990), pp. 276–9.

14. Richard Bradley, Chris Ball, Sharon Croft and Tim Phillips, 'The Stone Circles of Northeast Scotland in the Light of Excavation', *Antiquity*, 76, 2002, pp. 840–48.

15. Renfrew and Bahn (2004), pp. 90–91.

16. Hall and Coles (1994).

17. Tim Malim, 'Place and Space in the Cambridgeshire Bronze Age', in Brück (2001), pp. 9–22.

18. It would seem that the abandonment of houses in Bronze Age Cornwall was carefully planned and often attended by much ritual. See Jacqueline A. Nowakowski, 'Leaving Home in the Cornish Bronze Age: Insights into Planned Abandonment Processes', in Brück (2001), pp. 139–48.

19. Andrew Fleming, *The Dartmoor Reaves: Investigating Prehistoric Land Divisions* (B. T. Batsford, London, 1988).

20. Hazel Riley and Robert Wilson-North, *The Field Archaeology of Exmoor* (English Heritage, Swindon, 2001).

21. A. Fleming, 'Territorial Patterns in Bronze Age Wessex', *Proceedings of the Prehistoric Society*, 37, 1971, pp. 138–66.

22. Pryor (2006b), chs. 6 and 7.

23. C. A. I. French, *Excavation of the Deeping St Nicholas Barrow Complex, South Lincolnshire*, Lincolnshire Archaeology and Heritage Report Series, 1 (Heritage Trust of Lincolnshire, Sleaford, 1994).

24. For two examples see Pryor (1980), pp. 5 and 40.

25. Pryor (1974), pp. 14–15.

26. Mike Parker Pearson *et al.*, 'A New Avenue at Durrington Walls', *Past: The Newsletter of the Prehistoric Society*, 52, April 2006, pp. 1–2.

27. G. W. Abbott, 'The Discovery of Prehistoric Pits at Peterborough', *Archaeologia*, 62, 1910, pp. 332–52.

28. RCHM (1969), fig. 1, nos. 3–5.

29. Pryor (2001a), pp. 405–20. See also Pryor (2005).

30. Alex Bayliss and Francis Pryor, 'Radiocarbon and Absolute Chronology', in Pryor (2001a), pp. 390–99.

31. We have no solid evidence to support this idea, other than the fact that some of the smaller banks alongside possible field boundary ditches were too small ever to have been stock-proof, but would have provided a drier environment for hardwood cuttings over winter. Even sloe and hawthorn cuttings rot quite readily, if waterlogged for any length of time.

32. See, for example, Christopher Evans and Mark Knight, 'The "Community of Builders": The Barleycroft Post Alignments', in Brück (2001), pp. 83–98.

33. Richard Bradley, *The Passage of Arms: An Archaeological Analysis of Prehistoric Hoards and Votive Deposits*, p. 137 (Cambridge University Press, 1990).

34. The survey was carried out by Rog Palmer of Air Photo Services (Report No. 1999/02, March 1999).

35. For Fengate, see Pryor (2001a), pp. 405–20. See also Pryor (2005).

36. David Thomas Yates, *Land, Power and Prestige: Bronze Age Field Systems in Southern England* (Oxbow Books, Oxford, 2007).

37. I have deliberately chosen not to use 'co-axial', the accepted archaeological term to describe these distinctive rectangular fields.

38. Yates (2001); Bradley (2007), pp. 187–96.

39. H. C. Bowen, *Ancient Fields: A Tentative Analysis of Vanishing Earthworks and Landscapes*, p. 36 (British Association for the Advancement of Science, London, 1961); McOmish, Field and Brown (2002).

40. See, for example, Robert Johnston, ' "Breaking New Ground": Land Tenure and Fieldstone Clearance during the Bronze Age', in Brück (2001), pp. 99–109.

41. For a balanced view of the evidence, see Parker Pearson (2005), pp. 92–3. See also Cunliffe (2005), p. 29.

42. Sites of this period include Cladh Hallan, South Uist, recently excavated by Professor Parker Pearson and a team from Sheffield University.

43. R. W. Cowell and J. B. Innes, *The Wetlands of Merseyside*, p. 207 (Lancaster University Archaeological Unit, 1994).

44. Parker Pearson, Sharples and Symonds (2004), p. 59.

45. Rowan Whimster, *Burial Practices in Iron Age Britain*, British Archaeological Reports, British Series, 90 (Oxford, 1981).

46. Parker Pearson, Sharples and Symonds (2004), p. 64.

47. The recent example of Bradley Fen is a case in point. See Pryor (2003), pp. 290–91.

48. The only bona fide Bronze Age copper mine in England is at Alderly Edge, Cheshire. For an excellent overview of Bronze Age metalwork and mining, see Barber (2003).

49. Dennis Britton, 'The Isleham Hoard, Cambridgeshire', *Antiquity*, 34, 1960, pp. 279–82.

50. Brennand and Taylor (2003), p. 59.

51. However, mining is known to have continued into the later Bronze Age at Great Orme, if nowhere else.

52. W. O'Brien, *Mount Gabriel: Bronze Age Mining in Ireland*, pp. 207–28 (Galway University Press, 1994). Andrew Selkirk (with Tony Hammond), 'The Great Orme Mine', *Current Archaeology*, 130, 1992, pp. 404–9.

53. Simon Timberlake, 'Mining and Prospection for Metals in Early Bronze Age Britain: Making Claims Within the Archaeological Landscape', in Brück (2001), pp. 179–92.

54. A. Dutton and P. J. Fasham, 'Prehistoric Copper Mining on the Great Orme, Llandudno, Gwynedd', *Proceedings of the Prehistoric Society*, 60, 1994, pp. 245–86.

55. Sites like Dainton, Devon have produced good examples of Bronze Age moulds. See Barber (2003).

56. This was a specific response in a particular region. Further up the River Nene, at Raunds, near Northampton, Fengate-style Bronze Age fields continued in use until the end of the second millennium BC. See Jan Harding and Frances Healy, *The Raunds Area Project: A Neolithic and Bronze Age Landscape in Northamptonshire*, pp. 191–7 (English Heritage, Swindon, 2007).

57. Field and Parker Pearson (2003).

58. For a succinct explanation of dendrochronology, see Renfrew and Bahn (2004), pp. 137–41. For the Sweet track, see J. Hillam, C. M. Groves, D. M. Brown, M. G. L. Baillie, J. M. Coles and B. J. Coles, 'Dendrochronology of the English Neolithic', *Antiquity*, 64, 1990, pp. 210–20.

59. Most are probably medieval or post-medieval and were built for pack-horses; the Tarr Steps on Exmoor, although rebuilt many times, is possibly prehistoric. For an overview, see Mark Brayshay, 'Landscapes of Transport', p. 187, in Kain (2006), pp. 185–206.

60. Bradley (2007), pp. 232–3; F. M. M. Pryor, 'Welland Bank Quarry, South Lincolnshire', *Current Archaeology*, 160, November 1998, pp. 139–45.

61. A. J. Lawson, *Potterne 1982–5: Animal Husbandry in Later Prehistoric Wessex* (Trust for Wessex Archaeology, Salisbury, 2000).

CHAPTER 4. THE RISE OF CELTIC CULTURE: THE IRON AGE (800 BC–AD 43)

1. Professor Barry Cunliffe has labelled the eighth and seventh centuries BC the 'Earliest Iron Age' – an excellent academic solution to the problem of isolating change; see Cunliffe (2005), p. 32.

2. Mark Collard, Timothy Darvill and Martin Watts, 'Ironworking in the Bronze Age? Evidence from a 10th Century BC Settlement at Hartshill Copse, Upper Bucklebury, West Berkshire', *Proceedings of the Prehistoric Society*, 72, 2006, pp. 367–421.

3. Cunliffe (2005), p. 493; W. H. Manning, 'Ironwork Hoards in Iron Age and Roman Britain', *Britannia*, 3, 1972, pp. 224–50.

4. Renfrew and Bahn (2004), p. 342. Cast iron (discovered by the Chinese around 500 BC) requires no less than 1540 °C.

5. The range of prehistoric iron implements has been fully described by Sian Rees, *Agricultural Implements in Prehistoric and Roman Britain*, British Archaeological Reports, British Series, 69 (Oxford, 1979).

6. For an excellent, comprehensive debunking of the Celts, see Simon James, *The Atlantic Celts: Ancient People or Modern Invention?* (British Museum Press, London, 1999).

7. Cunliffe (2002); Cunliffe (2001), pp. 91–3, 306–8; Cunliffe (2005), pp. 470–71.

8. Liddiard (2005).

9. Some scholars maintain that trade at the very heart of the Roman Empire was indeed driven by market forces. Professor Martin Millet, however, disagrees; he concludes that even at the hub of the empire, exchange between Rome and the provinces was 'demonstrably embedded within the social and political system'. He goes on to point out that much of the large-scale movement of goods, such as the provision of supplies to the army, was actually motivated by factors more complex than free trade alone. 'These patterns develop in such a way as to demonstrate that the system was not simply a function of unbridled economic forces.' Quoted from Millett (1990), p. 6.

10. There is a large literature on prehistoric exchange systems. See, for example, Marcel Mauss, *The Gift: Forms and Functions of Exchange in Archaic Societies* (Cohen and West, London, 1969); Marshal Sahlins, *Stone Age Economics* (Tavistock Publications, London, 1974); Timothy K. Earle and Jonathon E. Ericson (eds.), *Exchange Systems in Prehistory* (Academic Press, London, 1977).

11. I discuss Iron Age slavery in Pryor (2003), pp. 424–7.

12. For example at Hod Hill, in Dorset. See Richmond (1968).

13. Strictly speaking, a rampart consists of a deep ditch on the downslope alongside a high bank upslope. The effect of the two is to provide a very much steeper slope, to deter potential attack.

14. For more on hillforts, see J. Forde-Johnston, *Hillforts of the Iron Age in England and Wales* (Liverpool University Press, 1976); Margaret Jesson and David Hill (eds.), *The Iron Age and Its Hillforts: Papers Presented to Sir Mortimer Wheeler* (Southampton University Archaeological Society, Southampton, 1971); Harding (1976).

15. Incidentally, the first excavation I ever took part in was at Ravensburgh Castle, in the summer of 1963, during my 'gap' year. It was directed by James Dyer. James is, and was, an inspired teacher of children and young adults, who has written extensively on the field archaeology and landscapes of southern Britain. James's excavations at Ravensburgh confirmed me in my intention of becoming an archaeologist. His indispensable book for the glove-box of your car, which is still in print, is *Southern England: An Archaeological Guide* (Faber and Faber, London, 1973). He has also written a fine introduction to British prehistory: *Ancient Britain* (Routledge, London, 1990).

16. B. W. Cunliffe, *Danebury: An Iron Age Hillfort in Hampshire*, vol. 6: *A Hillfort Community in Perspective*, Council for British Archaeology Research Report, 102 (York, 1995).

17. G. C. Guilbert, 'Planned Hillfort Interiors', *Proceedings of the Prehistoric Society*, 41, 1975, pp. 203–21.

18. Ann Woodward, 'Context, chronology, and history', in Barrett, Freeman and Woodward (2000), p. 116.

19. Cunliffe (2005), p. 34.

20. For southern Britain see the Gazetteer of the *Map of Southern Britain in the Iron Age* (Ordnance Survey, Chessington, 1962). For northern Britain, see R. W. Feacham, 'The Hill-Forts of Northern Britain', in A. L. F. Rivet (ed.), *The Iron Age in Northern Britain*, p. 60 (Edinburgh University Press, 1966).

21. The term is used throughout, in the standard account of the British Iron Age, Cunliffe (2005).

22. Liddiard (2005), pp. 131–40.

23. Ibid., pp. 21–36.

24. Romano-Celtic temples were constructed within other abandoned hillforts, for example Lydney, Monmouthshire; Lewes, Sussex (Harding, 1976, p. 44); and South Cadbury, Somerset (Barrett, Freeman and Woodward, 2000, pp. 176–8).

25. Strictly speaking, of course, power cannot be *de*volved unless it had

previous 'evolved' towards the centre, a process that did not finally happen until the Norman Conquest, in England – and somewhat later in Scotland and Wales.

26. Sharples (1991), pp. 259–63.

27. We also know about two undefended settlements at Quarry Lodden and Coberg Road, Dorchester, and there may well have been others.

28. In many pastoralist societies cattle raiding took place when the calves were sufficiently mature to be driven off and did not require constant attention from their mothers or owners.

29. For more on the development of tribal power, see Elman R. Service, *Origins of the State and Civilization* (W. W. Norton, New York, 1975).

30. Technically speaking, I should refer to the Maiden Castle/Marnhull style here. Marnhull was an undefended settlement north of Sturminster Newton, in northern Dorset.

31. By the late Iron Age occupation at Hambledon Hill may have transferred to nearby Hod Hill, which continued to be of importance into Roman times. See Richmond (1968).

32. Miles *et al.* (2003).

33. Payne, Corney and Cunliffe (2006), pp. 24–6.

34. Julie Rees-Jones and Mike Tite, 'Optically Stimulated Luminescence (OSL) Dating Results From the White Horse and Linear Ditch', in Miles *et al.* (2003), pp. 269–71.

35. Payne, Corney and Cunliffe (2006), pp. 89–96; Miles *et al.* (2003), pp. 243–68.

36. Payne, Corney and Cunliffe (2006), pp. 62–5.

37. Ibid., pp. 47–54.

38. Robert Van de Noort, Henry P. Chapman and John R. Collis (eds.), *Sutton Common: The Excavation of an Iron Age 'Marsh Fort'*, Council for British Archaeology Research Report, 154 (York, 2007).

39. Hall and Coles (1994), pp. 96–7; Tim Malim, *Stonea and the Roman Fens* (Tempus Books, Stroud, 2005).

40. French and Pryor (1993), p. 71.

41. Ibid., pp. 68–79.

42. Oswald, Ainsworth and Pearson (2006).

43. Max Adams, 'Iron Age Ridge and Furrow? So It Seems', *British Archaeology*, 13, April 1996 (summary on www.britarch.ac.uk).

44. Hope-Taylor (1977).

45. A. F. Harding, 'Excavations in the Prehistoric Ritual Complex Near Milfield, Northumberland', *Proceedings of the Prehistoric Society*, 47, 1981, pp. 87–135.

46. Excavations were carried out by *Time Team* in mid-April 2007.

47. J. E. Hodgkin, 'The Castles, Hamsterley', *Proceedings of the Society of Antiquaries of Newcastle upon Tyne*, 3rd series, 3, 1912, pp. 194–5; id., 'The Castles Camp, Hamsterley, County Durham', *Transactions of the Architectural and Archaeological Society of Durham and Northumberland*, 7, 1934, pp. 92–8.

48. I discuss the organization of Iron Age roundhouses, with references, in Pryor (2003), pp. 328–31.

49. The best introduction to Scottish crannogs is by the excavator of Oakbank crannog, Nicholas Dixon: *The Crannogs of Scotland: An Underwater Archaeology* (Tempus Books, Stroud, 2004).

50. Tom Williamson,' Early Co-axial Field Systems on the East Anglian Boulder Clays', *Proceedings of the Prehistoric Society*, 53, 1987, pp. 419–31; this paper used map regression to suggest that a large area of fields in south Norfolk had originally been laid out in the Iron Age. Its findings were refuted in David A. Hinton, 'The "Scole-Dickleburgh Field System" Examined', *Landscape History*, 19, 1997, pp. 5–12.

51. These were first brought to public attention by James Dyer: 'Dray's Ditches, Bedfordshire, and Early Iron Age Territorial Boundaries in the Eastern Chilterns', *Antiquaries Journal*, 41, 1961, pp. 32–43.

52. Cunliffe (2005), pp. 402–6.

53. Hod Hill boasted paved roads and it continued into Roman times. It is one of the best contenders for true Iron Age urban status.

54. Crummy (1997), pp. 16–17.

55. John Collis, *Defended Sites of the Late LàTene*, British Archaeological Reports, S2 (Oxford, 1975). Barry Cunliffe and Trevor Rowley (eds.), *Oppida in Barbarian Europe*, British Archaeological Reports, S11 (Oxford, 1976).

56. I have suggested that the earliest Neolithic landscape at Fengate might have been laid out along an earlier, Mesolithic, route between the upland and lower-lying ground, later to become fen. See Pryor (1993).

57. S. Harrison, 'The Icknield Way: Some Queries', *Archaeological Journal*, 160, 2004, pp. 1–22.

58. J. M. and B. J. Coles, *Prehistory of the Somerset Levels*, p. 49 (Somerset Levels Project, Exeter, 1989).

59. John Coles and Stephen Minnitt, *'Industrious and Fairly Civilized': The Glastonbury Lake Village* (Somerset Levels Project and County Council Museums Service, Exeter, 1995).

60. For a good introduction to the Somerset Iron Age lake villages, with many references, see Stephen Minnitt and John Coles, *The Lake Villages of Somerset* (Glastonbury Antiquarian Society, 1996).

61. For Fiskerton, see Field and Parker Pearson (2003); Beccles was excavated in September 2006 and July 2007; a report is currently in preparation for the Environment Agency who commissioned the work.

62. B. W. Cunliffe, *Hengistbury Head, Dorset*, vol. 1: *Prehistoric and Roman Settlement, 3500 BC–AD 500*, Oxford University Committee for Archaeology Monograph, 13 (Oxford, 1987).

63. J. D. Hill, 'The End of One Kind of Body and the Beginning of Another Kind of Body? Toilet Instruments and "Romanization" in Southern England During the First Century AD', in Adam Gwilt and Colin Haselgrove (eds.), *Reconstructing Iron Age Societies: New Approaches to the British Iron Age*, pp. 96–107, Oxbow Monograph, 71 (Oxford, 1997).

64. Jonathan Williams, 'New Light on Latin in Pre-Conquest Britain', *Britannia*, 38, 2007, pp. 1–12.

CHAPTER 5. ENTER A FEW ROMANS (AD 43–410)

1. Cunliffe (2002), pp. 94–5.

2. I discuss the survival of Iron Age and 'Celtic' cultural influences extensively in Pryor (2004), especially pp. 1–15.

3. Crummy (1997).

4. Earlier (Pryor, 2003, p. 414) I was more conservative and opted for a slightly lower figure of 1–1.5 million.

5. He was referring to his Pontic campaign, not to his two visits to Britain.

6. Peter Salway describes the Roman conquest as one of ebb and flow: Salway (1993), pp. 100–101.

7. Crummy (1997).

8. The long history of lead mining in Somerset and the south-west is fully described in a series of essays edited by Philip Newman, 'The Archaeology of Mining and Metallurgy in South-West Britain', *Bulletin: The Peak District Mines Historical Society*, 13/2, 1996.

9. Quoted from Harold Mattingly's translation of *Tacitus: The Agricola and the Germania*, revised ed. by S. A. Handford, pp. 72–3 (Penguin Books, 1970).

10. I. D. Margary, *Roman Roads in Britain*, 3rd edn. (John Baker, London, 1973).

11. Barry Cunliffe, 'Roman Danebury', *Current Archaeology*, 188, 2003, pp. 345–51.

12. A. Sargent, 'The North–South Divide Revisited: Thoughts on the Character of Roman Britain', *Britannia*, 33, 2002, pp. 219–26.

13. Margary's 1973 book is still the standard reference. For a more recent, and rather more accessible account, see Hugh Davies, *Roads in Roman Britain* (Tempus Books, Stroud, 2002).

14. Millett (1990), p. 55.

15. The Viatores, *Roman Roads in the South-East Midlands* (Victor Gollancz, London, 1964).

16. Ibid., p. 185.

17. Guy de la Bédoyère, *The Golden Age of Roman Britain* (Tempus Books, Stroud, 1999).

18. For a balanced and most readable account of Roman towns, see de la Bédoyère, (2003).

19. St Albans, Hertfordshire.

20. I use the word urbanity in the third meaning defined in the *Shorter Oxford English Dictionary*: the state, condition, or character of a town or city.

21. Richard Reece, *My Roman Britain*, p. 140 (Cotswold Studies, Cirencester, 1988).

22. Helena Hamerow, 'Hamwic', *British Archaeology*, 66, August 2002, pp. 20–24.

23. The archaeological profession's response to this new crisis was the founding of the Council for British Archaeology (CBA), in 1944. The CBA was originally set up to help organize and co-ordinate work on bomb sites. Today it is the public face of archaeology and it exists both to campaign and to assist the researches of professionals, amateurs and archaeological enthusiasts alike. For more on the CBA visit <www.britarch.ac.uk>.

24. See MoLAS (2000), preface (p. x).

25. For the Roman period in the Greater London area, see Dominic Perring and Trevor Brigham, 'Londinium and Its Hinterland: The Roman Period', in MoLAS (2000), pp. 120–70. See also de la Bédoyère (2003), pp. 41–4 and *passim*.

26. Southwark is a medieval name, derived from South Work (referring to the defensive works that secured the southern approaches to London Bridge).

27. I discuss Dr Mark Whyman's research into Dark Age York in Pryor (2004), pp. 172–3.

28. A. Clarke and M. Fulford, 'The Excavation of Insula IX, Silchester: The First Five Years of the "Town Life" Project, 1997–2001', *Britannia*, 33, 2002, pp. 129–66.

29. Two excellent general reviews of geophysics: Anthony Clark, *Seeing Beneath the Soil: Prospecting Methods in Archaeology*, revised edn. (Routledge, London 1996); Chris Gaffney and John Gater, *Revealing the Buried Past: Geophysics for Archaeologists* (Tempus Books, Stroud, 2004).

30. White and Barker (2002), colour plate 3.

31. The best popular book on Wroxeter is White and Barker (2002). Three major academic reports have been published by English Heritage, in 1997, 2000 and 2002.

32. White and Barker (2002), pp. 125–6.

33. M. Corney, 'A Field Survey of the Extra-mural Region of Silchester', in M. G. Fulford, *Silchester Defences 1974–80*, pp. 239–97, Britannia Monograph, 5 (London, 1984).

34. D. F. Mackreth, 'Durobrivae', *Durobrivae*, 7, 1979, pp. 19–21. For more on extra-mural *vici*, see Simon Esmonde Cleary, *Extra-Mural Areas of Romano-British Towns*, British Archaeological Reports, British Series, 169 (Oxford, 1987).

35. I discuss the role of late and post-Roman *Durobrivae*, in Pryor (2004), pp. 87–95.

36. Millett (1990), p. 185.

37. They were used as part of a barn – a fact supported by the discovery of burnt grain in the highest levels of the 1859 excavations. See White and Barker (2002), p. 147.

38. de la Bédoyère, (1989); Johnson (1989).

39. Frere (1991), p. 114.

40. Tim Gates, 'Hadrian's Wall Amid Fields of Corn', *British Archaeology*, 49, November 1999, p. 6; Tim Gates, 'Flying on the Frontier: Recent Archaeological Air Photography in the Hadrian's Wall corridor', in Frodsham (2004), pp. 236–45.

41. Dark (2000), pp. 100–109.

42. See, for example, Portchester Castle: Cunliffe (1975).

43. Tony Wilmott, 'Birdoswald and Its Landscape', *Current Archaeology*, 164, 1999, pp. 298–302.

44. My thanks to Guy de la Bédoyère who helped me with the references. See de la Bédoyère (1989), p. 21; see also Johnson (1989), p. 43.

45. It has been suggested that William I had the main keep, the White Tower, of the Tower of London, painted white when it was first built, to stand out as a mark of his authority.

46. David J. Breeze, *The Antonine Wall: The North-West Frontier of the Roman Empire* (Historic Scotland and Royal Commission on the Ancient and Historical Monuments of Scotland, Edinburgh, 2004).

47. Dark (2000), pp. 109–14.

48. Ibid., p. 11.

49. W. S. Hanson, 'Zones of Interaction: Roman and Native in Scotland', *Antiquity*, 76, 2002, pp. 834–40. This paper includes full references to the many sites concerned.

50. Patrick Ottaway, 'The Archaeology of the Roman Period in the Yorkshire Region: A Rapid Resource Assessment', in T. G. Manby, Stephen Moorhouse and Patrick Ottaway (eds.), *The Archaeology of Yorkshire: An Assessment at the Beginning of the 21st Century*, pp. 125–49, Yorkshire Archaeological Society, Occasional Paper, 3 (Leeds, 2003).

51. Taylor (2007).

52. Ibid., pp. 73–81.

53. The Romans constructed canals in northern Italy, for example, but none have yet been shown in Britain. The best contender, the Car Dyke, which runs along the western Fen margins, has been shown to have been used as a catch-water drain to divert run-off from the upland around low-lying areas.

54. Corney (2000).

55. Ibid., p. 37.

56. Fulford (1990), p. 27.

57. See papers by Fulford, French and myself, Robinson and Lambrick, in Michael Fulford and Elizabeth Nichols, *Developing Landscapes of Lowland Britain: The Archaeology of the British Gravels. A Review*, Society of Antiquaries of London, Occasional Papers, 14 (London, 1992).

58. T. W. Potter and R. P. J. Jackson, 'The Roman Site of Stonea, Cambs.', *Antiquity*, 217, 1982, pp. 111–20. For an opposing view, see Millett (1990), pp. 120–21.

59. Hall and Coles (1994), pp. 105–21; see also Phillips (1970).

60. P. J. Drury and Warwick Rodwell, 'Settlement in the Later Iron Age and Roman Periods', in D. G. Buckley (ed.), *Archaeology in Essex to AD 1500*, p. 64, Council for British Archaeology Research Report, 54 (London, 1980).

61. Warwick Rodwell, 'Relict Landscapes in Essex', in Bowen and Fowler (1978), pp. 89–98.

62. Simon Esmonde Cleary, 'Roman Britain: Civil and Rural Society', in Hunter and Ralston (1999), p. 172.

63. *Argentum* is the Latin word for silver.

64. Malcolm Todd has published interim reports on his work at Charterhouse on Mendip in *Proceedings of the Somerset Archaeology and Natural History Society* for 1993, 1994 and 2003.

65. Cunliffe (2005), p. 503.

66. Barrett, Freeman and Woodward (2000), p. 173.

67. A. Woodward and P. Leech, *The Uley Shrines: Excavations of a Ritual Complex on West Hill, Uley, Gloucestershire: 1977–9*, English Heritage Archaeological Report, 17 (London, 1993).

68. J. S. P. Bradford and R. G. Goodchild, 'Excavations at Frilford, Berks., 1937–8', *Oxoniensia*, 4, 1939, pp. 1–80.

69. Interim reports have appeared in the journal *South Midlands Archaeology* for the years 2002–4 (continuing). For a good summary, see C. Gosden and G. Lock, 'Frilford: A Romano-British Ritual Pool in Oxfordshire?', *Current Archaeology*, 184, 2003, pp. 156–9.

70. Stephen Johnson, *Later Roman Britain*, pp. 76–7 (Routledge and Kegan Paul, London, 1980).

71. I discuss the Saxon Shore fort controversy in Pryor (2004), pp. 135–43.

72. Cunliffe (1975).

73. Andrew Pearson, *The Construction of the Saxon Shore Forts*, British Archaeological Reports, British Series, 349 (Archaeopress, Oxford, 2003).

CHAPTER 6. NEW LIGHT ON 'DARK AGE' AND SAXON LANDSCAPES (AD 410–800)

1. The idea of an in-coming élite of less than 10,000 people was suggested by N. J. Higham, *Rome, Britain and the Anglo-Saxons* (Seaby, London, 1992).

2. Salway (1993), p. 388.

3. R. G. Collingwood and J. N. L. Myres, *Roman Britain and the English Settlements* (Oxford University Press, 1937).

4. Esmonde-Cleary (1989).

5. Dark (2000), pp. 130–56.

6. Millett (1990), pp. 227–30, has also suggested the departure of Roman forces may have followed a rebellion organized by the Romano-British élite.

7. Ibid., pp. 227–8.

8. For an excellent and up-to-date account of Scotland in the fifth to tenth centuries, see S. M. Foster, *Picts, Gaels and Scots* (Historic Scotland, Edinburgh, 2004).

9. Ibid., p. 73.

10. Campbell (2007).

11. The term 'Gaelic Church' – with its clear Irish attribution – is generally preferred to the older 'Celtic Church'.

12. Ibid., p. 55.

13. I discuss the principal discoveries made at Yeavering in Pryor (2006a), pp. 27–31.

14. And a remarkably fine report by the excavator, Hope-Taylor (1977).

15. Hoskins was probably the first person to draw this to the attention of the general public. See W. G. Hoskins and C. C. Taylor, *The Making of the English Landscape* (Guild Publishing, London, 1988), pp. 22–9.

16. Campbell (2007); Jonathan M. Wooding, *Communication and Commerce Along the Western Sealanes, AD 400–800*, British Archaeological Reports, International Series, 654 (Oxford, 1996); Anthea Harris, *Byzantium, Britain and the West: The Archaeology of Cultural Identity AD 400–650* (Tempus Books, Stroud, 2003).

17. I discuss Tintagel in Pryor (2004), pp. 178–81.

18. Campbell (2007).

19. Rippon (2000).

20. O. Rackham, *The History of the Countryside*, pp. 75–85 (Dent, London, 1986); Peter Murphy, 'The Anglo-Saxon Landscape and Rural Economy: Some Results From Sites in East Anglia and Essex', in J. Rackham (ed.), *Environment and Economy in Anglo-Saxon England*, pp. 23–39, Council for British Archaeology Research Report, 89 (York, 1994).

21. Millett (1990), pp. 181–211.

22. Rippon (2000), p. 52 (with references).

23. H. Williams, 'Ancient Landscapes of the Dead: The Reuse of Prehistoric and Roman Monuments as Early Anglo-Saxon Burial Sites', *Medieval Archaeology*, 41, 1997, pp. 1–32.

24. L. V. Grinsell, *The Ancient Burial Mounds of England*, pp. 40–56 (Methuen, London, 1936).

25. The large headland we excavated between Barnack and Bainton is a case in point, being aligned on ring-ditches 1, 6, 7, 8 and 9. Francis Pryor, Charles French, David Crowther, David Gurney, Gavin Simpson and Maisie Taylor, *Archaeology and Environment in the Lower Welland Valley*, vol. 2, p. 266, East Anglian Archaeology Report No. 27 (Cambridge, 1985).

26. Helena Hamerow, 'Great Sites: Hamwic', *British Archaeology*, August 2002, pp. 20–24.

27. For a superb overview of maritime links between Britain and Europe in the Saxon period, see Rodger (1997), pp. 1–30.

28. For more on early medieval relations between Britain and Europe, see Jacques Le Goff, *The Birth of Europe*, trans. Janet Lloyd (Blackwell, Oxford, 2005); Michael McCormick, *Origins of the EuropeanEconomy:Communications and Commerce AD 300–900* (Cambridge University Press, 2001).

29. For a general review, with references to all British prehistoric boat finds, see Peter Clark (ed.), *The Dover Bronze Age Boat in Context: Society and Water Transport in Prehistoric Europe* (Oxbow Books, Oxford, 2004).

30. For the Langdon Bay Bronze Age wreck, see S. Needham and M. Dean, 'La Cargaison de Langdon Bay à Douvres', in *Les Relations entre le Continent et les Isles Britanniques à l'age du Bronze*, pp. 119–24, Actes du Colloque de Lille, Supplément à la Revue Archéologique de Picardie (Amiens, 1987); for Iron Age cross-Channel and Atlantic coast contacts, see Cunliffe (2001), pp. 311–421; also Cunliffe (2005), pp. 446–84.

31. One thinks here of the great influence of Celtic monasticism from the mid-fifth century. See, for example, Cunliffe (2001), pp. 469–77.

32. 'Prittlewell: Treasures of a King of Essex', *Current Archaeology*, 190, February 2004, pp. 430–36; Martin Carver (ed.), *The Age of Sutton Hoo* (Boydell Press, Woodbridge, 1992).

33. Hodges (1989), p. 32.

34. A quern is a lighter form of millstone, similar to a heavy pestle and mortar. It usually involves top and bottom stones which are either rubbed together forwards and backwards (saddle querns) or are rotated with a pole handle (rotary querns).

35. Tim Pestell and Katharina Ulmschneider, 'Introduction: Early Medieval Markets and "Productive" Sites', in Pestell and Ulmschneider (eds.), *Markets in Early Medieval Europe: Trading and 'Productive' Sites, 650–850*, pp. 1–10 (Windgather Press, Macclesfield, 2003).

36. Many linguists prefer 'Early English' over 'Anglo-Saxon' to stress the close links between that language and the one in which I am writing.

37. The '-wich' ending of both Ipswich and Norwich derives from *wic*.

38. Hodges (1989), pp. 66–86.

39. Schofield (1999), p. 226.

40. For Lundenwic, see Malcolm, Bowser with Cowie (2003). For Eoforwic, see Hall (1996). For a summary of early Norwich, see Brian S. Ayers, 'The Urbanisation of East Anglia: The Norwich Perspective' in Gardiner (1993), pp. 117–43. For Ipswich, see Keith Wade, 'The Urbanisation of East Anglia: The Ipswich Perspective', in Gardiner (1993) pp. 144–51, .

41. For Lincoln and London at the close of the Roman period see Alan Vince, 'A Tale of Two Cities: Lincoln and London Compared', in Gardiner (1993), pp. 152–70.

42. James Rackham and Jane Sidell, 'London's Landscapes: The Changing Environment', in MoLAS (2000), pp. 11–27.

43. Barton (1993). I use the term City (with a capital C) specifically to refer to the original Roman walled area of *Londinium*, later to be termed the City of London or the Square Mile. The City is just a small part of the modern city that is London.

44. M. Atkin, 'The Norwich Survey 1971–1985: A Retrospective View', in Gardiner (1993), p. 131.

45. Hedley Swain, 'London's Last Roman?', *Current Archaeology*, 213, December 2007, pp. 35–9.

46. Malcolm, Bowser with Cowie (2003).

47. Ibid., p. 22.

CHAPTER 7. THE VIKING AGE (800–1066)

1. *Magnus's Saga: The Life of St Magnus, Earl of Orkney 1075–1116*, trans. Herman Pálsson and Paul Edwards (St Magnus' Cathedral, Orkney, 1996).

2. For a good summary of myths concerning the Vikings, see Julian Richards,

Blood of the Vikings, pp. 1–12 (Hodder and Stoughton, London, 2001).

3. The large arable fields held in common are known as 'Open' because they are not subdivided by walls or hedges.

4. The phasing that follows is based on Richards (1991).

5. Following the marriage in that year of Margaret of Denmark/Norway to James III of Scotland.

6. Richards (1991), p. 51.

7. Aston and Gerrard (1999). For an overview of monastic land management, see James Bond, 'Landscapes of Monasticism', in Hooke (2000), pp. 63–74.

8. Martin Biddle, 'Excavations at Winchester, 1971: Tenth and Final Interim Report: Part I', *Antiquaries Journal*, 55, 1975, pp. 96–126.

9. Martin Biddle, 'Excavations at Winchester 1962–63: Second Interim Report', *Antiquaries Journal*, 44, 1964, pp. 188–219. Imports are discussed on p. 217.

10. Martin Biddle and David Hill, 'Late Saxon Planned Towns', *Antiquaries Journal*, 51, 1971, pp. 70–85.

11. Colchester was re-founded as a *burh* by Edward the Elder in 917.

12. Hall (1996), p. 88.

13. Evidence for earlier Saxon occupation does, however, emerge from time to time, such as the five sunken-floored buildings revealed by the recent excavations at No. 1 Poultry. Rowsome (2000).

14. Thomas (2002), pp. 7–9.

15. Richard Hodges, 'Goodbye to the Vikings?', *History Today*, September 2004, pp. 29–30.

16. For a simple and straightforward account of the Open Field system, see Hall (1982), pp. 5–9.

17. For an excellent discussion of the historiography of Open Field studies, see Williamson (2003), pp. 8–27.

18. The word derives from the Elizabethan term 'champaine' (from the French *champ*, a field).

19. Aston and Gerrard (1999).

20. Hall (1982), p. 55.

21. A recent study suggests that the laying-out of these long strip fields amounted to an early, less formal and locally organized rationalization of the landscape, similar to that brought about by the process of nucleation. Mark Gardiner, 'Dales, Long Lands, and the Medieval Division of Land in Eastern England', *Agricultural History Review*, 57/1, 2009, pp. 1–14.

22. Ibid., pp. 48–9.

23. Hall (1995). Foard (2004), p. 102.

24. Brian Dix (ed.), 'The Raunds Area Project: Second Interim Report', *Northamptonshire Archaeology*, 21, 1986–7, pp. 3–30.

25. For an indispensable introduction to the subject, see Warwick Rodwell, *The English Heritage Book of Church Archaeology*, revised edn. (B. T. Batsford/English Heritage, London, 1989).

26. This figure is a rough estimate, based on the 12,000 listed parish churches in England. See Trevor Cooper, 'Keeping Parish Churches: Facts and Figures for Church of England Churches', *English Heritage Conservation Bulletin*, 46, autumn 2004.

27. I take a keen interest in the churches of Fenland and the more I visit them the more I am convinced that if it were not for the efforts of the Victorians, most would today be heaps of masonry rubble. Pevsner was too close to the Victorians to treat them fairly and his great series 'The Buildings of England' has tended to overstress the damage their restorations caused, at the expense of their very real achievements.

28. See various papers in English Heritage, *Conservation Bulletin*, 46, autumn 2004.

29. I am grateful to Maisie Taylor for first pointing this out to me.

30. D. Sutherland and D. Parsons, 'The Petrological Contribution to the Survey of All Saints Church, Brixworth, Northamptonshire: An Interim Study', *Journal of the British Archaeological Association*, 137, 1984, pp. 47–64.

31. I have more on Augustine and the British bishops in Pryor (2004), p. 174.

32. I have illustrated a map of diocesan boundaries in Pryor (2006a), p. 113.

33. I discuss minsters and early Church administration, ibid., pp. 113–14.

CHAPTER 8. STEADY GROWTH: LANDSCAPES BEFORE THE BLACK DEATH (1066–1350)

1. For a first-rate introduction to modern medieval archaeology, see Christopher Gerrard, *Medieval Archaeology: Understanding Traditions and Contemporary Approaches* (Routledge, London, 2003).

2. N. Pevsner and I. Richmond, *The Buildings of England: Northumberland*, 2nd edn. (Yale University Press, New Haven and London, 1992) p. 173.

3. I discuss this in Pryor (2006a), pp. 278–80. My thoughts there are based on Creighton and Higham (2005), pp. 217–18.

4. Paul Johnson, *Castles of England, Scotland and Wales*, pp. 61–5 (Seven Dials, London, 1989).

5. Liddiard (2005), pp. 89–91.

6. The discussion of Castle Acre draws heavily on Liddiard (2005), pp. 134–9.

7. Creighton and Higham (2005), p. 79.

8. Ibid.

9. F. A. Aberg and A. E. Brown, *Medieval Moated Sites in North-West Europe*, British Archaeological Reports, International Series, S121 (Oxford, 1981).

10. Bond (2004) and Hall (2006).

11. Bond (2004), pp. 277–9.

12. For an excellent and well-illustrated account of the town, see Vivien Bellamy, *A History of Much Wenlock* (Shropshire Books, Shropshire County Council, 2001).

13. Ibid., p. 176.

14. Ibid., p. 341.

15. Hall (2006), p. 17.

16. Historic Scotland has published excellent illustrated souvenir guides to these abbeys.

17. Hall (2006), pp. 32–8.

18. English Nature, *Barnack Hills and Holes National Nature Reserve* (English Nature, London, 2004).

19. Bond (2004), p. 332.

20. Readers of Pryor (2003) will recall the story of the Great Orme Bronze Age copper mines, Llandudno, pp. 270–77.

21. Granville Clay, Gerry McDonnell, Bonwell Spence and Robert Vernon, *The Iron Makers of Myers Wood* (Huddersfield and District Archaeological Society, 2004).

22. David Crossley, 'English Woodlands and the Supply of Fuel for Industry', *Industrial Archaeology Review*, 27/1, 2005, pp. 105–12.

23. Palmer and Neaverson (1994), p. 50.

24. David Gurney, 'Evidence of Bronze Age Salt-production at Northey, Peterborough', *Northamptonshire Archaeology*, 15, 1980, pp. 1–11.

25. For everything about early salt production, see Tom Lane and Elaine Morris (eds.), *A Millennium of Saltmaking: Prehistoric and Romano-British Salt Production in the Fenland*, Lincolnshire Archaeology and Heritage Reports Series, 4 (Heritage Lincolnshire, Heckington, 2001).

26. Hall and Coles (1994), pp. 143–5.

27. K. de Brisay, 'The Excavation of a Red Hill at Peldon, Essex, With a Note on Some Other Sites', *Antiquaries Journal*, 58, 1978, pp. 31–60.

28. J. M. Lambert, J. N. Jennings, C. T. Smith, C. Green and J. N. Hutchinson, *The Making of the Broads*, Royal Geographical Society Research Series, 3 (London, 1960).

29. Williamson (2006), p. 200.

30. For a good summary of Broadland history see Martin George, 'The Broads', in Peter Wade Martins (ed.), *An Historical Atlas of Norfolk*, 2nd edn., pp. 82–3 (Norfolk Museums Service, Norwich, 1994).

31. Fagan (2000).

32. There is a wealth of literature on royal and private hunting, parks and chases. I have found Muir (2004) very clear on the distinction between forests, chases and deer parks. For general information on parks, see Rackham (1976) and (1989) also Liddiard (2003). Birrell (1992) has provided a most excellent economic study of deer and deer farming in medieval England.

33. Hatfield Forest, Essex has been the subject of a classic study: Rackham (1989).

34. Ibid., p. 3.

35. Ibid., p. 41.

36. Liddiard (2003), p. 14.

37. Birrell (1992).

38. Roberts and Wrathmell (2000).

39. Ibid.

40. Today the Braunton Great Field comprises about 145 hectares with individually owned strips of land ranging in size from 0.3 to 2.4 hectares. Today there are fewer than 200 strips, but in 1840 there were 490. For various reasons the Great Field cannot be given statutory protection so its future remains uncertain. See Overton (2006), pp. 111–12.

41. This now seems beyond dispute. See two excellent recent studies: Jones and Page (2006) and Susan Oosthuizen, *Landscapes Decoded: The Origins and Development of Cambridgeshire's Medieval Fields* (University of Hertfordshire Press, Hatfield, 2006).

42. Delano Smith (1980), pp. 217–19.

43. Ibid.

44. John Beckett, *Laxton, Nottinghamshire: England's Last Open Field Village*, p. 20 (Laxton, 1989).

45. It is categorized today as Grade 3 (out of 5). For comparison, Grade 1 is top-quality silt and Grade 5 wet moorland.

46. M. M. Postan, *The Medieval Economy and Society* (Weidenfeld and Nicholson, London, 1972); Platt (1997), p. 14.

47. Williamson (2003), pp. 192–6.

48. Delano Smith (1980), p. 223.

49. Aston and Gerrard (1999).

50. Muir (2004), pp. 245–8.

51. Philip Rhatz and Lorna Watts, *Glastonbury, Myth and Magic*, pp. 67–8 (Tempus Books, Stroud, 2003).

52. For an excellent recent review, see Sam Turner (ed.), *Medieval Devon and Cornwall: Shaping an Ancient Countryside* (Windgather Press, Macclesfield, 2006).

53. Hoskins (1955), pp. 26–32.

54. Rippon (2006), p. 63.

55. Overton (2006), pp. 114–15.

56. For a full history of hedgerow dating and its demise, see Gerry Barnes and Tom Williamson, *Hedgerow History: Ecology, History and Landscape Character* (Windgather Press, Macclesfield, 2006).

57. The best example of the partitioning of the mound of a long barrow with wattle is by C.W. Phillips, 'The Excavation of the Giants' Hills Long Barrow, Skendelby, Lincolnshire', *Archaeologia*, 85, 1936, pp. 37–106.

58. For a good summary of run-rigg, see Muir (2004), pp. 227–8. The standard historical study, although somewhat outdated, is still that of R. A. Dodgshon, *Land and Society in Early Scotland* (Oxford University Press, 1981).

59. These dimensions are given by Muir (2004), p. 227.

60. Fagan (2000).

61. Yeoman (1995), pp. 108–20.

62. Royal Commission on the Ancient and Historical Monuments of Scotland, (1) *North-East Perth: An Archaeological Landscape*, (Edinburgh, 1990); (2) *South-East Perth: An Archaeological Landscape* (Edinburgh, 1994).

63. Yeoman (1995), p. 109.

64. Ibid., p. 110.

65. For a summary, see ibid., pp. 115–16. For a full report on excavation in the Peebles/Kelso area, see P. J. Dixon, J. R. Mackenzie, D. R. Perry and P. Sharman, *The Origins of the Settlements at Kelso and Peebles, Scottish Borders: Archaeological Excavations in Kelso and Floors Castle and Cuddygate/Bridgegate, Peebles by the Border Burghs Archaeology Project and the Scottish Urban Archaeology Trust, 1983–1994*. This is available online as Scottish Archaeological Internet Report, 2 (2003), at <www.sair.org.uk>.

66. Fiona Cooper, *The Black Poplar: Ecology, History and Conservation* (Windgather Press, Macclesfield, 2006).

67. Creighton and Higham (2005), p. 64.

68. Schofield (1999), pp. 210–12.

69. Yeoman (1995), p. 54.

70. The following discussion draws heavily on Aston and Bond (1976), pp. 96–108.

71. Schofield (1999), p. 210.

72. Creighton and Higham (2005), p. 218.

73. Dennison, Stronach and Coleman (2006); Dennison and Coleman (2000).

74. Owen (2002), p. 802.

75. Eleven burials, possibly battle victims, were found on the foreshore of the River Fleet. See Thomas (2002), p. 12.

76. Bruce Watson, Trevor Brigham and Tony Dyson, *London Bridge: 2000 Years of a River Crossing*, Museum of London Archaeology Service Monograph, 8 (London, 2001).

77. Thomas (2002), pp. 62–5.

78. D. Keene, 'Medieval London and Its Region', *London Journal*, 14, 1989, pp. 99–111.

79. From the Greek *orthos*, meaning 'right'.

80. T. R. Slater, 'Understanding the Landscape of Towns', in Hooke (2000), pp. 97–108.

81. We are now beginning to understand the role of the early Christian Church, too, in the Islamic world's accumulation of new scientific and mathematical knowledge. See Philip Jenkins, 'The Forgotten Christian Word', *History Today*, 59/4, April 2009, pp. 32–9.

82. Ibid., p. 104.

83. Ibid., pp. 104–5.

84. Beresford (1988).

85. Beresford (1988), p. 3.

86. Keith D. Lilley, Christopher D. Lloyd and Steven Trick, 'Design and Designers of Medieval "New Towns" in Wales', *Antiquity*, 81, 2007, pp. 279–93.

87. Beresford (1988), p. 13.

88. Ibid., pp. 290–315.

89. Queenborough (founded 1368) on the Isle of Sheppey was an exception, although not a successful one, as it never consisted of more than a single street. Aston and Bond (1976), p. 79.

90. Ibid., pp. 78–108. For a more recent review, see Schofield (1999).

91. Aston and Bond (1976), pp. 37–8.

92. Younger animals, such as lambs, are often reluctant to pass through a gate placed in the side of a field, away from the corner. See Pryor (2006b), p. 103.

93. Aston and Bond (1976), pp. 87–91.

94. Owen (2002).

95. Yeoman (1995), p. 59.

96. Schofield (1999), p. 211.

97. Dennison, Stronach and Coleman (2006).

CHAPTER 9. THE RISE OF THE INDIVIDUAL:
THE BLACK DEATH AND ITS AFTERMATH
(1350–1550)

1. Platt (1997).
2. The Black Death spread with extreme rapidity, which is not what one would expect of a disease spread by rats; there are also other aspects which do not altogether accord with modern observations of bubonic plague epidemiology. This might suggest that the disease was not caused by the bacterium *Yersinia pestis* but by an as yet unknown, but deadly, virus, perhaps similar to Ebola – that could possibly return. See Debora Mackenzie, 'Ring a ring o' roses, A pocket full of posies, Atishoo! Atishoo! We all fall down', *New Scientist*, 24 November, 2008.
3. Platt (1997), p. 193, quotes Rosemary Horrox (trans. and ed.), *The Black Death*, pp. 79–80 (Manchester University Press, 1994).
4. Platt (1997), p. 15.
5. Duncan Hawkins, 'The Black Death and the New London Cemeteries of 1348', *Antiquity*, 64, 1990, pp. 637–42.
6. Pevsner (1968), p. 296.
7. Bellcotes are a feature of Norman churches in the area and are also found at Peakirk and Werrington. See Steane (1974), p. 125.
8. Pevsner, Harris and Antram (1989).
9. Platt (1997), pp. 9–18.
10. Foard (2004), pp. 102–4.
11. Fagan (2000).
12. Muir (2004), p. 77.
13. Quoted ibid.
14. Ibid., p. 67.
15. A. J. L. Winchester, 'Hill Farming Landscapes of Medieval Northern England', in Hooke (2000), pp. 75–84.
16. Higham (2004), pp. 113–19.
17. The main areas where the two do not agree are north-east England and west Norfolk; these are partially explained by Roberts and Wrathmell (2000, p. 27) as earlier, non-Parliamentary enclosures. There are also problems in using a single source for Parliamentary Enclosure data (see John Chapman, 'The Extent and Nature of Parliamentary Enclosure', *Agricultural History Review*, 35, 1987, pp. 25–35).
18. For a well-written summary of the project, see Maurice Beresford and John Hurst, *Wharram Percy: Deserted Medieval Village* (English Heritage/ B. T. Batsford Books, London, 1990).

19. Hoskins (1955), p. 127.

20. Davison (1999).

21. Norman Davey, *A History of Building Materials*, p. 79 (Phoenix House, London, 1961).

22. Liddiard (2005), p. 64.

23. Hoskins (1955), p. 136.

24. Nicholas J. Moore, 'Brick', in John Blair and Nigel Ramsey (eds.), *English Medieval Industries*, pp. 211–36 (Hambledon Press, London, 1991).

25. Thomas (2002), p. 164.

26. Platt (1997), pp. 70–95.

27. Glyn Coppack, *Abbeys and Priories*, pp. 129–33 (Batsford/English Heritage, London, 1990).

28. I discuss the process of the Dissolution in Pryor (2006a), pp. 292–309.

29. Peter Yeoman, 'Medieval Rural Settlement: The Invisible Centuries', in W. S. Hanson and E. A. Slater (eds.), *Scottish Archaeology: New Perceptions*, pp. 112–28 (Aberdeen University Press, 1991).

30. This account of Rattray, and that of Finlaggan which follows, draw heavily on Yeoman (1995), pp. 111–19. For more on Finlaggan, see also David Caldwell, 'Urbane Savages of the Western Isles', *British Archaeology*, 13, April 1996 (internet summary at www.britarch.ac.uk).

31. R. A. Dodgshon, 'West Highland and Hebridean Settlement Prior to Crofting and the Clearances', *Proceedings of the Society of Antiquaries of Scotland*, 123, 1993, pp. 419–39.

32. Which reached Wales the year after England, in 1349.

33. Quoted in Wade Martins (1995), p. 42.

34. The administrative region known as the Scottish Borders was set up in 1973, comprising the counties of Berwick, Peebles, Roxburgh and Selkirk.

35. Richard Lomas and Richard Muir, 'The North East in the Medieval Period', p. 64, in F. H. A. Aalen and C. O'Brien (eds.), *England's Landscape: The North East* (English Heritage/Collins, London, 2006), pp. 53–76.

36. The report that summarizes the excavations appeared in two issues of the Northumberland county archaeological journal: D. H. Evans and M. G. Jarrett, 'The Deserted Village of West Whelpington, Northumberland: Third Report, Part One', *Archaeologia Aeliana*, 15, 1987, pp. 199–308; the second part of the report by Evans, Jarrett and S. Wrathmell, appeared in 16, 1988, pp. 139–92.

37. The original modern survey of bastles was by Ramm, McDowall and Mercer (1970). For a more recent review (with references), see Ryder (2004), pp. 262–71.

38. The following is based on Richard Tipping, 'Palaeoecology and Political

History: Evaluating Driving Forces in Historic Landscape Change in Southern Scotland', in Whyte and Winchester (2004), pp. 11–20.

39. For a brief history of the period and a detailed consideration of the reivers as fighting men, see K. Durham, *The Border Reivers* (Osprey Publishing, Oxford, 1995); see also Ryder (2004).

40. Ibid., p. 94.

41. From the Latin *palus*, a stake. Stakes were often used to defend the enclosure around the Pele.

42. Cruft, Dunbar and Fawcett (2006), pp. 40–51.

43. Ibid., pp. 576–81.

44. Ibid., p. 228.

45. Phythian-Adams (1987), pp. 19–26.

46. H. C. Darby, *The Medieval Fenland* (Cambridge University Press, 1940).

47. For a fine review of changing economies in the Fens, see H. C. Darby, *The Changing Fenland* (Cambridge University Press, 1983).

48. Phythian-Adams (1987), pp. 9–10.

49. Ibid., pp. 38–42.

50. Stocker (2006), p. 19.

51. Schofield (1999), pp. 210–12.

52. Thomas (2002), p. 116.

53. Hedley Swain *et al.*, 'Shakespeare's Theatres', *Current Archaeology*, 124, 1991, pp. 185–9.

54. Lloyd (2001).

55. Newman and Pevsner (2006), pp. 350–86.

CHAPTER 10. PRODUCTIVE AND POLITE: RURAL LANDSCAPES IN EARLY MODERN TIMES (1550–1750)

1. The main archaeological source is D. Gaimster and P. Stamper (eds.), *The Age of Transition: The Archaeology of English Culture 1400–1600* (Oxbow Books, Oxford, 1997). I also discuss the end of the Middle Ages in Pryor (2006a), ch. 8.

2. Thirsk (1987).

3. Hall and Coles (1994).

4. Phillips (1970).

5. R. J. Silvester, *The Fenland Project, Number 3: Marshland and the Nar Valley, Norfolk*, East Anglian Archaeology, 45 (Nortolk Archaeological Unit, Gressenhall, 1988).

6. For a readable if now rather outdated account of this unique region, see A.

K. Astbury, *The Black Fens* (originally published 1958, reprinted 1987 by Providence Press, Wardy Hill, Cambridge).

7. H. C. Darby, *The Draining of the Fens* (Cambridge University Press, 1940).

8. Richard Hills, *Machines, Mills and Uncountable Costly Necessities: A Short History of the Drainage of the Fens*, pp. 75–105 (Goose and Sons, Norwich, 1967).

9. Ibid., pp. 113–14.

10. The Latin word for a wood, forest or trees.

11. John Evelyn, *Silva: or a Discourse of Forest-Trees*, p. ii. I have used a facsimile of the 5th edition of 1729 (Stobart and Son, London, 1979).

12. Gilbert White, *The Natural History of Selborne*, ed. Richard Mabey (Penguin English Library, Harmondsworth, 1977).

13. Rackham (1976), p. 172.

14. Williamson (2000), p. 114.

15. Rodger (2004), p. 95.

16. Hoskins (1955), p. 158.

17. M. W. Barley, *The English Farmhouse and Cottage* (first published 1961; republished by 1987 Alan Sutton Publishing, Gloucester).

18. Ibid., pp. 57–128.

19. Ibid., pp. 129–79.

20. Although less serious than that of 1607, rural uprisings in the early modern period were not unknown, even in prosperous parts of the country, as witnessed by the Lincolnshire Rising of 1536; see Anne Ward, *The Lincolnshire Rising 1536* (Louth Naturalists, Antiquarian and Literary Society, 1996).

21. I use the example of Coppergate in York in Pryor (2006a), pp. 195–9. For a rapid succession of timber buildings – amounting to several local 'Great Rebuildings' – in an earlier medieval village, see Peter Wade Martins, *Excavations in North Elmham Park, 1967–1972*, 2 vols., East Anglian Archaeology Report, 9 (Norfolk Archaeological Unit, Gressenhall, 1980).

22. Tabraham and Grove (1995).

23. Excavations at Holyroodhouse Palace, Edinburgh, for *Time Team* in 2006 revealed a deposit of intensive burning in the ground-floor storage area beneath the Great Hall in what had been the south range of the Abbey cloisters. Stratigraphically this fire-reddened layer dated to the sixteenth century and it is tempting to suggest that it was a result of the 'rough wooing'.

24. Quoted in Tabraham and Grove (1995), p. 94.

25. R. A. Buchanan, *Industrial Archaeology in Britain*, p. 299 (Penguin Books, Harmondsworth, 1972).

26. Muir (2004), pp. 70–71, with references.

27. For a recent comprehensive account, see A. R. B. Haldane, *The Drove Roads of Scotland* (Berlinn, Edinburgh, 2008).

28. Cynthia Brown, 'Drovers, Cattle and Dung: The Long Trail from Scotland to London', *Proceedings of the Suffolk Institute for Archaeology and History*, 38, 1996, pp. 428–41.

29. Crosby (2006a).

30. Austen Wilks, 'Pioneers of Topographical Printmaking: Some Comparisons', *Landscape History*, 2, 1980, pp. 59–70.

31. R. Hyde, *A Prospect of Britain: The Town Plans of Samuel and Nathaniel Buck* (Pavilion Books, London, 1994).

32. N. Pevsner and B. Cherry, *The Buildings of England: Northamptonshire*, 2nd edn., pp. 400–402 (Penguin Books, Harmondsworth, 1973).

33. His brother Francis Tresham was one of the Gunpowder Plot conspirators. See Steane (1974), p. 206.

34. Richard Mabey's edition (Oxford University Press, 1988) has an excellent introduction and abundant illustrations.

35. Williamson (1995), p. 1.

36. See the Introduction, by the translator, Maurice Cranstone, to Jean-Jacques Rousseau, *The Social Contract* (Penguin Books, Harmondsworth, 1968).

37. Apart from individual house and garden guides, I have drawn on the following general works when considering country house landscapes: Williamson (1995); Strong (2000); Anthony Huxley, *An Illustrated History of Gardening* (Paddington Press, London, 1978); Jellicoe *et al.* (1986); Laurence Fleming and Alan Gore, *The English Garden* (Michael Joseph, London, 1979).

38. Adrian Tinniswood, *A History of Country House Visiting: Five Centuries of Tourism and Taste* (National Trust and Basil Blackwell, Oxford, 1989).

39. Christopher Morris (ed.), *The Illustrated Journeys of Celia Fiennes c.1682–c.1712* (Webb and Bower, Exeter, 1982).

40. Ingrams (2005), pp. 134–5.

41. One of the earliest was William Beckford's *Vathek* (1786). Beckford (1760–1844) made his own major impact on the landscape when he constructed a vast Gothic tower at the family house at Fonthill, Wiltshire (currently being restored by the Vivat Trust). *Nightmare Abbey* (1818) and *Crotchet Castle* (1831) are two satires on the Gothic novel by Thomas Love Peacock (1785–1866), published in a single volume by Penguin English Library (Harmondsworth, 1969).

42. Stuart Piggott, *William Stukeley: An Eighteenth-Century Antiquary*, 2nd edn. (Thames and Hudson, London, 1985).

43. Quoted in Burl (1976), p. 292.
44. George Lambrick, *The Rollright Stones* (Oxford Archaeological Unit, 1983).
45. Davison (1999), p. 19.
46. Miles *et al.* (2003), p. 7.

CHAPTER 11. FROM PLAGUE TO PROSPERITY: TOWNSCAPES IN EARLY MODERN TIMES (1550–1800)

1. Whyte (1999), p. 276.
2. MoLAS (2000), pp. 260–62.
3. Thomas (2002), pp. 162–6.
4. Short (2006), p. 176.
5. The original sources for the population statistics are given in MoLAS (2000), p. 261.
6. Aston and Bond (1976), pp. 113–17.
7. Whyte (1999).
8. Dennison, Stronach and Coleman (2006).
9. The tolbooth or toll house was the town's administrative building where taxes were collected; in many instances the tolbooth also acted as a temporary prison. Many still have barred windows.
10. E. Patricia Dennison and Russel Coleman, *Historic Forfar*, The Scottish Burgh Survey (Historic Scotland, Edinburgh, 2000).
11. E. Patricia Dennison and Russel Coleman, *Historic Dumbarton*, The Scottish Burgh Survey (Historic Scotland, Edinburgh, 1999).
12. Hunt (2006).
13. Bath also had a second season in the autumn.
14. For an excellent summary of Palladian Bath and its architectural contexts, see Nikolaus Pevsner, *An Outline of European Architecture*, pp. 344–9 (Penguin Books, Harmondsworth, 1943).
15. Hunt (2006), pp. 199–200.
16. Short (2006), p. 143.
17. According to the *Shorter Oxford English Dictionary*.
18. Fine memorials to the Le Stranges can also be seen in Hunstanton church. For the resort at Hunstanton, see Williamson (2006), pp. 124–5.
19. Nikolaus Pevsner, *The Buildings of England: Derbyshire* (2nd edn., revised by Elizabeth Williamson), pp. 112–18 (Penguin Books, Harmondsworth, 1978); Stocker (2006), p. 134.

20. Durie (2003), pp. 100–108.

21. Adrian Desmond and James Moore, *Darwin: The Life of a Tormented Evolutionist*, p. 374 (Michael Joseph, London, 1991).

22. Quoted in Durie (2003), pp. 102–3.

23. Dr Richard Russell's book, published in Oxford in 1753, *A Dissertation Concerning the Use of Sea Water in the Diseases of the Glands*, started the rapid growth of seaside resorts. The popularity of sea-bathing was increasing at Scarborough, for example, from 1730. See Pevsner (1966), p. 319.

24. For a first rate textbook of industrial archaeology, see Palmer and Neaverson (1998).

25. Palmer and Neaverson (1994).

26. Mike Hodder, 'Birmingham, "a towne maytayned by smithes"', *Current Archaeology*, 214, January 2008, pp. 9–17.

27. David Cranstone, 'The Whitehaven Coast 1500–2000: Post-Medieval, Industrial and Historical Archaeology', in Audrey Horning and Marilyn Palmer (eds.), *Crossing Paths or Sharing Tracks*, pp. 205–19 (Boydell and Brewer, Woodbridge, Suffolk, 2009).

28. Kate Clark, 'The Workshop of the World: The Industrial Revolution', pp. 280–81, in Hunter and Ralston (1999), pp. 280–96.

29. Thirsk (1970), pp. 148–77.

30. Frere (1991), p. 289.

31. I discuss medieval watermills in Pryor (2006a) pp. 140–43.

32. David Crossley, 'Water Power in the Landscape: The Rivers of the Sheffield Area', in Barker and Cranstone (2004), pp. 79–88.

33. Michael Nevell and John Walker, *Lands and Lordships in Tameside: Tameside in Transition 1348–1642* (Tameside Metropolitan Borough Council, 1998); Michael Nevell and John Walker, *Tameside in Transition: The Archaeology of the Industrial Revolution in Two North-West Lordships, 1642–1870* (Tameside Metropolitan Borough Council, 1999); Michael Nevell and John Walker, 'Industrialization in the Countryside: The Roles of the Lord, Freeholder and Tenant in the Manchester Area, 1600–1900', in Barker and Cranstone (2004), pp. 53–77, Michael Nevell, *Carrbrook: A Textile Village and Its Valley* (Tameside Metropolitan Borough Council, 2006).

34. Royal Commission on the Historical Monuments of England, *Thesaurus of Monument Types* (London, 1996).

35. The pioneering study is that by R. W. Brunskill, *Illustrated Handbook of Vernacular Architecture* (Faber and Faber, London, 1971).

36. Barnwell, Palmer and Airs (2004).

37. Leigh Alston, 'Late Medieval Workshops in East Anglia', ibid., pp. 38–59.

38. Alston (ibid., p. 57) quotes a surviving example: Cleo's Restaurant in the Market Place at Debenham, Suffolk.

39. P. S. Barnwell 'Workshops, Industrial Production and the Landscape', ibid., pp. 179–80.

40. Dr Barrie Trinder has been studying the squatter settlements of the area since the early 1970s. For a recent summary with references, see his 'Workshops and Cottages in the Ironbridge Gorge', ibid., pp. 173–8.

41. Ibid., p. 176.

42. M. Palmer, 'History', ibid., pp. 7–20.

43. David Cranstone (ed.), *The Moira Furnace: A Napoleonic Blast Furnace in Leicestershire* (North West Leicestershire District Council, Coalville, 1985).

44. Ibid., pp. 147–53. For a very useful handbook on turnpikes, see G. N. Wright, *Turnpike Roads* (Shire Books, Princes Risborough, 1992).

45. Christopher Taylor, *The Cambridgeshire Landscape*, p. 227 (Hodder and Stoughton, London, 1973).

46. Ibid., p. 228; Pevsner (1954), pp. 245–6.

47. Cannon (2001), p. 642.

48. The A5 in north Wales has been the subject of a thorough and beautifully illustrated survey, a model of its kind: Quartermaine, Trinder and Turner (2003).

49. Ibid., p. 80.

50. Rowley (2006), p. 13.

51. Palmer and Neaverson (1994), pp. 153–5.

52. Margaret Albright Knittl, 'The Design for the Initial Drainage of the Great Level of the Fens: An Historical Whodunit in Three Parts', *Agricultural History Review*, 55/1, 2007, pp. 23–50.

53. Palmer and Neaverson (1994), pp. 158–9, 172–8.

54. Hayman (2005), pp. 60–62.

55. Ibid., p. 159.

56. Rodger (1997 and 2004); Palmer and Neaverson (1994), pp. 179–82.

57. For a good general account of the archaeology of Britain's defences, see Saunders (1989).

58. Aston and Bond (1976), p. 110.

CHAPTER 12. RURAL RIDES: THE COUNTRYSIDE IN MODERN TIMES (1750–1900)

1. Williamson (2002), p. 110. He refers the reader to J. Caird, *English Agriculture in 1851* (London, 1852).

2. Williamson (2002), p. 111.

3. Barnwell and Giles (1997), p. 4.

4. Williamson (2002), p. 9.

5. Wade Martins (1995), p. 82.

6. John Peck, the diarist of Parson Drove, Cambridgeshire records how, as a magistrate, he had to separate long-established couples before sending them to the workhouse, and how this was the worst day's work of his life. The surviving thirty-six notebooks of the Peck diaries cover the years 1814–51, and are in the archives of Wisbech Museum.

7. Williamson (1995).

8. Ibid., p. 112.

9. Thirsk (1970).

10. In actual fact flax was a very ancient crop. I have excavated a piece of flax twine dating to the earlier Neolithic (3500 BC) from a waterlogged site at Etton, Cambridgeshire.

11. Wade Martins and Williamson (1999), p. 36.

12. Williamson (2000), p. 113.

13. Ibid.

14. Pat Stanley, *Robert Bakewell and the Longhorn Breed of Cattle* (Farming Press, Ipswich, 1995). For important later (nineteenth-century) breeds see Peter Wade Martins, *Black Faces: A History of East Anglian Sheep Breeds* (Norfolk Museums Service, 1993).

15. I have used the excellent summary of the agricultural revolution in Cannon (2001) and Wade Martins and Williamson (1999), pp. 1–9.

16. Ibid., pp. 99–119.

17. The word 'ley' is still used by farmers to describe grass or grass/clover mixtures that are planted for a fixed period of time. A ley is distinct from ancient pasture or long-term grazing.

18. The seed drill was made famous by Tull's book, *The Horse-Hoing Husbandry*, published in 1733.

19. Wade Martins and Williamson (1999), p. 205.

20. For references to Kerridge, see Thirsk (1987), pp. 67 and 72.

21. Thirsk (1987), pp. 57–8.

22. Norman Scarfe (trans. and ed.), *A Frenchman's Year in Suffolk, 1784: French Impressions of Suffolk Life in 1784*, p. xix (Boydell Press, Woodbridge. 1989). See also Norman Scarfe, *Innocent Espionage: The La Rochefoucauld Brothers' Tour of England in 1785* (Boydell Press, Woodbridge, 1995).

23. Hoskins (1955), p. 190.

24. Ibid., p. 207.

25. Wade Martins (1995), pp. 75–90.

26. Ibid., p. 76.

27. For a phased map of Parliamentary Enclosure, see Roberts and Wrathmell (2000), p. 30.

28. Wade Martins (1995), pp. 77–8.

29. Rowley (2006), p. 27.

30. Wade Martins and Williamson (1999), pp. 55–60.

31. 'If livestock are fed on a high plane of nutrition during their early life, then the final carcass will have the maximum proportion of muscle': quoted from Derek H. Goodwin, *Sheep Management and Production*, 2nd edn., p. 30 (Hutchinson, London, 1979).

32. For an excellent review, see Cook and Williamson (2007); for an earlier summary account see Christopher Taylor, *Fields in the English Landscape*, pp. 134–8 (J. M. Dent, London, 1975).

33. Grass generally starts into growth above 8 °C.

34. T. W. Beastall, *The Agricultural Revolution in Lincolnshire*, pp. 71–8, History of Lincolnshire, vol. 8 (History of Lincolnshire Committee, Lincoln, 1978).

35. Alexander Fenton and Bruce Walker, *The Rural Architecture of Scotland*, p. 20 (John Donald, Edinburgh, 1981). Today Auchindrain is an open-air museum and has been preserved as it might have appeared at the end of the nineteenth century. For more information visit <www.auchindrainmuseum.org.uk>.

36. The account of Scottish agricultural improvements relies heavily on Wade Martins (1995), pp. 95–7.

37. Ibid., p. 92.

38. The best account of the tragedy of the clearances is still that by J. Prebble, *The Highland Clearances* (Secker and Warburg, London, 1963).

39. Wade Martins (1995), p. 145.

40. Muir (2004), p. 52. For a historical account of crofting, see J. Hunter, *The Making of the Crofting Community* (John Donald, Edinburgh, 1976).

41. Wade Martins (1995), pp. 98–100.

42. Wade Martins (1995), pp. 91–3.

43. Ramm, McDowall and Mercer (1970).

44. Frodsham (2004), p. 86.

45. Whyte (1999), p. 266.

46. Barnwell and Giles (1997), pp. 3–5.

47. Wade Martins and Williamson (1999), pp. 49–67.

48. Williamson (2000), p. 115; Cook and Williamson (2007), pp. 54–6.

49. The following discussion is largely based on a study by Williamson (2002), pp. 155–8.

50. Short, Watkins and Martin (2007b), p. 6.

51. The nave of my own parish church at Sutton St James completely collapsed during the Commonwealth and today the chancel and tower are separated by grass.

52. Before the introduction of the water closet, privies were emptied by contractors overnight. This nightsoil was spread on fields surrounding the large cities. The vegetable-growing areas of Bedfordshire, for example, were greatly enriched by nightsoil brought from north London.

53. A rich source of potash consisting of the dropping of seagulls, shipped in bulk to Britain. Most guano was removed from islands off the coast of Peru, where the birds fed on the huge shoals of fish in the cold Humboldt Current. In the twentieth century artificial nitrate fertilizers were also known to farmers as guano.

54. J. B. Denton, *The Farm Homesteads of England* (London, 1863).

55. Barnwell and Giles (1997).

56. Not to be confused with the Gothic architect, James Wyatt, of Fonthill Abbey fame.

57. Thompson (1977).

58. Ibid., p. 79.

59. Hoskins (1955), pp. 197–8.

60. Jim Glasspool (ed.), *Chalk Streams: A Guide to Their Natural History and River Keeping* (The Test and Itchen River Association, 2006).

61. The 5th edn. of 1835 is the one generally reproduced. The latest available version is that published by Frances Lincoln (Kentish Town, London, 2004).

62. The description was applied to the Earl of Northumberland's estates in the western Lakes. The poem is quoted in Winchester (2006), pp. 197–210, which I have drawn upon extensively in this discussion of the Lake District.

63. Strong (2000), pp. 532–3.

64. *Fors Clavigera: Letters to the Workmen and Labourers of Great Britain*, vol. 5, letter 52 (published 1871–8).

65. Jellicoe *et al.* (1986), pp. 544–5.

66. In the mid-twentieth century it fell into disrepair, but it has been superbly restored by Bedfordshire County Council.

67. What little I know about English watercolours was taught me by my father, Robert Matthew Pryor (1917–2005), who accumulated a large and distinguished collection based around Peter De Wint. The collection was catalogued by Sotheby's for its sale (in London) on 4 July 2002.

68. Ronald Blythe, 'Foreword', in Peter Moyse, *John Clare: The Poet and the Place* (Crossberry Press, Helpston, 1993).

69. For a lively and very well written biography, see Ingrams (2005).

70. William Cobbett, *Cottage Economy*, p. 21 (Eco-logic Books, Bristol, 2005).

71. For a spirited defence of Victorian architecture and the lessons of its

conservation, see Jonathan Meades, 'Blind to the Test', *National Trust Magazine*, spring 2008, p. 17.

CHAPTER 13. DARK SATANIC MILLS? TOWNSCAPES IN MODERN TIMES (1750–1900)

1. Royal Commission on Historical Monuments, *The Town of Stamford*, p. xliv (HMSO, London, 1977).
2. Pevsner, Harris and Antram (1989), p. 687.
3. Pevsner and Cherry (1977), p. 137.
4. Stephen Grenter, 'The Bersham Ironworks', *Current Archaeology*, 141, December 1995, pp. 332–5.
5. It comes as a surprise to see 'Iron Rail Way' marked on the first edition of the Ordnance Survey 1-inch map of the area, published in May 1816.
6. Dick Sullivan, *Navvyman* (Coracle Books, London, 1983).
7. Freeman (1999), p. 1.
8. M. Robbins, *The Railway Age in Britain and Its Impact on the World*, p. 38 (Penguin Books, Harmondsworth, 1965).
9. Freeman (1999), pp. 1–9.
10. It is still open and passes through some of the grandest and most spectacular scenery in Britain.
11. Gerald Tyler, *The Railway Years in Chapel le Dale 1870–77* (Friends of St Leonard's Church, Chapel le Dale, North Yorkshire, n.d.).
12. Much of the architecture was the work of M. D. Wyatt. Paddington continued to be modified after 1854, culminating in the addition of a fourth span to the train shed in 1915.
13. Steven Brindle, *Paddington Station: Its History and Architecture* (English Heritage, Swindon, 2004).
14. I am thinking here, for example, of some of the Victorian terrace housing off Lincoln Road, Peterborough.
15. Swindon is now the home of English Heritage, in converted Victorian railway buildings in Kemble Drive. One of their constituent organizations, the one-time English Royal Commission for Historical Monuments, commissioned an outstanding survey of the town: Cattell and Keith Falconer, *Swindon: The Legacy of a Railway Town* (English Heritage, Swindon, 1995).
16. Palmer and Neaverson (1994), pp. 171–2.
17. Gustav and Chrissie Milne, *Medieval Waterfront Development at Trig Lane, London*, London and Middlesex Archaeological Society Special Paper, 5 (London, 1982).
18. Giles and Hawkins (2004), p. 7.

19. Ibid., p. 7.

20. For comparison, the process whereby large areas of Merseyside became urbanized is examined in Jennifer Lewis and Ron Cowell (eds.), *The Archaeology of a Changing Landscape: The Last Thousand Years in Merseyside*, whole issue of Journal of the Merseyside Archaeological Society, 11, 2002.

21. Carding and combing are processes that align fibres before they can be spun into yarns.

22. Giles and Hawkins (2004), p. 105.

23. The first census took place in the USA, in 1790. Britain and France, at war at the time, each held their first in 1801.

24. Hudson (1963), p. 51.

25. Palmer and Neaverson (2005), p. 31.

26. Ibid., p. 48.

27. Ibid., pp. 123–30.

28. Ian Forbes, Brian Young, Clive Crossley and Lesley Hehir, *Lead Mining Landscapes of the North Pennines Area of Outstanding Natural Beauty* (Durham County Council, 2003).

29. For a general review of early tin-working, see Sandy Gerrard, *The Early British Tin Industry* (Tempus Books, Stroud, 2000).

30. Marilyn Palmer and Peter Neaverson, *The Basset Mines: The History and Industrial Archaeology*, British Mining, 32 (Northern Mine Research Society, Sheffield, 1987); for an updated summary see Palmer and Neaverson (1998), pp. 127–40.

31. See, for example, Hoskins (1955), plate 56. For a more recent treatment, see Mark Brayshay, 'Landscapes of Industry', pp. 148–9 in Kain (2006), pp. 131–53.

32. The following account relies heavily on Palmer and Neaverson (1994), pp. 49–66.

33. Palmer and Neaverson (1998), pp. 6–7.

34. In actual fact Salts Mill was the second-largest cotton mill in Bradford. The largest was Manningham Mill, built between 1871–3 for the Bradford firm of Lister and Co. See Palmer and Neaverson (1998), p. 5.

35. Gary Firth, *Images of England: Salt and Saltaire* (Tempus Books, Stroud, 2001).

36. Hoskins (1955), p. 285.

37. Overton (2006), p. 112.

38. Thomas (2002), pp. 73–4.

39. Cannon (2001), p. 143.

40. Barton (1993), pp. 130–33.

41. The account of Brighton draws heavily on Short (2006), pp. 142–6.

42. It is 700 metres long.

43. Pevsner (1966), pp. 319–33.

44. Durie (2003), pp. 65–85.

45. See Aston and Bond (1976), pp. 136–75, for a good general review of Georgian and Regency urban development.

46. Fiona Cullen and David Lovie, *Newcastle's Grainger Town: An Urban Renaissance* (English Heritage, London, 2003).

47. This section relies heavily on Short (2006), pp. 168–76.

48. It was known as 'sweating'. See Henry Hodges, *Artifacts: An Introduction to Early Materials and Technology*, pp. 148–9 (Duckworth, London, 1989).

49. MoLAS (2000), p. 278.

50. My ancestor Samuel Hoare, treasurer of the original Quaker anti-slavery committee, lived in Heath House on Hampstead Hill, from where he regularly travelled to his bank in the City. See F. R. Pryor (ed.), *Memoirs of Samuel Hoare by his Daughter Sarah and his Widow Hannah. Also some Letters from London During the Gordon Riots* (Headley Brothers, London, 1911).

51. Short (2006), pp. 176–83; MoLAS (2000), pp. 274–81; Rowsome (2000), pp. 72–7.

52. The new Houses of Parliament are not, however, the sole candidates as symbols of Victorian London. Other contenders are the great railway termini and Sir Joseph Bazalgette's New Cross pumping station, without which Victorian Londoners could never have thrived.

53. For a comprehensive review of covered markets in Britain, see James Schmiechen and Kenneth Carls, *The British Market Hall: A Social and Architectural History* (Yale University Press, London and New Haven, 1999).

54. A 14-metre clinker-built boat was found on the foreshore at Graveney, in Kent. She was abandoned in the mid-tenth century and had been carrying a cargo of hops, presumably from Kent, weighing an estimated 6–7 tonnes. This indicates that beer (not ale, which is hop-less) was being brewed in later Saxon times on a near-industrial scale.

55. MoLAS (2000), p. 276.

56. Rowsome (2000), p. 73.

57. Quoted in Short (2006), pp. 176–9.

58. A. Seebohm Rowntree, *Poverty: A Study of Town Life* (1903).

59. Neil Rhind, *Blackheath Village and Environs 1790–1970*, vol. 2, pp. 43–53 (Bookshop Blackheath Ltd., 1983).

60. Crosby (2006b), pp. 150–51.

61. For a history of Birkenhead Park, see Clifford E. Thornton, *The People's Garden* (Department of Leisure Services and Tourism, Metropolitan Borough of Wirral, no date).

62. Quoted ibid., p. 3, from the *Report on the Select Committee on Public Works* (HMSO, 1833).

63. B. Lowry, *Discovering Fortifications from the Tudors to the Cold War* (Shire Books, Princes Risborough, 2006).

64. Ibid., pp. 60–107.

CHAPTER 14. THE PLANNER TRIUMPHANT: LANDSCAPES IN THE LATE NINETEENTH AND TWENTIETH CENTURIES

1. Written by Neil Innes and Viv Stanshall and released in 1968.

2. Barnwell and Giles (1997), pp. 6–7.

3. Many were planned before the First World War, but most were constructed just after.

4. Vic Mitchell, Keith Smith and Andrew C. Ingram, *Branch Line to Upwell* (Middleton Press, Midhurst, West Sussex, 1995).

5. Alistair Robertson, 'Railways in Suffolk', in David Dymond and Edward Martin (eds.), *An Historical Atlas of Suffolk*, pp. 108–9 (Suffolk County Council Planning Department, Ipswich, 1988).

6. This would have been the real 'purple sprouting' broccoli and not the flavourless calabrese that masquerades as that excellent vegetable in supermarkets today.

7. Barnwell and Giles (1997), p. 7.

8. Wright (1982), pp. 145–8.

9. They were made for him at the Great Western Railway works at Swindon by his friend Daniel Gooch, Locomotive Superintendent of the GWR. See Wright (1982), p. 145.

10. Brian Bell, *Farm Machinery*, 3rd edn. (Farming Press, Ipswich, 1989).

11. The definitive study is by William Foot, *Beaches, Fields, Streets and Hills: The Anti-Invasion Landscapes of England, 1940*, Council for British Archaeology Research Report, 144 (York, 2006).

12. For surviving pillboxes and other structures, see Ian Brown, David Burridge, David Clarke, John Guy, John Hellis, Bernard Lowry, Nigel Ruckley and Roger Thomas, *20th Century Defences in Britain: An Introductory Guide*, Practical Handbooks in Archaeology, 12 (Council for British Archaeology, York, 1996).

13. Pillboxes were built in a variety of shapes. For examples, see Ian J. Sanders *Pillboxes: Images of an Unfought Battle* (published by the author, 2005).

14. See Osborne (2004) for an excellent review of twentieth-century defensive structures in Britain.

15. In most instances this order would have amounted to a death sentence.

16. Cockroft, Thomas and Barnwell (2004); Clarke (2005).

17. Clarke (2005), pp. 199–200.

18. Cockroft, Thomas and Barnwell (2004), p. 225.

19. Ibid., p. 217.

20. For a fine collection of essays on farming in the Second World War, see Short, Watkins and Martin (2007a); quoted in Short, Watkins and Martin (2007b), p. 1.

21. This discussion draws heavily on Short, Watkins and Martin (2007b).

22. There were exceptions. Silage, for example, such a familiar part of the modern farming landscape, was a wartime introduction.

23. English Heritage, *Conservation Bulletin: Modern Times*, ed. John Schofield, 56 (2007), p. 15.

24. Ibid.

25. Rowley (2006), pp. 295–7.

26. The following is based on A. J. L. Winchester, 'The Freedom of the Hills', in Winchester (2006), pp. 205–7.

27. Winchester (2006), p. 207.

28. Quoted in Rowley (2006), p. 419.

29. The huge numbers of people who regularly walk through the area are causing damage to many of the more fragile peat surfaces. It should not be supposed that completely unfettered access is without its problems.

30. Quoted in Cole and Durack (1992), p. 101.

31. Linda Lear, *Beatrix Potter: A Life in Nature* (Allen Lane, London, 2007).

32. Ursula Buchan, *Garden People: Valerie Finnis and the Golden Age of Gardening*, p. 46 (Thames and Hudson, London, 2007).

33. These principles were defined in the previous century by William Robinson in *The Wild Garden* (1870).

34. MoLAS (2000), p. 226.

35. Rowley (2006), p. 61.

36. This strange suggestion was in an otherwise superb book by Trevor Rowley (2006), p. 249.

37. Winchester (2006), pp. 238–9.

38. I draw heavily on Rowley (2006) for material on planning in the twentieth century.

39. The Leyland cypress (*Cupressocyparis leylandii*) is a cross between the rare Nootka cypress (*Chamaecyparis nookatensis*) and the Monterey cypress (*Cupressus macrocarpa*). See George Drower, *Garden Heroes and Villains*, pp. 78–87 (Sutton Publishing, Stroud, 2006).

40. There is a large range of places of worship, apart from churches, in the modern urban landscape. For a good review of these see the English Heritage *Conservation Bulletin*, 46, autumn 2004.

41. Crosby (2006c), p. 183.

42. The discussion of Garden Cities and New Towns relies heavily on Rowley (2006), pp. 171–94.

43. It had not grown a great deal since Domesday, where it reportedly had nine villans and a priest, two sokemen, four cottars and a slave; also woodland for 100 pigs; Williams and Martin (2002), p. 381.

44. The term 'Greater London' was first used in the census of 1881 to include an area within 24 kilometres of central London. See Short (2006), p. 183.

45. The following paragraphs draw heavily on the excellent report by Taylor and Lovie (2004).

46. Pevsner and Cherry (1977), pp. 350–58.

47. Short (2006), pp. 99–104.

48. Without help from the Development Corporation in its final years (1987) the Bronze Age site at Flag Fen would probably never have become established as a popular visitor attraction.

49. For Telford, see Hooke (2006), pp. 202–9.

50. Stocker (2006), p. 111.

51. Owen (2002), p. 802.

52. Pevsner (1962), p. 221.

53. Helen Clarke and Alan Carter, *Excavations in King's Lynn 1963–1970*, Society for Medieval Archaeology Monograph Series, 7 (London, 1977).

54. For an excellent review of the town's history, written by an ex-mayor and historian, see Paul Richards, *King's Lynn* (Phillimore, Chichester, 1990).

55. Taylor and Lovie (2004).

56. Figures taken from Trevor Rowley, 'More of the Age than the Islands', *British Archaeology*, November–December 2006, pp. 11–15.

57. W. F. Grimes, 'Draughton, Colsterworth and Heathrow', in S. S. Frere (ed.), *The Problems of the Iron Age in Southern Britain*, pp. 21–8 (Institute of Archaeology, London, 1961).

58. Quoted in Rowley (2006), p. 66; taken from G. Maxwell, *Highwayman's Heath: The Story in Fact and Fiction of Hounslow Heath in Middlesex* (Thomasons Ltd., Hounslow, 1935).

59. Rowley (2006), pp. 67–73.

60. Both quotes ibid., p. 68.

61. Both quotes ibid., p. 72.

62. I have personally encountered thick deposits of alluvium on sites scheduled for housing and industrial development in the Fengate area of Peterborough and on housing estates on the fringes of Ely, Bedford and Lincoln and on many sites in or close to the floodplain of the Thames, near Oxford. For more about archaeological sites below alluvium, see Needham and Macklin (1992).

63. In August 2007 the citizens of Tewkesbury marched through their town, which had recently suffered catastrophic floods, in protest against proposals to build further housing estates in the floodplain of the River Severn.

64. The government's Index of Multiple Deprivation released this, in figures published for the year 2000; see Short (2006), p. 194.

65. For an excellent review of pubs and pub history, see Geoff Brandwood, Andrew Davison and Michael Slaughter, *Licensed to Sell: The History and Heritage of the Public House* (English Heritage, London, 2004).

66. Smith (2005).

67. Rowley (2006), p. 397.

68. Palmer and Neaverson (1994), p. 198.

69. Cole and Durack (1992), p. 149.

70. Williamson (2006), p. 125.

71. Hunt (2006), p. 204.

72. Rowley (2006), pp. 365–7.

73. Crosby (2006b), p. 147.

74. Walton and Wood (2006).

75. The origin of word is French and it was first used in English (1927) to describe military infrastructure, such as tunnels, gun-emplacement, etc. It remained in use as a military term during the Second World War and in the post-war decades, only acquiring a more general or civilian meaning from the early 1970s.

76. Rowley (2006), pp. 12–19.

77. Ibid., pp. 20–52.

78. Steane (1974) suggests that Faxton was abandoned somewhat earlier, but essentially for the same reasons. Today the site can only be reached by footpaths over the fields.

79. Some great landowners opposed the railways vigorously. The Marquis of Exeter had the unsightly railway sunk in a cutting and routed around his park at Burghley House, near Stamford, Lincs. His neighbour, however, the Earl Fitzwilliam, welcomed the arrival of the railway at Peterborough, near his country estate, Milton Park. Subsequently Peterborough thrived and Stamford stagnated. Today Stamford is regarded as an architectural gem, whereas Peterborough has a fine cathedral, and little else. The poet John Clare witnessed with horror the construction of the east coast main line through the unspoilt country around his native village of Helpston, near Peterborough.

80. Hooke (2006), p. 204.

81. Stocker (2006), pp. 27–8.

82. D. A. Ratcliffe (ed.), *A Nature Conservation Review: The Selection of Biological Sites of National Importance to Nature Conservation in Britain*, 2 vols. (Cambridge University Press, 1977).

83. For a good introduction to the scope of Landscape Characterization, with references, see English Heritage *Conservation Bulletin*, particularly issues 47 (winter 2004–5) and 54 (spring 2007).

84. The technique is explained well in a good 'how to do it' book by Stephen Rippon, *Historic Landscape Analysis: Deciphering the Countryside*, Council for British Archaeology, Practical Handbook, 16 (York, 2004).

85. A first step in this direction has recently been published by the English Heritage Characterization team. The report begins by dispelling the notion that anything built after 1950 does not count as heritage and quotes a MORI report of 2000 for English Heritage, which noted that most people disagreed with this suggestion. Incidentally, the same report also noted that 77 per cent of the people interviewed disagreed with the idea that that 'we already preserve too much of this country's heritage'. MORI Research Study Conducted for English Heritage, April–July 2000, *Attitudes Towards the Heritage*, p. 4.

CHAPTER 15. SAT NAV BRITAIN: WHAT FUTURE FOR THE LANDSCAPE?

1. George Lambrick, *Archaeology and Agriculture* (Oxford Archaeological Unit, 1977).

2. Information from Dominic Powlesland.

3. 'Gardeners' Digest', *The Garden (Journal of the Royal Horticultural Society)*, 131/11, November 2006, p. 726.

4. English Heritage, *Stonehenge World Heritage Site Management Plan* (London, 2000).

5. For the fascinating story behind the passing of the first Ancient Monuments Act, see Thompson (1977), pp. 58–74.

6. For an excellent summary of the various proposals in the white paper, see the *Council for British Archaeology Newsletter*, 2, April 2007, pp. 1–2.

7. Britain ratified the World Heritage Convention in 1984. See Timothy Darvill, 'Reeling in the Years: The Past in the Present', in Hunter and Ralston (1999), pp. 297–315.

8. For reviews of wetland research, see Bryony and John Coles, *People of the Wetlands: Bogs, Bodies and Lake-Dwellers* (Thames and Hudson, London, 1989); John M. Coles and Andrew J. Lawson (eds.), *European Wetlands in Prehistory* (Clarendon Press, Oxford, 1987). For plough-damage and modern farming, see J. Hinchliffe and R. T. Schadla-Hall (eds.), *The Past Under the Plough*, Directorate of Ancient Monuments and Historic Buildings, 3 (Department of the Environment, London, 1980); Keith Wilkinson, Andrew

Tyler, Donald Davidson and Ian Grieve, 'Quantifying the Threat to Archaeological Sites From the Erosion of Cultivated Soil', *Antiquity*, 80, 2006, pp. 658–70.

9. Steve Trow, Vince Holyoak and Fachtna McAvoy, 'Understanding Plough Damage: Research in Field and Lab', *Archaeologist*, 63, spring 2007, pp. 32–3.

10. George Lambrick (ed.), *Archaeology and Nature Conservation* (Oxford University Department for External Studies, 1985).

11. Clive Aslet, 'Design for Living', *Daily Telegraph*, 14 April 2007, pp. W1–W2.

12. English Heritage, *Low Demand Housing and the Historic Environment* (London, 2005).

13. English Heritage (2007).

14. In April 2008 it was announced that in future the covering of front gardens using impermeable materials, such as tarmac, paving or concrete, will require planning permission.

15. For a very useful review of climate change and its impact on the historic environment (with many references), see *English Heritage Conservation Bulletin*, 57, spring 2008.

16. English Heritage, *Wind Energy and the Historic Environment* (London, 2005).

17. Personal and anecdotal evidence for climate change can be too readily discounted. I found this reference particularly upsetting and very persuasive: Patrick Foster, 'Climate Change: A Threat to the Historic Environment', *Archaeologist*, 63, spring 2007, pp. 12–13.

18. Hulme *et al.* (2007).

19. The statistics are taken from ibid., pp. ii–v.

20. The picture in Scotland is complicated by the fact that some coastlines here are rising. The predicted rates for sea-level change therefore range between a fall of 2 centimetres and a rise of 58 centimetres, for the west coast.

21. The internationally respected Tyndall Centre for Climate Change Research (University of East Anglia) has suggested that sea-level rise by the end of the twenty-first century could be around 1.2 metres. This would be almost double what was suggested in the UKCIP02 Scientific Report and it would make the smooth management of change very difficult indeed.

22. We tend to underestimate the sheer horror of flooding and its effect on families. For a well-illustrated account of floods in the twentieth century, see M. G. and H. J. Harland, *The Flooding of Eastern England* (Minimax Books, Peterborough, 1980).

23. DEFRA is the ministry responsible for flood defences.

24. 'Adapting to Climate Change', *Natural World*, winter 2007, pp. 17–22.

25. For a review of possible future crops, see *Farming Link: DEFRA News for Farmers and Growers*, 6, November 2006, p. 5. See also <www.defra. gov.uk/agriculture/rccf/tor.htm> for news from DEFRA's Rural Climate Change Forum.

26. For the funding and archaeological implications of the Pathfinder Project, see Lynne Walker, 'Home and Heritage', *British Archaeology*, March 2004, pp. 24–5; Jason Wood, 'Team Effort', *British Archaeology*, November/December 2005, pp. 10–13. In early July 2008 a House of Commons Select Committee reported that the widespread demolition taking place as part of the Pathfinder Project was endangering the character of many northern cities. Demolition was also proceeding faster than building, partly as a result of the 'credit crunch'.

27. For the Thames Gateway, see Andrew Croft, 'The Thames Gateway', *English Heritage Conservation Bulletin*, 47, winter 2004–5, pp. 8–10. The Council for British Archaeology website, <www.britarch.ac.uk>, is an excellent source of information on current conservation issues.

28. RCHM (1969).

29. Enid Porter, *Cambridgeshire Customs and Folklore*, pp. 103–4 (Routledge and Kegan Paul, London, 1969).

30. A conference was organized at Christ Church, Oxford, in April 2008 on *W. G. Hoskins and the Modern World*, which examined his long-term influence on conservation and politics.

31. Pers. comm., February 2008.

32. i.e. animal feed, as opposed to milling wheats.

33. A report by Merrill Lynch, quoted on Radio 4, *Farming Today This Week*, Saturday, 1 June 2007.

34. Cauliflowers have been a staple in the British diet since the seventeenth century, but the largest grower of them, based Kent, has recently ceased production. Roger Welberry, 'Cauliflowers Face the Chop', *Lincolnshire Free Press*, 5 June 2007, p. 10.

35. For a well-thought-out paper on the future of rural landscapes within the EU, see Mark Blacksell, 'From Marx to Brussels: Agriculture and Landscape in Twenty-First-Century Europe', *Landscape History*, 28, 2006, pp. 77–87.

36. I wrote this before the 'credit crunch' and rapid oil price rises of 2008. Such vast buildings may really have a limited future.

37. British history can be perplexing. The excellent *Oxford Dictionary of British History*, for example, only mentions the eldest ironmaster, Abraham Darby I, and deals with his achievements in ten lines. By way of contrast, the various earls of Derby are together given approximately 100 lines.

Further Reading and Research

The writing of this book has been an interesting experience, as it has taken me into new and intriguing areas of knowledge. I have drawn heavily on the recently published (2006) English Heritage *England's Landscape* series for certain topics, such as the rise of resort towns from the mid-eighteenth century. It is probably still too early to assess the impact of these handsome books, but the volumes written by single authors (Tom Williamson, *East Anglia*; David Stocker, *The East Midlands*; Della Hooke, *The West Midlands*, and Brian Short, *The South East*) are exceptionally good. Without exception too, they are beautifully illustrated and I have used several of their aerial views in this book, through the courtesy of English Heritage. The publication, also in 2006, of Trevor Rowley's seminal work on *The English Landscape in the Twentieth Century* came as a godsend to someone whose expertise lies in the earlier third millennium BC, not AD. I have drawn on it extensively in Chapter 14. Incidentally, readers who are not familiar with the general run of archaeological literature can search for references and summaries on specific topics at the excellent British and Irish Archaeological Bibliography website (www.biab.ac.uk).

References are always a problem in a larger book intended for a general readership. The difficulties can be avoided by including a few significant sources in a series of chapter-by-chapter lists of further reading. In my experience, however, one normally wants to find something more specific and it can be very frustrating if the suggested reading list is too general. Academic books include references in the text using the Harvard (author/date) system, thus: (Pryor 1998, p. 305). However, even this abbreviated system does significantly break the reader's flow; so I have decided to adopt a hybrid system with endnotes, which I find easier to ignore when reading for pleasure. Works that are cited more than once are given in the author/date form, with full details in the List of References as below. I am aware that this system is slightly cumbersome, but after much thought I have failed to come up with anything better. I have also tried to keep spelling (never my strongest point) consistent with road maps, to make visiting the various places simpler. Most maps use the Ordnance Survey database so this is the spelling I have followed.

Hoskins and his contemporaries have been discussed in the text. Here I am concerned with current literature. The most important scholarly critique of present approaches to landscape history is *Ideas of Landscape* by Matthew Johnson (2007).[1] This book challenges the idea that landscapes can somehow be 'read' and suggests instead a theory-based approach in which ideas are tested against observable evidence. I have some sympathy for Johnson's approach, as it reflects my own experience as a prehistorian, but it does not invalidate the large body of work that has followed the more traditional, narrative-based, approach of Hoskins and others. These include a number of excellent textbooks and lexicons written in the tradition of landscape history which I have briefly discussed in the Introduction.[2] Even if it is believed by some to be theoretically questionable, I still like the idea of 'reading' a landscape, if only because it makes a day out looking for suitable clues more fun, especially if one is with youngsters. The best and most finely written of the 'reading the landscape' books are those by Richard Muir.[3] Such books use readily identifiable clues as a guide to what to look for: roads, for example, with wide verges and hedges set well back, often go with a later eighteenth- or nineteenth-century Parliamentary Enclosure landscape.

Recent years have seen something of an explosion of books and articles about various aspects of the British landscape. The English Heritage regional landscape already referred to must be the first port-of-call of any enquiry into the English landscape.[4] Anyone intent on becoming a serious student of the British landscape should refer to the two principal journals, *Landscape History* (published by the Society for Landscape Studies, since 1979) and *Landscapes* (published by Windgather Press, Macclesfield, since 2000). Both journals are also associated with a series of substantial books of essays and longer case studies.[5] Other papers and articles can be more technical and are often the result of recent changes in planning law and official advice, as laid down in *Planning Policy Guidance Note 16* for England and Wales (known as PPG-16) and in *Archaeology and Planning* (NPPG-5) for Scotland, published in 1989 and 1994, respectively.[6] In essence these guidance notes have said that developers must pay for any archaeological investigation their proposals might necessitate. It often takes years, but eventually the principal findings of the reports produced under current planning rules for the developer or client do filter into mainstream archaeological literature, usually by way of the Historic Environment Record maintained by the local authority in the relevant county or city.[7]

1. For a paper that successfully bridges the divide between the theoretical and historical approaches to landscape see: Andrew Fleming, 'Don't Bin Your Boots', *Landscapes*, 8, spring 2007, pp. 85–99.
2. See, e.g., Michael Aston and Trevor Rowley, *Landscape Archaeology: An Introduction to Fieldwork Techniques on Post-Roman Landscapes* (David and Charles, Newton Abbot, 1974).
3. Richard Muir, *The New Reading the Landscape: Fieldwork in Landscape History* (University of Exeter Press, 2000), and Muir (2004).
4. Published jointly with Collins, in 2006 and 2007 under the series title 'England's Landscape', the eight regions are: *The North East*, *The North West*, *The West Midlands*, *The East Midlands*, *East Anglia*, *The South East*, *The West* and *The South West*.
5. The Windgather Press (Macclesfield) series 'Landscapes of Britain' is particularly notable.
6. For a thorough review of archaeological legislation and practice in Britain, see John Hunter and Ian Ralston (eds.), *Archaeological Resource Management in the U.K.: An Introduction*, 2nd edn. (Sutton Publishing, Stroud, 2006).
7. Bradley (2007), for example, includes a wealth of material derived from commercially funded projects.

List of References

Ammerman, A. J., and Biagi, P. (eds.) (2003), *The Widening Harvest: The Neolithic Transition in Europe. Looking Back, Looking Forward* (Archaeological Institute of America, Boston).

Aston, M., and Bond, J. (1976), *The Landscape of Towns* (Dent, London).

Aston, M., and Gerrard, C. (1999), '"Unique, Traditional and Charming": The Shapwick Project, Somerset', *Antiquaries Journal*, 79, pp. 1–58.

Barber, M. (2003), *Bronze and the Bronze Age: Metalwork and Society in Britain c.2500–800 BC* (Tempus Books, Stroud).

Barker, D., and Cranstone, D. (eds.) (2004), *The Archaeology of Industrialization* (Maney, Leeds).

Barnwell, P. S., and Giles, C. (1997), *English Farmsteads, 1750–1914* (Royal Commission on the Historical Monuments of England, Swindon, 1997).

Barnwell, P. S., Palmer, M., and Airs, M. (eds.) (2004), *The Vernacular Workshop: From Craft to Industry, 1400–1900*, Council for British Archaeology Research Report, 140 (York).

Barrett, J. C., Freeman, P. W. M., and Woodward, A. (2000), *Cadbury Castle Somerset: The Later Prehistoric and Early Historic Archaeology*, Archaeological Report, 20 (English Heritage, London).

Barton, N. (1993), *The Lost Rivers of London* (BCA, London).

Bayliss, A., and Whittle, A. (eds.) (2007), 'Histories of the Dead: Building Chronologies for Five Southern British Long Barrows', *Cambridge Archaeological Journal*, 17/1 (Supplement).

Beresford, M. (1988), *New Towns of the Middle Ages: Town Plantation in England, Wales and Gascony* (Alan Sutton Publishing, Gloucester).

Birrell, J. (1992), 'Deer and Deer Farming in Medieval England', *Agricultural History Review*, 402, pp. 112–26.

Bond, J. (2004), *Monastic Landscapes* (Tempus Books, Stroud).

Bowen, H. C., and Fowler, P. J. (eds.) (1978), *Early Land Allotment*, British Archaeological Reports, 48 (Oxford).

Bowman, P., and Liddle, P. (2004), *Leicestershire Landscapes*, Leicestershire

Museums Archaeological Fieldwork Group Monograph, 1 (Leicestershire County Council, Leicester).

Bradley, R. J. (2000), *An Archaeology of Natural Places* (Routledge, London).

Bradley, R. J. (2007), *The Prehistory of Britain and Ireland* (Cambridge University Press).

Brennand, M., and Taylor, M. (2003), 'The Survey and Excavation of a Bronze Age Timber Circle at Holme-next-the-Sea, Norfolk, 1998–9', *Proceedings of the Prehistoric Society*, 69, pp. 1–84.

Brück, J. (ed.) (2001), *Bronze Age Landscapes: Tradition and Transformation* (Oxbow Books, Oxford).

Burl, A. (1976), *The Stone Circles of the British Isles* (Yale University Press, London).

Campbell, E. (2007), *Continental and Mediterranean Imports to Atlantic Britain and Ireland, AD 400–800*, Council for British Archaeology Research Report, 157 (York).

Cannon, J. (ed.) (2001), *The Oxford Dictionary of British History* (Oxford University Press).

Clark, J. G. D. (1971), *Excavations at Star Carr, an Early Mesolithic Site at Seamer near Scarborough, Yorkshire* (Cambridge University Press).

Clarke, B. (2005), *Four Minute Warning: Britain's Cold War* (Tempus Books, Stroud).

Cleal, R. M. J., Walker, K. E., and Montague, R. (1995), *Stonehenge in Its Landscape: Twentieth Century Excavations*, English Heritage Archaeological Report, 10 (London).

Cockroft, W. D., Thomas, R. J. C., and Barnwell, P. S. (2004), *Cold War: Building for Nuclear Confrontation 1946–1989*, paperback edn. (English Heritage, Swindon).

Cole, B., and Durack, R. (1992), *Railway Posters 1923–1947: From the Collection of the National Railway Museum, York* (Laurence King Publishing, London).

Cook, H., and Williamson, T. (eds.) (2007), *Water Meadows: History, Ecology and Conservation* (Windgather Press, Macclesfield).

Corney, M. (2000), 'Characterising the Landscape of Roman Britain: A Review of the Study of Roman Britain 1975–2000', in Hooke (2000), pp. 33–45.

Creighton, O., and Higham, R. (2005), *Medieval Town Walls: An Archaeology and Social History of Urban Defence* (Tempus Books, Stroud).

Crosby, A. G. (2006a), 'Moving through the Landscape', in Winchester (2006), pp. 53–72.

Crosby, A. G. (2006b), 'Townscapes and Cityscapes', in Winchester (2006), pp. 133–52.

Crosby, A. G. (2006c), 'The Quest for Utopia', in Winchester (2006), pp. 181–96.

Cruft, K., Dunbar, J., and Fawcett, R. (2006), *Borders*, The Buildings of Scotland (Yale University Press, New Haven and London).

Crummy, P. (1997), *City of Victory: The Story of Colchester – Britain's First Roman Town* (Colchester Archaeological Trust).

Cunliffe, B. W. (1975), *Excavations at Portchester Castle*, vol. 1: *Roman*, Society of Antiquaries Research Report, 32 (London).

Cunliffe, B. W. (2001), *Facing the Ocean* (Oxford University Press).

Cunliffe, B. W. (2002), *The Extraordinary Voyage of Pytheas the Greek* (Penguin Books, London).

Cunliffe, B. W. (2005), *Iron Age Communities in Britain*, 4th edn. (Routledge, London).

Cunliffe, B. W. (ed.) (2006), *England's Landscape: The West* (English Heritage/Collins, London).

Dark, P. (2000), *The Environment of Britain in the First Millennium* AD (Duckworth, London).

Darvill, T., and Thomas, J. (eds.) (1996), *Neolithic Houses in Northwest Europe*, Oxbow Monograph, 57 (Oxford).

Davison, B. K. (1999), *Old Wardour Castle, Wiltshire* (English Heritage, London).

de la Bédoyère, G. (1989), *Hadrian's Wall: History and Guide* (Tempus Books, Stroud).

de la Bédoyère, G. (2003), *Roman Towns in Britain* (Tempus Books, Stroud).

Delano Smith, C. (ed.) (1980), 'The Open Field Village of Laxton', papers published as *The East Midland Geographer*, 7/6, 54 (December).

Dennison E. P., and Coleman, R. (2000), *Historic North Queensferry and Peninsula*, The Scottish Burgh Survey (Historic Scotland, Edinburgh).

Dennison, E. P., Stronach, S., and Coleman, R. (2006), *Historic Dunbar*, The Scottish Burgh Survey (Historic Scotland, Edinburgh).

Durie, A. J. (2003), *Scotland for the Holidays: A History of Tourism in Scotland, 1780–1939* (Tuckwell Press, East Linton, East Lothian).

English Heritage (2007), *Suburbs and the Historic Environment* (Swindon).

Esmonde-Cleary, A. S. (1989), *The Ending of Roman Britain* (Routledge, London).

Fagan, B. (2000), *The Little Ice Age: How Climate Made History, 1300–1850* (Basic Books, New York).

Field, N., and Parker Pearson, M. (2003), *Fiskerton: An Iron Age Timber Causeway with Iron Age and Roman Votive Offerings* (Oxbow Books, Oxford).

Foard, G. (2004), 'Medieval Northamptonshire', in M. Tingle (ed.), *The

Archaeology of Northamptonshire, pp. 102–33 (Northamptonshire Archaeological Society).

Freeman, M. (1999), *Railways and the Victorian Imagination* (Yale University Press, New Haven and London).

French, C. A. I., and Pryor, F. M. M. (1993), *The South-West Fen Dyke Survey Project 1982–86*, East Anglian Archaelogy Report 59 (Fenland Archaeological Trust, Peterborough).

Frere, S. (1991), *Britannia: A History of Roman Britain*, 3rd edn. (Pimlico, London).

Frodsham, P. (ed.) (2004), *Archaeology in Northumberland National Park*, Council for British Archaeology Research Report, 136 (York).

Fulford, M. (1990), 'The Landscape of Roman Britain: A Review', *Landscape History*, 12, pp. 25–31.

Gaffney, V. (2007), 'Doggerland: Lost World of the Stone Age Hunters', *Current Archaeology*, 207, pp. 12–19.

Gardiner, J. (ed.) (1993), *Flatlands and Wetlands: Current Themes in East Anglian Archaeology*, East Anglian Archaeology, 50 (Norwich).

Giles, C., and Hawkins, R. (2004), *Storehouses of Empire: Liverpool's Historic Warehouses* (English Heritage, London).

Hall, D. (2006), *Scottish Monastic Landscapes* (Tempus Books, Stroud).

Hall, D. N. (1982), *Medieval Fields* (Shire Books, Princes Risborough).

Hall, D. N. (1995), *The Open Fields of Northamptonshire* (Northamptonshire Records Society).

Hall, D. N., and Coles, J. M. (1994), *Fenland Survey: An Essay in Landscape and Persistence*, English Heritage Archaeological Report, 1 (London).

Hall, R. A. (1996), *The English Heritage Book of York* (B. T. Batsford/English Heritage, London).

Harding, D. W. (1976), *Hillforts: Later Prehistoric Earthworks in Britain and Ireland* (Academic Press, London).

Hayman, R. (2005), *Ironmaking: The History and Archaeology of the Iron Industry* (Tempus Books, Stroud).

Higham, N. J. (2004), *A Frontier Landscape: The North West in the Middle Ages* (Windgather Press, Macclesfield).

Hodges, R. (1989), *Dark Age Economics: The Origins of Towns and Trade, AD 600–1000*, 2nd edn. (Duckworth, London).

Hooke, D. (ed.) (2000), *Landscape: The Richest Historical Record*, Society for Landscape Studies, supplementary series 1 (Society for Landscape Studies, Amesbury).

Hooke, D. (2006), *England's Landscape: The West Midlands* (English Heritage/Collins, London).

Hope-Taylor, B, (1977), *Yeavering: An Anglo-British Centre of Early*

Northumbria, Department of the Environment Archaeological Reports, 7 (HMSO, London).

Hoskins, W. G. (1955), *The Making of the English Landscape* (Penguin Books, London).

Hudson, K. (1963), *Industrial Archaeology: An Introduction* (Methuen, London).

Hulme, M., Jenkins, G. J., Lu, X., Turnpenny, J. R., Mitchell, T. D., Jones, R. G., Lowe, J., Murphy, J. M., Hassell, D., Boorman, P., McDonald, R., and Hill, S. (2007), *Climate Change Scenarios for the United Kingdom: The UKCIP Scientific Report*, Tyndall Centre for Climate Change Research, School of Environmental Sciences (University of East Anglia, Norwich).

Hunt, S. (2006), 'West Country Spas', in Cunliffe (2006), pp. 189–206.

Hunter, J., and Ralston, I. (eds.) (1999), *The Archaeology of Britain: An Introduction From the Upper Palaeolithic to the Industrial Revolution* (Routledge, London).

Ingrams, R. (2005), *The Life and Adventures of William Cobbett* (Harper Collins, London).

Jellicoe, G., Jellicoe, S., Goode, P., and Lancaster, M. (eds.) (1986), *The Oxford Companion to Gardens* (Oxford University Press).

Johnson, M. (2007), *Ideas of Landscape* (Blackwell Publishing, Oxford).

Johnson, S. (1989), *English Heritage Book of Hadrian's Wall* (B. T. Batsford/English Heritage, London).

Jones, R., and Page, M. (2006), *Medieval Villages in an English Landscape* (Windgather Press, Macclesfield).

Kain, R. (ed.) (2006), *England's Landscape: The South-West* (English Heritage/Collins, London).

Knight, D., and Howard, A. J. (2004), *Trent Valley Landscapes: The Archaeology of 500,000 Years of Change* (Heritage Publications, King's Lynn).

Lane, T., and Coles, J. (eds.) (2002), *Through Wet and Dry: Essays in Honour of David Hall* (Wetland Archaeology Research Project and Heritage Trust for Lincolnshire, Exeter and Sleaford).

Liddiard, R. (2003), 'The Deer Parks of Domesday Book', *Landscapes*, 4/1, pp. 4–23.

Liddiard, R. (2005), *Castles in Context: Power, Symbolism and Landscape, 1066–1500* (Windgather Press, Macclesfield).

Lloyd, D. (2001), *Broad Street, Its Houses and Residents Through Eight Centuries*, Ludlow Historical Research Group, Research Paper, 3 (Ludlow).

McOmish, D., Field, D., and Brown, G. (2002), *The Field Archaeology of the Salisbury Plain Training Area* (English Heritage, Swindon).

Malcolm, G., Bowser, D., with Cowie, R. (2003), *Middle Saxon London:*

Excavations at the Royal Opera House, 1989–99, Museum of London Archaeology Service Monograph, 15 (London).

Mellars, P., and Dark, P. (1998), *Star Carr in Context*, McDonald Institute Monographs (Cambridge).

Miles, D., Palmer, S., Lock, G., Gosden, C., and Cromarty, A. M. (2003), *Uffington White Horse and Its Landscape: Investigations at White Horse Hill, Uffington, 1989–95, and Tower Hill, Ashbury, 1993–4*, Thames Valley Landscapes, Monograph, 18 (Oxford Archaeology, Oxford).

Millett, M. (1990), *The Romanization of Britain* (Cambridge University Press).

Mithen, S. (2003), *After the Ice: A Global Human History 20,000–5000 BC* (Weidenfeld and Nicolson, London).

MoLAS (2000), *The Archaeology of Greater London: An Assessment of Archaeological Evidence for Human Presence in the Area Now Covered by Greater London*, Museum of London Archaeology Service (Museum of London).

Muir, R. (2004), *Landscape Encyclopaedia: A Reference Guide to the Historic Landscape* (Windgather Press, Macclesfield).

Needham, S., and Macklin, M. G. (eds.) (1992), *Alluvial Archaeology in Britain*, Oxbow Monograph, 27 (Oxford).

Newman, J., and Pevsner, N. (2006), *The Buildings of England: Shropshire* (Yale University Press, New Haven and London).

Osborne, M. (2004), *Defending Britain: Twentieth-Century Military Structures in the Landscape* (Tempus Books, Stroud).

Oswald, A., Dyer, C., and Barber, M. (2001), *The Creation of Monuments: Neolithic Causewayed Enclosures in the British Isles* (English Heritage, Swindon).

Oswald, A., Ainsworth, S., and Pearson, T. (2006), *Hillforts: Prehistoric Strongholds of Northumberland National Park* (English Heritage, Swindon).

Overton, M. (2006), 'Farming, Fishing and Rural Settlements', in Kain (2006) pp. 109–30.

Owen, O. (2002), 'Sound Foundations: Archaeology in Scotland's Towns and Cities and the Role of the Scottish Burgh Survey', *Antiquity*, 76, pp. 802–7.

Palmer, M., and Neaverson, P. (1994), *Industry in the Landscape, 1700–1900* (Routledge, London).

Palmer, M., and Neaverson, P. (1998), *Industrial Archaeology: Principles and Practice* (Routledge, London).

Palmer, M., and Neaverson, P. (2005), *The Textile Industry of South-West England: A Social Archaeology* (Tempus Books, Stroud).

Parker Pearson, M. (2005), *Bronze Age Britain*, 2nd edn. (B. T. Batsford/English Heritage, London).

Parker Pearson, M., Sharples, N., and Symonds, J. (2004), *South Uist: Archaeology and History of a Hebridean Island* (Tempus Books, Stroud).

Parker Pearson *et al.*, (2007), 'The Age of Stonehenge', *Antiquity*, 81, pp. 617–39.

Payne, A., Corney, M., and Cunliffe, B. W. (2006), *The Wessex Hillfort Project: Extensive Survey of Hillfort Interiors in Central Southern England* (English Heritage, London).

Pevsner, N. (1954), *The Buildings of England: Cambridgeshire* (Penguin Books, Harmondsworth).

Pevsner, N. (1962), *The Buildings of England: North-West and South Norfolk* (Penguin Books, Harmondsworth).

Pevsner, N. (1966), *The Buildings of England: Yorkshire, The North Riding* (Yale University Press, New Haven and London).

Pevsner, N. (1968), *The Buildings of England: Bedfordshire and the County of Huntingdon and Peterborough* (Yale University Press, New Haven and London).

Pevsner, N., and Cherry, B. (1977), *The Buildings of England: Hertfordshire*, 2nd edn. (Yale University Press, New Haven and London).

Pevsner, N., Harris, J., and Antram, N. (1989), *The Buildings of England: Lincolnshire* (Penguin Books, London).

Pevsner, N., and Williamson, E. (1979), *The Buildings of England: Nottinghamshire*, 2nd edn. (Yale University Press, New Haven and London).

Phillips, C. W. (1970), *The Fenland in Roman Times*, Royal Geographical Society Research Monograph, 5 (London).

Phythian-Adams, C. (1987), *Re-thinking English Local History* (Leicester University Press).

Platt, C. (1997), *King Death: The Black Death and Its Aftermath in Late-Medieval England* (University of Toronto Press).

Pryor, F. M. M. (1974), *Excavation at Fengate, Peterborough, England: the First Report*, Archaeology Monograph, 3 (Royal Ontario Museum, Toronto).

Pryor, F. M. M. (1980), *Excavation at Fengate, Peterborough, England: the Third Report*, Combined Royal Ontario Museum Archaeology Monograph, 6 and Northamptonshire Archaeological Society Monograph, 1 (Northampton and Toronto).

Pryor, F. M. M. (1993), 'Excavations at Site 11, Fengate, Peterborough, 1969', in W. G. Simpson, D. A. Gurney, J. Neve and F. M. M. Pryor (eds.), *The Fenland Project No 7: Excavations in Peterborough and the Lower Welland Valley, 1960–69*, pp. 127–40, East Anglian Archaeology Report, 61 (Cambridge).

Pryor, F. M. M. (1998), *Etton: Excavations at a Neolithic Causewayed Enclosure Near Maxey, Cambridgeshire, 1982–7*, English Heritage Archaeological Report, 18 (London).

Pryor, F. M. M. (2001a), *The Flag Fen Basin: Archaeology and Environment of a Fenland Landscape*, English Heritage Archaeological Report (London).

Pryor, F. M. M. (2001b), *Seahenge: New Discoveries in Prehistoric Britain* (HarperCollins, London).

Pryor, F. M. M. (2003), *Britain BC: Life in Britain and Ireland Before the Romans* (HarperCollins, London).

Pryor, F. M. M. (2004), *Britain AD: A Quest for Arthur, England and the Anglo-Saxons* (HarperCollins, London).

Pryor, F. M. M. (2005), *Flag Fen: Life and Death of a Prehistoric Landscape* (Tempus Books, Stroud).

Pryor, F. M. M. (2006a), *Britain in the Middle Ages: An Archaeological History* (HarperCollins, London).

Pryor, F. M. M. (2006b), *Farmers in Prehistoric Britain*, 2nd edn. (Tempus Books, Stroud).

Pryor, F. M. M., French, C. A. I., Crowther, D. R., Gurney, D. A., Simpson, W. G., and Taylor, M. (1985), *The Fenland Project, No. 1: Archaeology and Environment in the Lower Welland Valley*, 2 vols., East Anglian Archaeology Report, 27 (Cambridge).

Quartermaine, J., Trinder B., and Turner, R. (2003), *Thomas Telford's Holyhead Road: The A5 in North Wales*, Council for British Archaeology, Research Report, 135 (York).

Rackham, O. (1976), *Trees and Woodland in the British Landscape* (London, Dent).

Rackham, O. (1989), *The Last Forest: The Fascinating Account of Britain's Most Ancient Forest* (London, Dent).

Ramm, H. G., McDowall, R. W., and Mercer, E. (1970), *Shielings and Bastles*, Royal Commission on Historical Monuments (England) (HMSO, London).

RCHM (1969), *Peterborough New Town: A Survey of the Antiquities in the Areas of Development*, Royal Commission on Historical Monuments (England) (HMSO, London).

Renfrew, C., and Bahn, P. (2004), *Archaeology: Theories, Methods and Practice*, 4th edn. (Thames and Hudson, London).

Richards, C. (ed.) (2005a), *Dwelling Among the Monuments: The Neolithic Village of Barnhouse, Maeshowe Passage Grave and Surrounding Monuments at Stenness, Orkney* McDonald Institute Monographs (Cambridge).

Richards, C. (2005b), 'The Great Stone Circles Project', *British Archaeology*, March/April, pp. 16–21.

Richards, J. (1991), *Stonehenge* (English Heritage/B. T. Batsford, London).

Richards, J. C. (1990), *The Stonehenge Environs Project*, English Heritage Archaeological Report, 16 (London).

Richmond, I. A. (1968), *Hod Hill, vol. 2: Excavations Carried Out Between 1951 and 1958* (British Museum, London).

Rippon, S. (2000), 'Landscapes in Transition: The Later Roman and Early Medieval Periods', in Hooke (2000), pp. 47–61.

Rippon, S. (2006), 'Landscapes of Pre-Medieval Occupation', in Kain (2006), pp. 41–66.

Roberts, B. K. (1987), *The Making of the English Village* (Longman, London).

Roberts, B. K., and Wrathmell, S. (2000), *An Atlas of Rural Settlement in England* (English Heritage, London).

Rodger, N. A. M. (1997), *The Safeguard of the Sea: A Naval History of Britain, 660–1649* (Penguin, London).

Rodger, N. A. M. (2004), *The Command of the Ocean: A Naval History of Britain, 1649–1815* (Penguin, London).

Rowley, T. (2006), *The English Landscape in the Twentieth Century* (Hambledon Continuum, London).

Rowsome, P. (2000), *Heart of the City: Roman, Medieval and Modern London Revealed by Archaeology at 1 Poultry* (Museum of London Archaeology Service, London).

Ryder, P. (2004), 'Towers and Bastles in Northumberland National Park', in P. Frodsham (ed.), *Archaeology in Northumberland National Park*, pp. 262–71, Council for British Archaeology Research Report, 136 (York).

Salway, P. (1993), *A History of Roman Britain* (Oxford University Press).

Saunders, A. (1989), *Fortress Britain* (Oxbow Books, Oxford).

Schofield, J. (1999), 'Landscapes of the Middle Ages: Towns 1050–1500', in Hunter and Ralston (1999), pp. 210–27.

Sharples, N. M. (1991), *Maiden Castle: Excavations and Field Survey, 1985–6*, English Heritage Archaeological Report, 19 (London).

Short, B. (2006), *England's Landscape: The South-East* (English Heritage/Collins, London).

Short, B., Watkins, C., and Martin, J. (eds.) (2007a), *The Front Line of Freedom: British Farming in the Second World War* (British Agricultural History Society, Exeter).

Short, B., Watkins, C., and Martin, J. (eds.) (2007b), ' "The Front Line of Freedom": State-Led Agricultural Revolution in Britain 1939–45', in Short, Watkins and Martin (2007a), pp. 1–15.

Smith, J. (2005), *Liquid Assets: The Lidos and Open Air Swimming Pools of Britain* (English Heritage, London).

Steane, J. M. (1974), *The Northamptonshire Landscape: Northamptonshire and the Soke of Peterborough* (Hodder and Stoughton, London).

Stocker, D. (2006), *England's Landscape: The East Midlands* (English Heritage/ Collins, London).

Strong, R. (2000), *The Spirit of Britain: A Narrative History of the Arts* (Pimlico, London).

Tabraham, C., and Grove, D. (1995), *Fortress Scotland and the Jacobites* (Historic Scotland/B. T. Batsford, Edinburgh and London).

Taylor, J. (2007), *An Atlas of Roman Rural Settlement in England*, Council for British Archaeology Research Report, 151 (York).

Taylor, M. (1998), 'Identification of the Wood and Evidence for Human Working', in Mellars and Dark (1998), pp. 52–63.

Taylor, S., and Lovie, D. B. (2004), *Gateshead: Architecture in a Changing English Urban Landscape* (English Heritage, London).

Thirsk, J. (1970), 'Seventeenth-Century Agriculture and Social Change', in J. Thirsk (ed.), *Land, Church and People*, pp. 148–77, *Agricultural History Review*, vol. 18.

Thirsk, J. (1987), *England's Agricultural Regions and Agrarian History 1500–1750*, Studies in Economic and Social History (Macmillan Education, London).

Thomas, C. (2002), *The Archaeology of Medieval London* (Sutton Publishing, Stroud).

Thomas, J. S. (1991), *Rethinking the Neolithic* (Cambridge University Press).

Thompson, M. W. (1977), *General Pitt-Rivers: Evolution and Archaeology in the Nineteenth Century* (Moonraker Press, Bradford-on-Avon).

Wade Martins, S. (1995), *Farms and Fields* (B. T. Batsford, London).

Wade Martins, S., and Williamson, T. (1999), *Roots of Change: Farming and the Landscape in East Anglia, c.1700–1870*, British Agricultural History Society supplementary series, 2 (Exeter).

Walton, J. K., and Wood, J. (2006), 'World Heritage Seaside', *British Archaeology*, 90, pp. 10–15.

White, R., and Barker, P. (2002), *Wroxeter: Life and Death of a Roman City*, revised edn. (Tempus Books, Stroud).

Whyte, I. D. (1999), 'The Historical Geography of Britain from AD 1500', in Hunter and Ralston (1999), pp. 264–79.

Whyte, I. D., and Winchester, A. J. L. (eds.) (2004), *Society, Landscape and Environment in Upland Britain*, Society for Landscape Studies supplementary series, 2 (Amesbury).

Williams, A., and Martin, G. H. (eds.) (2002), *Domesday Book: A Complete Translation* (Penguin Books, London).

Williamson, T. (1995), *Polite Landscapes: Gardens and Society in Eighteenth-Century England* (John Hopkins University Press, Baltimore).

Williamson, T. (2000), 'The Rural Landscape: 1500–1900, the Neglected Centuries', in Hooke (2000), pp. 109–17.

Williamson, T. (2002), *The Transformation of Rural England: Farming and the Landscape 1700–1870* (University of Exeter Press).

Williamson, T. (2003), *Shaping Medieval Landscapes: Settlement, Society, Environment* (Windgather Press, Macclesfield).

Williamson, T. (2006), *England's Landscape: East Anglia* (English Heritage/Collins, London).

Wilson, B. (2002), 'Introduction to Norwich', in Nikolaus Pevsner and Bill Wilson, *The Buildings of England: Norfolk 1: Norwich and North-East*, pp. 179–88 (Yale University Press, New Haven and London).

Winchester, A. (ed.) (2006), *England's Landscape: The North West* (English Heritage/Collins, London).

Wright, N. (1982), *Lincolnshire Towns and Industry 1700–1914*, History of Lincolnshire, vol. 11 (History of Lincolnshire Committee, Lincoln).

Yates, D. (2001), 'Bronze Age Agricultural Intensification in the Thames Valley and Estuary', in Brück (2001), pp. 65–82.

Yeoman, P. (1995), *Medieval Scotland: An Archaeological Perspective* (B. T. Batsford/Historic Scotland, London).

Books to Keep in the Car Boot

The Buildings of England (and *The Buildings of Scotland, Ireland* and *Wales*), now published by Yale University Press. This series, the brainchild of the late Sir Nikolaus Pevsner, aims to publish every significant building, ancient or modern, in the British Isles. It is a major and continuing scholarly achievement. Landscape is discussed in the introductory chapter of each volume (rather more fully in the revised versions than in the Pevsner originals). The new and extensively revised and enlarged volumes are a considerable improvement on the smaller Pevsner versions, even if they lack some of the great man's enjoyable prejudices. They also tend to feature rather more non-ecclesiastical architecture, which is most welcome. Half a dozen volumes will help the rear wheels retain traction, but do not keep many more if you want to carry luggage or conserve fuel.

Simon Jenkins, *England's Thousand Best Churches* and *England's Thousand Best Houses* (Penguin Books, London, 2000 and 2004, respectively). I would carry these two books, even if I still owned a motorbike. The author has visited each building and has rated them with from one to five stars. His descriptions are succinct and intelligent and include personal touches that put one in mind of a benign Pevsner. The photographs, too, are superb. Most importantly, Jenkins only covers buildings that are accessible to public view, which the more exhaustive surveys of Pevsner cannot guarantee; over the years I have wasted much time and energy vainly trying to chase down keys for locked country churches that Pevsner has enthused over.

Douglas Greenwood, *Who's Buried Where in England* (Constable, London, 1999). Strictly speaking this book isn't about landscapes so much as the people who inhabited them. Even so, I consider it a must for the car boot.

John Kinross, *Discovering England's Smallest Churches* (Weidenfeld and Nicolson, London, 2003). An excellent, succinct county-by-county guide, but not without its humorous moments. For example, he mentions (p. 91) an account of a signpost in Lincolnshire which reads: 'To Mavis Enderby and Old Bolinbroke', under which some wag has added 'A son, both doing well'.

Various authors, *England's Landscape* (Collins and English Heritage, London, 2006). I would highly recommend keeping at least one of these volumes, each of which covers quite a large area, in the boot. The maps are excellent and if you have a co-operative passenger, who doesn't feel car-sick when map-reading, you can disentangle the landscape as you drive along. England is divided into eight regions, thus: *The South East* (vol. 1), *East Anglia* (vol. 2), *The South West* (vol. 3), *The West* (vol. 4), *The East Midlands* (vol. 5), *The West Midlands* (vol. 6), *The North East* (vol. 7), *The North West* (vol. 8).

The best cure for the sort of landscape blindness caused by satellite navigation is a good road atlas. I suggest Collins' *Discovering Britain Road Atlas and Guide*, which not only has excellent maps, but also includes a well-illustrated introduction entitled 'Discovering the Landscape'. My copy is already dog-eared and battered, but the binding has remained intact. A far more detailed atlas is *Philip's Navigator Britain*, at 1½ miles to 1 inch, it is almost the equivalent of a complete set of Ordnance Survey 1-inch (1 : 50,000,000) maps. The cover is less detailed for Highland Scotland, though. Like most archaeologists I carry battered coffee-stained and usually out-of-date copies of the relevant 1-inch (1 : 50,000) Ordnance Survey maps somewhere in the car.

This may sound somewhat eccentric, but the following idea was suggested to me by Professor Mick Aston and it makes plenty of sense. Mick has several copies of this dotted around his place, one of which lives in the car boot: *Domesday Book: A Complete Translation* (Penguin Books, London, 2002). As a matter of interest, very recent work suggests that Domesday Book was more about the people and the places where taxes were actually paid. We tend to forget that, rather like some developing countries today, a large part of the real eleventh-century English economy would now be regarded as 'black'.[1]

Finally, *The Good Pub Guide* (Ebury Press, London, published annually). Any foray into the landscape of Britain requires sustenance and I have found the many pubs listed in this guide nearly always live up to expectation.

1. David Roffe, *Decoding Domesday* (Boydell and Brewer, Woodbridge, 2007).

Glossary

Note: terms in italics are defined elsewhere in the Glossary.

ancient landscapes. See *woodland landscapes*.

ard. A form of chisel-like ancient plough which, unlike the *mouldboard plough*, lifts rather than turns the soil over.

assart. In medieval times assarts were clearings around the edges of woods or heaths which usually held a farmstead or smallholding.

barmkin. A defended farmyard usually attached to a fortified tower house.

bascule bridge. A counter-weighted lifting bridge, most commonly found in Holland today. When correctly balanced it can be operated by a single person.

bastle or **bastle house.** A thick-walled two-storey defended farmhouse, usually found in the Scottish Borders in the sixteenth and seventeenth centuries. The living area was on the first floor, with livestock below.

breck or **break.** A piece of steep or rough land often found between good arable ground, which could be taken into cultivation from time to time.

brickearth. A natural deposit of fine wind-sorted sandy silt which can be used for making bricks. When improved with manure, brickearths can form fertile soils.

broch. A form of drystone tower house accessed via stairs within the cavity walls. Brochs are found in the Western Isles and in adjacent parts of north-western Scotland. They were built or used from the *Iron Age* until the early centuries AD.

Bronze Age. The period characterized by the introduction of bronze, an alloy of copper with tin. It saw the construction of numerous henge monuments and round barrows and was followed by the *Iron Age* around 800 BC.

buddle. A tank or trough which made use of water to separate fine particles of lead or other minerals held in suspension.

burgage or **burgage plots.** The urban equivalent of *tofts* in the *Middle Ages*.

They occur in ancient boroughs and comprise a house and yard together with a narrow street frontage and a strip of land at the rear.

chaldron. A four-wheeled wooden wagon usually used for carrying heavy loads of coal or ore along a *waggonway*.

Champion landscapes. A medieval farming system based around collective holdings in which peasant farmers held strips within large *Open Fields*. The 'classic' Champion landscapes are on the heavier clay soils of the English Midlands.

clachan. The traditional form of rural settlement in Wales and western Scotland until the nineteenth century. They varied in size, but most were loosely organized hamlets with small houses and their yards clustered together.

cruck. A large curved beam which ran from the floor to the roof in many medieval houses and barns. They were often formed from the trunks of black poplar, a native tree which in windy areas grows naturally in a gentle curve.

dun. A defended homestead with characteristically thick walls, mostly built in the *Iron Age* and found in western Scotland.

enclosure. The process whereby land held by several people, whether as strips in *Open Fields*, as commons, shared heath, upland or meadow pasture, was taken into the control or possession of a single individual or estate. Enclosure was either voluntary ('by agreement') or statutory (by Act of Parliament).

fermtoun. A group of farms that operated a co-operative or *run-rigg* system, in the *Middle Ages* and in early *post-medieval* times. The western Scottish equivalent was the generally smaller *clachan*.

Iron Age. It followed the *Bronze Age,* around 800 BC, and was the period when iron came into common use. It saw the full development of the British landscape, including the construction of hundreds of hillforts. In southern Britain it ended with the *Roman* conquest of AD 43.

lynchet. A lynchet would build up at the foot of a ploughed strip or field on a hillside, after repeated ploughing with either an *ard* or a *mouldboard plough*. A bank (or positive lynchet) would accumulate on the upslope and a hollow (or negative lynchet), on the downslope.

machair. Large areas of sandy landscapes characteristic of the Western Isles, where many prehistoric sites are to be found. Machair contains numerous fragments of broken seashells and can be highly fertile, especially when enriched with manure or peat.

medieval. The period that covers all history from the end of *Roman* times until the Reformation of the mid-sixteenth century. It is generally divided into two: early medieval (from the fifth to the eleventh centuries) and late medieval, the equivalent of the *Middle Ages*, as defined here.

Mesolithic or **middle Stone Age.** The period between the *Upper Palaeolithic* and the *Neolithic*, from about 8000 BC to 4500 BC. It is characterized by hunters and gatherers who made tools and weapons from small flints known as microliths.

Middle Ages. Here the term is used to define the latter part of the *medieval* period, from the Norman Conquest (1066) until 1550. It is divided into two approximate halves: early (1066–1350) and late (1350–1550).

mouldboard plough. A form of plough (introduced to Britain in late *Saxon* times) in which a curved mouldboard behind the share, or cutting edge, inverts the soil to bury weeds and form a true furrow. Repeated ploughing with a mouldboard plough can give rise to *ridge-and-furrow*.

Neolithic or New Stone Age. The period between the *Mesolithic* and the *Bronze Age*. The Neolithic saw the introduction of farming and the construction of the first large communal monuments, such as long barrows. It spanned the period 4500–2500 BC.

nucleation. A process of the late *Saxon* period and the early *Middle Ages* in which a number of dispersed farmsteads in lowland Scotland and central England came together to form tighter communities in central villages; these often developed into *Open Field* and *run-rigg* farms.

Open Field landscapes. Open Field farms were organized around parishes and manors in the *Middle Ages* and many continued into *post-medieval* times. It was a form of communal farming where peasant farmers worked individual strips which were held in two to four large Open Fields – so named because the strips within them were open and never fenced, hedged or ditched.

Palaeolithic or Old Stone Age. The first and longest period in British prehistory. The earliest inhabitants of what was later to become the island of Britain settled around 600,000 years ago. The Palaeolithic (or *Upper Palaeolithic*) ends with the retreat of the Ice Age ice, around 8000 BC.

planned landscapes. Landscapes of larger regular rectangular fields, straight roads and large villages. These usually developed from *Champion* and *Open Field* systems in the *Middle Ages*, often, but not always, as a result of Parliamentary *enclosure*.

plantation towns. These are sometimes known as *medieval* 'new towns'. They were mostly planted in the landscape by order of the Norman kings from the eleventh to the thirteenth centuries, but later examples can also be found.

post-medieval. The period that follows the *Middle Ages*. It can be used to describe the entire span of time between 1550 and the present, or it can be subdivided into early modern (1550–1750) and modern (1750–the present).

reaves. Long fields defined by low drystone walls which were laid out in Dartmoor, Devon, in the Bronze Age. The Dartmoor Reaves are among the earliest, most complete and best preserved prehistoric fields systems in Europe.

ridge-and-furrow. A method of farming in which repeated ploughing in the same direction causes the build-up of high ridges, separated by deep furrows. Although characteristic of *Champion* landscapes, ridge-and-furrow is also commonly found in areas with poor surface drainage.

Roman and **Romano-British**. The term 'Roman' is used to define the period when large parts of Britain were in the Roman Empire (AD 43–410). The term 'Romano-British' describes the people and the culture of the time, thus: villas were constructed by leading Romano-British citizens in Roman times.

run-rigg. A Scottish form of *medieval* and early *post-medieval* infield–outfield farming based around a co-operative farm, usually under the control of a single landlord, as part of a multiple tenancy arrangement. The term 'run-rigg' refers to the fact that individual farmers could hold strips throughout the infield.

Saxon. The term used to describe post-*Roman* and early *medieval* times in England (410–1066). The eastern Scottish equivalent is Pictish. The period saw the reintroduction of towns and the development of the *Open Field* system.

toft. A plot of land that accompanied a house in a *medieval* village. In *Open Field* villages tofts did not form part of the co-operative system and provided the occupants of the house with grazing and/or produce, such as fruit and vegetables.

transhumance. A form of seasonal movement in which livestock (accompanied by some or all of the community) are grazed on upland or marsh in summer, and are returned to lowland pastures in winter. Transhumance was particularly important in Wales in the *Middle Ages* and in the Fens in the *Bronze Age* and *Middle Ages*.

Upper Palaeolithic. The final phase of the *Palaeolithic* marked by the appearance of modern humans (*Homo sapiens*), from about 40,000 years ago. It was succeeded by the *Mesolithic* around 8000 BC. Flint tools of the period were far smaller than those used previously.

waggonway. A horse-drawn railway. At first the tracks were wooden, later iron. The wagons pulled were often *chaldrons*. Waggonways were usually built in landscapes with steep hills and valleys, such as the coalfields of south Wales and north-eastern England, where canal construction was difficult or impossible.

woodland or **ancient landscapes**. These landscapes of winding lanes, hamlets and small irregular fields, grew from ancient patterns of individual farmsteads in areas where *nucleation* and the *Open Field* system did not develop.

Ancient or woodland landscapes were believed to have survived because the climate was wet, or the soils were not suited for intensive arable, but we now realize that social factors were also crucially important.

The Illustrations

Unless otherwise stated, photographs are by the author.

FIGURES

Index

Note: Page numbers in *italic* refer to illustrations in the text; those in **bold** refer to the Glossary